STUDIES IN CHRISTIAN HISTORY AND THOUGHT

The Westminster Confession of Faith and the Cessation of Special Revelation

The Majority Puritan Viewpoint on Whether Extra-biblical Prophecy is Still Possible

STUDIES IN CHRISTIAN HISTORY AND THOUGHT

A full listing of all titles in this series
will be found at the close of this book

STUDIES IN CHRISTIAN HISTORY AND THOUGHT

The Westminster Confession of Faith and the Cessation of Special Revelation

The Majority Puritan Viewpoint on Whether Extra-biblical Prophecy is Still Possible

Garnet Howard Milne

Foreword by Joel Beeke

WIPF & STOCK · Eugene, Oregon

Wipf and Stock Publishers
199 W 8th Ave, Suite 3
Eugene, OR 97401

The Westminster Confession of Faith and the Cessation of Special Revelation
The Majority Puritan Viewpoint on Whether Extra-Biblical Prophecy is Still Possible
By Milne, Garnet Howard
Copyright©2007 Paternoster
ISBN 13: 978-1-55635-805-0
ISBN 10: 1-55635-805-9
Publication date 1/15/2008

This Edition Republished by Wipf and Stock Publishers by arrangement with Paternoster

Paternoster
9 Holdom Avenue
Bletchley
Milton Keyes, MK1 1QR
Great Britain

STUDIES IN CHRISTIAN HISTORY AND THOUGHT

Series Preface

This series complements the specialist series of *Studies in Evangelical History and Thought* and *Studies in Baptist History and Thought* for which Paternoster is becoming increasingly well known by offering works that cover the wider field of Christian history and thought. It encompasses accounts of Christian witness at various periods, studies of individual Christians and movements, and works which concern the relations of church and society through history, and the history of Christian thought.

The series includes monographs, revised dissertations and theses, and collections of papers by individuals and groups. As well as 'free standing' volumes, works on particular running themes are being commissioned; authors will be engaged for these from around the world and from a variety of Christian traditions.

A high academic standard combined with lively writing will commend the volumes in this series both to scholars and to a wider readership.

Series Editors

Alan P.F. Sell, Visiting Professor at Acadia University Divinity College, Nova Scotia, Canada

David Bebbington, Professor of History, University of Stirling, Stirling, Scotland, UK

Clyde Binfield, Professor Associate in History, University of Sheffield, UK

Gerald Bray, Anglican Professor of Divinity, Beeson Divinity School, Samford University, Birmingham, Alabama, USA

Grayson Carter, Associate Professor of Church History, Fuller Theological Seminary SW, Phoenix, Arizona, USA

For Carol

CONTENTS

Foreword by Joel Beeke — xiii
Preface — xv
List of Abbreviations — xix

Introduction — 1

Chapter 1
The Westminster Assembly: Socio-political and Religious Context, Theological Inheritance and Constitution

1.1	Introduction	10
1.2	Socio-political and Religious Context	13
1.2.1	*European Context*	14
1.2.2	*English Context*	19
1.2.3	*English and Scottish Events in their British Context*	22
1.2.4	*Eschatological Fervour and the Interest in Prophecy*	35
1.2.5	*Challenges from Variant Theologies*	40
1.3	Theological Inheritance	42
1.3.1	*Augustine*	43
1.3.2	*Thomas Aquinas*	44
1.3.3	*John Calvin*	45
1.4	The Immediate Predecessors of the Assembly	48
1.4.1	*William Perkins*	49
1.5	Acknowledged Sources of the Westminster Theology	52
1.5.1	*William Whitaker*	52
1.5.2	*James Usher*	59
1.5.3	*John Ball*	60
1.6	Assessing the Contributions of the Westminster Divines	62
1.7	Conclusion	65

Chapter 2
The Necessity and Scope of Special Revelation

2.1	Introduction	67
2.2	The Limitations of General Revelation	68
2.3	Special Revelation and *WCF* 1:1	74
2.4	The Westminster Definition of Salvation	77
2.4.1	*Salvation in the Other Works of the Westminster Divines*	82
2.5	Salvation and the Necessity of Scripture	98
2.5.1	*The Scriptures are Necessary in Both an Absolute and a Conditional Sense*	99
2.5.2	*The Scriptures are Necessary for Both Personal and Holistic Redemption*	104
2.6	Conclusion	108

Chapter 3
The Obsolescence of the Former Modalities of Special Revelation

3.1	Introduction	109
3.2	An Exegetical Tradition	110
3.2.1	*Ephesians 1:17-18 and the Promise of New Revelations*	113
3.2.2	*Hebrews 1:1-2: Scripture the Sole Source of Special Revelation*	123
3.2.3	*Joel 2:28-32 and Acts 2:17*	133
3.3	Extra-biblical Modalities Relegated to the Past	140
3.4	Conclusion	145

Chapter 4
Clarifying the Claims to Continuationism

4.1	Introduction	146
4.2	Cessationism and Dreams	147
4.2.1	*Consigning Revelatory Dreams to the Past*	147
4.2.2	*Spiritualised Dreaming*	148
4.2.3	*Dreams and Puritan Providentialism*	149
4.3	Continuationism among the Reformed Orthodox	153
4.3.1	*Two Forms of Supernatural Revelation*	154
4.3.2	*The Inconclusive Witness of Some Claims to Revelation*	155
4.3.3	*Stricter Continuationists/Continuationism*	159

4.4	The Quaker Polemic – Reaction to the Westminster Cessationist View	166
4.5	Conclusion	176

Chapter 5
Prophecy and the Westminster Divines

5.1	Introduction	177
5.2	Other Puritan Forms of Discerning Secrets or the Future	180
5.3	Puritan Exegetical Conclusions Concerning New Testament Prophecy	188
5.3.1	*The Simple Assertion of the Cessation of Gifts*	193
5.3.2	*Why Prophecy is No Longer Necessary*	194
5.3.3	*Summary*	203
5.4	The Explanation of the Puritan Acceptance of Contemporary Prophecy	203
5.4.1	*The Possibility of Contemporary Prophecy*	206
5.5	Conclusion	217

Chapter 6
Prophecy and the Scots

6.1	Introduction: The Tradition of Miraculous Divine Intervention	219
6.2	John Knox	221
6.3	"Prophecy" and the Scottish Commissioners to the Westminster Assembly	224
6.3.1	*Robert Baillie, Archibald Johnston and Samuel Rutherford*	224
6.3.2	*Alexander Henderson and Robert Blair*	234
6.3.3	*George Gillespie*	237
6.3.3.1	INTERNAL CONTRADICTIONS	240
6.3.3.2	ON THE CESSATION OF THE OTHER MIRACULOUS GIFTS	241
6.3.3.3	A DISTINCTION BETWEEN MODERN AND BIBLICAL PROPHETS	241
6.3.3.4	A CONTINUATIONIST GILLESPIE IN A CESSATIONIST ASSEMBLY?	243
6.3.3.5	LINKING THE "MISCELLANY" TO THE ASSEMBLY DEBATES	244
6.3.3.6	GILLESPIE'S COMMITMENT TO WESTMINSTER ORTHODOXY	244
6.3.3.7	GILLESPIE AS PROPHET	246

6.4	An Enduring Legacy	247
6.4.1	*James Durham*	247
6.4.2	*Robert Fleming*	250
6.4.3	*James Hog*	252
6.4.4	*Edward Irving and the London Scottish Presbytery*	253
6.4.5	*John Kennedy*	255
6.5	Conclusion	256

Chapter 7
Subscription and the Westminster Confession of Faith

7.1	Introduction:	257
7.2	An Ambiguous Cessationist Clause?	258
7.3	Subscription in England	262
7.3.1	*Episcopalians*	263
7.3.2	*Non-conformists*	264
7.3.3	*The Westminster Divines*	267
7.3.4	*Presbyterians*	271
7.4	Subscription in Scotland	275
7.4.1	*The Use of Subscription Formulas*	277
7.5	Conclusion	283

Conclusion	**285**

Appendix
Private Spirits — **291**

8.1	Private Spirits as Personal Opinion	292
8.2	Private Spirits as the Private Revelations of the "Enthusiasts"	294

Bibliography	**299**
Index	**329**

Foreword

The battle between cessationism and continuatianism with regard to New Testament revelatory gifts rages on in the twenty-first century, often without mature, nuanced knowledge of the past. In *The Westminster Confession of Faith and the Cessation of Special Revelation,* Garnet Milne presents us with a much-needed study, detailing the confessional and individual Puritan views of this critical subject. He shows irrefutably that the Puritans as a whole—notwithstanding a few surprising exceptions, most notably, William Bridge—taught cessationism based on such texts as Ephesians 1:17-18, Hebrews 1:1-2, and Joel 2:28-32/Acts 2:17, even though they "believed that God 'continued' to speak in surprising and extraordinary ways, albeit not as directly as he had in biblical times" (p. 289).

Milne has done his homework well. He builds his case by presenting judicious and thorough evidence from a large number of both primary and secondary sources. In effect, he does for cessationism in Puritan thought what Ernest Kevan has done for Puritan thinking on the use of the law. At every turn and on every issue, Milne lets the Puritans speak for themselves, accurately explains what they were saying, and then provides balanced, objective, and, on occasion, surprising conclusions. Certain insights have far-reaching ramifications for Puritan soteriological studies in general, such as his conclusion that the Puritans use the term *salvation* as a concept that embraces not only personal redemption but also national and international temporal deliverance and reformation. Then, too, his presentation between immediate and mediate revelation in Puritan thinking is most helpful, for it shows how the Puritans could reject the possibility of a resurgence of the New Testament prophetic gifts while still occasionally tolerating several apparently revelatory forms (the use of the lot, angelic impressions, dreams, and prophetic insight) without severing any from the Scriptures and the accompanying illumination of the Holy Spirit. Ultimately, Milne shows that nearly all Puritans consistently rejected post-apostolic, extra-biblical revelation.

The Westminster Confession of Faith and the Cessation of Special Revelation ought to be read not only by those interested in Puritan theology, but also by pastors and lay people who wish to grow in their understanding of the debate between cessationism and continuationism. It is a fascinating, groundbreaking book for several reasons. It not only addresses a formidable subject never thoroughly studied before, but its conclusions are so transparent that the reader cannot but find himself repeatedly concurring with the author as he presents one new insight after another. Also, its treatment of individual Puritans and his comparative analysis between the English and the Scottish are most enlightening. Milne's book clarifies a remarkable amount of profound, theological detail that lies behind the cessationist clause of Westminster Confession of Faith, 1.1.

Joel R. Beeke
Puritan Reformed Theological Seminary,
Grand Rapids, Michigan.

Preface

Controversy in the church is usually considered in a negative light by most observers, because quite rightly, as social creatures, we prefer unity to disunity. There are also theological and political reasons which make the search for unity desirable. The Westminster Assembly was a political and ecclesiastical attempt to promote unity in seventeenth-century Britain, and produced documents which were intended to bind the kingdoms of England, Scotland and Ireland more closely together. While, perhaps predictably, this ambition was not fully realised, the Westminster Assembly did bequeath to the church documents that many denominations continue to find useful in their work and witness, and in a context of far more pluralistic societies than the Puritan British Isles. My study of this period has also, I trust, given me a wider understanding of the differences within the church of that time as well as a greater insight into how to deal with differences in viewpoint in a godly way in our own day and context.

The Westminster Confession of Faith (*WCF*), drawn up in London in the 1640s, has been one of the most influential confessions in the history of Reformed theology. It has occupied a very significant place in the life of a great many Protestant churches since the seventeenth century, and continues to serve as a chief subordinate standard in several major denominations today.

In the opening chapter of the Confession, the divines of Westminster included a clause which implied that there would no longer be any supernatural revelation from God for showing humankind the way of salvation. Means by which God had once communicated the divine will concerning salvation, such as dreams, visions, and the miraculous gifts of the Spirit, were said to be no longer applicable. However, many of the authors of the *WCF* accepted that "prophecy" continued in their time, and a number of them apparently believed that disclosure of God's will through dreams, visions, and angelic communication remained possible. How is the "cessationist" clause of *WCF* 1:1 to be read in the light of these facts? Was it intended as a strict denial of the possibility that any supernatural revelation for the purposes of salvation could take place after the apostolic period, or did its authors, as some modern scholars have argued, allow for a more flexible view, in which such divine revelation through extraordinary means might still take place? This book explores these questions in the light of the modern debates over the interpretation of the Confession's language and its implications for the church today. It considers the difference between "mediate" and "immediate" revelation as understood by the Westminster divines, and attempts to show that only "immediate" revelation was considered to have ceased, while "mediate" revelation, which always involved Scripture, was held to continue.

A detailed analysis of the writings of the Westminster divines reveals that these churchmen possessed both a strong desire to maintain the unity of Word and Spirit and a concern to safeguard the freedom of the Holy Spirit to speak to particular circumstances through the language and principles of Scripture. God still enabled predictive prophecy and spoke to individuals in extraordinary ways, but contemporary prophecy was held to be something distinct from the extraordinary prophecy of New Testament figures. In the minds of both the Scottish Presbyterians and English Puritans, prophecy was considered to be an application of Scripture for a specific situation, not an announcement of new information not contained within the Bible. The Scriptures always remained essential for the process of discerning God's will.

The Introduction to the book considers the debate over *WCF* 1:1 in its modern setting. Chapter One outlines the socio-political and theological context of the Westminster Assembly, and discusses the question of how to assess the respective contributions of the divines to the documents it produced. Chapter Two investigates the Westminster view of the necessity and scope of special revelation, and discusses the nature of the "salvation" which was conveyed by this means. Chapter Three surveys the exegetical traditions underpinning the teaching that former modalities of supernatural revelation had ceased. Chapter Four seeks to respond to modern claims that Puritan theology allowed for a "continuationist" position, by canvassing evidence both from seventeenth-century Reformed thinkers themselves and from their critics, who maintained that Westminster orthodoxy was indeed cessationist in style and intent. Chapters Five and Six explore the claims to and explanations for "prophecy" in Reformed theology in both England and Scotland in the seventeenth century. Chapter Seven examines the question of the theological status of the Westminster Confession in its own time. To what extent were subscription requirements envisaged by the Assembly and the governments of the day, and what form did these requirements take?

The book concludes that the Westminster divines intended the cessationist clause to affirm that there was to be no more extra-biblical, "immediate" revelation for any purpose now that the church possessed the completed Scriptures. The written Word of God was fully capable of showing the way of "salvation" in its wider scope as either temporal or eternal deliverance. At the same time the divines did not intend to deny that God could still speak through special providences that might involve

Preface xvii

dreams or the ministry of angels, for example, but such revelation was always to be considered "mediate". The primary means was held to be the written Scriptures, illuminated by the Holy Spirit. The unity of the Word and Spirit was maintained, and God's freedom to address individual circumstances remained intact.

Although a project like this involves calling on the advice of many, two men stand out as those who have contributed the most to the finished product. Dr. Ivor Davidson, Professor of Systematic Theology at Otago University was my thesis supervisor and his contribution cannot be overestimated. Dr. Rob Oxner, a Physician at Thames hospital was the other key contributor. Without his bibliographic knowledge and help, this book would not have been written. Any shortcomings in the work, of course, remain my own.

Garnet H Milne
Wanganui

LIST OF ABBREVIATIONS

ABD	David Noel Freedman et al. (eds.), *The Anchor Bible Dictionary*, 6 vols. New York: Doubleday, 1992.
ANF	Alexander Roberts and James Donaldson (eds.), *The Ante-Nicene Fathers*, 10 vols. Grand Rapids, MI.: Eerdmans, 1979-86.
CO	Wilhelm Baum, Edward Cunitz, and Edward Reuss (eds.), *Ioannis Calvini opera quae supersunt omnia*, 59 vols. Brunswick and Berlin: C.A. Schwetschke and Son, 1863-1900.
DNB	Edgar Williams et al. (eds.), *The Compact Edition of the Dictionary of National Biography*, 2 vols. London: Oxford University Press, 1975.
DPCM	Stanley M. Burgess and Gary B. McGee (eds.), *Dictionary of Pentecostal and Charismatic Movements*. Grand Rapids: Zondervan, 1996.
DPW	[Westminster] *Directory for the public worship of God.**
DSCHT	Nigel M. de. S. Cameron et al. (eds.), *Dictionary of Scottish Church History & Theology*. Edinburgh: T & T Clark, 1993.
EDNT	Horst Balz and Gerhard Schneider (eds.), *Exegetical Dictionary of the New Testament*, 3 vols. Grand Rapids: Eerdmans, 1990.
FPC	[Westminster] *The Form of Presbyterial Church-Government and of the ordination of Ministers.**
LC	[Westminster] *Larger Catechism.**
NBD	J. D. Douglas et al. (eds.), *New Bible Dictionary*. Leicester: IVP, 1982.
NDT	Sinclair B. Ferguson and David F. Wright (eds.), *New Dictionary of Theology*. Leicester, IVP, 1988.
NPNF	Philip Schaff and Henry Wace (eds.), *The Nicene and Post-Nicene Fathers of the Christian Church,* first series, 14 vols., repr. Grand Rapids, MI.: Eerdmans, 1988-91; second series, 14 vols., repr. Grand Rapids, MI.: Eerdmans, 1983-88.
SC	[Westminster] *Shorter Catechism.**
TDNT	G. Kittel and G. Friedrich (eds.), *Theological Dictionary of the New Testament,* 10 vols., Tr. G. W. Bromiley. Grand Rapids, MI.: Eerdmans, 1964-76.
TDOT	Johannes Botterweck et al. (eds.), *Theological Dictionary of the Old Testament*, 12 vols. Grand Rapids, MI.: Eerdmans, 1974-2003.
TWOT	R. Laird Harris, Gleason L. Archer, Jr., and Bruce K. Waltke (eds.), *Theological Wordbook of the Old Testament*, 2 vols. Chicago: Moody Press, 1980.
WCF	*Westminster Confession of Faith.***
WTJ	*The Westminster Theological Journal*.

*All citations of the *DPW*, *LC*, *SC*, and *FPC* are from *The Confession of Faith and Larger Catechism, Shorter Catechism, Directory of Public worship and Presbyterial Church Government*. Edinburgh: William Blackwood & Sons Ltd, 1969, reprint of the 1897 edition produced at the direction of the General Assembly of the Church of Scotland.

** *WCF* references are from the critical text by Samuel William Carruthers, The Westminster Confession of Faith, Being an Account of the Preparation and Printing of its Seven Leading Editions to Which is Appended a Critical Text of the Confession with Notes Thereon. Manchester: R. Aikman & Son, 1937.

Introduction

A vigorous discussion has arisen during recent years in Reformed Christianity over two questions bearing upon the work of the Holy Spirit and revelation. The first issue relates to the contemporary availability of supernatural or miraculous[1] gifts of the Holy Spirit as summarised in passages such as Rom. 12:4-8, 1 Cor. 12:28-31 and 14:1-39, and in particular to the gift of extraordinary prophecy. The second relates to the contemporary likelihood of God imparting his will through modes of communication such as dreams, visions, angels and the audible voice of the Divine Being. These two topics are explicitly connected in Scripture, as Num. 12:6-7 illustrates by summarising the means of divine disclosure for extraordinary prophets as visions, dreams, and face-to-face conversation.

In the modern debate the contemporary relevance of these related concepts is usually discussed within the broader framework of "cessationism" versus "continuationism". There is, however, some variation in the usage of this terminology.

A recent book edited by Wayne Grudem initially defines four positions integral to the controversy as "cessationist",[2] "Pentecostal",[3] "charismatic"[4]

---

[1] The definition of "miraculous" is, of course, controversial. See, for example, Colin Brown, "Miracle", *NDT*, 433-34, for one definition of "miracle", where Brown notes that the Latin word *miraculum* "suggests supernatural interference with nature or the course of events" (433). However, in Christian thought miracles have not only been understood as "extraordinary expressions of God's grace, but as divine attestation of the person or the teaching of the one who performs the miracle" (433). In addition, biblical miracles can be the "breaking into our present world-order of the order of the world to come"(433). See also M. H. Cressey, "Miracles", *NBD*, 782-84, where Cressey suggests that there are three defining attributes of biblical miracles – "wonder", "power" and "significance". While these characteristics are also evident throughout the created order, "miracles are events which dramatically reveal this living, personal nature of God, active in history not as mere Destiny but as Redeemer who saves and guides his people" (782). However Cressey's willingness to see a continuity between the extraordinary and the ordinary does not reflect the view of the seventeenth-century Protestant, John Owen, commenting on Heb. 2:4, which summarizes the New Testament categories of "miracle", links "signs", "wonders", "mighty works" and "Gifts of the Holy Spirit" through their common purpose and source. All are said to be supernatural works, which attest the truth of the gospel, and convey God's approbation of those who are doing the testifying. John Owen, *An Exposition of the Epistle to the Hebrews* (Edinburgh: Banner of Truth, 1991), vol. 3, 280-81. My use of the term "miraculous" will follow Owen's view, which also harmonizes with Brown above.

[2] For some examples of modern cessationist arguments, see Sinclair Ferguson, *The Holy Spirit* (Leicester: IVP, 1996), especially 214-37; O. Palmer Robertson, *The Final Word* (Edinburgh: Banner of Truth, 1993), especially 1-21 on prophecy. For general works on cessationism, see Richard Gaffin, *Perspectives on Pentecost. New Testament*

and "Third Wave".[5] The cessationist viewpoint denies the continuance of New Testament miraculous gifts such as prophecy, tongues and healing, and confines the exercise of those gifts to the apostolic era or even until the completion of the New Testament canon.[6] The remaining three stances are

---

Teaching On the Gifts of the Holy Spirit (Phillipsburg: Presbyterian and Reformed, 1979), especially 89-116. For the classic historical, though not exegetical, argument for the cessation of the charismata, see Benjamin Warfield, *Counterfeit Miracles* (London: Banner of Truth, 1972), especially 1-31. See also Richard Gaffin and Randall Fowler White, "Eclipsing the Canon? The Spirit, the Word, and 'Revelations of the Third Kind'," Gary Johnston and Randall Fowler White (eds.), *Whatever Happened to the Reformation?* (Phillipsburg: Presbyterian and Reformed, 2001), 133-57; Randall Fowler White, "Contrary to What You May Have Heard: On the Rhetoric and Reality of Claims of Continuing Revelation", Gary Johnston and Randall Fowler White (eds.), *Whatever Happened to the Reformation?*, 159- 84. For a critique of the Warfield thesis, see John Ruthven, *On the Cessation of the Charismata, The Protestant Polemic on Postbiblical Miracles* (Sheffield: Sheffield Academic Press, 1993), or Ruthven's PhD thesis, "On the Cessation of the Charismata: The Protestant Polemic of Benjamin B. Warfield" (unpublished PhD thesis, Marquette University, 1989), especially 107-98; John Wimber and Kevin Springer, *Power Evangelism* (San Francisco: Harper and Row, 1986), 119-21; and Gary Steven Shogren, "Christian Prophecy and Canon in the Second Century: A Response to B. B. Warfield", *The Journal of the Evangelical Theological Society* 40/4 (December 1997), 609-26.

[3] See Vinson Synan, "Classic Pentecostalism", *DPCM*, 219-22, for the history of classical Pentecostalism.

[4] See Peter Hocken, "Charismatic Movement", *DPCM*, 130-60.

[5] Wayne Grudem (ed.), *Are Miraculous Gifts for Today?: Four Views* (Leicester: IVP, 1996), 13. For a critique of the Signs and Wonders Movement, or the "Third Wave", see Michael Horton (ed), *Power Religion, the Selling Out of the Evangelical Church?* (Chicago: Moody Press, 1992), especially 80-91 on the Vineyard Churches. For Third Wave beliefs see Peter Wagner, "Third Wave", *DPCM*, 843-44. "The Third Wave" was a term coined by Peter Wagner, Professor Emeritus of church growth at the Fuller Theological Seminary's School of World Missions in Pasadena, California. In "A Third Wave?", *Pastoral Renewal* (July-August, 1983), 1-5, Wagner deems the first wave to have occurred at the beginning of the twentieth century with the founding of the Pentecostal movement. He identifies the second wave as the charismatic movement which can be traced from the 1950s in the major denominations. The third wave seems to date from the 1980s, and embraces those who cannot be labelled as Pentecostal and charismatic, but who have been traditionally known as evangelicals. See also Peter Wagner, *The Third Wave of the Holy Spirit* (Ann Arbor, MI: Vine Books, Servant Publications, 1988), especially 15 in relation to the historical significance of the movement.

[6] Grudem (ed.), *Are Miraculous Gifts for Today?: Four Views*, especially 25-64. See also Wayne Grudem, *The Gift of Prophecy in the New Testament and Today* (Eastbourne: Kingsway, 1988), especially 288-90 where he limits Heb. 1:1-2 to Scripture-producing revelation; Wayne Grudem, *The Gift of Prophecy in 1 Corinthians* (Lanham: University Press of America, 1982), especially 131-35 where he argues that

all opposed to the cessationist position and not only allow for but encourage the use of the miraculous spiritual gifts.[7]

Pentecostals trace their roots to the 1901 Pentecostal revival in the US, and among other distinctive characteristics hold that speaking in tongues is a sign of the baptism of the Holy Spirit, which follows conversion.[8] The second group, the charismatics, locate their origins in the charismatic renewal of the 1960s and 1970s and unlike Pentecostals have usually remained in existing denominations.[9] Charismatics do not necessarily hold that baptism of the Holy Spirit is a second experience following conversion. Neither do they regard tongues as an indispensable or essential sign of the baptism of the Spirit. The last group is the so-called Third Wave movement, associated with the Vineyard churches and the late John Wimber (1934-1997). It teaches that the baptism of the Holy Spirit happens to all Christians when they are converted, but stresses that miraculous signs and wonders should be concomitant with the proclamation of the gospel.[10]

Grudem goes on to identify a fifth and significant stance as the "open but cautious" position, of which he himself is an advocate. Those who hold this view are widely spread throughout the evangelical churches. They distinguish themselves from other continuationists by their emphasis on evangelism, Bible study and obedience, "rather than miraculous gifts", but they also allow for the continuance of the miraculous spiritual gifts.[11]

Whereas Grudem lists only one type of cessationism, another writer on the subject, Willem Berends, distinguishes different gradations of

---

dreams and visions are not usually associated with prophecy in the New Testament, and 231-55 where he considers that it is unlikely that the New Testament teaches that there was an office of prophet.

[7] Grudem (ed.), *Are Miraculous Gifts for Today?: Four Views*, 10-13.

[8] Grudem (ed.), *Are Miraculous Gifts for Today?: Four Views*, 11.

[9] Grudem (ed.), *Are Miraculous Gifts for Today?: Four Views*, 11. For a similar definition of "charismatic" to Grudem's, see Henry Lederle, *Treasures Old and New: Interpretations of "Spirit-Baptism" in the Charismatic Renewal Movement* (Peabody: Hendrickson, 1988), xiii.

[10] See John MacArthur, *Charismatic Chaos* (Grand Rapids, MI. Zondervan, 1992), 146 and 155-57 for Wimber's conversion to belief in the charismata. See also John Wimber and Kevin N. Springer, *Power Healing* (London: Hodder & Stoughton, 2001), especially 202 where Wimber claims to be able to impart the spiritual gift of healing, in apostolic fashion, by the laying on of hands.

[11] Grudem (ed.), *Are Miraculous Gifts for Today?: Four Views*, 13. The title mentions only four views, because Grudem elects to combine the charismatic and Pentecostal positions. For this combined viewpoint see Robert Saucy, "An Open but Cautious View", Wayne Grudem (ed.), *Are Miraculous Gifts for Today?: Four Views*, 98-99, where all believers are said to be baptized with the Spirit; on the argument that the Bible no where teaches cessationism, see 100; on the contemporary availability of prophecy, healing, tongues-speaking and exorcism, see 126-37.

cessationism. Berends proposes that cessationism should be differentiated as either "strong" or "weak", and subdivides "weak" cessationism into two further categories.[12] He cites the nineteenth-century theologians Augustus Strong and Charles Hodge as "strong" cessationists: they were of the opinion that all extraordinary works, such as miracles, healing, exorcism, prophecy and tongues have ceased.[13] This view limits miracles and the agency of miraculous gifts to the apostolic era, since the purpose of these miracles was either to attest new revelation, or to provide credentials for the teacher transmitting that revelation. Since it is assumed that no more revelation can be expected after the closure of the canon, there is no longer any reason for miracles, including the miraculous gifts of the Holy Spirit.[14]

In contrast, the primary position of "weak" cessationism is that "it is not God who has ceased to do supernatural works, but God's people".[15] Those who hold to the first variant of "weak" cessationism teach that miracles were limited to the early church to assist the spread of the Gospel during persecution and usually hold that the miracles ceased by the time of Constantine. The second group propose that miraculous gifts "were unique to the apostles and those who received the gifts directly from them through the laying on of hands".[16] Berends contends that John Calvin is representative of the former opinion,[17] while Benjamin Warfield is typical of the latter.[18]

More importantly, Berends postulates that some "weak" cessationists allow for a contemporary resurgence of the miraculous spiritual gifts, while stressing that these are not to be considered the norm for the modern church.[19] Berends' distinctions enable those within non-Pentecostal/charismatic traditions both to hold to the possible reappearance of miraculous spiritual gifts without making those gifts normative, and also to retain the designation "cessationist". This is effectively Grudem's "open but cautious view". However, it is doubtful whether Berends' distinction

---

[12] Willem Berends, "Cessationism", *Vox Reformata* 60 (1995), 44-54.

[13] Berends, "Cessationism", 45. See Augustus Strong, *Systematic Theology* (Old Tappan, N.J.: Fleming H. Revell, 1907), 118; Charles Hodge, *Systematic Theology* (Grand Rapids, MI: Eerdmans, 1993), vol. 1, 636.

[14] Berends, "Cessationism", 44-49.

[15] Berends, "Cessationism", 49.

[16] Berends, "Cessationism", 49.

[17] John Calvin, *A Harmony of the Gospels: Matthew, Mark and Luke* (Grand Rapids, MI: Eerdmans, 1989), vol. 3, 255.

[18] Warfield, *Counterfeit Miracles*, 6.

[19] Berends, "Cessationism", 50 and 53. Berends includes John Calvin, William Perkins and George Gillespie in this group, referring to another of his articles in the same edition of *Vox Reformata*: Willem Berends, "Prophecy in the Reformation Tradition", *Vox Reformata* 60 (1995), 30-43, at 33-40.

between "strong" and "weak" cessationism is helpful,[20] since both Strong and Hodge were open not only to special providence, but also to the possibility of God working in ways at least analogous to the miraculous.[21] They did deny, as Berends rightly points out, that there could be miracles to attest doctrine and teachers, but Calvin, allegedly a "weak" cessationist according to Berends, taught the same thing:

> But those miraculous powers and manifest workings, which were dispensed by the laying on of hands, have ceased; and they have rightly lasted only for a time. For it was fitting that the new preaching of the gospel and the new Kingdom of Christ should be illumined and magnified by unheard-of and extraordinary miracles.[22]

In view of the ambiguities in these classifications, it is less confusing to make a simple distinction between cessationists who deny the possibility of the return of the New Testament spiritual gifts and mediated miracles, and continuationists who allow for their return, whether in a normative or an extraordinary, non-normative sense. A further classification into "weak" or "strong" cessationism is unhelpful if not misleading, because, as Berends concedes, certain "weak" cessationists do believe in the "continuance" of the miraculous gifts of the Holy Spirit.

One additional significant distinction occurring within the modern debate needs to be highlighted. Some continuationists, while asserting that prophecy is still given, yet distinguish it from the type of prophetic insight given to the Old Testament prophets and to the apostles. Grudem endorses the contemporary recurrence of this type of New Testament prophecy, but differentiates between an infallible apostolic form and a lower, fallible form.[23]

Cessationist theologians have responded to the Grudem hypothesis with a number of counter-arguments. They have pointed out that the New Testament nowhere explicitly speaks of such a lower order of prophecy; that the Agabus prophecy of Acts 21:10-11 was not erroneous in part at all;

---

[20] Berends, "Cessationism", 49-50.

[21] See Hodge, *Systematic Theology*, vol. 1, 617-18, where he cites the *WCF* 5:3 as a prelude to his definition of miracle. He defines such a miracle, allowed by the Confession, as "an event in the external world, brought about by the immediate efficiency, or simple volition of God". Later Hodge distinguishes between miracles so defined and "providential miracles". The latter continue to be clear evidence of divine intervention (626). Strong's *Systematic Theology*, also allows for answers to prayer and other activities analogous to miracles (133,434).

[22] John Calvin, *Calvin: Institutes of the Christian Religion*, ed. John T. McNeill (Philadelphia: The Westminster Press, 1960), IV, 19, 6.

[23] See Wayne Grudem, *The Gift of Prophecy in the New Testament and Today*, especially 96-102.

and that even if some prophecies are less important in the history of redemption that does not make them any less inspired or infallible.[24]

The cessationist/continuationist dialogue is also taking place within confessional Reformed churches, which subscribe to Reformation symbols, and in particular to the *Westminster Confession of Faith (WCF)*. The first section of Chapter One of the *WCF* reads as follows:

> Although the light of nature, and the works of creation and providence do so far manifest the goodness, wisdom, and power of God, as to leave men unexcusable;[a] yet are they not sufficient to give that knowledge of God, and of His will, which is necessary unto salvation.[b] Therefore it pleased the Lord, at sundry times, and in divers manners, to reveal Himself, and to declare that His will unto His Church;[c] and afterwards, for the better preserving and propagating of the truth, and for the more sure establishment and comfort of the Church against the corruption of the flesh, and the malice of Satan and of the world, to commit the same wholly unto writing:[d] which maketh the Holy Scripture to be most necessary;[e] *those former ways of God's revealing His will unto His people being now ceased*[f] [emphasis added].
>
> [a] Rom ii. 14, 15; Rom. i. 19, 20; Ps.xix. 1, 2, 3; Rom. i. 32, with chap. ii. 1
> [b] 1Cor. i. 21; 1 Cor. ii. 13, 14
> [c] Heb. i. 1
> [d] Prov. xxii. 19, 20, 21; Luke i. 3, 4; Rom. xv. 4; Matt. iv. 4, 7, 10; Isa. viii. 19, 20
> [e] 2 Tim. iii. 15; 2 Peter i. 19
> [f] Heb. i. 1, 2[25]

The final clause in italics seems a straightforward statement: all miraculous modes of divine revelation have ceased now that Scripture is complete, and this is one reason why Scripture is indispensable. The proof-text of Heb. 1:1-2 refers to former methods of supernatural revelation, such as dreams, visions and the audible voice of God, all means whereby God conveyed prophetic revelations to both Old and New Testament prophets.

There has been, however, considerable discussion over this clause in recent years. "Continuationists" have disputed whether it is indeed a clear,

---

[24] See Ferguson, *The Holy Spirit*, especially 214-37; Robertson, *The Final Word*, especially 86-126. For a brief treatment on the cessation of prophecy, see George Knight III, *Prophecy in the New Testament* (Dallas: Presbyterian Heritage Publications, 1988), especially 7-8, n4; Kenneth Gentry, *The Charismatic Gift of Prophecy: A Reformed Response to Wayne Grudem* (Memphis: Footstool Publications, 1986), especially 75-107 for a survey of Reformed and Evangelical opinion on the cessation or continuance of New Testament prophecy.

[25] Carruthers' omission of the superscripted "[f]" before the proof-text Heb. 1:1-2 must be a printer's error. I have also provided the semicolons to separate the proof-texts.

unambiguous "cessationist" statement relegating all supernatural revelation, including New Testament prophecy and related miraculous revelatory gifts, to antiquity. Willem Berends, for example, points to the Scottish tradition, where, he maintains, "there are numerous accounts of miraculous escapes, many of which are attributed to dreams, visions and prophecies received by those who were persecuted".[26] Many of the Scots who had these experiences had received and approved the *WCF*, and Berends' appeal to the Scottish commissioner to the Westminster Assembly George Gillespie[27] as an example of someone who believed in the continuance of New Testament prophecy, places the debate firmly in this historical context of the *WCF* and its reception.[28] Berends also argues that the *WCF* permits contemporary miracles:

> The biblical record gives us no right to put God in a box. Rather with the Westminster Confession we must confess that: 'God, in His ordinary providence, maketh use of means, yet is free to work without, above, and against them, at His pleasure.(5,III)' Note the Confession's use of the present tense, there is no attempt to relegate acts of extraordinary providence, or miracles, to the past. God's continuing sovereign freedom is maintained.[29]

---

[26] Willem Berends, "Prophecy in the Reformation Tradition", 30-43, especially 38; "Cessationism", 44-54. Berends refers to a prophecy concerning Richard Cameron, described in John Howie, *The Scots Worthies* (Edinburgh: Oliphant, Anderson & Ferrier, n.d.), 423-24; and James Hewison, *The Covenanters* (Glasgow: John Smith and Son, 1908), 326.

[27] George Gillespie (1613-1648) was, in spite of the brevity of his life, one of Scotland's most influential seventeenth-century theologians. Son of the minister of Kirkcaldy, he evinced an early distaste for "prelacy" by his refusal to receive ordination at the hands of a Bishop. Following the 1638 signing of the National Covenant, Gillespie was then ordained a minister at Wemyss. In 1642 he became minister at Greyfriars, Edinburgh and was translated to the Westminster Assembly in 1643. Gillespie was known for both his piety and his debating ability. One famous incident in the Assembly was Gillespie's demolishing of the celebrated Erastian, John Selden. Following Gillespie's response in that debate, Selden remarked, "that young man, by this single speech has swept away the learning and the labour of ten years of my life": William Barker, *Puritan Profiles, 54 Personalities Drawn Together by the Westminster Assembly* (Fearn: Christian Focus Publications, 1996), 110-12, citing James D. Douglas, *Light in the North* (Grand Rapids, MI: Eerdmans, 1964), 41, who cites Robert Wodrow, *Analecta* (1834), vol. 3, 110 for this remark. Gillespie died tragically at thirty-five back in Edinburgh, having returned with the *WCF* for the Scottish Assembly to ratify. See also Louis Hodges, "George Gillespie", *DSCHT*, 359-60.

[28] Berends, "Prophecy in the Reformation Tradition", 38-40.

[29] Berends, "Cessationism", 52. Proof-texts to this clause do sanction miracles and since the clause in the *WCF* is in the present tense, the implication remains that miracles are still possible. 2 Ki. 6:6 refers to the axe head that Elisha caused to float. Dan. 3:27

Berends does not argue that this section of the *WCF* (5:3) supports the view that miraculous spiritual gifts continue, admitting that it is "quite a different question whether God's Spirit continues to give the power of miracles to his people".[30] However, in another essay, "Prophecy in the Reformation Tradition", Berends does signal an interest in the relationship between non-cessationism and the *WCF*. Berends introduces examples which he relates to the Westminster Assembly in different ways. He discusses William Perkins as someone "who taught most of the Westminster Divines"; he follows this discussion with reference to "George Gillespie as one who represented the Divines";[31] and he highlights Gillespie's and the Westminster divines' insistence that "no word of prophecy could be added to the Scriptures", over against Gillespie's acceptance of present-day prophets and prophecy.[32] Berends' final representative theologian, John Owen, is introduced as a figure who "fully subscribed to those Westminster articles which dealt with the sufficiency of Scripture", but also sanctioned ongoing divine "miraculous activity".[33] Berends is effectively asking whether subscription to the *WCF* is consistent with a view that allows for the contemporary possibility of supernatural gifts such as prophecy.

A second scholar, Byron Curtis, in a more recent article arguing for the continuance of private, extra-biblical revelation, quotes an English Westminster divine, William Bridge, as someone who supports his contention for the continuance of revelation through dreams, visions and prophecy.[34] Curtis concludes: "our evidence suggests that *WCF* §1 is more likely a compromise statement between various parties in the Westminster Assembly".[35]

On the other side of the debate are those who interpret the clause in *WCF* 1:1 to mean that there was a complete cessation of both former revelatory modes and extra-biblical prophetic revelations. Kenneth Gentry, for example, strongly disclaims the conjecture of those he labels "Presbyterian charismatics",

> [who] insist that this phrase [in *WCF* 1:1] refers only to redemptive-historical revelation, and not to "lower" forms of verbal, divine revelation. Such "lower planed" revelation does not, they aver, establish doctrinal truth or contradict Scripture, even though it is the voice of the

---

refers to the three Hebrews, Shadrach, Meshach and Abednego, who were unharmed even though they had been placed in a blazing furnace.

[30] Berends, "Cessationism", 52.

[31] Berends, "Prophecy in the Reformation Tradition", 30.

[32] Berends, "Prophecy in the Reformation Tradition", 38-39.

[33] Berends, "Prophecy in the Reformation Tradition", 40-41.

[34] Byron Curtis, "'Private Spirits' in the Westminster Confession §1.10 and in Catholic-Protestant Debate (1588–1652)", 58/2 *WTJ* (1996), 257-66.

[35] Curtis, "'Private Spirits' in the Westminster Confession", 265.

living God. It is given by God for personal and limited direction, as in a warning of impending disaster[...]and the like.[36]

Gentry directs attention to the debate within the Presbyterian Church of America, whose eighth General Assembly in 1980 adopted a cessationist reading of *WCF* 1:1.[37] Another Presbyterian theologian, O. Palmer Robertson, is no less emphatic in his explication of *WCF* 1:1:

> It is not just that the written canon is closed, meaning that no more words are to be added to the Bible. The end of revelation means that all those former ways of God's making his will known to his church have now ceased.[38]

Which reading of *WCF* 1:1 is more plausible, and what are the implications of reaching a verdict on this question? While the debate is a modern one, the issues on which it touches were elements in a very real controversy in the seventeenth century. The disputants of that age also locked horns on whether prophecy, dreams, visions, miracles and the miraculous gifts of the Spirit had endured following the closure of the canon of Scripture. The modern issues, therefore, insofar as they appeal to the views of the Westminster Assembly, can only be clarified through an analysis of the Westminster epistemology.

This thesis will endeavour to answer the question whether the Westminster divines, with special reference to the *WCF*, taught that extra-biblical supernatural revelation could have been bestowed on the church in their own day through prophecy, dreams and visions, or by means of other miraculous revelatory gifts of the Holy Spirit.

---

[36] Gentry, *The Charismatic Gift of Prophecy*, 119.

[37] Gentry, *The Charismatic Gift of Prophecy*, 124-29; Also see *Minutes of the Eighth General Assembly of the Presbyterian Church in America* (Savannah, GA: 1980), 83.

[38] Robertson, *The Final Word*, 60. Robert Reymond, writing in 1977, also assumes that the *WCF* clearly teaches cessationism. He notes: "It should hardly be necessary to make the point that the cessation of revelation is an integral part of the 'system of doctrine' set forth in the *Westminster Confession of Faith*". Robert Reymond, *"What About Continuing Revelation and Miracles in the Presbyterian Church Today?"* (Philadelphia: Presbyterian and Reformed, 1977), 2, n2.

Chapter 1

The Westminster Assembly: Socio-political and Religious Context, Theological Inheritance and Constitution

1.1 Introduction

The *Westminster Confession of Faith* is so named because of its place of composition – Westminster Abbey in London. This *Confession,* and the other documents produced by the Westminster Assembly,[1] *The Larger (LC)* and *Shorter Catechisms (SC), The Form of Church Government (FPC),* and *The Directory for the Public Worship of God (DPW),* were composed between 1 July 1643 and 14 April 1648, when the *Shorter Catechism* was presented with Scripture-proofs to the English Parliament.[2] The Assembly continued to meet up to 1649 preparing documents for publication, and until 25 March 1652 as a committee deciding on benefices and the licensing of candidates for the ministry.[3]

Our concern is primarily with the first chapter of the *WFC,* but the discussion of this text cannot be divorced from the wider context of all the completed documents produced by the Assembly, which were linked by an underlying Reformation theology and a common procedure of preparation. The *WCF* and *Catechisms* were a contribution to the hoped-for religious uniformity in the three kingdoms, but their authors did not presume that these documents introduced new theological insights. While more comprehensive than some earlier confessions, the *WCF* really contained no surprises. This held true for its distinction between divine communication through Scripture and other supernatural methods of revelation, as both the

---

[1] Hereafter sometimes "the Assembly". The reasons for the calling of the Westminster Assembly are set out below.

[2] The Assembly initially began to revise the *Thirty-nine Articles* of the Church of England, but did not finish that project. For a review of the Assembly's work on the Articles, see Robert M. Norris, "The Thirty-nine Articles at the Westminster Assembly" (unpublished PhD thesis, University of St. Andrews, 1977). See 43-62 for the detailed debate over the passive and active obedience of Christ as an example of a controversy continued during the composition of the *WCF.*

[3] Alexander G. Mitchell, *The Westminster Assembly: Its History and Standards* (Edmonton: SWRB, 1992), 442-43. There is the possibility that it continued to meet after that date until Oliver Cromwell's dismissal of the Long Parliament the following year 1653, but we have no information to conclude this one way or the other.

Waldensian Confession of Faith[4] and the *Second Helvetic Confession*[5] demonstrate. In *WCF* 1:1, the Westminster divines were simply elaborating on assumptions already implicit in earlier creedal summaries.

Benjamin Warfield highlights the protracted process required before final approval was obtained from Parliament for the *WCF*. It was a complex undertaking to produce documents whose teaching would reflect a united reformed witness in the three kingdoms.[6] The committee appointed to begin work on the *WCF* was established on 20 August 1644,[7] and it was not until 4 December 1646 that the completed *WCF* was presented to the House of Commons.[8] Three days later it went to the House of Lords,[9] but the Commons required proof-texts,[10] and so on 6 January 1647, Thomas Wilson, Adoniram Byfield and Stanley Gower were appointed as a committee to prepare them.[11] They returned the next day with the texts for the first paragraph of the chapter on Scripture, when these were debated. The whole first chapter was finalised on 15 January.[12]

The committee was supplemented on 5 March[13] and the whole process was completed by 5 April 1647. This was only the draft, however, and an

---

[4] Philip Schaff (ed.), *The Creeds of Christendom* (Grand Rapids, MI: Baker, 1985), vol. 3, 758. Article Two of the *Waldensian Confession* contrasts the transmission of God's Word by oracles in "diverse manners" with revelation through Scripture.

[5] Schaff (ed.), *The Creeds of Christendom*, vol. 3, 831. Chapter One of the *Second Helvetic Confession* contrasts God speaking directly to the fathers, the prophets and the apostles, with his speaking today through the Scriptures.

[6] Benjamin B. Warfield, *The Westminster Assembly and its Work* (Cherry Hill: Mack Publishing company, 1972), 107; Samuel William Carruthers, *The Westminster Confession of Faith, Being An Account of the Preparation and Printing of its Seven Leading Editions to Which is Appended a Critical Text of the Confession with Notes Thereon* (Manchester: R. Aikman & Son, 1937), 10-15.

[7] Mitchell, *The Westminster Assembly: Its History and Standards*, 357.

[8] Mitchell, *The Westminster Assembly: Its History and Standards*, 366.

[9] Mitchell, *The Westminster Assembly: Its History and Standards*, 366; *Journal of the House of Commons*, (London: 1803), vol. 4, 739. The chronology is somewhat complicated by the Journal's use of Regnal years which did not necessarily coincide with calendar years. Vol. 5, 461, for example, is said to be 23 Car. I., 9, 10, 11 February 1647, although the dates were actually 1648. 24 Car. I . did not start until the latter part of March 1648. When we consult the Journals we will cite the literal dates given in the Journal.

[10] *Journal of the House of Commons*, vol. 5, 2. Mitchell, *The Westminster Assembly: Its History and Standards*, 367.

[11] Alex F. Mitchell and John Struthers (eds.), *Minutes of the Sessions of the Westminster Assembly of Divines* (Edmonton: SWRB, 1991), 318-19.

[12] Mitchell and Struthers (eds.), *Minutes of the Sessions of the Westminster Assembly of Divines*, 322.

[13] Mitchell and Struthers (eds.), *Minutes of the Sessions of the Westminster Assembly of Divines*, 336.

attempt to append a caution about the use of proof-texts failed.[14] The final document, now with texts appended, was drawn up and presented to both houses on 29 April 1647.[15] However, it was not until 20 June 1648 that the House of Commons ordered that the *WCF* be printed, with this first edition omitting the fourth paragraph of Chapter 20, some of the fourth paragraph of Chapter 24 as well as the fifth and sixth paragraphs, part of the fourth paragraph of Chapter 23, and the whole of Chapters 30 and 31.[16]

The Assembly was not enthusiastic about the requirement to add proof-texts,[17] but it would be wrong to dismiss the proof-texts as irrelevant to the

---

[14] Mitchell and Struthers (eds.), *Minutes of the Sessions of the Westminster Assembly of Divines*, 345. See Mitchell, *The Westminster Assembly: Its History and Standards*, 367-68. In session 833 of the minutes on 29 April 1647, the Assembly is informed that both Houses had received the *WCF* and the revised *Thirty-Nine Articles* with Scripture proofs attached and that the House of Commons had ordered 600 copies of both to be printed. Alex F. Mitchell and John Struthers (eds.), *Minutes of the Sessions of the Westminster Assembly of Divines* (Edmonton: SWRB, 1991), 356. There are three extant sources of minutes. 1. *Minutes of the Sessions of the Assembly of Divines, from August 4th, 1643, to March 25th, 1652*, 3 volumes folio Ms. Held in Dr. Williams Library, Gordon Square, London. Mitchell and Struthers' "minutes" above are from the third (and most legible) volume. There is also a transcription of the three volumes of minutes (transcribed into 5 vols.) by E. Maunde Thompson, which are also available in microfilm, at New College Library, Edinburgh; 2. John Lightfoot, "The Journal of the Proceedings of the Assembly of Divines, from January 1, 1643 [actually 1 July 1643], to December 31, 1644", *The Whole Works of the Rev. John Lightfoot, D.D.*, ed. John Pitman (London: Printed by J. F. Dove, 1824), vol. 13, 1-344. 3. George Gillespie, "Notes of Debates and Proceedings of the Assembly of Divines and other Commissioners at Westminster. February 1644 to January 1645", *The Works of George Gillespie*, ed. David Meek (Edmonton: SWRB, 1991), vol. 2, 1-120. Gillespie's individual documents are paginated separately in both volumes. None of these sources constitutes full minutes and all contain gaps and cryptic comments, some of which are impossible to decipher.

[15] Mitchell and Struthers (eds.), *Minutes of the Sessions of the Westminster Assembly of Divines*, 356.

[16] Mitchell, *The Westminster Assembly: Its History and Standards*, 368-69; Mitchell and Struthers (eds.), *Minutes of the Sessions of the Westminster Assembly of Divines*, 416-17.

[17] Robert Baillie, *The Letters and Journals of Robert Baillie, A. M. Principal of the University of Glasgow M.DC.XXXVII.-M.DC.LXII.*, ed. David Laing (Edinburgh: Bannatyne Club, 1841-1842), vol. 2, 415. In a letter to his cousin William Spang, Baillie gives his view of this requirement. "Our Assemblie, with much adoe, at last have wrestled through the whole Confession, and all is now printed. The house of Commons requires to put Scripture to it[...]and what time that will take up, who knows" (vol. 2, 415). In another letter to George Young on October 13 1646, he writes, "others hes carried the putting of Scriptures to the margin of the Confession, which may prove a very long business, if not dexterouslie managed" (vol. 2, 403). See also Mitchell, *The Westminster Assembly: Its History and Standards*, 366-68. Robert Baillie (1602-1662) is

1.2. Socio-political and Religious Context

interpretation of the *WCF*.[18] Proof-texting, for seventeenth-century Protestants, was not a casual, simplistic or irrelevant matter, but a deliberate appeal to the authority of an exegetical tradition.[19] An extraordinary amount of political and ecclesiastical effort went into the preparation of the *WCF* and the other documents produced by the Assembly.

1.2. Socio-political and Religious Context

Two of the remarkable features of the Westminster Assembly, then, were its duration and the great care taken over its literary compositions. These points are particularly striking in view of the context of great socio-political and religious turmoil in which the Assembly took place. In seventeenth-century England, Scotland and Ireland, there was a pervasive political attachment to the ideal of a unity of religious and civil life. It was a unity, however, that was rapidly disintegrating, and, as Robert Paul and others

---

best known through his correspondence which survives in his published letters and journals. Known as a back-room negotiator rather than as a speaker at the Westminster Assembly, Scottish commissioner Baillie was nonetheless an important player. Educated at Glasgow University, his first church was at Kilwinning; he was appointed as a Professor of Divinity at Glasgow University, later becoming Principal in the final eighteen months of his life: William Barker, *Puritan Profiles, 54 Personalities Drawn Together by the Westminster Assembly* (Fearn: Christian Focus Publications, 1996), 106-109. For a recent biography of Robert Baillie, see Florence McCoy, *Robert Baillie and the Second Scots Reformation* (Berkeley: University of California Press, 1974), especially 94-111 for Baillie at the Westminster Assembly.

[18] Cornelius Burgess both shows that he understands that the *Thirty-Nine Articles* were included in the *WCF* and his appreciation of proof-texts: "Upon this season it was, that the late Assembly of Divines have taken so much pains to compose several *Articles* (which they call Chapters;) wherein both those of the *39 Articles* which are held to be indeed fit to be retained, are more fully cleared and explained; and the rest, added, with pertinent proofs of *Scripture*, to make it manifest that they are all evidently grounded upon the Word of God. But, all proofs are wanting in the 39 *Articles*: no text of Scripture being produced to make out any one of them". This is one of Burgess's several criticisms of the Thirty-nine Articles. Cornelius Burges, *Reasons Shewing the Necessity of Reformation [...]"* (London: 1660)[no further publishing details], 7. Burgess (1589-1665) of Presbyterian sympathies, appointed an assessor (vice-chair) at the Assembly was a strong minded individual who was at one point suspended from the Assembly because of objections he had to the Solemn League. Educated at Oxford and originally vicar of Watford, Hertfordshire, Burgess had been a chaplain to the King, but when the Long Parliament opened, he, along with Stephen Marshall, was chosen to preach the first fast-day, the two jointly preached for seven hours. Burgess later opposed the regicide of Charles I, but had his property confiscated at the Restoration and died in poverty, having been obliged to sell most of his books. Barker, *Puritan Profiles,* 25-29.

[19] Richard Muller, *Post-Reformation Reformed Dogmatics* (Grand Rapids, MI: Baker, 2003), vol. 2, 509-20.

have pointed out, the desire for such a bond of agreement was a factor behind the Civil War in England, as well as an explanation for the importance placed by the English Parliament on seeking advice from an Assembly of divines:

> The basic question at that time was not whether Parliament and the Assembly could produce a new and *different* sort of society and church, but whether they could restore a convincing semblance of the ancient unity of church and society, and in such a way that could convince people of its authority.[20]

The Westminster Assembly, established in 1643, was a proposed means to assist in the restoration of that unity in and between the churches of the three kingdoms. It was, at the same time, another consequence of the complex political, social and religious tensions which gave rise to the English Civil War (1642-1651). An understanding of the factors that produced the Civil War is of importance in assessing the particular shape that the Assembly took and the nature of the reforms it proposed. These factors need to be set within a range of broader contexts, in Europe, England and the British Isles as a whole. Such an analysis allows us to discern why it was that a particular epistemological position on the status of extra-biblical supernatural revelation became the subject of earnest debate in the Westminster Assembly and entered the text of the *WCF*, its most important confessional summary.[21]

1.2.1 European Context

The Assembly was instituted following a series of internecine conflicts that included two "Bishops' Wars", the establishment of two successive Parliaments, the "Short" and the "Long" Parliaments, and the outbreak of the "Civil War".[22] The seeds of civil war were political on a grand scale,

---

[20] Robert S. Paul, *The Assembly of The Lord* (Edinburgh: T. & T. Clark, 1985), 32. Paul highlights other reasons for the Assembly including the need for a new form of government to enable the ordination of ministers (44-45).

[21] *WCF* 1:1.

[22] For these terms, see Peter Newman, *Companion to the English Civil Wars* (Oxford: Facts on File, 1990): The Bishops' Wars were the two conflicts between England and Scotland (1639-1641), following attempted ecclesiastical reforms in Scotland and the Scottish abolition of episcopacy (13); The Civil War is often split into two periods. The first conflict between the Royalists and the forces of the Parliament extended from 1642-1646; the second occurred in 1648 when a coalition of Royalists, former Parliamentarians and Scots battled the forces of the Rump Parliament (28-29). Sometimes the Civil War is dated between 1642-1660 or 1642-1651(ix). The "Short Parliament" is so called because of its brevity, 13 April to 5 May, 1640 (141); the "Long Parliament" lasted from November 3, 1640 to 16 March, 1660 (92). The "Rump"

yet it was a politics inextricably tied to the individual personality of the Stuart king. The seeds of the conflict were also social and secular but were at the same time subject to irrevocable religious forces, so much so that John Morrill has designated the English revolution as "the last of the Wars of Religion",[23] a concept that hints at a link with the European Thirty Years War (1618-1648). Jonathan Scott, in his *England's Troubles*, reminds us that both religious and political ideals were involved in the seventeenth-century transformation of English institutions:

> Between 1603 and 1702 England saw its religious and political institutions destroyed by, then reconstructed through, the (European) ideas they were intended to contain.[24]

The influence of religion stands out when we consider the role played by Europe in the political and ecclesiastical affairs of the British Isles, for passion inspired by religious ideals was a major factor in the tumultuous environment in which the Westminster Assembly took place. Scott concludes that although religious and political fears were closely linked, "it was religious belief that was primarily responsible in England for driving participants in what became the civil war to take sides".[25] In a real sense the English church had historical links with the Reformation churches of Europe, and it is not to denigrate the importance of the English proto-reformer John Wycliffe (1324-1384),[26] the so-called "morning star" of the Reformation, to say that nationwide or city-state-wide Protestant church reform first occurred on the European continent, for it was there that a politically supported Protestantism had its birth. The location of important theologians in Europe meant that those enamoured with Calvinism in the English and Scottish churches naturally felt empathy for and retained contact with their European colleagues. This British identification with European Protestantism had another consequence when Reformed societies began to be attacked by Counter-Reformation political and religious forces. This was the role played in the English wars by an estimated 20,000 of Charles I's subjects who had fought as mercenaries for the Dutch and Swedish Protestant forces, and who had returned to the British Isles from the late 1630s. Indeed, Charles's defeat by the Scots in 1639 and 1641

Parliament comprised those members left following a purge of the Parliament in December, 1648 (134).

[23] John Morrill, *The Nature of the English Revolution* (London: Longman, 1993), 68.

[24] Jonathan Scott, *England's Troubles: Seventeenth-century English Political Instability in European Context* (Cambridge: Cambridge University Press, 2000), 24.

[25] Scott, *England's Troubles*, 94.

[26] For an introduction to Wycliffe's life, see David G. Fountain, *John Wycliffe: the Dawn of the Reformation* (Southampton: Mayflower Christian, 1984); Michael Wilks, *Wyclif: Political Ideas and Practice* (Oxford: Oxbow, 2000); Douglas C. Wood, *The Evangelical Doctor: John Wycliffe and the Lollards* (Welwyn: Evangelical, 1984).

could be attributed as much to the battle-hardened Scottish troops who returned from Europe to take on the menace Charles's belligerence posed, as to the military and logistic weakness of the English forces.[27]

Ironically, the inexperience of the English forces and their inevitable defeat were partly the fruit of the failure of royal leadership to discharge what was perceived by many to be their duty to fight for the vulnerable Protestants of Europe. A future Westminster divine, Thomas Gataker, raised the banner of a pan-European Protestant unity and solidarity in a rousing sermon in the 1620s, urging an English commitment to assist the European Reformed churches. According to Anthony Milton, this sermon was "prompted by a perceived *lack* of commitment to the international Calvinist cause, and this was among the 'godly' populace just as much as in government circles".[28]

Nonetheless, the government took the lead in this apparent complacency. Between 1559 to 1640, Elizabeth, James, and Charles would not approve a confessional foreign policy so that in James's time, for example, high-profile Calvinist preachers such as Thomas Gataker, William Gouge[29] and James Ussher[30] openly disagreed with James's refusal to allow the

---

[27] Scott, *England's Troubles*, 140.

[28] Anthony Milton, *Catholic and Reformed: the Roman and Protestant Churches in English Protestant Thought, 1600-1640* (Cambridge: Cambridge University Press, 1995), 505. See Thomas Gataker, *A Sparke Towards the Kindling of Sorrow for Sion* (London: William Sheffard, 1621). Born in London to a minister father, Gataker was educated at Cambridge, where he excelled in the biblical languages. His friends James Usher and John Selden considered him the most learned man in England. Rector of Rotherhithe, Surrey for 43 years, Gataker was one of the few at the Assembly who held to only Christ's passive obedience [his death upon the cross] as imputed righteousness, although the Assembly decided to include a reference to Christ's active obedience in *WCF* 17.2. Gataker was sick for much of the Assembly, but still produced the notes on Jeremiah, Isaiah and Lamentations for the English Annotations, along with other scholarly works. Although he sided with the Presbyterians, he probably preferred a moderate episcopacy. He died in 1654 and was buried at Rotherhithe. Barker, *Puritan Profiles*, 154-61.

[29] Gouge (1578-1653) was elected as an assessor at the Westminster Assembly following the death of Herbert Palmer. He was a Presbyterian leader among the London Puritans, and later President of Sion College. See Barker, *Puritan Profiles*, 35-38

[30] James Usher (or Ussher) (1581-1656), who declined a seat at the Westminster Assembly, was one of the most highly respected churchmen and theologians of his day. Though he responded to the invitation to attend the Westminster Assembly by preaching a sermon criticising its legality, his reputation among members of the Assembly has been assessed thus by his biographer: "All parties had confidence in his character, and marvelled at his learning". Usher was educated at the new Trinity College, Dublin, and is best known today for his biblical chronology, once often included in King James Version editions of the Bible. Usher was appointed first professor of Divinity at Trinity College, becoming Vice-Chancellor in 1615, and then bishop of Meath and

promotion of the palatine cause at home in England.[31] In the 1630s, with the ascent of the Laudian[32] policy of avoiding involvement in confessional conflicts abroad, those who held to a Protestant internationalism were further intimidated by the official view that any close religious ties with the continent could be considered treasonous.[33] The lack of interest of Laudian divines in participating in the collections for foreign churches is just one example of what appears to have been an outright hostility toward European Protestants.[34] Milton also reminds us that since Charles I considered Presbyterianism to be intrinsically subversive and since the Laudian divines believed Calvin to be a promoter of civil rebellion, it is little wonder that they did not seek to participate in a global Protestantism.[35]

It is a small leap of faith to believe that a lack of stomach for the protection of Protestant Calvinistic orthodoxy in Europe could translate itself into outright hostility to that same Calvinism in Britain given the right circumstances. Indeed, we can see the English rebellion of the 1640s as a response to the perceived incoming tide of the European Counter-Reformation to English shores. Many English Protestants feared what they considered to be the errors of Catholicism, not the least of which was the claim to infallibility by the papacy.[36] The English church understood this doctrine to mean that the Pope had replaced Scripture. Such a fear of other sources of revelation is a sub-theme threaded throughout this dissertation. However, as Jonathan Scott has pointed out, there was a clear-cut difference between the Reformation/Counter-Reformation conflict in

---

Clonmacnoise in 1621. John Knox Laughton, "James Usher", *DNB*, vol. 2, 2137. For an excellent overview of Usher's role in the Irish Church in the broader context of the political and ecclesiastical turmoil of seventeenth-century Ireland, see Crawford Gribben, *The Irish Puritans: James Usher and The Reformation of The Church* (Darlington: Evangelical Press, 2003), especially 119-27.

[31] Milton, *Catholic and Reformed*, 506-07.

[32] Laudianism refers to the polity and doctrine of the influential English churchman William Laud (1573-1645), Archbishop of Canterbury (1633-1645). For the Life of William Laud, see Hugh Redwald Trevor-Roper, *Archbishop Laud* (London: Macmillan, 1940). See 72-73 for Laud's clear enunciation of the divine right of Kings, with the King "God's immediate vicegerent on earth"; Charles Carlton, *Archbishop William Laud* (London: Routledge & Kegan Paul, 1987). On Laud and Puritanism, see 21-2, 42, 71, 122-23.

[33] Milton, *Catholic and Reformed*, 508.

[34] Milton, *Catholic and Reformed*, 514.

[35] Milton, *Catholic and Reformed*, 523. No doubt Charles's marriage to a Spanish Catholic was seen by the Calvinistic segment of the English church to be potentially damaging to the extirpation of popery within England. See Milton, *Catholic and Reformed*, 62 where he attributes the suppression of immoderate statements against Catholicism to Charles's increasing devotion to his wife.

[36] Milton, *Catholic and Reformed*, 219.

England and that occurring in Europe. Europe's battle was about Protestantism versus Catholicism, while the struggle in England was between a perceived Calvinistic Reformation and a Protestant hierarchical prelatism which was portrayed by many Calvinists to be Arminian,[37] ceremonial and sacramentalist – to all intents and purposes, to its enemies, popery by another name. Yet the fear of a Protestant version of popery was not unconnected to the belief that Catholicism itself was seeking to re-infect the English church. Scott writes that the 1641 *Grand Remonstrance* issued by Parliament to the king following the Irish rebellion demonstrates that Protestant fears were of a popish plot linked to Spain, which it was believed, intended the extirpation of Protestantism.[38]

When Scott observes that "it was religious belief that was primarily responsible in England for driving participants in what became the Civil War to take sides",[39] he suggests that Charles was intent on just such a protestantised Counter-Reformation. The Stuart monarch was only too well aware that a struggle between Parliaments and monarchy was happening all over Europe. A religiously inspired rebellion was what monarchs feared most.[40] This helps account for Charles's aversion to both Calvinism and Parliaments, and therefore to his eleven-year Personal Rule,[41] just as his anti-Calvinist viewpoint accounts for the fears of those who wanted a more thorough Protestant reformation along the lines of the Genevan template.

The *Ordinance of the Lords and Commons* of June 12, 1643 to establish the Westminster Assembly self-consciously associate the Reformed churches of Britain with the expressed desire that the English church not

---

[37] Arminianism is named after Dutch Reformed theologian Jakob Harmensen (or Harmenszoon. Latin: Arminius) (1560-1609), who contested John Calvin's teaching on predestination and election. Five points of a *Remonstrance* (1610) were signed by forty-five Dutch ministers and were answered at the Synod of Dort (1618-19) by what have become known as the Canons of Dort or the "five points of Calvinism", which assert the sovereignty of God in salvation and the bondage of the human will to sin. See Nicholas Tyacke, *Anti-Calvinists: The Rise of English Arminianism c.1590-1640* (Oxford: Clarendon, 1987), especially 185-87.

[38] Scott, *England's Troubles*, 94-95. This was just as real a fear among the Scots, who in their *National Covenant* of 1638, included the anti-papal 1581 confession of faith. They too feared the influence of European Catholicism (138). English House of Commons, *A remonstrance of the state of the kingdom. Die mercurii 15 Decemb. 1641. It is this day resolv'd upon the question, by the House of Commons; that order shall be now given for the printing of this remonstrance, of the state of the kingdom* (London: printed for Ioseph Hunscutt, 1641).

[39] Scott, *England's Troubles*, 94.

[40] Scott, *England's Troubles*, 80-81.

[41] On the Personal Rule, which was the period between the dissolution of Parliament in 1629 and the calling of the Short Parliament in 1640, see Christopher Daniels and John Morrill, *Charles I* (Cambridge: Cambridge University Press, 1988), 73-89.

Socio-Political and Religious Context 19

only be in "nearer agreement with the Church of Scotland", but also with "other Reformed Churches abroad".[42] The *Solemn League and Covenant*, which intended to unite the three kingdoms under one religion, appealed to the "example of GOD'S people in other nations" as a justification for their covenanting, just as the *Covenant* sought reformation after "the example of the best reformed Churches".[43] The *Covenant* concluded with a hope of a universal reformation. Not only did the Covenanters earnestly desire to repel "popery" and "prelacy"; they trusted their successful reformation would give

> encouragement to other Christian churches, groaning under, or in danger of, the yoke of antichristian tyranny, to join in the same or like association and covenant, to the glory of GOD, the enlargement of the kingdom of JESUS CHRIST, and the peace and tranquillity of Christian kingdoms and commonwealths.[44]

We cannot but notice that the signatories to this *Covenant* sought Reformation "according to the word of GOD".[45] That the Scriptures were to be the foundation of their epistemology - and therefore that any other source of authority, revealed or otherwise, was to be rejected - had already been decided before the Assembly began to compose its doctrinal symbols.

If the Civil War was caused in some measure by wider European factors, we must still look more closely at English internal developments in order to comprehend the forces at work in the dramatic religious and political transformation that occurred in England.

1.2.2 English Context

Ostensibly, in the reign of Charles I, English political life continued to operate much the same as it had in his father's day. But if this was so, we must revisit the reign of James I (James VI of Scotland)(1566-1625) and ask why the English Parliament did not revolt in the Jacobean era as it would in the time of Charles. To answer this question, we need to discern the way king and Parliament functioned in the Jacobean years. That Charles I asserted an absolutist power over his nation and Parliaments, while James did so in a far more restrained manner, is one possible argument that explains the civil chaos under Charles. Another way of stating such a thesis is to set off an English Parliament dominated by constitutionalists over against the absolutist rule of the monarch. Glenn Burgess, in his *The Politics of the Ancient Constitution*, and in his *Absolute Monarchy and the*

---

[42] *The Confession of Faith; the Larger and Shorter Catechisms[...]"* (Glasgow: Free Presbyterian Publications, 1988), 11.
[43] *The Confession of Faith; the Larger and Shorter Catechisms[...]"*, 358.
[44] *The Confession of Faith; the Larger and Shorter Catechisms[...]"*, 359.
[45] *The Confession of Faith; the Larger and Shorter Catechisms[...]"*, 359.

Stuart Constitution has examined this very question in considerable detail, adducing a coherent proposal that to see a simple constitutional/absolutist dichotomy is to misunderstand the background to the cataclysmic events of the 1640s.[46]

Burgess perceives that a consensus which had held in James' reign, over how the king exercised or applied the royal prerogative to rule, had broken down under Charles. It is agreed that the England of the seventeenth century did possess an "Ancient Constitution" derived from common law and was, therefore, an instrument of government which had developed over time.[47] Common law was considered adequate for providing a satisfactory method of handling all domestic political issues[48] - so much so that all local political activity, the king's included, was to be conducted in conformity to the law and subject to legal remedies if the law was transgressed. However, common law was not adequate for every political eventuality, because some things fell outside its boundaries. This required that the king possess a duplex authority - both an ordinary legal prerogative, subject to the Ancient Constitution, and an absolute prerogative reliant on the notion of the divine right of kings. While his ordinary prerogative was exercised in accord with common law and hence with the concurrence of Parliament, the monarch's absolute prerogative essentially operated in non-domestic matters such as dealing with foreign problems, or defending the realm from external threats. Even though Burgess perceives that there was no great ideological rift in the period under review, he discerns that conflict arose concerning how the royal prerogatives might be implemented.[49]

Under James I, the consensus held together because agreed principles were largely applied in an appropriate manner. As a means towards exploring how the Jacobean consensus broke down in the reign of his son, Burgess proposes a set of categories for defining the bases of Jacobean political debate. Discourse, he suggests, involves three particular dimensions: languages (conceptual assumptions), professions (social groups using the languages) and audiences. The group using the language in the seventeenth century were usually the learned professions (including the clergy), the gentry and Members of Parliament.[50]

---

[46] Glenn Burgess, *The Politics of the Ancient Constitution. An Introduction to English Political Thought, 1603-1642* (London: Macmillan, 1992); *Absolute Monarchy and the Stuart Constitution* (New Haven: Yale University Press, 1996).

[47] Burgess, *The Politics of the Ancient Constitution*, 19. For our purposes "common law" and "the Ancient Constitution" will function as synonyms.

[48] Burgess, *The Politics of the Ancient Constitution*, 87.

[49] Burgess, *The Politics of the Ancient Constitution*, 112-13.

[50] Burgess, *The Politics of the Ancient Constitution*, 117-18. It is important to notice that often where contradictory statements seem to occur in the debate, they only seem incompatible because they are addressed to *different* audiences in different contexts.

By far the most complex aspect of these bases of debate concerns the language used. Properly speaking, there were, as Burgess points out, three languages evident: that of common law, of civil law and of theology. Common-law discourse was the principal language for discussing political matters. Unsurprisingly, common lawyers were the dominant professional group, and they believed that common law could cope with all *domestic* political issues, which did imply nonetheless that common law had its limitations, hence the need for both civil and theological languages.[51] In contrast with their common-law colleagues, civil lawyers used language drawn from concepts based upon the moral principles of natural law, enabling them to critique common law objectively, but also to discuss external political questions not embodied in common-law conventions, such as the imperial nature of the Crown of England and the interrelationship of English polity with that of the Scots and Irish.[52]

The language of theology was by far the most intricate, because it involved three separate dialects or sub-languages. In Stuart England one imbibed political philosophy by listening to sermons in which one would hear of the necessity of submission to the sovereign, and the dogma of the divine right of kings. Another idiom resonated with the idea of the independence of the king from the papacy. A third theological sub-language concerned the duties of the godly prince, a subject that also shaded into the territory of millenarianism. These three idioms of theological language, Burgess suggests, can be summarised as "order theory", "patriarchalism", and "millenarianism", and in turn are addressed to three distinguishable audiences. The first sub-language was spoken for the benefit of the local population; the second was intended for an international audience, and asserted the autonomy of a monarchy over against allegiance to the papacy; while the third addressed the perceived obligations of the ideal of the "godly prince".[53]

A supremely important point of which we need to keep sight is that, when it encroached into the political arena, theological language had to be generalised. It was not considered the role of the preacher to preach a sermon asserting the king's right to impose taxation without parliamentary concurrence, for example. Therefore, because the law was the means of achieving the general goals of a theologically defined moral duty, one finds that when the consensus held into the 1620s, theological language was vague or non-specific when expressed in relation to political matters.[54]

---

[51] Burgess, *The Politics of the Ancient Constitution*, 119-20.
[52] Burgess, *The Politics of the Ancient Constitution*, 121-26.
[53] Burgess, *The Politics of the Ancient Constitution*, 130-31.
[54] Burgess, *The Politics of the Ancient Constitution*, 131-38.

Conflict was inevitable when the rules of discourse that had held together Jacobean political life began to be violated.[55] In Charles I's time, some sermons dealing with the divine right of kings began to fracture the conventions of discourse. It was a blatant transgression when theological language was used to attempt to resolve legal problems by an appeal to divine-right concepts,[56] but these homilies had been preceded by several novel applications of the royal absolute prerogative in secular affairs. One example involved the inappropriate use of the king's divine-right absolutism in the 1627 Five Knights' case (or Darnel's case), which involved the imprisonment of five gentry who would not pay the forced loan.[57] Granted writs of *habeas corpus*, the Privy Council responded that the five were to be kept in prison because of the king's "special commandment". This seemed to many an endeavour to use the royal absolute prerogative to prevent an investigation into an imprisonment which was illegal. The Privy Council postured that the king had a right to apply the absolute prerogative in the case of common-law court proceedings. This was a use of the absolute prerogative in domestic issues and politics and therefore outside the rules underlying the Jacobean consensus. It was not the convention of an absolute prerogative that caused the tensions; it was the wrong application of that prerogative, for now the Crown was attempting to place itself above the law. In this way, Parliament came to see that the common law was ambiguous and could no longer be relied upon to maintain its security.[58] It is possible the implosion of this long-established convention, which had in the past contributed to the stability of English society, was a factor in the Westminster Assembly's assertions that the Bible was the only unassailable and infallible authority for social as well as ecclesiastical reformation.[59]

1.2.3 English and Scottish Events in their British Context

If there is broad agreement in recent scholarship that religion played a significant role in bringing about civil war in England, this scholarly accord generally does not lay the blame for the war entirely upon religious

---

[55] Indeed James argued that "the King with his Parliament here are absolute...in making or forming of any sort of Lawes". James I, *Political Works of James,* ed. Charles McIlwain (New York: Russell & Russell, 1965), 311.

[56] Burgess, *The Politics of the Ancient Constitution,* 174-77. The breakdown of the consensus began to build from approximately 1625 as these more specific applications of the divine-right absolutism intruded into common-law territory.

[57] Forced loans were supposed to be levied in periods of crisis and were to be repaid by the Crown. See Newman, *Companion to the English Civil Wars,* 55.

[58] Burgess, *The Politics of the Ancient Constitution,* 190-94.

[59] In the "cessationist" clause of *WCF* 1:1, for example.

convictions. Anthony Milton, for example, in his important monograph *Catholic and Reformed*, argues expressly that it was not the religious climate in England that caused the Civil War. Milton attributes the war to "a host of cumulative political forces", but feels compelled to add:

> Nevertheless, the rise of the Laudians, and the eroded consensus of high Elizabethan Protestantism which their policies high-lighted in the country at large, left a nation fatally divided in its religion, at a time when a power vacuum at the centre led men increasingly to have recourse to religion to explain the political deadlock.[60]

John Morrill proposes, along similar lines, that though the Militia ordinance and the Nineteen Propositions of 1642 were the *"occasion"* of war, it was the lack of trust in the king that grew out of the religious perception of the Parliament which was its real *cause*.[61] Conrad Russell suggests that political instability in the seventeenth-century British Isles arose because of three distinct religious viewpoints, which British kings had to balance in their tripartite rule. Royal Supremacy governed the English and Irish churches' convocations and bishops, whereas in Scotland the concept of Royal Supremacy was foreign to a system which saw the Kirk as autonomous. While in England the approval of Parliament was needed to make religious decisions lawful, a Scottish General Assembly could make such judgements without recourse to Parliament.[62] Undoubtedly, an ecclesiastical decision which challenged the theological predilections of the king would emphasise the Scottish Kirk's claim to autonomy.

Arminianism was the theological linchpin which secured the wheel of revolution in the three Kingdoms. Nicholas Tyacke has written a compelling thesis that religion, specifically Arminianism, indeed played a major role in the outbreak of civil war in England.[63] An Arminianism that had been nascent in James and the Jacobean church came to fruition in his successor Charles I.[64]

Arminianism had also exercised successive English Parliaments. This was especially so in the inquiry into the anti-Calvinist writings of Richard Montagu (1577-1641)[65] dating from 1624, when John Pym (1583-1643)[66] had charged that Montagu's *"A Gagg for the New Gospell?"* taught Arminianism contrary to the affirmations of the Synod of Dort. By January

---

[60] Milton, *Catholic and Reformed*, 546.

[61] Morrill, *The Nature of the English Revolution*, 60.

[62] Conrad Russell, *The Fall of the British Monarchies, 1637-1642* (Oxford: Clarendon Press, 1991), 28-29.

[63] Tyacke, *Anti-Calvinists, The Rise of English Arminianism c. 1590-1640*.

[64] Tyacke, *Anti-Calvinists, The Rise of English Arminianism c. 1590-1640*, 106.

[65] William Hutton, "Richard Montagu", *DNB*, vol.1, 1402-1403.

[66] For an introduction to the life of Pym, see Sidney Reed Brett, *John Pym, 1583-1643. The Statesman of the Puritan Revolution* (London: John Murray, 1940).

26, 1629, Arminianism, according to Francis Rous (1579-1659),[67] had become a "Trojan horse" in England and was comparable to the threat of the Spanish Armada of 1588 and the Gunpowder Plot of 1605.[68] Between the dissolution of the Parliament of 1626 and the calling of the 1628 Parliament, Tyacke comments that "Arminianism [was] established as the highway to ecclesiastical preferment", a direct consequence of a proclamation issued by Charles in 1626.[69]

Parliament lost its initiative in pursuing concerns over the influence of Arminians when Charles forcibly closed the Commons in March 1629, heralding his eleven-year Personal Rule.[70] Because Arminians not only rejected aspects of Calvinism, but were also promoters of novel ceremonies and laid a greater stress on the sacraments, the polarisation of the church as perhaps inevitable.[71] Moreover, a correlation seemed to exist between Arminian sympathies and a more relaxed attitude to the Lord's Day. The *Book of Sports* was reissued in 1633 and imposed upon the church;[72] and private confession to a minister became increasingly common. By 1640 there were many disaffected clergy who were appalled at the Laudian/Caroline novelties. These ministers, unsurprisingly, included future Westminster divines like Stephen Marshall,[73] who in a sermon before

---

[67] James Rigg, "Francis Rous", *DNB*, vol.2, 1816.

[68] *Commons Debates for 1629*, W. Notestein and F. H. Relf (eds.) (Minneapolis: 1921), 12-13. Cited in Tyacke, *Anti-Calvinists, The Rise of English Arminianism c. 1590-1640*, 135.

[69] Tyacke, *Anti-Calvinists, The Rise of English Arminianism c. 1590-1640*, 157. On the proclamation, Tyacke cites J.P. Kenyon (ed.), *The Stuart Constitution 1603-1688* (Cambridge: Cambridge University Press, 1966), 154-55.

[70] Tyacke, *Anti-Calvinists, The Rise of English Arminianism c. 1590-1640*, 161-63.

[71] Tyacke, *Anti-Calvinists, The Rise of English Arminianism c. 1590-1640*, 199-201. An example of an innovation in worship was the transformation of the furniture of the church in the 1630s, when communion tables were converted into altars and permanently railed in the east of the chancel. The impetus for these changes came from Charles himself, although Laud also approved of such measures.

[72] The *Book of Sports* had been issued in 1617 and 1633 with royal approval, but was spurned by the Puritans as the "Morris Book". The *Book* sanctioned Whitsun Ales, May Day and other festival days which the Reformers had rejected as "popish". It also legitimated the "sports" such as dancing that were associated with those days. The Puritan Parliament ordered the burning of the *Book* by the public hangman on 5 May 1643. See Newman, *Companion to the English Civil Wars*, 14-15

[73] Marshall (1594-1665) was born at Godmanchester, Huntingdonshire, educated at Cambridge, and began his ministry at Wethersfield, Essex. He was one of the authors of *Smectymnuus*, a Presbyterian diatribe against Episcopacy, so titled after the first letters of its authors' names. Maintaining his Presbyterian views to the end, Marshall died in 1655 and was interred until the Restoration, when in 1661 his remains were exhumed by royal warrant and cast into a pit in St. Margaret's churchyard. The letters of Smectymnuus were the initials of the divines as follows. SM stands for Stephen

the Long Parliament in November 1940 highlighted five departures from orthodoxy now common in the English church. These were, respectively, doctrinal apostasy, Sabbath desecration, the suppression of preaching, superstitious and idolatrous worship, and indiscriminate admission to the Lord's Table.[74] However, were it not for the Scots, Marshall would not have been preaching that sermon before a Parliament, nor would he have played, together with his Scottish colleagues, such a pivotal role as a representative Presbyterian in a Westminster Assembly.

Before Scottish Presbyterianism could be exported to England, the English first had to export Laud's Arminianism to their northern neighbours. The Scots had long been aware of the influence of Arminianism in England, for as early as 1627 William Leslie had published an anti-Arminian treatise, *Vindiciae Theoligicae*.[75] Moreover, Arminianism was infiltrating Scotland, illustrated by Samuel Rutherford's banishment from Anwoth in 1636 following his publication of an anti-Arminian tract.[76] It was, however, the bold plan to impose a new discipline upon the Scottish Kirk (and which was first read publicly on July 23, 1637) that was to become the catalyst of the Scottish revolt. The new Prayer Book, a Scottish version of the English Book of Common Prayer, was one that was bound to

---

Marshall; EC for Edmund Calamy; TY for Thomas Young; MN for Matthew Newcomen; and W (UU) S for William Spurstowe. Barker, *Puritan Profiles*, 120-27; James Reid, *Memoirs of the Westminster Divines* (Edinburgh: Banner of Truth, 1982), vol. 2, 72-84. For a thorough discussion on Presbyterianism and the Assembly see J.R. de Witt, *Jus Divinum: The Westminster Assembly and the Divine Right of Church Government* (Kampen: J. H. Kok, 1969)

[74] Tyacke, *Anti-Calvinists, The Rise of English Arminianism c. 1590-1640*, 216-25. Stephen Marshall, *A Sermon Preached[...]November 17.1640, upon 2 Chron. 15.2* (London: Samuel Man, 1641), 32-35.

[75] William Leslie, *Vindiciae Theoligicae pro Perseverantia Sanctorum in Gratia Salvifica* (Aberdeen: E. Rabanus, 1627).

[76] Samuel Rutherford, *Exercitationes apologeticae pro divina gratia, in quibus vindicatur doctrina orthodoxa adversus Jacobum Arminium & Jesuitas* (Amsterdam: 1636). Cited in Tyacke, *Anti-Calvinists, The Rise of English Arminianism c. 1590-1640*, 232. Rutherford (1600-1661) was appointed to the Chair of Divinity at St. Mary's College, St. Andrews, in 1638 and served there until his death, apart from his four years in attendance at the Westminster Assembly. He was born in Nisbet and received his M.A. from Edinburgh University in 1621. He laboured in the ministry at Anwoth for nine years before being deprived of his office in 1636. See William Barker, *Puritan Profiles, 54 Personalities Drawn Together by the Westminster Assembly* (Fearn: Christian Focus Publications, 1996), 101-106. For an overview of Rutherford's importance to Scottish ecclesiastical history, see Sherman Isbell, "Samuel Rutherford", *DSCHT*, 735. For a recent biographical treatment and an analysis of Rutherford's thought, see John Coffey, *Politics, Religion and the British Revolutions: The Mind of Samuel Rutherford* (Cambridge: Cambridge University Press, 1997), especially 172-73 for Rutherford's view of the harmony of natural law with Scripture.

provoke a head-on clash between Arminianism and Calvinism and between Episcopacy and Presbyterianism, for the Scots considered that the Prayer book (also known as "Laud's liturgy") brought into close association Arminianism, the innovation of ceremonies and high sacramentalism.[77]

This incendiary situation was bound to explode. What had provoked Charles I to effectively tell the Scots to reject their own Reformation heritage? Various scholars have described Charles as impatient,[78] weak and inept,[79] insane or brainwashed.[80] To these failings, we can add Conrad Russell's assessment that Charles was "disgusted" by the less-structured worship practices of the Scots (for example, a lack of set prayers).[81] The king's lack of consultation with the Scots was a crucial error,[82] and Charles viewed any dissent towards his will as a personal attack upon his lawful authority.[83]

While Charles's character flaws no doubt contributed to his problems, the causes of the troubles were more complex. Morrill concludes that James had not sought a union of the English and Scottish churches, but merely desired to upgrade the Kirk's status and thus make the two churches more congruous. In this sense, Charles was continuing his father's desire for congruity. His concern was for order, not to anglicise the Scottish church.[84] But when Charles and Laud endeavoured to impose their new liturgy upon the Scots in 1637, the riot that followed the initial reading at St Giles in Edinburgh was the match that ignited a flame of ecclesiastical revolution in Scotland, which was to result in the restoration of Presbyterianism, two Bishops' Wars, the English Civil War, the Westminster Assembly, and ultimately the regicide of January 30, 1649 in London.[85]

---

[77] Tyacke, *Anti-Calvinists, The Rise of English Arminianism c. 1590-1640*, 234. For example, the new Prayer Book called baptised children regenerate, and added new ceremony to the rite.

[78] Burgess, *The Politics of the Ancient Constitution*, 200-201.

[79] John Kenyon, *Stuart England* (Harmondsworth: Penguin, 1985), 54-55.

[80] Morrill, *The Nature of the English Revolution*, 61-62.

[81] Russell, *The Fall of the British Monarchies*, 44.

[82] Russell, *The Fall of the British Monarchies*, 46.

[83] Russell, *The Fall of the British Monarchies*, 51.

[84] John Morrill, "The National Covenant in its British Context", John Morrill (ed.), *The Scottish National Covenant in its British Context* (Edinburgh: Edinburgh University Press, 1990), 1-30, at 8-11.

[85] Westminster divine, John Langely, minister of West-Tuderly, Southampton, ascribes the cause of England's political situation to this Edinburgh event. "who would ever have thought the throwing of a stool in the Church, out of indignation by a godly woman, a zealot, at the first broaching of the *English* Masse at *Edenbourough* [...]should have so mightily shaken the Popes chair". John Langely, *Gemitus Columbae: The Mournfull Note of the Dove* (London: Philemon Stephens, 1644), 28. Apart from his appointment to the Assembly and the place of his ministry, little more is known about

Scottish Privy Counsellors were as infuriated over the way the Prayer Book or service book was imposed as were the laity and most ministers. Between the public reading of the service book on 23 July 1637 and the subscribing of the *National Covenant*[86] on 28 February, 1638, there were attempts made to resolve the impasse by the Scots. The king, however, proved intractable.[87]

The *National Covenant* was a key component of Scottish resistance against the king's attempts to impose "Laud's liturgy". It had been co-authored by Alexander Henderson[88] and Archibald Johnston (Lord Warriston).[89] Both were later to become commissioners in the Westminster Assembly. This covenantal pact included the King's Confession of 1581, material added by Henderson, and an oath. It acclaimed Presbyterian government and the Reformed faith, but also required submission to the

---

Langley. See Reid, *Memoirs of the Westminster Divines*, vol. 2, 49. On the lady who threw the stool and started the riot, see David Calhoun, "Jenny Geddes", *DSCHT*, 352-53. See Russell, *The Fall of the British Monarchies*, 37-39, for the contrast between James and Charles in their application of the royal absolute prerogative and for Charles's view of the Royal Supremacy.

[86] For an analysis of the National Covenant, see Morrill, "The National Covenant in its British Context", 1-30. For the influence of the Covenanters on Scottish politics, see John Young, *The Scottish Parliament 1639-1661* (Edinburgh: John Donald, 1996).

[87] Russell, *The Fall of the British Monarchies*, 49-52.

[88] Henderson (1583-1646), who was already sixty at the time of the Assembly and who died before its adjournment, was not only the main drafter of the 1638 *National Covenant* but also of the *Solemn League and Covenant* itself. Converted under the preaching of the famous Robert Bruce in 1615 or 1616, Henderson, a quiet, grave and mild-mannered man, was highly esteemed by the Assembly, as their choice of him as preacher on the day of the subscription to the *Solemn League and Covenant* illustrates. He also played a major part in Assembly deliberations, being the acknowledged leader of the Scottish contingent. For biographical details, see Barker, *Puritan Portraits*, 96-101. For the influence of the Covenanters on Scottish politics, see John Young, *The Scottish Parliament 1639-1661* (Edinburgh: John Donald, 1996). On the 1640-41 Scottish constitutional settlement, as a pattern for the English Long Parliament, see 19-47.

[89] William Morison, *Johnston of Warriston* (London: Oliphant Anderson and Ferrier, 1901), 154. See also 93-103 for his time at the Westminster Assembly. The son of an Edinburgh merchant, Johnston was educated at the University of Glasgow. He took a leading part in drawing up the 1638 National Covenant with Alexander Henderson, and as an elder in the Church of Scotland was appointed a commissioner to the Assembly. Although he opposed the execution of Charles I, Johnston later accepted an appointment from Oliver Cromwell. Forced to flee to Europe following the Restoration, he was extradited to England from France, and was executed at Mercat Cross in Edinburgh within view of his own house. For more recent biographical information, see William Barker, *Puritan Profiles, 54 Personalities Drawn Together by the Westminster Assembly* (Fearn: Christian Focus, 1996), 112-14.

king, with the proviso that the people could resist the king himself if he did not live and rule according to the terms of the covenant. The *National Covenant*, in Russell's words, "told Charles, in barely veiled terms, that if he wanted to enforce the service book, he would have to fight for it".[90]

Condemning Arminianism and "popish" innovations in worship, the *National Covenant* also made explicit that changes in religion could only come about with the agreement of the General Assembly and Scottish Parliament. The Covenanters pledged loyalty to the monarch, but it was plainly a conditional loyalty. While Robert Baillie had been able to amend the *Covenant* so that Episcopacy was not condemned, in the next ten months the Covenanters had hardened their attitude to Episcopacy and asserted the necessity of Presbyterian church government. Charles rightly perceived that in rejecting bishops, the Scots were rejecting his own authority to dictate changes to the church.[91]

Realising that the king was intent on invading with an English army, the Scots began to gather a force of locals and expatriate mercenaries to resist him. The Covenanters, who felt a natural empathy with the godly in England, sought to enlist their support. A 1639 publication *An Information to All Good Christians within the Kingdome of England,* exemplified this.[92] This pamphlet and many others were circulated in England. *An Information* expressed the ideas that England and Scotland suffered a common disease of Arminianism and popery; that the enemy was seeking to bring England into conformity with Rome; and that England would benefit if she came to the aid of the Scots.[93] For their part the English also encouraged the Scots through personal contacts.[94]

Charles saw the demands of the *Covenant* as an affront to his honour, and with his control over the castles of Edinburgh and the port city of Dumbarton, the loyalty of some Scots, and the control of the navy, Charles considered himself well-resourced to tackle the recalcitrant northern Presbyterians. However, inexperienced in war himself, lacking necessary finance and with conflict in his own command structure, Charles and his

---

[90] Russell, *The Fall of the British Monarchies*, 53.

[91] Russell, *The Fall of the British Monarchies*, 53.

[92] Church of Scotland General Assembly, *An information to all good Christians within the kingdome of England, from the noblemen, barrons, borrows, ministers, and commons of the kingdome of Scotland, for vindicating their intentions and actions from the unjust callumnies of their enemies* (Edinburgh: Printed by James Bryson, 1639).

[93] Russell, *The Fall of the British Monarchies*, 60-68.

[94] Peter Donald, "The Scottish National Covenant and British Politics, 1638-1640", Morrill (ed.), *The Scottish National Covenant in its British Context*, 90-105, at 97-99.

forces were unable to withstand the Covenanters, who took the initiative and stormed Inverness in February 1639.[95]

Conrad Russell outlines the course of events that were to follow. The king's army and the Scottish army decided to negotiate rather than fight one another and met on 11 June 1639 at Berwick, thus ending the First Bishops' War. In the negotiations, Henderson asserted that the church had a *jure divino* authority which did not require the assent of civil lawmakers. Plainly the king's view that he ruled the church effectively through appointed bishops, and Henderson's view that the church ruled in its own sphere by divine right, were irreconcilable positions. Though further negotiations ensued, they were to prove fruitless.[96]

John Morrill has argued that at first the *National Covenant* was not intended to be meaningful outside Scotland: "the Scots had not yet seen their problem fully in British terms. A National Covenant, a bonding together of the Scottish nation, was an effective way of dealing with a Scottish king, but not with a king of Britain".[97] The Scottish insular viewpoint had changed by 1640 when the Scots sought to export the *National Covenant* in a desire to promote a Presbyterian ecclesiology in the English church, because they believed that the Scottish Kirk would not be secure "as long as prelacy prospered in England or Ireland; and no security for the constitutional guarantees exacted in 1639 unless the king was bound by similar restraints in those other kingdoms".[98]

Charles, still intent on using military force against the Scots, was forced to recall the English Parliament (the Short Parliament). Writs went out in March 1640, and by 13 April Parliament met ostensibly to raise subsidies to finance a second campaign against the covenanting Scots and ratify the "tunnage and poundage" backdated to 1625 which, like the controversial Shipmoney in the mid 1630s, required Parliament's endorsement. Led by John Pym, the Short Parliament used its appointment to highlight various grievances, until its dissolution by the Stuart king. Although the convocation of clergy should have ceased at the time of the dissolution of Parliament, Charles kept it in session to draw up canons to justify the ceremonial innovations by claiming their great antiquity. While there was clerical opposition to the canons or decrees (which became known as the *Etcetera oath*) the participants in the convocation itself, all subscribed. This

---

[95] John Kenyon with Jane Ohlmeyer, "The Background to the Civil War in the Stuart Kingdoms", John Kenyon and Jane Ohlmeyer (eds.) *The Civil Wars, A Military History* (Oxford: Oxford University Press, 1998), 3-40, at 16-22.

[96] Russell, *The Fall of the British Monarchies*, 63-68.

[97] Morrill, "The National Covenant in its British Context", Morrill (ed.), *The Scottish National Covenant in its British Context*, 13-14.

[98] Morrill, "The National Covenant in its British Context", Morrill (ed.), *The Scottish National Covenant in its British Context*, 15-16.

most likely had the effect of showing Laudian opponents outside the convocation that the Calvinist remnant in the church establishment hierarchy had crumbled, if not apostatised.[99]

Meanwhile, Charles's fiscal problems remained. Laud told the King that based on the teaching of Scripture he could raise the money without Parliament. Strafford[100] proposed that an Irish army could be used to defeat the Scots. However, rumours developed that the Irish army was meant for England and not Scotland. A shortage of equipment also meant that the plan could not be put into effect. Neither was Charles able to secure help from Spain. He was left with only the limited resources of England. Here too his endeavour to raise money met with stern refusals when many of the gentry opposed the war.[101] The strong undercurrent of pro-Scottish feeling added to the king's woes and he retained an unpaid and poorly armed military force made up of men who had theological concerns. These factors together explain the mutiny and desertions that took place.[102]

The Scots, using the English naval blockade as a pretext, decided to take pre-emptive action and invade England rather than remain on the border as they had done in the First Bishops' War. It was not a good omen that Newburn, the place the English chose to make their stand, was also difficult if not impossible to defend. Russell concludes:

> Newburn determined, first, that Scotland would not be Anglicized in religion: the Covenant, and the cause it represented, were there to stay. From this followed that any ultimate Act of Union could not be simply on terms of perfect union, but would have to allow for some form of unity in diversity.[103]

---

[99] Tyacke, *Anti-Calvinists, The Rise of English Arminianism c. 1590-1640*, 233-41. Conrad Russell observes that what provoked these canons was the king's dismay that many were opposing the ceremonies of the church. The first canon extolled the divine right of kings, and that the law of God, along with the laws of the nation and nature, sanctioned taxation. A canon against sectaries, condemning those who would not attend the service and sermons of the established church signalled persecution. Such an outcome may well have seemed more likely with the decision to condemn all books opposed to the English liturgy and ecclesiology. An oath, the infamous *Etcetera* Oath was also imposed, which required agreement with the doctrine and discipline of the English church adding that it embodied everything necessary for salvation. This implied that church ceremonies were necessary for salvation. Russell, *The Fall of the British Monarchies*, 136-38.

[100] Samuel Gardiner, "Sir Thomas Wentworth", *DNB*, vol. 2, 2230-231.

[101] Russell, *The Fall of the British Monarchies*, 125-34.

[102] Russell, *The Fall of the British Monarchies*, 141.

[103] Russell, *The Fall of the British Monarchies*, 143-45.

Ominously, in their victory, the Scots handed the English "an alternative political model and an alternative power-base.[...] No longer was the King the sole effective source of power".[104]

Charles was compelled to call another Parliament (the Long Parliament) to deal with the Scottish trouble; but once again, instead of approving the taxation he needed, the Commons quickly began discussing the now infamous canons. Tyacke observes that the terms "Arminianism and Popery were now used interchangeably and had secular as well as religious connotations – signifying absolutism in addition to heresy and idolatry".[105] Several petitions were presented to the parliamentary "Grand Committee of Religion" and grievances were recorded and reported to the House of Commons. The House of Lords also established a committee to consider innovation in religion. Composed of many who subsequently became members of the Westminster Assembly, the committee concluded that Tridentine doctrine[106] had been preached and sanctioned, and that Arminian and Socinian[107] errors had been tolerated. The same committee also exposed different ceremonies, rituals and impositions on extemporary prayer in church services. Furthermore, it reviewed the Book of Common Prayer in a bid to decide, among other things, whether legendary saints should be removed from the calendar and readings from the apocryphal books should be deleted.[108] In spite of its findings, the committee failed to recommend action and was disbanded in May.

To compound matters for Charles, the new Parliament was dominated by "Puritans". The definition of the label "Puritan" has a copious literature, and there is no consensus as to its precise meaning.[109] While the term is

---

[104] Russell, *The Fall of the British Monarchies*, 145.

[105] Tyacke, *Anti-Calvinists, The Rise of English Arminianism c. 1590-1640*, 243.

[106] "Tridentine doctrine" refers to the teaching of the Council of Trent (1545-1563), which met in Trento, Italy. This counter-Reformation council opposed the new Protestantism and sought to define the Catholic position more carefully. On Councils generally, see Heinrich Denzinger, *The Sources of Catholic Dogma*, Roy J. Deferrari (trans.) (St. Louis: Herder, 1957), especially 243-302 on Trent; Gerald Bray, "Councils", *NDT*, 172-73, for a brief summary of important church councils including Trent.

[107] Socinianism, named after the Italian leaders Fausto Sozini (or Sozzini) (Latin: Socinus) (1539-1604) and his uncle Lelio Sozini (1525-62), expressed a rationalistic theology. Although not denying revelation the Socinians downplayed it. Instead, they elevated the ability as well as the necessity of human reason in arriving at theological truth. Socinianism's most controversial tenet was its denial of the doctrine of the Trinity.

[108] Mitchell, *The Westminster Assembly: Its History and Standards*, 96-99.

[109] See Patrick Collinson, *English Puritanism* (London: The Historical Association, 1987), 7, 43. The term evolved in a series of religious conflicts within the Reformed Church of England. See also, John Harris, *The Puritanes Impurity: Or the Anatomie of a Puritane or Seperatist, by Name and Profession, Wherein is Declared the Differences*

problematic, it makes sense to use it as the Scottish commissioner to the Assembly, George Gillespie, did. Gillespie's acknowledged brilliance in debate was evident in his trenchant 1637 *Dispute against the English Popish Ceremonies*. Opposing Episcopalians, Gillespie says:

> they make godly and zealous Christians to be mocked and nick-named Puritans, except they can swallow the camel of conformity[...]we shrink not to be reproached for the cause of Christ. We know the old Waldenses before us, were also named by their adversaries, Catheres or Puritans[...]. But we are most sorry that such as are walking humbly with their God, seeking eagerly after the means of grace and salvation, and making good conscience of all their ways, should be made odious, and that piety, humility, repentance, zeal, conscience, &c., should be mocked, and all by occasion of the ceremonies.[110]

While the term "Puritan" was often used pejoratively, those Protestants who saw themselves as the despised Puritans owned the label, at least in principle, as a badge of honour.

The Long Parliament now found the language of the common law inadequate to deal with domestic issues because, as we have discussed, the king had intervened with his royal prerogative. Since the law could no longer be relied upon to preserve the liberties of Englishmen, the Parliament introduced new ways of discourse. The Parliament would now enact laws on its own initiative without reference to the king, signalling the death knell of the Jacobean consensus.[111] To avoid the fate of its predecessor, the Long Parliament took assiduous measures to ensure its own independence. Herbert Palmer illustrates how important religious leaders saw this step.[112] Palmer had seen special providential significance in

---

betwixt the True Protestant and a Puritane Made Manifest by the Sincerity of the One and Hypocrisie of the Other (London: printed by T. Fawcet, 1641): See 5-6 for a negative assessment and caricature of Puritans as hypocrites; Richard Heyricke (a Westminster divine), *Three Sermons Preached at the Collegiate Church in Manchester* (London: L. Fawne, 1641), Epistle dedicatory: "*My humble motion is, make us all* Puritans, *or to leave no* Puritan *amongst us*". Heyricke (1600-1667), educated at Oxford, became pastor of a church in Norfolk and was also appointed warden of Christ's College in Manchester. He was a faithful attender of the Assembly but was later implicated in a plot to raise money to enable Charles II to return to England. For biographical information on Heyricke see Reid, *Memoirs of the Westminster Divines*, vol. 2, 30-32.

[110] Gillespie, "A Dispute Against the English Popish Ceremonies", *The Works of George Gillespie*, vol. 1, 39. For the influence of the Civil war on the Puritans, see John Morrill, "The Impact of Puritanism", John Morrill (ed), *The Impact of the English Civil War* (London: Collins and Brown, 1991), 50-66.

[111] Burgess, *The Politics of the Ancient Constitution*, 224-30.

[112] Palmer (1601-1647) who replaced John White as assessor in September 1646 was born in Wingham, Kent, educated at Cambridge and appointed to St. Alphages's, Canterbury, in 1626. He later became a Presbyterian, was highly esteemed by his

the passing of the Act of Continuance: it was "(an Act of such wonder, as we can scarce beleeve our *senses*, our *experience*, our *understandings*, that it is *credible* or *possible*)".[113] If it had not been noticed before, this was plain evidence that Parliament had begun to wrestle the church from the hands of Laud and the king, asserting Parliament's duty and privilege to defend the true Reformed faith as the doctrine of the Church of England. The supremacy of the monarch was giving way to the supremacy of Parliament.[114]

A covenantal bond was forged between the two Houses of Parliament, according to which each member vowed to "maintain and defend, as far as lawfully I may, with my life, power, and estate, the true Reformed Protestant Religion, expressed in the doctrine of the Church of England, against all Popery and Popish innovation within this realm, contrary to the said doctrine".[115] Even though Charles signed laws which revoked the Court of High Commission and the Star Chamber,[116] he was implicated in plots against covenanting leaders in Scotland.[117] The Irish massacres further ensured increasing alienation between Parliament and people from the King's party.[118] By mid-1642, dark clouds of rebellion were gathering, civil war was imminent, and Parliament, needing the support of the Scots, wrote to the General Assembly of the Church of Scotland, expressing its wish to avoid a civil conflagration, to advance the reform of Church and State, and to "stirre up that Nation to send some Competent forces in aide of this Parliament and Kingdome, against the many Armies of the Popish and Prelaticall party".[119] The Scots' answer was to affirm a need for unity of faith through the vehicles of a common confession of faith, directory of worship, catechism and form of church government.[120] The Scottish

---

Westminster colleagues, and was also a major contributor to the Westminster catechisms. Barker, *Puritan Profiles*, 31-35.

[113] Herbert Palmer, *The Necessity and Encouragement of Utmost Venturing for the Churches Help: Together with the Sin, Folly, and Mischief of Self-Idolising* (London: John Bellamie, 1643), 67.

[114] Tyacke, *Anti-Calvinists, The Rise of English Arminianism c. 1590-1640*, 243-44.

[115] William Hetherington, *History of the Westminster Assembly* (Edinburgh: James Gemmell, 1890), 77.

[116] Hetherington, *History of the Westminster Assembly*, 78.

[117] Hetherington, *History of the Westminster Assembly*, 79.

[118] Hetherington, *History of the Westminster Assembly*, 80.

[119] See *A Declaration of the Lords and Commons in the Parliament of England, to the Generall Assembly of the Church of Scotland* (London: 1643)[no further publishing details given], 9.

[120] Hetherington, *History of the Westminster Assembly*, 84. See *A Declaration of the Lords and Commons in the Parliament of England, to the Generall Assembly of the Church of Scotland*; and the Scots' answer, *The Generall Assemblies Answer and*

Assembly also urged a "neere league and solemne Covenant for the maintenance of the truely reformed Protestant Religion" to unite the two churches and kingdoms.[121] *The Solemn League and Covenant*, which became the bedrock of the bond of union, was produced in draft form by 17 August 1643, some ten days after the arrival of Philip Nye, Henry Vane and Stephen Marshall, the visiting English commissioners. Probably composed chiefly by Alexander Henderson, it sought the reformation of church discipline, worship and government in the three kingdoms of England, Scotland and Ireland in conformity with the pattern of "the best reformed Churches" and, as we have noted,[122] "according to the Word of God" – the latter phrase added at the insistence of the English.[123] It would be a mistake to see English agreement to such a protocol as cynical pragmatism. Hetherington gives a balanced summary of the probity of the two parties in forming their alliance:

> England wished for a *civil league* with Scotland for the preservation of their mutual civil liberties, but was willing that it should have also a *religious* aspect and influence. Scotland desired a *religious covenant* for the preservation of their mutual religious liberties, but was willing that it should have also a *civil* aspect and influence.[124]

Charles's fate was sealed and a short-lived Puritan dominance in both church and government in England had begun.

Overall, the Westminster Assembly and the *Solemn League* alike were instruments for reformation which arose out of religious concerns in European, English and British contexts. Potent factors behind the establishment of the Assembly were the influences from Europe, especially the fear of Counter-Reformation forces, though in England and Scotland it was partly an apprehension of a Protestant Counter-Reformation. Not only, as we have noted,[125] did the Westminster Assembly see itself having an influence beyond the shores of the three kingdoms: it was also a key

---

Declaration to the Parliament of England (Edinburgh: 1643) [No further publishing details are available for these two documents], 12.

[121] *The Generall Assemblies Answer*, 12-13.

[122] See 19 above.

[123] *A Solemne League and Covenant* (London: Edw. Husbands, 1643).

[124] Hetherington, *History of the Westminster Assembly*, 99. But, as Paul points out, citing Richard Baxter, there were both religious and secular thinkers in the English Parliament. The latter agreed with the former, even though the concern of the latter was initially more over the imposition of arbitrary government than the reform of a corrupt church. Paul, *The Assembly of The Lord*, 53-54. See Richard Baxter, *Reliquiae Baxterianae: or, Mr. Richard Baxter's Narrative of the Most Memorable Passages of His Life and Times. Faithfully Publish'd from His Own Original Manuscript by Matthew Sylvester* (London: printed for T. Parkhurst, J. Robinson, J. Lawrence, and J. Dunton, 1696), I i, 18 (§27).

[125] See 19 above.

element in "the first serious efforts to create genuinely British institutions".[126] Rumours of a Popish plot played their part in agitations for change in the three kingdoms. At the heart of the seventeenth-century British conflicts stands the ambiguous figure of Charles I, together with William Laud, who had attempted to change the rules of discourse which had held together the Jacobean consensus of the bases for political debate. The Laudian zeal would ultimately be eclipsed by both English and Scottish Calvinists who became increasingly fearful that Calvinistic orthodoxy in the three kingdoms would be overturned. The Assembly was an attempt to make sure that this unthinkable result would never take place. In order to secure a thorough reformation, the Assembly would insist in its doctrinal conclusions that:

> The supreme judge by which all controversies of religion are to be determined, and all decrees of councils, opinions of ancient writers, doctrines of men, and private spirits, are to be examined; and in whose sentence we are to rest; can be no other but the Holy Spirit speaking in the Scripture.[127]

The Assembly's theology cannot be understood in detachment from a very specific set of political and cultural circumstances.

Although we have considered the role of religion in general terms, we must also consider in more detail the role played by reflection on eschatology during these years of crisis in particular.

1.2.4 Eschatological Fervour and the Interest in Prophecy

The Assembly was appointed at a time of great eschatological fervour,[128] for there was a belief widely held among Puritans that the world was entering its final phase and that certain chapters of the book of Revelation held a specific relevance for their own day. Puritan politics cannot be divorced from a deep interest in eschatology.[129]

---

[126] Arthur Williamson, "Patterns of British identity: 'Britain' and its Rivals in the Sixteenth and Seventeenth Centuries", Glenn Burgess (ed.), *The New British History. Founding a Modern State 1603-1715* (London: I.B.Tauris, 1999), 138-73, at 147-48.

[127] *WCF* 1:10.

[128] Samuel Logan, "The Context and Work of the Assembly", John Carson and David Hall (eds.), *To Glorify and Enjoy God* (Edinburgh: Banner of Truth, 1994), 32. The divines, as Samuel Logan puts it, "were called upon to create a model of theological stability and certainty in the context of considerable political and theological chaos".

[129] For a summary of the importance of eschatology in the thought of the Westminster divines, see John F. Wilson, *Pulpit in Parliament: Puritanism during the English Civil Wars 1640-1648* (Princeton: Princeton University Press, 1969), 193-94, 198-235.

Recent scholarship has concluded that John Foxe's *Acts and Monuments*, also known as Foxe's *Book of Martyrs*, had a defining role in the Puritans' perspective on history. Foxe had looked forward to the defeat of the papacy and of Islam, which he believed would be followed by a period of universal peace,[130] and he had promoted the idea that England was an elect nation, specially favoured as God worked out his purposes.[131] William Haller summarises Foxe's claims thus:

> All history[...]centred in the agelong struggle of Christ and Antichrist; the Pope was Antichrist; and England, the elect champion of the true faith, was his chosen enemy especially called by God to be the agent of his predestined overthrow.[132]

Even though, by the seventeenth century, *The Acts and Monuments* "had become detached from its established context and recruited to the Puritan and parliamentary cause[...]",[133] the Puritan appropriation of Foxe continued to underscore the reality that the "long tradition among the Puritans of interpreting all political events in an apocalyptic or millenarian sense", was not forgotten.[134] Since the Puritans' own day was believed to be of equal significance to the history already catalogued by Foxe,

---

[130] Bernard Capp, *The Fifth Monarchy Men. A Study in Seventeenth-Century English Millenarianism* (London: Faber and Faber, 1972), 25.

[131] William Haller, *Foxe's Book of Martyrs and the Elect Nation* (London: J. Cape, 1963), especially 224-50. But, see Crawford Gribben, *The Puritan Millennium: Literature and Theology, 1550-1682* (Dublin: Four Courts Press, 2000), 62-64 for the debate about whether Foxe was preoccupied with the "elect nation" concept over against Protestant internationalism. For a rejection of the "elect nation" perspective in Foxe, see David Loewenstein, *Milton and the Drama of History: Historical Vision, Iconoclasm and the Literary Imagination* (Cambridge: Cambridge University Press, 1993), 10.

[132] William Haller, *Liberty and Reformation in the Puritan Revolution* (New York: Columbia University Press, 1967), 19. See also Paul Kenneth Christianson, "English Protestant Apocalyptic Visions c. 1536-1642" (unpublished PhD thesis, University of Minnesota, 1971), especially 61-80 for John Foxe's eschatology.

[133] David Loades (ed.), *John Foxe and the English Reformation* (Aldershot: Scolar Press, 1997), 7. Loades explains that the first edition of 1554 was intended to give historical justification for the Reformation (1-2). See also Andrew Penny, "John Foxe, the Acts and Monuments and the Development of Prophetic Interpretation", David Loades (ed.), *John Foxe and the English Reformation*, 252-77, for a discussion of Foxe's eschatology; especially 256 for the way Foxe vacillated between the Papacy and Islam as candidates for the antichrist.

[134] Capp, *The Fifth Monarchy Men*, 35. See also Haller, *Foxe's Book of Martyrs and the Elect Nation*, 14, who observes that Foxe's book became "an expression of the national faith[...]and[...]an unanswerable defence of England's ideological position in the contemporary struggle for national independence and power".

Socio-Political and Religious Context

Westminster divine[135] Stephen Marshall urged Parliament to make a record of contemporary events as Foxe had done.[136] Puritan preachers constantly compared England with Israel or Judah. Thus, as Henry Scudder (d.1659?), for example,[137] warned, England was comparable to Judah in her sin, and could expect God's wrath in a similar manner to the ancient Israelite nations.[138] England not only had the privileges granted a covenanted nation, but also its responsibilities.

Another Westminster divine, Peter Sterry (d. 1672), preaching before Parliament in 1651, confidently called upon the conclusions of a certain "gentleman of understanding" that in the prophecy of Isa. 24:13-16: "*The place, said he, on which this Prophesie is fixed by the constant Reception of the Rabbins, is this Ile of Great Brittain*".[139] One of Cromwell's chaplains, he was known at Cambridge as a Platonist and was considered by some to be "mystical and obscure", but his sermons were thought by others "excellent both in matter and style", and his prose was held to be comparable to John Milton's. He was a vociferous opponent of Presbyterianism, and willing to proclaim his opposition to Presbyterian views with great vigour.[140] Sterry's political and eschatological interests met in this sermon, for he was confident that political events suggested that Christ himself would soon return to England.[141]

---

[135] We will discuss how to assess the contribution of individual divines at 62-65 below.

[136] He urged "that you would provide that some worthy, faithfull heart, and heads, and pens bee set on work, who may undertake this Work, and have leave (as Mr. *Fox* had in Queen *Elizabeths dayes*.)[...]". Stephen Marshall, *A Sacred Record to be Made of Gods Mercies to Zion* (London: Stephen Bowtell, 1645), 35.

[137] Scudder, educated at Cambridge, became minister at Drayton in Oxfordshire. He was chosen for the Assembly in 1643 and was constant in his attendance at its sittings. He was esteemed by John Owen and Richard Baxter for his *Christians Daily Walk in Holy Security and Peace*, which ran to eleven editions by 1674. Reid, *Memoirs of the Westminster Divines*, vol. 2, 133-36. Henry Scudder, *The Christians Daily Walk in Holy Security and Peace* (London: Henry Cripps and Lodowick Lloyd, 1652).

[138] Henry Scudder, *Gods Warning to England by the Voyce of His ROD* (London: Philemon Stephens and Edward Blackmore, 1644), 3. A precedent for this kind of warning had already been entrenched in Puritan homiletical practice through John Foxe's labours. John Foxe, *Actes and Monuments of these Latter and Perilous Dayes, Touching Matters of the Church* [...] (London: R.B. Seeley and W. Burnside, 1839). See vol. 8, 600-47, where Foxe gives an extensive discussion of God's blessing that attended both the godly Queen Elizabeth and England, and of God's curse upon the persecuting Queen Mary and her subordinates.

[139] Peter Sterry, *England's Deliverance from the Northern Presbytery, Compared with its Deliverance from the Roman Papacy* (London: Peter Cole, 1652), 36.

[140] Born in Surrey and educated at Cambridge, Sterry was chosen Fellow of Emmanuel College in 1636. Reid, *Memoirs of the Westminster Divines*, vol. 2, 175-77.

[141] Sterry, *England's Deliverance from the Northern Presbytery*, 44-45.

National politics, therefore, were believed to be matters of profound cosmic and eternal importance. However, it is true that some Westminster divines were more cautious than Sterry in relating political events to an eschatological scheme. Anthony Burgess (or Burgesse) (c.1607-c.1663) was one.[142] Burgess acknowledges that "many sober Divines" think the day of judgement not far off, and look "for mighty alterations in the world". "But these", he says, "seem only conjectures".[143]

An eschatological signpost often cited by less cautious Puritans was that of the "two witnesses" of Rev. 11:3.[144] Joseph Caryl (1602?-1673), unlike Burgess, maintained that the prophetic timetable was a matter beyond conjecture in 1644 when he told Parliament: "I beleeve the providence of God is now about to open and give the unerring interpretation" of this

---

[142] Anthony Burgess (or Burgesse) (c.1607-c.1663), unrelated to the other Burgess (Cornelius) of the Assembly, was born to a schoolmaster in Watford, Hartfordshire. He was educated at Cambridge, where he also taught, and later became pastor at Sutton-Coldfield, Warwickshire from which he was ejected under the Act of Uniformity in 1662. His preaching and writing ministry was widely appreciated and, during his time at the Assembly, he frequently preached before Parliament. Reid, *Memoirs of the Westminster Divines*, vol. 1, 147-54. For the Act of Uniformity, see Charles Whiting, *Studies in English Puritanism from the Restoration to the Revolution, 1660-1688* (London: Frank Cass by arrangement with the Trustees of the Society for Promoting Christian Knowledge, 1968), 1-42.

[143] Anthony Burgess, *A Demonstration of the Day of Judgment, Against Atheists & Hereticks* (London: T. Underhill, 1657), 52-53.

[144] Herbert Palmer notes enthusiastically that if the witnesses had been killed as prophesied, their predicted resurrection symbolises a glorious English reformation for the near future. Palmer, *The Necessity and Encouragement of Utmost Venturing for the Churches Help: Together with the Sin, Folly, and Mischief of Self-Idolising*, 64. Also note the Westminster divine, William Reyner, in *Babylons Ruining-Earthquake and the Restauration of Zion* (London: Samuel Enderby, 1644), who was concerned with the misreading of the Revelation 11 prophecy: "A mistake concerning the two Witnesses, may peradventure make us looke for the earth-quake that shall ruine the Beast's Kingdome as a thing a farre off, when yet our selves may be in the middest of it" (40). William Reyner (d. 1666) was educated at Cambridge and was one of the Westminster divines in constant attendance at the Assembly. Minister of Eggham, Surrey for about forty-six years, Reyner was ejected under the Act of Uniformity and died in poverty. It seems that the one cited above was his only printed sermon. Reid, *Memoirs of the Westminster Divines*, vol. 2, 127-28. For a thorough discussion of the Revelation 11 prophecy, see Rodney Lawrence Petersen, "Preaching in the Last Days: The Use of the Theme of 'Two Witnesses,' as Found in Revelation 11:3-13, With Particular Attention to the Sixteenth and Early Seventeenth Centuries" (unpublished PhD thesis, Princeton Theological Seminary, 1985), especially 330-68 for John Foxe's exposition of the two witnesses.

prophecy.[145] Though one of the less prominent debaters at the Assembly, Caryl sided with the Independents, but the general respect given to him is illustrated by his appointment as Licenser of Books on Divinity.[146] Caryl lent the weight of his considerable reputation to the heightened eschatological aspirations in a sermon delivered on a day of thanksgiving for parliamentary military victories in April 1644:

> The actions of these times are now a making, and will shortly make a full exposition of this Scripture. I am sure the businesse of this day, will be as a Comment upon that of it, read unto you.[147]

Thomas Hill (1602-1653),[148] one of the seven daily preachers at Westminster Abbey during the sitting of the Assembly, was only stating what seemed obvious when he optimistically noted: "Yea, we have reason to hope, most of the *bitter passages* [of the book of Revelation] concerning the *Churches* of *Christ*, are already *fulfilled*".[149] Hill added "that there was much *Sugar* at the *bottome* [of the prophecies of the book of Revelation] reserved for these last ages, which may animate us to seeke (with all humble sobriety) a *revelation* of the *Revelation*".[150]

---

[145] Joseph Caryl, *The Saints Thankful Acclamation of Christ's Resumption of His Great Power and the Initials of His Kingdome* (London: Giles Calvert, 1644), 4. Another Westminster divine, Francis Woodcock, assured his congregation that the pouring of the third vial (Rev. 16:4) was "when in the times of Queen *Elizabeth* this State made a Law against *Priests* and *Jesuites*, enacting it Treason for any to seduce this People to the Romish Religion". Francis Woodcock, *The Two Witnesses* (London: Luke Fawne, 1643), 24. Woodcock (1614-1649 or 1651) was born in Chester, Cheshire and educated at Oxford, entering the ministry there with a reputation as a Puritan. Chosen as a Westminster divine, Woodcock later became Proctor of the University of Cambridge. Reid, *Memoirs of the Westminster Divines*, vol. 2, 265-66.

[146] Caryl, a preacher of some repute, was born in London and educated at Oxford. Firstly curate of Battersea, Surrey, he later became preacher to Lincoln's Inn in London. He was appointed to the Westminster Assembly, but was also chaplain to the commissioners sent to arrange peace with the king in 1647. He also, along with John Owen, accompanied Cromwell to Scotland. He was ejected from the ministry following the Restoration. Barker, *Puritan Profiles*, 127-30.

[147] Caryl, *The Saints Thankful Acclamation of Christ's Resumption of His Great Power*, 4.

[148] Hill was born at Kington, Worcestershire and educated at Cambridge. He was ordained in 1633 and became a noted preacher. Hill was elected Master, firstly of Emmanuel College and later of Trinity College, Cambridge, and also served as Vice-Chancellor of the University. Barker, *Puritan Profiles*, 140-44.

[149] Thomas Hill, *The Militant Church Triumphant over the Dragon and His Angels* (London: John Bellamie and Ralph Smith, 1643), 3.

[150] Hill, *The Militant Church Triumphant over the Dragon and His Angels*, 3.

1.2.5 Challenges from Variant Theologies

Ironically, in the late sixteenth and early seventeenth centuries, the quest for the Puritan ideal of a unified orthodoxy coincided with the spawning of a variety of sects, such as the Familists,[151] and the Seekers or Schwenkfeldians,[152] who often compromised the Protestant principle of *sola Scriptura* by appealing to immediate revelations of the Holy Spirit, and thus further threatened the Puritan ideal of a Calvinistic unified orthodoxy. The Puritans were equally dismayed over what they perceived

---

[151] Established about 1540, the European Familists or "Family of love" followed the teachings of Dutch spiritualist Henry Nicholas, whose goal was to establish perfect love on earth. Christopher Marsh, *The Family of Love in English Society, 1550-1630* (Cambridge: Cambridge University Press, 1994).

[152] The "Seekers" was a name given to various small sects that mushroomed in the early seventeenth century and which gave rise to the later Quaker movement. Dating from the 1620s, the Seekers were "seeking" a new church, believing all contemporary churches were corrupt. They were influenced by Kaspar Schwenckfeld of Lower Silesia, and usually conducted their meetings in silence, only speaking when they felt inspired by the Holy Spirit. The earlier Schwenckfeldians were the followers of Kaspar Schwenckfeld von Ossig (1490-1561), a German theologian who led the Protestant Reformation in Silesia. He made a distinction between the outward word of the Scriptures and the inward spiritual word, anticipating Quaker views. For the history and thought of Schwenckfeldianism, see George Huntson Williams, *The Radical Reformation* (Kirksville: Sixteenth Century Journal Publishers, 1992), especially 199-211 and 1237. On the Seekers in England, see Ted LeRoy Underwood, *Primitivism, Radicalism, and the Lamb's War. The Baptist-Quaker Conflict in Seventeenth-Century England* (Oxford: Oxford University Press, 1997), 12-14; 25-26; 65-66. For a contemporary analysis of the many sects at the time of the Assembly, see Thomas Edwards, *The First and Second part of Gangraena: or a Catalogue and Discovery of Many of the Errors, Heresies, Blasphemies and Pernicious Practices of the Sectaries of this Time, Vented and Acted in England in these Four Last Years* (London: Ralph Smith, 1646). See 1-109 for a catalogue of the "many errours of the sectaries"; Thomas Edwards, *The Third Part of Gangraena or, a New and Higher Discovery of the Errors, Heresies, Blasphemies, and Insolent Proceedings of the Sectaries of these Times; with Some Animadversions by Way of Confutation upon Many of the Errors and Heresies Named* (London: Ralph Smith, 1646); or Robert Baillie, *A Dissuasive from the Errours of the Time: Wherein the Tenets of the Principall Sects, Especially of the Independents, are Drawn Together in One Map, for the Most Part, in Words of Their own Authours, and Their Maine Principles are Examined by the Touch-stone of the Holy Scriptures* (London: Samuel Gellibrand, 1645); see also Robert Baillie, who casts his net wide in *Anabaptism, the True Fountaine of Independency, Antinomy, Brownism, Familisme, and Most of the Other Errours, which for the Time doe Trouble the Church of England, Unsealed* (London: Samuel Gellibrand, 1647). See 89-128 where he charges the Anabaptists with "Antipaedobaptisme, Arminianisme, Arianisme, Familisme, and other wicked Errours" (89).

to be theological aberrations, such as Antinomianism[153] and Socinianism, which they regarded as threats to a pure church.

These matters weighed heavily on the mind of the Assembly, to the degree that its documents self-consciously addressed the "errors" taught by these contemporary sects and theological diversions.[154] Nevertheless, even though they were broadly unified under a Puritan umbrella, it is important to notice that there was some variety in the thinking of the Westminster divines in their discussions on revelation and on the gifts of the Holy Spirit. William Bridge, for example, whom we shall discuss below,[155] argued in a series of sermons for the validity of contemporary visions, dreams and prophecy, and, as we have already noticed, Scottish commissioner George Gillespie accepted the possibility of contemporary prophecy.[156] Even though, as will become clear, the overwhelming majority of Westminster divines held to a cessation of the miraculous gifts of 1 Cor. 12: 28-29 and the former modes of supernatural revelation, a question that still remains to be answered is this: did the Westminster Assembly, as a body, seek to define by the way it framed the first paragraph of the *WCF* its position on the subject of the cessation of supernatural or extra-biblical revelation?

---

[153] Antinomianism was a denial of the validity of biblical moral law in Christian experience. In its English form, the Antinomians argued that the Spirit told the soul directly that it was in a state of grace, and therefore it was not necessary to seek evidence of obedience to the law in one's life when looking for assurance of salvation. William Dell (d. 1664) and John Saltmarsh (d. 1647) were seventeenth-century Antinomians frequently criticised by Westminster divines and other Puritans. For a modern treatment of Dell and a survey of his life and teaching, see Eric C. Walker, *William Dell Master Puritan* (Cambridge: Heffer, 1970). On Antinomianism, see 66, 69, 923, 226. For a survey of the Antinomian debate in the seventeenth century, see David D. Hall (ed.), *The Antinomian Controversy, 1636-1638: A Documentary History* (Durham: Duke University Press, 1990). For contemporary attacks on the Antinomians, and in particular on John Saltmarsh, see Samuel Rutherford, *A Survey of the Spirituall Antichrist.[...]*"(London: Andrew Crooke, 1648), especially 194-297 for "Discoveries of Familisme in M Saltmarsh"; Thomas Gataker, *Shadowes without Substance, or, Pretended New Lights[...]*" (London: Robert Bostock, 1646). See 74-75 for Gataker's attack on the Antinomian appeal to an immediate voice of the Spirit; John Ley, *Light for Smoke or a Cleare and Distinct Reply]...]to a Darke and Confused Answer in a Booke Made, and Intituled The Smoke in the Temple, by John Saltmarsh [...]*"(London: Christopher Meredith, 1646). See 86-87 for Ley's criticism of Antinomian claims to extra-biblical revelation; Thomas Fuller, *Truth Maintained [...]*" (Oxford: 1643)[no further publishing details], especially 32-33, where he pleads the cessation of miracles and "sensible impressions" of the Spirit against the Antinomians.

[154] Hetherington, *History of the Westminster Assembly*, 143.

[155] See Chapter Five, 160-66 below.

[156] See Chapter Six, 237-247 below.

1.3 Theological Inheritance

The Westminster divines were the recipients of an essentially Augustinian epistemology, mediated through both the Reformers and subsequent English and Scottish theologians. They came to the Assembly with a background profoundly influenced by a polemical Protestantism which owed much to such scholars as Martin Luther, John Calvin, Huldrich Zwingli, Henry Bullinger and Peter Martyr Vermigli. While John Calvin was arguably the dominant theological force among the Puritans and the Scots, he was by no means the only one.[157] Furthermore, "Calvinism" was represented by a spectrum of theological opinions within recognizable parameters. This was evident at the Assembly itself, where debates on the doctrine of the atonement exposed radically different interpretations of its extent and application.[158] We should not assume that because Calvin held certain views on the cessation of supernatural revelation, these were necessarily mirrored in the Westminster Assembly documents. While John Calvin's theology was indebted to Augustine,[159] so too was Peter Martyr Vermigli's. And, while Martyr and Calvin took differing views on the continuance of prophecy, both could appeal to Augustine. It is worth looking in brief at Augustine's own view of the place of miracles and supernatural revelation in the post-apostolic church.

---

[157] It is also simplistic to look for exclusively foreign sources behind the *WCF*. Mitchell makes the point well in Mitchell, *The Westminster Assembly: Its History and Standards*, 370-71.

[158] For a discussion on Amyraldianism in the Assembly, see Chapter Three below, 135, n111. For the modern debate on Calvin and the atonement, see Robert T. Kendall, *Calvin and English Calvinism to 1649* (Carlisle: Paternoster, 1997), especially 205 where Kendall claims the Westminster divines came close to making works the ground of salvation. For a response to Kendall's interpretation, see Paul Helm, *Calvin and the Calvinists* (Edinburgh: Banner of Truth Trust, 1982), especially 71-81, which refutes the claim that the Westminster divines "in effect" taught salvation by works. For alleged differences between Calvin and Westminster on the doctrine of assurance, see Charles Bell, *Calvin and Scottish Theology. The Doctrine of Assurance* (Edinburgh: Handsel Press, 1985), especially 124-30.

[159] Gordon R. Payne asks: "Where, then, is Calvin to be located theologically and philosophically? The answer is that he is the heir and follower of the Augustinian tradition flowing from Augustine through Anselm of Canterbury, Bernard of Clairvaux, William of Auvergne, Bonaventure, Thomas Bradwardine, Gregory of Rimini and John Wycliffe": Gordon R. Payne, "Augustinianism in Calvin and Bonaventure", *WTJ* 44/1 (Spring 1982), 1-30, at 2. Richard A. Muller notes that Calvin and his contemporary Protestants were part of "a developing Augustinian theology, the roots of which extend into the middle ages, indeed, back to Augustine": Richard A. Muller, *Christ and the Decree, Christology and Predestination in Reformed Theology from Calvin to Perkins* (Grand Rapids, MI: Baker, 1986), 13.

1.3.1 Augustine

Although in his earlier writings Augustine had denied the validity of modern miracles, he later accepted the possibility of revelatory dreams, visions, and miracles.[160] Indeed, dreams concerning an individual who had demanded baptism were one type of revelation.[161] Augustine apparently believed that revelations came via angelic spirits.[162] Reflecting on the miracles that occur at martyrs' memorials, he wonders whether angels might be involved, but he leaves such questions to those who have the gift of discerning spirits and refers to the extraordinary story of one John the Monk. In his narrative, he tells of a vision given to a woman which had been prophesied by this John. Here too he opens up the possibility that perhaps an angel had been involved.[163] Since he concluded that such prophetic insights had not ceased, Augustine can be classified as a

---

[160] Augustine, *City of God*, 22, 8. (*NPNF* first ser., 2, 484-90). For a discussion on Augustine's acceptance of miracles of healing, see Peter Brown, *The Cult of the Saints: Its Rise and Function in Latin Christianity* (London: SCM Press, 1981), 77-78.

[161] Peter Brown notes, "Augustine had once mocked Donatist claims based on such revelations (*ep.ad cath*, xix, 49-50). Now, he was the object of just such excitements: a poor man from an outlying village had come to Hippo to be baptised by Augustine as the result of just such a dream. (*de cura ger. pro mort.* xii, 15) Augustine knew that he had played a role in the dreams of many people. (*Serm.* 322 and 323, 2.) In his reaction to this, he shows himself very much the son of his mother Monica. On his deathbed, a sick man was brought to him to be healed. His first reaction was to joke: 'If I had the gift you say I have, I would be the first to try it on myself'; but, as soon as he heard that the man had been told to come to him by a dream, he laid his hands on him (*Vita*, xxix, 5)". Peter Brown, *Augustine of Hippo, A Biography* (London: Faber and Faber, 1967), 413. Later Brown argues that Augustine "seems to accept the validity of his mother's earlier dream regarding his conversion as true. *Conf.* VIII, xii, 28-30" (109). And further: "[W]hen Augustine wrote On the True Religion in 390, he had stated, explicitly, that miracles such as had happened in the times of the Apostles were no longer allowed to take place; and he had repeated this view, by implication, in many other books and sermons. At the same time, however, he had actually witnessed and accepted the cures associated with the spectacular discovery of the bodies of Gervasius and Protasius in Milan [ ] modern miracles which had once been peripheral, now became urgently important as supports to faith" (415).

[162] Augustine, *City of God,* 16, 6 (*NPNF* first ser., 2, 313-14). See also Susan Schreiner, *The Theatre of His Glory* (Grand Rapids, MI: Baker, 1991), 42, who notes that Augustine taught that demons and unfallen angels could know the future. Demons could only know it fallibly, whereas the good angels had a more certain understanding of what was to come: Augustine says: "And therefore they [the good angels] have a more certain knowledge even of those temporal and mutable things, because they contemplate their principles and causes in the word of God, by which the world was made": Augustine, *City of God,* 9, 22 (*NPNF* first ser., 2, 177).

[163] Augustine, *De Cura pro Mortuis*, 21 [from *The Retractions* 2, 64] (*NPNF* first ser., 1, 549-50).

"continuationist", in broad terms, although he did not propose that a renewal of miraculous spiritual gifts could be expected or was normative for the church of his time.

1.3.2 Thomas Aquinas

Although an analysis of the complex evolution of medieval theology is beyond the scope of this thesis, the Augustinian inheritance in Puritan times had, of course, been mediated through a rich tradition spanning a millennium. Thomas Aquinas (1224/5 –1274) is arguably the most important example from this legacy and his influence should not be overlooked.[164] In a discussion on prophecy in his massive *Summa Theologiae*, Aquinas shows an obvious reliance upon Augustine, frequently referring to him as an authority to sustain his position. Aquinas distinguishes between two types of foreknowledge. He is not happy with the Platonist idea that souls can foreknow the future the more they are separated from their bodies, but he affirms a natural prophetic ability in which human experience can discern future events from analysing their causes.[165] Nevertheless, he is willing to concede that when the soul is less bound by the body (presumably near the point of death), it is more able to be influenced by "spiritual substances" and is more open to

> subtle impressions which natural causes leave upon the human imagination. The soul cannot receive any such impressions when it is taken up with sense objects.[166]

Similarly, dreams can be brought about through natural or "corporal" causes, or through "spiritual" causes. These "spiritual" causes are either revelation conveyed from God through angels, or the actions of demons

---

[164] For Calvin's reception of the Church Fathers and the Medievals, see Anthony Lane, *John Calvin: Student of the Church Fathers* (Edinburgh: T. & T. Clark, 1999), especially 21, where Lane discusses and questions the claim that medieval thinkers including Aquinas influenced Calvin indirectly through John Major; For the suggestion that Calvin might have read Aquinas in intermediate sources, or that he refrained from naming him often, because this was his practice with most other scholastics, see 44-45. See the critique of Aquinas in Arvin Vos, *Aquinas, Calvin, and Contemporary Protestant Thought* (Washington, D.C.: Christian University Press, 1985), especially 1-17 on the similarity between Calvin and Aquinas on the meaning of faith. Also see 161-71 where Vos outlines common Protestant misrepresentations of Aquinas. For a major study of Calvin's thought in its sixteenth-century context, examining the theological and philosophical themes of Calvin's works in the light of his medieval predecessors, see Richard A. Muller, *The Unaccommodated Calvin: Studies in the Foundation of a Theological Tradition* (New York; Oxford: Oxford University Press. 2000).

[165] Thomas Aquinas, *Summa Theologiae* (London: Blackfriars; and Eyre & Spottiswoode; New York: McGraw-Hill, 1970), vol. 45, 31.

[166] Aquinas, *Summa Theologiae*, vol. 45, 33.

who can also reveal future events.[167] Divination through revelation from angels, designated "prophetic revelation", is lawful, but not that from demons.[168] Prophecy by supernatural means can also be imparted in two ways. It can arrive either by express revelation, or in another way by an "inward instinct" to "which human minds submit to sometimes even unknowingly".[169] When prophecy comes by "inward instinct", occasionally it is difficult for the prophet to distinguish between this and his own spirit. Therefore, prophecy brought about in this manner provides less certainty that the matter spoken by the prophet is indeed from God and not of his own spirit.[170] While Aquinas believes that the prophets of Eph. 4:11 were the Old Testament prophets whose prophetic role had been assumed by the apostles,[171] he also teaches that prophecy is available to the modern church to the degree that "at each period there were always some who had the spirit of prophecy, not for the purpose of setting out new doctrine to be believed, but for the governance of human activities".[172] Aquinas asserts both the necessity of miracles[173] and an ongoing gift of miracles,[174] believing that he was being faithful to Augustine in allowing for modern prophecy, revelatory dreams and visions, and miracles, while disallowing new revelation for doctrine.

1.3.3 John Calvin

John Calvin did not follow Augustine and Aquinas in this direction; in marked contrast, he associated claims to new revelation with a violation of the unity which joins the Scriptures and the Holy Spirit.[175] He cautioned against driving a wedge between the Word and the Spirit by seeking the Spirit's guidance elsewhere than in the Word, stressing it as an inviolable rule that the Spirit and the Word must not be separated.[176] The presence of

---

[167] Aquinas, *Summa Theologiae*, vol. 40, 59.
[168] Aquinas, *Summa Theologiae*, vol. 45, 35.
[169] Aquinas, *Summa Theologiae*, vol. 45, 23.
[170] Aquinas, *Summa Theologiae*, vol. 45, 23.
[171] Thomas Aquinas, *Commentary on Saint Paul's Epistle to the Ephesians* (Albany: Magi Books,1966), 162-63.
[172] Aquinas, *Summa Theologiae*, vol. 45, 93.
[173] Aquinas, *Summa Theologiae*, vol. 45, 141.
[174] Aquinas, *Summa Theologiae*, vol. 45, 143.
[175] For Calvin's teaching on the knowledge of God, see Edward Dowey, *The Knowledge of God in Calvin's Theology*, 3rd edn. (Grand Rapids, MI: Eerdmans, 1994); T. H. L. Parker, *The doctrine of the Knowledge of God: A Study in the Theology of John Calvin* (Grand Rapids, MI: Eerdmans, 1994).
[176] "Therefore the Spirit, promised to us, has not the task of inventing new and unheard-of revelations, or of forging a new kind of doctrine, to lead us away from the received doctrine of the gospel, but of sealing our minds with that very doctrine which is

the "Libertines", "certain giddy men" who sought to establish doctrine apart from the Scriptures, made it essential for Calvin to articulate a distinct and clear rejoinder.[177] He disapproved of the Libertines' elevation of "the teaching office of the Spirit", to the degree that they "despise[d] all reading".[178] The Genevan Reformer denied that the Spirit imparted new doctrine, and affirmed that the contemporary role of the Holy Spirit was to confirm doctrines already revealed in Scripture.[179]

Certainly, Augustine and Aquinas would have agreed with Calvin that there would be no more revelation for doctrine, but was Calvin also excluding the possibility of other non-doctrinal revelations from the Spirit? Some appeal to him as a theologian who allowed for the continuation of revelatory prophecy.[180] Statements can certainly be marshalled from Calvin's writing which seem to indicate that he did concede the possibility of new prophetic revelation. For example, Calvin can write:

> Those who preside over the government of the church in accordance with Christ's institution are called by Paul as follows: first apostles, then prophets, thirdly evangelists, fourthly pastors, and finally teachers [Eph.4:11]. Of these only the last two have an ordinary office in the church; the Lord raised up the first three at the beginning of his Kingdom, and now and again revives them as the need of the times demands.[181]

However, it would be a thorough misunderstanding of Calvin to assume he means that the office of prophet, with its capacity to deliver extraordinary, extra-biblical revelations, might be revived. Such a reading of Calvin would have him likewise allowing a restoration of extraordinary apostles, together with their miraculous powers, for according to Calvin the office of apostles, together with evangelists and prophets, would occasionally be reconstituted in subsequent church history. Beth Langstaff is correct in concluding that here,[182] as well as in his commentary on Eph. 4:11, Calvin means by an "apostle" a figure such as Martin Luther or his fellow-reformers. Langstaff cites Calvin's treatise against Albert Pighius,[183]

---

commended by the gospel": John Calvin, *Institutes of the Christian Religion,* ed. John T. McNeill (Philadelphia: The Westminster Press, 1960), I, 9, 1.

[177] Calvin, *Institutes*, I, 9, 1.

[178] Calvin, *Institutes*, I, 9, 1.

[179] John Calvin, *Treatises Against The Anabaptists and Against The Libertines* (Grand Rapids, MI: Baker, 1982), 224. Calvin's view of the Anabaptists is summarised by Richard Gamble, "Calvin's Theological Method: Word and Spirit, A Case Study", Richard Gamble(ed.), *Articles on Calvin and Calvinism* (New York: Garland, 1992), vol. 7, 61-73, at 70.

[180] Calvin, *Institutes*, IV, 3, 4. See Willem Berends, "Prophecy in the Reformation Tradition", *Vox Reformata* 60 (1995), 30-43, at 35.

[181] Calvin, *Institutes,* IV, 3, 4.

[182] Calvin, *Institutes,* IV, 3, 4.

[183] CO, vol. 6, 250.

Socio-Political and Religious Context 47

where Calvin explicitly calls Luther an "apostle". She also highlights interesting verbal parallels of the terms used for Luther's role in the Reformation, comparing those in Calvin's treatise *The necessity of Reforming the Church*,[184] with his definitions of "apostle" and "evangelist" in the *Institutes*.[185]

Moreover, Calvin did make unambiguous statements about the cessation of predictive prophecy. In his commentary on Acts 21:9, where Philip's prophesying daughters are mentioned, Calvin gives an historical and progressive survey of prophecy: it had almost ceased with the Jews, was revived "to give lustre to the beginnings of the Gospel", and became a sign of a more complete dispensation.[186] Its cessation in the early church was caused by the need to remove the uncertainty that would arise if new revelations were still expected. The cessation of prophets also prevented people always looking for "something new". While it was possible that God had withdrawn prophecy because of the perversity of human beings, the main reason prophecies ceased was that God was testifying that their "end and fulfilment were present in Christ".[187] Calvin also often interprets the gift of prophecy in the New Testament as a gift of expounding the Bible in preaching,[188] and so binds prophecy to Scripture, because "[...]we are to expect nothing more from his Spirit than that he will illumine our minds to

---

[184] CO, vol. 6, 459.

[185] Beth Langstaff, "Temporary Gifts: John Calvin's Doctrine of the Cessation of Miracles" (unpublished PhD thesis, Princeton Theological Seminary, 1999), 296-99. Langstaff's comprehensive analysis concludes that Calvin taught that miracles "ceased with the end of the apostolic era[...]. The class of miracles which have ceased encompasses all those extraordinary, visible, and material signs by which God in biblical times displayed his power and manifested his presence: not only miraculous gifts such as healing, exorcism, and speaking in tongues, but supernatural revelation through prophecy and visions; voices from heaven and the appearance of angels; miracles of nature (the multiplication of bread, for example), confirmation (Gideon's fleece) and judgment (Ananias and Saphira). God no longer reveals himself in these ways and such miracles should not be sought"(338). See Calvin, *Institutes*, IV, 3, 4.

[186] John Calvin, *The Acts of the Apostles* (Grand Rapids, MI: Eerdmans, 1991), vol. 7, 194-95.

[187] Calvin, *The Acts of the Apostles*, vol. 7, 195.

[188] Commenting on Rom. 12:6, "[...]*whether prophecy, let us prophesy according to the proportion of our faith"*, Calvin writes that rather than see this gift as predicting the future: "I prefer, however, to follow those who understand the word in a wider sense to mean the peculiar gift of revelation by which a man performs the office of interpreter with skill and dexterity in expounding the will of God. In the Christian Church, therefore, prophecy at the present day is simply the right understanding of Scripture and the particular gift of expounding it, since all the ancient prophecies and all the oracles of God have been concluded in Christ and His gospel". John Calvin, *The Epistles of Paul to the Romans and the Thessalonians* (Grand Rapids, MI: Eerdmans, 1991), vol. 8, 268-69.

perceive the truth of his teaching".[189] Even if one seeks guidance, he or she should do so from the Word.[190] Neither can we see angels today;[191] God no longer reveals himself by visions,[192] nor does he impart the miraculous gifts of the Spirit.[193]

While Calvin was sceptical about a recurrence of New Testament miraculous gifts, other theologians who had an impact on the English and Scottish Reformations were, like Augustine and Aquinas, more open to the miraculous. Calvin represents only one of two strands of thought among Augustine's heirs concerning ongoing immediate revelation. Peter Martyr Vermigli (1499-1562), also firmly in the Augustinian theological tradition, patently taught the continuance of predictive prophecy: "Yet in mine opinion, it is not to be denied, but that there be still prophets in the church, although not so famous as in times past".[194] When we compare Calvin's lack of a chapter on prophecy in the comparison between Vermigli's *Common Places* and the second edition of Calvin's *Institutes,* we can see a graphic and definitive contrast between Vermigli's pronouncements on the continuation of prophecy and Calvin's cessationism.[195]

1.4 The Immediate Predecessors of the Assembly

This tradition, which contained both cessationist and continuationist elements, is also evident in the thought of both the immediate predecessors of the Westminster divines and their contemporaries, which perhaps demonstrates a lack of the same rigorous consistency that we see in Calvin in his conflict with the Libertines. Alternatively, perhaps those who still advocated supernatural, extra-biblical revelations for guidance were less concerned by, or conscious of, the danger that such a concession

---

[189] Calvin, *Institutes,* IV, 8, 13.

[190] "Let it be observed that two things are here connected, the word and the Spirit of God, in opposition to fanatics, who aim at oracles and hidden revelations without the word[...]. [E]verything that relates to the guidance of our life is contained in them[the Scriptures]abundantly": John Calvin, *Commentary on the Book of the Prophet Isaiah* (Grand Rapids, MI: Baker Book House, 1993), vol. 7, 347-48.

[191] John Calvin, *The Gospel according to St John 1-10* (Grand Rapids, MI: Eerdmans, 1993), vol. 4, 43.

[192] CO, vol. 46, 27, a sermon on Luke 1:11-15.

[193] CO, vol. 7, 631. Calvin had underscored his views on cessationism in his earliest writings, such as his 1536 *Institutes*: "But those miraculous powers and manifest workings, which were dispensed by the laying on of hands, have ceased[...]": John Calvin, *Institutes of the Christian Religion 1536 Edition* (London: Collins, 1975), 126.

[194] Peter Martyr Vermigli, *The Common Places, of the Most Famous and Renowned Divine Doctor Peter Martyr*[...]*Translated and Partlie Gathered by Anthonie Marten* [...]" (London: 1583)[no further publishing details have been given], 1, 3, 24.

[195] Calvin, *Institutes,* vol. 2, 1628.

represented to the unity of the Word and Spirit, and to the Protestant principle of *sola Scriptura*.[196]

1.4.1 William Perkins

William Perkins (1558-1602) was one of England's most important Protestant theologians. Appointed lecturer at Great St Andrews', Cambridge in 1584,[197] his influence was still evident in the city a generation later, when Independent and Westminster divine Thomas Goodwin, who had gone to Cambridge in 1613, noted: "the town was then filled with the discourse of the power of Mr. Perkins' ministry, still fresh in most men's memories".[198]

Even after his death Perkins' influence persisted in spite of the fact that he was only a fringe member of the early Puritan movement, and was a supporter of neither Presbyterian government nor separatism.[199] How thoroughly his own theological ideas were transferred to a later generation

---

[196] For the *WCF* on the Word and Spirit see Wayne Spear, "Word and Spirit in the Westminster Confession", Ligon Duncan (ed.), *The Westminster Confession into the 21st Century* (Fearn: Christian Focus, 2003), vol. 1, 39-56. Spear focuses, in this brief essay, on the Westminster view of the inspiration of Scripture and the internal testimony of the Holy Spirit.

[197] William Perkins, *The Work of William Perkins*, ed. Ian Breward (Appleford: The Sutton Courtney Press, 1970), 8.

[198] Samuel Clarke, *A General Martyrologie* (London: 1677)[no further publishing details given], 23, cited by Breward in Perkins, *The Work of William Perkins*, 9. Exiled Scottish minister Robert Fleming, in his 1669 work, *The Fulfilling of Scripture*, calls Perkins "that excellent man of God" and is obviously acquainted with his works. Robert Fleming, *The Fulfilling of The Scripture Complete in Three Parts* (London: J. and B. Sprint, Aaron Ward, Richard Ford, and John Oswald, 1726, [originally published in Rotterdam, 1669]), 103. Thomas Goodwin (1600-1680), born at Rollesby in Norfolk, was one of the five dissenting brethren (the others were Philip Nye, Jeremiah Burrough[e]s, William Bridge and Sidrach Simpson) and like the other four had served a Congregational church in the Netherlands. Educated at Cambridge, he became an important minister during the interregnum. He was one of Oliver Cromwell's main religious advisors and was present at Cromwell's deathbed with John Owen and other close counsellors. He was also one of the most active speakers of the Assembly, making 357 speeches between August 1643 and November 1644. This exceeded in number the speeches of all others and was twice as often as all but six of the Assembly. Goodwin along with Owen was a major influence behind the Savoy conference, where the Congregational Churches produced their doctrinal and church polity statements in 1658. Ousted at the Restoration of 1660, Goodwin founded a Congregational church in Fetter Lane, London. Enhanced by a somewhat gloomy countenance, Dr. Goodwin is said to have terrified a student who was being examined at Oxford with the question expressed in doleful tones, "Are you prepared for death?" Barker, *Puritan Profiles*, 70-77.

[199] Perkins, *The Work of William Perkins*, 10-12.

is hard to say. Ian Breward, in his analysis of Perkins, concludes that not only is it "notoriously difficult to assess influence in the spiritual and theological realm", but:

> although Perkins was one of the most widely quoted authors prior to 1660, his users normally used him as they used the fathers and the schoolmen – to support their own opinions and to provide a further link in the chain of argument.[200]

Nonetheless, Perkins' influence indirectly extended to the Westminster Assembly, through the evident reliance of James Usher's *Body of Divinitie* upon Perkins' *Armilla Aurea*.[201] Perkins' views on the manner of supernatural revelation in his own day are somewhat ambiguous. While he held that modern-day preachers of the gospel could be immediately called by God, he also maintained that the call through the "immediate voice" of God or by angels was not how the first Reformation preachers in England received their vocation. Instead they were called by "instinct" and did not need to perform miracles to attest their immediate calling, because they only taught the "old & auntient doctrine of the Prophets and Apostles".[202] Furthermore, these gospel preachers were pastors and teachers and not "Apostles or Evangelists", and they only preached the "doctrine of the word".[203] In his *An Exposition upon Christs Sermon on the Mount*, Perkins is unequivocal that all extraordinary calling of prophets and teachers is now ceased. This includes calling by "instinct".[204] Now the modern prophets concern themselves with the "wholsome handling of the Word [which] stands in two things; in a right interpretation: and opening of the true sense of Scripture, and in a due and sound collection of wholsome doctrine from the same[...]".[205]

---

[200] Perkins, *The Work of William Perkins*, 101-102.

[201] Perkins, *The Work of William Perkins*, 102. Breward, in fact, considers that both the *Irish Articles* and the *Body of Divinitie* were influenced by Perkins. Breward sees a "broad similarity of structure"; a "similarity of method and tone"; and an "almost verbatim quotation" from Perkins in Usher's work on the love of God. He considers that Usher's discussion of the Lord's Supper is also "largely [taken] over [from] Perkins' account".

[202] William Perkins, *A Commentarie or Exposition, upon the Five First Chapters of the Epistle to the Galatians [...] by [...] W. Perkins. Now Published for the Benefit of the Church, and Continued with a Supplement upon the Sixth Chapter, by Rafe Cudworth* (Cambridge: John Legat, 1604), 34.

[203] Perkins, *A Commentarie or Exposition, upon the Five First Chapters of the Epistle to the Galatians*, 34.

[204] William Perkins, *The Workes of that Famous and Worthy Minister of Christ in the Universitie of Cambridge, M. W. Perkins* (London: printed by John Haviland, 1631), vol. 3, 239.

[205] Perkins, *The Workes of that Famous and Worthy Minister of Christ* [1631], vol. 3, 239.

In addition, in his *A Discourse of Witchcraft* he notes that revelatory dreams, one of the ways God used to reveal his will to his prophets, have now ceased.[206] This view is consistent with that expressed by Perkins in his commentary on Hebrews 11, where he clearly distinguishes infallible apostles and fallible post-apostolic ministers, noting that "no Ministers at this day have such a priviledge" as to be guided by the Holy Spirit without error.[207] This would seem to exclude the possibility of modern-day prophets who could receive extra-biblical revelation.

In another work, *A Fruitfull Dialogue Betweene the Christian and the Worldling Concerning the End of the World*, Perkins gives a list of six marks by which one might recognize a true prophet and a further five tests which enable one to accept a prophecy as true. His conclusions are consistent with his denial in his Hebrews commentary that ministers in his day might possess infallible extra-biblical knowledge. While he is open to the possibility of modern-day "prophets", his qualification of their credentials show that these are "prophets" of a quite different stamp than New Testament prophets of the early church.[208] As the details demonstrate, Perkins' definition of authentic "prophets" and "prophecies" contradict the qualifications of New Testament prophets in Scripture. For example, gender and age are issues for Perkins, who claims women and young men are disqualified from becoming authentic modern prophets, whereas both classes were obviously sanctioned as legitimate prophets in the New Testament church.[209]

The ambiguity of Perkins, however, becomes apparent when we turn back to his commentary on Hebrews 11, where he sanctions extraordinary revelations of blessings and judgements concerning individuals, churches and states. Although he gives cautions about heeding such revelations, he is clear that God may give extraordinary revelation apart from the Scriptures:

> And yet we tie not the Lord in such strait bonds, but that he may sometime extraordinarily reveale his purpose therein, to some [of] his selected servants: yet provided, that that revelation be examined and allowed of the Church.[210]

Presumably the Church would examine such revelation in the light of Scripture, but here Perkins is clearly accepting an extraordinary revelation

---

[206] Perkins, *The Workes of that Famous and Worthy Minister of Christ* [1631], vol. 3, 625.

[207] William Perkins, *A Commentary on Hebrews 11* (New York: Pilgrim Press, 1991, [1909 edition]), 184.

[208] William Perkins, *The Workes of that Famous and Worthie Minister of Christ in the Universitie of Cambridge, Mr. W. Perkins* (Cambridge: University of Cambridge, 1609), vol. 3, 465-77, especially 468-69.

[209] See, for example, Acts 2:17 and Acts 21:19.

[210] Perkins, *A Commentary on Hebrews 11*, 38.

apart from it. While "selected servants" might receive an extraordinary revelation like Noah, the more usual expectation was guidance by means of Scripture and providence for specific circumstances, which was available to all. Even though, in that case, God guided his faithful people, not only by the Scriptures, but also by "counsell of some others of his, or else by his owne secret inspiration", the guidance was not an extraordinary revelation. Instead, Perkins concludes:

> How often shall a Christian man finde in the course of his life, that God put it into his minde, to answer thus or thus, or to foresee this or that; by which his so doing, he escaped some great danger: so that *(though not in the same manner as Noah was)* all faithfull men doe daiely finde, that they are warned by God of such things as doe concerne them [emphasis added].[211]

Perkins therefore leaves open the possibility that a revelation, similar to that afforded to Noah, is possible for non-doctrinal matters in his own day. However, the church has to approve it, which means that such a revelation must be subordinate to the Bible, and is of such a character that an uninspired church can pass judgement on its validity. His rejection of extra-biblical prophecy elsewhere would seem to contradict this allowance for extraordinary revelation. Moreover, that this revelation must be tested by the church illustrates that it is not of the same order of importance or certainty as that granted to Noah. While we can be sure that Perkins' views were known to the Westminster divines, the majority of them followed only one strand of his logic or religious epistemology. As we shall see, the divines embraced the idea that God was still able to forewarn and guide people in specific circumstances of their lives, but, for the most part, they did not follow Perkins in allowing extra-biblical revelation. Significantly, Perkins was also out of step with another prominent and influential contemporary, ten years his senior.

1.5 Acknowledged Sources of the Westminster Theology

1.5.1. William Whitaker

William Whitaker (1547/8-1597), Professor of Divinity at Cambridge from 1579 to 1595, has recently been suggested as the most significant influence upon Chapter One of the *WCF*.[212] Whitaker had lectured on, and given an

---

[211] Perkins, *A Commentary on Hebrews 11*, 39.

[212] Wayne Spear, "The Westminster Confession of Faith and Holy Scripture", Carson and Hall (eds.), *To Glorify and Enjoy God*, 87-100, at 88. Wayne Spear concludes in his essay that "[...]the Confession follows the thought of William Whitaker very closely in its statements" (88).

Socio-Political and Religious Context

extensive rebuttal of, the Tridentine view of Scripture, articulated by Robert Bellarmine (1542-1621) and Thomas Stapleton (1535-1598), both of the Society of Jesus.[213] Of the several Protestants who presented arguments in answer to Tridentine doctrine, Whitaker was one of those most respected by Robert Bellarmine.[214] In his published lectures entitled *Disputation on Holy Scripture*,[215] Whitaker's views expressly foreshadow Chapter One of the *WCF*. He is also the most frequently quoted theologian in the extant Assembly minutes.[216] Spear concludes from his reading of both documents that "[t]here is hardly a concept in Chapter One of the Confession which does not have a parallel in Whitaker's *Disputation*".[217]

Whitaker, in his *Disputatio,* proves to be a faithful interpreter of the cessationist elements of the Augustinian epistemology as it was mediated through John Calvin in particular.[218] He demonstrates this in a number of ways, taking a firm stance, for example, on the necessity of Scripture,

---

[213] See Thompson Cooper, "Thomas Stapleton", *DNB*, vol. 2, 1988; Anthony Lane, "Robert Bellarmine", *NDT*, 84-85.

[214] The editor of the Parker Society volume includes a report in his preface: "'I have', says the writer of his life, in Lupton's Protestant Divines, 'I have heard it confessed of English Papists themselves, which have been in Italy with Bellarmine himself, that he procured the true portraiture and effigies of this *Whitaker* to be brought to him, which he kept in his study. For he privately admired this man for his singular learning and ingenuity; and being asked of some of his friends, Jesuits, why he would have the picture of that heretic in his presence? he would answer, *Quod quamvis haereticus erat et adversarius, erat tamen doctus adversarius:* that, 'although he was an heretic, and his adversary, yet he was a learned adversary'": Whitaker, *Disputation*, x. Whitaker interacts with Robert Bellarmino, *Disputationum Roberti Bellarmini [...] de Controuersiis Christianae Fidei, Aduersus Huius Temporis Haereticos, Tomus Secundus (tertius) [...]* (Ingolstadii: Dauidis Sartorii, 1588); and Thomas Stapleton, *Principiorum Fidei Doctrinalium Demonstratio Methodica, per Controversias Septem in Librie Duodecim Tradita*, (Paris: 1578)[no further publishing details].

[215] Guilielmo Whitakero, *Disputatio de Sacra Scriptura* (Cantabrigia: 1588). The English version to which we refer is, William Whitaker, *Disputation on Holy Scripture* (Cambridge: The University Press, 1849).

[216] In 1642, Thomas Hill complained to the House of Commons that Whitaker would blush to see the departure from truth that had occurred in their day. Thomas Hill, *The Trade of Truth Advanced* (London: John Bellamie, Philemon Stephens, and Ralph Smith, 1642), 49.

[217] Spear, "The Westminster Confession", Carson and Hall (eds.), *To Glorify and Enjoy God,* 88.

[218] Whitaker, *Disputation*, 181 and 340. Whitaker appeals to Calvin's authority against his Catholic opponents.

because God had ceased to impart new revelation through visions and dreams and other extraordinary means.[219]

Whitaker lists the Schwenckfeldians[220] and Libertines[221] among others in his catalogue of those who have a heretical doctrine of Scripture and who:

> despise the whole scripture, and insult it with many reproaches holding that we should attend not to what the scriptures speak, but to what the Spirit utters and teaches us internally.[222]

His criticism is aimed squarely at their denial of the necessity for Scripture, but he does not say any more about their extra-biblical revelations at this juncture. Certainly his disapproval of their revelations is obvious, but later he not only condemns but also unreservedly outlaws any such spiritual afflatus. The Scriptures are needful, according to Whitaker, because they contain the doctrine, both Law and Gospel, that is requisite if one is to be saved. As a further argument for the necessity of Scripture he adds:

> Besides, God does not teach us now by visions, dreams, revelations, oracles, as of old, but by the scriptures alone; and therefore, if we will be saved, we must of necessity know the scriptures.[223]

Whitaker's repudiation of any revelation apart from the Scriptures comes into sharper focus as he expounds the Protestant shibboleth of the inner testimony of the Holy Spirit.[224] Whitaker pointedly rejects the argument that the church is needed to decide what constitutes Scripture: "The voice of Christ and true and genuine scripture", can be known, "without the judgement of the church".[225] The correct way to judge Scripture is twofold.

---

[219] "If anyone objects that the Lord does not speak in a vision today, I reply that, since the authority of Scripture is more established for us, God must be heard out of it": Calvin, *The Acts of the Apostles*, vol. 6, 265.

[220] See 30, n66.

[221] See 35, n85.

[222] Whitaker, *Disputation*, 36.

[223] Whitaker, *Disputation*, 521.

[224] "For as God alone is a fit witness of himself in his Word, so also the Word will not find acceptance in men's hearts before it is sealed by the inward testimony of the Spirit. The same Spirit, therefore, who has spoken through the mouths of the prophets must penetrate into our hearts to persuade us that they faithfully proclaimed what had been divinely commanded". Calvin, *Institutes*, I, 7, 4. For discussions of Calvin's doctrine of the inner testimony of the Spirit, see George Hendry, *The Holy Spirit in Christian Theology* (London: SCM Press, 1957), 72-85; Francois Wendel, *Calvin* (Glasgow: William Collins Sons and Co, 1976), 156-65; Ronald Wallace, *Calvin's Doctrine of the Word and Sacrament* (Tyler: Geneva Divinity School Press, 1982), especially 101; Wilhelm Niesel, *The Theology of Calvin* (Grand Rapids, MI: Baker, 1980), 37-38.

[225] Whitaker, *Disputation*, 287.

Firstly, "the authority of God himself shines forth" in Scripture. The Scriptures then can be understood as Scripture out of Scripture itself, because God's authority shines through it.[226] Secondly, this personal judgement emerges through "the internal witness of the Holy Spirit".[227] Although there are also external testimonies,[228] these evidences will not have any effect "unless the testimony of the Holy Spirit be added". Indeed, the only argument that can thoroughly persuade us is the testimony of the Holy Spirit.[229]

In his defence of the inner testimony or witness of the Spirit, Whitaker discloses his rejection of extra-biblical revelation.[230] The case of the recognition of genuine Scripture is distinct from doctrine as such and, while the Holy Spirit testifies privately to the Christian that Scripture is indeed the voice of Christ, it is erroneous to conclude that Protestants lay claim to extra-biblical revelation of the Spirit when they argue for an inner testimony. Whitaker's Catholic opponents contended that this testimony of the Spirit must be something external to the Scriptures and not inherent in the Word, because it is "not taken from the books themselves".[231] Whitaker agrees that it is not

> the same as the books themselves; yet it is not external, nor separate, or alien from the books, because it is perceived in the doctrine delivered in those books; for we do not speak of any enthusiastic influence of the Spirit.[232]

He does not reserve use of the pejorative adjective "enthusiastic" for those who claimed to be inspired in the doctrinal matters that are necessary

---

[226] Whitaker, *Disputation*, 289.

[227] Whitaker, *Disputation*, 290.

[228] "[I]f any pious persons have yet doubts concerning the scriptures, much more certain evidences may be gathered from the books themselves, to prove them canonical, than from any authority of the church". He cites Calvin (Inst. I, 8) and proceeds to list qualities recognised by the pious, such as the majesty of the doctrine and the fulfilment of prophecy. Whitaker, *Disputation,* 292-93.

[229] Whitaker, *Disputation*, 295.

[230] The role of the "inner testimony" was assumed by most Puritans to be a mediate one and it carries this sense in the *WCF* . A later Scottish theologian, William Cunningham, interprets the *WCF* teaching on the testimony of the Spirit in *WCF* 1:5 to imply a mediate rather than an immediate revelatory function: "This is all that the word [bearing witness] necessarily implies,[...]. [T]here is no reason why we should regard it as implying that by a distinct intimation or explicit assertion he [the Spirit] directly or immediately tells or assures any believer that the Scriptures are the word of God". William Cunningham, *Theological Lectures on Subjects Connected with Natural Theology, Evidences of Christianity, the Canon and Inspiration of Scripture* (London: James Nisbet, 1878), 328.

[231] Whitaker, *Disputation*, 295.

[232] Whitaker, *Disputation*, 295.

for salvation. Rather he repudiates an "enthusiasm" which would claim that revelation was involved in the inner testimony of the Holy Spirit, and in the recognition of and assent to certain books being holy Scripture. Not only does God not teach doctrine by vision and dream today, but anyone who lays claim to an external work of the Spirit is under the influence of "enthusiasm", an influence which Whitaker will not countenance for a moment.

In spite of clear rebuttals by Protestant theologians, it was at this point that the Reformed orthodox position was believed vulnerable to attack, at least by Stapleton.[233] Whitaker reacts to Stapleton's charge that Protestants claim they know the Scriptures to be the Word of God by an immediate revelation of the Holy Spirit. He reiterates what he has already said: "This is no extraordinary or immediate revelation separate from the teaching of the books themselves".[234] Turning the objection back onto Stapleton, how, he asks, does the Catholic Church know that the Scriptures are the Word of God?

> If they say by a private revelation; then they conclude that extraordinary and private revelations are still employed, and so they establish and confirm enthusiasm; for this authority they attribute even to the present church.[235]

This is evidence that Whitaker associates "enthusiasm" with claims to new or extra-biblical revelation. For Whitaker, it is obvious that "extraordinary and private revelations" are no longer available. His argument is simple and unambiguous. One cannot know that the Scriptures are the Word of God by extra-biblical revelation, since such extra-biblical revelations have ceased. If Whitaker had conceded that there are still such private revelations, he could not have in such an unqualified manner dismissed an argument for such private revelation to confirm Scripture as Scripture, any more than he could have dismissed the same argument for matters of doctrine.

---

[233] I use the term "Reformed orthodox" as a description for those who stood in the Protestant Augustinian tradition, acknowledging the particular, though not exclusive, importance of the Genevan Reformation. My use of the term "Reformed orthodoxy" encompasses the previous generation of classical Reformers as well as Richard Muller's category, "High orthodoxy". Muller says: "High orthodoxy (ca. 1640-1685-1725) spans the greater part of the seventeenth and the first quarter of the eighteenth century[...]. It represents a still broader theological synthesis than early orthodoxy: it rests upon a confessional summation of the faith, has a somewhat sharper and more codified polemic against its doctrinal adversaries, and possesses a broader and more explicit grasp of the tradition, particularly of the contribution of the Middle Ages": Muller, *Post-Reformation Reformed Dogmatics*, vol. 1, 31.

[234] Whitaker, *Disputation*, 297.

[235] Whitaker, *Disputation*, 297.

Another way he reinforces his cessationist argument is to deny revelations that are "beside" the Scriptures:

> If they answer [that they establish the canon], by some internal impulse or revelation of the Spirit, we entirely reject such revelations which are beside the word, as fanatical and anabaptistical and utterly heretical.[236]

Any revelation which is "beside the Word" (not necessarily *opposed* to the Word, but *extra* to it) is rejected. It is *"beside"* the Word that the Church has the authority to decide the canon of Scripture. We must reject the Catholic position which relies upon a revelation of the Spirit to sanction its magisterium to authorise the canon, because there can be no new revelation from God apart from the Scriptures.[237] For Whitaker, the Protestant "inner testimony" is no extra-biblical revelation; instead the Tridentine claim that the church establishes the canon of Scripture is itself contingent upon novel revelation. Indeed, Whitaker thinks those claims are absurd, because they correlate with "fanatical and anabaptistical and utterly heretical" inspirations or revelations.

Not only does the ability to *know* Scripture *as* Scripture require the illumination, or the inner testimony, of the Holy Spirit, but the semantic content of Scripture itself can only be known from the Holy Spirit speaking in the Scriptures:

> For if scripture cannot otherwise be known but by scripture and the Holy Spirit, which was the conclusion we have arrived at already, in the third question [concerning the authority of Scripture[238]]; then certainly neither should we seek the sense of scripture from any other source than from scripture and the Holy Spirit speaking in scripture.[239]

---

[236] Whitaker, *Disputation*, 333. According to Whitaker, tradition cannot appeal to promises of further revelation to the apostles either. In John 16:12, where the Lord Jesus says that he has many things yet to tell, is, says Whitaker quoting Augustine, the text that most "foolish heretics" use to authorise their doctrine. In Augustine's (tract.96.) response, the clear indication is that the powers of prophets and apostles are no longer available: "Who of us can do this, destitute of the extraordinary authority of a prophet or an apostle, without incurring the severest blame for his temerity"(544-45)? See Augustine, *Tractate 96*, 2. (*NPNF* first ser., 7, 372).

[237] He adds that if popes contained traditions in their minds, when a pope dies, therefore "traditions would perish with him[...]. Besides, when a person is chosen pope, he brings no other mind with him to the papacy than he had formerly when he was a cardinal or a monk; whereas this hypothesis would require that his mind should be immediately illuminated with the ideas of these traditions". Whitaker does not countenance that the mind of a pope, like any other mind, could now receive immediate illuminations or revelations. Whitaker, *Disputation*, 653-54.

[238] Whitaker, *Disputation*, 275.

[239] Whitaker, *Disputation*, 447.

There is no possibility of extra-biblical revelation in order to apprehend the sense of Scripture. Rather, the impossibility of further immediate revelation now requires the use of means for interpreting Scripture:

> For since scripture hath no audible voice, we must use certain means to investigate what is the sense and what [is] the mind of the scriptures.[240]

Whitaker does, at times, use vocabulary that might seem to suggest that revelation is still available to the contemporary Christian. However, we should interpret his use of such language in the light of his more pervasive and unambiguous cessationist arguments. For example, when he allows that the Holy Spirit can give people the words to pray, Whitaker cannot mean that this involves an immediate extra-biblical revelation unless he is directly contradicting his otherwise salient and transparent position.[241] The inner testimony of the Holy Spirit himself, which is necessary to force heretics to acknowledge the true Scriptures, can also be called "revelation".[242] Faith too can be depicted as "revelation". Whitaker observes that when Peter confessed Jesus as the Christ,[243] "Peter nevertheless could not believe before a divine revelation was added to all this; and therefore Christ attributes the whole of Peter's faith to revelation".[244] Here we see the inner testimony again termed revelation, because substantially faith consists of the inner testimony as revelation:

> For what else is that infused faith but the testimony of the Holy Spirit, on account of which we believe even the scriptures and the doctrine of the scripture, and which seals the whole saving truth of scripture in our hearts?[245]

While Whitaker does not address how God imparts individual personal guidance, his emphatic denial of the likelihood of genuine revelation apart from Scripture – a denial which involves his rejection of "enthusiastical" spirits - suggests that he leaves no room for extra-biblical direction in life's circumstances. Even if the Holy Spirit can "dictate" words to us, that "dictation" must presumably be compatible with the assumption that God has ceased to give revelation *besides* the Scriptures.[246]

In summary, when Whitaker assigns a dictating role to the Holy Spirit, making the praying subject the amanuensis, he does not compromise his cessationist stance. He suggests, rather, that the Holy Spirit works in the

---

[240] Whitaker, *Disputation*, 466.

[241] "[T]he Holy Spirit will suggest and dictate words to us, and guide us in our prayers": Whitaker, *Disputation*, 267.

[242] Whitaker, *Disputation*, 317-18.

[243] Matt. 16:17.

[244] Whitaker, *Disputation*, 355.

[245] Whitaker, *Disputation*, 355.

[246] Whitaker, *Disputation*, 267.

believer, supervising and leading the thought-processes in harmony with Scripture, providence and the will of God. The fact that he repudiates the idea that the inner testimony of the Spirit is a "private spirit"[247] imparting extra-scriptural revelation strongly suggests the assumption that he is committed to the inviolable bond of Word and Spirit. It is precisely in his rejection of the authority of a "private spirit" that he disavows the possibility of an immediate or direct "dictation" by the Holy Spirit:

> We do not say that each individual should acquiesce in that interpretation which his own private spirit frames and dictates to him; for that would be to open a door to fanatical tempers and spirits.[248]

1.5.2 James Usher

A generation on, the Reformed doctrine of the unity of the Word and Spirit, exemplified in Whitaker, was evident in the writing of others whose work is agreed to lie behind the documents of the Westminster Assembly. Usher is universally recognised as a primary source for the *WCF*, through the influence of two of his compositions. He was responsible for both the drafting of the *Irish Articles*[249] whose echo is heard in the *WCF*,[250] and for *A Body of Divinity, or, The Summe and Substance of the Christian Religion*, where he discusses the subject of revelation at length.[251] In Benjamin

---

[247] Whitaker, *Disputation*, 433-34.

[248] Whitaker, *Disputation*, 433.

[249] Barker, *Puritan Profiles*, 44-47. Mitchell concludes: "In regard to the important chapters of the Confession on the Holy Scriptures [among others][...] the resemblance to the Irish Articles both in expression and general arrangement is so close, that not the slightest doubt can be entertained about the main source from which the materials in these chapters have been derived". Mitchell, *The Westminster Assembly: Its History and Standards*, 379.

[250] For the Irish Articles, see Philip Schaff (ed.), *The Creeds of Christendom* (Grand Rapids, MI: Baker, 1985), vol. 3, 526. Mitchell and Struthers (eds.), *Minutes of the Sessions of the Westminster Assembly of Divines*, xlvii-l. Warfield accepts Alex F. Mitchell's conclusion, in the introduction of *Minutes of the Sessions of the Westminster Assembly of Divines*, that the Irish Articles were a source for the *WCF*, but also suggests this caveat: "But it is no more clear that they used it than that they used it very freely and only so far forth as served their purpose; they looked to it for advice, not authority": Warfield, *The Westminster Assembly and its Work*, 175.

[251] Douglas F. Kelly, "The Westminster Shorter Catechism", Carson and Hall (eds.), *To Glorify and Enjoy God*, 105-26, at 107-108. James Usher, *A Body of Divinity, or The Summe and Substance of Christian Religion; Catechistically Propounded, and Explained, by Way of Question and Answer: Methodically and Familiarly Handled. Collected long since out of Sundry Authors, and Reduced unto One Common Method by James Usher B. of Armagh* (London: T. Downes and G. Badger, 1649). Warfield notes that while the *Body of Divinity* may not have been before the Westminster Assembly

Warfield's harmony,[252] Usher's statement, which corresponds to *WCF* 1:10, affirms the epistemic priority of holy Scripture: "[T]hese holy Scriptures are the rule, the line, the square, and light, whereby to examine and try all judgements and sayings of men and Angels[...]. All traditions and revelations[...]are to be embraced so far forth as they may be proved out of the divine Scriptures, and not otherwise".[253] We should not think, though, that since "revelations" are to be tried by Scripture, that genuine extra-biblical revelations are to be expected, for visions through dreams and "all other extraordinary Revelations, are ceased".[254] Nevertheless, while Usher takes a cessationist position in his writings, mirroring Calvin and Whitaker, we shall later consider the claim that Usher himself was said to have uttered several prophecies which subsequently came to pass.[255]

1.5.3 John Ball

Another acknowledged influence on Westminster theology was John Ball (1584-1640), singled out by Daniel Neal as one of "three considerable

---

committee prior to its framing the chapter on Scripture, we cannot be sure of its precise date of publication. Usher wrote to John Downame concerning the work on 12 May, 1645, so it must have predated that May. The Assembly committee, on the other hand, was appointed in 20 August 1644, although the actual drafting of the chapter on Scripture was not initiated until 12 May 1645. A report on progress was only made on 7 July 1645, so it is likely that they did possess the *Body of Divinity* (the earliest extant version is 1645) when they were composing the initial drafts of that chapter: Warfield, *The Westminster Assembly and its Work*, 176-77. Douglas Kelly suggests it might have been composed as early as 1614. Kelly, "The Westminster Shorter Catechism", Carson and Hall (eds.), *To Glorify and Enjoy God*, 317. For a full discussion of the proximate sources of the *WCF*, see Jack Rogers, *Scripture in the Westminster Confession: A Problem of Historical Interpretation for American Presbyterianism* (Grand Rapids, MI: Eerdmans, 1967), 257-64. For the importance of the *Body of Divinity* as a source, see 261-64. Rogers notes: "The headings of chapters in the Westminster Confession which cannot be traced to the Irish Articles can generally be found in *A Body of Divinitie*, and its much fuller treatment of many of the themes of the Confession help us to understand the background of the more terse confessional formulae" (261).

[252] Benjamin B. Warfield, *The Westminster Assembly and its Work*, 190.

[253] Warfield quotes the London 1702 reprint of James Usher's, *A Body of Divinity*, 1702 edition (15); 1649 edition (18).

[254] Usher, *A Body of Divinity*, 7. He adds that the Scriptures are now necessary, "because then God immediately by his voice and Prophets sent from him, taught the Church his truth which now are ceased, *Heb*.1. 1, 2" (7).

[255] James Usher, *The Strange and Remarkable Prophecies and Predictions of the Holy Learned and Excellent James Usher etc* (London: 1780) [no further publishing details are given]. On Usher's "prophecies", see 209 below.

divines" of his period.[256] A minister at Whitmore in Staffordshire, and one whom Richard Baxter identified as "the best Bishop in England",[257] Ball wrote an influential catechism, *A Short Treatise Contayning all the Principall Grounds of Christian Religion*,[258] which was most likely a source of the *WCF*, if only because it was, along with Usher's *Body of Divinity*, one of the "chief popular dogmatic handbooks of its day".[259] Furthermore, Alexander Mitchell believes that Ball's covenant theology "contains all that has been admitted into the Westminster standards",[260] and that Ball was also a source for the Westminster catechisms.[261]

Ball's doctrine of Scripture has much in common with that of the *WCF*. For example, Ball refers to the principle that the Scriptures were *immediately inspired* (*WCF* 1:8), a designation that was also common currency in English and European Reformed theology.[262] Ball relegates diverse modes of revelation to the past when he explains that the Word of God had been once made known through visions, dreams, inspiration, engraving on the heart, Urim and Thummim, signs, audible voice and lastly by writing. Using the same proof-text as the *WCF* (Heb. 1:1), he emphasises the scope of the application of Scripture,[263] and is thoroughly convinced that everything indispensable for faith and life is written there:

---

[256] Daniel Neal, *The History of the Puritans* (London: Thomas Tegg and son, 1837), vol. 1, 635. The two other "considerable" divines were Dr Lawrence Chadderton, a Calvinist, and Dr Richard Neile, an Arminian.

[257] Neal, *The History of the Puritans*, vol. 1, 635. Neal does not give a reference for Baxter's opinion.

[258] John Ball, *A Short Treatise Contayning all the Principall Grounds of Christian Religion* (London: Edward Brewster and Robert Bird, 1633).

[259] Warfield, *The Westminster Assembly and its Work*, 176. Warfield has also created a harmony between Ball's *Catechism*, Usher's *Body of Divinity* and *WCF* Chapter One (177-90).

[260] Mitchell, *The Westminster Assembly: Its History and Standards*, 377. John Ball, *A Treatise of the Covenant of Grace: Wherein the Graduall Breakings out of Gospel-grace from Adam to Christ are Clearly Discovered, the Differences Betwixt the Old and New Testament are Laid Open, Divers Errours of Arminians and Others are Confuted; the Nature of Uprightnesse, and the Way of Christ in Bringing the Soul into Communion with Himself, Together with Many Other Points, both Doctrinally and Practically Profitable, are Solidly Handled* (London: Simeon Ash, 1645). This treatise received written recommendations from five Westminster divines at the very time that the Assembly began to compose the *WCF*. See Mitchell, *The Westminster Assembly: Its History and Standards*, 377.

[261] Mitchell, *The Westminster Assembly: Its History and Standards*, 420.

[262] Warfield, *The Westminster Assembly and its Work*, 204. He cites, for example, the Lutheran Abraham Calov, *Systema Locorum Theologicorum* (Witebergea: Sumptibus A Hartmanni, 1655-1677), vol. 1, 463.

[263] Ball, *A Short Treatise*, 4-5.

> Whatsoever was, is, or shall bee necessary, or profitable to bee knowne, beleeved, practised, or hoped for, that is fully comprehended in the bookes of the Prophets and Apostles.[264]

The Scriptures are complete and perfect; so much so that:

> In the whole body of the Scripture, al doubts and controversies are perfectly decided[...]. Unwritten traditions 1. Cor. 4. 9. new articles of faith, Jer. 7. 31. and 19. 5. and new visions and revelations, are now to bee rejected Heb.1.1[...].[265]

That Ball separates new articles of faith from new visions and revelations indicates that he has more in mind than merely the cessation of revelation for new doctrine.

1.6 Assessing the Contributions of the Westminster Divines

While we have noticed the likely sources of Westminster theology, the related question concerning the influence of the individual Westminster divines also needs attention.[266] Is it possible to ascertain which contributors to the Assembly were the most important?

The Long Parliament originally appointed 30 lay assessors and 121 divines to constitute the Westminster Assembly. The Scots appointed another two lay assessors and five divines to sit at the Assembly. In addition, five peers, nine commoners, eighteen English divines and six Scottish commissioners were subsequently included. Of the total number appointed, only 69 were present on the opening day, with the average attendance settling between 60 and 80. Only 12-20 spoke frequently, and some appointed never attended, while several died or were excused during the period of the Assembly.[267]

Deciding who might have been most influential in the framing of the documents is not a straightforward task. Jack Rogers, in his thesis, *Scripture in the Westminster Confession: A Problem of Historical Interpretation for American Presbyterianism,* gives his conclusions about the most important contributors from among the divines and commissioners to the Westminster Assembly. "The Committee of the few" was probably

---

[264] Ball, *A Short Treatise,* 33.

[265] Ball, *A Short Treatise,* 34-35.

[266] Simeon Ash[e] had advised the Commons in 1642 to choose men who were pious, impartial and well acquainted with Scripture. Simeon Ash, *The Best Refuge, for the Most Oppressed* (London: Edward Brewster and John Burroughs, 1642), 62. Ashe (c.1597-1662) was one of the London clergy appointed to the Westminster Assembly. He was an important Presbyterian and was also one of those instrumental in supporting the restoration of the monarchy and later was appointed a Royal Chaplain by Charles II. Barker, *Puritan Profiles,* 218-24.

[267] Hetherington, *History of the Westminster Assembly,* 102-17.

the committee established to prepare the initial draft of the *WCF*.[268] This committee consisted of Thomas Gataker, Robert Harris, Thomas Temple, Cornelius Burges (or Burgess), Edward Reynolds, Joshua Hoyle, Charles Herle and the Scottish commissioners. A committee of three, consisting of Edward Reynolds, Charles Herle and Matthew Newcomen,[269] was also established to fine-tune the wording of the *WCF* after it had been debated on the floor, and to report back any recommendations for changed phraseology.[270] This smaller committee, instituted on 8 July 1645, which was to consult the Scots, also had a change of personnel when on 8 December 1645, Anthony Tuckney and Jeremiah Whitaker replaced Charles Herle. On 17 June 1646, John Arrowsmith was added, and, on 1 September 1646, Daniel Cawdry, a late addition to the Assembly, was included also. This committee became known as the committee for rewording and reworking the Confession of Faith.[271]

On 7 July 1645 the drafting committee reported its deliberations on the doctrine of Scripture. This marked the beginning of the work on the *WCF* of the Assembly as a whole and on 11 July a debate was held over whether the remaining chapters of the *WCF* should be allocated to the entire body of the Assembly in three committees. The drafting committee was charged with the task of dividing the chapters between the three committees of the Assembly. The chairmen of these committees, which had been instituted as early as 8 July 1643, were, respectively, William Gouge, Thomas Temple and Nicholas Prophet.[272]

There are various ways of assessing the contribution of individuals. Rogers concludes his analysis thus:

> [T]he chief authorship of the Confession of Faith may be assigned to a few: Reynolds, Burges, Temple, Herle, Hoyle, Gataker, and Harris.

---

[268] Rogers, *Scripture in the Westminster Confession*, 160.

[269] Born at Colchester, Essex and educated at Cambridge, Matthew Newcomen (c. 1610-1669) served as curate at both Messing, Essex and Stoke-by-Nayland, Suffolk. He later became lecturer and curate at Dedham, Essex, where he remained until 1662. Newcomen, one of the youngest members of the Westminster Assembly, was of the Presbyterian majority and another of the "Smectymnuans". During the Assembly he was a vocal opponent of the Independents, of Antinomianism and of the Erastians. As one of its editors, he played a leading role in producing the *WCF*. Following his ejection in 1662, he left for Leiden in the Netherlands to be pastor of an English church. Barker, *Puritan Profiles,* 234-39. See also William Beveridge, *A Short History of the Westminster Assembly* (Edinburgh: T. & T. Clark, 1904), 105-17 on the committee structures of the Assembly in the preparation of the *WCF*.

[270] Rogers, *Scripture in the Westminster Confession*, 163.

[271] Rogers, *Scripture in the Westminster Confession*, 175.

[272] Rogers, *Scripture in the Westminster Confession*, 163. Rogers arrives at his selection of names by making credible assumptions based on the minuted names of those who usually reported back for the committees. See 163, n236.

Newcomen, Tuckney, Whitaker and Arrowsmith played the largest supporting roles. To these English members of the Westminster Divines must be added the constant influence of the four Scottish Commissioners: Henderson, Baillie, Gillespie and Rutherford.[273]

On the other hand, Wayne Spear shows in his thesis, *Covenanted Uniformity in Religion*, another means of assessing the comparative influence of individuals in the Assembly. He counts the number of times the divines appear in the minutes as speakers.[274] While it is possible, as Rogers and Spear have done, to draw conclusions about the comparative influence of each member, such a conclusion can never be definitive. After all, each part of the *WCF* was debated in the plenary sessions of the Assembly before acceptance, giving everyone present an opportunity to address its various sections. Rogers himself admits that the small committee for reworking the *WCF* did so "to correspond to the Assembly's will".[275] This is an admission that the entire Assembly was involved in and responsible for the final wording of the *WCF* to go to Parliament.

We should not ignore those who were appointed but failed to take their seats, because the fact of their selection is an indication that they were perceived to be orthodox in their opinions. It is also likely that certain individuals felt more strongly about some aspects of the Assembly deliberations than about others. The Scots, for example, were very keen to see their form of church government established in the three kingdoms. So Robert Paul understands Robert Baillie: "the Scottish cause and the Presbyterian cause were one".[276] It is also true that a frequent contributor in a debate need not necessarily be the most effective. In any debate, one person may convince others by speaking only once. Furthermore, those working behind the scenes, although they may be silent in a public debate, can have a great influence on the outcome.

While we have taken the suggested influences of prominent members into account, we are more concerned to discern if there is an overall consensus on the subject of the cessation or the continuance of supernatural revelation. We also include representatives from the different ecclesiological or confessional positions in the Assembly. The key parties defined by their ecclesiology were the Erastians, the Independents, the Presbyterians and the Episcopalians. The latter group was only briefly

---

[273] Rogers, *Scripture in the Westminster Confession*, 176.

[274] Wayne Spear, "Covenanted Uniformity in Religion: The Influence of the Scottish Commissioners upon the Ecclesiology of the Westminster Assembly" (unpublished PhD thesis, University of Pittsburgh, 1976), appendix C, 362. Not all members are listed, however. Spear uses only the first two volumes of the manuscript minutes for the 243 sessions from February 1643 to November 1644.

[275] Rogers, *Scripture in the Westminster Confession*, 175.

[276] Paul, *The Assembly of The Lord*, 444.

represented, while the Erastians and Independents were a decided minority. However, there is no evidence that ecclesiological preference, in this context, influenced an adherent's doctrine of Scripture. We have also taken into account whether or not members contributed to the discussion of divine revelation in their other writings, and whether or not they were considered by their contemporaries to be influential in the debates.[277]

As our subsequent discussion will show, many of the most prominent divines gave much attention to the doctrine of Scripture, both at the Assembly and in their sermons and treatises, and they often responded to claims of extra-biblical revelation in their own day.

1.7 Conclusion

Religious differences played a major part in catapulting the three kingdoms into civil war, but without a doubt political and military events were seized upon by the English Puritans and Scottish Presbyterians to advance the cause of ecclesiastical and national reformation. The Scottish covenanting tradition now found its echo in the *Solemne League*, and in the wake of a heightened eschatological fervour the Westminster Assembly sought to clarify the obligations specified in that document with new doctrinal commitments, including the *WCF*.

Westminster's literature needed to respond to the theological, ecclesiastical and social problems that arose from the mushrooming sects throughout the three Kingdoms which threatened a national Reformed unity, but the resulting doctrinal productions of the Assembly also owed much to former generations of Reformed thinkers.

The key features of an identifiable Augustinian religious epistemology are present in a representative sample of the Reformed orthodox. A commitment to the Bible as the essential rule of faith and conduct, a concomitant stress on the unity of Word and Spirit, and the necessity for the inner testimony of the Holy Spirit are the pervasive components. The ambiguities we have seen in the writings of William Perkins are not discernible in the more immediate sources of the *WCF*: Whitaker, Usher and Ball. In these latter authors, we find a rigorous and stringent cessationist view. The older theologian William Whitaker has nothing positive to say about new extra-biblical revelations, but seeks to demolish the claims of both "enthusiasts" and his Catholic adversaries to any such

---

[277] For other select biographies of the divines, see the relevant articles in *DNB*; Larry Holly, "The Divines of the Westminster Assembly: A Study of Puritanism and Parliament" (unpublished PhD thesis, Yale University, 1979), 282-366; also Thomas Smith, *Select Memoirs of the Lives, Labours and Sufferings of Those Pious and Learned English and Scottish Divines [...] who Ultimately Crowned the Venerable Edifice with the Celebrated Westminster Confession of Faith* (Glasgow: D. Mackenzie, 1828).

revelation, while at the same time vehemently denying that Protestants claim any new revelations in addition to the inscripturated Word. It is fundamental to Whitaker's support of Protestantism's *sola Scriptura* that he denies the Catholic charge that Protestants relied upon extra-biblical revelation to confirm the canon.

Usher and Ball were equally unambiguous, teaching a complete cessation of extra-biblical revelation. These theologians were more in step with Calvin's cessationist views and we will argue that it was this cessationism that underpins the Westminster theology and not the more open continuationist views of the later Augustine, Aquinas and an early Protestant reformer like Peter Martyr. Indeed, we find the majority of the Reformed orthodox of the seventeenth century in line with Calvin's more sceptical approach, although, as we shall see, there are still those who accept the possibility of extra-biblical revelations, such as the eminent Richard Baxter.[278] While the Westminster Assembly itself was composed of individuals of varying theological acumen, different levels of debating participation and rhetorical skill, and greater or lesser reputations as theologians, the democratic committee structure employed at the Assembly suggests that the responsibility for the final documents should be evenly apportioned to all of its members.

---

[278] See Chapter 4, 159 below.

Chapter 2

The Necessity and Scope[1] of Special Revelation

2.1 Introduction

The cessationist clause of *WCF* 1:1 can only be interpreted in the light of the basic assumptions of the religious epistemology adopted by the divines represented at Westminster. These assumptions include particular conceptions of the original method or methods of divine revelation, the content of this disclosure, and the purposes for which it was given. The concern of the cessationist clause[2] is obviously explained ultimately in the

---

[1] We do not use the word "scope" in the same technical sense in which it has been used in Protestant scholasticism, but rather to imply the extent of the utility and function of Scripture as special revelation. For the formal distinctions concerning the foundation and scope of Scripture in the Reformed orthodox, see Richard Muller, *Post-Reformation Reformed Dogmatics* (Grand Rapids, MI: Baker, 2003), vol. 2, where he concludes that the early Reformers wrote of the foundation (*fundamentum*) and the scope (*scopus*), meaning the goal or centre of Scripture (208-13). While Christ is both the foundation and scope of Scripture, "Christ does not point out the meaning of all doctrine" (212). Christ is at the core of the Christian message, but Christ is not "the overarching meaning of all Scripture" (212). Edward Leigh, a contemporary of the Westminster divines is another who adopts the notion that Christ is the *fundamentum Scripturae*: "The Scriptures are *fundamentum quo*, the fundamental writings which declare the salvation of Christians, *John* 5.37. Christ [the] *fundamentum quod*, the fundamental means and cause which hath purchased and doth give it, *John* 4.42": Edward Leigh, *A Systeme or Body of Divinity: Consisting of Ten books. Wherein the Fundamentals and Main Grounds of Religion are Opened: The Contrary Errours Refuted [...]*"(London: William Lee, 1654), Prolegomena [not paginated]. Similarly Westminster divine Jeremiah Burroughs uses the concept of *scopus Scripturae*. He understands the *scopus* of the whole of Scripture to involve the declaration of God's mercy and goodness, but also applies the term to the various exegetical conclusions that arise out of discrete chapters. Jeremiah Burroughs, *An Exposition of the Prophecy of Hosea* (Edinburgh: James Nichol, 1865), 461-62. Cited in Muller, *Post-Reformation Reformed Dogmatics*, vol. 2, 221.

[2] *WCF* 1: 1 "[…]yet are they not sufficient to give that knowledge of God, and of His will, which is necessary unto salvation. Therefore it pleased the Lord, at sundry times, and in divers manners, to reveal Himself, and to declare that His will unto His Church; and afterwards, for the better preserving and propagating of the truth, and for the more sure establishment and comfort of the Church against the corruption of the flesh, and the malice of Satan and of the world, to commit the same wholly unto writing: which

role of Scripture as the means by which the way of salvation was held to be made known, since the Scriptures are now deemed to be "most necessary". In order to discern the import of the cessationist clause, we need to answer four questions especially:

i. In what sense are God's "former ways" of revelation said to have ceased?
ii. What is "will"?
iii. What is the "salvation" in question?
iv. What is the necessity of Scripture for gaining access to salvation?

We take up the first question in the next chapter. The second question is answered clearly in *WCF* 1:1, as the information for attaining salvation: for it is the "knowledge of God, and of His will, which is necessary unto salvation", something the *WCF* is going to summarise and clarify from Scripture. The remaining two questions will be addressed in the body of this chapter.

The divines contextualise the discussion of where God's will leading to salvation was thought to be located, and it is an analysis of this context which must preface our discussion of the final two questions. The source of the "will" of God that leads the knower to salvation is clarified in a discussion in *WCF* 1:1 of the two categories of revelation which the divines perceived were available to humankind. The first of these we will term general revelation.[3]

2.2 The Limitations of General Revelation

The Westminster Assembly inherited the doctrine of *sola Scriptura* from the classical Reformers. This doctrine was not muted in any way in Westminster theology when its authors strategically located their doctrine of Scripture at the very head of the *WCF*.

In their opening chapter, the divines propose two fountainheads for knowledge of the transcendent God. The first of these, the tripartite source of creation, God's government of the universe, and the law of God written on the heart, is dismissed as soteriologically inadequate. As their prooftexts show, the divines believe that these means of unveiling, termed respectively creation,[4] providence, and the light of nature,[5] do convey

---

maketh the Holy Scripture to be most necessary; *those former ways of God's revealing His will unto His people being now ceased*" [cessationist clause emphasised].

[3] The virtue of using the term "general revelation" and its counterpart "special revelation" in the Westminster epistemology is treated below at 71.

[4] Typically in Reformed orthodoxy, providence was grouped with creation. See, for example, Article Two of the French and Belgic Confessions of Faith in Philip Schaff, *The Creeds of Christendom* (Grand Rapids, MI: Baker, 1985), vol. 3, 360 and 383.

authentic information about the Creator, including such realities as God's "goodness, wisdom and power".[6] These revelatory phenomena also teach all human beings something about creaturely "concupiscence". As the divines understood it, when one perceives a knowledge of God through the world or by the light of nature, the intuitive ethical impulse of the law of God exposes an inherent unwillingness and inability to obey. As a result, every person is rendered inexcusable, since although people know about God's ethical demands, they fail to respond to them in an acceptable and appropriate manner. For the Westminster divines, humankind's moral dilemma lies here: we recognize enough about God, ourselves and our duty to God to condemn us, yet we lack both the capacity and the willingness necessary to satisfy God. Instinctive knowledge of God, dismissed by the *WCF* as insufficient to "save" the human race, is held to be universally available, and has been conveniently termed a "natural" or "general" revelation.[7]

The divines teach that the innate limitations of this public knowledge of God logically create an urgent need for further enlightenment. To

---

[5] See Jack Rogers, *Scripture in the Westminster Confession: A Problem of Historical Interpretation for American Presbyterianism* (Grand Rapids, MI: Eerdmans, 1967), 265. Rogers correctly points out that accepted proximate sources of the *WCF*, James Usher (or Ussher), *A Body of Divinity, or The Summe and Substance of Christian Religion; Catechistically Propounded, and Explained, by Way of Question and Answer: Methodically and Familiarly Handled. Collected long since out of Sundry Authors, and Reduced unto One Common Method by James Usher B. of Armagh* (London: T. Downes and G. Badger, 1649), and *The 1615 Irish Articles*, [See Schaff, *The Creeds of Christendom*, vol. 3, 526] do not use the phrase "the light of nature". The term appears four times in the *WCF* and is allowed a positive role in the determining of some matters of worship and church government (*WCF* 1:6.). It also surfaces in the Canons of Dort. See "Canons of the Synod of Dort" in Schaff, *The Creeds of Christendom*, vol. 3, 557 (Primum Doctrinae Caput, Paragraph 4, rejectio errorum) and vol. 3, 565 (Tertium et Quartum Doctrinae Caput, Article 6.). The light of nature was "*the knowledge which God hath given unto man in their natural estate since the fall of men, whereby he hath in some degree made known unto them himself, and the good they ought to do, and the evils they ought to shun*": John Maynard (or Mainard), *The Law of God Ratified*[...]"(London: Francis Tyton, 1674), 176. Because it declared right and wrong in this way, the Puritans sometimes identified the light of nature with the "candle of the Lord" (Prov. 20:27), or conscience. See Westminster divine Anthony Burgess, *Vindiciae Legis: Or, A Vindication of the Morall Law and the Covenants, from the Errours of Papists, Arminians, Socinians, and More Especially, Antinomians* (London: Thomas Underhill, 1647), 61.

[6] Rom. 2:14-15; 1:19-20; Ps. 19:1-3 and Rom. 1:32 with Rom. 2:1.

[7] "Although the light of nature and the works of creation and providence do so far manifest the goodness, wisdom, and power of God, as to leave men unexcusable; yet are they not sufficient to give that knowledge of God and of His will, which is necessary unto salvation". *WCF* 1:1.

distinguish this further type of knowledge from "general revelation", it has been helpfully classified as "supernatural" or "special", because of its more limited availability, its supernatural manner of transmission, and its specialised content. While this "general/special" terminology is not found in the *WCF*, it was beginning to be used in the seventeenth century.[8] It was used in the 1619 Canons of Dort. In Article Five of the discussion of the "Perseverantia Sanctorum", "speciali revelatione" is said to be unnecessary for the assurance of salvation. The article adds that the Scriptures do not attribute assurance to "speciali et extraordinaria revelatione".[9] It can be seen in the sermons of Westminster divine John Maynard[10] on the law of God. Maynard, in one homily, having canvassed Rom. 1:19-21 and 2:14-15, distinguishes between Scripture as "special revelation" and the "common general light of Nature".[11] His contemporary Andrew Perne (1596-1654) contrasts the natural knowledge of God and the saving knowledge of God by stressing that the latter is the "speciall favour of God".[12] Thus, although the exact phraseology of "general" and "special" revelation is absent from the *WCF*, the distinction made by the divines themselves can be safely categorised in this historical context as a division

---

[8] George Hendry in his commentary on the *WCF* simply assumes the category of special revelation in his discussion, using the term freely to describe the revelation of saving knowledge as distinguished from general revelation. George Hendry, *The Westminster Confession for Today: A Contemporary Interpretation* (Richmond, VA: John Knox Press, 1960), 22-24. Robert Shaw prefers "supernatural revelation" in his commentary on the *WCF*: Robert Shaw, *The Reformed Faith* (Inverness: Christian Focus Publications, 1973), 5.

[9] See Schaff, *The Creeds of Christendom*, vol. 3, 575.

[10] Maynard preached before Parliament on 26 February 1644 and 28 October 1646. See John Wilson, *Pulpit in Parliament: Puritanism during the English Civil Wars, 1640-1648* (Princeton: Princeton University Press, 1969), 244. Maynard (d. 1665), born at or near Riverfield in Sussex, was a minister at Mayfield, Sussex when he preached this series of sermons. He was educated at Oxford and his sympathy for Parliament's cause in the Civil War is one factor that accounts for his presence in the Assembly of divines and as one invited by the Long Parliament to preach fast-day sermons. Ejected by the Act of Uniformity, Maynard continued to live in Mayfield until his death. For a summary of Maynard's life, see James Reid, *Memoirs of the Westminster Divines* (Edinburgh: Banner of Truth, 1982), vol. 2, 84-85.

[11] Maynard, *The Law of God Ratified*[...]", 179.

[12] Andrew Perne, *Gospell Courage, or Christian Resolution for God, and His Truth* (London: Stephen Bowtell, 1643), 11. Perne, a frequent preacher before Parliament was a regular attender at the Westminster Assembly. Educated at Cambridge, Perne was offered attractive preferments following the Assembly, but returned to Wilby, Northamptonshire, where he laboured in total for 27 years. Reid, *Memoirs of the Westminster Divines*, vol. 2, 118-20.

between such types of divine disclosure.[13] The conventional terminology has a certain utility for our present purpose since it helps to accentuate the *WCF's* differentiation between God's intervention in history to redeem the elect, and the more limited, general and less efficacious witness to God of nature itself.

Those who make such a distinction do not imply that general revelation is without value. James Usher, for example, had espoused the worth of the light of nature "to further unto salvation".[14] Scottish commissioner to the Assembly Samuel Rutherford also held a positive view of the light of nature.[15] Rutherford lays stress on the harmony between the light of nature as the law written on the heart, and the moral code as recorded in Scripture.[16] Maynard's position concurs to the extent that he agrees that far from being worthless, God might still use the light of nature "*as a remote preparative for the receiving of the Gospel in some to whom the word of salvation was tendred*".[17] His position demonstrates that the Puritans were willing to re-evaluate the usefulness of general revelation in the light of Scripture, and indicates that Westminster orthodoxy did allow this natural and universally accessible unveiling of the divine will an important place in its religious epistemology.

WCF 20, for example, gives the light of nature an authoritative function, while creation and providence receive their own individual treatments.[18] As we shall see in more detail in due course, with Scripture in hand, general revelation became a place where God's mind could be discerned, particularly in matters of personal and national temporal significance.[19]

---

[13] Benjamin Warfield holds: "The one [Natural/General] has in view to meet and supply the natural need of the creatures for knowledge of their God; the other [Supernatural/Special/Soteriological] to rescue broken and deformed sinners from their sin and its consequences". Benjamin Warfield, *The Works of Benjamin B. Warfield* (Grand Rapids, MI: Baker, 1991), vol. 1, 6. Bruce Milne, *Know the Truth* (Leicester: Inter-Varsity Press, 1982), defines special revelation as "the ways God makes himself known with a clarity and fulness which far surpasses general revelation. It is centred in the miracle of the incarnation and mediated through the God-inspired words of the Bible" (24-27, at 24). His "material form" of special revelation is the Scriptures.

[14] Usher, *A Body of Divinity*, 5.

[15] John Coffey, *Politics, Religion and the British Revolutions: The Mind of Samuel Rutherford* (Cambridge: Cambridge University Press, 1997), especially 172-73 for Rutherford's view of the harmony of natural law with Scripture.

[16] Samuel Rutherford (or Rutherfurd), *The Divine Right of Church-Government and Excommunication [...]*"(London: Christopher Meredith, 1646), 76-77.

[17] Maynard, *The Law of God Ratified*, 185.

[18] *WCF* Chapters Four and Five respectively.

[19] Puritan providentialism and the relation of Scripture to contemporary events were thus linked.

The Westminster view of the comparative utility of what amounted to general and special revelation is duplicated in the works of various Westminster divines. Daniel Featley (1582-1645), for example, noted in the English Annotations[20] that however valuable the light of nature in human

---

[20] *Annotations upon All the Books of the Old and New Testament: This Third, above the First and Second, Edition so Enlarged, As They Make an Entire Commentary on the Sacred Scripture: The Like Never before Published in English. Wherein the Text is Explained, Doubts Resolved, Scriptures Parallel'd, and Various Readings Observed; By the Labour of Certain Learned Divines Thereunto Appointed, and Therein Employed, As is Expressed in the Preface* (London: Evan Tyler, 1657), Romans 1:19-20. Hereafter, sometimes the Annotations. The English or Westminster Annotations, as they are variously called, prepared by English Westminster divines and others appointed by Parliament and first printed in 1645, give a good insight into the standard Reformed exegesis of the day. Although not lauded by all the Westminster divines, Scottish commissioner Robert Baillie gives a strong endorsement to the Annotations. Baillie writing to Robert Ramsey on 15 January 1646 urged, "When Thomas Young comes home[...]He will give yow and Mr. George the Annotations, which I pray yow accept without any scrupulositie". Robert Baillie, *The Letters and Journals of Robert Baillie, A. M. Principal of the University of Glasgow M.DC.XXXVII.-M.DC.LXII.*, ed. David Laing (Edinburgh: Bannatyne Club, 1841-1842), vol. 2, 336. According to Daniel Neal the following were the authors of the Annotations. The Pentateuch, Ley; 1 Kings to Esther, Gouge; Psalms, Casaubon; Song, Smalwood; Isaiah to Lamentations, Gataker; Ezekiel to Malachi, Pemberton in the first edition and Richardson in the second; gospels, Ley; Paul's epistles, Featley; with two others, Downham and Reading, probably addressing the remaining books: Daniel Neal, *The History of the Puritans; or, Protestant Nonconformists; from the Reformation in 1517, to the Revolution in 1688* (London: Thomas Tegg and Sons, 1837), vol. 2, 505. The preface to the Dutch Annotations, translated by Theodore Haak (or Haake) in 1648, suggests that there were other authors of the English Annotations than those mentioned above: "And here in *England* it soon got into such a repute, that when, not long after, Parliament found good, to get New *Annotations* made upon the whole Bible for general Edification, by those Reverend and able Divines, Mr *Leigh*, Mr *Downham*, Dr *Gouge*, Mr *Taylour*, Mr *Gataker*, Mr *Pemberton*, Mr *Abbot*, Mr *Reading*, Dr *Featly* and Mr *Tooker*, (placed here in order of the parts of the Bible which they were to undertake) they (the Parliament) did then in especial manner recommend *this very Bible and Notes* unto them) (As well as Deodates Italian) causing Copies of each to be divided and sent respectively unto them, for to make use thereof, which also they did. And my Lord *Primate* of *Armagh*, Dr *Usher*, of happy memory, was often heard to wish very heartily, both before and after that time, that the whole work might be *Englished*, as finding it the *plainest* and *impartionalest*, and *freest of Escursions* and *Impertinencies*, of any he knew, that knew so many:[...]What value the principal Members of the late *Assembly of Divines*, together with the Scotish Church-Commissioners, did set upon it, their own words best express in that subscribed free *Attestation* of theirs[...]". [In this attestation, the divines explain that they have already had access to these annotations and commend them. Thirty-five divines including the four Scottish ministers subscribed this attestation. Although other independents are there, Bridge is missing.] Theodore Haak (translator), *The Dutch*

consciences" might be, its net result was to render all human beings without excuse in God's sight. Daniel Featley, an Episcopalian, attended the Assembly, albeit briefly (he was expelled for allegedly acting as a spy on Assembly proceedings for the king).[21] Featley concluded, in agreement with the *WCF*,[22] that general revelation leaves human beings in a hopeless position without some other source of truth.[23] It is the inadequacy of this knowledge of God in nature and conscience that establishes the necessity of a special way to discover God's mind, both to apprise humankind of the way into God's Kingdom, and to show how to exist and persevere as citizens of heaven.[24]

Annotations upon the Whole Bible: Or, All the Holy Canonical Scriptures of the Old and New Testaments, Together with, and According to Their Own Translation of All the Text: As Both the One and the Other were Ordered and Appointed by the Synod of Dort, 1618, and Published by Authority, 1637 (London: John Rothwell, Joshua Kirton, and Richard Tomlins, 1657), vol. 1, preface.

[21] See Barker, *Puritan Profiles*, 47-51. Featley was born at Charlton-upon-Otmoor, Oxfordshire and contributed the annotations on Paul's Epistles to the English Annotations. He spoke out against the *Solemn League and Covenant*, which would have resulted in his expulsion in any case.

[22] *WCF* 1:1.

[23] Featley, *Annotations*, Romans 1:20. Other Westminster divines concur. See Thomas Goodwin, *The Works of Thomas Goodwin, D.D.* (Edinburgh: James Nichol, 1863), vol. 6, 234; or William Bridge, *The Works of the Rev. William Bridge, M.A.* (London: Thomas Tegg, 1845), vol. 1, 259, 434; Maynard suggests two reasons why general revelation renders human beings inexcusable. First, they "*shut their eyes against the light*" by not seeking to build upon the light they already possess. Secondly, he suggests that they do not live up to the light received, "according to those natural abilities which they had". Maynard, *The Law of God Ratified*, 185-86. Featley more cautiously explains that human beings are inexcusable because they fail to respond to a knowledge of God, though he does not suggest that people possess an ability to respond adequately to that knowledge. Featley, *Annotations*, Romans 1:19.

[24] *WCF* 1:1. Those confessions which do not begin with the doctrine of Scripture include the 1530 Lutheran *Augsburg Confession*, the 1523 *Articles or Conclusions of Ulrich Zwingli*, the 1559 *French Confession*, the 1561 *Belgic Confession*, the 1560 *Scotch Confession*, the 1562 *Thirty-Nine Articles of the Church of England*, and the 1655 *Confession of the Waldenses*. Those confessions which begin with the doctrine of Scripture include the 1576 *Formula of Concord*, the 1536 *First Helvetic Confession*, the 1566 *Second Helvetic Confession*, the 1580 *Second Scotch Confession or National Covenant* (although this was appended to the first Scotch Confession), the 1586 *An Harmony of the Confessions of the Faith of the Christian and Reformed Churches*, and the 1615 *Irish Articles of Religion*. The most accessible compendium of Protestant confessions, catechisms and articles of faith is Philip Schaff's, *The Creeds of Christendom*.

2.3 Special Revelation and *WCF* 1:1

Westminster divine John Arrowsmith's (1602-1659) biblical theology serves as an example of those which see the need for a disclosure of God's will beyond that present in general revelation. Arrowsmith was a noted scholar and theologian, who later became Master of St John's College, Cambridge; Vice Chancellor of the University; and Master of Trinity College.[25] He posited two basic ways of knowing God: first, by natural knowledge, which he associated with the light of nature; secondly, through knowledge of God in Scripture, which conveys far more than the light of nature.[26] The light of nature can inform us that there is a God, but it fails to impart the knowledge of "*who and what he is*, in regard of his Essence, Subsistence, and Attributes".[27] The fullness of knowledge requires a "Scripture-revelation".[28] However, this bare "Scripture-revelation" is not saving on its own, but requires a transfer of this revealed knowledge to the inner man. Therefore since more than a basic reading of the word of Scripture is needed, the more complete form of Scripture as revelation is:

> A knowledge of God[...]proceeding[...]from effectual irradiations of *the Spirit of wisdom and revelation* [Eph. 1:17], accompanied with purging and cheering influences from the same spirit.[29]

Such revelation remains a knowledge firmly tied to Scripture, for:

> Since the Canon of Scripture was perfected, the things which the Holy Ghost discoverth are no other for substance, but those very things which are contained in the written word.[30]

---

[25] In that order. Arrowsmith was born near Newcastle-upon-Tyne, took his M.A. at Cambridge in 1623 and became vicar of St. Nicholas Chapel in King's Lynn, Norfolk in 1644. Ironically one of his eyes had been put out by an arrow when a boy, making his name particularly appropriate. For a brief account of Arrowsmith's life and work, see Larry Holly, "The Divines of the Westminster Assembly: A Study of Puritanism and Parliament" (unpublished PhD Thesis, Yale University, 1979), 282.

[26] John Arrowsmith, *Armilla Catechetica. A Chain of Principles; Or, An Orderly Concatenation of Theological Aphorismes and Exercitations*[...]" (Cambridge: Cambridge University, 1659), 150.

[27] Arrowsmith, *Armilla Catechetica*, 128.

[28] Arrowsmith, *Armilla Catechetica*, 128.

[29] Arrowsmith, *Armilla Catechetica*, 150.

[30] Arrowsmith, *Armilla Catechetica*, 150-51. For recent discussions on the Reformed orthodox doctrine of Scripture, see Scott Thomas Murphy, "The Doctrine of Scripture in the Westminster Assembly" (unpublished PhD thesis, Drew University, 1984); Jack Rogers, *Scripture in the Westminster Confession: A Problem of Historical Interpretation for American Presbyterianism* (Grand Rapids, MI: Eerdmans, 1967); and Geoffrey Nuttall, *The Holy Spirit in Puritan Faith and Experience* (Oxford: Basil Blackwell, 1947), 21-33.

The way to salvation itself is accordingly to be found in Scripture, which "is so framed, as to deliver all things necessary to salvation in a clear and perspicuous way".[31] Nonetheless "the effectual irradiations" of the Holy Spirit must accompany the knowledge found in Scripture in order to render that knowledge efficacious. This latter claim of Arrowsmith's, namely the enabling of the Holy Spirit, was an integral component of the epistemology of the Westminster Assembly. While special revelation was revealed outwardly and objectively to the church, it did not become the knowledge of God unto salvation for the individual without the efficacy of the Spirit in applying it.[32] Equally, the knowledge applied by the Spirit was to be found only in the written Word.

The divines introduce their foundational presuppositions concerning God's supernatural revelation at the head of the *WCF*. *WCF* 1:1, makes *three* initial statements concerning the motive, the necessity and the intended recipients of this further revelation. First, God's motive in granting it is described as his pleasure. Special revelation was a voluntary decision on God's part to convey extra information. Secondly, the content of the revelation itself was God's will, which human beings need to know in order to be saved. Thirdly, the revelation was given specifically to "His Church". These three features emphasise the personal nature of the more special and focused revelation, the intention of which is to save, and thereby to establish a personal relationship between God and the saved which could be instituted in no other way.

The remainder of *WCF* 1 tells us a good deal more about the identity and design of this second category of divine revelation. In the past, such revelation was given at different times and in different ways,[33] but now it is restricted to the "Holy Scripture".[34] Secondly, it is committed "wholly" to the Scriptures (*WCF* 1:1). Thirdly, these Scriptures are called the "Word of

---

[31] Arrowsmith, *Armilla Catechetica*, 96.

[32] *WCF* 1:6. "Nevertheless we acknowledge the inward illumination of the Spirit of God to be necessary for the saving understanding of such things as are revealed in the Word".

[33] The divines were in perfect accord with James Usher's authentic Protestantism who had enquired: "*Where then is the saving knowledg[e] of God to be had perfectly?*" The simple answer is: "In his holy Word". Usher, *A Body of Divinity*, 6.

[34] Another renowned English theologian, William Gouge, likewise confines God's special revelation to the completed canon. Gouge compared the communication of divine counsel in the two defining epochs of redemptive history in his commentary on the book of Hebrews: "This manifesting of Gods will by parts, is here noted by way of distinction and difference from Gods revealing of his will under the Gospel: which was all at one time, namely the time of his Sonnes being on earth: for then the whole counsell of God was made known, so farre as was meet for the Church to know it while this world continueth". William Gouge, *A Learned and Very Useful Commentary on the Whole Epistle to the Hebrewes* (London: Joshua Kirton, 1655), 8.

God written",[35] consisting of sixty-six canonical books which are "to be the rule of faith and life" (*WCF* 1:2). Fourthly, since the whole Bible constitutes this "rule of faith and life" and since this rule is at once in its entirety the complete Scripture, the Word of God, and the way of salvation, an inevitable conclusion follows: the totality of the Bible is concerned with human salvation.[36]

The two proof-texts (1 Cor. 1:21 and 2:13-14)[37] for the clause on the limitations of general revelation in *WCF* 1:1("yet they are not sufficient to give that knowledge of God and of His will, which is necessary unto

---

[35] When they qualified the "Word of God" as written, the divines probably wanted to signal that there was formerly an "unwritten" Word of God also. Richard Muller notes: "The Reformed Orthodox did not, as is commonly assumed, make a rigid equation of the Word of God with Holy Scripture": Richard Muller, *Post-Reformation Reformed Dogmatics*, vol. 2, 182. As Scott Murphy determined in his dissertation on the Westminster doctrine of Scripture: "In theory the Divines believed God's Word to comprise more than Scripture. It is God's total revelation to man-kind". Scott Thomas Murphy, "The Doctrine of Scripture in the Westminster Assembly" (unpublished PhD thesis, Drew University, 1984), 70. Also see Henry Wilkinson Sr. (1566-1647) who speaks for Reformed orthodoxy when he asks in his 1629 catechism, "*What is the word of God?*" The catechumen was supposed to answer: "The Bookes of the holy Canonicall Scriptures, containing the covenants both of our obedience to God, and of his saving grace in Christ to us". Wilkinson, like Usher, typically restricted the "Word of God" to the Scriptures as the sole contemporary source of saving information. Henry Wilkinson, *A Catechisme, Contayning a Short Exposition of the Points in the Ordinary Catechisme, with Proofes of the Same out of the Scripture [...]* (London: Robert Birde, 1629), not paginated. There were two Henry Wilkinsons, a father and son, at the Assembly who need to be distinguished. Wilkinson senior was one of the oldest members of the Assembly and probably did not take a very active part in the debates and committees. See Reid, *Memoirs of the Westminster Divines*, vol. 2, 247-49. Henry Wilkinson junior (1609-1675), at one time Lady Margaret Professor at Oxford, was ejected at the Restoration, and lived out his days as a non-conformist in Clapham, Surrey. See Reid, *Memoirs of the Westminster Divines*, vol. 2, 249-51.

[36] *WCF* 1:6 asserts that nothing is to be added to the whole counsel of God (which is now set down in Scripture) - either by "new revelations of the Spirit, or traditions of men". See Bellarmine's arguments for tradition as part of the Word of God and Whitaker's response in William Whitaker, *Disputation on Holy Scripture* (Cambridge: The University Press, 1849), 551-62.

[37] Featley exegetes the text (1 Cor. 1:21) to refer to the limitations of general revelation for attaining a knowledge of God for salvation. Featley understands this text to be about knowing God for salvation, in contrast with the knowledge of God gleaned through general revelation which makes humans inexcusable. He comments: "*knew not God*} That is, knew him not to salvation, for otherwise the Apostle teacheth, Rom. the first, vers. 20. that they knew so much of the eternal power and Godhead by the creation of the world as made them unexcusable": Featley, *Annotations,* 1 Cor. 1:21. 1 Cor. 2:13-14 contrasts spiritual understanding with unspiritual, and can be applied to the totality of the Bible's teaching.

The Necessity and Scope of Special Revelation 77

salvation")³⁸ confirm this specific design of special revelation. They contrast the apprehension of God's mind obtained through natural or general revelation with that acquired through the preaching of the gospel, and demonstrate that the divines have in mind a knowledge of God which provides requisite information for attaining salvation - in Gouge's language, "meet for the Church to know".³⁹ Thus the limitations of general revelation have been overcome, so that human beings can not only *know about* God, but also *know* God savingly.

However, an important question invites further discussion. Was the "whole counsel of God", described in *WCF* 1:6, limited to a certain *class* of redemptive-historical information, and did it therefore leave open the possibility of God granting his counsel through extra-biblical means for other matters such as temporal guidance? In other words, are the modern-day "Presbyterian charismatics", chided by Kenneth Gentry, correct in their claim that the concept of salvation in *WCF* 1:1 merely refers to "redemptive-historical revelation",⁴⁰ or is the distinction between redemptive-historical revelation and revelation for personal guidance itself a false dichotomy?

To attempt a resolution of this question, we need first to understand in some detail the Reformed orthodox definition of "salvation". A precise sense of the term as used by the Westminster divines is necessary in order to determine the burden of the cessationist language of *WCF* 1:1.

2.4 The Westminster Definition of Salvation

When *WCF* 1:1 assumes the necessity of further revelation for salvation, it uses a word with a semantic range in biblical Hebrew and Greek as wide as that in ordinary English usage.⁴¹ It is not a simple task to discern how the divines mean to characterise this salvation, partly because a major purpose

---

³⁸ "Although the light of nature and the works of creation and providence do so far manifest the goodness, wisdom, and power of God, as to leave men unexcusable; yet are they not sufficient to give that knowledge of God and of His will, which is necessary unto *salvation* [emphasis added]": *WCF* 1:1.

³⁹ Gouge, *A Learned and Very Useful Commentary on the Whole Epistle to the Hebrewes*, 8.

⁴⁰ Kenneth Gentry, *The Charismatic Gift of Prophecy: A Reformed Response to Wayne Grudem* (Memphis: Footstool Publications, 1986), 119.

⁴¹ The concept of salvation is of course prominent in both the Old and New Testaments. For the semantic range of "salvation" in the Old Testament, see John Hartley, "ישׁע", *TWOT*, 1, 414-16. See also J. Schüpphaus, J. F. Sawyer and H. J. Fabry, "ישׁע", *TDOT*, 6, 441-63. For the New Testament definition of "salvation" and its context, see Karl Schelkle, "σωτηρία, σωτήριος, σωτήριον and σωτήρ", *EDNT*, 3, 327-29. See also Walter Radl, "σῴζω", *EDNT*, 3, 319-21; see Werner Foerster and George Fohrer, "σωτηρία, σῴζω and σωτήρ", *TDNT*, 7, 965-1024.

of a confession of faith might be said to be its capacity to summarise the way to salvation rather than to describe the nature of that salvation itself; partly because the *WCF* itself gives no explicit definition; and partly because "salvation" terminology in Puritan theology was often characterised by the Bible's own fluidity of meaning and lack of precision in its use of language.[42] Sometimes, for example, an element of human experience might be claimed as an aspect of the *means* or *way* to salvation; at other times, it might be used of salvation *itself*. To give just one example: Sanctification is usually considered by Reformed orthodoxy to be one of the non-causal means to future salvation, yet Samuel Rutherford, for one, proposes in his catechism that sanctification is also an authentic experience of salvation which is already possessed and which entails a positive living out of God's ethical demands both by the individual believer and by the church as a whole.[43] Nonetheless, bearing these caveats in mind, it is possible to discover what the divines meant by "salvation" from a close perusal of the *WCF* and Westminster *Catechisms*. A survey of the *WCF* and of the Westminster *Catechisms* reveals that the noun, the verbal forms, and the concept of "salvation" appear many times throughout each of these documents, but the definition of the conception is not uniform.

The *WCF* makes a distinction between salvation as personal redemption and salvation as a more broadly conceived category. This is implied in *WCF* 1. On the one hand, *WCF* 1:7 asserts that not all Scripture needs to be understood for salvation;[44] on the other, the proof-text for *WCF* 1:6 (2 Tim. 3:15-17) affirms that Scripture makes "wise for salvation" and that "all Scripture" is useful for that purpose.

---

[42] The Puritans themselves were well aware that the term "salvation" and its cognates covered a wide semantic range. See the Annotations on the following texts for various meanings of salvation: (author Meric Casaubon) Ps. 3:8: Safety; Ps. 18:5: Defence from danger; Ps. 78:22: Providence, (author Thomas Gataker) Isa. 26:1 and Isa. 49:8: Physical deliverances a type of spiritual redemption; (author John Ley) Luke 1:71: Salvation from spiritual enemies, life, sin and Satan; Luke 2:30: Christ himself; Luke 19:9. The means to and assurance of eternal life; (author Daniel Featley) 1 Tim. 4:10, where salvation extends to all men in their temporal and natural existence; Phil. 2:12. Sanctification; Heb. 2:3. Spiritual in contrast to temporal deliverances; (authors for the remaining books unconfirmed) Acts 13:26. The gospel; 1 Pet. 1:9. Peace and joy begun in this life and perfected in heaven, and the restoration of the body at the resurrection; Rev. 12:10. Deliverance from tyrants, the putting down of heathen emperors, setting up Christian ones and removing their accuser.

[43] Samuel Rutherford, *Rutherford's Catechism Containing the Sum of Christian Religion* (Edinburgh: Blue Banner Productions, 1998), 45-46. Also see 54, where Rutherford equates sanctification with regeneration.

[44] Also see *LC* Q&A 72, where "justifying faith" is used instead of saving faith. This terminology suggests a distinction between the two.

In support of the contention that the *WCF* makes such a distinction, we can see how complex is its definition throughout the *WCF*. We will look at the definition under the headings of "salvation for personal redemption" and "holistic salvation". The first phrase, "salvation for personal redemption", refers to personal salvation from the judgement of God, and while such a condition is assumed to be a present possession for the Christian, it clearly cannot be divorced from ultimate eschatological salvation. The second term, "holistic salvation", includes salvation as personal redemption, but also encompasses both deliverance from temporal judgements and the provision of mercies which are mediated through Scripture in different ways. Thus, "personal redemption" might be regarded as a subset of "holistic salvation".

In *WCF* 2: 1 (*Of God and the Holy Trinity*) salvation is conceived of as forgiveness and reward, since God's judicial condemnation of sin is contrasted with these two gifts. The passage states that forgiveness of sins and the rewarding of those who diligently seek God constitute salvation, though just what the reward might be the text does not make clear other than to indicate that it is something separate from forgiveness.[45]

In the next chapter, *WCF* 3:5 (*Of God's Eternal Decree*), personal redemption as eschatological salvation is discussed. The elect are described as "chosen, in Christ, unto everlasting glory". The proof-text (1 Thess. 5:9) refers to salvation as deliverance from God's wrath to heaven's glory: "For God did not appoint us to suffer wrath but to receive salvation through our Lord Jesus Christ". *WCF* 3:6 defines the elements of this salvation in the body of the chapter, and also cites proof-texts which refer to sanctification, justification, obedience, holiness, adoption as sons, and good works. It concludes that this *ordo salutis,* summed up in the proof-text 1 Pet. 1:5, leads to personal eschatological salvation.

In *WCF* 7:3 (*Of God's Covenant with Man*), there is a further distinction between salvation as personal redemption and the end-result of salvation, which is eternal life. Both "life" *and* "salvation" are said to be offered through a covenant of grace.[46] It is unlikely that "salvation" here is loosely epexegetical, in view of the extreme care taken in the composition of the *WCF*.[47] "Life" therefore must mean "eternal life", since the previous

---

[45] Neither is it clear from the proof-text, Heb. 11:6.

[46] "Man by his fall having made himself incapable of life by that covenant, the Lord was pleased to make a second, commonly called the covenant of grace; wherein He freely offereth unto sinners life and salvation by Jesus Christ, requiring of them faith in Him that they may be saved, and promising to give unto all those that are ordained unto life His Holy Spirit, to make them willing and able to believe". *WCF* 7:3.

[47] Mitchell says of the care that was taken in the composition of the first chapter: "The Westminster divines, like the Irish, place this Article at the head of their Confession. This, and not the doctrine of the Decree, is the point from which their whole

section talks about the eternal life offered to Adam – a life that Adam failed to attain through the covenant of works. That spiritual life which is consummated in heaven is nevertheless to some degree a present possession, as the proof-texts illustrate.[48] Although the predominant and most common use of "salvation" in the *WCF* is to describe deliverance from sin to eternal life in heaven,[49] it does not exhaust the semantic content of the term "salvation" in Westminster theology.

Within the chapters of the *WCF* we find internal evidence for a broader definition of salvation that transcends personal redemption or eschatological salvation and which offers the believer benefits which include temporal blessing. Such a holistic salvation indeed comes into sharp focus in the vital Chapter 14 (*Of Saving Faith*), which is devoted to describing the acts of trust and volition which lay hold of the promises leading to salvation.[50] In this chapter, it is said that not only is a person who experiences saving faith obedient to God's will, but also that faith accepts promises which will be fulfilled in this life as well as in the one to come. At this point the *WCF* is codifying a broader construal of salvation, for it expressly states that this saving faith (which by definition "saves") may be

---

system is sought to be evolved, although that doctrine is placed by them, as it had been by the Irish divines, in its logical rather than in its natural order. If any chapter in the Confession was more carefully framed than another, it was this, 'of the Holy Scripture.' It formed the subject of repeated and earnest debate in the House of Commons as well as in the Assembly[...]". Alex Mitchell and John Struthers (eds.), *Minutes of the Sessions of the Westminster Assembly of Divines* (Edmonton: Still Water Revival Books, 1991), xlix.

[48] First, in Mark 16:15-16, salvation is offered those who believe and are baptised; secondly, John 3:16 describes faith leading to eternal life; and thirdly, Rom. 10:6 and 9 teach that salvation occurs when a person both confesses that Christ is Lord and believes in him.

[49] *WCF* 7:5 says that the OT Jews had "eternal salvation" through faith in the Messiah which was mediated though OT types and ordinances. In *WCF* 8:5, *Of Christ the Mediator*, Christ is said to have purchased reconciliation and an "everlasting inheritance". In *WCF* 10:1, *Of Effectual Calling*, "Grace and salvation" are contrasted with the "state" of sin and death, which defines salvation as life, since it is contrasted with death. In *WCF* 12, *Of Adoption*, salvation equates to eternal life. In *WCF* 17:1, *Of Perseverance*, perseverance leads to eternal salvation. In *WCF* 18:1, *Of Assurance of Grace and Salvation*, the "estate of salvation" equates to a state of grace, which the proof-text, 1 John 5:13, says is the same as eternal life.

[50] John Gerstner, Douglas Kelly and Philip Rollinson agree, in their commentary on the *WCF*, that all acts of faith responding to the Word are related intimately to salvation in Christ: "In a sense, all Christian responses to the word worked by the Holy Spirit are directly or indirectly, immediately or reflexively, a resting on Christ alone for salvation". John Gerstner, Douglas Kelly and Philip Rollinson, *A Guide: The Westminster Confession of Faith* (Signal Mountain: Summertown Texts, 1992), 72.

The Necessity and Scope of Special Revelation

exercised in contexts not directly related to or limited to personal redemption:

> By this faith, a Christian believeth to be true whatsoever is revealed in the Word [...] embracing the promises of God for this life, and that which is to come. But the principal acts of saving faith are accepting, receiving, and resting upon Christ alone for justification, sanctification, and eternal life, by virtue of the covenant of grace.[51]

Even though the principal intent of salvation is spiritual deliverance, saving faith is said to lay hold of promises of temporal assistance. Therefore, it conjoins earthly privileges or blessings to the Puritan concept of salvation, and thus links temporal deliverance to Scripture promises.[52]

The same point is elaborated emphatically in *WCF* 19:6 (*Of the Law of God*), where the redeemed are said to receive earthly blessings stemming

---

[51] *WCF* 14:2. Although the wording was altered slightly in the final editing, the minutes of 9 September 1646 record: "It [saving faith] likewise resteth upon every other promise of God even for this life also". Mitchell and Struthers (eds.), *Minutes of the Sessions of the Westminster Assembly of Divines*, 277. William Goode elaborated on the same theme when he linked the preaching of the Gospel and the other ordinances to temporal and spiritual happiness which flowed from reformation. Goode shows how he understood the complexity of the concept of salvation when he defined the broad parameters of gospel blessing: "Gospel Truth, and the Ordinances of Jesus Christ are the Churches Treasures, and upon the Restauration, Preservation and Propagation of these being the means of godlinesse, depends both our Spiritual and Temporal happiness; Godlinesse *having the promises of the life* that now is, and that which is to come, 1 *Tim.* 4.8". Goode's use of 1 Tim. 4:8 confirms that the Puritans understood saving faith to apprehend blessings for this life as well as for a future eternity. William Goode, *Jacob Raised: Or, the Means of Making a Nation Happy Both in Spiritual and Temporal Priviledges* (London: Nath. Webb and Will. Grantham, 1647), 15. Later he identifies the "security" of the nation with "Salvation". Goode, *Jacob Raised*, 20-21. Little is known of Goode who was born around 1599, but we do know that he served continuously as a divine, being one of those "superadded" following the establishment of the Assembly. For biographical information, see Reid, *Memoirs of the Westminster Divines*, vol. 1, 319

[52] William Spurstowe calls the promises of Scripture, such as peace and joy and quieting of the soul, the "wells of salvation": William Spurstowe, *The Wels of Salvation Opened: Or, A Treatise Discovering the Nature, Preciousness, Usefulness of Gospel-Promises, and Rules for the Right Application of Them* (London: Ralph Smith, 1655), 142. William Spurstow[e] (1605-1666) was a convinced Presbyterian (one of the authors of Smectymnuus) and a regular participant in the Assembly. Spurstow's father had once been a member of Parliament. His son, the divine, though opposed to Episcopal government in the church was appointed as chaplain to the King. He resigned his charge at the passing of the Act of Uniformity and retired to Hackney, Middlesex. Barker, *Puritan profiles*, 189-92; Reid, *Memoirs of the Westminster Divines*, vol. 2, 148-51.

from their obedience to the moral law.[53] While the chapter stresses that these rewards do not flow from the covenant of works, which was fulfilled by Christ, nevertheless "[t]he promises of it [the law], in like manner, show them God's approbation of obedience, and what blessings they may expect upon the performance thereof". Obedience to the moral law is required, because, as section 6 states, it is a "rule of life informing them of the will of God, and their duty". We can also discern from the proof-texts that the fruits of obedience to the law flow from the covenantal relationship.[54]

Both eschatological salvation (conceived of as personal redemption from sin and equipping for heaven's glory) and a holistic salvation that includes temporal blessings are evident in the development of the *WCF*.

2.4.1 Salvation in the Other Works of the Westminster Divines

This same understanding of salvation is apparent in the wider writings of the divines, as we might expect. The meaning of a doctrine is best discovered by analysing not only the sermons, but also the theological treatises of its adherents. Just as the nuances of John Calvin's thought can be fully appreciated only when we go outside his *Institutes* to his letters, sermons and commentaries, so too in order to comprehend the Westminster concept of salvation more fully we must scan the wider horizon of the

---

[53] We are hard pressed to find a modern commentator on the *WCF* who acknowledges this controversial claim in *WCF* 19:6. Gerstner, Kelly and Rollinson, for example, contradict the very intent of the *WCF* at this point: "Finally, the law does not bring us blessing but shows us the way we must behave in this life as the grace of God brings us eternal blessings". Gerstner et al, *A Guide: The Westminster Confession of Faith*, 95. For a more candid explanation, see David Dickson's seventeenth-century commentary. Dickson notes that one of the reasons Antinomians err in denying the contemporary validity of the law is "[b]ecause Paul adjoineth and proposeth to believers under the New Testament, both a command and a promise of the decalogue, as properly belonging to them, Eph. vi. 2, 3". The Ephesians text promises long life to obedient children for New Testament believers and is also a proof-text for the relevant clause in *WCF* 19:6. David Dickson, *Truth's Victory over Error: Or, the True Principles of the Christian Religion, Stated and Vindicated Against the Following Heresies, viz. Arians, Arminians, Anabaptists, Antinomians, Brownists, Donatists, Epicureans, Eutychians, Erastians, Familists, Jesuits, Independents, Libertines, Manicheans, Pelagians, Papists, Quakers, Socinians, Sabellians, Sceptics, Vaninians, &c. The Whole being a Commentary on All the Chapters of the Confession of Faith, by Way of Question and Answer: In which, the saving Truths of our Holy Religion are Confirmed and Established; and the Dangerous Errors and Opinions of its Adversaries Detected and Confuted.* (Kilmarnock: Printed by John Wilson, 1787), 119.

[54] Notice the allocation of Lev. 26:1-4 (with 2 Cor. 6:16) as a proof-text, both of which, in context, imply blessings in return for obedience.

authors' explanatory homiletical comments as well as their confessions and catechisms.

Here too we encounter their use of the idea of salvation in a variety of contexts. These range from a very narrow and limited concept to a conception which provides a broad and inclusive use and which reaches into all areas of life.[55]

Thus Sydrach Simpson (c1600-1655) restricts the meaning of the word to justification. Simpson's own Christian life was not only focused on the pious hope of heaven, as demonstrated by his public opposition to the radical Fifth Monarchy men[56] and his brief imprisonment, which was a result of his expressed hostility towards Cromwell's government.[57]

---

[55] Archibald Hodge understands the scope of Scripture to encompass all of life. In his commentary on the *WCF*, he writes: "The inspired Scriptures of the Old and New Testaments are a *complete* rule of faith and practice: they embrace the whole of whatever supernatural revelation God now makes to men, and are abundantly sufficient for all the practical necessities of men or communities[...] as a matter of fact, the Scriptures do teach a perfect system of doctrine, and all the principles which are necessary for the practical regulation of the lives of individuals, communities, and churches. The more diligent men have been in the study of the Bible, and the more assiduous they have been in carrying out its instructions into practice, the less has it been possible for them to believe that it is incomplete in any element of a perfect rule of all that which man is to believe concerning God, and of all that duty which God requires of man". Archibald Alexander Hodge, *The Confession of Faith: A Handbook of Christian Doctrine Expounding the Westminster Confession* (Edinburgh: Banner of Truth Trust, 1978), 37-38.

[56] The Fifth Monarchy men were a political and religious grouping at the time of the Interregnum who hoped to usher in the rule of the saints – the fifth monarchy of the prophet Daniel (Dan. 2:44 and 8:26-28), on which they based their desire to reform Parliament. They foresaw a golden age, but, unlike the more moderate Puritans, believed that this hope warranted political and military intervention by those who were not in authority. They were finally crushed following an uprising in 1661 under the leadership of Thomas Venner when they tried to overthrow the new government in London. For a comprehensive study of the Fifth Monarchy men, see Bernard Capp, *The Fifth Monarchy Men. A Study in Seventeenth-Century English Millenarianism* (London: Faber and Faber, 1972), especially 30-31 and 78-79 for Independent Westminster divine William Bridge's millenarian influence on Fifth Monarchy ministers. See also Iain Murray, *The Puritan Hope* (London: Banner of Truth Trust, 1971), especially 48, for a summary of the phenomenon.

[57] Simpson was probably born in Lincolnshire, was educated at Cambridge, and became curate and lecturer at St. Margaret's, London, where his preaching was well received. Having spent some time in the Netherlands because of his unwillingness to conform, he later returned to London in 1641 where he took up his old lectureship and added another at St. Anne's. He was a key Independent member of the Westminster Assembly and in 1650 was appointed Master of Pembroke Hall, Cambridge. Simpson was one of five leading "dissenting brethren", known as such because of their

Simpson subsumes the declaration of righteousness, or the Protestant concept of forensic justification, under the heading of salvation and refers to these interchangeably: "Scripture makes Justification and Salvation all one".[58] Fellow-divine Obadiah Sedgewick extends its definition to include other categories of the *ordo salutis*: "Vocation, and Justification, and Adoption, and Sanctification, and Glorification".[59] However, the term "salvation" was not always considered synonymous with spiritual redemption.

Leland Ryken concludes in his study of the Puritans: "For the Puritans, to limit the authority of the Bible to narrowly religious issues would violate the principle that all of life is religious".[60] So all-encompassing was biblical redemption in Puritan thought[61] that, as Obadiah Sedgwick put it to Parliament in 1644, it was the position of heretics that God confined himself to "matters of eternal life": for God's providence "doth not onely manage the great monuments of eternall salvation, but also disposeth the least moments of our temporall safety".[62]

For the Puritan, the great promises of temporal salvation were indeed to be identified in Scripture. Thus William Lyford stated:

---

ecclesiastical preference for Independency and dissent from Presbyterianism. He died after having been through a period of spiritual darkness. Barker, *Puritan Profiles*, 87-90.

[58] Sydrach Simpson, *Two Books of Mr Sydrach Simpson[...]I. Of Unbelief, or the Want of Readiness to Lay Hold on the Comfort Given by Christ, II. Not Going to Christ for Life and Salvation is an Exceeding Great Sin, Yet it is Pardonable* (London: Peter Cole, 1658), 10.

[59] Obadiah Sedgewick, *The Bowels of Tender Mercy Sealed in the Everlasting Covenant [...]* "(London: Adoniram Byfield, 1661), 74. Sedgewick (or Sedgwick) (1600-1658), a popular preacher, and himself the son of a vicar, studied at Oxford becoming firstly a private chaplain. He entered the ministry in 1630 and was appointed to the Westminster Assembly, where his Presbyterian views were evident. He resigned St. Paul's in 1656, because of ill health. Barker, *Puritan Profiles*, 130-32.

[60] Leland Ryken, *Worldly Saints* (Grand Rapids, MI: Zondervan, 1990), 142. See also Allen Carden, "The Word of God in Puritan New England: Seventeenth-Century Perspectives on the Nature and Authority of the Bible", *Andrews University Seminary Studies* 18, 1 (Spring 1980), 1-16, at 9-11.

[61] For a comprehensive definition of holistic salvation, see, for example, Simeon Ashe: The individuals who are pious Christians will be saved by Christ (Ps. 85:8) with a fourfold salvation. It is firstly, salvation from sin; secondly, security from "all externall grievances and annoyances" in so far as it is to their best advantage; thirdly, deliverance from all afflictions that come their way in their earthly life; fourthly, eternal salvation or life after death. Simeon Ash, *The Church Sinking, Saved by Christ* (London: Edward Brewster, 1645), 22-23.

[62] Obadiah Sedg[e]wick, *A Thanksgiving-Sermon [...]* "(London: Samuel Gellibrand, 1644), 5-6.

You will need direction out of the Word for every estate and condition of life, for times of Health & Sickness, for Affliction & Prosperity, for good and ill Report - This *Word of the Lord is exceeding large.*[63]

The Westminster divines linked this temporal salvation with spiritual redemption in different ways.[64] First, William Bridge connected the temporal mercies of the Christian life and spiritual salvation by associating both with the idea of "redemption":

> The Saints and people of God, they are called the 'Redeemed of the Lord,' Isa. lxii. 12., not only because they are redeemed from hell and from wrath, but because that they have their mercies and blessings in a way of redemption; there is a line of that great mercy of redemption that runs through all the mercies which they have; they have health redeemed out of the hand of sickness, they have liberty redeemed out of the hand of straitness, they have peace redeemed out of the hand of war, they have assurance redeemed out of the hand of doubting and unbelief, they have mercy redeemed out of the hand of misery, they have joys and comforts redeemed out of the hand of grief: they are the redeemed of the Lord; whatsoever great mercy of blessing they have, they have it in a way of redemption.[65]

---

[63] William Lyford, *The Plain Mans Senses Exercised to Discern Both Good and Evil: Or, A Discovery of the Errors, Heresies, and Blasphemies of These Times, and the Toleration of Them as They are Collected and Testified Against by the Ministers of London [...]"* (London: Richard Royston and Edward Forrest, 1655), 63. William Lyford, (1598-1653) was one of several who, though appointed, never sat at the Assembly for reasons we have no knowledge of. Educated at Oxford, Lyford was a nonconformist and an avowed Calvinist in his theology. He sees himself as representative of doctrinal orthodoxy, when he answers the question: why do ministers differ in their expositions, obtaining different doctrines for the same text? In response he makes this rather astounding claim: "I answer, that for the substance of Doctrine there is sweet Harmony among the Reformed Churches, so that you may go into a thousand Congregations, where our old sound Ministers are the Lights that shine, and you shall finde that they all speak the same thing, preach the same Jesus Christ, and walk after the same Spirit". Lyford, *The Plain Mans Senses,* 55-56. See William Archbold, "William Lyford", *DNB,* vol. 1, 1259.

[64] For typical examples of the term "redemption" used beyond personal salvation, see, for example, Samuel Rutherford's sermon preached in 1645: "[T]he *Lord Jesus* is a Saviour not onely of persons, but also a nationall redeemer, *hee sprinkleth many nations, Esay 52.15. with his blood, he sprinkles cleane water upon nations the house of Israel, and cleanseth them from all their filthinesse and idols, for his names sake, Ezek.36.22.25*". Samuel Rutherfurd [sic], *A Sermon Preached before the Right Honorable House of Lords,[...]Wednesday the 25. day of June, 1645* (London: Andrew Crook, 1645), 60.

[65] Bridge, "The Spiritual Actings of Faith through Natural Impossibilities", *The Works of the Rev. William Bridge*, vol. 2, 286.

In other words, according to Bridge, it is not just that God blesses with temporal deliverance, but that he also exercises spiritual redemption *in* physical redemption. Thomas Goodwin gives a more detailed explanation of just how this connection may be deemed to function. In his series of expositions on Christ as mediator he explains how temporal and spiritual salvation are bound together. Goodwin concedes that the promise in John 17:12, "those that thou gavest me I have kept, and none of them is lost", seems to refer to the salvation of souls, while in John 18:9 it is a similar phrase applied to physical deliverance.[66] Goodwin's answer to the puzzle of why Christ's words refer principally to souls in one passage and yet are applied to temporal deliverance in another demonstrates how the Puritans linked the two aspects of redemption. For Goodwin, a kind of reverse typology is operative. Whereas normally we think of Old Testament types such as David, or the Land of Canaan, symbolising spiritual realities or anti-types such as a Christ and heaven, Goodwin uses spiritual promises of the salvation of the soul to "typify" temporal deliverance. While Bridge connected the spiritual and the temporal with little explanatory comment, Goodwin explained how and why this occurred:

> God that saves thy soul, out of the same love saves thy body too[...]Will God save thy soul? Certainly he will deliver thy body.[67]

Thus Christ's resurrection saves the soul and "by virtue of the same resurrection we shall be preserved here in the world".[68]

Secondly, the divines linked both temporal salvation and salvation as personal redemption to the preaching of the gospel.[69] The evangelical

---

[66] Goodwin, *The Works of Thomas Goodwin*, vol. 5, 214. Even if Goodwin has not considered the link between John 18:9 and John 6:39, that latter text is also a reference to the resurrection and therefore eschatological salvation rather than the deliverance of the apostles from temporal danger, while John 17:12 does indeed appear to refer to the physical survival of the apostles up to the point of Christ's death and resurrection.

[67] Goodwin, *The Works of Thomas Goodwin*, vol. 5, 214.

[68] Goodwin, *The Works of Thomas Goodwin*, vol. 5, 214.

[69] George Gillespie has a similar insight when he explains that national temporal salvation is a mercy arising from the gospel: "[A]s the promises of spirituall and eternall blessings, so the promises of peace and temporall deliverances, are not legall but even Evangelicall". Thus national temporal salvation is something that flows from the gospel, and is not to be confined to the Old Testament era. Temporal salvation in the Old Testament was not only a type of spiritual salvation in the New, but occurs identically for the faithful Christian nation. If the atonement itself meant temporal salvation for ancient Israel, then surely it must mean the same for modern England or Scotland – a point made emphatically by Gillespie before the House of Lords: "A land is accepted, and a peoples peace made with God, not by their repentance and humiliation, but by Christ beleeved on[...]. There were Sin-offerings, and Burnt-offerings appointed in the Law for a Nationall atonement[...]which did typifie pardoning of Nationall sinnes through the merit of Jesus Christ. We must improve the office of the Mediator, and the

The Necessity and Scope of Special Revelation

graces of repentance and faith are the two actions required for spiritual salvation, which are usually considered to arise in response to preaching. In a sermon based on Heb. 11:7, a text which describes God's warning to Noah to save his family in the ark, Obadiah Sedgwicke understands as an example of how temporal national salvation may be obtained. Just as Noah was saved by faith, so too "nothing will save us without faith".[70]

If faith is exercised for both temporal and eternal salvation, for Edmund Calamy, so too is repentance. Preaching before the Commons in 1644, he thundered that repentance can bring salvation of the soul from hell and "*save thy body also from ruine*".[71] Furthermore: "As a *personall repentance* is a meanes to obtain a *personall salvation*; so a *nationall repentance* is a meanes to obtain *a national salvation*".[72]

Edward Reynolds (1599-1676) related temporal blessing to the gospel directly in his treatise *The Vanity of the Creature*, where he calls the Word of God the "*Gospell of Salvation*", which

> is the Fountaine not onely of Eternall, but of Temporall Blessings. And therefore wee find CHRIST did not onely say unto the sicke of the Palsie, *Thy sinnes are forgiven thee* but Also *Arise and walke*, intimating, That Temporall Blessings come along with the Gospell[..]".[73]

Reynolds, considered one of the seven most important divines in the composition of the *WCF*, was ironically one of only four of the divines who later conformed.[74] He also owns this very Puritan notion that this temporal deliverance was a salvation that flowed from the "*Gospell of Salvation*".

---

promise of free grace, in the behalf of Gods people": George Gillespie, *A Sermon Preached[...]27th. of August, 1645* (London: Robert Bostock, 1645), 27.

[70] Obadiah Sedgwicke, *An Arke against a Deluge: Or Safety in Dangerous Times* (London: Samuel Gellibrand, 1644), 19.

[71] Edmund Calamy, *Englands Antidote against the Plague of Civil Warre* (London: Christopher Meredith, 1645), 14. Edmund Calamy (1600-1666), a frequent speaker at the Assembly, was sternly Presbyterian in his views from the outset. Strongly intolerant, he did not shrink from reminding Parliament of their need to suppress error and heresy. Calamy was born in Walbrook, London, was educated at Cambridge and became a favourite preacher among the Parliamentarians. A "Smectymnuan", Calamy was appointed curate of St Mary Aldermanbury in London, which had a tradition of Puritan sympathy. He was ejected at the Restoration, spent some time in prison, and died in 1666, apparently heartbroken by the devastation caused by the great London fire of that year. Barker, *Puritan Profiles*, 208-18.

[72] Calamy, *Englands Antidote against the Plague of Civil Warre*, 28.

[73] Edward Reynolds, *Three Treatises of the Vanity of The Creature. The Sinfulnesse of Sinne. The Life of Christ* (London: Rob. Bostocke and George Badger, 1642), 26.

[74] Once a leader among the Presbyterian Puritans, following the Restoration Reynolds became bishop of Norwich. Born at Southampton, he was a successful scholar at Oxford whose development as a Calvinist coincided with his moderate views on church government. Although he did not take a very active role in the debates, his work

A third way in which these different strands of salvation were said to be connected was through their mutual dependence upon the work of Christ as Saviour. Since Christ's benefits, which included promises for this world and the world to come, were conveyed in the gospel, then plainly temporal salvation could not be divorced from a relationship with Christ. Jeremiah Burroughs in his sermon *"Christ is all in all"*, based on Col. 3:11, annexes the enjoyment of earthly blessings to union with Christ. He establishes his main doctrine that:

> Christ is the only means of conveyance of good that God the Father intends to communicate unto the children of men in order to eternal life; He is all in all.[75]

This, he suggests, is the "sum of the gospel, the great mystery of godliness",[76] through which Christ supplies mercy and goodness to both soul and body.[77] He ascribes justification, adoption, peace and reconciliation with God to the realisation that Christ is "all in all", but he also affirms that for the alleviation of our worldly discomforts, Christ is "all in all in the enjoyment of all". This can include blessings in this temporary existence, because since it flows from the "blood of the covenant" comfort extends to everything the believer enjoys in this life:

> A believer can look upon every bit of meat he has, and upon all the good he enjoys, and can see it all come streaming to him in the blood of Christ. And so it comes more sweetly[...]. Therefore, there are no people in the world who can enjoy outward comforts with as much fulness of contentment as do the people of God, because they all come to them through Christ. Christ is all in all in the enjoyment of all.[78]

---

in the committees was influential. Later as bishop, he was known for his tolerance of, and moderation towards, dissenters. Barker, *Puritan Profiles*, 179-85.

[75] Jeremiah Burroughs, *The Saints' Treasury* (Ligonier, PA: Soli Deo Gloria, 1991[reprint from 1656]), 43. Burroughs was educated at Cambridge and became minister at Edmunds in Suffolk and later rector in Twitshall, Norfolk, from where he was suspended for refusing to read the *Book of Sports*. After a period in the Netherlands, Burroughs returned to England in 1641 and became a lecturer at St Giles and Stepney in London. Known as a moderate, Burroughs died tragically having fallen from his mount in 1646, before the Assembly had finished its work. Barker, *Puritans Profiles*, 80-84.

[76] Burroughs, *The Saints' Treasury*, 43.

[77] Burroughs, *The Saints' Treasury*, 91.

[78] Burroughs, *The Saints' Treasury*, 65. In another sermon, "the glorious enjoyment of heavenly things by faith" in *The Saints' Treasury*, 95-96, Burroughs links the promise of Ps. 91:7 with a concrete faith that the plague will not kill a believer. Also see the link Burroughs makes between temporal and eternal blessing, in Jeremiah Burroughs, *A Sermon Preached [...] 26. Novemb. 1645.*[On Phil. 4:12](London: R. Dawlman, 1646), especially 34-36.

The divines were also aware of the obvious differences between temporal and eternal salvation, although these were essentially variations of genre rather than totally separate and unrelated categories. Thomas Case (1598-1682)[79] says of temporal salvation that it is *for the sake of God's people*; it *finds* them already the people of God; and *finds* them already qualified persons. Whereas, spiritual salvation is ultimately *for God's sake*; and "*bestow*[s] these *qualifications* upon them".[80] However, they are also intimately yoked:

> After he hath bestowed a *Christ* upon them, he thinks nothing too good or too much for their sake. *He that spared not his own Son, but delivered him up for us all, how shall he not with him also freely give us all things?* After he hath redeemed them from *eternall death*, with the *Blood of his Son*, he will not stick to redeem them from *temporall Destruction*, with the *blood* of his and their *enemies*.[81]

While all temporal and spiritual salvation flowed from the same good news about Jesus Christ, the Puritans also clearly understood temporal salvation in political and even nationalistic terms. Their appeal to Scripture to justify a role for the state in national salvation reinforces the argument that salvation in its complete sense could not be confined to personal spiritual redemption. Their differences with the opponents of moral and ecclesiastical reformation and national salvation turned upon Scripture interpretation.

The Puritans sometimes used typology in rather striking ways. Reference to Christ's atonement was commonplace in discourse on questions of national security and deliverance,[82] but John Dury (or Durye) (1596-1680), who exemplifies the more tolerant face of the Westminster Assembly, went one step further in a sermon on Isa. 52:11 before the House

---

[79] Case had a reputation for being the most outspoken Presbyterian in the Assembly, a reputation which he earned by his earnest appeals to Parliament. He was implicated in a conspiracy against Cromwell and was imprisoned for five months, but Case survived to outlive all the other active members of the Assembly. Barker, *Puritan Profiles*, 224-29.

[80] Thomas Case, *A Sermon Preached before the Honourable House of Commons at Westminster, August 22. 1645* (London: Luke Fawne, 1645), 14.

[81] Case, *A Sermon Preached before the Honourable House of Commons at Westminster, August 22. 1645*, 13.

[82] Jeremiah Burroughs comments: "[W]e are to look upon outward deliverances, as the fruit of Christs bloud". Jeremiah Burroughs, *Sions Joy* (London: R. Dawlman, 1641), 42. See also Stephen Marshall, who exhorts: "You are met to seek the good of the Land[...]. It may bee not only our welfare, and peace, and Religion: but even the welfare of all Christendome, under God, depends upon your meeting". Stephen Marshall, *A Sermon Preached[...]November 17.1640, upon 2 Chron. 15.2.* (London: Samuel Man, 1641), 46.

of Commons in 1645.[83] Not only was England parallel with Israel,[84] he argued, but the Levitical vessel-bearers represent Christians, ministers and civil rulers.[85] The task of the vessel-bearers, as with all Christians, is to flee from Babylon to Jerusalem and to ensure the correct service of the Lord.[86] Three principles can be discerned in Dury's exposition of this text. First, use of typology confirms that the Puritans did not consider Old Testament temporal deliverances solely as types of a future eschatological salvation.[87] "Spiritual Babylon", therefore, rather than being the world in contradistinction to heaven, comprises "humane worldly societies", which are characterised by "disorder" and reliance upon human reason rather than upon the Word of God.[88] Similarly, rather than heaven being "Spiritual Jerusalem", that privilege was granted to "the frame and nature of the

---

[83] John Dury was born in Scotland and later based in England, but travelled widely in Europe. He was ordained in Europe, and had his ordination confirmed by Bishop Hall of Exeter. His great wish was to see reconciliation between Lutherans and Calvinists. Dury, of Presbyterian sympathy, was a "superadded" divine who was a regular attender at the Assembly. Reid, *Memoirs of the Westminster Divines*, vol. 1, 269.

[84] The identification between Israel and England is also made in a sermon by Westminster divine Richard Vines, who compared the wilderness experience of Israel with the current socio-religious turmoil in England, rather than perceiving the wilderness as a type of sin or worldliness. For Vines, just as God dealt miraculously with Israel in the wilderness, causing the Israelites to sing, so too can the English have happiness in their wilderness. Richard Vines, *The Happinesse of Israel[...]March 12th 1644*(London: Abel Roper, 1645), 10-11. In Vines' thinking, the promises which were not received by the heroes of the faith in Hebrews 11, were not (as is the usual interpretation) promises of heaven, but promises which the church will enjoy on earth in the latter days (17). God saves unto everlasting salvation through temporal salvation – "the Salvation of Salvation it selfe". We are saved from our enemies so that we will be saved eternally (13). Vines (c.1600-1656), one of Parliament's favourite preachers was also one of the more frequent contributors to the Assembly debates. A graduate of Magdalene College, he was at first a schoolmaster at Hinckley, Leicestershire, later becoming a rector of both Weddington and Caldecote in Warwickshire. Appointed as a Westminster divine, he also laboured at St. Clement Danes, London. Later Master at Pembroke Hall, Cambridge, Vines was of the Presbyterian majority at the Assembly. Barker, *Puritan Profiles*, 132-36.

[85] John Dury (or Durye), *Israels Call to March out of Babylon unto Jerusalem* (London: Tho. Underhill, 1646), 10. Dury admits that the civil magistrate is not properly represented by the Levites, but that, nevertheless, there is a "similitude and resemblance between the Levites and the Magistrates".

[86] Dury, *Israels Call to March out of Babylon unto Jerusalem*, 6-10.

[87] Dury, *Israels Call to March out of Babylon unto Jerusalem*, 4-5.

[88] Dury, *Israels Call to March out of Babylon unto Jerusalem*, 34-35. See also Burroughs, *Sions Joy*, 49: "[T]hat deliverance from A*Egypt* was a type of deliverance from [the] *Antichrist*".

Church of God" on earth, and was characterised by "peace" and a reliance upon divine oracles.[89]

A second principle which can be discovered from Dury's sermon is the assertion that the civil government has spiritual responsibilities, and is to be intimately involved in the spiritual prosperity of the spiritual Jerusalem. Civil magistrates in such a society, like the sons of Levi and the vessel-bearers of the Temple, can be distinguished from the rulers of spiritual Babylon who rely upon the idol "reason" or the "interest" of the state, and who seek temporal happiness as their end and as the end of their nation.[90]

The civil and spiritual government of the City of God (Jerusalem/ the New Testament church), on the other hand, desires above all else as its purpose to see its citizens in communion with God. The civil magistrates as vessel-bearers in this temple are to do everything in their power first to make sure the establishment of the church in the land[91] by ensuring that those guilty of scandalous behaviour are prevented from taking the Lord's Supper; secondly, by purging the universities of "scholastical Divinity";[92] thirdly, by training sufficient ministers; and finally by inspecting and supervising all schools and curricula for children.[93]

The third principle is the precise means used by respective spiritual cities to achieve their avowed ends. Spiritual Babylon uses the means of political strategy and the exercise of social power, which include craft, subtlety, deceit, witchcraft, sorcery, and enchantments[94]- divination is an integral component of such a government.

The governors of spiritual Jerusalem use quite different means. According to Dury, England and Scotland were without peer among nations since biblical times, because all of their citizens had covenanted "to walk in the waies of his Word, to maintain the Cause of Religion". Thus Dury exclaims to this uniquely privileged civil government of the spiritual Jerusalem:

> Your charge is not only the outward safety of three Kingdomes, to settle them in such a way as you have covenanted: but the care of the Protestant Religion, and Cause [...] is committed unto you.[95]

The vessel-bearers must accordingly do their part to bring about "the joyfull promise of deliverance, and salvation" of God's people.[96] Moreover, just as true piety replaces the policy and power of "Babylon", so too does the

---

[89] Dury, *Israels Call to March out of Babylon unto Jerusalem*, 34-35.
[90] Dury, *Israels Call to March out of Babylon unto Jerusalem*, 36.
[91] Dury, *Israels Call to March out of Babylon unto Jerusalem*, 47.
[92] Dury, *Israels Call to March out of Babylon unto Jerusalem*, 48.
[93] Dury, *Israels Call to March out of Babylon unto Jerusalem*, 48-49.
[94] Dury, *Israels Call to March out of Babylon unto Jerusalem*, 37-38.
[95] Dury, *Israels Call to March out of Babylon unto Jerusalem*, 24.
[96] Dury, *Israels Call to March out of Babylon unto Jerusalem*, 21.

Word and the Spirit supplant deceit and pagan divination.[97] While Dury has in mind the responsibility of the state to assist its citizens towards spiritual salvation, these principles first pointed the way to national political and social liberty, which in turn would facilitate spiritual salvation.

In the pre-Christian era, a full-orbed salvation was considered to be mediated through the various modalities of special revelation which according to *WCF* 1:1 had now ceased. The precise identity of the "former ways" of revelation should tell us much about the kind of "salvation" the divines had in mind. When Usher implies that a *"saving knowledg[e] of God"* had also been conveyed through the Urim and Thummim in a verbal way, he links salvation with corporate divine guidance, at least for Old Testament times.[98] Cornelis Van Dam, in his comprehensive modern study on the enigmatic device of the Urim and Thummim, also concludes that the high priest's efficacious use of these means required a divine verbal response, which suggests that the divine communication was more extensive than monosyllabic "yes" and "no" answers analogous to the casting of lots.[99] John Ley (1583-1662) had come to a similar conclusion three centuries earlier.[100] Ley, in his annotations on Ex. 28:30, likewise determines that while there might be some concurrent mechanical function in the use of the Urim and the Thummim, "[t]hese answers [to enquiries of the Urim and the Thummim] were sometimes made by audible voice, sometimes by secret inspiration[…]".[101] Intelligible cogent verbal

---

[97] Dury, *Israels Call to March out of Babylon unto Jerusalem*, 35, 39 -41.

[98] Usher, *A Body of Divinity*, 6. In 1 Sam. 28:6, Saul sought an answer to a military dilemma through dreams and visions and through the Urim and the Thummim. Because God did not answer his request, he turned to the spiritual medium or witch of Endor.

[99] Cornelis Van Dam, *The Urim and Thummim. A Means of Revelation in Ancient Israel* (Winona Lake: Eisenbrauns, 1997), 221-22. The guidance given by the Urim and Thummim included military wisdom (Judg. 1:1, 1 Sam. 14:36-37) , the humbling and punishment of his people (Judg. 20:18-36), the confirmation of a king (1 Sam. 10: 22), matters of state (1 Sam. 22:15) and help for David to attain the throne (1 Sam. 22:10; 23: 2,4,10-12; 30:8; 2 Sam. 2:1-4.).Van Dam, *The Urim and Thummim*, 269.

[100] Ley was born in Warwick, educated at Oxford, became vicar of Great Budworth, Cheshire in 1616 and later prebendary at Chester Cathedral. His final ministry was as rector in Solihull, Warwickshire, after which he retired to Sutton Coldfield, Warwickshire, where he spent his last days. He was enamoured of Presbyterian ideas, and rejected Episcopacy, but is understood by some to have been swayed to the Independent position during the sitting of the Assembly, where he also chaired the committee for the examination of ministers. He was an important member of the First Committee of the Assembly which was one of three which composed the Assembly documents. See Barker, *Puritan Profiles*, 239-44. For Ley's Independency, see Robert Henderson, *The Teaching Office in the Reformed Tradition* (Philadelphia: Westminster Press, 1962), 199.

[101] John Ley, *Annotations*, Ex. 28:30.

communication was transmitted simultaneously with the operation of this mysterious apparatus for temporal guidance.

More commonly, as Usher highlighted, God divulged his mind through dreams and visions, such as those granted to Joseph and Daniel, which were instances of "Revelations whereby God signified his will".[102] Yet, just as with the Urim and the Thummim, those divine revelatory dreams which were given to pagans or non-Israelites had a "temporal" salvific significance for the people of God.[103] The dream given to the pagan soldier in the camp of Midian, for example, made Gideon confident of victory,[104] inviting the comment from the *Annotations*: "Divine dreams are always either clear and evident of themselves, or else opportunity interprised for the benefit of Gods people".[105]

Since the Urim and Thummim and other obsolete revelatory media for conveying salvific data are grouped as joint supernatural means for discovering that salvation, the information conveyed by dreams, visions or the Urim and the Thummim should tell us something of what was meant by "salvation".[106]

For English and Scottish Puritans, the Scriptures now functioned to provide the same assistance to the modern Christian nation as dreams, visions and the Urim and the Thummim once had for ancient Israel. Therefore, these revelatory devices were not thought to be only vehicles of special revelation to teach the way of personal redemption. Neither was the divine revelation mediated through these former modes considered only as types or shadows of spiritual matters. Certainly, the Puritans did teach that Old Testament promises foreshadow spiritual things,[107] but they were far

---

[102] Usher, *A Body of Divinity*, 7.

[103] As Ley comments in his annotations on this verse: "This dream was not so much for Pharaoh, as to be a meanes to deliver Joseph, and to provide for Gods Church". Ley, *Annotations,* Gen. 41:1. Of the butler's dream, he remarks in the same chapter: "yet this forgetfulness of his [the butler's] was serviceable to the divine providence, for thereby Josephs knowledg of interpretation of dreams, was reserved to the best occasion to make use of it[…]". Ley, *Annotations,* Gen. 41:9.

[104] Judg. 7:13-14.

[105] *Annotations,* Judg. 7:14.

[106] Thomas Case in a sermon before Parliament in 1644 concludes: "Some cases were so *Criticall* under the Law, that God was faine to set up an *infallible Oracle of Urim* and *Thummim,* to which the Non-plust judges of inferiour Courts might appeale[…]. And therefore your condition is so much the harder, by how much God hath erected no such Office now in the times of the Gospel". Thomas Case, *Jehoshaphats Caveat to His Judges* (London: Luke Fawn, 1644), 11.

[107] The divines did hold to the typological importance of physical redemption. Ebenezer Erskine and James Fisher in their catechism on the *SC* so interpret the Shorter Catechism Q&A 44. Ebenezer Erskine and James Fisher, *The Assembly's Shorter Catechism Explained* (Edinburgh: Oliver and Boyd, 1835), 238. For the classic

from spiritualising every concept in the Old Testament because they held that God gave temporal deliverances to the modern Christian nation, just as he had to Israel.

While William Gouge teaches that "[t]emporall good things" prefigure "spirituall and heavenly good things",[108] he also makes it explicit that he regards the contemporary availability of divine advice through Scripture as analogous to the function of the Urim and Thummim, or the role of dreams and visions. He contends that the Scriptures have replaced other now obsolete means of supernatural illumination as a source of effectual divine direction in the difficult non-doctrinal choices which still confront the new covenant church, individuals, and nations. This guidance, now available in the pages of holy Writ, is still a valid experience of God's saving will and purpose. In a sermon on a pressing matter of physical suffering that afflicted his society entitled *Dearth's Death: Or, a Removall of Famine, Gathered out of II Sam. XXI.I.*, Gouge poses the question: "How may we now seeke of God? The meanes of old used, are now no more of use".[109] He makes it clear that he does not believe in the efficacy of any prophecy, dreams, visions or the Urim and Thummim and believes that he can demonstrate that the *WCF* and *Catechisms'* proof-texts, 2 Pet. 1:19 and Isa. 8:20, teach the availability of guidance through Scripture, which is "as sure and certaine a meanes for enquiring of God, as ever the Church had".[110] In other words, the Scriptures have now taken over the function of imparting guidance for life's varied circumstances, which was previously the prerogative of the other modes. These former modalities have now ceased, though they were once ordained vehicles of immediate divine disclosure.

Gouge acknowledges God's equal interest and involvement in the seventeenth-century national and political context, while clearly relegating the older channels of dreams and the like to past. He is therefore far from

---

Protestant discussion of typology, see Patrick Fairbairn, *The Typology of Scripture* (Grand Rapids, MI: Kregel, 1989), especially vol. 2, 50, where the overthrow of the Antichrist is also considered a fulfilment of the "typological" redemption from Egypt, thus bringing the lessons and promises of the wilderness to bear on the contemporary culture.

[108] William Gouge, *The Progresse of Divine Providence* (London: Joshua Kirton, 1645), 8.

[109] William Gouge, *Gods Three Arrowes: Plague, Famine, Sword, In Three Treatises* (London: Edward Brewster, 1631), 161.

[110] Gouge, *Gods Three Arrowes*, 161. In Question and Answer Three of the *LC*, Isa. 8:20 is a proof-text for the Scriptures being "the only rule of faith and obedience", whereas 2 Pet. 1:19 is a proof-text in *WCF* 1:1 proving the necessity of the Scriptures for salvation, because the former supernatural ways of revelation had ceased. The cessationist clause in the *WCF* immediately follows the "necessity" clause, which uses the text from 2 Peter.

sanctioning the contemporary use of those archaic ordinances for temporal guidance. He concludes his advice by an appeal to David:

> Let this therefore be the generall use and close of all, that in famine and other like judgements we do as *David* is here noted to do, *enquire of the Lord*: enquire of him in and by his word: and withall, as *David* here also did, follow the directions prescribed by the Lord in his Word; then shall we be sure to have such an issue as David had, expressed in these words, *God was intreated for the land*.[111]

The message preached by John Bond (d. 1680) on 22 August 1645 to the House of Commons, is perhaps the most remarkable of its type from the years of the civil war, and dates from the occasion when he preached a thanksgiving sermon for the Parliamentary victories at Bridgewater and Sherborn Castle. According to his biographer James Reid, who characterises Bond as a zealous Covenanter, the sermon was still being read in England and Scotland in the early nineteenth century. Bond, a minister at Savoy in London during the sitting of the Assembly, retired at the inception of the Restoration, dying some twenty years later in Lutton, Dorsetshire.[112] In this particular sermon, on Isa. 25:9, entitled *Ortus Occidentalis: Or, a Dawning in the West*, (which also happened be the point of the compass where Parliament's armies had routed the king's forces) Bond's design is to demonstrate how these military successes were really God's salvation. In doing so, he also underscores how the Puritan mind links not just personal but national, temporal and eternal salvation by basing all of these on Scripture. He suggests that while some restrict his text to mean "*spirituall* salvations" and some to "*temporall* salvations", in reality it refers to both:

> for every victory which God now a-dayes gives to his great cause in *England*, doth bring with it double mercies, namely, a *spirituall step* or advance towards a pure Reformation; and a civill and *temporall step* or furtherance towards outward peace and tranquilitie.[113]

---

[111] Gouge, *Gods Three Arrowes*, 162. For a Scottish example of identical teaching, see William Guild (1586-1657), *The Throne of David* (Oxford: Rob. Blagrave, 1659), especially 21-22, where the Word and the Spirit are said to take the place of the Urim and the Thummim for specific guidance of non-doctrinal matters. See also 25-27 for a further discussion on how the Bible as the "sacred Oracle" guides the believer in life's circumstances.

[112] Reid, *Memoirs of the Westminster Divines*, vol. 1, 132-34. John Bond (c. 1610-c.1680) was educated under fellow Westminster divine John White and was later appointed as Master of Trinity Hall in Cambridge.

[113] John Bond, *Ortus Occidentalis: Or, A Dawning in the West* (London: Fr. Eglesfield, 1645), 2. John Bond gave a definition of salvation in another sermon: "*Salvation* is nothing else but the *putting* of a thing into a *safe condition*". John Bond, *Salvation in a Mystery: Or A Prospective Glasse for Englands Case* (London: Francis Eglesfeild, 1644), 7 [There are conflicting spellings of "Eglesfield"].

Bond also indicates that while non-believers, as the Exodus illustrates, shared in Israel's "Temporall" salvation, there is also a spiritual aspect for God's true people to such a deliverance; hence temporal salvation for the non-believer and for the true believer contains several differences. In the first instance, believers obtain:

> higher benefits by those deliverances; for they sucked inward sweetness, and spirituall good out of all that chaine of mercy and salvation.[114]

Secondly, spiritual people profit permanently from such mercies, because their faith is nurtured in experiences of God's gracious temporal deliverances, thus equipping them further for their walk as believers.[115] Spiritual individuals such as Moses can discern spiritual things in such deliverances, for he "got extraordinary *familiarity with God*, by his long march in the wilderness".[116]

In illustrating his claims John Bond finds these temporal saving experiences promised in the Word. While he can discern God in such salvific events for various reasons, one in particular stands out:

> "[...]when deliverances do flow in upon us *in the channell of the promises*, then you may be sure they are mercifull mercies, and that they have in them *much of God*: For the promises they are the *buckets* belonging to these *wels* and fountaines of *salvation. Therefore with joy shall they draw water out of the wels of salvation.*[117]

The "*channell of the promises*" is of course the Bible, but where, Bond inquires, are such promises for military victory in England? Two may be discovered in Scripture. First,

> promises made to *Joshua*, or any other holy man in Scripture for provisions, and protections in the Lords worke and cause, may very well be applied to us, and all others, in like works and causes.[118]

Any "*generall promise* of the Lords presence, and assistance for us in his service, is as sufficient for all *particulars* whereof we stand in need".[119] Secondly, we can discern God's promises to England as particular, not just as the application of a general promise. 1 Cor. 1: 25-29 and Deut. 32:36-39 are examples of such specific promises.[120] It was considered perfectly justifiable for a Puritan divine to infer from the pages of Holy Scripture

---

[114] Bond, *Ortus Occidentalis: Or, A Dawning in the West*, 23.
[115] Bond, *Ortus Occidentalis: Or, A Dawning in the West*, 23-25.
[116] Bond, *Ortus Occidentalis: Or, A Dawning in the West*, 23.
[117] Bond, *Ortus Occidentalis: Or, A Dawning in the West*, 27-28.
[118] Bond, *Ortus Occidentalis: Or, A Dawning in the West*, 29.
[119] Bond, *Ortus Occidentalis: Or, A Dawning in the West*, 29.
[120] Bond, *Ortus Occidentalis: Or, A Dawning in the West*, 29-30.

such a remarkable explanation for the military perplexities facing the modern nation of England.[121]

Not just national but international deliverance could be grounded in scriptural material. Richard Byfield associated international temporal salvation in eschatological terms.[122] Byfield (1598-1664), a later addition to the Assembly and brother of the more celebrated Nicholas Byfield, had been suspended before the establishment of the Assembly for refusing to read the *Book of Sports*, and was also ejected from his long-time charge at Long Ditton, Surrey for declining to conform to the Act for Uniformity at the Restoration.[123] He no doubt reflected at the time of his ejection and retirement on the failure of his prayer in this epistle dedicatory: "[T]hat these Kingdoms may be the Lords and his Christs; Crownes with Gospel-blessings remaining to our posterities for ever: Which is the Prayer of [...]Richard Byfield".[124] Byfield's *Zion's Answer* has all the ingredients of the Puritans' bold optimism that the kingdoms of the earth were about to become the Kingdom of Christ.[125] This radical hope and anticipation was predicated on three suppositions. First, many prophecies in the Old Testament predicted such a victory.[126] Secondly, Byfield perceived an identity between Zion and both the Christian church and the nation in which it resides: "This Nation of *England* at this day is Gods *Zion*".[127] Or to put it more accurately: "every Society, City, Common-wealth, Nation and Kingdom, that hath that which made *Zion Zion*, is fitly called *Zion*".[128] He adds that all nations will come to worship the Lord[129]; it is not so much that the church goes into the nations, but that the nations enter into the church.[130] Both church and civil government come from heaven; therefore civil government is also part of the Jerusalem which comes down from

---

[121] See also Case, *A Sermon Preached [...]August 22. 1645*, especially 18-19. Thomas Case followed Bond on the same fast day with a similar message, and a similar national and military soteriology.

[122] Richard Byfield, *Zion's Answer to The Nations Ambassadors, According to Instructions Given by Isaiah From God's Mouth* (London: Ralph Smith, 1645).

[123] See Reid, *Memoirs of the Westminster Divines*, vol. 1, 162-64.

[124] Byfield, *Zion's Answer to The Nations Ambassadors*, epistle dedicatory (not paginated).

[125] Rev. 11:15.

[126] The text of the sermon itself - Isa. 14: 32, and Isa. 3:26 for just two examples among many.

[127] Byfield, *Zion's Answer to The Nations Ambassadors*, 8.

[128] Byfield, *Zion's Answer to The Nations Ambassadors*, 20.

[129] Byfield, *Zion's Answer to The Nations Ambassadors*, 12.

[130] Byfield, *Zion's Answer to The Nations Ambassadors*, 14.

heaven,[131] and Christian magistrates are part of the foundation of the church.[132]

Byfield's third supposition is that Scripture (Isa. 14:32) also teaches that the poor will find "all manner of Salvations" in Zion.[133] A cascade of deliverances comprises God's determined blessings for his fallen world. Since the victory of Zion is assured in God's Word,[134] salvation will surely come to Zion.[135] But what is that salvation? There are many salvations, yet they are all of a piece. Byfield lists ten varieties, without exalting one over another; they are configured as essentially one salvation.[136] They include; pardon of sins; the Holy Spirit; soul feastings and divine teaching; protection and preservations; the ministry; power with God in prayer; kings and queens and whole nations serving the churches; afflictions sanctified; good news for both this life and the one to come; and finally, knowledge that God has commanded blessing in Zion and life evermore: "This is the salvation that may be had in *Zion*".[137]

"Salvation", for the Puritan, was a concept that included personal, national and international temporal deliverance and reformation, and was not therefore confined to personal redemption from sin and the wrath of God. It was this concept, so boldly explored in the sermons of the Westminster divines, that made its way into the *WCF*.

2.5 Salvation and the Necessity of Scripture

For the Westminster Assembly, the manner in which a knowledge of *Scripture* was necessary for salvation was quite a different issue from the question of why special revelation was necessary *per se*. As we have seen, the divines predicated the necessity of special revelation on the inadequacy of general revelation as a source of saving knowledge. We now turn our attention to the more precise question of the sense in which the Bible, and therefore also its confessional summation,[138] is so necessary, even essential,

---

[131] Byfield, *Zion's Answer to The Nations Ambassadors*, 21.

[132] Byfield, *Zion's Answer to The Nations Ambassadors*, 22.

[133] Byfield, *Zion's Answer to The Nations Ambassadors*, 10.

[134] Byfield, *Zion's Answer to The Nations Ambassadors*, 26.

[135] Byfield, *Zion's Answer to The Nations Ambassadors*, 26.

[136] Byfield, *Zion's Answer to The Nations Ambassadors*, 26-27.

[137] Byfield, *Zion's Answer to The Nations Ambassadors*, 27.

[138] Anthony Burgess notes: "There is no building of any confessions of faith, but the materials must be sercht from this mountain[Scripture]". Anthony Burges, *The Difficulty of, and The Encouragements to a Reformation* (London: Thomas Underhill, 1643), 9; For Anthony Tuckney a confession of faith is a "short modell of the *Principles of the doctrine of Christ, Heb.6.1*". Anthony Tuckney, *A Good Day Well Improved[...]to Which is Annexed a Sermon on 2 Tim. 1.13* (London: I. Rothwell, 1656), 247. The *WCF* was also described as "an admirable summary of Christian faith and practice".

for salvation in its full scope and extent, in the light of the Puritan supposition that this special revelation was now confined to Scripture.

The *WCF* teaches that the preaching of the Scriptures is the primary means God uses to impart, or make possible a saving interest in God's covenant of grace. "[T]he ordinances in which this covenant is dispensed are the preaching of the Word, and the administration of the sacraments of Baptism and the Lord's Supper".[139] However, it is important to discuss the parameters of that necessity under two rubrics. First, we can discern that the divines believed that Scriptures were essential in both an *absolute* and a *conditional* sense; and secondly, that they were believed necessary for both *personal redemption* and *holistic salvation*.

2.5.1 The Scriptures are Necessary in Both an Absolute and a Conditional Sense[140]

While *WCF* 1:1 introduces the necessity of a more special revelation to furnish what general revelation lacked, it is obvious that much of the content of articles of faith was not held to be strictly indispensable in order to attain personal redemption.[141] Yet even if the references in the *WCF* to the scope of salvation *were* thought to be confined to personal redemption, those matters not absolutely necessary for personal redemption could hardly be considered superfluous. When the Reformed orthodox stress the necessity of Scripture for salvation, they usually do not only have in mind an absolute exigency to enable salvation; they also make scholastic distinctions between different types of necessity.[142] This is illustrated in the

---

Alexander G. Mitchell, *The The Westminster Assembly; Its History and Standards* (Edmonton: SWRB, 1992), 371.

[139] *WCF* 7: 6

[140] For a comprehensive survey where he links Federal theology with the scope of Scripture, and where he concludes that later orthodoxy affirms "that the goal of Scripture in whole and in part was the redemption of believers", see Muller, *Post-Reformation Dogmatics*, vol. 2, 206-23, especially 223.

[141] See, for example, John Selden who asserts that much of the Thirty-nine Articles "do not contain matters of faith". He includes how churches are to be governed and whether infants should be baptised as examples of statements that are not matters of faith. John Selden, *Table-Talk: Being the Discourses of John Selden Esq; or His Sence of Various Matters of Weight and High Consequence Relating Especially to Religion and State* (London: E. Smith, 1689), 2.

[142] For a survey of Protestant Scholasticism in general, see Carl Trueman and Scott Clark (eds.), *Protestant Scholasticism: Essays in Reassessment* (Carlisle: Paternoster, 1999), especially Philip Ryken, "Scottish Reformed Scholasticism", 196-210 at 204-07, where Ryken contrasts scholasticism proper with the homiletic method of the Scots. Note also Muller, *Post-Reformation Reformed Dogmatics*, especially, vol. 2, 87: the

Puritan insistence that both faith *and* obedience were obligatory for salvation.[143] Although faith was fundamentally essential, obedience was its inevitable consequence. It did not *cause* salvation – but it was still necessary.

John White summarises what the Puritans had in mind in his important work, *A Way to the Tree of Life*,[144] where he describes two types of necessity in Scripture:

> Now when wee say, the grounds and rules of faith and obedience; contained in Scripture, are necessary to salvation, we mean not that all are of like necessity. Ignorance, or unbeleef in God, or Christ, excludes absolutely from salvation, *John* 3. 18. so doth not ignorance, or unbeleef in some temporall promise, although it cannot be excused from sinne[...][T]he things written therein are necessary to that end [salvation]; although not alike necessary, and that there is nothing necessary to that end, that is not to be found there.[145]

For White, the whole of Scripture, "the things written therein", is necessary for salvation, and there is nothing necessary that is not found there. These two truths undergird the Westminster insistence that nothing is to be added to or taken away from Scripture.[146]

Edward Reynolds makes a different though related distinction, when he discriminates between the "cause" of salvation and the "way" to salvation. Good works are not "proper causes on which we may depend for salvation"; they are "good in *genere via* as paths to Heaven, not in *genere*

WCF was "the greatest confessional document written during the age of Protestant scholasticism".

[143] Obadiah Sedgewick explains: Christ "discovers unto us infallibly the reality, and the quality of our salvation so there is not any one truth, nor any one path necessary unto that salvation, but he opens it, and reveales it, whether it respect our faith, or our obedience". Sedgewick, *The Bowels of Tender Mercy Sealed in the Everlasting Covenant [...]"*, 57.

[144] Born in Stanton Saint John, Oxfordshire, White (1574-1648) was educated at New College, Oxford. He became persuaded of Presbyterianism at the Westminster Assembly where he was also an officer, being appointed assessor, along with Cornelius Burgess, to take the place of the prolocutor when he was absent, although White himself had to be relieved of his duties as assessor because of ill health. Rector at Dorchester, Dorset for thirty-seven years, White, along with Twisse, was one of the older members of the Assembly. The esteem in which Parliament and Assembly held White was illustrated by his appointment to lead the prayer at the initial subscription of the *Solemn League and Covenant* in 1643. Barker, *Puritan Profiles*, 22-24.

[145] John White, *A Way to the Tree of Life Discovered in Sundry Directions for the Profitable Reading of the Scriptures: Wherein is Described Occasionally The Nature of a Spirituall Man* (London: R. Royston, 1647), 65.

[146] *WCF* 1:6.

causa".[147] In a similar vein, the *WCF* makes the attainment of heaven contingent on moral rectitude, because Christians are quickened and strengthened "to the practice of true holiness, without which no man shall see the Lord".[148] Even though it is underlined in Chapter Sixteen (*Of Good Works*) that even the best deeds cannot merit pardon or eternal life, it is equally asserted that everyone needs to possess "fruit unto holiness, [so that] they may have the end, eternal life".[149]

As we find in William Twisse,[150] this mandatory obedience was sometimes termed a "necessitie of Commandment". While Twisse concedes that there are "but few" things necessary for passing from spiritual death to spiritual life, there is a *"necessitas praecepti"* which requires a striving after perfection. If, because of negligence, a Christian fails in his or her obedience to this "necessitie of Commandment[...]this is a very pardonable sin upon our confession of it",[151] although those negligent in striving for a perfection of knowledge still jeopardise their salvation. Twisse encourages the individual to see that the life lived by faith is on a pathway to heaven, and consequently that the highest attainments of faith draw one nearer to glory:

> There is a plerophory and fulness of faith that we should strive unto, and of knowledge as well as of holiness: For this life is our way to heaven, and still we must draw neerer thitherwards, by knowing all that we can know by the Word, *Deut* 29.29.[152]

The necessity of command was formally differentiated from the "necessity of means", the latter being the *sine qua non* of spiritual redemption, as Samuel Rutherford enunciates in his *Due Right of Presbyteries*, where he expounds his perspective on fundamentals of the faith. Although Rutherford closes his discussion by admitting how difficult it is to arrive at

---

[147] Edward Reynolds, "Brotherly Reconciliation", *Twenty Sermons Preached upon Several Occasions* (London: George Thomason, 1660), 13. Later Reynolds discusses three classes of "fundamentall Doctrines"– faith, practice and worship (30-31).

[148] *WCF* 13:1.

[149] *WCF* 16:2

[150] William Twisse (1578-1646) died during the sitting of the Assembly. He was prolocutor or chair of the Assembly and combined a big reputation as a theologian with a mild manner. Educated at Oxford, he was also widely regarded as the most accomplished debater in England, although his supralpasarianism was a minority view. Twisse who had been rector of Newbury, Berkshire until his appointment to the Assembly, was buried in Westminster Abbey, but was later disinterred with his remains being cast into St. Margaret's churchyard. Barker, *Puritan Profiles*, 18-21.

[151] William Twisse, *The Scriptures Sufficiency To Determine All Matters of Faith, Made Good against the Papist: OR, That a Christian May be Infallibly Certain of His Faith and Religion by the Holy Scriptures* (London: Matthew Keynton, 1656), 122.

[152] Twisse, *The Scriptures Sufficiency*, 119.

a definitive body of non-negotiable doctrine which one must believe,[153] he nevertheless attempts to explain the essential principles required to obtain salvation, which also implies keeping communion with a true church.[154]

Salvation, Rutherford asserts, is Christocentric, because the foundation of matters basic to redemption is specifically knowledge of Christ: "*Jesus Christ* is the foundation of faith reall or personall and the knowledge of Christ is the dogmaticall foundation of faith".[155] A share in this foundation is not automatic, but requires an understanding of "matters of faith". Rutherford differentiates these into three categories: "fundamentall points", superstructures built upon fundamentals, and "circa-fundamentalia", or things "about" fundamental matters of faith.[156] Although he gives no examples for the second category, he believes (as was also true with fundamentals) that their repudiation invites condemnation, because to deny such a "superstructure built on fundamentals" is to undermine the foundational or primary fundamentals. The third category, "circa-fundamentalia", describes aspects that are still matters of faith, but ignorance of which does not automatically condemn. Examples include historical and chronological details, such as the record that Paul left his coat in Troas.[157] A knowledge of this third type is not compulsory for salvation, because such matters do not comprise a necessity of means (*necessitas medii*): "Many are in glory[...]and yet knew never that *Sampson* killed a Lion".[158] True believers may even hold erroneous opinions about these features and yet still not be damned, though a "malicious opposing" of such elements in Scripture becomes a fundamental error.[159]

In addition, fundamentals which are arrived at by consequence from Scripture may be fundamentals for one person, but to those who are less intelligent, less educated or less knowledgeable, the same points appear less important.[160] Rutherford avers that even when the Apostles doubted Christ's resurrection,[161] which is a "fundamental" point, they were

---

[153] Samuel Rutherford, *The Due Right of Presbyteries or, A Peaceable Plea for the Government of the Church of Scotland* (London: Richard Whittaker and Andrew Crook, 1644), 229.

[154] Rutherford, *The Due Right of Presbyteries*, 223.

[155] Rutherford, *The Due Right of Presbyteries*, 221. He later explains: "The specifice and essentiall forme of a fundamentall article is not taken from the authoritie of God speaking in the Word[...]but from the influence that the knowledge of an article hath to unite us to God in Christ, and bring us to salvation". Rutherford, *The Due Right of Presbyteries*, 222.

[156] Rutherford, *The Due Right of Presbyteries*, 221.

[157] 2 Tim. 4:13.

[158] Rutherford, *The Due Right of Presbyteries*, 221-22.

[159] Rutherford, *The Due Right of Presbyteries*, 222.

[160] Rutherford, *The Due Right of Presbyteries*, 222-23.

[161] See Matt. 28:17, for example.

The Necessity and Scope of Special Revelation

nonetheless still true believers.[162] Furthermore, Rutherford concedes that an uneducated "Papist" or Lutheran who believes that Christ is both a true man and physically present in the Lord's Supper, and therefore in many different places on the earth, is not necessarily condemned for it, because the "error may be meerely philosophick".[163] Rutherford reasons that attitude is very important: a deficit of understanding or knowledge concerning fundamentals does not condemn if there is a willing disposition to believe anything clearly revealed in the Bible.[164] Under these circumstances the believer holds a legitimate implicit faith.[165]

Plainly, there is, for Rutherford, nothing superfluous in Scripture or in special revelation because the whole of Scripture is either *necessitas praecepti* or *necessitas medii*, which means that no part of Scripture is an indifferent matter.[166] The wrong attitude to the material of Scripture might condemn a believer, but those dogmas that are obligatory as the means of salvation are naturally the ones which are absolutely necessary - though Rutherford admits that culpability through weakness in understanding fundamentals is dependent upon intellectual or academic ability. Rutherford is anxious not to be misunderstood on this matter. He is concerned that some might think he is endorsing a willingness to be content with belief in only primary fundamentals. In his perspective, those who never strive to grow in grace merely show that they have never laid hold of Christ as their

---

[162] Rutherford, *The Due Right of Presbyteries*, 224.

[163] Rutherford, *The Due Right of Presbyteries*, 224-25.

[164] Rutherford, *The Due Right of Presbyteries*, 225. On this point, see also Samuel Rutherford, *A Free Disputation against Pretended Liberty of Conscience Tending to Resolve Doubts Moved by Mr. John Goodwin, John Baptist, Dr. Jer. Taylor, the Belgick Arminians, Socinians, and Other Authors Contending for Lawlesse Liberty, or Licentious Toleration of Sects and Heresies* (London: Andrew Crook, 1649), 59.

[165] See also Rutherford, *The Due Right of Presbyteries*, 226, where Rutherford also further refines his classification of fundamentals, the first "matter of faith", by suggesting two types, thereby slightly adjusting his earlier scheme. He proposes a class of primary fundamentals, which are summarised as *"Credenda"* (points to be believed in the Apostles' Creed), *"Petenda"* (things we ask God in the Lord's Prayer), and *"Agenda"* (things to be done which are found in the Decalogue). The second division is indeed secondary, although these elements too can be found in the Apostles' Creed. While Christ's incarnation and death exemplify primary fundamentals, clauses such as *"conceived by the holy Ghost, and borne of the Virgin Mary"* or *"he suffered under Pontius Pilate, was crucified &c"* are representative of lesser or secondary fundamentals. They are necessary to be believed, because God commanded them (*necessitas praecepti*), but they are not absolutely essential because they are not a required means of salvation (*necessitas medii*). It is enough that believers would not deny them, were they explained to them in a clear way. Rutherford probably means that there are some believers who have not been taught these lesser fundamentals, but that their lack of knowledge does not keep them from attaining heaven.

[166] Rutherford, *The Due Right of Presbyteries*, 222.

foundation in the first place. Thus, he warns, to suggest that people should rest on those primary fundamentals is only an abuse of the doctrine.[167]

Rutherford's English colleagues also made attempts to define which articles of faith were considered absolutely indispensable for personal redemption, although none of them offers a complete list. Jeremiah Burroughs is convinced that recognising one's need for Christ as mediator is such a necessary means:

> That which I shall this day endeavor is to show you something of the glory of God shining in this truth: that God communicates Himself through a Mediator, through His Son. This is the great point of theology that is absolutely necessary for you to know if you would have eternal life. It is possible to be ignorant of many other truths and still be saved, but there must be something of this or there can be no salvation.[168]

Burroughs' colleague Thomas Goodwin detects a plenary "pith" of gospel truth, which is further refined in the "kernel" as knowledge necessary for obtaining eternal salvation:

> You see, my brethren, what is *the pith of the gospel*. It is the mystery of God's will; to know but this, that God will save sinners in the blood of Christ, this is the pith of the gospel. This is that which is essential to salvation[...]. But this is the kernel of all, God will save sinners[...]. If the gospel lay all in great hidden wisdom and rationalities, and that a man must know all the depths of wisdom in it, all the rationalities of it, the coherence of one truth with another, before he can be saved, many poor weak understandings should have been undone, and never should have come to be saved.[169]

The gospel thus can be distilled down to bare essentials and still be the means of personal redemption from God's wrath. This truth is not, however, to be divorced from the necessity of command.

2.5.2 The Scriptures are Necessary for Both Personal and Holistic Redemption

When the divines assert the necessity of the Scriptures for salvation in *WCF* 1:1 they may thus be understood to imply (a) that the Bible is necessary for personal redemption from sin and eschatological salvation, and (b) that it also transcends such a use. This broader purpose of Scripture is stressed in other writings by the authors of the *WCF*, suggesting that it is unlikely that the *WCF*'s summation of Scripture would preclude the means of obtaining what God imparted in the way of earthly blessing and temporal salvation or deliverance.

---

[167] Rutherford, *The Due Right of Presbyteries*, 229.
[168] Burroughs, *The Saints' Treasury*, 44.
[169] Goodwin, *The Works of Thomas Goodwin*, vol. 1, 143.

The Necessity and Scope of Special Revelation

The Puritans underscore the necessity of Scripture for temporal salvation in two ways: first, they attribute both personal redemption and holistic salvation to the same grounds of faith in Scripture;[170] secondly, they affirm that Scripture is the rule of faith and life for attaining a holistic salvation.[171] Since such a comprehensive salvation entails all of human experience, Stephen Marshall urges Christians to make "Gods Word the Rule of all our actions in our bent and purpose".[172] Therefore, as a "rule" it contains

---

[170] According to Joseph Caryl, for spiritual salvation, there are promises of free grace whereby God pardons sin; promises of grace, whereby God gives faith and repentance; and promises "unto" grace - that if a believer exercises faith and repentance, that person will be saved. All these hold true as well for temporal salvation, for in this category there are also promises of free grace, promises of grace and promises "unto" grace for nations. See Joseph Caryl, *The Arraignment of Unbelief, as the Grand Cause of our Nationall Non-establishment* (London: Giles Calvert, 1645), 42.

[171] In *WCF* 1:2 it is baldly stated: "All [the canonical books] which are given by inspiration of God to be the rule of faith and life". In *WCF* 1:9, we learn: "The infallible rule of interpretation of Scripture is the Scripture itself". If Scripture is "the" rule of faith and life, and if the "infallible rule of interpretation of Scripture" is also Scripture, then without question, to be consistent *WCF* 1:10 must conclude that the whole of Scripture, or more accurately the Holy Spirit speaking in the entire Scripture, is "supreme judge" in all religious controversies – which, of course, it does. In *WCF* 19, *Of the Law*, the Law is said to be "a rule of life informing them of the will of God" only because it is part of Scripture. Thus in *WCF* 31:4, the most pious collection of theologians cannot be the rule: "All synods or councils, since the Apostles' times, whether general or particular, may err; and many have erred. Therefore they are not to be made the rule of faith or practice; but to be used as a help in both". *LC* 3 puts it thus: "Q3: What is the word of God? A3: The holy scriptures of the Old and New Testament are the word of God, the only rule of faith and obedience". *SC* 2 puts it so: " Q2: What rule hath God given to direct us how we may glorify and enjoy him? A2: The word of God, which is contained in the scriptures of the Old and New Testaments, is the only rule to direct us how we may glorify and enjoy him".

[172] Stephen Marshall, "The Life of Christ or the Great Mystery of Spiritual life", *The Works of Mr Stephen Marshall* (London: printed by Peter Cole and Edward Cole, 1661), 28. See also Anthony Burgess who is equally certain that the Scriptures have this comprehensive necessity. The Scripture he notes is "the *primum principium cognoscendi*, the first principle to teach and inform us". He means here to "inform us" unto salvation including political salvation, for he adds: "This is the Standard of all Truth, all Truth (I say) necessary to Salvation, It is the Christians Metaphysicks, Ethicks, and Politiques, the Rule of all Speculative and Practicall Truth, *To the Law and to the Testimony* [...] Isaiah 8.20.": Anthony Burgess, *CXLV Expository Sermons Upon the Whole 17th Chapter of the Gospel According to St John: or Christ's Prayer Before His Passion Explicated, and Both Practically and Polemically Improved* (London: Thomas Underhill, 1656), 474-75.

"promises for every condition that can be",[173] and thus is not restricted to justification.

This willingness to make the Scriptures the rule of faith and life for all of life was a common Puritan ideal. Henry Wilkinson (1616-1690), who, though not a member of the Assembly, was a favourite of Parliament,[174] preached a sermon on Hab. 2:3, entitled *The Dark Vision*, in St Mary's Oxford on 31 January, 1648. It has as its theme the task of waiting for God's answer to prayer in dark times.[175] In this sermon, Wilkinson's obvious goal is to make his text relevant for his audience. Alluding to the *WCF* proof-text Heb. 1:1-2, Wilkinson dismisses the possibility of using visions in his own day for temporal deliverance:

> You know, God spake at sundry times, and in divers manners [...] so that Dreams, Visions and Revelations cease, which were extraordinary, and only *pro tempore*.[176]

The only visions believers wait for are revelations of "Admonition and Instruction", which now only come by the Scriptures.[177] The Word of God is the "Umpire, guide, [and] rule of thy life",[178] and thus Wilkinson specifically prescribes the use of Scripture as the rule of faith and life in contradistinction to "extraordinary impulses upon our spirits and revelations",[179] for the purpose of obtaining temporal deliverance – in this instance the deliverance of the church from her enemies.[180] The Word of God is thus the only rule for temporal deliverances.[181]

A little-known Westminster divine, Thomas Carter (d. 1646), minister of Dynton in Buckinghamshire,[182] in a sermon called *Prayers Prevalencie for*

---

[173] Marshall, "The Life of Christ or the Great Mystery of Spiritual life", *The Works of Mr Stephen Marshall*, 42-44, at 42.

[174] As Principal of Magdalen College, Oxford, he was responsible for training many Puritan preachers during the Interregnum, and had also entertained Cromwell and Fairfax and preached before them at Oxford. He was ejected by the Act of Uniformity, and was later excommunicated for not reading a divine service according to the rubric. He maintained his Presbyterian views all his life. He was known as "Dean Harry" to distinguish him from the other two Henry Wilkinsons who were Assembly divines. Charlotte Fell-Smith, "Henry Wilkinson", *DNB*, vol. 2, 2268.

[175] Henry Wilkinson, *Three Decad[e]s of Sermons Lately Preached to the University at St Mary's Church in Oxford* (Oxford: Thomas Robinson, 1660), 118.

[176] Wilkinson, *Three Decads of Sermons*, 116.

[177] Wilkinson, *Three Decads of Sermons*, 116.

[178] Wilkinson, *Three Decads of Sermons*, 115.

[179] Wilkinson, *Three Decads of Sermons*, 132.

[180] Wilkinson, *Three Decads of Sermons*, 114-16.

[181] The promises one rests on as one waits for deliverance are found in Scripture texts such as Rom. 8:28, Mal. 4:2, Isa. 54:7, and Mat. 28:20. Wilkinson, *Three Decads of Sermons*, 122.

[182] Reid, *Memoirs of the Westminster Divines*, vol. 1, 192.

Israels Safety also prescribes Scripture as a rule for temporal salvation. He exhorts the House of Commons on 28 June 1643, from Ex. 32: 9-10, to pray for the sins of the nation and thus to save the nation from God's wrath. He lists four sins prevalent in England, which for him ought to be enough for Parliament to realise that there may be an impending judgement in the nation. Not only can such a fate be discerned by reason: there is also evidence from Scripture (Gen.15: 15).[183] Parliament's important task is to identify the sin correctly and to judge the status of sins in the nation.[184] But there has to be a rule by which to judge, and that rule (here Carter cites Isa. 8:20) is the "Word of God", where "all opinions and practices are to be tried".[185] When the situation is thus correctly tested, the obligation is for Parliament to pray in order "to save a Nation from ruine".[186]

Carter's Westminster colleague Herbert Palmer exhorted the same Parliament, reminding it of its obligation under the *Solemne League and Covenant* to reform the church according to the "Word of God[which] *is the only Rule*" for church reformation.[187] This responsibility to live by the rule of the Word with a view to reformation was extended by Westminster divine William Reyner to be a rule by which civil government is guided in its punishment of sin.[188] *WCF* 23 (*Of the Civil Magistrate*), incorporates these salvific functions of the civil government. We cannot avoid the conclusion that for the Westminster Puritans, the concept of holistic salvation, which includes temporal deliverance, earthly blessing and reformation, renders the Scriptures necessary as a rule of faith and life.

---

[183] Thomas Carter, *Prayers Prevalencie for Israels Safety* (London: John Bellamie and Ralph Smith, 1643), 1-4.

[184] Carter, *Prayers Prevalencie for Israels Safety*, 5-11.

[185] Carter, *Prayers Prevalencie for Israels Safety*, 8-9. There are though secondary rules, such as civil law, the example and custom of the people of God and the human conscience, but they also should be regulated by the Scriptures (9).

[186] Carter, *Prayers Prevalencie for Israels Safety*, 22.

[187] Herbert Palmer, *The Glasse of Gods Providence towards His Faithfull Ones* (London: Th. Underhill, 1644), 50-51. For Scripture as the rule for reformation, also see Alexander Henderson, *A Sermon Preached[...]December 27. 1643* (London: Robert Bostock, 1644), 19. See also Burges[s], *The Difficulty of, and The Encouragements to a Reformation*, 10-14, where he categorizes seven competing rules for Reformation, which can all be identified under the four listed in *WCF* 1:10: church councils, opinions of ancient writers, doctrines of men and private spirits. Burgess's use of Scripture as a rule for reformation, therefore, has this link with *WCF* 1:10. In the *WCF*, the rule of the Holy Spirit speaking in the Scripture is an article of faith which teaches that the way of salvation requires an adequate judge for controversies that would jeopardise that salvation. This is further proof that the Puritans saw reformation as salvation. Thus, naturally the Scriptures were the rule.

[188] William Reyner, *Babylons Ruining-Earthquake and the Restauration of Zion* (London: Samuel Enderby, 1644), 44-45.

2.6 Conclusion

The Westminster Assembly made a distinction between a universal revelation of God which rendered human beings inexcusable, and a more specific revelation, which was tied to the way of salvation. Although the divines never used these precise terms in their documents, the later distinction between "general" and "special" revelation is a helpful one when seeking to understand the Puritans' religious epistemology. Special revelation was formerly imparted through dreams, visions, the Urim and Thummim and other supernatural manifestations, but following the completion of the canon, the saving revelation, known as the Word of God, ceased to be given and was now fully contained in the sixty-six books of Scripture. The "salvation" referred to in *WCF* 1:1 cannot be taken to be confined to personal eschatological salvation: both in the *WCF* itself and in the usage of its authors in their other works it is displayed in ways that encompass both personal redemption from the consequences of sin and temporal deliverances from danger. "Salvation" captures the biblical promises which are both for this life and for the life to come.

Furthermore, there are propositions to be known and duties to be performed, which are necessary for salvation. These entail "faith" and "life" - matters to be believed and actions to be done. This fact ensured, for the divines, that the whole of Scripture was necessary for salvation, for the scope of God's special revelation encompassed both a necessity of means and a necessity of command.

The Westminster view that the former modes of special revelation had ceased and given way to Scripture alone invites some further reflection. What *exactly* did the Assembly mean to say had actually ceased and why were these other modalities no longer operative? Such questions take us to the heart of the subject in this thesis. To them we now turn.

Chapter 3

The Obsolescence of the Former Modalities of Special Revelation

3.1 Introduction

The obvious difference between the *WCF* and the older Reformed confessions on the doctrine of Scripture was the addition of an explanatory clause concerning the cessation of former modalities of revelation– the cessationist clause of *WCF* 1:1.[1] But what did this statement signify? Were all other forms of supernatural revelation, apart from revelation in Scripture, excluded absolutely, or did God still impart information to humankind through other modalities in some limited sense?

The vast majority of published commentators on the *WCF* do not help us in this enquiry, because mostly they fail to indicate whether these "former ways" were deemed by the *WCF* to have ceased absolutely or ceased only as means to convey new doctrines or ethical stipulations.[2] Edward Morris,

---

[1] *WCF* 1:1 "[...]those former ways of God's revealing His will unto His people being now ceased".

[2] For comments on *WCF* 1:1, see Hugh Martin, *The Westminster Doctrine of the Inspiration of Scripture* (London: J. Nisbet, 1877), 49-50; Francis Beattie, *The Presbyterian Standards: An Exposition of the Westminster Confession of Faith and Catechisms* (Richmond: The Presbyterian Committee of Publication, 1896), 49; For the more accessible works, see Robert Shaw, *The Reformed Faith* (Inverness: Christian Focus, 1973), 1-7; Archibald Alexander Hodge, *The Confession of Faith: A Handbook of Christian Doctrine Expounding the Westminster Confession* (Edinburgh: Banner of Truth Trust, 1978), 25-43. See especially 38, where he comments: "private revelations have been professed only by vain enthusiasts"; Rowland Ward, *The Westminster Confession for the Church Today: A Modernised Text and Commentary Commemorating the 350th Anniversary of the Westminster Assembly 1643-49* (Melbourne: Presbyterian Church of Eastern Australia, 1992), 6-8; George Hendry, *The Westminster Confession for Today: A Contemporary Interpretation* (London: SCM Press, 1960), 19-26. Hendry sees special revelation as God acting in history as well as in words (24); and John Gerstner, Douglas Kelly and Philip Rollinson, *A Guide - The Westminster Confession of Faith* (Signal Mountain: Summertown Texts, 1992), 1-6; Richard Muller, *Post-Reformation Reformed Dogmatics* (Grand Rapids, MI: Baker, 2003), vol. 2, 88; James Philip, *The Westminster Confession of Faith. An Exposition, Part 1 Chapters 1-8* (Edinburgh: Holyrood Abbey Church, 1966). Philip does not discuss the cessationist clause at all. We have already discussed the likely meaning of

however, writing at the end of the nineteenth century, is one notable exception. In his *Theology of the Westminster Symbols*, he comments:

> The work of the Spirit both in revelation and in inspiration is viewed as finished and complete. He graciously illuminates, teaches, educates, edifies, but he no longer reveals - he no longer inspires. All assumption of prophetic functions or of apostolic authority is hereby condemned: false communications claiming divine warrant are cast out: even the inner light of faith, contemplated as supplying to the believer any further or higher knowledge than that here contained, is set aside.[3]

Although Morris does not elucidate his conclusions on the *WCF's* religious epistemology any further, we need to ask whether the majority of the seventeenth-century Reformed orthodox would have concurred with his interpretation of the cessationist clause. While the Westminster Puritans believed that the church would receive a clearer understanding of Scripture, in particular for a greater insight into the meaning of the intricate details of the book of Revelation,[4] our analysis will show that most of the Reformed orthodox who taught on this subject expressed views on the cessation of extra-biblical revelation that concur with Morris's interpretation of the cessationist clause found in *WCF* 1:1.

3.2 An Exegetical Tradition

There always have been two sides in Protestantism to the debate over the availability of extra-biblical revelation and, as we have noted in the Introduction, two opposing views remain to this day. Jer. 31:31-34 prophesied New Covenant blessings which were to include a greater effusion of the Holy Spirit,[5] but for the Reformed orthodox these promises did not extend to contemporary miracles and extra-biblical methods of revelation. James I, no less, stated the matter baldly in 1597: since

---

the content of revelations "necessary unto salvation" proscribed by the cessationist clause in the previous chapter.

[3] Edward Morris, *Theology of the Westminster Symbols* (Columbus: 1900) [No further publishing details are given], 92.

[4] See, for example, Thomas Goodwin: Though God revealed all "for the matter contained in the New Testament, that shall be revealed until the end of the world, yet in regard of the light whereby this is discerned, God hath gone on by piecemeal": Thomas Goodwin, *The Works of Thomas Goodwin, D.D.* (Edinburgh: James Nichol, 1863), vol. 5, 528; or Edward Reynolds, *Self-Deniall* (London: George Thomason, 1659), 36.

[5] *WCF* 7:6 and 20:1.

the establishing of his Church by the Apostles, al miracles, visions, prophecies & appearances of Angels or good Spirits, are ceased; which served only for the sowing of faith, and planting of the Church.[6]

O. Palmer Robertson rightly points out that the *FPC*, completed before the *WCF*, teaches the cessation of the extraordinary offices of apostle, evangelist and prophet. He concludes "It would seem clear from this distinction that the Westminster Assembly had determined at its earliest stage to register its opinion that the foundational offices by which revelation was brought to the church no longer were functional in the church's life".[7]

Those who did not agree with such a stance in the days of the Westminster Assembly provoked a vigorous response from polemicists like Thomas Edwards (1599-1647). Edwards was an indefatigable Presbyterian minister and controversialist, although he was not a member of the Westminster Assembly. He penned a three-part onslaught against the sectaries or ecclesiastical Independents of the day entitled *Gangraena*, a work which illustrates the invective and passion that the claim to continuing immediate revelation, among other "errors", could inspire.[8] While Edwards' disputatious style may seem unattractive today, Scottish commissioner Robert Baillie was much taken with the *Gangraena*.[9] When

---

[6] James I, *The Workes of the Most High and Myghtie Prince* (London: [printed by] Robert Barker and John Bill, 1616), 127. Or as one Westminster divine put it: "[T]hough I cannot speak to you, as he [Paul] did to them, by an immediate revelation from God, yet by good prognosticks and signes drawn out of the book of Gods Providence, I shall[...]shew good grounds of strong hopes". John Langley, *Gemitus Columbae: The Mournfull Note of the Dove* (London: Philemon Stephens, 1644), 28.

[7] O. Palmer Robertson, "The Holy Spirit in the Westminster Confession", Ligon Duncan (ed.), *The Westminster Confession into the 21st Century* (Fearn: Christian Focus, 2003), vol. 1, 96. The Form states: "The officers which Christ hath appointed for the edification of his church, and the perfecting of the saints, are, some extraordinary, as apostles, evangelists, and prophets, which are ceased": *FPC*, 172.

[8] Thomas Edwards, *The First and Second part of Gangraena: or a Catalogue and Discovery of Many of the Errors, Heresies, Blasphemies and Pernicious Practices of the Sectaries of this Time, Vented and Acted in England in these Four Last Years* (London: Ralph Smith, 1646). Thomas Edwards, *The Third Part of Gangraena or, a New and Higher Discovery of the Errors, Heresies, Blasphemies, and Insolent Proceedings of the Sectaries of these Times; with Some Animadversions by Way of Confutation upon Many of the Errors and Heresies Named* (London: Ralph Smith, 1646).

[9] Baillie, for example, writes: "Their ministrie are faithful watchmen; and some late books have done them good; especiallie Mr. Edwards's Gangraena; which must either waken the Parliament, and all others, to lay to heart the spreading of the evil errors, or I know not what can doe it": Robert Baillie, *The Letters and Journals of Robert Baillie, A. M. Principal of the University of Glasgow M.DC.XXXVII.-M.DC.LXII.*, ed. David Laing (Edinburgh: Bannatyne Club, 1841-1842), vol. 2, 352. And later in 1646: "I MARVELL that Mr. Edwards's book is not yet come abroad: its stay is hurtfull" (vol. 2, 358).

he published his own tracts against the pretensions to new revelations by Independents of various stripes, Baillie showed an obvious reliance on Edwards' research.[10]

In his *Dissuasive from the Errours of the Time,* Baillie opposes the view of the Independents, that 1 Cor. 14: 29 provided biblical precedent for the unordained to preach in church, by countering that the prophets mentioned in the text were "extraordinary" prophets, but still those who held an office in the church. As a result, in his view, the biblical example can form no precedent, because "these gifts are ceased, That it is so, vers.30. makes cleare, where the Prophets doe preach extemporary Revelations".[11]

Edwards and Baillie were both reacting to "enthusiasts" from the vantage-point of an impressive and authoritative exegetical tradition. One common cessationist text used in the Westminster symbols evident in this tradition is Rev. 22:18-19, which was interpreted to prove that the completed Scriptures are the sole rule of faith and life.[12] Westminster orthodoxy, as Thomas Goodwin represents it, concludes from this text:

---

[10] These claims to new inspirations were denounced in Edwards' work. Edwards, *The First and Second Part of Gangraena.* Error 144 is typical: "That there are Revelations and Visions in these times, yea to some they are more ordinary, and shall be to the people of God, generally within a while" (28). Or number 145: "That the gift of miracles is not ceased in these times, but that some of the Sectaries have wrought miracles, and miracles have accompanied them in their baptism, &c. and the people of God shall have power of miracles shortly" (28). Later, in an additional catalogue of errors, he writes: "Some of the Sectaries do affirm and hold they have not only had Revelations, but they have seen Visions also". Furthermore, they claim that the "means of God revealing himself and his mind and will to his servants in reference to their salvation, is immediately by himself, without Scripture, without Ordinances, Ministers, or any other means". Edwards, "A Fresh and Further discovery of the Errours and Pernicious Practises of the Sectaries in England", *The First and Second Part of Gangraena*, 2.

[11] Robert Baillie, *A Dissuasive from the Errours of the Time: Wherein the Tenets of the Principall Sects, Especially of the Independents, are Drawn Together in One Map, for the Most Part, in Words of Their own Authours, and Their Maine Principles are Examined by the Touch-stone of the Holy Scriptures* (London: Samuel Gellibrand, 1645), 178. Again relying on the *Gangraena* extensively as an authority and source for the tenets, Baillie footnotes that those who deny that the Scriptures are the Word of God send people "from the word to seek revelations above and contrary to it". Robert Baillie, *Anabaptism, the True Fountaine of Independency, Antinomy, Brownism, Familisme, and Most of the Other Errours, which for the Time doe Trouble the Church of England, Unsealed* (London: Samuel Gellibrand, 1647), 99.

[12] It is held to support *WCF* 1:2 : "All which are given by inspiration of God, to be the rule of faith and life", and *LC* 3, which also confines the Word as a rule of faith and life to the Scriptures.

"these words were singled out to be his [Christ's] last, and that he meant to speak no more till the day of judgement".[13]

However, the four key texts which form the basis of the wider Protestant contemporary perspective confining special revelation to the Bible, are found in Eph. 1:17-18, Heb. 1:1-2, and Acts 2:17-18 (with Joel 2:28). The first two are Westminster proof-texts, while Acts 2:17-18 and its Old Testament source yield similar exegetical conclusions in the sermons and writings of the Reformed orthodox, where there are direct associations of this passage with the same "last days" referred to in Heb. 1:2. We will consider the Puritan treatment of each of these texts in turn to see how they were understood to support a cessationist stance.

3.2.1 Ephesians 1:17-18 and the Promise of New Revelations

The Westminster symbols use the three separate citations, Eph. 1:17, or 1:18 and the whole passage Eph. 1:17-19, six times in all as proof-texts, always in a context which assumes that the Word and the Spirit function together in the process of "revelation".[14] These verses were in effect a litmus test of cessationism for Westminster orthodoxy, and in addition were the occasion to contrast two categories of divine disclosure – "immediate" and "mediate" revelation. To anchor this discussion in its correct context, therefore, we need to preface this analysis of Puritan exegesis by bringing into sharper focus this crucial dichotomy that was central to the Puritan doctrine of the Holy Spirit. Any resolution of the basic question in this thesis requires an appreciation of how these discrete types of revelation were held to function.

Scott Murphy, in his dissertation on the Westminster doctrine of Scripture, defines "immediate" revelation as "an act occurring directly without an intervening agency and apart from all human means or

---

[13] Thomas Goodwin, *The Heart of Christ in Heaven, Towards Sinners on Earth. Or, a Treatise Demonstrating the Gracious Disposition and Tender Affection of Christ in His Humane Nature Now in Glory, unto His Members under all Sorts of Infirmities, Either of Sin or Misery* (London: R. Dawlman, 1642), 39.

[14] In Chapter 10 of the *WCF, Of Effectual Calling*, Eph. 1:17-18 are cited in support of the clause: "enlightening their minds spiritually and savingly to understand the things of God". In Chapter 14, *Of Saving Faith*, in the first section, the same verses serve to support the clause: "the work of the Spirit of Christ in their hearts". This clause refers back to the faith that embraces the gospel promises. For the authors, *LC* Answer 67, Eph. 1:18-20 confirms: "Effectual calling is the work of God's almighty power and grace". In *LC* Answer 72, they establish the work of the Spirit in the application of justifying faith. In *LC* Answer 190, they demonstrate the work of God in response to prayer to "[p]revent and remove[...]ignorance". In *LC* Answer 192, the third petition of the Lord's Prayer includes asking "that God would by his Spirit take away from ourselves and others all blindness".

cooperation".[15] "Mediate" revelation, on the other hand, is, by definition, illumination through some means, understood by Reformed orthodoxy to involve at least human agency and the Scriptures.[16] Westminster orthodoxy repeatedly denied that "immediate" revelation was still possible.[17] Anthony Burgess provides a typical instance of this view. Burgess wrote on the subject in a series of sermons on Christ's High Priestly prayer in John 17. In these homilies, he sketches his doctrine of Scripture, maintaining that meaningful communion with Christ is still available to the New Testament believer.[18] Notwithstanding other reasons for limiting the source of the voice of God,[19] he concludes that God's voice is now only heard in the Scriptures because God has ceased to convert, sanctify and impart prophecy by "immediate revelation".[20] "God who could convert immediately", Burgess urges, "and reach home to our souls, as he did to the Prophets by an immediate Revelation, hath taken this away".[21] God's will must be sought in the Bible, because "in this latter Age he guides it [the church] by the Scriptures only".[22] The *WCF* does locate the sole authority in the

---

[15] Scott Thomas Murphy, "The Doctrine of Scripture in the Westminster Assembly" (unpublished PhD thesis, Drew University, 1984), 47.

[16] James Usher reasons that the Word of God is now accessible only in the Holy Scriptures, simply because God no longer speaks "immediately by his voice and Prophets sent from him". James Usher (or Ussher), *A Body of Divinity, or The Summe and Substance of Christian Religion; Catechistically Propounded, and Explained, by Way of Question and Answer: Methodically and Familiarly Handled. Collected long since out of Sundry Authors, and Reduced unto One Common Method by James Usher B. of Armagh* (London: Tho. Downes and Geo. Badger, 1649), 7.

[17] Richard Muller in his erudite *Post-Reformation Reformed Dogmatics* simply assumes that the *WCF* cessationist clause teaches "the cessation of immediate revelations". Muller, *Post-Reformation Reformed Dogmatics*, vol. 2, 88.

[18] Anthony Burgess, *CXLV Expository Sermons Upon the Whole 17th Chapter of the Gospel According to St John: or Christ's Prayer Before His Passion Explicated, and Both Practically and Polemically Improved* (London: Thomas Underhill, 1656).

[19] Burgess, *CXLV Expository Sermons Upon the Whole 17th Chapter of the Gospel According to St John:* First, revealed truth is the foundation of all truth (474); secondly, God reveals himself now in no other way, for there now "is no other Word of God, but what is written" (473); thirdly, God has ordained all spirits to be measured against the rule of Scripture, "which could not be, if the voice of the Spirit could be heard any other way, but in and by the Scriptures[...]" (471); fourthly, God himself wisely joined the Scriptures with the Spirit, and although in extraordinary cases God may choose to sanctify without the Word, we remain bound by Scripture (471).

[20] Burgess, *CXLV Expository Sermons Upon the Whole 17th Chapter of the Gospel According to St John*, 471.

[21] Burgess, *CXLV Expository Sermons Upon the Whole 17th Chapter of the Gospel According to St John*, 471.

[22] Burgess, *CXLV Expository Sermons Upon the Whole 17th Chapter of the Gospel According to St John*, 473.

Scriptures for "all controversies of religion", because they have been both "immediately inspired" and providentially preserved by God.[23] However, do the divines leave open the possibility that God might still give immediate inspirations, perhaps for some other purpose than as a rule of faith and life? If the Puritan divines maintained that this was possible, it is difficult to see how they could deny that such inspirations could become part of Scripture. The Apocryphal books were specifically excluded as an authority, because they were not held to be divinely inspired,[24] and this strongly suggests that if any divinely inspired utterance could be found and written down, it could not be rejected as part of the canon of Scripture. However, the divines also excluded the possibility of other additions to Scripture in *WCF* 1:6, which they could not do unless they believed there was to be no more immediate inspiration.

In his late nineteenth-century commentary on the Westminster standards Francis Beattie correctly recognised that the divines intended that Christ no longer spoke immediately to his church, because the Word of God was no longer available except in Scripture:

> It is now through the inspired word alone, and by the Holy Spirit speaking therein, that the will of God, in all that pertains to life and salvation, is made known. In no case is the administration [of Christ's prophetic office] now immediate; it is mediate, through the word, by the Spirit.[25]

The denial that there could be any ongoing immediate revelation was not a novel claim nor was it evidence of some growing rationalism or rigid scholasticism; it was a perspective inherited from Protestant scholars with impeccable credentials, such as the important Scottish Federal theologian Robert Rollock, who had also a generation earlier insisted in his *Treatise of Effectual Calling* that the immediate voice of God was now limited to Scripture.[26]

Later subscribers to Westminster orthodoxy continued to attach importance to the cessation of "immediate" revelation, which they too detected in the Westminster theology. We can see this position, for example, in an early eighteenth-century Scottish commentary on the *WCF*,

---

[23] *WCF* 1:8.

[24] *WCF* 1:3.

[25] Beattie, *The Presbyterian Standards: An Exposition of the Westminster Confession of Faith and Catechisms*, 144. Of course, this did not mean that the Word was not available through preaching, but that preaching could only be efficacious if based upon a text of Scripture.

[26] Robert Rollock, *A Treatise of Effectual Calling* (London: 1603) [no further publishing details given], 64; cited in Muller, *Post-Reformation Reformed Dogmatics*, vol. 2, 204. I cite a later edition, although the pagination matches the earlier one: Robert Rollock, *Select Works of Robert Rollock,* ed. William Gunn (Edinburgh: 1849) [no further publishing details given], 64.

which understands the *WCF* to deny the availability of any extra-biblical immediate revelation in its discussion on Chapter 18:1, *On Assurance of grace and salvation*.[27] The author affirms that "we do not require of such ane assurance as is gote by immediate revelation".[28] While admitting that some extraordinary confirmatory events can happen, there is no "immediate" verbal revelation,[29] and any appeals to "God speaking immediately to us" are deceptive at best. The author further derides Antinomian Tobias Crisp, who he claims:

> attempts to bring in the Spirit of God as a sharer in that persuasion which may deceive or bring people under such an immediate enduit of the Spirit as is now ceased.[30]

---

[27] Two separate Edinburgh University libraries have classified and filed this particular unpublished commentary as three discrete and apparently unrelated collections of manuscripts. An examination of each of them, however, shows that they are all part of the same commentary and written by the same hand. Although anonymous, they give us a useful insight into the way the *WCF* was interpreted in the early eighteenth century when the Scottish church demanded a strict subscription to the *WCF* (on the matter of subscription, see Chapter Seven below). Below is a summary of each of the manuscripts classified as three separate works in Edinburgh University Central Library and New College Library, Edinburgh.

New College Library: Edinburgh University:
MS. Wes. 3.3. 1-2, "Exposition of the Westminster Confession of Faith", Quarto. 2 v. 1718. V.1. Chapter 1. Section 1 to Chapter 2. Section 3; V.2. Chapter 7. Section 6 to Chapter 8. Section 8.
Central Library: Edinburgh University:
MS. Dc.2.68, "Westminster Assembly. Explication of the Westminster Confession of Faith. Central Library Manuscript. 1 vol.". Ch. 9 *Of free will* (begins 12 September 1719) to Ch. 13 *Of Sanctification*
MS Dc.6.64-66 (3 vols.), "Westminster Assembly. Sermons on the Westminster Confession 1716 to 1725".
 i. MS. Dc. 6.64. Chapter 2 *Of God and the Trinity* to *Of God's Eternal decree*. Begins 7 June 1716 to 14 January 1717.
 ii. MS. Dc.6.65. The front page reads "3rd volume comprehending Chapter 4th, 5th and 6th [i.e. from *Of Creation* to *Of the Fall of Man, of Sin, and of the Punishment Thereof*] April 26, 1717 to Aug 20, 1717".
 iii. MS. Dc.6.66. Begins 25 May 1725. Chapters 17 to 19. [i.e. Chapter 17- *Of the perseverance of the Saints;* Chapter 18- *Of the Assurance of Grace and Salvation;* Chapter 19- *Of the Law of God.*].

[28] MS. Dc. 6.66, "Sermons on the WCF", 173.
[29] MS. Dc. 6.66, "Sermons on the WCF", 173-74.
[30] MS. Dc. 6.66, "Sermons on the WCF", 174. He does not give the reference to Crisp. Tobias Crisp (1600-1643), a man of means, a Doctor of Divinity and graduate of

The author thus rejects the Antinomian claim to immediate revelation of the Spirit for the purpose of assurance. In his earlier analysis of *WCF* 1:6, however, he is just as sceptical about claims to authentic direct revelation for *any* reason:

> "[...]since then New Revelations are needlesse and if we are to expect from God the sustainer of light by way of immediate Revelations, already delivered: then we may be very much satisfied such Revelations are not from His, and consequently must be[...]deceiving meteors designed by Satan to seduce.[31]

Despite such contentions, Puritan writings are also replete with mystical claims concerning the "immediate *work*" of the Spirit, a term which potentially renders the "immediate/mediate" distinction confusing. It appears that the Reformed orthodox generally understood the "immediate *work*" of the Spirit and "immediate *revelation*" to be two distinct processes. While they taught more precisely that now God mediated special revelation solely through Scripture, they did not deny an "immediate work" of the Holy Spirit so long as this work was closely tied to the content of the scriptural canon. John Howe (1630-1705), for example, in discussing the work of the Spirit in ushering in a golden age for the church, contends:

> There are many scriptures also, that speak of the great improvement and growth of christians by the *immediate* work of the Spirit of God. When I say, *immediate*, I do not mean, as if it did work without means; but that by the means it doth itself immediately reach its subject; and therefore, that all the operations of the Spirit, whether in converting or in building up of souls, lie not in the instruments, but strike through all, so as to reach their subject.[32]

Thomas Case, in a sermon preached before Parliament in 1644, interprets the prophecies of the New Covenant in Jer. 31:34 and Isa. 54:13 to imply an "immediate" work of the Spirit. Nonetheless, when those prophets predicted that no one would need a teacher and that children would be taught of the Lord, this was not a justification, he reasoned, for rejecting the authority and function of ministers. Rather these prophesies meant that New Covenant believers would be taught by ministers and, "*inwardly* and

---

Cambridge, was considered an Antinomian, but also gave offence with his rigid Arminianism. Augustus Bickley, "Tobias Crisp", *DNB*, Vol. 1, 468.

[31] MS. Wes. 3.3. 1-2, "Exposition of the Westminster Confession of Faith", I, 261-62.

[32] John Howe, *The Whole Works of John Howe* (London: F. Westley, 1822), vol. 5, 265-66.
Howe is cited in Iain Murray, *The Puritan Hope* (London: Banner of Truth Trust, 1971), 241-55, especially 249. John Howe was a later contemporary of the Westminster divines, though he was too young to be a member of the Assembly.

experimentally [experientially], and immediatly by the *Spirit of Christ*".[33] Here the use of "immediate" is applied to the inward conviction or work of the Holy Spirit which leads into truth, but which does not preclude the need for a "mediating" teacher of the Scriptures.

Samuel Rutherford likewise proposes in his *Survey of the Spirituall Antichrist*, that while it is the "immediate breathing of the spirit" which rank petitions for prayer,[34] "the dumbe knockings of revelations without, or contrary to the word", should be rejected.[35] Plainly, the immediate activity of the Spirit did not operate *without* the "word", just as the Spirit equally did not work *contrary* to it.

With this "mediate/immediate" distinction in mind, when we come to examine the Reformed orthodox exegesis of Eph. 1:17-18, we quickly discover that these Reformed interpreters insist that the ἀποκαluψίv mentioned in this text is always to be drawn from Scripture. When Rutherford defines "revelations and inspirations", citing Eph. 1:17-18, he identifies such a disclosure as "a speciall internall revelation, made of things in scripture".[36] This knowledge too can be "immediate", and yet these revelations "are not to be thought unlawfull revelations, and destitute of the word[...]".[37] An "immediate" revelation in this sense, though, is an application by the Spirit of the words of Scripture immediately, and hence is in line with the distinction above: "It is the knowledge of no new Article which is not conteined in the word in the Generall".[38] Any immediacy is focused on the work of the Spirit in applying Scripture, not on initiating some new revelation external to Scripture.

The utility of this text as a point of contrast between immediate and mediate revelation extended beyond prohibiting new articles of faith or ethics. A major theme in the expositions of Westminster divines when they appeal to Eph. 1:17-18 to rule out immediate revelation is the frequent assertion that supernatural guidance external to Scripture is not available, even for non-doctrinal purposes.

The Reformed orthodox denied that there could be new revelations for understanding or interpreting the Scriptures. Extra-biblical manifestations of the divine mind were being claimed in the seventeenth century, as

---

[33] Thomas Case, *Jehoshaphats Caveat to His Judges* (London: Luke Fawn, 1644), 4-5.

[34] Samuel Rutherford, *A Survey of the Spirituall Antichrist. [...]"* (London: Andrew Crooke, 1648), 332.

[35] Rutherford, *A Survey of the Spirituall Antichrist*, 337. See also Samuel Rutherford, *A Sermon preached [...]Janu. 31.1643* (London: Richard Whittakers and Andrew Crooke, 1644), especially 32-36 where he contradicts the Antinomian claim of an immediate witness of the Spirit in assurance of salvation.

[36] Rutherford, *A Survey of the Spirituall Antichrist*, 40.

[37] Rutherford, *A Survey of the Spirituall Antichrist*, 41-42.

[38] Rutherford, *A Survey of the Spirituall Antichrist*, 41.

Thomas Goodwin intimates in his sermon on Eph. 1:17; for Goodwin, however, these verses do not teach ongoing extra-biblical revelation:

> It is not *extraordinary revelation* that he meaneth here, such as Paul had[...]he doth not mean the extraordinary revelations of those times.[39]

Why is the possibility of "extraordinary revelations" excluded? Goodwin notes simply that the epistle was addressed to all the Ephesians, whereas extraordinary revelations were meant only for a few.[40] This enables him to deny that immediate revelation is in view, but he also adds that visions no longer occur:

> By revelation you must not understand as if there were *visions* made. No, brethren; 'Henceforth, though we have known Christ after the flesh, we know him no more'.[41]

In the allusion to 2 Cor. 5:16, the Protestant hermeneutical principle of the analogy of Scripture comes into play. Bolstering the interpretation of one text by identifying supporting texts elsewhere in Scripture is an appeal to the infallible witness of the living voice of God in the Word itself.[42] Arguing from the general to the particular, Goodwin builds on his insight that there are to be no more visions, and asserts that there can be no extra-biblical revelation as an aid to biblical exegesis. The apostle, he contends, does not pray

> that they may have the Spirit of wisdom and revelation in the *knowledge of truths*, to open Scripture, to have an immediate light thus from heaven; to be able to say, This I know by divine revelation to be the meaning of such a place: or in matters of controversy to be able to say, This I know by divine revelation immediately that this is the truth. No, there is no such revelation now.[43]

Even though Goodwin's dissent on the subject is transparent enough, he does not preclude personal or subjective insight when the Spirit applies the Word directly to privileged individuals. In a final rhetorical flourish, he exclaims:

> It is not a revelation to draw men from the Word. No, but usually God cometh down upon the wings of some promise, or some word of his; and in that promise, putting an immediate beam of light from heaven into it, revealeth himself to a man's soul, that a man knoweth more of God in half an hour than he hath done in all his life.[44]

---

[39] Goodwin, *The Works of Thomas Goodwin*, vol. 1, 289.
[40] Goodwin, *The Works of Thomas Goodwin*, vol. 1, 289.
[41] Goodwin, *The Works of Thomas Goodwin*, vol. 1, 294.
[42] A principle set down as an article of faith in *WCF* 1:9.
[43] Goodwin, *The Works of Thomas Goodwin*, vol. 1, 294.
[44] Goodwin, *The Works of Thomas Goodwin*, vol. 1, 294. The same rejection of revelation for disclosing meaning is emphatically proclaimed by Edward Reynolds in

Thus Goodwin concludes that this text supports the notion that no further immediate light divorced from Scripture promises is to be expected from heaven. Goodwin was representative of a standard Reformed orthodox view that neither such ability as the prophet Daniel utilised to interpret divinely inspired dreams through revelation,[45] nor the use of a "Gideon's fleece" to confirm the mind of God was any longer possible in the modern church. Goodwin probably would have rejected any claim to an "Abrahamic" type of revelation or to any "immediate" divinely inspired exposition of Scripture, and dismissed it as enthusiasm.[46]

According to John Lightfoot, another fallacious exegetical conclusion derived from Eph. 1:17 was the belief that God might give immediate revelations for assurance of salvation. Lightfoot (1602-1675), who wrote copiously on the doctrine of Scripture was, along with John Selden[47] and Thomas Coleman[48], one of the impressive triumvirate of Erastians at the Westminster Assembly. Lightfoot was a Hebrew scholar and a prolific writer who brought considerable theological ability to Assembly deliberations. Lightfoot's own minutes of the Assembly are an invaluable resource for students of the Westminster Assembly, which testify to his commitment to attend the daily workings of the Assembly.[49]

---

his sermon on Phil. 3:15-16 entitled *Brotherly Reconciliation*. In an identical manner, he expounds that the "*Spirit of Wisdom and Revelation*" of Eph. 1:17 "both openeth the heart to the Word, giving an understanding to know the Scriptures, and openeth the Scriptures to the heart". He warns, as Goodwin did, that this does not imply that one can comprehend the meaning of Scripture "by divine and immediate Inspiration, or in a way of simple Enthysiasme". Rather, rejecting "*Dreams or Visions*, or any other immediate way", "the *only light*" for understanding was "*the Word*". Edward Reynolds, "Brotherly Reconciliation", *Twenty Sermons Preached upon Several Occasions* (London: George Thomason, 1660), 26-27.

[45] Dan. 2:3-45 and Judges 6:37-40.

[46] Edmund Hall is another witness to this view who had written in 1650 that there can be no "Abrahamic" type of revelations such as the one concerning Isaac (Gen. 22:2.), "because God hath given us his revealed will in writing, since which immediate revelations have ceased in the Gospel Churches, there being no need of them at all". Edmund Hall, *Digitus Testium, or a Dreadful Alarm to the Whole Kingdom* (London: 1650) [No further publishing details are given], 25.

[47] John Selden (1584-1654), was one of the Erastians of the Assembly and an acknowledged authority on Jewish and classical antiquity. William Barker, *Puritan Profiles, 54 Personalities Drawn Together by the Westminster Assembly* (Fearn: Christian Focus Publications, 1996), 54-58.

[48] Thomas Coleman (1598-1646) was twice reprimanded for offending the Assembly. Entering Magdalen College, Oxford, Coleman became so proficient in Hebrew that he was known as Rabbi Coleman. Notably Coleman and George Gillespie had an extended literary interchange over Coleman's Erastianism. Barker, *Puritan Profiles*, 58-60.

[49] Born at Stoke, Lightfoot received his theological education at Christ's College, Cambridge. Ordained as a curate in 1623, Lightfoot left a ministry in Ashley,

Lightfoot uses Eph. 1:17 to disprove the availability of immediate revelation for personal assurance of salvation. The "illumination" referred to in this text is, he notes, "not in the same manner by new or immediate revelation, but by the mediate divine word[...]".[50] Rather, God gives:

> 'the spirit of wisdom and revelation in the knowledge of Christ;' as it is [in] Ephes. i.17. But how? Revealing to him, by experimental feeling, that which he knew, indeed, before in Scripture, but only by bare theory.[51]

In a later sermon on Jude 12, he dismisses the possibility that there might be any God-given immediately inspired messages to the saints, although he allows that God does still transmit a certain type of revelation:

> The spirit of revelation is given indeed to saints, but means little that sense that these men speak of, but is of a clean different nature.- The apostle prays, Ephes, i.17 [...] And God gives this spirit; but in what sense? Not to foresee things to come[...]".[52]

While this text affirms a type of prophetic ability, it does not imply that human beings come to assurance by "immediate whispers from heaven". Rather there is "another way:[...], 'Through patience and comfort of the Scriptures we have hope[...]'".[53] The Antinomians taught otherwise, and while many Puritans talked of an immediate witness of the Spirit they denied immediate revelation as a confirmation of one's interest in the estate of salvation.

Joel Beeke also comes to the same conclusion in his discussion of the Puritan and Westminster Assembly doctrine of assurance. Beeke considers the subjective and objective elements in the matter of assurance of salvation and concludes that the divines always base the subjective on the objective:

> Consequently, *subjective* evidence must always be based upon the promise [in Scripture] and be regarded as secondary, for such is often mixed with *human* convictions and feelings even when it gazes upon the work of God.[54]

Staffordshire, to move to London in 1642 where he lectured at St. Bartholomew's. He was later appointed a master of St. Catherine Hall, Cambridge, and received his D.D. in 1652. Although he sided with the Presbyterians in the Savoy conference of 1661, he complied with the Act of Uniformity the following year. His final charge was as a prebend at Ely, Cambridgeshire. Barker, *Puritan Profiles*, 61-65.

[50] "At hoc itidem non per novam aliquam immediatam revelationem, sed mediante verbo divino[...]".

John Lightfoot, *The Whole Works of the Rev. John Lightfoot, D.D.*, ed. J. R. Pitman (London: Printed by J. F. Dove, 1822), vol. 5, 461.

[51] Lightfoot, *The Whole Works of the Rev. John Lightfoot, D.D.*, vol. 6, 211.

[52] Lightfoot, *The Whole Works of the Rev. John Lightfoot, D.D.*, vol. 6, 238.

[53] Lightfoot, *The Whole Works of the Rev. John Lightfoot, D.D.*, vol. 6, 239.

[54] Joel Beeke, *Assurance of Faith* (New York: Peter Lang, 1991), 156. Also published as Joel Beeke, *The Quest for Full Assurance, The Legacy of Calvin and his*

Beeke's assessment is in line with the views of the seventeenth-century Puritans, on the basis of the evidence we have canvassed. If the Puritans had been open to immediate extra-biblical revelation in any sense, we would surely have found evidence of it here in this question of assurance. Instead, they express their extremely intense spirituality, evident in someone like Goodwin, in a way that claims a certain mystical encounter with the divine, but which usually includes the disclaimer that we must go to the Scriptures if we would have God address us.

While Goodwin and Lightfoot made specific applications of a general principle, a third use of the Ephesians text was to argue comprehensively for the total cessation of immediate revelation for any purpose. Though the Puritans often only condemn claims to extra-biblical revelation for doctrine, this does not mean that they affirm the Spirit's immediate teaching for any other purpose. The argument from silence is not especially convincing in such instances since it has to be applied very selectively. If one concludes that the Holy Spirit will neither "immediately" clarify the semantic content of Scripture nor divulge an immediate revelation of one's spiritual condition, it is a formidable exegetical challenge to discover biblical support for similar revelations for other purposes.

Anthony Tuckney represents most of the Westminster divines, and Reformed orthodoxy in general, in his undisguised antipathy towards claimants to immediate revelation. Tuckney (1599-1670), who had chaired the committee for the *Shorter Catechism*, was an important member of the Assembly, and sometimes considered to have played the largest supporting

---

successors (Edinburgh: Banner of Truth, 1999), 129. The primary and objective ground of assurance is, of course, held to be the promise of God in Scripture. See also Goodwin who addressing the teaching on the sealing of the Spirit, warns that subjective experience without the written Word is delusional: "Therefore let me tell you this, all your revelations that are without the Word, or would draw you from the Word, are naught and dangerous. We do not speak for enthusiasms; it is the Spirit applying the Word to the heart that we speak of": Goodwin, *The Works of Thomas Goodwin*, vol. 1, 250. In a separate discussion of the theme, Joel Beeke, "Personal Assurance of Faith: The Puritans and Chapter 18.2 of the Westminster Confession", *WTJ* 55/1 (Spring 1993), 1-30, puts things thus: "Generally speaking, Puritans of the stature appointed to draft the *WCF* would not teach that assurance is obtainable from trusting in the promises alone, by self-examination alone, or by the witness of the Holy Spirit alone. Rather, most Puritans taught that the believer cannot truly trust the promises without the aid of the Holy Spirit, and that he cannot with any degree of safety look upon himself without the enabling enlightenment of the Spirit" (28). He also concludes: "In every sense, however, these three groups [with different understandings of how assurance works] are united in asserting that the Spirit's testimony is always tied to, and may never contradict, the Word of God. 'The Spirit is promised in the Word, and that promise is fulfilled in experience.' On the one hand, Antinomianism must be avoided, and on the other, the freedom of the Spirit must be protected" (28).

role in the preparation of the *WCF*.[55] In his *Good Day Well Improved,* Tuckney is dismissive, referring to: "The darkest and *blindest* times [which] have talked much of such *visions*". Such pretensions, he concludes, find no support in Scripture, because the only type of revelation still available is the mediate revelation of Eph. 1:17 by the Spirit "which onely sealeth that, which Scripture writeth".[56]

In summary, the Reformed orthodox used Eph. 1:17 apologetically to defend the unity of Word and Spirit, and as an opportunity to deny the possibility of further extra-biblical revelation. Inspired dispatches from heaven for the purpose of opening up the sense of Scripture, for assurance of personal redemption, or for any other purpose, were considered to be no longer possible.

3.2.2 Hebrews 1:1-2: Scripture the Sole Source of Special Revelation

Another text frequently deployed by the Reformed orthodox as a serviceable weapon against the sectaries was the first two verses of the Epistle to the Hebrews. The *WCF* argues from the same proof-text in 1:1 that since the saving will of God is committed "wholly" to writing, all other methods of divine communication have given way to the written Word of God. As the *WCF* summarises it: "those former ways of God's revealing His will unto His people being now ceased".[57] This single clause was the subject of debate in both Assembly and Parliament as has already been pointed out. The record of the debate over this section in Parliament implies that it was a controversial inclusion in the *WCF*, for not every clause of the *WCF* is isolated in the Journal records:

---

[55] He was a Professor of Divinity at Cambridge and one of the Presbyterian majority in the Assembly. Barker, *Puritan Profiles*, 175-79.

[56] Anthony Tuckney, *A Good Day Well Improved[...]to Which is Annexed a Sermon on 2 Tim. 1.13* (London: I. Rothwell, 1656), 305-07. See also Thomas Hill, *Truth and Love Happily Married in the Saints, and in the Churches of Christ* (London: Peter Cole, 1648), 32. William Jenkyn, who preached before the House of Lords in 1645, warned the peers of the danger of waiting on revelations for directions to reform the church: "Beware therefore of going any whither else to know his minde: *Tis learned ignorance, to want the knowledge of that which the word teacheth not.* It's high presumption for any to pretend his will without bringing his word[...]. [L]et nothing passe for the will of God, unlesse it brings *a ticket* from the word of God": William Jenkyn, *Reformation's Remora; or Temporizing the Stop of Building the Temple* (London: Christopher Meredith, 1646), 6.

[57] *WCF* 1:1.

And the Question being put, Whether these Words, "Those former Ways of God's revealing his Will unto his People.....now ceased", should stand; It passed with the Affirmative [abbreviated in the source of the quote].[58]

Parliament probably passed the clause by majority vote, as there was by no means perfect unanimity in the Commons for the wording of the *WCF*, as the voting figures recorded in both the debate on Chapter Twenty-four, *Of Marriage and Divorce*, and on the title of the *WCF* demonstrate. On 18 February 1647 there was a 40/71 split vote over a consanguinity clause,[59] and on 17 March the same year the Commons voted down the title "Confession of Faith" 61/41, in favour of the alternative "Articles of Christian Religion".[60]

The parliamentary review of the cessationist clause followed the appending of the proof-texts. When the House endorsed and passed the wording and proof-texts unchanged,[61] it ratified a Reformed interpretive tradition that had consistently affirmed the plenary finality of the canon of Scripture as indicated in Heb. 1:1-2 and therefore the cessation of further immediate revelation.

John Flavel, a later commentator on the *SC*, also understood this text to disallow any "extraordinary visional appearances, or oraculous and immediate voice of God to men". He argues:

> God indeed hath so appeared unto some, Numb. xii. 8. Such voices have been heard from heaven, but now these extraordinary ways are ceased, Heb. i. 1, 2. and we are no more to expect them; we may sooner meet with satanical delusions than divine illuminations in this way[...]. We are now to attend only to the voice of the Spirit in the scriptures: this is a more sure word than any voice from heaven, 2 Pet. i. 19.[62]

Flavel, in support of his exegesis of Heb. 1:1-2, refers to an occasion when Satan impersonating Christ, told a believer that he was Christ in person and claimed that the man was worthy and merited such a privilege. Although this occurrence was not a purported disclosure of new doctrine,

---

[58] *Journal of the House of Commons* (London: 1803) [no further publishing details are given], vol. 5, 177.

[59] *Journal of the House of Commons*, vol. 5, 467.

[60] *Journal of the House of Commons*, vol. 5, 502.

[61] These verses occur as proof-texts in four places in the Westminster symbols. Apart from *WCF* 1:1, verse two is used to confirm *WCF* 4:1, creation by the triune God; and in *WCF* 8:1 that Christ is heir of all things. Heb. 1:1-2 also support *LC* Answer 43, the "diverse ways of administration" whereby God reveals his whole will for "edification and salvation". As in *WCF* 1:1, the *LC* alludes to the multiple modes of revelation God has used.

[62] John Flavel, *The Works of John Flavel* (London: Banner of Truth Trust, 1968), vol. 2, 308.

Flavel still believes one must reject this sort of claim to inspired "revelation".[63]

One of the ways in which the Puritans revealed that they understood Heb. 1:1-2 to be a cessationist text was by insisting that a preacher's homiletical subject-matter must be grounded in the canon of Scripture. They base their premise on two presuppositions. One is a straightforward appeal to the evident fact that God has withdrawn the former diverse modalities of divine disclosure. James Usher, as we have already seen, is unequivocal in his cessationist exegesis of the text.[64] Other later commentators such as David Dickson are equally unambiguous. He asks: "Are these former ways of God's revealing his will unto his people now ceased?" Answering "yes", he concludes that enthusiasts and Quakers "err, who maintain, that the Lord hath not ceased yet to reveal his will as he did of old[...]". He gives as the reason Heb. 1:1-2. What has ceased includes inspiration, visions, dreams, the Urim and the Thummim, signs, and audible voices: "All which do end in writing[...]".[65] John Ball's catechism concludes a similar list with the phrase, "and lastly by writing".[66]

The Assembly was almost unanimous in affirming a cessationist exegesis of Heb. 1:1-2. In the discussions of visions and oracles in the light of Hebrews 1 we do not find, with one possible exception, a straightforward clarification that dreams and visions as immediate revelation still continue for other "non-Scripture-producing" purposes.[67] What we do discover, however, is a claim by seventeenth-century minority sects that immediate revelation or inspiration, whether in the form of dreams, visions, an internal

---

[63] Flavel, *The Works of John Flavel*, vol. 2, 308. Flavel does not identify the subject who had the vision described.

[64] See Chapter One above, 60, n254. See also Usher, *Body of Divinity*: The gift of exorcism has ceased, though praying for God to remove a demon is legitimate (227). "prayer is the voice of Gods spirit in us" (348); "there is no more need of miracles; and ther[e]fore we keeping the same doctrine of Christ and his Apostles, must content our selves with the confirmation which hath already been given" (442).

[65] David Dickson, *Truth's Victory over Error: Or, the True Principles of the Christian Religion, Stated and Vindicated Against the Following Heresies, viz. Arians, Arminians, Anabaptists, Antinomians, Brownists, Donatists, Epicureans, Eutychians, Erastians, Familists, Jesuits, Independents, Libertines, Manicheans, Pelagians, Papists, Quakers, Socinians, Sabellians, Sceptics, Vaninians, &c. The Whole being a Commentary on All the Chapters of the Confession of Faith, by Way of Question and Answer: In which, the saving Truths of our Holy Religion are Confirmed and Established; and the Dangerous Errors and Opinions of its Adversaries Detected and Confuted*. (Kilmarnock: Printed by John Wilson, 1787), 26-27.

[66] John Ball, *A Short Treatise Contayning all the Principall Grounds of Christian Religion* (London: Edward Brewster and Robert Bird, 1633), 5.

[67] The exception is William Bridge, whose position will be discussed in the next chapter.

voice or impulse, does continue.[68] Although Protestants of the seventeenth century still felt threatened by the Church of Rome and its religious epistemology (which also implied extra-scriptural revelation via tradition, and the authority of the church over Scripture[69]), Cromwell's tolerance had compounded the perceived threat from fringe Protestant sects and their claims to extra-biblical revelation.[70] With the advent of the Quaker movement, these opinions became increasingly entrenched in England and Scotland.

A second presupposition in the Puritan exposition of Heb. 1:1-2 concerned the nature of Christ's mediatorial prophetic role. The Puritans were already familiar with the view that Christ is the only source of special revelation and that he no longer communicates with human beings apart

---

[68] For example, George Fox, *Gospel Truth Demonstrated, in a Collection of Doctrinal Books [...]*" (New York: Isaac T. Hopper, 1831), vol. 3, 394. For a discussion of Fox and the early Quakers, see Richard Bailey, *New Light on George Fox and Early Quakerism: The Making and Unmaking of God* (San Francisco: Mellen Research University Press, 1992). For Quaker views on revelation, see especially 28-35 and 221-71. The Quaker movement received official, if negative, recognition in 1654. The *Parliamentary History* records the beginning of the Quakers: "a sect which made its first Appearance about this Time". *The Parliamentary and Constitutional History of England from the Earliest Times to the Restoration of King Charles 2nd* (London: 1751-1762) [no further publishing details are given], vol. 20, 402. For a thorough discussion of Quaker theology and epistemology, see Ted LeRoy Underwood, *Primitivism, Radicalism, and the Lamb's War. The Baptist-Quaker Conflict in Seventeenth-Century England* (Oxford: Oxford University Press, 1997), especially 101-19 on the "inner light"; Barry Reay, "Quakerism and Society", J. McGregor and Barry Reay (eds.), *Radical Religion in the English Revolution* (Oxford: Oxford University Press, 1984), 141-64; Robert Acheson, *Radical Puritans in England, 1550-1660* (London: Longman, 1990), especially 69-74 on the social and theological distinctives of the Quaker movement; for early Quaker eschatology, see Ted LeRoy Underwood, "Early Quaker Eschatology", Peter Toon (ed.), *Puritans, the Millennium and the Future of Israel: Puritan Eschatology 1600-1660* (Greenwood: Attic Press, 1970), 91-103. For Quakers as Puritans, see Hugh Barbour, *The Quakers in Puritan England* (New Haven: Yale University Press, 1964), especially 1-32. For a Scottish seventeenth-century rebuttal of Quaker theology, and especially that of Robert Barclay, see John Brown, *Quakerisme the Path-way to Paganisme. Or a View of the Quakers Religion: Being An Examination of the Theses and Apologie of Robert Barclay [...]* (Edinburgh: John Cairns, 1678), especially 19-50 on the Quaker position of "immediate" revelation. For a detailed apologetic for Quakerism, see Robert Barclay, *An Apology for the True Christian Divinity* (Glasgow: R. Barclay Murdoch, 1886), especially 11-46 on "immediate" revelation, and 46-65 on the Scriptures.

[69] As we saw with Whitaker: See Chapter One, at 51-59 above.

[70] Henry Gavin Alexander, *Religion in England 1558-1662* (London: University of London Press, 1975), 193-97; or Baillie, *The Letters and Journals of Robert Baillie*, vol. 2, 230.

from Scripture. This was an exegetical conclusion highlighted in the influential Geneva Bible notes on Heb. 1:1-2:

> the sonne of God is in deed that Prophet or teacher which hath actually now performed that that God after a sort & in shadowes signified by his Prophets, and hath fully opened his Fathers wil to y world. *So that the former declaration made by the Prophets was not ful & nothing must be added to this latter.*[71]

Thus, the cessation of revelation was an implication that flowed from the belief that Christ had fully disclosed his Father's will which was now completely set down in Scripture. This is not to say that Christ only began to function as a prophet at his incarnation. On the contrary, the Puritans understood the pre-incarnate Christ to be the one who conveyed Old Testament revelation as the great pre-eminent prophet, and the one who spoke through dreams, visions and angelic visitations to Old Testament people, thus asserting Christ's revelatory role in both Testaments. George Walker (d. 1651), for example, teaches this. Considered one of the more aggressive debaters of the Westminster Assembly, Walker had already been imprisoned for preaching sedition, until he was released by the Long Parliament in 1641.[72] In his catechism Walker avers that it was Christ who:

> spake also at sundry times, and in divers manners, as apparitions, dreames and visions to the Fathers in times past, and by his Spirit inspiring and moving the Prophets, *Heb.* i.1. And in the dayes of his flesh he preached the Gospell with his own mouth. And as after his Ascension, he sent down the Holy Ghost upon his Apostles, and gave them the gifts of Tongues, and of Knowledge to Prophecy and Preach the Gospell to all Nations.[73]

The Revealer is the same in the three dispensations mentioned – before the incarnation, during Christ's earthly ministry, and following his ascension in the foundational period of the New Testament church. Even after the prophets and apostles died, Christ still speaks to their successors, "Ministers of the Gospell", and:

> by his Spirit gives them knowledge and utterance, to teach and expound the Scriptures, and to bring men to the saving knowledge of the truth.[74]

Walker concludes that now:

---

[71] Gerald T. Sheppard (ed.), *The Geneva Bible. The Annotated New Testament 1602 Edition* (Cleveland: The Pilgrim Press, 1989), Heb. 1:1-2.

[72] A Presbyterian, Walker was born at Hawkshead, Furness, Lancashire and educated at Oxford. He was the seventeenth most frequent speaker in the Assembly debates on church government. Barker, *Puritan Profiles,* 244-48.

[73] George Walker, *The Key of Saving Knowledge, Opening out of the Holy Scriptures, the Right Way, and Straight Passage to Eternal Life [...]*" (London: 1640) [no further publishing details are given], 45.

[74] Walker, *The Key of Saving Knowledge*, 46.

no other Prophets or Preachers, are to be heard, but those which Preach in his Name, truly according to his Word conteined in the holy Scriptures.

Any modern prophets who claim to speak with immediate revelation should be rejected as false prophets.[75]

Walker's unequivocal identification of Christ as revealer in both eras should not obscure another valid distinction. John Lightfoot points out that Heb. 1:1-2 contains a contrast between the teaching of the prophets and priests in the Old Testament and the preaching of Christ in the New.[76] This distinction highlights the more glorious nature of the final revelation that comes through the incarnate and then glorified Christ.

Lightfoot also elaborated the point that preaching matter must be derived from the Scriptures, when he defended his doctoral thesis at Cambridge, *Post Canonem Scripturae Consignatum non sunt Novae Revelationes Expectandae*, in 1652.[77] He suggests that the contrast shown in Heb. 1:1-2 was between a former method of immediate revelation transmitted mediately by humans, and the personal teaching of the Saviour himself.[78] Lightfoot responds to an assertion that visions, heavenly voices, divine dreams and other kinds of revelation are still possible.[79] He gives a three-pronged rebuttal,[80] signifying what preaching, and therefore the content of the Bible, for him entails.

1. "After the canon of Scripture was sealed new dogmas of faith may not be expected beyond what is in the Scripture or above the sense of Scripture".[81]
2. "New revelations are not to be expected in this sense, to elicit the sense of Scripture or explain the dogmas of faith".[82]
3. "[N]o other revelations should be expected for the purpose of directing the actions of life, for moral training, for consoling and steadying the

---

[75] Walker, *The Key of Saving Knowledge*, 46.
[76] Lightfoot, *The Whole Works of the Rev. John Lightfoot, D.D.*, vol. 6, 286.
[77] Lightfoot, *The Whole Works of the Rev. John Lightfoot, D.D.*, vol. 5, 455.
[78] Lightfoot, *The Whole Works of the Rev. John Lightfoot, D.D.*, vol. 5, 465-66.
[79] Lightfoot, *The Whole Works of the Rev. John Lightfoot, D.D.*, vol. 5, 460.
[80] "Non me latet, quam multa dicantur ab historiagraphis, de visionibus, vocibus coelestibus, insomniis divinis, et aliis istiusmodi revelationum generibus, per saecula plurima post illud tempus exhibitis: qualia etiam de se ipsis garrire non erubescunt hodieque nonnulli e nostro saeculo, e nostra gente[...]Tria sunt, quae in hac quaestione praecipue volumus". Lightfoot, *The Whole Works of the Rev. John Lightfoot, D.D.*, vol. 5, 460.
[81] "Quod post consignatum Scripturae canonem, non sint expectanda nova dogmata fidei, quae vel praeter Scripturam obtineant, vel supra Scripturam sapiant[...]". Lightfoot, *The Whole Works of the Rev. John Lightfoot, D.D.*, vol. 5, 460.
[82] "[...]quod ad eliciendum Scripturae sensum, aut ad fidei dogmata, in ea comprehensa, explicandum, non expectandae sint novae revelationes". Lightfoot, *The Whole Works of the Rev. John Lightfoot, D.D.*, vol. 5, 461.

mind weighed down with anxiety, for understanding the spiritual state of the soul; rather, all these things should be sought from Scripture".[83] Furthermore, he later adds, "[w]hen the revelations cease the expectation of revelations ought also to cease".[84] Lightfoot is sure that preaching should take its doctrinal information from Scripture alone; that there is no immediate revelatory assistance to understand the meaning of Scripture; and that ethical stipulations, guidance in life and spiritual comfort must also now be sought in Scripture.

Thomas Goodwin preached three sermons on Heb. 1:1-2 in which he also contrasts the "visions, dreams and types &c", which God has laid aside, with the sole source of God's revelation today: "the word and sacrament unto the hearts of men".[85] Preaching finds its "matter" in the Scriptures, and because the full revelation has come through Christ, the revealer continues to speak to Jews and Gentiles. Though Christ is now in heaven, this speaking by the Son persists "[b]ecause he is with us ministers in delivering of it to the end of the world; yea, Jesus Christ hath his pulpit in heaven to this day".[86]

An interesting side-light to the contention that the Assembly probably meant by its use of Heb. 1:1-2 as a proof-text to indicate a complete cessation of the former modalities of divine disclosure, can be found in comments by William Carter (d.1658) that closely parallel the wording of *WCF* 1:1. If we see such evidence of wording similar to the cessationist clause in an exposition of Heb. 1:1-2 by a Westminster divine, while it might not be conclusive on its own, the elucidation of its meaning by the author may offer support to an understanding of the sense of *WCF* 1:1.

William Carter, a popular preacher in London and as an active member of the Westminster Assembly one who had adequate opportunity for input into the wording of the *WCF*,[87] wrote words similar to the *WCF* 1:1

---

[83] "[...]quod ad dirigendas vitae actiones, ad mores instruendos, ad animum, anxietate pressum, solandum et stabiliendum, ad statum animae spiritualem congnoscendum, non sint expectandae ullae revelationes, sed omnia haec a Scriptura sint quaerenda". Lightfoot, *The Whole Works of the Rev. John Lightfoot, D.D.*, vol. 5, 462.

[84] "Ubi desiit finis revelationum, desinat etiam oportet expectatio revelationum". In 200-02, Chapter Five below, we will evaluate Lightfoot's views on prophecy as presented at this point in his thesis. Lightfoot, *The Whole Works of the Rev. John Lightfoot, D.D.*, vol. 5, 466. Lightfoot adds elsewhere that the purpose of other revelatory activities was to produce Scripture, although not every inspired word was written: Lightfoot, *The Whole Works of the Rev. John Lightfoot, D.D.*, vol. 3, 368.

[85] Goodwin, *The Works of Thomas Goodwin*, vol. 5, 537.

[86] Goodwin, *The Works of Thomas Goodwin*, vol. 5, 538.

[87] Although little biographical information has survived on Carter, we know that he came to adopt the Independent position on church government and had a reputation as a

cessationist clause in 1654 based upon the same text. Just as James Usher had concluded that God's "immediate" revelations by Old Testament supernatural transactions "now are ceased, *Heb*.1.1, 2",[88] Carter uses very similar wording to the *WCF* cessationist clause, concluding from the same text: "Those wayes of speaking now are ceased since God hath *spoken to us by His Sonne*".[89] In his detailed exegesis of Heb. 1:1-2, contained in his *Short Discourse Concerning the Manifestations of God unto His People in the Last Dayes,* Carter produces three cessationist arguments to attempt to prove why one should "look not after extraordinary visions or revelations", thus helpfully explaining the precise meaning of his cessationist clause.[90]

First, he contends "your labour will be lost" because those ways have ceased. Secondly, by them, the believer risks delusions. If anyone requires ordinary guidance in "the compass of *nature and reason*", then reason and sense are to be one's guide. For "matters above nature" the believer should refer to the Bible. He leaves no middle category for the use of dreams and visions. Thirdly, he asserts, one will be distracted from where one's true advantage lies if one relies on extra-biblical revelation.[91] There can be no doubt that Carter's own "cessationist clause" comprehensively proscribes all miraculous modes of extra-biblical revelation.[92]

Overall, there is a solid body of evidence to suggest that the Reformed orthodox cessationist exegesis of Heb. 1:1-2 makes the Bible the unchallenged source-book for preaching. The fact that William Carter in his similar cessationist language understands the text to prohibit extra-biblical revelation for any purpose, adds strength to a comprehensive cessationist reading of the clause in *WCF* 1:1, for which it is a proof-text.

---

diligent preacher, preaching twice on Sunday to two large congregations as well as lecturing on weekdays. Reid, *Memoirs of the Westminster Divines*, vol. 1, 190-91.

[88] Usher, *A Body of Divinity*, 7.

[89] William Carter, *The Covenant of God with Abraham Opened [...] Together with A Short Discourse Concerning the Manifestations of God unto His People in the Last Dayes. Wherein is Shewed the Manner of the Spirits Work Therein to be in the Use of Ordinary Gifts, not by Extraordinary Revelations* (London: John Rothwell, 1654), 155.

[90] Carter, *The Covenant of God with Abraham Opened [...] Together with A Short Discourse Concerning the Manifestations of God unto His People in the Last Dayes*, 156.

[91] Carter, *The Covenant of God with Abraham Opened [...] Together with A Short Discourse Concerning the Manifestations of God unto His People in the Last Dayes*, 155-58.

[92] Carter also answers the objection that after Christ's ascension there were still extraordinary ways of revelation manifested in the early church. He answers simply that Christ was speaking through these apostles and prophets, even though Christ was in heaven. Carter, *The Covenant of God with Abraham Opened [...] Together with A Short Discourse Concerning the Manifestations of God unto His People in the Last Dayes*, 132-33.

Heb. 1:2 also refers to the "last days", the extent of which was the subject of much discussion among the Puritans. When they identified the "last days" in which the "Son" preached, the Puritans usually understood the term to confirm their cessationist stance. The political and ecclesiastical upheavals in early seventeenth-century Britain gave ready impetus to the idea that God was beginning to work out his final intentions for the world and for the church. Sermons of the period are replete with the themes of biblical eschatology, as we noted in Chapter One. The assumption was widely spread that the church was living in the "last days", but Puritan writers evince three distinct interpretations of this phrase. Sometimes it refers to the entire church age; elsewhere, it applies to the apostolic era; and in yet other instances, it describes the last days of the Jewish economy, concluding in AD 70 with the destruction of Jerusalem and the Temple. All three senses were proposed when texts such as Heb. 1:2 were under discussion.

When they interpreted the phrase the "last days" to refer to the entire gospel age, Puritan exegetes did not suppose that "speaking by the Son" also continued in the present through extraordinary revelations. William Gouge notes in his commentary on Hebrews:

> The new Covenant of Grace is in these last dayes fully revealed by the Gospel: and ratified by the death of Christ; so as no clearer revelation, nor former ratification can be expected: and in this respect also they are fitly stiled the *last dayes*.[93]

The last days, for Gouge at least, cover the period between Christ's Advent and the Day of Judgement.[94]

Those who limited the last days to the apostolic era, such as the important English Episcopalian theologian Edward Leigh (1602-1671), also denied that new revelations would be given.[95] In the preface to his *Body of Divinity*, Leigh distinguishes between different modes of revelation:

---

[93] William Gouge, *A Learned and Very Useful Commentary on the Whole Epistle to the Hebrewes* (London: Joshua Kirton, 1655), 12.

[94] Featley in the Annotations on Heb. 1:1-2 also argues that since these "last days" are the days of the Gospel, believers are to receive no further revelation. Featley, *Annotations upon All the Books of the Old and New Testament: This Third, above the First and Second, Edition so Enlarged, As They Make an Entire Commentary on the Sacred Scripture: The Like Never before Published in English. Wherein the Text is Explained, Doubts Resolved, Scriptures Parallel'd, and Various Readings Observed; By the Labour of Certain Learned Divines Thereunto Appointed, and Therein Employed, As is Expressed in the Preface* (London: Evan Tyler, 1657), Heb. 1:2.

[95] The esteem in which Leigh was held by Assembly divines was evident in their commendation of his book *Critica Sacra*. Seven of the Assembly divines were ordered to express their appreciation of this work. Alex Mitchell and John Struthers (eds.), *Minutes of the Sessions of the Westminster Assembly of Divines* (Edmonton: Still Water Revival Books, 1991), 191.

> *All extraordinary wayes of revelation are now ceased, we are to pray for a further Discovery of Gods minde in his Word*, Ephes.1.17. *not to expect new Revelations* ex parte objecti, *but* ex parte Subjecti[...]".[96]

By adopting this scholastic distinction, Leigh is denying the contemporary possibility of objective, and therefore of immediate extra-biblical revelation. Citing Heb. 1:2 in his first book *On Scripture*, he notes:

> The time wherein God spake unto us by his Sonne, is called the last dayes or the last time. *Heb*.1.2. 1 *Pet.* 1.20. to note that we are not hereafter to expect or look for any fuller or more clear *Revelation* of Divine Mysteries then that which was then delivered.[97]

John Owen disagrees with "[m]ost expositors [who] suppose this expression, 'The last days,' is a periphrasis for the times of the gospel".[98] Rather, Owen argues, the phrase signifies:

> the last days of the Judaical church and state, which were then drawing to their period and abolition, that are here and elsewhere called 'The last days,' or 'The latter days,' or 'The last hour'[...]".[99]

John Lightfoot endorses Owen's chronology in a sermon on Jude 12:

> [T]he last days of the old world, are the last days of the old economy[...]. To all we might add, that, at the fall of Jerusalem, all Scripture was written, and God's full will revealed; so that there was no farther need of prophecy and revelation.[100]

While the Reformed orthodox defined the "last days" in Heb. 1:2 in different ways, they largely agreed that new revelations did *not* occur following the apostolic age. At the same time, they also held that Christ continued to speak *viva voce* in the completed Scripture until the end of time, so that one may still say that God speaks now by his Son in the days of the gospel.

For Reformed orthodoxy, a cessationist interpretation of "last days" terminology is, perhaps paradoxically, compatible with the prophecy of Joel 2:28-32, quoted in Acts 2:17. At first sight, it seems to stretch credibility to suggest that a Scripture prophecy which talks so expansively about the dynamic and universal work of the Spirit in such exalted and "immediate" terms might bolster a cessationist apologetic. That the Reformed orthodox understood these texts in this way dramatically illustrates how firmly

---

[96] Edward Leigh, *A Systeme or Body of Divinity: Consisting of Ten books. Wherein the Fundamentals and Main Grounds of Religion are Opened: The Contrary Errours Refuted [...]"* (London: William Lee, 1654), preface.

[97] Leigh, *A Systeme or Body of Divinity,* 89.

[98] John Owen, *An Exposition of the Epistle to the Hebrews* (Edinburgh: Banner of Truth Trust, 1991), vol. 3, 11.

[99] Owen, *An Exposition of the Epistle to the Hebrews,* vol. 3, 11.

[100] Lightfoot, *The Whole Works of the Rev. John Lightfoot, D.D.*, vol. 6, 241-42.

opposed they were to the continuationist claims of the "enthusiasts", and how solid the Puritan commitment was to the finality, sufficiency and authority of Scripture as the foundational presupposition of their religious epistemology.

3.2.3 Joel 2:28-32 and Acts 2:17

These two key texts, Joel 2:28-32 and Acts 2:17, talk about the effusive activity of the Spirit – a torrent of prophecy, dreams and visions – in the "last days" of the New Covenant dispensation. Not surprisingly, those who accepted ongoing revelatory visions and oracles often appealed to both passages.[101] In marked contrast, most of the Reformed orthodox were of the opinion that the literal fulfilment of these texts, insofar as they were interpreted to promise miraculous and immediate revelation, was confined to the apostolic era. It is true that some Puritan contemporaries of the Assembly such as Ed Hyde did restrict the prophecy *in toto* to the days of the apostles,[102] but this was the exception rather than the rule.[103]

Reformed orthodoxy solved the paradox, that a text which overtly prophesies "immediate" extra-biblical revelation could also be used to lend support to cessationism, by moving in a surprising direction in its exegesis. Joel 2:28 and Acts 2:17 were still considered relevant prophecies for the seventeenth-century Christian, because they were understood analogically or typologically. They were commonly taken to be a promise to the contemporary church of non-miraculous gifts, including, for example, the ability to interpret Scripture. A brief survey of this exegetical tradition is instructive, because it demonstrates that this view was not an anomaly.

The typological use of these texts is widely attested in international Calvinism, including another source which influenced English and Scottish ministers and theologians of the seventeenth century: the Dutch Annotations. This collection had been prepared in Holland by 1637; it was translated into English by Theodore Haak (or Haake) and printed in London

---

[101] For example, see Sydrach Simpson's criticism of those who "have thought indeed that they had such [a] kind of Revelation as the Prophets of old, and have applied unto themselves those Scriptures, Acts 2.17 [...] whereas all this while it hath been nothing else but a work of fancy[...]": Sydrach Simpson, *Two Books of Mr Sydrach Simpson[...] I. Of faith, Or, Beleeving is Receiving Christ; And Receiving Christ is Believing. II. Of Covetousness* (London: Peter Cole, 1658), 189-90.

[102] Ed Hyde, *Christ and His Church: or, Christianity Explained, under Seven Evangelical and Ecclesiastical Heads* (Oxford: Rich Davis, 1658), 285.

[103] David Dickson, a later commentator on the *WCF*, is able to embellish the Westminster view that immediate revelation ceased in the "last days" of Heb. 1:2 by using Acts 2:17 as a supporting text. Dickson, *Truth's Victory over Error*, 27.

in 1657.[104] The 1618 Synod of Dort was authorised by the government to prepare the notes, and though the Dutch Annotations were not "englished" until forty years later, we know that they were accessible to the English, because the authors of the English Annotations were urged by Parliament to consult them and the Westminster divines subscribed an attestation in 1645 seeking to have them translated into English.[105]

The international Reformed commitment to a standard exegesis of Joel 2:28 is evident in these Dutch comments:

> "[...]*and your sons and your daughters shall prophesie and your old men shall dream dreames, and your young men shall see visions* [that is to say; They shall be enabled through the operation and revelation of the spirit, both to understand & explain the mysteries of the holy Gospel. See *Hos*.12.11 with the annot. These expressions are borrowed from the state and condition of the old Testament, wherein God used to reveal himself to the Prophets by dreams and visions, See *Num*.12.6].[106]

Another influential commentary, the Italian Diodati Annotations, understands the Joel prophecy in similar terms:

> By the inward virtue of my *Spirit*, I will enlighten the understanding of all mine elect [...] and will give them a lively and supernatural light of the mysteries of the Gospel; accompanied at certain times, and in certain persons, with prophetick and divine revelations, *Acts* 2:17.[107]

John Diodati does not here sanction contemporary immediate revelation, because his exegesis of the Acts reference assumes that God has literally fulfilled the miraculous aspect of the Joel prophecy in the early church, something that was evident in the record of the Acts of the Apostles. Instead, he highlights the figurative meaning:

---

[104] In the preface to the (English or Westminster) Annotations, the fact that the English appreciated two other Bible commentaries is acknowledged: "We have made use of the Italian Annotations of Deodat, and of the Dutch Bibles, the one lately again set forth at Geneva, the other in Holland". *Annotations*, preface.

[105] Theodore Haak (translator), The Dutch Annotations upon the Whole Bible: Or, All the Holy Canonical Scriptures of the Old and New Testaments, Together with, and According to Their Own Translation of All the Text: As Both the One and the Other were Ordered and Appointed by the Synod of Dort, 1618. and Published by Authority, 1637 (London: John Rothwell, Joshua Kirton, and Richard Tomlins, 1657), vol. 1, preface. See the preface also for the participants who prepared this Dutch translation of the Bible and notes. Although Haak's letter to Baillie, probably written in 1647, complains of a lack of encouragement in his work (Baillie, The Letters and Journals of Robert Baillie, vol. 3, 7.), its importance and eventual acceptance by the English were not in question.

[106] *Dutch Annotations*, Joel 2:28.

[107] John [or Giovanni] Diodati, *Pious and Learned Annotations upon the Holy Bible* (London: Nicholas Fussell, 1664), Acts 2:17.

v.17. *shall prophesie*] *viz*. Shall have such grace and understanding as to declare the good will of God. *Dream dreams*] he speaks by such figures as were usual in those days and as God revealed himself to his servants.[108]

The *Geneva Bible* notes also echo this tradition,[109] and the English Annotations give an almost identical interpretation of Acts 2:17:

> Dreames, and visions, were one ordinary meanes whereby God revealed his will to the Prophets. Numbers 12.6. So we must understand the Prophets speaking of things to come, attemperated to the capacity of the present times wherein they preached and wrote: so when they speak of Gods service, they name; *altars, sacrifices,* gold, silver, incense, &c. all which when they relate to times of the Gospel, are to be understood, as allusions to legal rites, not proprieties of the Gospel: so that here, dreames, and visions import excellent gifts of the Spirit, and understanding of things revealed by the Holy Ghost[...]. God still offereth, and respectively bestoweth now on his Church, in the Spirit of sanctification, though not in the faith of miracles.[110]

According to these influential commentaries, therefore, the correct interpretation of this text teaches that the promise of miraculous abilities is at the same time a pledge of the availability of ordinary gifts of the Spirit when the extraordinary have ceased.

The international nature of this particular exegesis is also evident from the work of Frenchman Moïsé (Moïse or Moses) Amyraut (1596-1664) who wrote a *Discourse Concerning the Divine Dreams Mentioned in Scripture*, where he takes a strong cessationist position on Heb. 1:1-2. Amyraut, whose name is more commonly associated with the soteriological theory often called "hypothetical universalism",[111] had his supporters in the Assembly, and he may have been partly responsible for the moderate Calvinism expressed in its documents.[112]

---

[108] Diodati, *Pious and Learned Annotations upon the Holy Bible,* Acts 2:17.

[109] Sheppard (ed.), *The Geneva Bible,* Joel 2:28.

[110] *Annotations*, Acts 2:17.

[111] "Amyraldianism" contends that Christ died for every individual, at least hypothetically, which is a view at odds with "limited atonement", where Christ is understood to have suffered and died redemptively for the elect only. See Alan Clifford, *Atonement and Justification: English Evangelical Theology 1640-1790: An Evaluation* (Oxford: Clarendon Press, 1990), especially 26-27 for Amyraldianism in the Westminster Assembly and Richard Baxter's belief that it was allowed for. For a sympathetic and comprehensive discussion on Amyraldianism, see Brian Armstrong, *Calvinism and the Amyraut Heresy: Protestant Scholasticism and Humanism in Seventeenth-Century France* (Madison: University of Wisconsin Press, 1969), especially 159-221 on predestination.

[112] In the Assembly minutes of Session 547, 4 December 1645, we read the intriguing entry: "Upon a motion made by Mr. Dury, according to the desire of Mr. Rivett, that the Assembly would purge him from a charge of complaining against Amyraldus to this

Amyraut concludes on the subject of Heb. 1:1-2: "He [God] now only reveals himself in one way, *viz*. By the preaching of the Gospel, whereas then he did it in divers manners".[113] Amyraut poses the question: *"Whether God doth make use of this kind of Revelation by Dreams, now under the Dispensation of the Gospel*[?]"[114] In answering, he cites Joel's prophecy (Joel 2:28), noting that it embraces the time of the gospel, though he also queries:

> that not withstanding this, we see by experience that those miraculous gifts of the Spirit of God are ceased long ago[...]how then shall we reconcile our experience with this prophesy?[115]

He affirms that the miraculous gifts were indeed evident in the early church, but:

> though the words of *Joel* seem only to design the extraordinary and miraculous gifts of the Spirit, yet under them are also compris'd, those more ordinary ones, which consist in the illumination of the understanding of the faithful, in knowledge of the Divine truth[...]".[116]

It is not surprising, then, to find that this explanation has its precursor in John Calvin's works, which also foreshadow the English Annotations' typological interpretation of the Old Testament sacrificial cultus, and at the same time teach the cessation of miraculous gifts:

Assembly". Mitchell and Struthers (eds.), *Minutes of the Sessions of the Westminster Assembly of Divines*, 167. Carruthers explains that: "At Dury's request (4th December, 1645) Rivet was given a certificate clearing him of the charge that he had complained to the Assembly against Amyraut. The latter, a kindly man, willing to find a theological *via media*, had issued in 1644 a dissertation '*De gratia universali*,' which Rivet, an orthodox Calvinist, criticised in a pamphlet in 1648". Samuel William Carruthers, *The Everyday Work of the Westminster Assembly* (Philadelphia: The Presbyterian Historical Society (of America) and the Presbyterian Historical Society of England, 1943), 186. Robert Baillie writes in complaint to William Spang on 24 October 1645: "Unhappilie Amiraut's Questions are brought in on our Assemblie. Many more love these fancies here than I did expect. It falls out that Spanheim's book is so long a-coming out, whileas Amiraut's treatise goes in the Assemblie from hand to hand; yet I hope this shall goe right". Baillie, *The Letters and Journals of Robert Baillie*, vol. 2, 324. On the *WCF* in general, see Armstrong, *Calvinism and the Amyraut Heresy*, 141 and 236. Armstrong identifies the offender who had given Amyraut's paper to the Assembly as a son (Louis) of Amyraut's nephew Pierre du Moulin (105).

[113] Moses (or Moïse or Moisé) Amyraldus, *A Discourse Concerning the Divine Dreams Mention'd in Scripture, Together with the Marks and Character by which They Might be Distinguished from Vain Delusions. In a Letter to Monsieur Gaches by Moses Amyraldus*, Ja. Lorrde (translator) (London: Walter Kettilby, 1676), 42.

[114] Amyraldus, *A Discourse Concerning the Divine Dreams*, 101.

[115] Amyraldus, *A Discourse Concerning the Divine Dreams*, 103-104.

[116] Amyraldus, *A Discourse Concerning the Divine Dreams*, 104-105.

[L]et us understand that the words spoken then to the Jews are true for us today for, although the visible gifts of the Spirit have ceased, God has not yet withdrawn His Spirit from His Church.[117]

The Westminster divines largely followed this exegetical tradition. Some used the Joel prophecy in a purely cessationist way, arguing that the extraordinary gifts referred to in the prophecy were given for the confirmation of the gospel. Anthony Burgess, for example, in his commentary on 1 Cor. 3, notes concerning the events of Joel and Acts 2:

> These were extraordinary. But because such extraordinary gifts were in the nature of Miracles to confirm the Apostles Doctrine and their Mission from God, they now cease[...]. The former [*"wonderfull and miraculous operations"*] did especially belong to the Church in its first plantation. Hence *Acts* 2. we reade of the accomplishment of that glorious Prophecy, Joel 2, *To pour out his Spirit*, &c. but now these miraculous operations are ceased.[118]

Even George Gillespie, who argues for the continuation of a form of extraordinary prophecy, avoids using this text to sanction it, for he understands Acts 2:17-18 to be a record of the fulfilment of Joel 2:28 on the day of Pentecost. Gillespie distinguishes between the prophesying referred to in these texts and "[e]xtraordinary prophesying from immediate and miraculous inspiration", thus departing somewhat from the standard exegesis. This Acts 2:17-18 prophesying was a gift given to all the "disciples, men and women", and Gillespie links it to speaking "with other tongues".[119]

For most, the contemporary use of Joel's prophecy was consistent with cessationism. This is true in Thomas Manton (1620-1677). Although he was apparently only appointed a Westminster divine (as one of the scribes of the Assembly) following the completion of the Westminster symbols, Manton was held in such esteem that he was asked to write the official preface to the *WCF*.[120] Commenting on Acts 2:17, he asserts:

---

[117] John Calvin, *Calvin's New Testament Commentaries. The Acts of the Apostles*, eds. David Torrance and Thomas Torrance (Grand Rapids, MI: Eerdmans, 1977), vol. 6, 59.

[118] Anthony Burgesse (or Burgess), *The Scripture Directory, for Church-Officers and People or, a Practical Commentary Upon the Whole Third Chapter of the First Epistle of St Paul to the Corinthians* [...]" (London: Thomas Underhill, 1659), 75-76.

[119] George Gillespie, "Miscellany Questions", *The Works of George Gillespie*, ed. David Meek (Edmonton: SWRB, 1991), vol. 2, 30.

[120] Charlotte Fell-Smith, "Thomas Manton", *DNB*, vol. 1, 1315. Born in Lawrence, Somerset and educated at Oxford, Manton would become one of the leading Puritans of his day.

These are but figurative expressions, to signify the gifts of the Holy Ghost, which we receive by virtue of Christ's ascension, abundance of knowledge, faith, and holiness.[121]

Just as the prophets of the Old Testament used the terminology of the Temple to prophesy concerning the New Testament church, so too Joel's prophecy (Joel 2:28) should be interpreted analogically, according to Manton: "By prophecy you may understand the gifts of illumination; by vision gifts of consolation; and by dreams, the gifts of sanctification".[122]

John Lightfoot also links the Joel prophecy to another Old Testament cessationist text. While he uses the two texts from Joel and Acts to support his cessationist view in his doctoral thesis,[123] in a sermon on John 11:51 he associates the outpouring of the Spirit in Acts 2:18 with Dan. 9:24:

> 'That year' was the great year of 'pouring down the spirit' of prophecy and revelation, as in Acts ii;- the great year of 'sealing vision and prophecy'.[124]

The fact that the Annotations concur with Lightfoot's exegesis of Dan. 9 demonstrates that, for the Puritans as a whole, cessationism was embedded in their systematic theology. They believed that threaded through the Old and New Testaments is the idea that God would cease to give special revelation following the completion of the initial period of the primitive New Testament church:

> All the visions and prophetical predictions, concerning Christ, were fulfilled, in and by him[...]they [the Jews] have had no Vision, Prophet, nor Prophecies, never since our Saviour Christ Jesus came[...]. Christ by his prophetical office, shut up, and sealed up all former Visions, Prophets, and prophecies.[125]

The Puritans did not only use typological arguments when they expounded these texts to support their cessationism. William Carter, for example, explains that the cessationist interpretation arises from the context of Acts 2:17-18:

---

[121] Thomas Manton, *The Complete Works of Thomas Manton, D.D.* (London: James Nisbet, 1873), vol. 14, 182.

[122] Manton, *The Complete Works of Thomas Manton*, vol. 14, 183. Richardson in his notes on Joel 2:28 in the Annotations has this to say: "*your old men*] By an allusion to the visible manner of Gods gracious gifts and dealings with his people and Prophets, in dreams, and visions, before the coming of Christ. He describes the Spiritual worship of God, and the abundant gifts of his grace in the days of the Gospel: so applying here his speech to the better capacity of the present people, not yet confounding or disannulling the distinct orders of Ministers in the Church of Christ". John Richardson, *Annotations*, Joel 2:28.

[123] Lightfoot, *The Whole Works of the Rev. John Lightfoot, D.D.*, vol. 5, 458-59.

[124] Lightfoot, *The Whole Works of the Rev. John Lightfoot, D.D.*, vol. 7, 308.

[125] *Annotations*, Dan. 9:24.

this must be meant of ordinary gifts, because it is made a distinct thing to the former, as that which God would do for all his servants[...]. Therefore every beleever hath the spirit of prophesie[...]yet to understand the prophesies, which the Saints of the Old Testament ordinarily had not[...]".[126]

In summary, for Reformed orthodoxy, whether the "last days" were deemed to have been completed in AD 70 at the time of the destruction of Jerusalem, or whether they embraced the apostolic period, or whether they encompassed the entire gospel age, there was overwhelming agreement that the visions and dreams of the prophecy of Joel were to be applied figuratively in the period subsequent to the apostolic era.

Edward Reynolds summarises the standard Puritan approach to all these texts when he integrates insights from Acts 2:17-18 (with Joel 2:28), Heb. 1:1-2 and Eph. 1:17, in his sermon on the first verse of Psalm 110. Reynolds' argument has four main steps: First, he proposes that Heb. 1:1-2 teaches that God speaks more fully and plainly now than he did to the fathers. Visions and dreams are inferior, because the fathers only "saw in glimpses and morning starres and prefigurations",[127] making their revelations inferior to ours in that sense. Secondly, Reynolds appeals to Eph. 1:17 to assert that the way of revelation must be distinguished:

> To the old Church *in dreams and vision, in figures and latent wayes*: But to the Evangelicall Churches, *in power, evidence and demonstration,* 1. *Cor.*2. 4, 5.[128]

Thirdly, Joel 2:28 is a reference to the greater and more extensive effusion of the Spirit: "but now is the Spirit powred upon *all flesh*; and this heavenly dew falleth not upon the fleece, but upon the whole earth".[129] And finally, there is no disadvantage to the New Testament believer because God restricts his will and comfort to Scripture:

> for though there be no Prophetical, or extraordinary revelations, by dreames, visions, extasies, or enthusiasmes; yet according to the measure of spiritual perspicacie, and diligent observation of Holy Scriptures, there are still manifold revelations or manifestations of Christ unto the soule, The secret and intimate acquaintance of the Soule with God, [...]are Heavenly and constant revelations out of the Word manifested to the soules of the faithful by the Spirit.[130]

---

[126] Carter, *The Covenant of God with Abraham Opened [...] Together with A Short Discourse Concerning the Manifestations of God unto His People in the Last Dayes*, 86.

[127] Edward Reynolds, *An Explication of the CX. Psalm [...] Being the Substance of Several Sermons Preached at Lincolns Inne* (London: R[obert?]. B[ostock?]., 1656), 38.

[128] Reynolds, *An Explication of the CX. Psalm*, 39.

[129] Reynolds, *An Explication of the CX. Psalm*, 39.

[130] Reynolds, *An Explication of the CX. Psalm*, 48.

The spiritual privileges of the contemporary believer exceed those of the Old Testament saints, despite the fact that miraculous categories of inspiration have ceased.

The Westminster divines' supposition that all immediate inspiration has ended was not limited to the exegesis of these three texts. It arose also in other exegetical contexts either as distinct arguments or in the form of plain assertion.

3.3 Extra-biblical Modalities Relegated to the Past

In the first place, extra-biblical modalities were simply relegated to the past by some. William Gouge, for example, in his comments on Job 33:15, contrasts God's communication in the Scriptures with God's communication through dreams and visions, consigning the latter to the past:

> Now he sets out the several wayes God used to make his will known to his people by, before the Scriptures were written[...][t]hat God did use to teach men by dreams, and night visions.[131]

His phraseology assumes that the Scriptures have superseded the function of dreams and visions.

Thomas Valentine (1585/6-1665?), as one of those suspended for refusing to read the *Book of Sports*, had indicated his willingness to take a public stand against the established church and therefore exhibited the right credentials for appointment to the Puritan Westminster Assembly.[132] He similarly identifies the era of the patriarchs, prophets and apostles as the epoch of supernatural revelation, in a sermon to the House of Lords in 1647. Valentine assigns "visions, dreams or apparitions in bodily shapes" to "former times, to Patriarchs, Prophets, and Apostles".[133]

Other theologians explained that extra-biblical revelation for the governance of the church has ceased because we now have all such information we need in Scripture. For Anthony Burgess, there can be no more immediate revelation, because God has ordained that his church must be governed through the ordinary ministry and through ordinary preaching from Scripture. While Burgess admits that God could continue to govern his church through immediate revelations and apparitions, God does not do so because he has appointed an ordinary ministry in place of the former

---

[131] William Gouge, *Annotations*, Job 33:15. See also on Job 4:12.

[132] Reid, *Memoirs of the Westminster Divines*, vol. 2, 190-91. Valentine, was educated at Cambridge. He later became minister of Chalfont St. Giles, Bucks. He was a constant attender at the Assembly and, according to Reid, was a popular preacher.

[133] Thomas Valentine, *A Charge against the Jews, and the Christian World, for not Coming to Christ who would have Freely Given them Eternall Life* (London: John Rothwell, 1647), 17.

which used extra-biblical revelations.[134] Burgess is, accordingly, certain that the office of apostle and prophet, and the gift of miracles were for the "first constituting of the Church".[135]

Westminster orthodoxy was also belligerent towards claimants to new revelation, because the orthodox feared the inherent danger of appeals to inspirations. Warnings of false revelation without the Word formed a constant refrain in Puritan literature, for the simple reason that such "inspiration", purporting to be immediate revelation apart from Scripture, could lead one away from the Scriptures.

Edmund Calamy, commenting on 2 Pet. 1:19,[136] rejects as dangerous any claimed extra-biblical revelation of God's will from heaven, apart from the Scriptures, for instruction on worship:

> And if God should now at this day discover his way of Worship, and his Divine Will by Revelations, how easily would Men be deceived, and mistake Diabolical Delusions, for Divine Revelations.[137]

William Spurstowe, in his treatise, *The Wels of Salvation Opened*, warns against seeking spiritual consolation from outside Scripture: "take heed of *groundless and wild fancies concerning the manner of receiving comfort*".[138] He also gives two reasons why the way of extra-biblical revelation is so dangerous. First, because the Word of God and its promises are thereby devalued; secondly, such revelations are dangerous, because they are deceitful and illusory, for Satan takes advantage of people who are open to revelations by giving them false revelations.[139] The danger of any "obtruding his *fancies* upon others" is also uppermost in his mind when he relegates visions and revelations to the past in *The Spiritual Chymist*.[140]

Anthony Tuckney, in a sermon on 2 Tim. 1:13, *The Form of Sound Words*, is realistic about how difficult it is to stem the tide of claims to new revelation. He is well aware that the "evils" which flow from such claims

---

[134] Burgess, *CXLV Expository Sermons Upon the Whole 17th Chapter of the Gospel According to St John*, 558.

[135] Burgess, *CXLV Expository Sermons Upon the Whole 17th Chapter of the Gospel According to St John*, 558.

[136] Another proof-text for *WCF* 1:1.

[137] Edmund Calamy, *The Godly Mans Ark, or City of Refuge in the Day of His Distress* (London: Thomas Parkhurst and John Hancock, 1693), 58.

[138] William Spurstowe, *The Wels of Salvation Opened: Or, A Treatise Discovering the Nature, Preciousness, Usefulness of Gospel-Promises, and Rules for the Right Application of Them* (London: Ralph Smith, 1655), 153.

[139] Spurstowe, *The Wels of Salvation Opened*, 153-62.

[140] William Spurstow, *The Spiritual Chymist: Or, Six Decad[e]s of Divine Meditations on Several Subjects* (London: 1666) [no further publishing details are given], 163.

are solidly entrenched in England itself.[141] Augustine's advice had appealed to Tuckney: "Let us beware of such dangerous temptations of pride",[142] but Tuckney does not deny that "sometimes, possibly there may be some more then [*sic.* than] an ordinary intimation of Gods will[...]". He qualifies this with the following statement: "*For the things declared*, it may be they may be helped to apply some generall word in Scripture to a particular case".[143] The Puritans were truly fearful of the threat of claims to a spiritual afflatus, and sometimes they condemned such claims by association, aligning what they conceived were modern pretensions to dreams and visions with astrology and the "*invocation of damned spirits*".[144]

Another argument for the cessation of immediate special revelation, exemplified by Sydrach Simpson, was to link the cessation of revelation to the cessation of miracles.[145] Simpson's logic is straightforward enough. Since Scripture is complete and since miracles are for the confirmation of doctrine, both special revelation and miracles intended to confirm doctrine have ceased. In his book, *Of Unbelief or the Want of Readines[s] to Lay Hold on the Comfort Given by Christ*, he insists that the miraculous confirmation of faith "is wholly ceased as to the introducing, or confirming of any Doctrine".[146] The reason is simply that all doctrine that has now been given is recorded in Scripture and has already been confirmed by miracles. When such faith in miracles was available, it required a "special revelation that God will put forth his power to do such things as he hath foretold shall come to pass".[147] Although miracles would still be required if there were other doctrines to be received,[148] with the Scriptures now

---

[141] Tuckney, *A Good Day Well Improved[...]to Which is Annexed a Sermon on 2 Tim. 1.13*, 307.

[142] Tuckney, *A Good Day Well Improved[...]to Which is Annexed a Sermon on 2 Tim. 1.13*, 305, where he cites Augustine: "Caveamus tales tentationes superbissimas & periculosissimas". Augustine, *On Christian Doctrine*, preface, 6 (*NPNF* first ser., 2, 520).

[143] Tuckney, *A Good Day Well Improved[...]to Which is Annexed a Sermon on 2 Tim. 1.13*, 307.

[144] Thomas Gataker, *His Vindication of the Annotations by Him Published Upon these Words, Thus Saith the Lord, Learn not the Way of the Heathen, and be not Dismayed at the Signes of Heaven, for the Heathen are Dismayed at them. Jer. 10.2* (London: Richard Thrayle, 1653), 86.

[145] See also Anthony Burgess on this point. He includes all extraordinary gifts such as those listed in 1 Cor. 12 as well as those which Acts 2:17 implies have ceased, because such gifts are miracles: "to confirm the Apostles Doctrine, and their Mission from God, they now cease". Burgess, *The Scripture Directory for Church-Officers and People*, 75.

[146] Simpson, *Two Books of Mr Sydrach Simpson[...]I. Of Unbelief*, 9.

[147] Simpson, *Two Books of Mr Sydrach Simpson[...]I. Of Unbelief*, 8.

[148] Simpson, *Two Books of Mr Sydrach Simpson[...]I. Of Unbelief*, 9-10.

complete the only miracles that still occur are "invisible ones: such as are the opening of blind understandings and raising dead hearts and the like".[149]

Perhaps the Westminster Puritans' most common cessationist argument was the frequently used hermeneutical application of Old Testament categories, institutions and narrative in an analogical sense. This was something that is widely attested in their interpretation of Acts 2:17, as we have seen, but it was not restricted to that text. Stephen Marshall, in a sermon on 2 Chron. 15:2, suggests that God's covenantal presence in Old Testament ordinances is useful now only as a didactic analogy. While he avers that Scripture has taken over the revelatory function of the former modalities, Old Testament ordinances can still be useful teaching tools when spiritually understood:

> To the Nation of the *Jews* it [God's presence in his Covenant] implyed something which concernes not us, but mystically or analogically: As to have the *Arke, Urim* and *Thummim*: To have God to reveale himselfe in *Visions* and *Dreames*: To answer by *Thunder, &c.*[150]

For Edward Reynolds, in a sermon on the text Zech. 4:6, Zerubbabel's vision serves a similar analogical purpose. The prophet's uncertainty over the meaning of the vision teaches us "by the way not to despond or be discouraged by the difficulty of the Scriptures[...]".[151] Old Testament visionary experiences can instruct us on how to approach biblical texts by applying their lessons to the more restricted epistemological boundaries of Scripture alone.

Westminster orthodoxy appealed to the plenitude of Scripture as God's revelation for all purposes as conclusive proof that all immediate revelation has ceased. Anthony Burgess confines the "Word of God" to Scripture, asserting that since Scripture has replaced the immediate revelations which came to the patriarchs: "There is no other Word of God, but what is written".[152] If, Burgess proposes, people had only realised that the Bible was the true Word of God:

> Neither Superstitious Traditions on the one hand, nor subtle Delusions of pretended Revelations on the other hand could ever have molested or troubled the Church.[153]

---

[149] Simpson, *Two Books of Mr Sydrach Simpson[...]I. Of Unbelief*, 9.

[150] Stephen Marshall, *A Sermon Preached[...]November 17.1640, upon 2 Chron. 15.2.* (London: Samuel Man, 1641), 10.

[151] Edward Reynolds, *Divine Efficacy without Humane Power* (London: George Thomason, 1660), 2.

[152] Burgess, *CXLV Expository Sermons Upon the Whole 17th Chapter of the Gospel According to St John*, 473.

[153] Burgess, *CXLV Expository Sermons Upon the Whole 17th Chapter of the Gospel According to St John*, 475.

This same sentiment resonates in the *WCF*.[154] Samuel Rutherford agrees, refusing to listen to the notion that the Spirit's revelations could have an effect without the Word. In a sermon in manuscript on Rev. 3:20, Christ's "knocking", according to Rutherford, is the calling of the gospel, and can be distinguished from false revelation by the very fact that it is accompanied by the Word of God, for "the Lord now goes along with his word; and he hath in a manner tied himself to it".[155]

Therefore, when the *WCF* concludes in 1:6, that "nothing at any time is to be added [to Scripture], whether by new revelations of the Spirit[...]", we must conclude that the divines most likely intended that there is now no possibility of other immediate revelation being sanctioned. One of the authors of the *WCF*, Francis Cheynell, repeats what was considered a truism: *"Our faith is not built upon [...] the Revelations of Angells, but upon the Word of God, that Word that stands for ever"*.[156] "We", he urges:

> must not expect such *unwritten Revelations* as were vouchsafed to *Abraham*, because *the whole Counsell of God*, his Royall Will and Pleasure doe now stand upon record as his perfect Law[...]".[157]

The Puritans, as we have already noted from their exposition of other texts, did not limit their denial that new revelation occurred only in matters of doctrine and ethics. When Thomas Hill (1602-1653) consigns extra-biblical revelation to history, he is not just referring to revealed doctrine, but also to the manner in which the intention of the divine mind was conveyed immediately for daily life. The esteem in which his colleagues held Hill was illustrated by his choice as one of the seven daily preachers at Westminster Abbey during the sitting of the Assembly.[158] In one of his more important homilies, Hill calls into question any claimed novel revelations for ordinary life and guidance:

---

[154] *WCF* 1:6.

[155] Samuel Rutherford, MS. Dc.S.30, "Sermon on Revelation 3:20" (Edinburgh: Edinburgh University), 68. I have modified the spelling and expanded the text which is in a degree of shorthand.

[156] Francis Cheynell, *A Plot for the Good of Posterity* (London: Samuel Gellibrand, 1646), 22-23. Cheynell(1608-1665) may have had a violent temper and earned the reputation of being a fanatic, according to his biographer, but he was trusted enough in his own day to be both a member of the Assembly and an examiner for heresy. Cheynell, born in Catstreet, Oxford, a Fellow of Merton College, Oxford, later became parson of Petworth, Sussex and was a frequent preacher before Parliament. Augustus Bickley, "Francis Cheynell", *DNB,* vol. 1, 363.

[157] Cheynell, *A Plot for the Good of Posterity,* 13.

[158] Hill, who was born at Kington, Worcestershire, was educated at Cambridge where he was later elected a Fellow of Emmanuel College. He was ordained in 1633, and became a noted preacher. Hill was elected Master, first of Emmanuel College and later of Trinity College, Cambridge, and also served as Vice-Chancellor of the University. Barker, *Puritan Profiles,* 140-44.

Do not thou decline the word of God, and flie to Revelations; know thou there is, and do thou carefully *maintain, that sweet harmony that is between the word of God and the Spirit of Revelation*; and if the same Spirit that did endite the word, do speak in thy mind and work in thy heart, then indeed thou hast a great deal of cause to rejoyce, and then thou mayest safely go on; but cursed will they be in their practises, that do divide those things, separate them that God hath conjoyned together, *word and Spirit, do not thou advance*[the] *Spirit, to the disparagement* of the word: make use of the word in a concurrence with *the light of the Spirit*, and *improve the Spirit for a more full discovery of the word.*[159]

Although his main point is that there will be no more revelation for truth, he extends his application to any work of the Spirit in the mind and heart for daily living. In harmony with this view, John Lightfoot, in a sermon on Judges 20:27-28, agrees "that there is now no other way to inquire of God, but only from his word[...]".[160]

3.4 Conclusion

An analysis of the writings of the Westminster divines reveals their pervasive commitment to a cessationism of a rather comprehensive kind. In their exposition of the key texts of Eph. 1:17-18, Heb. 1:1-2, and Joel 2:28-32/Acts 2:17, a large proportion of the divines contend that the possibility of further revelation has ceased, both for the purposes of doctrinal insight and for ethical guidance. They repeatedly contrast the role of Scripture with phenomena such as dreams and visions as means of divine communication, and argue that the latter modalities are firmly confined to the past.

From a range of other biblical texts the divines adduce further reasons as to why the church ought no longer to expect revelation from a source outside of Scripture itself. Extra-biblical revelation is restricted to the eras of the patriarchs, prophets, and apostles. Special revelation for the governance of the church is said to have ceased. Warnings are issued against the inherent dangers of appeals to immediate inspiration, and the cessation of such revelation is linked to the cessation of miracles. Old Testament texts in particular tend to be read analogically. The Scriptures as a whole are presented and appealed to as the final supernatural revelation of God for all purposes.

Such a weight of testimony from the wider writings of the divines strongly suggests that a similar perspective on cessationism is implicit in *WCF* 1:1. There were, however, some exceptions to this point of view both within and outside the Assembly. To these we shall turn our attention next.

---

[159] Thomas Hill, *The Best and Worst of Paul and his Character in Both Conditions* (Cambridge: 1648) [no further publishing details are given], 16.

[160] Lightfoot, *The Whole Works of the Rev. John Lightfoot, D.D.,* vol. 6, 286.

Chapter 4

Clarifying the Claims to Continuationism

4.1 Introduction

As we have seen, a large majority of seventeenth-century Puritans believed that those who claimed to find revelation in dreams and visions subscribed to a view which was no longer valid. Nevertheless, it is clear that some thought otherwise. It is plainly important to explore these differences in order to clarify the claims to continuationism among the Reformed orthodox.

In this chapter, we shall take the following steps. First, it will be helpful to consider the cessationist/continuationist divide in the seventeenth century with further reference to the subject of dreams. Dreams in particular provide a significant test-case for the debate, in so far as they were obviously one of the more common modalities of supernatural revelation both in the Old Testament and in the apostolic era. What precisely was their status in the evaluation of those on both sides of the argument in Reformed circles?

In the second place, we shall consider some of the more explicit claims to extra-biblical revelation among the Puritans, and examine how these claims are to be assessed in the light of the strongly cessationist arguments presented by so many Reformed preachers and theologians of the period. What kinds of continuationism may have been in mind, and how precise are some of the descriptions that imply a continuationist mindset?

Finally, we shall turn to the seventeenth-century Quaker polemic against strict cessationism. The arguments of those most vigorously opposed to a resolutely cessationist position are of considerable importance, because they expose the ways in which Reformed orthodoxy in general and Westminster theology in particular was perceived by its opponents. Those who favoured the possibility of experiencing the freedom of the Spirit apart from the Word were resistant to the pneumatology of Westminster precisely because they understood it to deny the possibilities of such liberty. Claims to continuationism among the Reformed orthodox can only be rightly assessed in the context of a wider consideration of arguments for and against the possibility of extra biblical revelation in the seventeenth century.

4.2 Cessationism and Dreams

A belief in the revelatory nature of divinely inspired dreams was the most obvious and frequent exception to the Puritan cessationist stance, but even those who were strict cessationists thought that God sometimes used dreams to guide his people. If Thomas Gillespie's (1708-1774) view a generation later faithfully reflected his Puritan predecessors, then some may have held that a dream was quite distinct from a revelation, although the dream could convey previously unknown information. Gillespie was a Scottish minister, founder of the Relief Church and a strict cessationist.[1] In his *Essay on the Continuance of Immediate Revelations of Facts and Future Events*, he distinguishes "divine dreams that excite to duty, and are premonitions of dangers to be avoided" from "immediate revelations of facts and future events". The former in his view are available to his contemporaries, but the latter have ceased.[2] However, did Puritans and Scottish Presbyterians of the previous century also make similar or related distinctions?

We can discern three cessationist perspectives on dreams among the seventeenth-century Reformed orthodox, two of which gave dreams experienced by the godly a certain legitimacy as ways of revealing new information. There were those who
1. simply consigned revelatory dreams to the past.
2. understood revelatory dreams from Scripture in a spiritualised way for the new covenant epoch.
3. reasoned that dreams were an element of God's providential government, and therefore a means that God could use to direct the steps of life in the light of Scripture.

We will consider these categories in turn.

4.2.1. Consigning Revelatory Dreams to the Past

There is little doubt that the most common position among Westminster divines was to deny the validity of contemporary extra-biblical revelation through dreams. William Gouge in the Annotations on Job 33:14-15, for example, when speaking of God's ethical instructions given in dreams and visions of the night, says that they are the way "God *used to* make his will known to his people by, before the Scriptures were written [emphasis added]".[3] This stance was compatible with the second category of the

---

[1] For details on Gillespie, see David Lachman, "Thomas Gillespie", *DSCHT*, 360-61.

[2] Thomas Gillespie, *An Essay on the Continuance of Immediate Revelations of Facts and Future Events* (Edinburgh: W. Gray, 1771), 15.

[3] William Gouge, *Annotations upon All the Books of the Old and New Testament: This Third, above the First and Second, Edition so Enlarged, As They Make an Entire Commentary on the Sacred Scripture: The Like Never before Published in English.*

cessationist view of dreams since Samuel Rutherford says something similar while making dreams still relevant means of grace to the believer.[4]

For John Arrowsmith, dreams were ways of revelation revealing truth to the Patriarchs, but God gathered "all" the truth revealed this way and inscripturated it.[5] William Carter admits that God could still speak "to us by dreams, visions and revelations extraordinary and by persons infallibly inspired", but concludes that he now denies to "his people that which formerly he granted".[6] William Spurstow is equally certain that in the infancy of the church God made himself known by visions, dreams and oracles, now he speaks by his written word.[7]

4.2.2 Spiritualised Dreaming

We have already canvassed the near consensus of Reformed orthodoxy, which interpreted the promise in Joel 2:28-32, that the believer would dream and see visions, as a metaphor for non-miraculous spiritual gifts, such as the gift of understanding the teaching of Scripture. However, the Reformed orthodox themselves also allegorised Old Testament records of actual dreams in order to make them relevant to the New Testament believer.

Thus Samuel Rutherford, in a series of three sermons on Jacob's dream (Gen. 28:10-15), interpreted revelatory dreams in the Old Testament as types of spiritual graces in the New. In his second sermon, he makes a typically cessationist comment that the former modes were something evident in Old Testament history when God:

> thought most good [to communicate] in his infinite wisdom by immediate inspirations, by apparitions, by dreams, and the Lord speaks to

---

Wherein the Text is Explained, Doubts Resolved, Scriptures Parallel'd, and Various Readings Observed; By the Labour of Certain Learned Divines Thereunto Appointed, and Therein Employed, As is Expressed in the Preface (London: Evan Tyler, 1657), Job 33:14-15; or see Henry Wilkinson, *Three Decad[e]s of Sermons Lately Preached to the University at St Mary's Church in Oxford* (Oxford: Thomas Robinson, 1660), 116.

[4] See 149, n9 below.

[5] John Arrowsmith, ΘΕΑΝΘΡΩΠΟΣ; *or, God-Man*, (London: Humphrey Moseley and William Wilson, 1660), 91.

[6] William Carter, *The Covenant of God with Abraham Opened [...] Together with A Short Discourse Concerning the Manifestations of God unto His People in the Last Dayes. Wherein is Shewed the Manner of the Spirits Work Therein to be in the Use of Ordinary Gifts, not by Extraordinary Revelations* (London: John Rothwell, 1654), 141.

[7] William Spurstow, *The Spiritual Chymist: Or, Six Decad[e]s of Divine Meditations on Several Subjects* (London: 1666) [no further publishing details are given], 163.

Moses face to face as a man doth to his friend he being familiar with Moses in those times when this history was.[8]

According to Rutherford, this ancient record of the modes of special revelation still had much to teach his generation. Rutherford discerns a principle in Scripture that God's grace is present in the hearts and minds of believers during sleep, because in a way that the ungodly do not, God's people have him in their hearts while they are awake:

> [i]t will sometimes be so with you in the night also, for grace hath room in the sensitive appetite as well as it hath in the rational and so if there is little of God in the day time, there will be nothing of him in the time of sleep.[9]

Thus, the congregation should understand that God's presence in a dream provides sanctifying grace rather than revelation.

4.2.3 Dreams and Puritan Providentialism

While Rutherford implied that dreams recorded in Scripture were important evidence that God's grace can be present in sleep, his fellow Scottish commissioner to the Assembly, the intense and zealous Archibald Johnston (or Lord Warriston, 1611-1663), was sure that God mediated his grace through dreams to provide concrete divine guidance. Johnston exemplifies the third grouping of cessationists, who saw dreams as a component of a holistic providentialism.[10] He was a man whose ambition often got in the way of his happiness, for he regularly found himself in straitened circumstances caused by the political machinations of the Interregnum. His religious commitment, however, was beyond doubt. As his biographer puts it, in his "involuntary self-revelation[…]we have, I think the best confession of all that his life had its sources in the convictions and inspirations of the Christian Faith".[11]

---

[8] Samuel Rutherford, MS Dc.S.30, "Sermon on Genesis 28:13, 14" (Edinburgh: Edinburgh University), 25. Spelling modernised and the shorthand in which these sermons were recorded is transcribed.

[9] Samuel Rutherford, MS Dc.S.30, "Sermon on Genesis 28:10-15" (Edinburgh: Edinburgh University), 22.

[10] For a comprehensive analysis charting the shifting perspective on providence among American Puritans into the eighteenth century, see Michael Winship, *Seers of God. Puritan Providentialism in the Restoration and Early Enlightenment* (Baltimore: John Hopkins University Press, 1996), especially 125-52 for the decline and eventual extinction of Puritan providentialism.

[11] William Morison, *Johnston of Warriston* (London: Oliphant Anderson and Ferrier, 1901), 154. See also 93-103 for his time at the Westminster Assembly. The son of an Edinburgh merchant, Johnston was educated at the University of Glasgow. He took a leading part in drawing up the 1638 National Covenant with Alexander Henderson, and

Johnston's published diaries are heavily edited and exclude much of the personal religious struggle that defines this passionate Scot. The editing procedure has partially obscured the expression, so evident in the manuscripts, of his intimate belief in and reliance upon the God of all providence. If he recalls a conversation, for example, Johnston gives God the credit for the recollection or for the fact of its presence in his consciousness.[12] He is also aware that some fellow Christians considered his profound commitment to providentialism to be idiosyncratic. Remembering a prophetic warning from a female acquaintance, he notes in his diary:

> I remembered that Janet Arnot told me of [...] dangers intended for me xx I thought if any knew what I had written on the 10 days would they not call it jolye and a romance and at the best as Spotswood wrytes of Knox a devout imagination.[13]

Johnston saw no contradiction between his belief that an omnipresent God constantly attended to the minutiae of his daily existence and his commitment to the Protestant belief in the unity of Word and Spirit. This is especially evident in his doctrine of divine guidance. On the Lord's Day, 23 January 1659, he records how he heard a sermon from a Mr Case (probably Thomas Case, the Westminster divine), then met with John Owen who had enquired after friends in Scotland, and later listened to a "revelation" from a visiting Quaker:

> The Quaker came into me and would dissuade me from going to the House of Lords and would have me beleive that God would destroye that Kingship and the House of Lords. I asked what warrand he had. He told

---

as an elder in the Church of Scotland was appointed a commissioner to the Assembly. Although he opposed the execution of Charles I, Johnston later accepted an appointment from Oliver Cromwell. Forced to flee to Europe following the Restoration, he was extradited to England from France, and was executed at Mercat Cross in Edinburgh within view of his own house. For more recent biographical information, see William Barker, *Puritan Profiles, 54 Personalities Drawn Together by the Westminster Assembly* (Fearn: Christian Focus, 1996), 112-14.

[12] "The Lord was pleased to bring to my mynd an word that Mr J. Neison spak[e]" (2 May 1655): Archibald Johnston, "The Diary of Archibald Johnston", MS 6247 (Edinburgh: National Library of Scotland, 17 April 1655 to 10 June 1655), 14. The *National Library of Scotland Catalogue of Manuscripts Acquired since 1925 iv.* (Edinburgh: Her Majesty's stationery office, 1982), notes: "20th Century abridged transcription. Transcript of parts of volumes xiv-xxiv,xxvi – xliii of the diary of Archibald Johnston of Warriston, 1655-61, used in the preparation of Diary of Sir Archibald Johnston of Wariston, vol. iii, Scottish History Society, 1940, ed. James D. Ogilvie. Only entries relating to Johnston's public life appear in the printed text; the transcript, though incomplete, contains, in addition, prayers, religious meditations, and particulars of the health and establishment of his family".

[13] Johnston, "The Diary of Archibald Johnston", MS 6248 (27 December 1655 to 15 January 1656), 13 January 1656, 76.

me of a revelation. I asked the Word that goeth alongst with the Spirit and that I would not beleive him if he came without the Law and Testimony which God had joyned with their inspirations and bidden me trye the spirits by it.[14]

Johnston expected a providentially relevant "Word" to accompany any alleged divine leading.

In spite of his classic Reformed piety, Johnston frequently engaged in divination by lot, although the answers he obtained seldom helped to solve the perplexities of life, especially in matters that directly involved his family.[15] We might expect someone of such a mystical tendency to take cognisance of his dreams; yet when he did so, his conclusions did not violate a view that the Word and Spirit should not be separated. Johnston was a vocal champion of the *WCF*, which he embraced with unbridled enthusiasm and commitment, exhibiting at the same time an awareness of the danger of not making the Scriptures the guiding rule of life, itself a transparent confirmation of the extent to which the Word functions as the only rule of faith and life.[16]

At the same time, Johnston employs the insights of his dreams when they harmonise with providentially relevant Scripture texts and suggests that if a text of Scripture seems apposite to the occasion and if a dream concurs with the written Word, then the dream can be considered legitimate illumination:

> I fell asleepe and therin dreamed that God gaive order to a senate of grave counselors whom I saw to provyde me my 7 or 8000 marks be year, and when I was wakened by ones incoming, and upon that I thought agayn on my wyfes lighting on 1 Ki. 17ch. and on my dreame backing it, a good token that God might move the Protector and his Counsel to give us some of our owen.[17]

---

[14] Johnston, "The Diary of Archibald Johnston", MS 6254 (9 November 1658 to 23 January 1659), 76.

[15] Johnston, "The Diary of Archibald Johnston", MS 6247, 46.

[16] He not infrequently urges people to read the *WCF* daily along with the Scriptures. Johnston, "The Diary of Archibald Johnston", MS 6248 (27 December 1655 to 15 January 1656), 84 and 91. Furthermore, he plainly sees that, as a rule of faith, the Bible could be misused as a source of daily guidance, not just in matters of doctrine: "In the ryding down to Kirkliston I urged the first Chapter of the Confession of Faith about the Scriptures as the perfect reule of our fayth and lyfe and so wee should not believe by fancyes and vayne hoopes above what is written not by feares and jealousyes beneath what is written". Johnston, "The Diary of Archibald Johnston", MS 6248 (27 December 1655 to 15 January 1656), 92.

[17] Johnston, "The Diary of Archibald Johnston", MS 6250 (1 July to 27 July 1656), 89.

He regards dreams as both "providences",[18] and "impressions" from God,[19] while acknowledging the difficulty of ascertaining their source. Nevertheless, he is content to attribute to God those dreams which accord with Scripture and are providentially connected to the occasion. Therefore, when he dreams that Samuel Rutherford is consoling him by means of a Bible text that his situation will reach a satisfactory conclusion, Johnston is satisfied that this is divine guidance.[20] Thus Johnston adhered to the advice that he proffered his Quaker acquaintance; he refused to separate the Word from the Spirit in his use of lots, dreams and impressions while he frantically tried to make sense of his crumbling world, even though he did not explain clearly how dreams could guide and yet not be new revelations.

Johnston's Westminster colleague William Strong, in his large treatise on the doctrine of providence, similarly, attributed dreams to providence, but gave a more precise explanation of how he believed God's personal guidance could be discerned in "casual providences":

> There are also some things which are *contingent* or *fortuitous*, that is , though all things be governed by the determinate counsel in God, and there be nothing casual unto him[...]yet in respect of us there are some things which are contingent[...]*without humane election*, and wonderful, and those casual providences are for the good of the Saints in dreams, in lots, in ordering the wills and affections of men, in the slip of a horse, the fall of an house, the meeting of a friend, a man is casually cast upon such places, persons, occasions, as *Saul* when he went forth to seek Asses and found a Kingdom.[21]

In the same way that one might bump into an old friend, God might use dreams to direct the lives of individuals. Just as meeting a friend is not a miracle or a special revelation, so an ordinary dream can have a purely human origin and still be part of God's "determinate counsel" for the individual. Strong's acceptance, in the same treatise, that God spoke to Augustine's mother Monica in a dream should be understood in the light of

---

[18] "At supper wee had many instances of strange providences as[...]Lady Busbyes dream how to cure her palsy[...]". Johnston, "The Diary of Archibald Johnston", MS 6251 (8 October 1656 to 3 November 1656), 104-105.

[19] Johnston, "The Diary of Archibald Johnston", MS 6259 (14 June 1661), 48.

[20] Johnston, "The Diary of Archibald Johnston", MS 6259, 51-52.

[21] William Strong, *A Discourse of the Two Covenants: Wherein the Nature, Differences and Effects of the Covenant of Works and of Grace are Distinctly, Rationally, Spiritually and Practically Discussed; Together with the Considerable Quantity of Practical Cases Dependent Thereon* (London: Francis Tyton, 1678), 428. William Strong (d. 1654) was an Independent who received his education from Cambridge, and became rector at Moore Critchell, but was forced out of his office by royalists and escaped to London, where he became a Westminster divine. Later, in 1647, he was appointed as minister for St. Dunstans-in-the-West. Edward Carlyle, *DNB*, vol. 2, 2021.

this explanation of dreams as providence.[22] This should alert us to be wary of designating such divine speaking in dreams as immediate or special revelation. Thomas Coleman sees biblical dreams functioning in this way also:

> Dreaming, and telling a dreame to ones bedfellow, and neighbour, what more ordinary? Yet *Gideon* from such a relation observed a Divine providence, and an answer from the Almighty.[23]

In summary: Gouge simply consigns revelatory dreams to the past, Rutherford allegorises them, and Johnston and Strong regard them as the workings of providence. Each of these positions is compatible with a cessationism which denies that the Holy Spirit will impart extra-biblical revelation immediately to the soul by way of dreams. The latter two approaches still deserve to be labelled "cessationist", even though they continue to regard dreams as relevant for the contemporary Christian. Explanations given by other Puritans, however, may also imply a continuationist revelatory role for contemporary dreams.

1.1 Continuationism among the Reformed Orthodox[24]

There were five varieties of potential continuationists, though the categorisation of each is only tentative and subject to discussion. There were those who:

1. supposed that angels communicated to human beings through dreams.
2. believed that pious individuals when dying had a unique insight into the divine will.
3. maintained a belief in the divinatory nature of dreams but recognised that this was not the view of Reformed orthodoxy.
4. were ambiguous toward the whole matter of revelatory dreams.
5. were openly and decidedly continuationists.

---

[22] "And so did Austin after his conversion take a great deal of comfort in his mothers covenant interest, and in all the prayers that she did put up to God for him[…]till the Lord in a dream gave her great hopes concerning his salvation". Strong, *Discourse of the Two Covenants*, 204.

[23] Thomas Coleman, *The Christians Course and Complaint, Both in the Pursuit of Happinesse Desired, and for Advantages Slipped in that Pursuit* (London: Christopher Meredith, 1643), 49-50.

[24] Geoffrey Nuttall's seminal study allows for the existence of a strand of Puritan thought which considered extra-biblical revelation possible: Geoffrey Nuttall, *The Holy Spirit in Puritan Faith and Experience* (Oxford: Basil Blackwell, 1947), 24. However, John Murray's review rightly criticises Nuttall's conclusion and shows that the usual Puritan view was that Word and Spirit could not be separated: John Murray, *Collected Writings of John Murray* (Edinburgh: The Banner of Truth Trust, 1982), vol. 3, 325-26.

4.3.1 Two Forms of Supernatural Revelation

The prominent French theologian Moïse Amyraut is representative of the first variety, although his position highlights the quandary of those seventeenth-century theologians who attempted to categorise the role of dreams. Amyraut makes a distinction between revelatory dreams from God[25] and those that come through angels, denying the possibility of the former but allowing the existence of the latter.[26] This distinction makes him a cessationist as far as divine revelation is concerned, but a continuationist with respect to the ongoing function of angelic, uninspired disclosures. John Owen also considers that angels might still speak with men. When Owen comments on Heb. 1:14, he allows angels still to have a revelatory function in the church. While he questions how far God might continue to use the ministrations of angels, noting that this is "hard to determine",[27] he concludes nonetheless:

> so to say that God doth not or may not send his angels unto any of his saints, to communicate his mind unto them as to some particulars of their own duty, according unto his word or to foreshow unto them somewhat of his own approaching work, seems, in my judgement, unwarrantably to limit the Holy One of Israel.[28]

Of course, the challenge for this viewpoint is to explain how one can allow angelic revelations, which presumably proceed from God's will (and which were one of the former modes of revelation), but still deny that they are *divine* or *immediate* revelations.[29] It was more common to attribute dreams to the influence of fallen angels. When Peter Sterry notes that Satan can inspire dreams, this explains for him a source of human rebellion.[30]

The second type of continuationist adopts the position, relatively common in the seventeenth century, of attributing to the dying a mysterious ability to receive divine communication, which according to conventional wisdom became possible as the soul became increasingly detached from the body. Edmund Calamy wrote a series of sermons, published as the collection *The Godly Mans Ark*, the first inspired by the death of one of his godly parishioners, a Mrs Elizabeth Moores. In a postscript to this sermon, he

---

[25] Moses (or Moïse or Moisé) Amyraldus, *A Discourse concerning the Divine Dreams mention'd in Scripture, together with the marks and character by which they might be distinguished from vain Delusions. In a letter to Monsieur Gaches by Moses Amyraldus*, Ja. Lorrde (translator) (London: Walter Kettilby, 1676), 42.

[26] Amyraldus, *A Discourse concerning the Divine Dreams*, 119-28.

[27] John Owen, *An Exposition of the Epistle to the Hebrews* (Edinburgh: Banner of Truth Trust, 1991), vol. 3, 250.

[28] Owen, *An Exposition of the Epistle to the Hebrews*, vol. 3, 250.

[29] We shall discuss the matter of prophecy delivered by angels in Chapter Five, 182-188 below.

[30] Peter Sterry, *The Clouds in which Christ Comes* (London: R. Dawlman, 1648), 19.

recollects the comments he made at her burial. Calamy recounts a revelation Mrs Moores had on the day of her death:

> In the morning of that day in which she dyed she fell into a slumber which she heard (as she thought) one saying to her, *This day thou shalt be with me in Paradise* [...]. When she can hardly speak to express the greatness of her joy, then to hear a voice (as it were) saying to her, This day shalt thou be with me in Paradise. This (in all probability) was *the voice of God and not of Man*.[31]

Calamy qualifies this account in six ways which differentiate the perceived difference between this type of experience and immediate special revelation. First, he tempers the report of her dream with notes in parenthesis: "as she thought", "as it were" and "in all probability". Next, he observes that some might dream of heaven yet go to hell: the point is presumably made in order to emphasise the ambiguity of such experiences. Thirdly, he warns that dreams are not a sufficient evidence of salvation, for they can be of diabolical origin. Fourthly, he notes that the lady in question had been an active Christian for many years. Fifth, he stresses that her sufferings had gone on for over a year. Finally, he underscores that this divine encounter happened when the deceased was "on the brink of eternity".[32] It is unlikely that Calamy would have wished to call Mrs Moores' dream "immediate revelation", partly because the experience hardly qualified as an infallible Word from God, and partly because the words that she heard as the "*voice of God*" were themselves drawn from Scripture (Lk. 23:43). At least, however, we can conclude that something analogous to immediate revelation did occur, although not so unambiguously as to imply a resurgence of the spiritual gift of inspired prophecy which was formerly given for the edification of the church.

4.3.2 The Inconclusive Witness of Some Claims to Revelation

The third group of continuationist includes those in the Reformed tradition who could not quite bring themselves to deny that dreams provided some certainty, even though they knew that their position contradicted the conventional line. The anonymous eighteenth-century Scottish commentary on the *WCF* exhibits the same tension when it explains that dreams are a point of contact between the human and the divine. The author admits that while the *WCF* teaches that revelatory dreams have ceased, in his opinion they remain channels of revelation. It is clear from this example that, paradoxically, a confessional Presbyterian could simply overlook the clear meaning of the subordinate standard on the cessation of revelation - even in

---

[31] Edmund Calamy, *The Godly Mans Ark, or City of Refuge in the Day of His Distress* (London: Thomas Parkhurst and John Hancock, 1693), 130-31.

[32] Calamy, *The Godly Mans Ark*, 130-31.

an age where strict subscription was required.[33] While unsure of precisely how God might use "natural dreams",[34] the author of the Scottish commentary candidly asserts that although "the sense of our confession here does more than insinuate, this method of Revelation is ceased", God nevertheless still communicates through nocturnal visions.[35] Although more certain that other forms of immediate revelation have ceased,[36] the writer nevertheless recognises that one objective of the *WCF* was to deny authenticity to claims of revelatory dreams. Perhaps his ambivalence on the subject highlights the dynamic tension between a firm belief in pervasive providentialism on the one hand, and the cessationism so central to the commitment of Reformed orthodoxy to *sola Scriptura* on the other.

The fourth category comprises those who were ambiguous when they discussed the possibility of contemporary revelatory dreams. John Hacket (1592-1670), who only briefly attended the Assembly,[37] was one of these. He draws a distinction between visionary dreams and revelations:

> "[...] *Pharaoh* and *Nebuchadeneser* had Visions, and understood not what they meant, but when the intelligence of the thing is opened as it was to *Joseph* and *Daniel*, it became a Revelation.[38]

His comments suggest that people may have visionary experiences which are not revelations until a true prophet interprets them. However, if true prophets no longer exist, then presumably we should conclude that visions and dreams can no longer become revelatory in this fashion because they lack a qualified interpreter. Hacket himself does not draw that conclusion and while he cannot ignore the claims of ancient authorities to revelatory dreams, he is frankly sceptical about claims to new visions:

---

[33] See Chapter Seven below for a discussion of the relevance of subscription to the cessationist/continuationist debate.

[34] MS. Wes. 3.3. 1-2 "Exposition of the Westminster Confession of Faith" (Edinburgh: Edinburgh University [New College Library], 1718): "But however great use the author of our being may make of these: yet we are not to dwell on such. Neither also diabolicall dreams[...]" (34).

[35] MS. Wes. 3.3. 1-2 "Exposition of the Westminster Confession of Faith", 37-38.

[36] MS. Wes. 3.3. 1-2 "Exposition of the Westminster Confession of Faith": "[...]Voyces from Heaven[...]. Those to whom such revelations were made had need to know that they were indeed truly from God, and though such ane inquiry may appeare not so material now this Method of Revelation being ceased[...]" (39-42).

[37] Hacket was a convinced Episcopalian and champion of the Prayer Book. He later became Bishop of Coventry and Lichfield following the Restoration. George Perry, "John Hacket", *DNB*, vol. 1, 863.

[38] John Hacket, *A Century of Sermons upon Several Remarkable Subjects* (London: Robert Scott, 1675), 993. See also William Gouge who implied that all visions were revelations: "Visions did differ from bare revelations, because what was in them revealed, came from some visible shape presented to men". Gouge, *Annotations*, Job 4:12.

Let it deter any one that is not possessed with the spirit of Arrogance, to think that he is possessed with the spirit of Divination [...]. There is no hope that we vile sinners should see such Visions[...]".[39]

However, his scepticism did not descend into a thorough going agnosticism, for he seems to have believed that Augustine's mother Monica had genuine revelatory dreams. Part of his argument against those of his contemporaries who claimed to have received revelation is that Monica was that rare class of person who "knew when *God* gave her a supernatural inspiration in her sleep, and when it was but a common dream".[40] Hacket might possibly have limited such dreams to the time of the early church or he may have believed that what was possible for Monica was also possible in his day, but he says neither of these things.

John Ley, too, appears to have asserted in his dispute with Antinomian John Saltmarsh that contemporary visions and dreams could be revelatory, in spite of Ley's statement elsewhere that miracles were limited to the early church.[41] In *Light for Smoke,* Ley rejects Saltmarsh's interpretation of Joel 2:28 and Acts 2:17. Saltmarsh concludes that visions are superior to dreams and that the worth of young men, therefore, exceeds that of old men.[42] Specifically, Saltmarsh develops the theory that young men have visions concerning church reformation, while old men merely dream about such a renovation. Ley responds that revelations imparted through visions are not more excellent than those given by dreams because dreams too appear in Scripture as bearers of revelation. He cites biblical examples, and dreams given to Jerome and Zwingli, placing special emphasis on the Swiss Reformer's dream because it revealed or at least clarified doctrine.[43]

---

[39] Hacket, *A Century of Sermons upon Several Remarkable Subjects*, 994.

[40] Hacket, *A Century of Sermons upon Several Remarkable Subjects*, 994. See Augustine, *The Confessions*, 6, 13, 23: "At my request and at her own desire she petitioned you every day with a strong cry from her heart, that by a vision you would show her what was to happen after my coming marriage. But you never willed to grant this. She saw certain illusory and fantastic images, the product of the human spirit's efforts in its urgent concern for an answer. The account which she gave me was not marked by the confidence she normally showed when you disclosed the future to her, but she spoke contemptuously of what she saw. She used to say that, by a certain smell indescribable in words, she could tell the difference between your revelation and her own soul dreaming". Translation from Henry Chadwick (tr.), *Saint Augustine*: *Confessions* (Oxford: Oxford University Press, 1992), 108.

[41] See Ley, *Annotations*, Luke 9:2 and Mark 16, where Ley restricts miracles to the early church. Ley may have seen miracles and divine dreams as different categories.

[42] See John Saltmarsh, *The Smoke in the Temple, Wherein is a Designe for Peace and Reconciliation of Believers* [...](London: G. Calvert, 1646), 29.

[43] John Ley, *Light for Smoke or a Cleare and Distinct Reply]...]to a Darke and Confused Answer in a Booke Made, and Intituled The Smoke in the Temple, by John Saltmarsh [...]"* (London: Christopher Meridith, 1646), 26-27. The doctrine clarified

Contending that great matters too may be unveiled in dreams, Ley adds that old men such as the author of the book of Revelation see visions and that therefore Saltmarsh's conclusions are erroneous.

In an apparent about-face, Ley then denounces Saltmarsh's claims that revelations may come to the young visionaries and to elderly dreamers. Ley calls such revelations "a vapour of a young mans bragge, or the vanity of a sick mans dreame".[44] Had he not already cited the revelatory dreams of Jerome and Zwingli, we might conclude that he was unsympathetic towards the possibility that such revelations could appear after the final book of Scripture was written rather than understand him to be endorsing claims to revelation.

In addition to dismissing Saltmarsh's view of the status of visions and dreams, Ley also criticises Saltmarsh's opinion that ecclesiastical government will be reordered according to instructions received through an angelic revelation:

> [I]f you refuse the Scripture light in expectation of Evangelicall Revelations, take heed you comply not with the Papists[...]making Propheticall light or revelation a note of the Church, and pretending Revelations from Angels[...]".[45]

He concedes that he does not doubt that such revelations "for the most part" offer smoke for light.[46] But he does not dismiss *in toto* Saltmarsh's hope that extra-biblical revelation persists for believers. Rather, Ley challenges him:

---

was that of Christ's alleged presence in the elements of the Eucharist. For Zwingli's dream, see Abraham Ruchat who describes Zwingli's experience of being directed in a dream to Exodus 12:11 in the LXX, where the same Greek verb (ἐστί) is found as that used in the institution of the Lord's Supper: "qui lui indiqua le passage du Livre de l'Exode, C. XII.v.11. *C'est la Pâque de l'Eternel*. A son reveil il courut à la Bible Grecque, où il trouva ces paroles, πάσχα ἐστί κυρίῳ qui signifient la même chose" (303). Zwingli himself was uncertain about the colour of the figure that revealed this to him: "*ater fuerit an albus non memini*" (303). Abraham Ruchat, *Histoire de la Réformation de la Suisse, où l'on voit tout ce qui s'est Passé de plus Remarquable, depuis l'An 1516. jusqu'en l'An 1556., dans les Églises des XIII. Cantons, & des États Confédérez qui Composent avec eux le L. Corps Helvétique* (Geneva: Marc-Michel Bousquet, 1727), tom. 1, at 301-303. For Jerome's famous dream, in which he was accused of being a Ciceronian and not a Christian, see Jerome, *To Eustochium*, Letter 22, 30 (*NPNF* second ser., 6, 35-36). J. N. D. Kelly, *Jerome: His Life, Writings and Controversies* (London: Gerald Duckworth, 1975), 41-44, concludes that Jerome had an actual experience, but that it arose from deep psychological tensions; see also Harald Hagendahl, *Latin Fathers and the Classics: A Study on the Apologists, Jerome, and other Christian Writers* (Gothenburg: Gothenburg University Press, 1958), 318-28.

[44] Ley, *Light for Smoke*, 28.
[45] Ley, *Light for Smoke*, 87.
[46] Ley, *Light for Smoke*, 87.

[I]f you have any warrant, any good ground for such a vision and revelation from heaven, shew it; it is a matter of too great a moment to be taken upon trust, upon your bare word[...]".[47]

At this juncture, Ley is unlikely to be suggesting the possibility of new revelations, because Saltmarsh's own riposte suggests that it highly improbable that Ley believed that immediate revelation continued in his day. In Saltmarsh's response to what Ley had said about the superiority of old men's dreams over young men's visions, he accuses Ley of joking, or as he puts it, "Jeasting":

Why are you so much in the defence of Jeasting, and so serious in your Scripture proofes for it? Take heed of strengthening corrupt nature by Scripture[...]".[48]

The best explanation of this surprising comment is that Saltmarsh knew Ley to be sceptical towards modern claims to immediate revelation, for he seems to have thought that Ley's interpretation made illicit use of Bible texts to ridicule his opponent.[49]

The views of both Hacket and Ley invite caution when we consider whether some Puritans could be classified as cessationists or continuationists. The ambiguity we see in these divines, however, is not present in those who were stricter continuationists.

4.3.3. Stricter Continuationists/Continuationism

Although few, a minority of eminent Puritans did exhibit an unequivocal continuationism. For example, the famous, if theologically idiosyncratic, Richard Baxter (1615-1691), in his *Christian Directory*, plainly allows that God may yet bring new revelations:

It is *possible* that God may make new Revelations to particular persons about their particular duties, events or matters of fact, in subordination to the Scripture, either by inspiration, vision, or apparition or voice.[50]

---

[47] Ley, *Light for Smoke*, 88.

[48] John Saltmarsh, *An End of One Controversie: Being an Answer or Letter to Master Ley's Large Last Book Called Light for Smoke* (London: G. Calvert, 1646), 9.

[49] See also Ley, *Annotations*, Matt. 27:19, where he proposes that the dream experienced by Pilate's wife was most likely a "special providence".

[50] Richard Baxter, *A Christian Directory: Or, A Summ of Practical Theologie and Cases of Conscience* (London: Nevil Simmons, 1678), 185. Baxter taught a novel doctrine of the atonement, called by its detractors "neonomianism". Christ's death was said to have brought about a "new law" which was obeyed through repentance and faith, which in turn became one's personal righteousness: James Packer, "Richard Baxter", *NDT*, 82-83. For biographical information, see Barker, *Puritan Profiles*, 288-94; for Baxter's ministry at Kidderminster, see Nigel Knowles, *Richard Baxter of Kidderminster* (Bewdley: Star and Garter, 2000), especially 61. On Baxter's polemic

Baxter's views were echoed in Westminster divine, William Bridge (1600-1671). Bridge believed that new inspiration was still possible through miraculous revelatory modalities. As we shall see, he classifies those supernatural modes chronologically, distinguishing between their status before and after the completion of the New Testament Scriptures. In the Old Testament era and during the foundational period of the church, these modes were God's "standing" ordinances or the officially appointed means for conveying God's will. Today, however, they are *non*-standing ordinances, though they remain operative. We could describe the distinction as "normative" and "non-normative" ordinances.

One of five prominent dissenters at the Assembly, Bridge was an active participant and debater.[51] He appears in Wayne Spear's list as the thirteenth most regular speaker at the Assembly during the debates over church government, so his contribution was significant.[52] Among his colleagues at Westminster, Bridge held a minority position in the debate concerning whether or not God still communicates his will through dreams, visions and voices. Bridge reveals his unequivocal continuationism in a series of three sermons on 2 Pet. 1:19.[53] Ironically, these sermons, entitled *"Scripture Light the Most Sure Light"*, were designed to promote the importance of Scripture. Published in 1656, they were probably preached near this date, close to a decade after the completion of the *WCF* but two years before the composition of the *Savoy Declaration*. In his first sermon, Bridge rejects the view that his text teaches "a revelation and light which God doth set up in the soul, which when a man hath obtained, then he is to take heed to the written word no longer".[54] He adds: because Isa. 8:20 points us to the law

---

against Antinomianism, see Tim Cooper, *Fear and Polemic in Seventeenth-Century England* (Aldershot: Ashgate, 2001), especially 60-68. On Baxter's own claim to spiritual insight bordering on a "revelation", see 96-98.

[51] Bridge's life had followed a path similar to that of his Independent colleagues. He was born in Cambridgeshire and educated at Emmanuel College Cambridge, later becoming a Fellow of the same College. He was granted a lectureship at St Peter's, London in 1630 and later at both Colchester, Essex and St. George's Tombland, Norwich. He was appointed rector at St. Peter's, Hungate, Norwich in 1636. Suspended and excommunicated for not conforming to Bishop Wren's demands, he went to Holland and on his return was appointed to the Westminster Assembly. Bridge continued in active ministry until a final illness led to his death. Barker, *Puritan Profiles*, 84-87.

[52] Wayne Spear, "Covenanted Uniformity in Religion: The Influence of the Scottish Commissioners upon the Ecclesiology of the Westminster Assembly" (unpublished Ph.D thesis, University of Pittsburgh, 1976), 362.

[53] A proof-text for the *WCF* phrase in Ch.1:1: "which maketh the Holy Scripture to be most necessary".

[54] William Bridge, *The Works of the Rev. William Bridge, M.A.* (London: Thomas Tegg, 1845), vol. 1, 401.

and the testimony, "if therefore any man do pretend light[...]so as to lay by the word written, that light is no true light".[55] Moreover, it is not valid to interpret Isaiah to promise believers more light which will supersede the Scriptures.[56] Bridge assures his listeners that Scripture light is true light, while false lights "do lead men into fens and bogs".[57] The refrain in these sermons[58] is that Scripture provides full and sufficient light and is a "rule for life".[59]

The substance of Bridge's three sermons comprises a discussion of eight "lights" which he detects in Christian experience. The "lights" are respectively revelations or visions, dreams, impressions made upon the heart with or without the Word, experience, the law and light within, providence, reason and astrology. With numerous qualifications, he subordinates them to Scripture and thus makes them of limited practical value without a link to the Word written. In all of them, "there is no more light in them than what they do borrow" from the Scriptures,[60] whose light exceeds or goes beyond "revelations or visions, and the light thereof".[61] Thus visions and dreams for revelation are not limited to the Old Testament or the primitive New Testament church, even though they suited those periods when the people of God were in their infancy.[62] Now, however, their usefulness is impeded, because they can be counterfeits originating from the Devil, as can be demonstrated from Martin Luther's personal experience.[63]

---

[55] Bridge, *The Works of the Rev. William Bridge,* vol. 1, 401.

[56] Bridge, *The Works of the Rev. William Bridge,* vol. 1, 401-402.

[57] Bridge, *The Works of the Rev. William Bridge,* vol. 1, 412.

[58] Bridge, *The Works of the Rev. William Bridge,* vol. 1, 433.

[59] Bridge, *The Works of the Rev. William Bridge,* vol. 1, 412.

[60] Bridge, *The Works of the Rev. William Bridge,* vol. 1, 413.

[61] Bridge, *The Works of the Rev. William Bridge,* vol. 1, 413.

[62] Bridge, *The Works of the Rev. William Bridge,* vol. 1, 414.

[63] For Luther on the Devil, see Heiko Oberman, *Luther: Man between God and the Devil* (New Haven: Yale University Press, 1989), especially 102-106. Luther's wariness concerning visions is found throughout his writings: "One must rely solely on the testimony which Jesus Christ, God's Son, brought down from heaven and believe it. This Christians do. They could, of course, make much of the revelation and visions of God. But they listen only to the testimony of this Man and believe Him". Martin Luther, *Luther's Works*, ed. Jaroslav Pelikan (Saint Louis: Concordia Publishing house, 1970), vol. 22, 322. Or again, "Christ has been prepared, revealed, and placed to be seen by all flesh. Thus in the New Testament the Holy Spirit has been poured into the hearts of the godly, yet He has also been declared openly by very obvious signs to confirm the Word. Therefore it is nothing that our prophets are looking for support for their own error from this text when they say that they have the Holy Spirit and that it is necessary that a person feel the Holy Spirit, although they themselves have not yet given evidence of the Spirit. To such we must respond in this way: 'It is not enough to have the Spirit poured in. Indeed, this benefits you alone. But you must show and openly give evidence of that manifestation and outpouring of the Spirit in order that all flesh may see it.' Because

Bridge draws the lesson from Luther that just as the reformer had concluded, "I know no picture of Christ but the Scripture", so, "[t]herein is Christ lively pictured, described, and set forth before our eyes: it is not so in revelations and visions".[64] This very negative assessment of visions and revelations is compounded when Bridge goes on to ask:

> [I]f God should now speak unto you by visions, or visional revelations, how would you know that this were the voice of God, and not a delusion of Satan?[65]

Even if the Christian gains truth in keeping with Scripture from such an encounter, "who doth not know that the devil will speak an hundred truths that he may croud in one lie amongst them[?]".[66] Neither should we conclude that a revelation comes from God because of its exalted content, for Satan tempted Eve with a matter of extreme importance. Furthermore, even if some future event is revealed and it subsequently comes to pass, there is still no way to be sure that the revelation was not a Satanic delusion.[67] Neither can one know from a "taste" or subjective evaluation that such an incident was genuinely of divine origin.[68]

Moreover, the act of seeking revelation may lead a person away from the Scriptures, as happened to those in Luther's day who "pretended unto great discoveries and revelations".[69] The same thing has happened to those who lead one into "popery and superstition".[70] Furthermore, asks Bridge, if Luther had "hearkened to revelations and visions, and not kept close to the Scripture, what had [i.e. would have] become of his reformation?"[71] And, he adds, revelations may make one an atheist, because the only difference between an "atheist, or a pagan infidel, and a Christian [...][is] that the Christian is for the Scripture".[72]

---

they cannot do this, just as our prophets never can, let them with us remain students of Holy Scripture. We now have no revelation of the Holy Spirit other than Holy Scripture". Luther, *Luther's Works*, vol. 18, 107.

[64] Bridge, *The Works of the Rev. William Bridge*, vol. 1, 414. Luther says something similar. "In his epistles, therefore, Paul sets forth and urges Jesus Christ in almost every verse. He sets Him forth through the Word, since Christ cannot be set forth any other way than through the Word and cannot be grasped any other way than through faith". Luther, *Luther's Works*, vol. 26, 356.

[65] Bridge, *The Works of the Rev. William Bridge*, vol. 1, 414.

[66] Bridge, *The Works of the Rev. William Bridge*, vol. 1, 414.

[67] Bridge, *The Works of the Rev. William Bridge*, vol. 1, 414-15. (415 is wrongly numbered as 416).

[68] Bridge, *The Works of the Rev. William Bridge*, vol. 1, 415.

[69] Bridge, *The Works of the Rev. William Bridge*, vol. 1, 415.

[70] Bridge, *The Works of the Rev. William Bridge*, vol. 1, 416. Mohammed is an example.

[71] Bridge, *The Works of the Rev. William Bridge*, vol. 1, 416.

[72] Bridge, *The Works of the Rev. William Bridge*, vol. 1, 416.

Notwithstanding his negative assessment of such a search for additional revelation, Bridge poses a telling question: "but, you will say, may not God speak by extraordinary visions and revelations, in these days of ours?" He responds in the affirmative: "Yes, without all doubt he may: God is not to be limited, he may speak in what way he please".[73] This astonishing answer concedes that God may grant even a revelation such as God's instruction to Abraham to sacrifice his son Isaac.[74] Nonetheless, even in a case like this, the commandment in Scripture, "thou shalt not kill", is a surer and more certain rule.

As we can see from his scepticism about visions and revelations and from this example, Bridge does not explain why a believer should heed visions and revelations, even though he admits that God may give them. Of the latter he cites accounts from Foxe's *Book of Martyrs* and a prophecy allegedly given to Luther, as examples of authentic divine revelations.[75] Bridge takes a less agnostic stance, concluding:

> The Lord may work a miracle, and being wrought, I am bound to receive it; but I may not put God upon the working of a miracle[...]without tempting him.[76]

[Richard] Greenham is the only near contemporary Bridge cites as an authority to endorse his view that God may still give a vision agreeable to the Word.[77]

Having acknowledged that visions may be God-given, it is not surprising that Bridge allows that God may also speak both in dreams and directly to

---

[73] Bridge, *The Works of the Rev. William Bridge*, vol. 1, 416-17.

[74] Bridge, *The Works of the Rev. William Bridge*, vol. 1, 417.

[75] Bridge, *The Works of the Rev. William Bridge*, vol. 1, 417. Again, Bridge gives no references for these allusions. Parenthetically, we should notice here the difference between Bridge and others who endorsed Lutheran "prophecy" as legitimate. Samuel Rutherford, for example, interprets Luther's "prophecy" to be the leading of Scripture and the Spirit rather than a vision or any other type of immediate revelation. Samuel Rutherford, *A Survey of the Spirituall Antichrist.[...]*" (London: Andrew Crooke, 1648), 42.

[76] Bridge, *The Works of the Rev. William Bridge*, vol. 1, 417. God will even commend someone who is very backward in listening to or in acknowledging any revelation or vision. Bridge, *The Works of the Rev. William Bridge*, vol. 1, 418.

[77] Bridge, *The Works of the Rev. William Bridge*, vol. 1, 419. Bridge gives no reference, but he could have had in mind this statement by Richard Greenham: "To one that said she had a thing told her in the spirit that should undoubtedly come to passe[...]we must trie these motions by the word, whether they be fore spirituall or temporall things: if they be of God and according to his word beleeve them for the words sake and not onely because of the revelations". Richard Greenham, *The Workes of the Reverend and Faithfull Servant of Jesus Christ M. Richard Greenham* (London: Cuthbert Burbie, 1605), 473. On Greenham (1535?-1594?), see Alexander Gordon, "Richard Greenham", *DNB*, vol. 1, 834,

the soul.[78] Bridge bases his conclusions upon his novel exegesis of the *WCF* cessationist proof-text Heb. 1:1-2, an interpretation that parts company with the standard expositions of his Westminster colleagues. As we noted above, Bridge's explanation of these verses centres on the status of ordinances, which are God's instituted methods of imparting grace to his church.[79] In the Old Testament era, dreams, visions and other miraculous events were God's standing ordinances, but Scripture, preaching, prayer and the New Testament sacraments have replaced them in the new dispensation. Furthermore, though their status has changed, God can still convey revelation through dreams and visions in an *ad hoc* or non-standard manner. At this point, rather than using the language of cessation which is more usual, Bridge asks:

> If there be such an ordinance still, wherein we are still to wait on God, why doth the apostle make this difference between times past, and the present time of the Son?[80]

Bridge's answer is to transfer the role of settled ordinance to Scripture, without abrogating any of the former miraculous methods of revelation, even though he advises that we should no longer look for God's mind in the earlier modes. It is not so much, for Bridge, that Scripture renders visions and dreams obsolete, as that Scripture has replaced them as the standard, formal and normative vehicle of God's will, although God may still reveal his mind occasionally through these now uncommon and subordinate methods. It appears that Bridge at this point feels that his contemporaries will not agree, for once again he invokes the assistance of Martin Luther, implying that Luther's words are a commentary on Heb. 1:1-2 and are in harmony with Bridge's opinion:

> Nay, says Luther, but there is such a sufficiency in the Scripture, that though some men should have visions, dreams and voices; yet the Scripture is so full, that *nec curo, nec desidero*, I neither care for nor desire them.[81]

---

[78] Bridge, *The Works of the Rev. William Bridge,* vol. 1, 421.

[79] See 161 above.

[80] Bridge, *The Works of the Rev. William Bridge,* vol. 1, 422.

[81] Bridge, *The Works of the Rev. William Bridge,* vol. 1, 422-23. Bridge, who gives no reference here, may be thinking of Luther's commentary on Genesis 37:10: "Therefore the Holy Spirit is first accustomed to suggest dreams, then to show an explanation, and thirdly, to carry them out, and this can be beautifully applied to the Trinity of Persons. The Father gives the dreams, the Son interprets them, and the Holy Spirit carries them out. I call these true and prophetic dreams which do not deceive. But concerning these I do not assume the power of judgment for myself, except *a posteriori;* the rest of the throng of dreams I completely despise. I do, indeed, have dreams from time to time, which move me somewhat, but I think little of them and I have made a pact with my Lord that I want to believe Moses and the prophets. I do not desire dreams for

In spite of Bridge's careful attempt to justify contemporary extra-biblical modes of revelation and to qualify them so comprehensively that they are practically irrelevant, his discussion radically reinterprets the standard Puritan definition of revelatory visions and dreams in two ways. First, most Puritans believed that revelations from Old Testament times were self-authenticating, so that it was left to the prophet to know if he had received the infallible word of God. A true prophet, it was believed, could readily distinguish God-given signs from those derived from Satanic or human influence.[82] Secondly, Bridge's position which concedes that God may still reveal himself as he did when ordering Abraham to sacrifice Isaac, effectively makes God's revelations contradictory and therefore error-prone. Bridge demands that whoever believes he has received such a vision must submit the revelation to the judgement of Scripture.

It is tempting to think here that Bridge speaks hypothetically or even ironically, because of his denial that such revelations are useful – indeed he avers that claims to revelations through the modalities external to Scripture should be ignored. Yet later, having conceded that immediate revelations have continued, he agrees that those revelations such as Abraham experienced are still possible. While this is foreign to the Reformed orthodox of Bridge's generation, his idiosyncrasy on this matter was even recognised by opponents of orthodoxy.

The Quakers were to be the most vocal opponents of the cessationist stance they perceived in the Westminster theology, believing that the Reformed orthodox made a fundamental mistake in confining the Word of God to Scripture. Bridge's difference on this point was highlighted by George Whitehead (1636?-1723), an important early English Quaker, who shows how Bridge's position was seen by those who maintained that contemporary immediate revelation could be both valid and authoritative. In his critique of these sermons by Bridge, Whitehead takes issue with Bridge's emphasis on the superiority of "Scripture-light" and with his appeals to the apostles who:

> hoped through the word or spirit of prophecy in them, and such did not deny the giving place to the dawning of the special Light and Revelation in the heart, as *W. Bridge* in his blindness hath done[ ]".[83]

---

this life and have no need of them for the life to come". Luther, *Luther's Works*, vol. 6, 333.

[82] See, for example, William Jamison, *Verus Patroclus: Or, the Weapons of Quakerism, the Weakness of Quakerism* (Edinburgh: 1689) [no other publishing details given], 65.

[83] George Whitehead, *The Law and Light Within, The most sure Rule or Light, which Sheweth the Right Use and End of the Scripture, Manifested in Opposition to Several False Principles Inserted in a Book Intituled Scripture Light the Most Sure Light, by William Bridge, the Great Pastor and Reverend Father, so Accounted, of the Church at*

Whitehead criticises Bridge's teaching that the Spirit within is not the *"rule of our goodness and lives"*,[84] but also recognises correctly that Bridge is not fully in tune with Reformed orthodoxy, and he charges Bridge with being in conflict with his fellow "priests" in two respects. First, Bridge's opinion that Scripture is superior to other modes of revelation contradicts the opinion of "his brethren the Priests [*viz.* clergy]".[85] Whitehead recognises that Bridge's colleagues believe revelatory visions and dreams conveying the Word of God in the Old Testament dispensation and in the apostolic era were equal to the revelation of Scripture. Whitehead also detects a second conflict between Bridge and his colleagues. Many, unlike Bridge, "do not own revelations to be manifest in these dayes".[86] Whitehead is broadly accurate on this latter point. He also takes exception to Bridge's scepticism about on-going revelation and accuses Bridge of "gross ignorance" in claiming that today no one can discern whether a revelation is from God or from the Devil.[87]

Whitehead has correctly recognised Bridge's difference from his colleagues at crucial points. The exegetical conclusions Bridge draws from Heb. 1:1-2 demonstrate his divergence from the overwhelming cessationist commitment of most Reformed orthodox. In this matter, Bridge is isolated from his co-religionists by his espousal of a continuationist stance. Whitehead, naturally for his part, believed that Bridge did not go far enough.

Whitehead also had other colleagues who stood directly against the Westminster theology and who wrote polemical critiques of the *WCF*, its authors and its adherents. These opponents of the *WCF* provide a valuable insight into how antagonists towards Reformed orthodoxy comprehended Puritan religious epistemology in general and the meaning of the cessationist clause in *WCF* 1:1 in particular.

4.4 The Quaker Polemic – Reaction to the Westminster Cessationist View

The sects of "enthusiasts" which flourised in the 1640s were a direct threat to those Presbyterians who sought a unified church under Presbyterian

---

Yarmouth in Norfolk (London: 1662) [no further publishing details], 2. For a sympathetic biography of Whitehead, see John Barlow, *George Whitehead: The Last of the Early Friends* (London: Headley Brothers, 1908), especially 38-39 for the relief from persecution which followed the accession of William and Mary.

[84] Whitehead, *The Law and Light Within*, 6.

[85] Whitehead, *The Law and Light Within*, 5. Bridge did not contradict Reformed orthodoxy at this point, because the Reformed orthodox and he both agreed that in the Old Testament dispensation visions and dreams were on a par with Scripture, because they were in the place of Scripture, and often became Scripture.

[86] Whitehead, *The Law and Light Within*, 5.

[87] Whitehead, *The Law and Light Within*, 5-6.

government. The tolerance of the English army infuriated those who, like Rutherford, had hoped for a "pure" reformation. We sense his antipathy and frustration in *A Survey of the Spirituall Antichrist*:

> And now the *Army* send Laws to *Parliament* to remove the penall statutes against all hereticks, what ever they bee, *Arrians, Libertines, Davi[d] Georgians, Familists, Antiscripturists,* such as deny *there is a God, a Saviour who bought them, Antinomians*[…]".[88]

Later Quakers, however, proved to be the greatest challenge to a Reformed orthodox spiritual hegemony in England, Scotland and New England.[89] Quakers questioned the central Protestant doctrine of the unity of the Word and Spirit when they argued that the *WCF* improperly denied the possibility of "immediate revelations". George Fox himself denounced the claims of the *Savoy Confession* and the *WCF* that revelation had ceased, which he understood to mean that all new extra-biblical immediate revelation had concluded.[90] Some Quakers considered the *WCF* was simply inconsistent on this subject, but when they engaged confessional Presbyterians and Independents in debate they did so believing that it was in fundamental error. The manner in which the Reformed orthodox responded suggests that the Quakers had understood the *WCF* correctly.

William Parker may have been an early Quaker, because his opposition to the Westminster religious epistemology is similar to that of later members of the same movement. His published comments on the Assembly and the *WCF*, however, predate the establishment of the Quaker movement in England. Parker wrote the first detailed critical appraisal of the *WCF*, entitled *The Late Assembly of Divines Confession of Faith Examined*.[91] An extensive critique, it provoked a vigorous response from Richard Baxter. In

---

[88] Rutherford, *A Survey of the Spirituall Antichrist*, 336.

[89] Even the nineteenth-century commentator John MacPherson sees the need to emphasise that the *WCF* excludes claims of the Quaker type concerning revelation. John MacPherson, *The Westminster Confession of Faith. With Introduction and Notes by the Rev. John MacPherson, M.A., Findhorn* (Edinburgh: T& T Clark, 1881), 37.

[90] See George Fox, *Something in Answer to that Book Called the Church-Faith Set Forth by Independents and Others; Agreed upon by Divine Messengers, Meeting at the Savoy in London. And also, to that Book, Intituled, the Confession of Faith, Approved on by the Church of Scotland* (London: Robert Wilson, 1660), 17 and 19. In Fox's view, *WCF* 1 denies all new revelation including prophecy.

[91] W[William?]. Parker, *The Late Assembly of Divines Confession of Faith Examined. As it was Presented by Them unto the Parliament. Wherein Many of Their Excesses and Defects, of Their Confusions and Disorders, of Their Errors and Contradictions are Presented, Both to Themselves and Others* (London: 1651) [no further publishing details are given]. For interaction with Parker's work, see the Presbyterian scholar William Jamison's, *Verus Patroclus: Or, the Weapons of Quakerism, the Weakness of Quakerism*. Jamison calls William Parker an Arminian and refutes his commentary on *WCF* 3 (237-72).

his own confession of faith, Baxter argues that it is not necessary to subscribe to the *WCF*, although, unfortunately, he does not shed any light on how he understands the cessationist clause.[92] Parker, who addresses his treatise to Parliament, takes issue with every chapter of the *WCF*. His first criticism is the subject of this thesis and illustrates not only how well he understands the *WCF*'s strict cessationism, but also that therein lies its initial and primary error:

> For first, you say, *Section* 1. That those former ways of Gods revealing his will unto his people are now ceased; where, if you by those former wayes, understand such wayes and meanes whereby God either ordinarily instructed the people, as he taught the Families of the Patriarches, by the Patriarches themselves, *Gen.*18.19. and the people of the old world by the preaching of *Noah*, 2. *Pet.*2.5 or extraordinarily, by Angels, Dreams, Visions, Inspirations, and the like, revealed his will to the Prophets and Apostles of old, you are very much mistaken.[93]

Parker uses two arguments against the *WCF* cessationist stance. The first cites the appearance of an angel in Germany in his own day who prophesied an invasion of the "Turks"; the second is based upon texts of Scripture which he contends are contrary to the *WCF*'s position. He appeals to several passages (including Num. 12:6 and Joel 2:28-29) which he believes contradict the *WCF* cessationist clause, and which prove instead that revelational prophecy continues.[94] Parker does not seem conscious of a view that the divines argued only that "Scripture-producing" prophecy had ceased, as he believes that *WCF* 1: 2 uses Rev. 22.18 as a proof-text to suggest that all miraculous methods of divine disclosure have ceased, a position which he opposes. Nevertheless, Parker understands that new extra-biblical revelation would not contradict Scripture, but rather would vindicate it and clarify existing doctrine based upon it.[95] Furthermore, Parker wishes

---

[92] Baxter writes: "And though I have read over the exceptions of one William Parker, against the Assemblies confession of Faith, which whosoever reads, may see with half an ey[e] that the author was a Papist. He sets up the main body of Popish doctrine; only instead of the Popes supremacy and Infallibility, he draws people to receive that Doctrine from some new inspired prophets; but if these cheaters could draw people once to receive the Doctrine, it were easie to disgrace those pretended Prophets, and to take them down out of the chair at their pleasure, and so set up the Pope again". Richard Baxter, *Rich: Baxter's Confession of His Faith, Especially Concerning the Interest of Repentance and Sincere Obedience to Christ, in Our Justification & Salvation* (London: Thos. Underhil and Fra. Tyton, 1655), 23.

[93] Parker, *The Late Assembly of Divines Confession of Faith Examined*, 6.

[94] Parker, *The Late Assembly of Divines Confession of Faith Examined*, 6-8. The others are Gen. 18:19; 2 Pet. 2:5; Isa. 59:21; Amos 3:7; Matt. 28:34; Rev. 6:9-11; Rev. 12:17; and Wisdom 7:27 from the Apocrypha. Parker's use of the Apocrypha may have partly given rise to Baxter's comment that Parker was a "Papist".

[95] Parker, *The Late Assembly of Divines Confession of Faith Examined*, 10-12.

to supplement *WCF* 1:10 with "public Spirits" as well as "private Spirits", and intends the Holy Spirit to be the judge of both – a judgement that could, in Parker's view, either be concomitant with Scripture or not.[96] Finally he adds:

> The only exception that we take against your tenth and last section, is this, That you limit the holy Ghost, as if he was inherent in the Scriptures.[97]

Parker's opposition to the *WCF's* binding of the Word and Spirit foreshadows later Quaker opposition to what the *WCF* taught about the cessation of immediate revelation. Quakerdom's most extensive rebuttal of Westminster religious epistemology, however, would come from the pen of George Keith.

Although it would be profitable to undertake a detailed study of what the Quaker luminary Robert Barclay has to say about the *WCF*,[98] we will attempt to address the more extensive rebuttal produced by George Keith (1639?-1716) of Westminster's teaching concerning the cessation of immediate revelation. Keith covers the same ground as Barclay, but also interacts with the *WCF* more copiously. Keith was born into a Presbyterian home in Aberdeenshire, but became a Quaker in 1662.[99] In 1700, after a tumultuous career during which he was imprisoned several times and was finally disowned by other Quaker leaders, he conformed to the established Church in England, having publicly retracted his former opinions.[100] As one initially intent on entering the Presbyterian ministry, Keith presumably would have been acquainted with the *WCF* and with the general construal of the cessationist clause in *WCF* 1:1.

---

[96] Parker, *The Late Assembly of Divines Confession of Faith Examined*, 15.

[97] Parker, *The Late Assembly of Divines Confession of Faith Examined*, 16.

[98] See Chapter Three, 126, n68 above.

[99] In 1702, Keith became one of the first missionaries to America for the *Society for the Promotion of the Gospel*. It was his second visit, as he had already lived there for a time as a Quaker. He returned to England in 1704 and, forced to sell his books, lived the rest of his life in comparative poverty. Keith was an important and able Quaker controversialist, as well as an Oriental scholar and mathematician with an M.A. from Marischal College, Aberdeen. For biographical details, see Alexander Gordon, "George Keith", *DNB*, vol. 1, 1112.

[100] He writes, that he (Keith) has asserted: "both in Speech and Print, too frequently, that the Spirit within, meaning the inward Evidence of the Spirit, as touching the great Matters of the Christian Faith and Practise, was the principal Rule of Faith and Life, wherein, I acknowledge my Error and great Mistake[…]". George Keith, *The Deism of William Penn and his Brethren, Destructive to the Christian Religion, Exposed and Plainly Laid Open, in The Examination and Refutation of His Late Reprinted Book […]"* (London: Brab. Aylmer, 1699), 3. See also George Keith, *George Keith's Explications of Divers Passages Contained in his Former Books[…]"* (London: B. Alymer and Rich. Baldwin, 1697).

One of Keith's most important works, *Immediate Revelation Not Ceased*, was first published in 1668.[101] In it, he discusses the view of the *WCF* and the Assembly on this matter. Although Keith denies that there will be any further gospel revelation, like Parker he believes that the canon might conceivably be supplemented.[102] Nevertheless, he does not plead the "necessary continuance" of audible voices, visible appearances of angels or of Christ, nor of dreams and visions or external miracles. In this he makes an important concession, knowing that the "national way", as he calls the position of the Reformed orthodox, denies the continuance of these types of revelation.[103]

The "immediate revelation" which Keith understands to continue is a work of the Holy Spirit, presenting the "substance" of a revelation to the mind or the soul. We can characterise his view of this kind of revelation as objective rather than subjective, because he implies that the revelation has added some external substance to the soul. The rationale for this position may be that it preserves his contention that revelation comes from without rather from within.[104]

Keith teaches that immediate revelation still guides Christian lives. Since his examples include such matters as believers choosing marriage-partners or deciding where to live, he has in mind more than matters of doctrine or ethics.[105] In the new birth which a believer undergoes, Keith asserts that

---

[101] George Keith, *Immediate Revelation (or Jesus Christ the Eternal Son of God, Revealed in Man. Revealing the Knowledge of God, and the Things of his Kingdom, Immediately) Not Ceased, but Remaining a Standing and Perpetual Ordinance in the Church of Christ, and being of Indispensable Necessity, as to the Whole Body in General, so to Every Member thereof: Every True Believer in Particular, Asserted and Demonstrated. And the Objections that Have any Seeming Weight Against it Answered* (London: 1675) [no further publishing details are given].

[102] Keith, *Immediate Revelation*, 3-5.

[103] Keith, *Immediate Revelation*, 6-7. Keith shows in another work that he understands the cessationist clause to deny "immediate" revelation: "and your Church Confession of Faith saith, *The former way of God's revealing himself by Prophecy and immediate Revelation, is ceased*". George Keith, *Help in Time of Need, from the God of Help. To the People of the (so called) Church of Scotland, Especially the Once more Zealous and Professing, Who Have so Shamefully Degenerated and Declined from that Which their Fathers the Primitive Protestants Attained unto [...] Being Certain Particulars Very Weighty, and of Great Concernment for Them to Consider Seriously [...]"* (Aberdeen: 1665) [no other publishing details are given], 23.

[104] Keith, *Immediate Revelation*, 26. Keith's position suggests that revelation is something solid or substantial, but in a spiritual sense. The propositional content of revelation directly impresses itself upon the soul.

[105] Keith, *Immediate Revelation*, 6. Although the principles by which one may choose a marriage-partner naturally arise in the realm of ethics, guidance in choosing a particular mate among a number ethically qualified may be seen as an essentially non-ethical choice. Even if the latter decision is considered an ethical one, the key difference

God implants an "organ" which is the faculty for apprehending "immediate forms, properties, qualities and ideas".[106] He describes the process as "spiritual seeing, hearing, tasting, smelling and feeling the word of life".[107] Though Keith clearly speaks analogically here, he also employs Aristotelian categories: his opponents "conceive regeneration to be but an accidental (though supernatural) change of mind", whereas in contrast, Keith "know[s] it to be a substance, and feel[s] it to be so".[108] He uses other terms to help to explain this contrast. Keith maintains that immediate revelation is "intuitive", whereas his opponents only allow for that kind of knowledge which is "abstractive and not intuitive".[109] "Intuitive" knowledge, he says, is analogous to a human being hearing the voice of another person or smelling flowers, whereas "abstractive" knowledge is like receiving a report from a third party, or perceiving a painting of bread and meat as opposed to possessing the real thing.[110]

Keith therefore rejects the Episcopal and Presbyterian traditions in Scotland which claim that spiritual knowledge is "*ex parte subjecti, medium incognitum*", that is, only subjective. In this Keith alludes to a treatise of Robert Baron, the "Aberdeen Doctor", as a case in point.[111] Keith also makes reference to the Scottish commissioner to the Assembly: "*George Gillespie* a man most famous in the Presbyterian way, in his book of *Miscellanies*, cap. 21. pag. 261".[112] Keith thinks that the same error continued later into the seventeenth century:

---

between Keith and is opponents is clear. Whereas Keith could expect direction to a marriage-partner through an immediate revelation, Puritan orthodoxy would consider such a course illegitimate. Further, Puritan wisdom would typically have seen a decision to marry a particular scripturally qualified individual as a matter of providence, not subject to the immediate direction of God.

[106] Keith, *Immediate Revelation*, 9.
[107] Keith, *Immediate Revelation*, 9.
[108] Keith, *Immediate Revelation*, 10.
[109] Keith, *Immediate Revelation*, 13.
[110] Keith, *Immediate Revelation*, 13-14.
[111] Robert Baron [or Barron], *Ad Georgii Turnebulli Tetragonismum Pseudographum Apodixis Catholica, Sive Apologia pro Disputatione de Formali Objecto Fidei* (Aberdeen: 1631) [no other publishing details are given]. For biographical details of Baron, see Henry R. Sefton, "Aberdeen Doctors", *DSCHT*, 1-2. Such a sense of spiritual knowledge as subjective is to be found also in England. See Edward Leigh, *A Systeme or Body of Divinity: Consisting of Ten books. Wherein the Fundamentals and Main Grounds of Religion are Opened: The Contrary Errours Refuted [...]*" (London: William Lee, 1654), "To the Candid and Christian Reader".
[112] Keith, *Immediate Revelation*, 31. In the passage Keith cites George Gillespie arguing with Antinomians who believed in direct assurance from the Spirit, without the Word and without sanctification. Gillespie is of the opinion that there are, on the contrary, two avenues for assurance. First, believers may reflect on the evidence of their sanctification. Secondly, the Holy Spirit, like a teacher, may assure the believer that

[T]he National Teachers to day, both Episcopal and Presbyterial much use it, affirming all Objective Manifestations of the very truths of the Gospel, and essentials of Religion to be ceased, and no other way to be objectively Revealed, but by the Scriptures outward Testimony[...]".[113]

Keith sees a correspondence between "objective" and "immediate" revelation. He perceives that Heb. 1:1-2 distinguishes subjective and mediate revelation from that which is immediate and objective, for God, he suggests, spoke "mediately" to the Fathers through the prophets in Old Testament times, but now speaks to us "in his Son, or by his Son, *Heb*.1.1. That is more immediately".[114] He shores up his continuationist assertions by appealing to texts in Jeremiah 31, Hebrews 8 and, as we would expect, Joel 2:28-29.[115]

---

reasoning based on the evidence presented (his sanctification) is accurate: "Without this evidence of the Spirit of God the soul doth but grope after a full assurance, as it were in the dark; but when the Holy Ghost cometh to do the office of a comforter, then there is light and liberty": George Gillespie, "Miscellany Questions", *The Works of George Gillespie*, ed. David Meek (Edmonton: SWRB, 1991), vol. 2, 106. Gillespie also makes the point that the Spirit does not work apart from the Word, and therefore he must himself make use of the internal marks of sanctification. The Spirit witnesses along with our conscience and so, "if the witness of our conscience be blank", and still a voice speaks peace to the soul, then the spirit is a spirit of delusion. Plainly, what Keith would object to here is the idea that the Spirit must use the Word if one is to have an effective testimony of assurance. Gillespie does not allow objective knowledge of the Spirit nor of the Spirit's assurance. The knowledge must be subjective – that is, the mind must compare a subjective experience with the Word of God. Only then can the Holy Spirit come and give an informed assurance. Gillespie, "Miscellany Questions", *The Works of George Gillespie*, vol. 2, 108. He adds: "the ground and reason of our assurance, or that for which we are assured, is not his act of revealing, but the truth of the thing itself which he doth reveal unto us from the word of God". Even the testimony of the Holy Spirit can be effectual only with reference to the Word. Gillespie, "Miscellany Questions", *The Works of George Gillespie*, vol. 2, 110. Although Gillespie does not use the precise technical language which Keith employs, he does deny that the Spirit works in the matter of assurance in an immediate, intuitive and objective way.

[113] Keith, *Immediate Revelation*, 31-32. For insight into this Quaker subjective/objective distinction, see William Jamison who observes in his *Verus Patroclus* that objective revelation was imparted "immediately" to the patriarchs, prophets and apostles and passed on by them mediately. Subjective revelation is the same as "illumination" and is an application of a revelation already received (18-19). From a Reformed standpoint, the Scriptures are now the objective revelation, and when the Spirit applies that to the soul, it is done to the subject and is therefore a subjective revelation or illumination (20-23). Jamison, *Verus Patroclus: Or, the Weapons of Quakerism, the Weakness of Quakerism*, 18-23.

[114] Keith, *Immediate Revelation*, 80.

[115] Keith, *Immediate Revelation*, 81.

Keith's opponents did not deny the part of his exegesis of Heb. 1:1-2 which asserts that God spoke "mediately" through the prophets (although, of course, they would say God spoke immediately *to* the prophets). However, Keith's claim to the contemporary immediacy of revelation set him apart from his co-religionists. Although Keith does not argue that dreams and visions necessarily continue, he still urges that there can be revelation apart from Scripture which is the common property of all believers. He states his position, fully aware that he is at odds with the *WCF*:

> [T]hey say There is need of an Illumination, (they are afraid to call it a Revelation, as may be seen in their Confession of Faith 1 *Cap*.6. *Art.* where denying all New Revelations of the Spirit, they add, nevertheless, we acknowledg[e] the inward Illuminations of the Spirit of God, to be necessary for the saving understanding of such things, as are Revealed in the Scriptures, for therein (say they) the whole Counsel of God concerning all things is revealed yet,)[...]".[116]

Keith goes on to contend that the *WCF* denies all new objective and immediate revelation and he also heaps opprobrium upon its authors:

> *who call themselves an Assembly of Divines, but in effect are but Diviners and Guessers, having so plainly denyed that which makes the Divine, to wit, The Mind and Spirit of Christ, Revealing in Man, the things of his Kingdom.*[117]

Keith's view is that the *WCF* teaches that "the Spirit of Prophecy is Ceased",[118] that "all new Revelations are Superfluous",[119] and that any extra-biblical voice of God is effectively excluded: "The word proceeding from Gods mouth, is Ceased; he speaks not from word of mouth now, as he did of old, but from the Scriptures".[120]

The significant difference between Keith and his opponents is that Keith insists that truth can be revealed "immediately" to the soul in a way that bypasses Scripture. The Puritans did not deny that the Spirit of Christ impresses truth upon the soul; what they did deny is that such truth is external to Scripture. Keith insists that "immediate" revelation may come directly from the Godhead, while the Puritans taught that the Spirit applies the truths of Scripture "mediately" to the soul.

While his treatise was aimed at the Scots and thereby was an indictment of the cessationism that Scottish Presbyterians confessed, during Keith's

---

[116] Keith, *Immediate Revelation*, 133.

[117] Keith, *Immediate Revelation*, 204.

[118] Keith, *Immediate Revelation*, 206.

[119] Keith, *Immediate Revelation*, 207. Keith does concede that his opponents allow for predictive prophecy, a concession which we will discuss in Chapter Six below, but he draws a clear distinction between it and the biblical prophetic gift he asserts the divines have proscribed.

[120] Keith, *Immediate Revelation*, 210.

first American sojourn (1688-1694) he engaged the attention of the "Church of *New-England*" which had "espoused [the *WCF*] to be her Confession of Faith also".[121] Keith thought that he had discovered a contradiction between *WCF* 1:1 and 1:6 - the latter section of which apparently admits immediate revelation.[122] Although Keith does not suggest that the divines really intended to approve contemporary immediate revelation, he does see an unintentional inconsistency between the assertions contained in these two paragraphs. At the same time, Keith has not moderated his allegation that the *WCF* maintains a comprehensive cessationism:

> But because it is taken for granted, and laid down for a Fundamental among Presbyterians and Independent Teachers, as well as many others, That all inward divine Revelation and Inspiration such as Believers had in the times of the Apostles is ceased[...]all these gifts are now ceased[...]".[123]

If Keith was looking for a reaction, he was not disappointed. Puritan heavyweights Cotton Mather, James Allen, Joshua Moody and Samuel Willard collaborated on The Principles of the Protestant Religion Maintained, a vigorous rejoinder which supports the cessationist interpretation of the *WCF*. Though spirited, their response is also measured, for they understand the *WCF*'s assertion that "extraordinary inspiration" is not needed because "the Canon is perfected".[124] The *WCF* implies, they hold, that "new divine Revelations & Inspirations of the Spirit of God be now ceased", while their Quaker adversary is imposing "meer Legerdemain".[125] The problem is, in their view, that Keith has confused the terms "inspiration", "revelation" and "new": "Inspiration" means an "Inward, extraordinary Discovery of the mind of God, made by the Holy Ghost in the hearts of His servants";[126] "Revelation" is "any Discovery

---

[121] George Keith, *The Presbyterian and Independent Visible Churches in New England and Else-where, Brought to the Test, and Examined According to the Doctrine of the Holy Scriptures, in Their Doctrine, Ministry, Worship, Constitution, Government, Sacraments and Sabbath Day, and Found to be No True Church of Christ* (Philadelphia: Will. Bradford, 1689), 62.

[122] Keith, *The Presbyterian and Independent Visible Churches in New England and Else-where*, 27.

[123] Keith, *The Presbyterian and Independent Visible Churches in New England and Else-where*, 43.

[124] Cotton Mather, James Allen, Joshua Moody and Samuel Willard, *The Principles of the Protestant Religion Maintained, and Churches of New-England, in Profession and Exercise thereof Defended, Against All the Calumnies of One George Keith, a Quaker, in a Book Lately Published in Pensilvania, to Undermine Them Both* (Boston: Richard Pierce, 1690), 18.

[125] Mather *et al*, *The Principles of the Protestant Religion Maintained*, 21.

[126] Mather *et al*, *The Principles of the Protestant Religion Maintained*, 22.

which is made to us of the Will of God".[127] Revelations are either mediate or immediate. The latter term is synonymous with inspiration, while mediate revelations are synonymous with "illumination". "New" can refer "either to the kind of the things revealed or to the Act of Revealing".[128] Therefore, "Saving Illuminations" are common to Christians today, and "in this sence, there are new Revelations made from time to time, to God's Children, i.e. subjectively, 2 Pet. 3. 18.".[129] The Americans still do not, however, admit the possibility of new immediate, objective or extra-biblical revelation, for their concession to new revelation precludes "such inspirations as the Prophets and Apostles of old had, by which God discovered His mind to them immediately".[130] Thus, citing Heb. 1:1-2 and 2 Tim. 3:16-17, they conclude:

> That the Scriptures do so fully contain the mind of God in all things necessary for Faith and Salvation, that there need no such *Inspirations* to be afforded to any and therefore they are now ceased.[131]

The widely accepted belief they share, that mediate revelations continue, affirms their cessationist stance:

> We have already told the world, that we deny not *new Revelations, subjective* and *mediate*, i.e. that the Spirit of God blesseth the Use of means, Reading, Hearing, &c with His Influence, opening the eyes of their minds, and giving them a spiritual Illumination[...]".[132]

Keith tries another approach, another bid to disprove the Puritan perspective, in *The Pretended Antido[t]e Proved Poyson*,[133] where he attempts to negate the force of cessationist proof-texts 2 Tim. 3:16, Heb. 1:1-2 and Prov. 22:19. However, Mather and his colleagues apparently did not feel the need to continue the argument.[134] Keith was not pleading new revelations for new doctrines,[135] but Mather and his fellow-ministers understood the *WCF* to preclude all immediate revelation, conceding that only those contemporary revelations of the mediate variety suggested by Eph. 1:17 were valid.

---

[127] Mather *et al*, *The Principles of the Protestant Religion Maintained*, 22.

[128] Mather *et al*, *The Principles of the Protestant Religion Maintained*, 23.

[129] Mather *et al*, *The Principles of the Protestant Religion Maintained*, 23. Mather *et al* had already defined mediate revelations as illuminations. See also 172, n113 above for the association of mediate revelations with illuminations.

[130] Mather *et al*, *The Principles of the Protestant Religion Maintained*, 23.

[131] Mather *et al*, *The Principles of the Protestant Religion Maintained*, 23.

[132] Mather *et al*, *The Principles of the Protestant Religion Maintained*, 26-27.

[133] George Keith, *The Pretended Antido[t]e Proved Poysen* (Philadelphia: Will. Bradford, 1690).

[134] Keith, *The Pretended Antido[t]e*, 43.

[135] "I do not [...] hold forth any *New Revelation* of any *new Doctrine* [...] but a *new Revelation* of *antient Doctrine* [...]". Keith, *The Pretended Antido[t]e*, 47.

4.5. Conclusion

It is clear from the evidence we have canvassed in Chapters Three and Four that as far as most Reformed orthodox were concerned, earlier modes of special revelation had completely ceased. Some did equivocate over the precise place of dreams in the Christian life, but only a few Puritans were continuationists in any thoroughgoing sense of the word. The two obvious exceptions to the Puritan cessationist consensus are Richard Baxter and William Bridge. Westminster divine William Bridge departed most radically from the predominant cessationism, and this was pointed out by a critic of Reformed orthodoxy, English Quaker George Whitehead. Quaker polemic against the cessationist view held by the *WCF* dismissed the Puritan insistence on the unity of the Word and Spirit. In their defence of Westminster orthodoxy, Puritan theologians reaffirmed that the cessationist clause of *WCF* 1:1 excluded the possibility of any new immediate revelation. In the next chapter, we shall discuss in detail another related contentious matter – the place of extraordinary prophecy in the Westminster theology.

Chapter 5

Prophecy and the Westminster Divines

5.1 Introduction

Recently a number of scholars have attempted to categorise and explain the theological and historical impetus for Christian prophecy and explore the reasons for its alleged cessation in the New Testament churches. David Hill, David Aune and Wayne Grudem, in particular, are perhaps the most widely attested writers who have produced insights into the past and present status of Christian prophecy.[1]

David Hill suggests that the repudiation of Montanism[2] signalled the end of prophecy in the church, when it ceased for two reasons: first, a decline in the number of prophets was linked to the process whereby "appointed office-bearers and Scripture took the place of pneumatic inspiration".[3]

---

[1] David Hill, *New Testament Prophecy* (London: Marshall, Morgan and Scott, 1979); David E. Aune, *Prophecy in Early Christianity and the Ancient Mediterranean World* (Grand Rapids, MI: Eerdmans, 1983); Wayne A. Grudem, *The Gift of Prophecy in 1 Corinthians* (Washington, D.C.: University Press of America, 1982). See also Wayne A. Grudem (ed.), *Are Miraculous Gifts for Today?: Four Views* (Leicester: Inter-varsity Press, 1996). Of the four views canvassed in *Are Miraculous Gifts for Today?*, Richard Gaffin's seems closest to the predominant view among the Reformed orthodox in the seventeenth century: Richard Gaffin, "A Cessationist View", Wayne A. Grudem (ed.), *Are Miraculous Gifts for Today?: Four Views*, 25-64; cf Wayne A. Grudem, *The Gift of Prophecy in the New Testament and Today* (Eastbourne: Kingsway, 1988). For other modern discussions on whether New Testament prophecy has continued or ceased, see Jack Deere, *Surprised by the power of the Spirit* (Eastbourne: Kingsway, 1994), 133-43; Gordon Fee, *God's Empowering Presence: The Holy Spirit in the Letters of Paul* (Peabody: Hendrickson Publishers, 1994), especially 174-75. For an analysis of New Testament prophecy in which it is argued that prophecy should be explained and understood as theology, see Thomas W. Gillespie, *The First Theologians. A Study in Early Christian Prophecy* (Grand Rapids, MI: Eerdmans, 1994), who writes: "The task of the prophets, as Paul understands it, is to explicate through divine revelation the implications, theological and behavioural, of the apostolic kerygma" (262).

[2] On Montanism, see briefly Trevor A. Hart (ed.), *The Dictionary of Historical Theology* (Grand Rapids, MI: Eerdmans, 2000), 380-81; and especially Christine Trevett, *Montanism: Gender, Authority and the New Prophecy* (Cambridge: Cambridge University Press, 1996).

[3] Hill, *New Testament Prophecy*, 190.

Secondly, the presence of false prophets undermined the status of true prophets and prophecy.[4]

Hill also concludes that the idea that New Testament charismatic gifts were no longer given following the inauguration of the new age is foreign to Paul's thought.[5] While he rejects the idea of a "second blessing", Hill contends that the practice of prophecy (including visionary experiences and the like) within the contemporary worshiping community is in accord with the practice in the New Testament churches.[6] In his view, while modern Pentecostals incorrectly identify "tongues-speaking" as prophecy[7] they do genuinely participate in the same prophetic gifts as those described in the New Testament. However, their tendency to repeat phrases from the King James Version of the Bible suggests that, in these instances, the Pentecostals engage in a kind of "'second hand' inspiration".[8] Nonetheless, Hill in his conclusion does not espouse the idea that extra-biblical predictive prophecy continues. Instead he perceives that the gift of prophecy is now tied to the exposition of Scripture:

> Perhaps - and we can put it no stronger than that - it is those who have grasped the meaning of Scripture, perceived its powerful relevance to the life of the individual, the Church and society, and declare that message fearlessly who are the true successors not only of the Old Testament prophets but also of the prophets in the New Testament.[9]

This conclusion is surprising in the light of Hill's apparent conviction that New Testament charismatic gifts continue in the church because, even if unconsciously articulated, Hill's understanding of continuing prophecy in the church is strongly reminiscent of explanations we will find among the seventeenth-century English Puritans and Scottish Presbyterians.

Wayne Grudem's insights are similar to Hill's.[10] However, Grudem argues that two separate grades of prophecy can be found in Scripture.[11] In addition, he also sees a difference between the authority of Old Testament prophets and that of those leaders in the New Testament who were not apostles. In the former dispensation, the prophet was examined and if he was a true prophet then his words were taken as true, whereas in the New Testament each "lower order" prophecy had to be weighed carefully by the

---

[4] Hill, *New Testament Prophecy*, 191-92.
[5] Hill, *New Testament Prophecy*, 202 and 206.
[6] Hill, *New Testament Prophecy*, 210.
[7] Hill, *New Testament Prophecy*, 211.
[8] Hill, *New Testament Prophecy*, 212-13.
[9] Hill, *New Testament Prophecy*, 213.
[10] See the Introduction above, 1-3, n5 and n6 for Grudem's writings on modern prophecy and continuationism.
[11] Grudem, *The Gift of Prophecy in 1 Corinthians*, 21-32.

church.[12] Prophecies given by persons described in 1 Cor. 14:37-38 did not rank with Old Testament prophecies; only the apostles were capable of giving Christian equivalents.[13]

Grudem believes that a fallible, lower-order prophecy continues in the contemporary church. A text such as 1 Cor. 13: 8-12, according to Grudem, does not imply that prophecy would cease when the canon of Scripture was complete. The "perfect" mentioned in this text refers to the consummation of world history and the ushering in of a new reality at the end of time.[14] Grudem's analysis of prophets and prophecy in Scripture is not without its problems and detractors, as we saw in our Introduction,[15] but his conclusion that there is a lower order of prophecy was also the position of the Reformed orthodox in the seventeenth century. Unlike Grudem, however, these theologians denied that the revelation in question was extra-biblical.

One of the most widely cited studies on prophecy, that by David Aune, concludes from an analysis of five surveys of New Testament prophecy and prophets,[16] including that of Hill, that:

1. The New Testament prophet was "the functional equivalent of the OT prophet".[17]

2. The prophet "was never integrated into the organizational structure of local churches".[18]

3. Prophets only exercise their gifts within the context of worship services, according to the Pauline letters.[19]

4. Prophets such as Agabus in Acts are no different from John who wrote the book of Revelation.[20]

---

[12] Grudem, *The Gift of Prophecy in 1 Corinthians*, 58-66. Texts he refers to include 1 Cor. 14:29 and 1 Thess. 5:20.

[13] Grudem, *The Gift of Prophecy in 1 Corinthians*, 72.

[14] Grudem, *The Gift of Prophecy in 1 Corinthians*, 211.

[15] See introduction, 6, n24 above.

[16] Aune, *Prophecy in Early Christianity and the Ancient Mediterranean World*, 1-14, discussing Harold Guy, *New Testament Prophecy: Its Origin and Significance* (London: Epworth Press, 1947); Gerhard Friedrich, "Prophets and Prophecies in the New Testament", *TDNT*, vol. 6, 828-61; Éduard Cothener, "Prophétisme dans le Nouveau Testament", Fulcran Vigouroux [main author], *Dictionnaire de la Bible: Supplément / Commencé par Louis Pirot et André Robert, Continué sous la Direction de Henri Cazelles et André Feuillet Tome 8: Pithom-Providentissimus* (Paris: Letouzey & Ané, 1972), vol. 8, 1222-1337; Theodore M. Crone, *Early Christian prophecy: A Study of its Origin and Function* (Baltimore: St. Mary's University Press, 1973). Crone suggests that the most common function of the early Christian prophet was preaching rather than prediction (294-95).

[17] Aune, *Prophecy in Early Christianity and the Ancient Mediterranean World*, 202.

[18] Aune, *Prophecy in Early Christianity and the Ancient Mediterranean World*, 203.

[19] Aune, *Prophecy in Early Christianity and the Ancient Mediterranean World*, 205.

5. Prophets are thought to be leaders, not because they hold an office, but because they are believed to give divinely inspired messages.[21]

6. Finally, as the church becomes more institutionalised, the prophets become increasingly superfluous and are excluded from active guidance of the community.[22]

Aune's conclusion that Agabus and the Seer of the Book of Revelation share a common status differs from Grudem's view, highlighting the lack of agreement among modern scholars over the identity and role of the New Testament prophets. This ambivalence is less obvious in the seventeenth-century Puritan analysis of New Testament prophecy and prophets.

We shall explore the Puritans' perspectives on claims to sixteenth- and seventeenth-century prophecy by a threefold route. Firstly, we shall consider how they viewed other forms of guidance such as astrology, the use of lots, and angelic agencies. Secondly, we shall examine their exegetical conclusions of the key passages cited on the subject of prophecy. Thirdly, we shall investigate the Puritan rationale for accepting the legitimacy of modern forms of predictive prophecy, and Puritan definitions of what prophecy was. We shall briefly discuss the relationship between prophecy and providentialism in Puritan theology, but this chapter will focus mainly on the role of Scripture in Reformation and post-Reformation prophecy.[23]

5.2 Other Puritan Forms of Discerning Secrets or the Future

The question of ongoing prophecy in the seventeenth-century Puritan milieu is complicated by the prevalent idea that God communicated in a variety of ways that sometimes bordered on revelational prophecy and sometimes did not. Astrology, lots and Satanic infusions fit into the latter category, while the guidance of elect angels appears to bear some relation to the imparting of prophetic insight. We will look at these views in the same order.

The Puritans realised this whole notion of inquiring after secret knowledge was dangerous. According to John Lightfoot, this included seeking prophecy:

> [A]nd now they are able to be ministers, and to teach the congregation. But, after that generation, when the gospel was settled in all the world[...] then was study of the Scriptures the way to enable men to unfold the

---

[20] Aune, *Prophecy in Early Christianity and the Ancient Mediterranean World*, 207-209.

[21] Aune, *Prophecy in Early Christianity and the Ancient Mediterranean World*, 211.

[22] Aune, *Prophecy in Early Christianity and the Ancient Mediterranean World*, 211.

[23] Providentialism and prophecy is an area of Puritan thought which still has much to yield.

Scriptures, and fit them to be ministers to instruct others: and revelations and inspirations neither needful nor safe to be looked after, nor hopeful to be attained unto.[24]

Lightfoot's caution is also adopted by Stephen Marshall who adds that claims to predictive prophecy were anachronistic. Marshall condemns those who:

> itch after it, and many doe as *Nebuchadnezzar* did, when his thoughts troubled him in the night, that hee might know what should come to pass over it[…]".

For these would-be seekers after prophecy, Marshall cites Acts 1:7 as a reason why such knowledge is not available: *"That it is not for us thus to know the times and seasons, which the Father hath kept in his own hand[…]"*.[25]

Most Puritans believed, like Marshall, that claims to an astrological knowledge of the times were equally unlawful.[26] Astrology[27] had a firm grip on some Puritan congregations, often provoking a pastoral rebuke,[28] though by no means all Puritan ministers rejected it. Henry Wilkinson Junior even wondered aloud whether the Westminster Assembly was possibly the fulfilment of an astrological prediction when he addressed the Long Parliament in 1643.[29] After all, Johannes Kepler had deduced from the appearance of a star in 1604, that "Ecclesiasticall Discipline shall be

---

[24] Lightfoot, *The Whole Works of the Rev. John Lightfoot, D.D.*, vol. 3, 369-70.

[25] Stephen Marshall, *The Right Understanding of the Times* (London: Stephen Bowtell, 1647), 6-7.

[26] Marshall, *The Right Understanding of the Times*, 6.

[27] For a useful discussion of the church's interaction with astrology in earlier times, see M. L. W. Laistner, "The Western Church and Astrology During the Early Middle Ages", *Harvard Theological Review, Harvard Theological Review* 34 (1941), 253-75.

[28] Marshall, *The Right Understanding of the Times*, 6-7. See also Stephen Marshall, *Reformation and Desolation* (London: Samuel Gellibrand, 1642), 26-27, in which Marshall criticizes those who think that predictions made by preachers from the Scriptures are of "no more certainty, than the judgement of *judiciall Astrology*".

[29] Henry Wilkinson, *Babylons Ruine, Jerusalems Rising* (London: Chr. Meredith and Sa. Gellibrand, 1644). Perhaps we should be surprised that astrology is so rarely affirmed by Westminster divines, given the widespread acceptance of a Christianised astrology in both England and New England. See David Hall, "A World of Wonders: The Mentality of the Supernatural in Seventeenth-Century New England", David D. Hall and David Grayson Allen (eds.), *Seventeenth-Century New England* (Boston: The Colonial Society of Massachusetts, 1984), 239-74, at 249-50. Wilkinson's Westminster colleague, Thomas Gataker, however, believed that the Assembly had been unanimous in rejecting astrology: Thomas Gataker, *His Vindication of the Annotations by Him Published Upon these Words, Thus Saith the Lord, Learn not the Way of the Heathen, and be not Dismayed at the Signes of Heaven, for the Heathen are Dismayed at them. Jer. 10.2* (London: Richard Thrayle, 1653), 6.

restored by publike Councell[...]", causing Wilkinson to suggest that Kepler may well have been referring to the Synod of Dort in 1618 or perhaps to *"The Assembly of Divines now called"*.[30] Such an open appeal to astrology is striking in the light of the general distaste apparent among other Puritan divines of its influence in society.

Less contentious was the use of lots. Lots were generally held to be a more acceptable form of discerning God's will although, as Thomas Gataker (1574-1654) pointed out, extraordinary or "divinatory" lots had become unnecessary, even though they had once served useful functions "either for the discovery of some hidden matter past, or present; or for the presaging and foretelling of some future event".[31] Gataker, one of the oldest members of the Assembly, published 48 works, making him among the most industrious members of the Assembly and allowing him to enter the lists of debaters with both formidable experience and an impressive reputation as a scholar. Gataker concludes that in his own day "none of them [extraordinary and divinatory lots] are now lawfull".[32] Nor could lots serve as a precedent because we "must walke by ordinarie precepts, not by extraordinary practises".[33] Evidently Gataker presupposes that only what Scripture sanctions can be lawful. Therefore, the lots in question are not lawful, "without expresse warrant or speciall revelation from God".[34]

Even though Satanic prophecy granted through such means as the Delphic oracle was generally considered to be no longer available,[35] the Puritans retained a belief that Satan possessed the power to counterfeit God's means of special revelation. For this reason they needed to explain the differences between Satanic revelations and the ongoing ministry of the Holy Spirit. It was believed that Satan, unlike God, had no power over the will of a human subject, as Charles Herle explains:

> No mans heart is immediately in the hands of the Devill, it is our selves that put the weapon into his hands, whereby he wounds us[...]. So farre is the Divell from being able irresistibly to worke upon, or incline our hearts, as he cannot without our helps, fasten any the least impression on

---

[30] Wilkinson, *Babylons Ruine, Jerusalems Rising*, 24.

[31] Thomas Gataker, *Of the Nature and Use of Lots; a Treatise Historicall and Theologicall* (London: William Bladen, 1619), 269.

[32] Gataker, *Of the Nature and Use of Lots*, 298.

[33] Gataker, *Of the Nature and Use of Lots*, 299.

[34] Gataker, *Of the Nature and Use of Lots*, 301.

[35] John Arrowsmith, *Armilla Catechetica. A Chain of Principles; Or, An Orderly Concatenation of Theological Aphorismes and Exercitations*[...]" (Cambridge: Cambridge University, 1659), 101-102.

them, should he *come and find nothing in me*[...]he could get nothing out of us, work nothing in us[...]".[36]

Herle is certain that those who claim that the Devil can tempt with an immediate impression affecting the will "give to the Divell more then his due[...]".[37] The danger of demonic temptation is therefore avoidable.[38]

Satan was believed to be limited because his manner of communication was considered to differ from that adopted by the Holy Spirit. The Puritans typically embraced Aristotelian faculty-psychology as a working theory, believing that it accurately described the process of mental life. God's method of communication, and that of other spirits, was often explained in the light of this analysis. The higher or more cerebral faculties were held to be the understanding and the will; while the lower faculties were deemed to be the senses and imagination. It was thought that when God communicates with human beings, he first impresses the understanding and the will, beginning with the higher faculties, "and thence upon the affections and senses".[39] The descent from the higher to the lower faculties is, however,

---

[36] Charles Herle, *Ahab's Fall by His Prophet's Flatteries* (London: J. Wright, 1644), 20-21. Herle (1598-1659) became prolocutor on the event of the death of William Twisse. Though he preferred Presbyterian church government, Herle was known for his tolerance and support of the Independents in the Assembly. Educated at Exeter College, Oxford, and appointed to represent Lancashire at the Assembly, he was associated from 1626 with the Rectory of Winwick in Lancashire. He was buried in the chancel of the church in 1659. Barker, *Puritan Profiles,* 29-31. William Spurstowe agreed with Herle that while God "works by *divine infusions* of grace, which effectually sway the soul to an assent or consent, Satan [works] only by *moral perswasions*, which may be powerful to sollicite, but not to constrain". William Spurstow[e], *ΣATANA NOHMATA: Or, the Wiles of Satan in a Discourse upon 2. Cor.2.11.* (London: 1666) [no further publishing details are given], 14.

[37] Herle, *Ahab's Fall by His Prophet's Flatteries,* 22

[38] Edward Reynolds, another avowed cessationist, believed that revelations as categorised in Num. 12:6 have ceased, but he asserted that Satan could still mimic God's former ways of revelation. Reynolds delineates some methods of Num. 12:6 revelations as "by true *Voices*, by real *access* of *Angels*, and by immediate *Ilapse* of Truth into the Understanding". However, because revelations were mostly given by visions and dreams, the Devil, Reynolds notes, imitates God and affects the imagination in an attempt to delude: Edward Reynolds, *A Treatise of the Passions and Faculties of the Soul of Man. With the Several Dignities and Corruptions Thereunto Belonging* (London: Robert Boulter, 1678), 621. This work is a classic treatment of the Puritan use of faculty psychology. See especially 621 for an illustration of how the fancy or imagination can produce concrete material changes. Reynolds cites a white woman giving birth to a black child because she had a painting of an Ethiopian on her wall. The same procedure explains Jacob's mottled sheep and goats in Gen. 30:30-39: when the coloured branches were perceived by the animals' fancy during the mating process, this ensured that the female animals would give birth to speckled offspring.

[39] Herle, *Ahab's Fall by His Prophet's Flatteries,* 23.

reversed when the agent of the impressions is Satan. Satan ascends to the higher faculties from the lower "carelesse senses, disordered affections, or a troubled fancy, he ascends to the will; and thence back againe to the others".[40] Yet even with this qualification, Satan is still, in the view of William Strong, capable of counterfeiting and persuading an individual "that surely this is a fellowship with God, and this is communion with him[...]".[41]

It is not hard to find examples of Westminster divines who admitted the ongoing ministry of revelation from the elect angels. Even William Strong, who denies that special revelation is still given,[42] believes in such a ministry:

> [F]or the Churches sake they have many discoveries made to them; that they might also teach them to us; they receive a spirit of Prophecy from Christ for the Churches sake, *Rev.* 19.10. the god of this world blinds the eyes of men, and the Angels that are imployed by the Spirit of God do inlighten them.[43]

---

[40] Herle, *Ahab's Fall by His Prophet's Flatteries*, 23.

[41] William Strong, *Communion with God in Ordinances[...]*"(London: Fra. Tyton, 1656), 249. For other expression of concern regarding Satanic revelations, see William Gouge, *A Learned and Very Useful Commentary on the Whole Epistle to the Hebrewes* (London: Joshua Kirton, 1655), 137; Anthony Burgesse, *Spiritual Refining: Or, a Treatise of Grace and Assurance, The Use of Signs in Self Examination [...]*" (London: T[homas] U[nderhill], 1658), 132. Burgess[e] avers in another sermon on John 17:12: "Although God only doth originally and by his own property know things to come, yet the *devils they may foretell some things*; Not that the devils can of themselves foreknow any future casuall thing, for they know not the hearts and free wils of men, yet some things they certainly foreknow, some things with great conjectures, certainly they know such things which God revealeth to them[...]": Anthony Burgess, *CXLV Expository Sermons Upon the Whole 17th Chapter of the Gospel According to St John: or Christ's Prayer Before His Passion Explicated, and Both Practically and Polemically Improved* (London: Thomas Underhill, 1656), 395. See also William Carter, *The Covenant of God with Abraham Opened [...] Together with A Short Discourse Concerning the Manifestations of God unto His People in the Last Dayes. Wherein is Shewed the Manner of the Spirits Work Therein to be in the Use of Ordinary Gifts, not by Extraordinary Revelations* (London: John Rothwell, 1654), 158; Samuel Rutherford, *Influences of the Life of Grace. Or, a Practical Treatise Concerning the Way, Manner, and Means of Having and Improving of Spiritual Dispositions, and Quickning Influences from Christ the Resurrection and the Life* (London: Andrew Crook, 1659), 190; and Samuel Rutherford, *A Survey of the Spirituall Antichrist.[...]*"(London: Andrew Crook, 1648), 45.

[42] William Strong, *A Treatise Shewing the Subordination of the Will of Man unto the Will of God* (London: Francis Tyton, 1657), 77.

[43] William Strong, *A Discourse of the Two Covenants: Wherein the Nature, Differences and Effects of the Covenant of Works and of Grace are Distinctly, Rationally, Spiritually and Practically Discussed; Together with the Considerable*

Two important elements distinguished contemporary angelic communications from the special revelation which had become the rule of faith and life. The belief that angels still communicate through the anonymous intrusion of "suggestions" or "motions" into the imagination is the first of these elements. William Spurstowe used faculty psychology to explain the modern transmission of angelic knowledge: like a painter who arranges the colours of his pallet on the canvas, the angel can order the existing "*Species* and Signatures of things" in the imagination so that the understanding and the will can then act. Spurstowe calls this ordering of objects in the imagination a "suggestion".[44] The "will" may then accept the "suggestion" which is now in the fancy, because the imagination affects the will by exciting "its desires towards some convenient and pleasing object".[45] The Puritans usually believed that these "suggestions" were either secret, or impossible to distinguish from the working of one's own mind. Thus, John Maynard proposes:

> As for the godly, I am perswaded, they are many times directed strongly, by the secret suggestions of the Angels, for the avoiding of dangers, and the obtaining the good.[46]

By "secret" Maynard implies that the person who received the suggestion to avoid some unforeseen danger could not identify or distinguish the source of that impulse from one's inner mental life. Belief in this continuing ability of spirits to impart suggestions is sanctioned by *WCF* 21:2, thereby distinguishing such suggestions from former ways of special revelation which have now ceased (*WCF* 1:1).[47]

Quantity of Practical Cases Dependent Thereon (London: Francis Tyton, 1678), 401; William Gouge also accepts that angels may communicate with human beings because they are God's messengers "to declare and execute his will": Gouge, *A Learned and Very Useful Commentary on the Whole Epistle to the Hebrewes*, 63.

[44] Spurstow, ΣΑΤΑΝΑ ΝΟΗΜΑΤΑ: *Or, the Wiles of Satan*, 12.

[45] Spurstow, ΣΑΤΑΝΑ ΝΟΗΜΑΤΑ: *Or, the Wiles of Satan*, 12-13. The impact on the will can often be more successful than on the understanding, because of "a natural aptness in men to be moved by such inducements[...]"(13).

[46] John Maynard, *The Beauty and Order of the Creation* (London: Henry Eversden, 1668), 209. He also concluded: "For I cannot conceive, but that the good Angels should as well suggest good thoughts, as the evil Angels do evil thoughts" (208). Also see Isaac Ambrose, who concludes that although angels have ceased to appear to people, they still work among us even though their "converse is not so sensible": Isaac Ambrose, *Ministration of and Communion with Angels* (London: Rowland Reynolds, 1673), 127. For biographical details, see John Bailey, "Isaac Ambrose", *DNB*, vol. 1, 30.

[47] The proof-text, which refers to Satan, is the record of Christ's temptation in Matt. 4:9-10. The use of this particular text need not imply that Satan might appear in person and hold a conversation, but it at least suggests that Satan might still communicate ideas to a human being. Elect angels were also active, according to the Assembly, though the ministry of good angels was tied to their role in providence. *LC* answer 16 cites Ps.

The second element of angelic activity related to angels' role in the administration of providence. William Greenhill(1591-1671) has an extended discussion on the function of angels in providence. Greenhill was minister at Stepney and one of the "dissenting brethren" at the Assembly.[48] He summarises angelic activity as having "a great part under God in the government of the world".[49] Amongst other functions, Greenhill describes angels as rational creatures who have "prophetical knowledge" as well as knowledge of the past and to those whom God reveals matters which are contingent and which relate to the church.[50]

The angels' role in providence still continues, and even if angelic visions and appearances have ceased,[51] angels still communicate with human

---

103:20-21 to prove that "God created all the angels[...]to execute his commandments, and to praise his name". This execution is the work of angels in providence. William Carter is a strong cessationist, but still allows for the "suggestions of Satan". Even though one does not receive revelations for ordinary guidance, the Devil can still counterfeit God's now obsolete means of revelation. God gives revelation only through the Word, but Satan is still able to "make powerfull impressions upon the phansie, and much resembling those of the spirit of God": Carter, *The Covenant of God with Abraham Opened [...] Together with A Short Discourse Concerning the Manifestations of God unto His People in the Last Dayes*, 156-57. See also Spurstow, *ΣΑΤΑΝΑ ΝΟΗΜΑΤΑ: Or, the Wiles of Satan*. According to Spurstow, Satanic suggestions often cannot be distinguished from heaven-sent "illapses" (15-16). In addition, the subject often cannot distinguish Satanic insinuations from "the lustings and ebullations of depraved nature" (33). Not only can Satan counterfeit genuine revelations, he can even enable a human being to know something about the future which would then come to pass (77).

[48] Greenhill was a diligent Puritan and a faithful attender at the Assembly. He received his education at Magdalen College, Oxford. For context, see James Reid, *Memoirs of the Westminster Divines* (Edinburgh: Banner of Truth, 1982), vol. 1, 365-67.

[49] William Greenhill, *An Exposition of Ezekiel* (Edinburgh: Banner of Truth Trust, 1994), 27.

[50] Greenhill, *An Exposition of Ezekiel*, 27-28. Edward Corbet[t] (1602-1657) concurs that angels can only "discover bad thoughts, by wicked actions", whereas God alone can know one's thoughts: Edward Corbett, *Gods Providence* (London: Robert Bostock, 1642), 8. This Westminster divine was expelled from Oxford for refusing to support the royal cause. Archbishop Laud declined to grant him a living, but the tables were turned when Corbett acted as a witness against Laud at Laud's trial. Corbett was a regular attender at the Assembly and served on the committee for examining and ordaining ministers. He also completed a Latin commentary in four volumes folio on the Letter to the Romans. See Reid, *Memoirs of the Westminster Divines*, vol. 1, 264-67.

[51] This was the predominant view of Westminster divines. Joseph Caryl in his commentary on the Book of Job notes that one of the diverse ways that God spoke mouth to mouth was through angels. He goes on to say that this way of revelation, however, along with all the other miraculous modes, has been replaced by a *"clearer light"*, by which he means Christ: Joseph Caryl, *An Exposition with Practicall Observations Continued upon the Fourth, Fifth, Sixth and Seventh Chapters of the*

beings. The secret suggestion of angels, part of God's special providence towards his church, was the usual and received explanation for the discovery of the Gunpowder Plot. In 1605 one of the plotters, Francis Tresham, tipped off his Catholic brother-in-law, Lord Monteagle, and advised him not to attend Parliament on 5 November. Puritans frequently attributed the plan's thwarting to angelic intervention, but never as far as we can discover to a visit from an angel in a vision, dream or as a personal visible presence of which the human subject was conscious.

Ralph Brownrig suggests that one of the similarities between the deliverance in Dan. 6:21-22 and the detection of the Gunpowder Plot was the intervention of "an *Angel*, An *extraordinary* discovery, by an *over-ruling providence*".[52] Brownrig does not explain exactly how the angel brought about the "discovery", but in his view the intervention which resulted produced a letter exposing the conspirators: "That *Pen*", Brownrig writes:

> by which that *Letter* was written, which first gave notice of this *horrid Treason*, being thereto *over-ruled* by God's *great Providence*, was made of a *Quil* of an *Angel's wing*.[53]

The author of the letter exposing the plot presumably had a secret impulse or inner compulsion to write it, and thus averted a dreadful tragedy. Brownrig's appeal to the role of angels in providence was mirrored by John Strickland, who also put discovery of the plot down to a special providence,[54] and by Francis Cheynell, who attributed the discovery to "a wonderfull providence".[55]

It is clear, then, that Puritans believed that both good and bad angels guided human beings under the providence of God. Though special

---

Booke of Job (London: H. Fawne, H. Overton, L. Fawne, I. Rothwell and G. Calvert, 1645), 84 and 87.

[52] Ralph Brownrig, *Fourty Sermons* (London: John Martyn, James Allestry, and Thomas Dicas, 1661), 63. Brownrig (1592-1659), bishop of Exeter, was both a convinced Episcopalian and a strict Calvinist. He did not sit at the Assembly, though appointed, and was a strong royalist. See John Overton, "Ralph Brownrig", *DNB*, vol. 1, 237-38. Although the ministry of angels was accepted among Reformed orthodox, it was typically believed to be "mediate" rather than "immediate". See, for example, on this point John Arrowsmith, *Englands Ebenezer or, Stone of Help*[...]" (London: Samuel Man, 1645), 5-6.

[53] Brownrig, *Fourty Sermons*, 63.

[54] John Strickland said that it was discovered by the "eye of heaven": John Strickland, *Immanuel, or The Church Triumphing in God with Us* (London: Henry Overton, 1644), 15. Strickland (d. 1670), educated at Oxford, was later to be put out of his charge of Edmund's parish in New Sarum at the time of the Act of Uniformity. Reid, *Memoirs of the Westminster Divines*, 2, 177-79.

[55] Francis Cheynell, *A Plot for the Good of Posterity* (London: Samuel Gellibrand, 1646), 3.

revelation had ceased, this did not mean that God no longer used angels, but it did mean that their activity became more discreet so that the motions or secrets they conveyed to the imagination merged with human self-consciousness.

5.3 Puritan Exegetical Conclusions Concerning New Testament Prophecy

A major strand of Puritan exegesis of those biblical texts, including Acts 13:1-2; 19:6; 21:9; Rom. 12:6; 1 Cor. 12:28; 1 Corinthians 14; and Eph. 4:11, which refer to prophecy concludes that while the extraordinary prophecy of the Old and New Testament prophets is not reproduced in the later church, an analogous prophetic function continues.

John Owen (1616-1683), arguably the greatest English theologian of his time, was not a member of the Assembly, although he had the respect of the Puritan Parliament and was chaplain to Oliver Cromwell. A prolific author whose works are still in print, Owen was a towering theological influence in his own day. He is associated with Westminster theology in that, at the very least, he was a major contributor to the recension of the *WCF*, the *Savoy Declaration* of 1658, whose statement on Scripture was almost identical to its more famous predecessor and which also retained the cessationist clause of *WCF* 1:1.[56] One of the most careful of modern students of Owen's work, Carl Trueman, believes that Owen was profoundly influenced by the *WCF*:

> The significance for Owen of the Westminster Confession, and of the international theology which it embodied can scarcely be overestimated[...]. [H]is substantial agreement with the Westminster Confession is clear from the Savoy Declaration of 1658, for the drafting of which he was largely responsible.[57]

---

[56] Born into an old Welsh family, Owen's father Henry was vicar of Stadham and Chiselhampton, Oxfordshire. Owen himself was educated at Oxford, but left the university because he refused to submit to William Laud's statutes. See Barker, *Puritan Profiles*, 295-300. See also William Orme, *Memoirs of the Life, Writings, and Religious Connexions, of John Owen, D.D., Vice-Chancellor of Oxford, and Dean of Christ Church, during the Commonwealth* (London: T. Hamilton, 1820); John Owen, *The Correspondence of John Owen (1616-1683): with an Account of his Life and Work*, ed. Peter Toon (Cambridge: James Clark, 1970); Peter Toon, *God's Statesman: The Life and Work of John Owen, Pastor, Educator, Theologian* (Exeter : Paternoster Press, 1971); Sinclair B. Ferguson, *John Owen on the Christian Life* (Edinburgh: Banner of Truth, 1987); Steve Griffiths, *Redeem the Time: The Problem of Sin in the Writings of John Owen* (Fearn : Mentor, 2001).

[57] Carl Trueman, *The Claims of Truth: John Owen's Trinitarian Theology* (Carlisle: Paternoster Press, 1998), 17-18.

Owen, for whom extraordinary "*prophesy* is nothing but to declare hidden and secret things by virtue of immediate revelation",[58] gives a useful summary of the diverse meanings "prophets" and "prophecy" can have in Scripture:

> But the names of *prophets* and *prophecy* are used variously in the New Testament: for, -1. Sometimes an *extraordinary office* and *extraordinary gifts* are signified by them; and 2. Sometimes *extraordinary gifts* only; and 3. Sometimes an *ordinary office* with *ordinary gifts*, and sometimes *ordinary gifts* only. And unto one of these heads may the use of the word be everywhere reduced.[59]

Although we meet divergent understandings of individual texts among the Westminster divines themselves, Owen's distribution is fairly typical. He believes that Eph. 4:11, 1 Cor. 12:28 and Acts 13:1-2 refer to extraordinary prophets in office; Acts 21:9, 19:6, and 1 Corinthians 14 to extraordinary prophets out of office; and Rom. 12:6 to an ordinary office carrying with it an ordinary gift.[60]

Owen held that some gifts analogous to those miraculous gifts of the Spirit continue in the contemporary church.[61] Westminster divines also understood that meaning is fluid in some of these texts, for the same texts were thought to provide for both extraordinary and ordinary prophets.[62] We can see in the Assembly debate over proof-texts for *FPC* how some texts

---

[58] John Owen, *The Works of John Owen* (Edinburgh: The Banner of Truth Trust, 1979), vol. 4, 452.
For modern discussions on whether New Testament prophecy has continued or ceased, see the following: Deere, *Surprised by the power of the Spirit*, 133-43; Fee, *God's Empowering Presence: The Holy Spirit in the Letters of Paul*, especially 174-75; "A Cessationist View", Wayne A. Grudem (ed.), *Are Miraculous Gifts for Today?: Four Views*, 25-64. See also Grudem, *The Gift of Prophecy in the New Testament and Today*. See also Introduction 2, n2 above.

[59] John Owen's views are particularly accessible because his works have been reprinted in recent decades. He was also the Puritan who wrote most extensively on the work of the Holy Spirit. Owen, *The Works of John Owen*, vol. 4, 451. On the Holy Spirit, see also Origen, *De Principiis*, 1, 3. (*ANF* 4, 251-56); Sinclair Ferguson, *The Holy Spirit* (Leicester: IVP, 1996).

[60] Owen, *The Works of John Owen*, vol. 4, 451-53.

[61] Owen, *The Works of John Owen*, vol. 4, 475.

[62] Vern Poythress argues for a distinction between discursive and non-discursive knowledge. While the latter, or a combination of both kinds of knowledge, is analogous to the apostolic gifts of the New Testament, it is not the same as that imparted through the miraculous gifts. See especially 83-92 where Poythress attempts to classify modern claims to charismatic gifts and integrate those claims into a view that Scripture is complete: Vern Sheridan Poythress, "Modern Spiritual Gifts as Analogous to Apostolic Gifts: Affirming Extraordinary Works Of The Spirit Within Cessationist Theology", *Journal of the Evangelical Theological Society* 39/1 (March 1996), 71-102.

yield different conclusions for different exegetes. Records of the debate show that a minority wished to limit "prophecy" in 1 Cor. 14:3 to extraordinary prophecy. Lightfoot's *Journal* of the Assembly deliberations records the discussion on the proof-text clause: "though these different gifts may meet in, and accordingly be exercised by, one and the same minister". He also notes on Tuesday 21 November 1643:

> Then was some exception at 1 Cor. xiv.3; and among the rest I challenged it as speaking of prophecy in its proper sense: and this was somewhat agitated and Sir *Benjamin Rudyard* desired that in regard of the doubtfulness it might be waved; but it was voted against us.[63]

Obviously, a majority of Assembly divines had no difficulty in applying this text to both extraordinary prophets and ordinary "prophets" set apart for ministry.

Further, sectaries used the same New Testament texts to claim a biblical precedent for preaching out of office. In response, a twofold application of these texts allowed some, such as William Rathband, to argue for the extraordinary nature of biblical prophets in order to overturn the Independents' conclusion. Rathband (d.1695), who was a late addition to the Assembly, made up for missed opportunities by being a frequent attender.[64] He also cited 1 Corinthians 14 against the Brownist separatists and argued that in that passage Paul referred either to extraordinary prophets or to those set apart for the ministry.[65]

Therefore, while most Puritans believed that God had ceased to appoint extraordinary prophets,[66] they could still draw lessons for their own day

---

[63] John Lightfoot, "Journal of the Proceedings of the Assembly of Divines from January 1, 1643, to December 31, 1644", *The Whole Works of the Rev. John Lightfoot, D.D.*, ed. J. R. Pitman (London: Printed by J. F. Dove, 1824), vol. 13, 59.

[64] Reid, *Memoirs of the Westminster Divines*, vol. 2, 125-26.

[65] William Rathband, *A Most Grave, and Modest Confutation of the Errors of the Sect, Commonly Called Brownists or: Separatists* (London: Edward Brewster and George Badger, 1644), 65-66. In another treatise, he repeats the same argument and denies that 1 Corinthians 14 can be used as a justification for lay-preaching: William Rathband, *A Briefe Narration of some Church Courses Held in Opinion and Practise in the Churches Lately Erected in New England* (London: Edward Brewster, 1644), 46. Samuel Rutherford sums up the common viewpoint: "All Prophets are either ordinary or extraordinary, as is cleare in *Gods* Word; extraordinary now are not in the Church, and the ordinary Prophets now are not gifted to preach the Word, except as *Timothy*, from their youth they have been trained up in the Scriptures [...]": Samuel Rutherford, *The Due Right of Presbyteries or, A Peaceable Plea for the Government of the Church of Scotland* (London: Richard Whittaker and Andrew Crook, 1644), 280.

[66] Samuel Rutherford (or Rutherfurd), *The Divine Right of Church-Government and Excommunication [...]*" (London: Christopher Meredith, 1646), 39 and 64. Or Samuel Rutherford, *Rutherford's Catechism Containing the Sum of Christian Religion* (Edinburgh: Blue Banner, 1998), 50-51. For a collection of Reformed catechisms,

from texts which were properly applicable to inspired prophets, and so maintain the relevance of those same passages for the modern church. The idea that inspired this hermeneutic was the observation that extraordinary and ordinary expressions of the same gift advance the health of the church.[67] Manifestations of similar gifts were united by their utility. William Lyford demonstrates how the Puritans could distil the two classes of prophecy from one text, and so justify the continuance of one in a non-miraculous sense:

> These Gifts may either be *acquired*, or *infused*; *At first* they were *infused* immediately, both for the honour of the Gospell, and the speedier spreading of it; afterwards they are *continued* for the good of the Church by the Help *of study or prayer*: Even as the Gift of *Healing* is now continued by the study and Art of Physick.[68]

In a similar vein, Samuel Rutherford concludes: "these extraordinary Prophets, and our ordinary Prophets and Pastors differ not in *specie* and nature".[69] Therefore, God's regulation of the extraordinary office is likewise a pattern for regulating the office of ordinary prophet or pastor.[70] Thus, not only did the gifts themselves become applicable, but the modern church could also make use of the general principles regulating such "extraordinary" offices or gifts by applying them to the "ordinary" gifts of the Spirit.

While the Reformed orthodox appropriated texts which referred to extraordinary prophets and made those texts apply to ordinary prophets in the modern church, at the same time they usually maintained that immediately inspired New Testament prophecy had ceased.

The two types of extraordinary prophets in the early churches were identified by the Puritans as those who could predict the future and those who could apply Scripture by means of immediate revelation.[71] According

---

including those of William Gouge, Herbert Palmer, James Ussher, Samuel Rutherford and Robert Blair, see Alexander F. Mitchell, *Catechisms of the Second Reformation* (London: James Nisbet, 1886).

[67] In his discussion of analogous gifts John Owen highlights the common principle of "edification" in the original gift and its analogous replacement. Owen, *The Works of John Owen*, vol. 4, 475.

[68] William Lyford, *An Apologie for our Publick Ministerie and Infant-Baptism* (London: Richard Royston, 1657), especially 7-8.

[69] Rutherford, *The Due Right of Presbyteries*, 466.

[70] Rutherford, *The Due Right of Presbyteries*, 466-67.

[71] But see Earle Ellis who describes the New Testament prophets in Acts performing several functions including prediction (Acts 11:28); declaration of divine judgements (Acts 13:11); engaging in symbolic actions (Acts 21:11); and expounding the Scriptures (Acts 15:32): Earle Ellis, *Prophecy and Hermeneutic in Early Christianity* (Grand Rapids, MI: Baker Book House, 1993), 130-31. However, the third category really relates to the manner of prophesying, while the declaration of judgements is also

to the majority of Reformed orthodox, both of these types had ceased to operate. Anthony Burgess's words on the subject appear to suggest that God had arbitrarily made a decision to withdraw the immediate miraculous gifts of 1 Corinthians 14 so that now he only gives ordinary gifts mediately, which he explains, as William Lyford had, are utilised through study and the use of means, including prayer and preaching.[72] For Burgess, the issue divided Protestants from Catholics, for the Catholic opposition (who in Burgess's view made "prophetical light, a mark of the true Church[...]"[73]) charged that "we have no Prophets, or Revelations amongst us as they have". As far as Catholics were concerned, cessationism rendered Protestantism a false church.[74]

If Burgess addressed the issue of predictive and extra-biblical revelatory prophecy, Richard Byfield focused on the second category of extraordinary prophecy, asserting that the ability to apply the Scriptures by means of revelation had ceased because God had limited the office of the New Testament prophet "for the first plantation of the Gospell and the settling of Christian Churches".[75] Those prophets whose gift was for "[*t*]*elling forth* the written word, by immediate assistance of the Holy Ghost, dexterously unfolding and applying Scripture", have ceased to appear along with inspired foretellers.[76] While contemporary pastors and teachers do something similar, "that is, to open and apply the Scripture to edification, exhortation and comfort, and to convince gainsayers [...]",[77] now a presbytery consists of pastors and elders only, "extraordinary gifts now being ceased".[78] Byfield would not have concurred with Aune that the

---

predictive in nature and is more properly a power of the apostle to perform wonders rather than a prophetic function.

[72] Burgesse, *Spiritual Refining*, 111.

[73] Burgesse, *Spiritual Refining*, 134.

[74] Burgesse, *Spiritual Refining*, 134. William Gouge makes the same point in his commentary on the book of Hebrews: "In regard of the want of miracles among Protestants: whence they infer, that we have neither true Church nor true Ministry": Gouge, *A Learned and Very Useful Commentary on the Whole Epistle to the Hebrewes*, 138.

[75] Richard Byfield, *The Power of the Christ of God, Or a Treatise of Power, as It is Originally in God the Father, and by Him given to Christ His Sonne* (London: Jo. Bellamie, and Ralph Smith, 1641), 12.

[76] Byfield, *The Power of the Christ of God*, 12.

[77] Byfield, *The Power of the Christ of God*, 13

[78] Byfield, *The Power of the Christ of God*, 20. Westminster divine Richard Capel concurs that the gift for interpreting Scripture by extraordinary revelation has ceased because prophets and apostles are no longer present: Richard Capel, *Capel's Remains, Being An Useful Appendix to His Excellent Treatise of Tentations. Concerning the Translations of the Holy Scriptures* (London: John Bartlet, 1658), 33-34. See also 12-13. Capel (1586-1656) a fellow of Magdalen College, voluntarily resigned his charge at

extraordinarily gifted prophets were not integrated into the formal structures of the church; only that there were no longer any present and therefore could not exist as members of sessions or presbyteries.

When the Puritans discussed the claims that inspired prophets still existed, they advanced a number of cessationist arguments as compelling reasons to reject claims to immediate revelation through gifted prophets. It is worth considering these arguments in a little detail, such as the link believed evident between the cessation of prophecy and the cessation of miracles; a standing ministry; and Scripture's sufficiency.

5.3.1 The Simple Assertion of the Cessation of Gifts

Though not a formal argument, the Westminster divines frequently simply asserted that prophecy as a miraculous gift has terminated. William Greenhill is typical in his statement that "extraordinary, prophets, apostles, evangelists [...] are ceased.[79] While Christ, Greenhill notes, "spake immediately to Ezekiel, he speaks in his word to us".[80]

We may see in the unpublished minutes of the Assembly that many participants in its debates supported as a general category the viewpoint that miraculous gifts had ceased. A little-known Westminster divine, Thomas Baylie (or Bayly) (1586-1663), who was rector of Maningford Crucis near Marlborough and later of Mildenhall in Wiltshire,[81] asserts that "[...]miraculous faith ceased long ago".[82] Joshua Hoyle (1590-1664), said to be one of the most influential members of the Assembly, was the only sitting Irish divine present. A Fellow and Professor of Trinity College,

---

Eastington, Herefordshire, when required to read the Book of Sports. He practised medicine until 1641 when he began preaching at Pitchcombe, Gloucestershire. Thomas Cooper, "Richard Capel", *DNB*, vol. 1, 308.

[79] Greenhill, *An Exposition of Ezekiel*, 109.

[80] Greenhill, *An Exposition of Ezekiel*, 111.

[81] Baylie was educated at Oxford and became a zealous Puritan and covenanter. While he was ejected from his church by the Act of Uniformity, the rumour that he was a "fifth-monarchy man" has not been substantiated. Reid, *Memoirs of the Westminster Divines*, vol. 1, 130-31.

[82] "Minutes of the Sessions of the Assembly of Divines, from August 4th, 1643, to March 25th, 1652", 3 vols. in folio Ms. are held in the Dr Williams Library, London. We have used the transcribed minutes, prepared by E. Maunde Thompson, "Minutes of the Sessions of the Assembly of Divines from August 4th, 1643 to April 24th 1652". The transcribed volumes are held at New College Library in Edinburgh. Vol. 1, f45b, 90. [The folio number is the original and the next number is the page number of the transcribed volume]. Hereafter, *Transcribed Minutes*.

Dublin, Hoyle was one of the impressive scholars of his day.[83] He adds his voice to the conclusion that extraordinary gifts are "now ceased".[84] William Bridge and Stephen Marshall concur in the same debate[85]- a surprising development in Bridge's case because, on the basis of the evidence from his sermons we have discussed above, he can be categorised as a continuationist.[86] These bare cessationist statements, of course, usually presupposed other exegetical assumptions of which we can discern three categories.

5.3.2 Why Prophecy is No Longer Necessary

Prophecy was understood to be a miraculous gift which had ceased at the same time as other miraculous New Testament spiritual gifts.[87] For example, representative Puritan writers assert:

1. That there are no longer people qualified to pass on miraculous gifts.[88]
2. That it is a matter of sobriety to teach that miracles have ceased, presumably to counteract "enthusiasm".[89]

---

[83] Hoyle fled to London in 1641 because of the slaughter of Protestants in Ireland. In 1648 he was appointed as Master of University College, Oxford. Barker, *Puritan Profiles*, 170-72.

[84] *Transcribed Minutes*, vol. 1, f190, 373.

[85] *Transcribed Minutes*, vol. 1, f191, 374-75. It is, therefore, highly unlikely that Bridge, whose continuationist views were considered in our previous chapter, was arguing for the contemporary availability of miraculous spiritual gifts.

[86] See 161-167 above.

[87] For an example of a commentator on the *WCF* affirming the cessation of miracles, see John Brown who asks: "Q. Wherein doth a counterfeit miracle differ from a true one? A. Beside a difference in their nature, all true miracles confirm some doctrine, leading to a virtuous life; but counterfeit miracles always confirm trifles, falsehoods, and wicked practices. Why doth not God still work miracles for the confirmation of the Scriptures? A. Because they are only necessary to establish truth at first, and to awaken the world to consider and receive it; and, if always wrought, would make little impression on men's minds": John Brown [of Haddington], *Help for The Ignorant Being an Essay Towards an Easy Explication of The Westminster Confession of Faith and Catechisms* (Edinburgh: William Gray, 1758), 9. Others were sure miracles were ceased, but were not so sure when they had ceased. "Thus we see when it should cease; but when miracles did cease is not easy to be defined. If the story be true in Tertullian, they continued some two hundred years after Christ[...]": Thomas Manton, *An Exposition of the Epistle of James* (London: The Banner of Truth Trust, 1962), 449. For a modern discussion on why Old Testament prophecy ceased, see Frederick Greenspahn, "Why Prophecy Ceased", *Journal of Biblical Literature* 108/1(1989), 37-49.

[88] Thomas Goodwin reasoned that miraculous gifts have ceased because they could no longer be conveyed through the laying on of hands. *Transcribed Minutes*, vol. 1, f339, 665.

Prophecy and the Westminster Divines 195

3. That there has been a change in the measure of the Holy Spirit imparted to the settled church.[90]

4. That supernatural miracles are no longer necessary to establish the church by using such a divine validation or authentication of its teaching. This fourth argument was the most common.

Francis Cheynell limited miracles to the foundational era of the church. Appointed to examine heresy, in an account of one investigation, Cheynell links miracles and prophecy, and affirms that the prophetic gift so evident at Corinth was "as extraordinary as the gifts of Tongues or Miracles".[91] Cheynell, along with the other investigating ministers, affirms that "Prophets and Apostles were extraordinary officers & *pro tempore* for the first planting and founding of the Church[...]".[92] The church has been

---

[89] Thomas Ford (1598-1674 or 76), a minister at Exeter, whose suffering at Laud's hands was a useful credential for participation in the Assembly, said simply that as a matter of sobriety one must deny the contemporary availability of extraordinary gifts of the Spirit. Ford, applying the claim that the spiritual songs of 1 Cor. 14:26 were immediately inspired, sarcastically proposes: "But I suppose no sober man will now pretend to any such extraordinary gift, which ceast in the Church long since, as the gift of Tongues, and other effects of the Spirit extraordinary". Thomas Ford, *Singing of Psalmes the Duty of Christians under the New Testament or a Vindication of that Gospel-Ordinance* (London: F. Eaglesfield, 1659), 16.

[90] Obadiah Sedgwick, *The Bowels of Tender Mercy Sealed in the Everlasting Covenant [...]"* (London: Adoniram Byfield, 1661), 589. See also John Conant, *Sermons Preach'd on Several Occasions. The Third Volume* (London: Thomas Cockerill and H. Walwyn, 1698), at 310-11, where Conant notes that we cannot expect a miracle of healing as Christ performed in his incarnation. Although we cannot be certain, the John Conant (1587-?) of the Assembly was probably the uncle of the younger Conant cited here. The *DNB* suggests that the younger Conant could not have been the Assembly divine, because he failed to sign the Solemn League and Covenant. William Hunt, "John Conant", *DNB*, vol. 1, 421-22. Thomas Wilson concurred that miraculous faith was unavailable in his day. Thomas Wilson, *Jerichoes Down-Fall* (London: John Bartlet, 1643), 25. Wilson (1601-1653), studied at Cambridge and became a school teacher but later served as a minister in several congregations. Wilson was suspended for a time for refusing to read the Book of Sports, but later was granted a charge at Otham, Kent, when he also attended the Westminster Assembly. Reid, *Memoirs of the Westminster Divines*, 251-64.

[91] Francis Cheynell, *An Account Given to the Parliament by the Ministers Sent by Them to Oxford [...] The Chief Points Insisted on in Those Conferences are, 1. Whether Private Men might Lawfully Preach. 2. Whether the Ministers of the Church of England were Antichristian. Both which Questions were Disputed, Objections Answered, and the Truth Confirmed. 3. And Lastly, Divers of M. Erbury's Dangerous Errours which He hath Broached and Maintained, are Recited and Refuted* (London: Samuell Gellibrand, 1647), 15.

[92] Cheynell, *An Account Given to the Parliament by the Ministers Sent by Them to Oxford*, 19.

founded, planted and sufficiently authenticated so that, as Christopher Tesdale (b.1591) explains, miracles are quite simply obsolete because their apostolic, foundational and confirmatory function has now concluded:

> Miracles, say some, were the bells that tolled in hearers to the Apostles Sermons, good conversation comes in now in the place of Miracles [...]".[93]

The sanctified life of the believer has assumed the role that miracles once had in confirming the apostles' doctrine. When revelation ended, so too did any need for the miraculous. In this context, William Gouge explains the correlative function between the revelatory and the other extraordinary gifts mentioned in 1 Cor. 12:28 (which included prophecy), when he expounds Heb. 2:4, the *locus classicus* of the corroborative instrumentality of miracles. The extraordinary gifts are those alluded to in Joel 2:28-29 and demonstrated in the Acts 2:17-18, as well as in 1 Corinthians 12:[94]

> That extraordinary gifts are here intended, is evident, in that they are here joyned with Signes, Wonders and Miracles: and because they are brought in for the very same end: namely for confirmation of the Gospel.[95]

Gouge's colleague Anthony Burgess makes the same Protestant cessationist point in his commentary on 1 Cor. 3:5, noting that:

> because such extraordinary gifts were in the nature of Miracles to confirm the Apostles Doctrine, and their Mission from God, they now cease.[96]

A similar cessationist argument was also applied to the miraculous authentication of the gospel ministry. Since no more doctrine will be revealed (a premise unquestioned by the orthodox), miraculous gifts are obviously no longer needed to authenticate a standing ministry, for such validation is only necessary when a teacher brings new revelation. Thus Lazarus Seaman,[97] for example, asserts that there have been no apostles,

---

[93] Christopher Tesdale, *Hierusalem: Or a Vision of Peace* (London: Phil. Stephens, 1644), 4. Tesdale was an Assemblyman and one-time pastor of Husborne-Tarrant, Southampton county. See Reid, *Memoirs of the Westminster Divines*, vol. 2, 183-85.

[94] Gouge, *A Learned and Very Useful Commentary on the Whole Epistle to the Hebrewes*, 142. For Gouge's cessationism, see also William Gouge, *Gods Three Arrowes: Plague, Famine, Sword, In Three Treatises* (London: Edward Brewster, 1631), 161.

[95] Gouge, *A Learned and Very Useful Commentary on the Whole Epistle to the Hebrewes*, 142.

[96] Anthony Burgess, *The Scripture Directory, for Church-Officers and People or, a Practical Commentary Upon the Whole Third Chapter of the First Epistle of St Paul to the Corinthians [...]"* (London: Thomas Underhill, 1659), 75.

[97] Seaman (1607-1675) though one of the younger divines at the Assembly, was one of its most frequent speakers. Educated at Emmanuel College, Cambridge, he became a deacon and was later appointed rector at All Hallows, Bread Street, London. A staunch opposer of the Independents and Erastians at the Assembly, Seaman was ejected

evangelists or prophets for sixteen hundred years, yet God still makes good his Word through pastors and teachers.[98] A connection is accordingly established between the adequacy of a standing ministry of the Word and the irrelevance of miraculous prophecy.

In a similar fashion, Henry Hammond contrasts the now-defunct provision of miracles with the continuous ordinary task of ministry.[99] The modern prophet only declares what God has already revealed in Scripture. Preaching on Luke 9:55, Hammond compares the *"Prophetick Spirit"* of Elijah with the *"Gospel-Spirit"* of the post-apostolic age.[100] Modern "prophets" now work with the content of Scripture only:

> [prophecies] proceed from some peculiar incitations of God; I mean not from the ordinary, or extraordinary, general, or special *direction*, or influence of his grace, cooperating with the Word, as in the breast of every regenerate man, (for the Spirit of Sanctification, and the Spirit of Prophecy, are very distant things) but from the extraordinary *revelations* of God's Will, many times against the setled rule of duty[...]. Consequent to which is, that because the prophetick office was not beyond the *Apostles* time to continue constantly in the Church, any further, than to interpret, and superstruct upon what the Canon of Scripture hath setled among Christians.[101]

The phrase "continue constantly in the Church" does not imply a continuing though intermittent gift, because Hammond adds in parentheses "(Christ and his Word in the New Testament, being that Bath-Col [*sic*], which the

---

following the Restoration. He is said to have possessed a library of some 5000 books. Barker, *Puritan Profiles*, 229-33.

[98] Lazarus Seaman, *A Glasse for the Times* (London: John Rothwell, 1650), 29.

[99] Henry Hammond (1605-1660), though appointed a Westminster divine, like James Usher and William Lyford, did not sit in the Assembly. Robert Harrison, "Henry Hammond", *DNB*, vol. 1, 885. Hammond was charged with universalism, works justification and a false interpretation of the Third Commandment by the authors of: *A Testimony to the Truth of Jesus Christ, and to our Solemn League and Covenant; as also Against Errours, Heresies and Blasphemies of These Times, and the Toleration of Them* (London: Thos. Underhill, 1648). See 15, for example. The *Testimony* was subscribed by fifty-two London ministers, including a significant number of Westminster divines. Hammond's *A Brief Vindication* denies the charges, although he attempts to argue for a hypothetical universalism. Henry Hammond, *A Brief Vindication of Three Passages in the Practical Catechisme, from the Censures Affixt on Them by the Ministers of London, in a Book Entitled, A Testimony to the Truth of Jesus Christ &c.* (London: Richard Royston, 1648), 3-13. Nevertheless, he was unquestionably orthodox on the doctrine of Scripture.

[100] Henry Hammond, *Sermons Preached by that Eminent Divine Henry Hammond, D.D.* (London: Robert Pawlet, 1675), 63-64.

[101] Hammond, *Sermons Preached*, 64.

Jews tell us, was alone to survive all other ways of Prophecy:)".[102] Hammond allows a continuing "prophetic" ability in the ordinary function of the pastor or teacher, but denies revelatory powers beyond the apostolic era.[103]

William Strong, likewise, contends for the cessation of prophets and of the gift of prophecy, while allowing for modern "prophets":

> *Eph.* 4.11. *he gave gifts to men*: that is, the office, and the gifts that did qualifie for the office: officers that are set in the Church are of two sorts: some temporary, as *Apostles*, *Prophets* and *Evangelists*: and their gifts were but for a time: the gifts did cease with the office[...]".[104]

Since Strong also holds that Luther had (predictive) prophetic abilities,[105] consistency requires us to believe that Strong understood Luther's prophetic gift to be something other than that of an immediately inspired New Testament prophet.[106] Surprisingly, one could, therefore, see even foretelling as a function of the modern uninspired prophet. This was further evidence that Westminster divines accepted the validity of predictive prophecy which fell outside the definition of prophecy by immediate revelation. The latter was a New Testament miraculous gift which had now

---

[102] See also Hammond, *Sermons Preached*, 64, in which he goes on to denounce all "*enthusiasts*" in orthodox fashion. He also links such "enthusiasm" with epilepsy, melancholy (often associated with epilepsy in his day) and "phanatick phansie". Rabbinic scholars held that God had communicated through a "bath qol" (literally the "daughter of the voice"; hence the echo of the voice of God) from time to time throughout Israel's history, but that when prophecy had ceased all that remained as a source of new revelation was the "bath qol". On the "bath qol", see Otto Betz, "φωνή", *TDNT*, vol. 9, 288-90.

[103] Abraham Kuyper believed that the Reformers sought to revive the office of prophet as "prophesying, in the general sense". Kuyper probably meant the proclamation of the gospel utilising ordinary gifts. Abraham Kuyper, *The Work of the Holy Spirit* (Grand Rapids, MI: Eerdmans, 1975), 159.

[104] William Strong, *XXXI. Select Sermons, Preached on Several Occasions* (London: Francis Tyton, 1656), 94-95. See also 681; and Strong, *A Treatise Shewing the Subordination of the Will of Man unto the Will of God*, 6.

[105] William Strong, 'Ημερα' Αποκαλυψεως. *The Day of Revelation of the Righteous Judgement of God*. (London: I. Benson, and I. Saywell, 1645), 11-12.

[106] This is Beth Langstaff's conclusion in her comprehensive study: "Numerous collections of his [Luther's] prophecies were published and his prophetic gifts were cited as evidence of his divine authority, despite his own denial that he possessed such powers[...]. Moreover, it is certain that when Calvin calls Luther and his colleagues 'prophets', he does not mean that they are foretellers of the future or endowed with supernatural knowledge". See Beth Langstaff, "Temporary Gifts: John Calvin's Doctrine of the Cessation of Miracles" (unpublished PhD thesis, Princeton Theological Seminary, 1999), 299.

ceased and yet a gift that effectively fulfilled a similar function continued.[107]

This sufficiency of the standing ministry with its "ordinary gifts" was derived from another cessationist plank - the doctrine of *sola Scriptura*. It seemed necessary to limit God's voice to Scripture if he had already finished speaking through immediate extraordinary prophecy or other supernatural means.[108] Westminster divine John de La Marche (or Delamarche), the minister of a French congregation in London,[109] compares revelation given through the ephod[110] worn by the ancient Israelite high priest with revelation mediated through modern ministers who no longer have access to the same kind of oracle. This was a standard comparison, as we have already noted in Chapter Two:

> And thus the true and faithfull Ministers of the Gospel having first consulted the true Oracles of God onely, that is, his sacred word ought to informe in the name of the Lord, the King and his Nobles[...]".[111]

Obviously a dishonest and unfaithful minister could falsely claim to go beyond the only oracle now in existence. De La Marche has in mind the teaching of Scripture on the responsibility of the civil magistrate to preserve the true religion in the land.

Joseph Caryl likewise earnestly pleaded before the Commons in 1645 for a thoroughgoing reformation in England. He admits that reformation was by then no longer possible through the instruction of inspired prophets: "Tis granted, We have no such revelations as *Isaiah* brought to *Ahaz* and his

---

[107] Acts 11:28.

[108] For the Radical Reformation on Scripture, see Stuart Murray, "Anabaptists", in Hart (ed.), *The Dictionary of Historical Theology*, 13-16, at 15 where he sees the difference over Scripture between the Anabaptists and the Reformers one of hermeneutics and application rather than over authority. For the theology of perhaps the most influential leader of the Anabaptists, see F. H. Little, *A Tribute to Menno Simons: A discussion of the Theology of Menno Simons and its Significance for Today* (Scottdale, Pa: Herald Press, 1971).

[109] The House of Commons appointed de La Marche (dates unknown) to represent Guernsey and Jersey, but in 1643 he petitioned Parliament to release him for pressing pastoral needs on Guernsey. See Larry Holly, "The Divines of the Westminster Assembly: A Study of Puritanism and Parliament" (unpublished PhD thesis, Yale University, 1979), 297-98.

[110] By metonymy this refers to the Urim and Thummim which were attached to the linen ephod. See Lev. 8:8; Num. 27:21; Deut. 33:8; 1 Sam. 28:6; Ezra 2:63; Neh. 7:65. Carol Meyers, "Breastpiece", *ABD*, vol. 1, 781. and Carol Meyers, "Ephod", *ABD*, vol. 2, 550.

[111] John de La Marche, *A Complaint of the False Prophets Mariners upon the Drying up of Their Hierarchicall Euphrates. As it was Preached Publickly in the Island of Garnezey before a Sett Order of Ministers* (London: Thomas Payne, 1641), 46.

people".[112] Yet, England can still discover in Scripture what "amounts to a particular promise",[113] and thus can appropriate those of God's blessings previously bestowed only upon his Old Testament people.[114] "These promises are ours, as well as this was *Jerusalems*".[115]

The sufficiency of Scripture was itself an argument for the cessation of prophecy, and it rendered claims to any immediate revelation external to Scripture both false and unnecessary. As we have seen in William Strong's appeal to Luther's gift, the limitation of God's voice to Scripture did not necessarily preclude an ability to predict the future, because promises in Scripture that pertained to the future could be harnessed as promises for England. The Scriptures themselves were a kind of heuristic device that enabled the Puritan to make predictions about particular, but otherwise unforeseen, events.

Such foretelling had a long-established history which involved illustrious names from the time of the Reformation. The phenomenon has caused many students of church history to consider carefully examples of predictive prophecy which have been claimed for Reformed orthodox "prophets". John Lightfoot discusses the phenomenon in his doctoral thesis, where he raises a series of questions meant to affirm both the cessation of special revelation and the sufficiency of Scripture:

"[...]is it lawful to expect revelations? For explaining Scripture? It [Scripture] bears its own key with it. For begetting new articles of faith?[...]. For guidance in life? 'The law of God is a light to our feet[...].' For predicting the future? Here some hesitate and here we may check our step a little.[116]

---

[112] Joseph Caryl, *The Arraignment of Unbelief, as The Grand Cause of Our National Non-establishment* (London: Giles Calvert, 1645), 42.

[113] Caryl, *The Arraignment of Unbelief*, 42.

[114] Stephen Marshall, for example, in a treatise on infant baptism, takes the position on the Great Commission of Matt. 28:16-20 that the nations are to be discipled *as* nations. He thinks a national covenanted church is necessary if God's purposes are to be realised: "[N]ow their Commission was extended to make *all* Nations Disciples, every Nation which should receive *the faith* should be to him now, as the peculiar Nation of the *Jewes* had beene in time past". Stephen Marshall, *A Sermon of the baptizing of Infants* (London: Stephen Bowtell, 1644), 38.

[115] Caryl, *The Arraignment of Unbelief*, 43.

[116] "[...]ad quod expectare liceat revelationes? An ad explicandam Scripturam? Clavem suam ipsa secum portat. An ad novos articulos fidei generandos?[...]An ad dirigendam vitam? 'Lex Dei est lux pedibus nostris'[...]An ad praedicenda futura? Hic haesitant nonnulli: et hic paullum nos sistamus gressus". John Lightfoot, *The Whole Works of the Rev. John Lightfoot, D.D.*, ed. J. R. Pitman (London: Printed by J. F. Dove, 1822), vol. 5, 467. This work was published two years before the edition which contains the minutes of the Assembly.

Lightfoot then cites the standard claim that Martin Luther, John Hus and John Knox foretold events which subsequently came to pass. He describes the predictions of all three men as divine revelations: "so that they were not able to teach these things unless they were taught by some divine revelation".[117] Lightfoot gives a carefully considered response to these claims and suggests that even if the prophecies attributed to Huss, Luther, and Knox and others were revelations:[118] "Let it not be denied. But this hardly undermines our investigation",[119] and affirms that his thesis addresses claims to new or future revelations for a rule of faith and manners:

> We speak in our investigation about new revelations, that is, as to whether the Scripture may be supplemented in the future by any means, either as a rule of faith or as a rule of morals.[120]

He concludes:

> Now even if it be granted that these revelations of which we speak were true and pure, they have nevertheless ceased from this use, so unusual and strange, as it is easy to observe from the very things which were predicted and proclaimed.[121]

Even though Lightfoot's scepticism is evident, he makes a clear distinction between the revelation that is Scripture and the predictions of unusual events. Is this difference a solution to the claims of Reformation prophecy? Is lower-order "immediate" prophecy still possible as long as it is not placed on the same level as Scripture? There are at least six reasons why we cannot conclude that Lightfoot's distinction between revelation for faith and manners on the one hand and Knoxian predictions on the other legitimises new immediate revelations as long as they are not considered part of the rule of faith and life:

1. Lightfoot does not call these supposed revelations "immediate".

---

[117]"[...] ut non, nisi divina aliqua revelatione edocti, edocere haec possent" Lightfoot, *The Whole Works of the Rev. John Lightfoot, D.D.*, vol. 5, 467.

[118] Lightfoot, *The Whole Works of the Rev. John Lightfoot, D.D.*, vol. 5, 467.

[119] "I. Non negetur. At parum hoc facit adversus quaestionem nostram". Lightfoot, *The Whole Works of the Rev. John Lightfoot, D.D.*, vol. 5, 467.

[120] "Loquimur in quaestione nostra de novis revelationibus, hoc est, ac si vicem Scripturae ullo modo suppleturis, vel pro norma fidei, vel pro norma morum, futuris". Lightfoot, *The Whole Works of the Rev. John Lightfoot, D.D.*, vol. 5, 467.

[121] "Jam ergo si concedatur, veras et meras fuisse has, quas loquimur, revelationes, minime tamen in usum cesserunt talem, tam insolitum, tam insolentem, ut facile et ex ipsis rebus praedictis et praedicatis observare". Lightfoot, *The Whole Works of the Rev. John Lightfoot, D.D.*, vol. 5, 467-68.

2. When he writes: "we may check (*sistamus*) our step a little", Lightfoot is pausing to consider a possible explanation, not stopping to affirm modern predictive prophecy.

3. His qualification that he is talking only about revelations added to Scripture can be explained as an argument that other claims to prediction do not contradict his thesis, irrespective of their validity, and it therefore makes them irrelevant to his purpose. He is probably, therefore, speaking hypothetically.

4. Lightfoot stresses that looking for such revelations is unlawful, which would hardly be the case if Scripture sanctioned them. Such illegality also devalues the alleged "revelations" and means that they cannot bear the same authority or certainty as similar revelatory experiences in Bible times. Thus they cannot equate to the New Testament extraordinary prophetic gift which enabled both the exposition of Scripture by revelation, and prediction for the edification of the Church.

5. Lightfoot elsewhere specifically states that there are no modern revelations for predicting the future. In a sermon on Jude 12, *The feasts of Charity*, Lightfoot dismisses the argument of contemporary claimants to prophecy and excludes the gift of the Spirit for revelation in a similar list to that in his thesis. His statement is unequivocal here that God does not give the spirit of wisdom and revelation to "foresee things to come".[122]

6. Finally, he gives an entirely different explanation in his thesis when he reclassifies modern foretelling as an applying of Scripture to providence – the standard Reformed orthodox clarification of such phenomena:

> Very many future events have been predicted by very many men, correctly and with a consonant outcome. Not from some immediate afflatus, or revelation, but out of the reading of the scriptures, and observation, and experience, as could be demonstrated in many of these examples, if it were not too much. But we are interested in brevity. Therefore let this be enough for the present.[123]

This final word in the thesis concludes with a degree of scepticism that modern predictive prophecy could be legitimately construed as extra-biblical extraordinary revelation.

---

[122] Lightfoot, *The Whole Works of the Rev. John Lightfoot, D.D.*, vol. 6, 238.

[123] "Praedicta sunt quamplurima futura ab hominibus quamplurimis, vere et eventui consone, non ex immediato aliquo afflatu, aut revelatione, sed ex lectione Scripturae, et observatione, et experientia, ut in plurimis horum exemplorum demonstrari posset, si non nimium esset. Sed brevitati studemus. Haec ergo in praesentiarum sunto satis". Lightfoot, *The Whole Works of the Rev. John Lightfoot, D.D.*, vol. 5, 468.

5.3.3. Summary

The Puritans raised a number of arguments against suggestions that immediate prophecy could be available in their own day. They proposed that when miracles, whose role was to authenticate and attest the doctrine of the apostles, ceased, so too did prophecy, which was one of those miracles. Furthermore, the standing ministry had no need of miracles, because the purpose for which God had given them was now fulfilled. This idea, not surprisingly, went hand-in-hand with the notion that Scripture was sufficient as a supernatural revelation for faith leading to eternal life and for direction in this life.

5.4 The Explanation of the Puritan Acceptance of Contemporary Prophecy

Before turning to the explanations the Puritans gave for contemporary prophecy, it is important to notice how they viewed the role of Scripture in the area of guidance generally.[124] Human reason was a highly valued source of guidance in ordinary human decision-making, as Jeremiah Burroughs urged in a sermon preached in 1645.[125]

> [God] hath given two Lights to man, to guide his course; the Scriptures the greater, to guide man, especially in his spirituall condition, in these more immediate references he hath to God, for his worship and enjoyment of communion with him; The other the lesse, the light of Reason, to be his guide in naturall and civill things, in the ordering his life for his naturall and civill good[...]".[126]

Notwithstanding the valuable direction of reason in the light of Scripture, the Bible itself was the primary guide for Puritan divines. When Stephen Marshall defines several types of accessible knowledge in his *The Right Understanding of the Times*, he illustrates how practical Puritans found biblical guidance to be. One who has a biblical or "theological" knowledge of the times, he says, will respond by living an authentic Christian life in obedience to the will of God, which is:

> to observe all Gods administrations, wherewith the present time is filled, his providences, his mercies, his judgements, his words, his workes, to observe them (I say) so as thereby to bee inabled seasonably and timely to

---

[124] For an introduction to the Puritan view that Scripture takes over the rule of the Urim and Thummim in non-doctrinal guidance, see also Chapter Two, 92-94 above.

[125] Jeremiah Burroughs, *Irenicum, to the Lovers of Truth and Peace* (London: Robert Dawlman, 1645).

[126] Burroughs, *Irenicum, to the Lovers of Truth and Peace*, 98.

performe their own duties, and to regulate their conversations according to the exigence and juncture of times[...]".[127]

Puritans conducted their lives for "the salvation of their owne soules",[128] but in such complex and important matters the *"Booke"* is always primary:

> *That the Booke of God, and onely the Booke of God, is able to informe them who faithfully study it, in all the duties that doe belong to every new posture or face of time[...]onely Gods Booke* can do it.[129]

In Puritan perspective, the Bible is not relevant just as a source of general moral principles: it serves to give the Christian ethical guidance in all particular circumstances – *"every new posture or face of time"*. What added lustre to the ordinance of preaching by the *"Booke"* was Scripture's assumed efficacy and power which, in turn, was held to derive from divine authority.[130] Effectively, biblical preachers were mouthpieces of God himself and therefore delivered prophetic oracles in the sense that they proclaimed the contemporary will of God to his people. Richard Love (1596-1661), who was appointed a Westminster divine although we have

---

[127] Marshall, *Right Understanding,* 10.

[128] Marshall, *Right Understanding,* 10.

[129] Marshall, *Right Understanding,* 17. See also Stephen Marshall, "The Life of Christ or the Great Mystery of Spiritual life", *The Works of Mr Stephen Marshall* (London: printed by Peter and Edward Cole, 1661), 27-28. Later he notes: "The Grace of Faith wrought in us by the Spirit of God, and acted in us by the Spirit of God, it immediately hath its whol[e] application to the Word [...]. [T]he Spirits proper and immediate work is to deal with the will of Christ revealed in his Word, it looks not at Heaven immediately, it looks not to Christ immediately; but it looks at God, and Christ, and Heaven mediately through the Word" (43). He adds: "but you shall find in the Word Promises for every condition it is possible for you to fal into[...]" (69).

[130] For a wide-ranging discussion on the Puritan view of the Bible in which five representative Puritans from different strands of Protestantism are discussed, see John R. Knott, *The Sword of the Spirit.Puritan Responses to the Bible* (Chicago: The University of Chicago Press, 1980), especially 13-41, for an overview of the ideas of English Reformers, such as John Rogers' dynamic view of the Bible as the living Word. See also Kenneth Shipps, "The 'Political Puritan'", *Church History* 45 (1976), 196-205, at 203, who discusses the political influence of Puritan preaching: "Between 1625 and 1640 citizens in at least one-fourth of the parliamentary boroughs had paid for or could hear a puritan lecturer and/or minister: The ten largest boroughs hired lecturers or had puritan ministers. Thus it was possible for puritans to have influence over a far greater number of parliamentary elections than a peer of the realm"; Horton Davies, *The Worship of the English Puritans* (Westminster: Dacre Press, 1948), suggests: "The preacher was the man of God, the prophet, who declared to the congregation the 'mystery' of the Gospel, unfolding the whole plan of salvation, under compulsion to bring men to the parting of the ways that lead to salvation or to damnation[...]. The preaching of the Word was neither a moral homily nor a philosophical disquisition; it was the authoritative declaration of the will of the Blessed God" (185).

no evidence of his participation in the Assembly, explains that "a true Minister of the Gospel (whatsoever the world now thinketh) is an Angel of light, an Herauld of heaven, and Embassadour of God".[131]

Love and his fellow-Puritans did not suggest that God gave extraordinary inspiration to the modern preachers so that they might become inspired prophets such as Jeremiah or the Apostle Paul.[132] As we have already considered, the exegetical stance of the Reformed orthodox led them to distinguish between immediately inspired prophets and those who were uninspired.[133] For example, Westminster divines Philip Nye,[134] Thomas Goodwin,[135] and William Carter[136] all taught that while prophecy refers in some biblical texts to ordinary preaching, in others it signals the presence of extraordinary prophets and prophetesses who received immediate revelations in the early church. Thus Carter allows for extraordinary

---

[131] Richard Love, *The Watchmans Watchword* (Cambridge: Cambridge University, 1642), 17. Love had formerly been chaplain to Charles I and was to become master of Corpus Christi College. For biographical details, see Emily Bradley, "Richard Love", *DNB*, vol. 1, 1246.

[132] See the Antinomian William Dell, *The Tryal of Spirits Both in Teachers and Hearers, Wherein is Held Forth the Clear Discovery, and Certain Downfal of the Carnal and Antichristian Clergie of These Nations. Testified from the Word of God to the University-Congregation in Cambridge. Whereunto is Added A Plain and Necessary Confutation of Divers Gross Errors Delivered by Mr Sydrach Simpson in a Sermon Preached to the Same Congregation at the Commencement, Anno 1653 [...]"* (London: Giles Calvert, 1660), in which he attacks Westminster divine Sydrach Simpson for teaching that universities were the equivalent of the Old Testament school of the prophets (80). Another of Simpson's errors, according to Dell, was that "*men now, are not to receive the* Spirit, *in that immediate way to* understand *the Scriptures*" (114).

[133] See, for example, Henry Scudder who teaches in a sermon, preached before the Commons, that while ministers are not immediately inspired or commissioned by God, in so far as their word is consistent with the Bible, Christians should receive it as the Word of God as much as they would the words of the prophets themselves: Henry Scudder, *Gods Warning to England by the Voyce of His ROD* (London: Philemon Stephens and Edward Blackmore, 1644), 6-7. He warns that prophets as ministers of the Word have spoken to his audience, and he threatens that if they fail to heed the warning, God will apply his "Judgements, Spirituall, Temporall, and Eternall" (11).

[134] Philip Nye, *A Case of Great and Present Use* (London: Jonathan Robinson, 1677), 1-2. Nye (1596-1672), next to Goodwin was the most frequent Independent speaker. Nye, educated at Oxford, became the tactical leader of the Independents in the Assembly. He held a ministry position at Acton in Middlesex and also held lectureships in London. Treated harshly at the Restoration, Nye resumed the ministry in 1672 at Cutters' Hall, Cloak Lane, Queen Street, London. Barker, *Puritan Profiles*, 77-80.

[135] Thomas Goodwin, *The Works of Thomas Goodwin, D.D.* (Edinburgh: James Nichol, 1863), vol. 11, 542-43.

[136] Carter, *The Covenant of God with Abraham Opened [...] Together with A Short Discourse Concerning the Manifestations of God unto His People in the Last Dayes*, 29.

prophetesses lawfully to exercise their gifts in the church in those days.[137] With the centrality of Scripture as a source of guidance in view, we now turn to consider the Puritan acceptance of the possibility of contemporary prophecy.

5.4.1 The Possibility of Contemporary Prophecy

It is important to explore more deeply the predominant Puritan view that the application of Scripture still qualifies as genuine divine prophecy, demonstrating that they did not restrict the term *prophecy* to just uninspired preaching *per se*.[138] Premonitory dreams and premonitions while awake, a traditional belief we have already seen Thomas Gillespie maintain in the eighteenth century,[139] were one type of "prophetic" experience that still occurred. Yet, as Gillespie also explained, they were distinguishable from "immediate revelation". The Puritan John Flavel, a sympathetic commentator on the *SC*, also acknowledged that both pagans and Christians had genuine premonitions of death. As examples of the latter, he mentions John Knox and James Usher.[140]

The Quaker George Keith implies that both Quakers and Reformed orthodox alike share a common belief in a prophetic facility. At the same time Keith, though representative of Quaker resistance and opposition to Westminster orthodoxy, does not automatically see widespread acceptance of foretelling as proof of a claim to the New Testament prophetic gifts of immediate revelation. He opposes the way the contemporary Scottish Presbyterians denied the modern possibility of immediate extra-biblical revelation, but at the beginning of his essay he acknowledges that a Christian may have the "accidental" ability to predict the future. He also

---

[137] Carter, *The Covenant of God with Abraham Opened [...] Together with A Short Discourse Concerning the Manifestations of God unto His People in the Last Dayes*, 145-46.

[138] There was, nonetheless, a strong tradition that defined preaching as prophecy. The early Puritan Thomas Cartwright not only assumes that "the use of extraordinary gifts in tongues & revelation of things to come, be ceased", but that "those meanes from the Church, whereby it may have edifying, exhortation, and consolation, and have them abundantly", have remained. He refers here to the ordinary gifts and includes the prophecy mentioned in Rom. 12:6, and 1 Cor. 14:3, while he sees 1 Thess. 5:20-21 as referring to both extraordinary and ordinary prophets. Thomas Cartwright, *A Confutation of the Rhemists Translation* (Amsterdam: Theatrum Orbis Terrarum Ltd, 1971), 431-32. The frequent identification of "prophesying" with uninspired preaching makes it important to be wary of misinterpreting Puritan use of the term.

[139] Refer to Chapter Four, 147, n2 above.

[140] John Flavel, "A treatise of the soul of man", *The Works of John Flavel* (London: Banner of Truth, 1968), vol. 3, 67-72. For his commentary on the *SC*, see vol. 6, 140-317.

believes that a non-Christian may have it, which indicates that Keith does not consider that the predictive facility is a gift of the Holy Spirit only:

> [The] Lord at times reveals unto whom he pleaseth, both for the comfort of the Godly and the terror of the Wicked. This many of the National-way acknowledge, and experience proveth[...]the Controversie is not at all stated, betwixt these of the national way and us, for none of us plead its absolute and indispensable necessity to any, and they acknowledge, it may be given to some.[141]

We cannot construe Keith's concession as Westminster allowing for "immediate" revelational prophecy, because he sees a clear disjunction between the religious epistemology of the *WCF* and the predictions of Christian worthies such as John Hus, George Wishart and John Knox. According to Keith, the *WCF* had departed from orthodoxy and had erred in its claim that God no longer reveals himself through immediate prophetic revelations of the Knoxian type.[142] Keith reiterates this distinction in another work in which he asserts that the *WCF*'s cessationist clause precludes foretelling as immediate revelation:

> "[...]and your Church Confession of Faith saith, *The former way of God's revealing himself by prophecy and immediate Revelation, is ceased; and God hath committed his counsel wholly into writing (or to the Scriptures) and nothing is to be added thereto by any new revelation of the Spirit.*[143]

Keith's diatribe makes it plain that by "prophecy" he means foretelling, because once more he marshals Knox and Wishart to illustrate his point as examples of extraordinary prophecy, adding an appeal to evidence in Foxe's *Book of Martyrs*.[144] Those who take the same cessationist view as the *WCF* have, he charges:

> degenerated and apostatized from the primitive Protestants and Reformers, who not only affirmed, that there were immediate Revelations

---

[141] George Keith, *Immediate Revelation (or Jesus Christ the Eternal Son of God, Revealed in Man. Revealing the Knowledge of God, and the Things of his Kingdom, Immediately) Not Ceased, but Remaining a Standing and Perpetual Ordinance in the Church of Christ, and being of Indispensable Necessity, as to the Whole Body in General, so to Every Member thereof: Every True Believer in Particular, Asserted and Demonstrated. And the Objections that Have any Seeming Weight Against it Answered* (London: 1675) [no further publishing details are given], 2-3.

[142] Keith, *Immediate Revelation*, 193-97.

[143] George Keith, *Help in Time of Need, from the God of Help. To the People of the (so called) Church of Scotland, Especially the Once more Zealous and Professing, Who Have so Shamefully Degenerated and Declined from that Which their Fathers the Primitive Protestants Attained unto [...] Being Certain Particulars Very Weighty, and of Great Concernment for Them to Consider Seriously [...]"* (Aberdeen: 1665) [no further publishing details are given], 23.

[144] Keith, *Help in Time of Need, from the God of Help*, 23-24.

from God, and that the Spirit of Prophecie was not ceased, but witnessed the same in themselves, and foretold many things of consequence by the spirit of Prophecie, which came to pass.[145]

Keith was certainly not alone in his opinion. An earlier critic, William Parker, in the first published critique of the *WCF*, similarly argued that the *WCF* was erroneous in teaching the cessation of prophecy and prophets.[146]

However, what can we make of Keith's presumption that among both Christian and non-Christian there is a commonly (though not universally) accepted facility of prediction? He was certainly correct in his assertion that belief in predictive prophecy was widespread among the Reformed orthodox. That belief seems not to fit with the Westminster Puritans' equally vigorous commitment, previously discussed, to the cessation of "immediate revelation". How do we resolve the paradox?

In point of fact, Keith is not quite correct in saying that the Reformed orthodox generally denied that any form of immediate knowledge could still come from God. Sometimes the premonitions of a believer could be labelled "immediate". Meric Casaubon, the author of the English Psalms' Annotations, though not a Westminster divine, teaches in his scholarly *Treatise Concerning Enthusiasme* that prophecy by immediate divine inspiration was widely accepted by Christians in his day. Although Casaubon goes to great lengths to give a naturalistic explanation for "enthusiasm", he claims that there is a general belief in prophetic foresight:

> Most that have written of Divination, to prove that it proceeds of naturall causes, insist upon the divination of some dying men, upon which they inferre a naturall aptitude of the Soul to it when loose and free from the body. That holy men when near to death, have often prophesied by *immediate divine Inspiration*, is not a thing to be disputed among Christians [emphasis added].[147]

What distinguishes this type of prophecy from the early Christian extraordinary gift is obviously that it is attributed, as a "naturall aptitude", only to the souls of holy men near death.[148] Casaubon here articulates a

---

[145] Keith, *Help in Time of Need, from the God of Help*, 23.

[146] W[William?]. Parker, *The Late Assembly of Divines Confession of Faith Examined. As it was Presented by Them unto the Parliament. Wherein Many of Their Excesses and Defects, of Their Confusions and Disorders, of Their Errors and Contradictions are Presented, Both to Themselves and Others* (London: 1651) [no further publishing details are given], 6-8: he lists several Bible texts which, he claims, argue against the *WCF* for the continuation of such prophecy.

[147] Meric Casaubon, *A Treatise Concerning Enthusiasme, as It is an Effect of Nature: But is Mistaken by Many for Either Divine Inspiration, or Diabolical Possession* (London: Thomas Johnson, 1656), 59.

[148] Women are not necessarily excluded. See Chapter Four, 155, n31 above for an example of a woman who it is purported received a revelation at the point of death.

widely held superstition, we have already met, that as long as the soul is earthbound, its attachment to the non-spiritual material of the body limits its ability to receive spiritual messages from God, but, as the soul becomes detached from the body, it can communicate more easily with other spirits.[149] While this view certainly existed, it neither constituted a claim to the miraculous New Testament gift nor did it describe how modern prophets in normal health functioned.

The cessationist controversy centres upon another category of predictive prophecy which is not limited to the dying. In the seventeenth century, assertions were rife that orthodox and unorthodox alike exhibited prophetic powers.[150] These claims were often linked by a common fear of papal persecution. While little attempt was made to reconcile the prevalent view that the New Testament prophetic gift had ceased with the phenomenon of these modern claims to "prophecies", unquestionably orthodox persons were frequently identified as foretellers. James Usher was, according to many, just such a prophet. In one published account it is reported that he foretold the rebellion in Ireland, the confusions and miseries of the English Church and State, the death of King Charles I, his own poverty, the divisions in England over religion, and finally a papal persecution inflicted upon the Reformed churches of England.[151]

John Selden (1584-1654), one of the Erastians of the Assembly and an acknowledged authority on Jewish and classical antiquity,[152] allegedly also prophesied against Rome, predicting that "Happy dayes return".[153] Richard Baxter's *Fair Warning or XX Prophesies*, which foresees the "return of Popery", includes a "prophesie" attributed to another Westminster divine, Edward Reynolds.[154] Baxter assigns other prophecies respectively to John Selden, Archbishops Whitgift, Laud and Bancroft, and Bishops Sanderson, Gauden and Hooker.[155] As his title implies, those prophecies serve to ensure Protestant uniformity and to repel a recrudescent Catholicism. Thus their propaganda intent is quite transparent. Other prophecies, such as those allegedly from Martin Luther and Andreas Musculus which predict the

---

[149] See Aquinas on this at 44-45 above.

[150] The Antinomian John Saltmarsh was one of the latter. John Saltmarsh, *Twelve Strange Prophesies, besides Mother Shiptons. With the Predictions of John Saltmarsh* (London: 1648) [no further publishing details are given].

[151] James Usher, *Strange and Remarkable Prophesies and Predictions of the Holy, Learned, and Excellent James Usher, Late L. Arch-Bishop of Armargh, and Lord Primate of Ireland* (1681) [no further publication details are given].

[152] Barker, *Puritan Profiles*, 54-58.

[153] John Selden, *A Prophecy, Lately Found Amongst the Collections of Famous Mr John Selden* (Lon[d]on: 1659) [no further publishing details are given], 4.

[154] Richard Baxter, *Fair Warning: The Second Part. Or XX Prophesies Concerning the Return of Popery* (London: H. Marsh, 1663), 29.

[155] Baxter, *Fair Warning*, 1-5 and 29.

downfall of the Roman Church and the victory over Germany by the "Turks" or Muslims, suggest another use. In the latter prophecies, threat of a Turkish invasion is a call to repentance and reformation.[156]

Among Westminster divines, William Bridge, in his sermon, *Scripture Light the Most Sure Light*, also accepts that prophecy is still possible in his day, but he is sceptical about its usefulness,[157] though in another sermon he clearly accepts that a prophecy uttered by Bishop Cooper during the Marian persecution was valid.[158]

The widespread belief in contemporary prophecy is surprising given the equally prominent view that extraordinary New Testament prophets had died out together with their gift. Apparently, for the seventeenth-century Puritan these discordant ideas were reconcilable. However, it is a belief in mediate prophecy, in which Scripture plays the central role, which explains why the cessation of immediate prophecy was not seen to nullify the availability of insight into the future for those who lived by the written Word of God.

The general hermeneutical principle lying behind the Puritan acceptance of contemporary prophecy was summarised by John White in a fast-day sermon delivered before the English Parliament:

> Whatsoever things were written aforehand, were written for our learning, saith the Apostle, *Rom.* 15.4. The Lawes for our Direction: The Prophecies for Observation of their Accomplishment in answerable Events: The Promise for our Comfort and consolation: The Examples of Evil for Caution, of Good for Imitation: And lastly the Events, ordered by the Wisdome, and Providence of God, for Precedents and Patternes, representing our State and Condition, either What it is at Present, and why so, or what wee are to Expect it may be hereafter.[159]

---

[156] *Several Choice Prophecyes of the Incomparable and Famous Dr Martin Luther, as also, the Remarkable Prophecy of the Learned and Reverend Dr Musculus. Collected by R.C.* (London: Edward Thomas, 1666). The author is not identified. For a perspective on eschatological prophecy in the Lutheran Reformation, where he refers to John Hus' prophecy concerning Luther, see Robin Barnes, *Prophecy and Gnosis, Apocalypticism in the Wake of the Lutheran Reformation* (Stanford: Stanford University Press, 1988), 47. For a study of how the interpretation of eschatology developed, see Le Roy Froom, *The Prophetic Faith of our Fathers* (Washington: Review and Herald, 1950), especially vol. 2, 513-79.

[157] William Bridge, *The Works of the Rev. William Bridge, M.A.* (London: Thomas Tegg, 1845), vol. 1, 417.

[158] Bridge, *The Works of the Rev. William Bridge*, vol. 4, 339.

[159] John White, *The Troubles of Jerusalems Restauration, or, the Churches Reformation* [...] (London: 1646) [no further publishing details are given]. 1. Or consider John Arrowsmith: "Such is the course of divine providence: where Iniquities breaks fast, calamatie will be sure to dine". John Arrowsmith, *The Covenant Avenging Sword Brandished* (London: Samuel Man, 1642), 1-2.

Some collections of prophecies circulating in the seventeenth century were patently warnings based on the example of Scripture.[160] This is the best explanation of the prophecies discussed in Richard Baxter's *Fair Warning*.[161] The small section Baxter quotes of Reynolds "prophecy" is a diatribe against those sympathetic to "Rome", not a prediction as such at all.[162] Edward Reynolds' "prophecy" does not purport to be an immediate and extra-biblical revelation but is a segment from a 1657 sermon.[163] Had someone told Reynolds that he was uttering a prophecy by immediate revelation, he would certainly have been surprised. Thomas Gillespie explained Usher's prophecies in the same way.[164] Gillespie, answering the

---

[160] See also, for example, Edmund Calamy, *Englands Looking-Glasse* (London: Chr. Meredith, 1642). Citing Amos 3:8, he comments: "He hath spoken unto us by the voice of his Ministers, that with one mouth and lip, have foretold us of desolation, and destruction. It hath beene the constant voice of Gods faithfull Servants, from the Pulpit, for these many years early and late" (13-14). He also stresses that, in his own warning of judgement in the sermon, he is not saying what God will do, but only what he should do in the light of their spiritual condition (20).

[161] See 211-12 above.

[162] For a recent thorough discussion of Puritan providentialism, see Michael P. Winship, *Seers of God. Puritan Providentialism in the Restoration and Early Enlightenment* (Baltimore: John Hopkins University Press, 1996), who ascribes this kind of "prophecy" to John Calvin: "With Providence inserting itself so lucidly in the sectarian strife of the sixteenth century, it is perhaps not surprising that Calvin's grasp of Providence could even lead him into prophecy. He foresaw divine vengeance on Henry VIII for his arrogance[...]" (15). Winship cites *Letters of John Calvin Compiled from The Original Manuscripts and Edited with Historical Notes by Dr. Jules Bonnet*, (Philadelphia: n.d.) [No further publishing details are given], vol. 2, 190; vol. 4, 32; vol. 1, 417; vol. 1, 376.

[163] Baxter, *Fair Warning*, 29. Although we have been unable to trace this sermon, which Baxter only identifies as preached in 1657 before Parliament, Reynolds' strict cessationism is well attested in his other works. See, for example, Edward Reynolds, *An Explication of the CX. Psalm [...] Being the Substance of Several Sermons Preached at Lincolns Inne* (London: R[ob]. B[ostocke]., 1656), 48; Edward Reynolds, "Brotherly Reconciliation", *Twenty Sermons Preached upon Several Occasions* (London: George Thomason, 1660), 27; Edward Reynolds, *Three Treatises of The Vanity of the Creature. The Sinfulnesse of Sinne. The Life of Christ* (London: Rob Bostocke and George Badger, 1642), 411; Edward Reynolds, *The First Sermon upon Hosea* (London: Robert Bostock, 1649), 78.

[164] Usher himself said that Christians offend against the Third Commandment when they call into question God's wisdom by prying "into the hidden counsels of God. As when a man undertaketh to foretel future things & events, &c". The erudite Irish bishop does not here forbid attempts to seek God's direction in individual circumstances. However, he does advocate a healthy scepticism towards claims that humans can gain infallible access to the future through divination, while at the same time he precludes any modern notion that God still discloses his mind through infallible prophets. James Usher, *A Body of Divinity, or The Summe and Substance of Christian Religion;*

claim "*that immediate divine revelations of secret things, and future events, have continued to be given to the Christian church after the apostolical age*", responds:[165]

> Many if not almost all, supposed predictions of future events by holy and intelligent men, it is more than probable, were only applications of scripture-prophecies and examples to nations, persons, circumstances, and events, declaring how it was to be expected the Lord would act[...]. It is affirmed that Archbishop Usher foretold things to come: but he only told what appeared to him likely to happen to the church[...]in consequence of his carefully studying the book of Revelation.[166]

Gillespie was not sanitising an unacceptable idea for a more sceptical and scientific age, but merely reiterating the Puritans' own explanation of such phenomena. William Gouge in *Gods Three Arrows* gives the same teaching and explicitly aligns prophetic foresight with a concomitant denial that extraordinary immediate prophecy continues. In *A Plaister for the Plague*, he appeals to Amos 3:7: "*Surely the Lord God will doe nothing, but he revealeth his secrets to his servants the Prophets*".[167] Building on a previous point that "*God fortels what he intends against sinners*", Gouge offers a potential objection, which he promptly qualifies:[168]

> Ministers have not now such certaine knowledge of Gods minde, as of old the Prophets and Apostles had, to whom God did immediately and infallibly make knowne his minde.[169]

Instead, the Scriptures, which are both inspired and a surer word of prophecy, tell us the sorts of sins which cause God to respond in judgement:

> So as when Ministers see such sinnes impudently and impenitently committed, they may well inferre that God purposeth to send some judgement to such a people.[170]

Gouge laments that many ministers had recently warned about an impending plague, but their "threatening was little regarded; little or no amendment followed thereupon: now therefore is the plague among us".[171]

Catechistically Propounded, and Explained, by Way of Question and Answer: Methodically and Familiarly Handled. Collected long since out of Sundry Authors, and Reduced unto One Common Method by James Usher B. of Armagh (London: T. Downes and G. Badger, 1649), 240.

[165] Thomas Gillespie, *An Essay on the Continuance of Immediate Revelations of Facts and Future Events* (Edinburgh: W. Gray, 1771), 13.

[166] Gillespie, *An Essay on the Continuance of Immediate Revelations of Facts and Future Events*, 13.

[167] Gouge, "A Plaister for the Plague", *Gods Three Arrowes*, 12.

[168] Gouge, "A Plaister for the Plague", *Gods Three Arrowes*, 11.

[169] Gouge, "A Plaister for the Plague", *Gods Three Arrowes*, 13.

[170] Gouge, "A Plaister for the Plague", *Gods Three Arrowes*, 13.

Thomas Carter in *Prayers Prevelancie for Israels Safety* broadens the application of the same principle to the whole nation.[172] The ruin of a nation is "discernible by parallel cases, and upon spirituall grounds in the *Word of God*".[173] For, when a nation has many prodigious sins:

> the Lords *Daniels* can read and interpret them, by helpe of the Word, as letters written in unknowne Characters, cannot be understood without a rule from the Writer.[174]

This discovery of secrets was not the product of theological reflection alone; rather, it occurred especially in the act and drama of preaching. The Puritans were first and foremost preachers whose primary interest was the cure of souls. They usually constructed their sermons in such a way that the message gleaned from the Bible passage under examination was applied or contextualised for the listeners with a view to piercing the heart.[175] This they attempted to do by first using Ramist logic to create dichotomous subdivisions of the Bible text.[176] In addition, the homily was separated into sections, usually those of doctrine, reason and use.[177] Ordinarily, several doctrines, reasons and uses were expounded,[178] with the result that the

---

[171] Gouge, "A Plaister for the Plague", *Gods Three Arrowes,* 13.

[172] Thomas Carter, *Prayers Prevalencie for Israels Safety* (London: John Bellamie and Ralph Smith, 1643).

[173] Carter, *Prayers Prevalencie,* 3.

[174] Carter, *Prayers Prevalencie,* 4.

[175] For a sympathetic analysis of Puritan pastoral preaching, see James Packer, *Among God's Giants* (Eastbourne: Kingsway, 1991), 365-81.

[176] See Perry Miller, *The New England Mind. The Seventeenth Century* (New York: Macmillan, 1939), vol. 1, 116-53; Leon Howard, *Essays on Puritans and Puritanism* (Albuquerque: University of New Mexico Press, 1986), 79-81; Jack B. Rogers, *Scripture in the Westminster Confession. A Problem of Historical Interpretation for American Presbyterianism* (Grand Rapids, MI: Eerdmans, 1967), 87-95; Bryan Spinks, "Brief and Perspicuous Text; Plain and Pertinent Doctrine: Behind 'Of the Preaching of the Word' in the Westminster Directory", Martin Dudley (ed.), *Like a Two-Edged Sword, the Word of God in Liturgy and History* (Norwich: The Canterbury Press, 1995), 91-112, at 100-102. Wilbur S. Howell, *Logic and Rhetoric in England, 1500-1700* (Princeton: Princeton University Press, 1956), 146; Walter Ong, *Ramus: Method and Decay of Dialogue: From the Art of Discourse to the Art of Reason* (Cambridge: Harvard UP, 1958); Donald McKim, *Ramism in William Perkins' Theology* (New York: P. Lang, 1987). For a helpful analysis of the themes and texts of American Puritan sermons, see Allen Carden, "Biblical Texts and Themes in American Puritan Preaching, 1630-1700", *Andrews University Seminary Studies* 21/2 (Summer 1983), 113-28.

[177] See O. R. Johnston, "The Puritan Use of the Old Testament," *Evangelical Quarterly* 23/3 (July 1951), 183-209.

[178] The *DPW* also produced by the Assembly, specifically lists under its subheading "*Of the preaching of the Word*" the use of doctrines, reasons and uses as the correct homiletic method: *DPW,* 145-47. See also, 147, where the method is said only to be recommended and need not be precisely followed. Philip Nye, in an argument against

highly structured homiletical method was meant to deliver contemporary guidance. Texts from historical sections of Scripture were often applied to modern England, but miraculous events from Scripture were also contextualised by the imaginative Puritan preacher.

Thomas Hill's sermon on 2 Cor. 12:1-11 is typically Ramist in approach.[179] Hill makes a general application from the outset, drawing out the example of other biblical characters who saw visions or who had a close spiritual relationship with Christ, concluding that those closest to God were able to discover his deepest mysteries.[180] Verses 2 and 3[181] have as their *doctrine* that God surprises his servants with discoveries. The *reason* is that God sometimes seeks us before we seek him. The *use* is that when Christians are humble, God may surprise them with his "com[ing] in upon thee"[182] with "most glorious discoveries".[183] The latter term describes God's experiential communication with his people and is an important and charged expression for the Reformed orthodox.[184] Although for Paul "discoveries" in context were immediate revelations, in Hill's day they have become insights into Scripture.[185] Hill applies the revelatory experiences of inspired prophecy found in the Scriptures to his narrower contemporary epistemological boundaries.

While mediate prophecy, if we can describe it in that way, made a more dramatic impact if it was applied to public figures of national importance or was uttered in a politico-religious context by someone comparable to John Knox or Martin Luther, it evidently operated in the private lives of

---

subscription, denies that this document tied him to this specific method. Philip Nye, *Beames of Former Light, Discovering how Evil it is to Impose Doubtfull and Disputable Formes or Practises upon Ministers; Especially under the Penalty of Ejection for Nonconformity unto the Same. As also Something about Catechizing* (London: Adoniram Byfield, 1660), 57.

[179] Thomas Hill, *The Best and Worst of Paul and his Character in Both Conditions* (Cambridge: 1648) [no further publishing details are given].

[180] Hill, *The Best and Worst of Paul*, 1.

[181] Hill, *The Best and Worst of Paul*, 6. 2 Cor. 12:2-3.

[182] Hill, *The Best and Worst of Paul*, 7.

[183] Hill, *The Best and Worst of Paul*, 7.

[184] Hill, *The Best and Worst of Paul*, 7-8. It can refer to *discoveries* in Scripture, or it may refer to alleged revelations apart from Scripture. See also Thomas Hill, *The Good Old Way Gods Way, to Soule-refreshing Rest* (London: John Bellamie and Philemon Stephens, 1644), epistle dedicatory, where he suggests that those who say "*there is* no need of Ministry or Ordinances, [are] *flattering us with hope of* new Apostles, & glorious discoveries *by them*". The term also occurs in connection with providence: "Who knowes but the *providence of God* may now be making the same *discovery* in England[…]": Thomas Hill, *The Militant Church Triumphant over the Dragon and His Angels* (London: John Bellamie and Ralph Smith, 1643), 29.

[185] Hill, *The Best and Worst of Paul*, 8.

individual believers as well. Quoting Heb. 12:13 and 4:12-13, Hill explains that dynamic power is inherent in the preaching of Scripture, as it functions normatively.[186] The first of these two texts describes the living and active qualities of the "Word of God", while the second stresses God's omniscience. The two actualities conspire together to convey remarkable information to the listener:

> There are many people wonder when they come to hear a Sermon, how the Minister comes to know their secrets; and sometimes you shall have a hearer, as he goes out of the Assembly, say, This man, though a stranger to me, hath read over the *story of my life*, and as if he had been acquainted with my *bosom secrets* all my time, I had them discovered to me in this Sermon; how comes this to pass?[187]

Hill explains that "the Minister brings the *word that is quick and piercing* as the *all-seeing God himself*[...]". God's knowledge of an individual's heart is revealed through the preaching of the Bible's texts and existentially coincides with secret thoughts, thus exposing hidden faults such as hypocrisy - the example Hill goes on to describe.[188] In this manner the omniscient God has even exposed murderers. Hill notes in parentheses "(I had almost said) in a *miraculous way*".[189] He illustrates how the Reformed orthodox believed that they were open to God's personal communication without compromising the Augustinian inseparability of Word and Spirit. God could and did speak through the preached Word so that, after prayer and study, the preacher expounded a passage of Scripture in such a way that it became a personal message from God to each individual member of the congregation, sometimes revealing otherwise secret information.

The Reformed orthodox equally stressed that "prophetic" insights were not "inspired revelation" and were not to be believed on the same level as Scripture. Anthony Tuckney, for example, disputing with "enthusiasts" who

---

[186] Thomas Hill, *Six Sermons, of Thomas Hill D.D. Master of Trinity Colledge in Cambridge* (London: Peter Cole, 1649).

[187] Hill, *Six Sermons*, 10. In the nineteenth century, London Baptist preacher Charles Spurgeon was criticised for claiming something similar in his own ministry, when, also appealing to God's omniscience, he allegedly pointed to a man during a sermon and not only charged him with working on Sunday as a shoemaker, but knew exactly how much profit the man had made that day and how much his takings amounted to. The shoemaker, who later admitted that he had indeed both taken nine pence and made the four pence profit claimed by Spurgeon, was promptly converted and never traded again on the Lord's Day. See Henry Christmas, *Preachers and Preaching in Ancient and Modern Times* (London: Ward, Lock, & co., 1878), 206-209. Christmas gives no reference.

[188] Hill, *Six Sermons*, 10-11.

[189] Hill, *Six Sermons*, 12.

claimed special revelation, warns against glorifying legitimate spiritual insight:

> I deny not, but that sometimes possibly there may be some more then [than] ordinary intimation of *Gods* will to some of his servants; *For their persons*, holy, humble, faithfull, and Orthodox. *For the things declared*, it may be they may be helped to apply some generall word in Scripture to a particular case. But never thereby put upon others either to believe or do anything above, much lesse contrary to the Scripture[...]".[190]

Such a mediate prophetic phenomenon generated its own vocabulary. English divines used a variety of expressions to explain the function of applying Scripture, including terms such as "secret suggestions", "motions", "instincts" and "impulses". Thomas Manton illustrates how one of these terms was used. Even though all divine miraculous communication has ceased, Manton says, God still infuses a "strong instinct" - something distinct from immediate prophecy.[191] While God does not reveal his secrets concerning events of the new dispensation as often as he did in the days of the Old Testament, yet God can and does warn people of Manton's own day through that very "strong instinct":

> But now, God having opened his good treasure to us, we have higher arguments of piety, a larger measure of gifts, clearer discerning and understanding of the truths of the word, therefore prophecy ceaseth. Yet now, in the times of the gospel, he doth not altogether fail his people; for though they can have no certain knowledge of future contingencies, yet he begets some strong instinct in the mind of his children, puts it into their hearts to avoid this and avoid that: we have no infallibility of the event, yet we may discern much of the providence of God.[192]

Manton not only binds providence to the Word, but yokes it as well to the Holy Spirit.

> When the church was destitute of outward helps, God used the way of miracles and oracles; but that dispensation is not continued, because we have a better way: providence, the Spirit, and the word, take them all together, do exceedingly open the mind of God to us.[193]

---

[190] Anthony Tuckney, *A Good Day Well Improved[...]to Which is Annexed a Sermon on 2 Tim. 1.13* (London: I. Rothwell, 1656), 307. Anthony Tuckney also believes that "inspiration" exists in his own day, but plainly does not mean immediate inspiration. "In the Ministry of his Word God *holds out his Hand*, Rom. 10.21. and by the Inspirations of his Spirit he has *hold* on our *Hearts*": Anthony Tuckney, *Forty Sermons upon Several Occasions [...]"* (London: Jonathan Robinson and Brabazon Aylmer, 1676), 536.

[191] Heb. 11:7. Thomas Manton, *The Complete Works of Thomas Manton, D.D.* (London: James Nisbet, 1873), vol. 14, 173.

[192] Manton, *The Complete Works of Thomas Manton*, vol. 14, 179.

[193] Manton, *The complete Works of Thomas Manton*, vol. 14, 181. Like Manton, John Conant had put these concepts together: "Now God calls upon us by his Word, by his

The English Westminster divines were convinced that God could reveal secrets and future events, but they chose to explain these "revelations" as something distinct from prophetic immediate inspiration. The centre of such revelations for them was Scripture, and they continued to stress that immediate revelation or inspired prophecy had ceased.

5.5 Conclusion

Seventeenth-century English Puritans believed in the efficacy of various types of divination as diverse as angelic impressions, astrology, lots and human reason, but the primary source of otherwise hidden knowledge was the Scriptures. Most Reformed orthodox rejected the possibility of a resurgence of the New Testament prophetic gifts, consigning them to the past by a number of arguments, yet they acknowledged that prophetic insight in their own day remained possible.

When Puritans needed to explain these predictive phenomena, having denied the availability of that immediate prophecy granted New Testament apostles and prophets, some of them invoked the interference of good and bad angels, while others allowed a facility for pious persons near death to receive personal revelations. Most commonly of all they clarified their views on contemporary prophecy by saying that the modern preacher was able to determine the true meaning of providential events by drawing on Scriptural principles or examples.

Although Westminster theologians denied that general revelation could provide redemptive knowledge of God, providence took on a positive role in the light of the efficacy of Scripture and the work of the Holy Spirit. Even the "revelation" of the Gunpowder Plot was considered a special providence involving secondary causes, rather than special immediate revelation.[194] Among the vast majority of the Westminster divines' sermons which deal with the subject of guidance, we discern an unwillingness to claim any sort of inspired extra-biblical revelation for guidance. Instead, we see a tendency to deny that there is still immediate revelation for both matters of religious truth and for daily living, whether in the life of the individual or nation.

Although this chapter has focused on English theologians, it is important also to analyse the views on modern prophecy held by the Scottish commissioners to the Assembly, and to glance briefly at the position of their countrymen who were committed to Westminster orthodoxy. We shall

---

Spirit, and by his Providences". Conant, *Sermons Preach'd on Several Occasions. The Third Volume*, 330.

[194] See Arrowsmith, *Englands Ebenezer or, Stone of Help*, 5-6: As we have noted above, although the ministry of angels was accepted among the Reformed orthodox, that ministry was understood to be "mediate" rather than "immediate". See 187, n52 above.

endeavour to discern whether the Scots, who had a long history of prophetic claims, agreed with the insights enunciated by their English counterparts.

Chapter 6

Prophecy and the Scots

6.1 Introduction: The Tradition of Miraculous Divine Intervention

Any inquiry into the colourful lives and views of the sixteenth- and seventeenth-century Covenanting Scots, including those of the Scottish commissioners to the Westminster Assembly, cannot but conclude that these northern Presbyterians firmly believed that God still revealed secrets. Some would add that the Scots equally believed that God performed miracles of healing and sent angelic visitors to his chosen servants. The mythology from these times has been kept alive by the sympathetic efforts of that avid nineteenth-century collector of biographical information, the Scottish historian Robert Wodrow.[1] In the traditions recorded by Wodrow, events in the lives of Scottish reformers and Covenanters are transformed into contemporary miracles, where, for example, an angelic being rescues four-year-old Samuel Rutherford from certain death down a well,[2] or Alexander Gordon dreams of the future beheading of the Marquis of Argyle.[3] Other historians would suggest, as Patrick Walker does in his *Six Saints of the Covenant*, that persecuted preachers such as Alexander Peden uttered many extraordinary prophecies in the course of their lives.[4] These

---

[1] For a biography of Wodrow (1679-1734), see David Lachman, "Robert Wodrow", *DSCHT*, 881. See also Edward Cowan's brief essay on the prophetic heritage of the Scots: "Prophecy and Prophylaxis: A Paradigm for the Scotch-Irish?" in Tyler Blethen and Curtis Wood (eds.), *Ulster and North America: Transatlantic Perspectives on the Scotch-Irish* (Tuscaloosa: University of Alabama Press, 1997), 15-23, especially 17, where Cowan claims that the religious elite tried to suppress folk seers and popular predictions but continued to describe figures such as John Knox as prophets.

[2] Robert Wodrow, *Analecta: Or Materials for a History of Remarkable Providences; Mostly Relating to Scotch Ministers and Christians* (Edinburgh: Maitland Club, 1842), vol. 1, 57. Clifford Button points out that the "bonnie white man" referred to in the event in question may have been a passing baker. Clifford Button, "Scottish Mysticism in the Seventeenth Century. With Special Reference to Samuel Rutherford" (unpublished PhD thesis, University of Edinburgh, 1927), 27-28.

[3] Wodrow, *Analecta: Or Materials for a History of Remarkable Providences; Mostly Relating to Scotch Ministers and Christians*, vol. 1, 22-23.

[4] Patrick Walker, *Six Saints of the Covenant: Peden: Semple: Welwood: Cameron: Cargill: Smith* (London: Hodder and Stoughton, 1901), e.g. vol. 1, 87 on Peden's prophetic vision.

prophecies were understood to be predictions of contingent events which could not have been otherwise known without supernatural assistance.

What stands out in these hagiographical accounts is that a strong tradition of the persecuted prophet dominated the religious landscape of post-Reformation Scotland. The practice of foretelling was, in a sense, nothing new. As Shari Cohn has argued, "second sight" in particular was part of the Scottish experience from earliest times.[5] Cohn notices a difference, however, between the Lowland Scots on the one hand, and the residents of the Highlands and Islands on the other: the latter maintained a belief in fairies, while the former saw such claims as pure superstition.[6] Seventeenth-century minister and Gaelic scholar, Robert Kirk (1644-1692), confirms in his sympathetic account of some of their practices that the inhabitants of the Highlands were indeed superstitious. Kirk too believed that he had a natural gift of healing and second sight, though his explanation of how one gains these abilities demonstrates that they bear no relation to a New Testament spiritual gift.[7]

Margo Todd has discussed the Scottish prophetic tradition in her recent book, *The Culture of Protestantism in Early Modern Scotland*.[8] Todd distinguishes between the technical sense of the term προφήτης and the popular view. The technical meaning for the Reformers was that of a preacher interpreting God's will in sermons, while the popular viewpoint connected "preachers with supernatural powers of telling the future, not to mention other miraculous potential".[9] Todd also connects the popular opinion of the laity to pre-Reformation superstition and explains the elevated importance of the Protestant minister as a relic of the status of the old priest, in spite of the democratising potential of Presbyterian church

---

[5] Shari Ann Cohn, "The Scottish Tradition of Second Sight and other Psychic Experiences in Families" (unpublished PhD thesis, University of Edinburgh, 1996), 8-53. See also John MacQueen, "The Saint as Seer: Adomnan's Account of Columba", Hilda Davidson (ed.), *The Seer in Celtic and Other Traditions* (Edinburgh: John Donald, 1989), 37-49, on Columba as seer and miracle worker.

[6] Cohn, "The Scottish Tradition of Second Sight", 12. Cohn cites Thomas Smout, *A History of the Scottish people 1560-1830* (London: Fontana, 1985), 184-92.

[7] Cohn, "The Scottish Tradition of Second Sight", 13-15. One of the ways to become a seer was to place one's foot on the seer's foot and look over the seer's right shoulder, while the seer puts his hand on the other person's head (15). Sometimes those with second sight sought to have the clergy somehow remove the ability, although others did not see the facility as a burden (18-19). Both children and animals could have second sight (21). Cohn also lists two eighteenth-century ministers and one nineteenth-century minister who were well-known seers (28).

[8] Margo Todd, *The Culture of Protestantism in Early Modern Scotland* (New Haven: Yale University Press, 2002); see especially 358, 362, 370, 386, and 391-400 on prophecy.

[9] Todd, *The Culture of Protestantism in Early Modern Scotland*, 392.

government.[10] Todd's thesis argues that Scottish Protestantism sought to "rebaptise magic as miracle",[11] and she gave a sociological rather than a theological explanation for the Scottish acceptance of contemporary miracles. One of the dangers in applying such an analysis to any particular society is a possible temptation to generalise one's conclusions, and so to ignore evidence that invites other interpretations. Perhaps Todd falls into this trap when she offers Samuel Rutherford as an example of one who encouraged a correspondent to believe (Todd labels such correspondents as Rutherford's "groupies") that she would hear the voice of God.[12] There is no warrant in Rutherford's writing to suggest that he meant any more than that the individual would be spiritually strengthened by God's grace through the voice of God in Scripture, because Rutherford, as much as any in his day, rejected out of hand the idea that God still spoke with an audible voice.[13] Had Todd explored the Reformed orthodox explanation of prophetic claims she might have come to a different opinion about their alleged origin.

Clearly something more than a sociological analysis is required for the purposes of clarifying the Scottish attitude towards prophecy. We must look more closely at the phenomenon of prophecy in order to discover how the Scottish church itself viewed these claims. To this end, it is helpful to consider a first-hand account of the abilities of a "prophet". As it happens, the "prophet" in question is the archetypal foreteller from the time of the Reformation in Scotland – John Knox himself.

6.2 John Knox

John Knox gave a clear explanation for the genesis of his prophetic insight long before the second Reformation in Scotland:

> My assurances are not the Mervallis of Merlin, nor yit the dark sentences of prophane Prophesies; But (1.) the plane treuth of Godis Word; (2.) the invincibill justice of the everlasting God; and (3.) the ordinarie course of his punishmentis and plagues from the begynning, ar my assurance and groundis. Godis Word threatneth destructioun to all inobedient; his immutabill justice must requyre the same. The ordinary punishmentis and plagues schawis exempillis.[14]

---

[10] Todd, *The Culture of Protestantism in Early Modern Scotland*, 385-92.
[11] Todd, *The Culture of Protestantism in Early Modern Scotland*, 398.
[12] Todd, *The Culture of Protestantism in Early Modern Scotland*, 399.
[13] See 226-34 below for Rutherford's position.
[14] John Knox, *The Works of John Knox*, ed. D. Laing (Edinburgh: James Thin, 1895), vol. 3, 168-69. Dale Johnson in his PhD thesis "Prophecy, Rhetoric and Diplomacy: John Knox and the Struggle for the Soul of Scotland", unpublished PhD thesis (Georgia State University, 1995), argues that Knox developed his claims to prophetic prescience

Pierre Janton, in his essay *Prophétie et Prophesying chez John Knox et dans La Tradition Puritaine*, concludes that both Knox and the English Puritans taught that any prophetic insight in their time had to be grounded in Scripture:

> Prophecies of Knox are applications of the biblical texts to the concrete situation[...]. This attitude defines the strict framework within which a prophecy is possible. The Holy Spirit does not speak to the prophet apart from Scripture[...]. *Prophecy thus becomes a commentary and application of Scripture.*[15]

Richard Greaves, in his thorough *Theology and Revelation in the Scottish Reformation*, also interprets Knox's "revelations" in this way:

> Emphasizing that he did not speak as one privy to God's secret wisdom, he insisted that he was called to preach about 'the sentence of Godis law' on those who violated it[...]. Basic to Knox's sense of prophetic vocation was his firm conviction of biblical authority and his personal sense of divine election.[16]

Aaron Kester in his thesis, "The Charismata in Crisis: The Gifts of the Holy Spirit in the Reformation Church of England", argues that, as his title

---

over time and "wore the prophet's mantle but held it in tension with the leading Protestant reformers, who believed that prophetic powers ended with the Apostles" (54-55). For a succinct survey of Knox's life and thought, see Richard Kyle, "John Knox", *DSCHT*, 465-66. See also W. Stanford Reid, *Trumpeter of God* (Grand Rapids, MI: Baker, 1974), especially 284, where the author introduces a note of scepticism about Melville's claims that Knox made prophetic predictions; Henry Sefton (ed.), *John Knox* (Edinburgh: Saint Andrew Press, 1993), which is a brief biography and compendium of Knox's writings; Thomas M'Crie, *The Life of John Knox* (Caithness: Free Presbyterian Church of Scotland, 1960), especially 282-85, where the author accepts Knox's own explanation that his alleged prophecies were applications of Scripture apart from instances which M'Crie puts down to lawful "premonitions" (285). For Knox as reformer, see Roger A. Mason (ed.), *John Knox and the British Reformations* (Aldershot: Ashgate, 1998).

[15] "Les prophéties de Knox sont des applications des textes bibliques à la situation concrète. [...]Cette attitude définit le cadre strict dans lequel une prophétie est possible. L'Esprit-Saint ne parle pas au prophète en dehors de l'Ecriture [...]. *La prophétie devient donc commentaire et application de l'Ecriture*". [The italicised sentence is attributed to "John Philpot, Lettre XII, Examinations and Writings, Parker Soc., Cambridge, 1842, p.252".] Pierre Janton, "Prophétie et Prophesying chez John Knox et dans La Tradition Puritaine", Geneviève Demerson et Bernard Dompnier (eds.), *Les Signes de Dieu aux XVIe et XVIIe Siècles: Actes du Colloque Organisé par le Centre de Recherches sur La Réforme et La Contre-Réforme* (Clermont-Ferrand: Faculté des Lettres et Sciences humaines de l'Université Blaise-Pascal, 1993), 37-44, at 41.

[16] Richard L. Greaves, *Theology and Revolution in the Scottish Reformation* (Grand Rapids, MI: Christian University Press, 1980), 1. Also see 4-24 for Knox's use of Scripture as his basic authority.

implies, there was a shift of perspective during the sixteenth century in England. An acceptance that supernatural spiritual gifts were still available to the contemporary church was replaced by the belief that there had been a comprehensive cessationism:

> By the close of Elizabeth's reign, theologians of the Church of England could dismiss all claims of direct, extraordinary operations of the Holy Spirit as evidence of fanaticism and heresy, latent or patent.[17]

Though Kester theorises that Knox is a pre-cessationist prophet, he still concludes that:

> Knox was a true prophet only in that he was a scriptural prophet, relying heavily upon the revelation once given in Holy Writ and applying that revelation to his own situation under the guidance of the "spreat of trueth".[18]

Dean Smith, however, is a dissenting voice to this interpretation. While we argue, with Greaves and Janton, that Knox's own explanation of his prophetic powers is fully in line with that of Samuel Rutherford in the second Reformation, Smith suggests that Knox's explanation of his "prophecies" was not a denial that Knox received immediate revelations. Smith refers to the explanation given by Knox above and dismisses it on the grounds that Knox also refers to specific prophecies by other ministers.[19] This is hardly an explanation of Knox's cessationist claims. Knox's very point is that we must explain a specific prophecy as an application of Scripture presumably in reliance upon the Holy Spirit, but not as an extra-biblical revelation.

---

[17] Aaron Kester, "The Charismata in Crisis: The Gifts of the Holy Spirit in the Reformation Church of England" (unpublished PhD thesis, Miami University, 1990), 237. Kester concludes that cessationism in the English church grew out of theological controversy and not out of biblical exegesis. He proposes that it was really the threat of alleged prophets to the social and political order that gave rise to cessationism in the English church (294-95). Kester cites John Rogers as a cessationist, for example. For his cessationist stance, see John Rogers, *The Displaying of an Horrible Secte of Grosses and Wicked heretiques, and what Doctrine they Teach in Corners. Newely Set Foorth by J. R. 1578. Whereunto There is Annexed a Confession of Certain Articles, Which was Made by Two of the Familie of Love, being Examined before a Iustice of the Peace, the 28 of May 1561, Touching Their Errours Taught Amongest Them in Their Assemblies* (London: John Day, 1579), preface [preface not paginated], where he denies that predictive prophecy remains in the church.

[18] Kester, "The Charismata in Crisis: The Gifts of the Holy Spirit in the Reformation Church of England", 200.

[19] Dean Smith, "The Scottish Presbyterians and Covenanters: A Continuationist Experience in a Cessationist Theology", *WTJ* 63 (2001), 39-63, at 41-42.

6.3 "Prophecy" and the Scottish Commissioners to the Westminster Assembly

When we examine the views of the Scottish commissioners appointed to represent the Scottish church at the Westminster Assembly, it is quickly apparent that these theologians in general accepted post-apostolic foretelling. We also find that they, and others in subsequent Scottish history, usually explained contemporary prophetic foresight in a manner consistent with a cessationist reading of the *WCF*. Their explanations are, in principle, compatible with that given by John Knox.

For the purpose of discerning whether or not both cessationism and continuationism were represented by the Scottish commissioners to the Assembly, we can classify the Scottish commissioners to the Assembly somewhat loosely and tentatively into two categories. The first, represented by Robert Baillie, Archibald Johnston and Samuel Rutherford, unambiguously taught the cessation of immediate prophecy. The latter, comprising Alexander Henderson, Robert Blair and George Gillespie, present us with a far more complex picture.[20]

6.3.1 Robert Baillie, Archibald Johnston and Samuel Rutherford

Reformed orthodox views on the continuance or cessation of inspired foretelling are usually expressed in a context that is not directly concerned with proving or disproving the availability of prophetic gifts. Robert Baillie affirms his cessationism in such a milieu when he dismisses the Independents' claims of exegetical support for preaching by the unordained. Although Baillie uses the language of "prophecy" to include uninspired exposition of the Scriptures,[21] he believes that it is the

---

[20] Blair may have sat in the Assembly in 1648; John Maitland attended, but neither Robert Douglas nor John Earl took his seat. See Alexander G. Mitchell, *The Westminster Assembly: Its History and Standards* (Edmonton: SWRB, 1992), xx and 442. There seems to be no relevant material for John Maitland, the other Scottish elder who attended the Assembly. James Hewison summarises the circumstances thus: "John, sixth Earl of Cassillis[...] never took his seat at Westminster. John, first Earl of Loudoun [...] attended meetings, but did not contribute any suggestions of moment. Similarly, Sir Charles Erskine is just mentioned in the minutes, while Robert Blair of St. Andrews, appointed in 1648, does not seem to have sat. Maitland, Henderson, and Gillespie took their seats[...] on 16th September and Maitland sat till 1647[...]. Balmerino came in place of Cassillis [...] Argyle succeeded Balmerino[...]. He was succeeded by Winram of Liberton. Warriston, admitted 1st February 1644, attended few meetings. Robert Meldrum, a political agent was a member from the beginning": James Hewison, *The Covenanters* (Glasgow: John Smith and Son, 1908), vol. 1, 385. Hewison earlier mentions Rutherford and Baillie (380-82).

[21] Robert Baillie, *A Dissuasive from the Errours of the Time: Wherein the Tenets of the Principall Sects, Especially of the Independents, are Drawn Together in One Map,*

prerogative of ordained ministers only.[22] Thus, New Testament miraculous prophetic gifts must not be automatically appropriated as precedents for uninspired and unordained preachers. Baillie accordingly denies that a verse such as 1 Cor. 14:30 can be used by the Independents to justify their practices of prophesying, because the prophets spoken of in that particular text are:

> [m]en endued with extraordinary gifts, whose practice can be no pattern to the Churches now a dayes, where these gifts are ceased. That it is so, vers. 30. makes cleare, where the prophets doe preach extemporary revelations.[23]

While this seems effectively to deny the view we have already seen among English Puritans that such a text could still be used to prove that a gift analogous to that of extraordinary prophecy continued in the church, Baillie does adopt such a stance vis-à-vis another text. He argues that the words of 1 Thess. 5:20, "do not treat prophecies with contempt", can refer either to extraordinary prophets or to ordinary ordained preachers, but not to a class of unordained prophets. Therefore, Independents, according to Baillie, cannot claim support from this text either.[24]

Even so, God is still held to reveal the future in some sense for the majority of the Reformed orthodox. Baillie's colleague Archibald Johnston is certainly open to the idea of prophetic revelation. In his diary, Johnston reveals a deep admiration for Margaret Michelson (or Mitchell), a Scottish woman who was thought to experience prophetic raptures.[25] He also

---

for the Most Part, in Words of Their own Authours, and Their Maine Principles are Examined by the Touch-stone of the Holy Scriptures (London: Samuel Gellibrand, 1645), 118. See also George Henderson, *Religious Life in Seventeenth-Century Scotland* (Cambridge: Cambridge University Press, 1937), especially 17-18 for Baillie's opposition to the prophetic claims of Anabaptists and Quakers.

[22] Baillie, *A Dissuasive from the Errours of the Time*, 174 and 176.

[23] Baillie, *A Dissuasive from the Errours of the Time*, 178.

[24] Baillie, *A Dissuasive from the Errours of the Time*, 179. He also demonstrates how these terms were flexible when he uses them in a loose and imprecise way. Writing to Lord Lanerick in 1646, he makes a prediction with the disclaimer: "Albeit I be no prophet". Robert Baillie, *The Letters and Journals of Robert Baillie, A. M. Principal of the University of Glasgow M.DC.XXXVII.-M.DC.LXII.*, ed. David Laing (Edinburgh: Bannatyne Club, 1841-1842), vol. 2, 355. On another occasion, he claimed to give a prophecy. Addressing the General Assembly in a report of the labours of the Scottish commissioners in the Westminster Assembly, he warns those who would cause division and trouble for the Kirk of Scotland: "Let me speak prophecie unto him: Were he this day of never so high a price, and great fragrancie among us, yet he shall become a cursed soule, and his memory shall stinck to all generations". Baillie, *The Letters and Journals of Robert Baillie*, vol. 3, 13.

[25] Archibald Johnston, *Diary of Sir Archibald Johnston of Wariston 1632-1639*, ed. George Morison Paul (Edinburgh: Scottish History Society, 1911), 393.

claimed prophetic powers himself as the mid 1660s approached, in the belief that 1666 was an important year in the prophetic calendar.[26] His diary entry for 25 May 1661 notes:

> Hier my friend cam in and told me sundry prophecyes of the overturning the papistical religion and party in 1666, which I told him was coincident with something I had written yesterday which I read to him.[27]

However, such "prophecies" differed from the extraordinary prophecy of New Testament gifted prophets in that they required the concurrence of a Bible text. As we have already noticed, Johnston is not prepared to accept a Quaker prophetic revelation at face value without an accompanying Scripture text.[28] In spite of the highly charged and experiential nature of his Christianity, Johnston still requires the conjunction of the Word and Spirit before he will acknowledge any prediction as authentically God-given.[29]

Johnston's more celebrated colleague Samuel Rutherford was undoubtedly a cessationist. Vern Poythress, in an essay designed to bridge the divide between cessationism and continuationism, suggests that there are three types of processes functioning in the exercise of spiritual gifts. There are "discursive processes, nondiscursive processes and mixed processes". While the Apostles received revelations through non-discursive processes, contemporary believers, while also receiving non-discursive insights, have gifts which are only analogous to the New Testament miraculous gifts of the Spirit.[30] Though he implies that Rutherford belongs to the cessationist camp, Poythress suggests that Rutherford accepts that revelation may still come in a non-discursive manner.[31] Nonetheless, Poythress stresses both the analogous function of modern dreams and visions and their reliance on Scripture: "Modern impressions or visions, to

---

[26] The date contained the number 666 – the number of the "beast" in Rev. 13:8.

[27] Archibald Johnston, "The Diary of Archibald Johnston (1655-1661)", MS 6247-6259. Edinburgh: National Library, 1940. MS 6259, 32.

[28] Johnston, "The Diary of Archibald Johnston, MS 6254, 9 November 1658 to 23 January 1659, 76.

[29] Sydney Burrell gives this interpretation of Johnston's view of God's communication as well: Sydney Burrell, "The Apocalyptic Vision of the Covenanters", *The Scottish Historical Review* 135 (April 1964), 1-24, at 17.

[30] Vern Sheridan Poythress, "Modern Spiritual Gifts As Analogous To Apostolic Gifts: Affirming Extraordinary Works Of The Spirit Within Cessationist theology", *Journal of the Evangelical Theological Society* 39/1 (March 1996), 71-102, at 77.

[31] Poythress, "Modern Spiritual Gifts As Analogous To Apostolic Gifts: Affirming Extraordinary Works Of The Spirit Within Cessationist theology", at 95-96. Rutherford's own explanation does fit into Poythress's categories, as we will see in Samuel Rutherfurd [or Rutherford], *A Survey of the Spirituall Antichrist.[...]"* (London: Andrew Crooke, 1648), 42-44.

be valid, must not add to the Bible but be wholly derivative from it".[32] Poythress proposes an explanation of modern revelatory phenomena in line with that offered by English Puritans and Scottish Presbyterians of seventeenth-century Britain.

However, at least one near-contemporary of Rutherford's held that he had once been a fully-fledged continuationist in respect of immediate revelation, but that his views on prophecy had changed at the time of the Westminster Assembly. Quaker George Keith, who so vigorously rejected the cessationist argument of the *WCF*, liked to find contradictions in the other writings of its authors. Keith analyses what he considers are anomalies in Rutherford's thought in his *Way Cast Up*, where he also claims that the *WCF* teaches the cessation of all extraordinary revelation in *WCF* 1:1 and 1:6.[33] Rutherford, he asserts, originally allowed that there could be modern extra-biblical revelation but changed his views to mirror the *WCF* during the sitting of the Assembly.[34]

A survey of Rutherford's own writings only reveals that Keith was correct that Rutherford was a cessationist at the Westminster Assembly. There is no evidence that he was ever a continuationist. Rutherford takes the common position that biblical "prophecy" terminology can refer to both

---

[32] Poythress, "Modern Spiritual Gifts As Analogous To Apostolic Gifts: Affirming Extraordinary Works Of The Spirit Within Cessationist theology", at 78.

[33] George Keith, *The Way Cast Up, and the Stumbling-blockes Removed from Before the Feet of Those, Who are Seeking the Way to Zion, with Their Faces Thitherward: Containing an Answere to a Postscript, Printed at the End of Samuel Rutherford's Letters, Third Edition, by a Nameless Author [...]*' (Aberdeen: 1677) [no other publishing details are given], 9-10.

[34] Keith, *The Way Cast Up*, 18-19 and 185-86. Keith's examples of Rutherford's earlier allegedly continuationist position are not very convincing. He cites a third edition of Rutherford's letters from 1675. The references in Keith match Samuel Rutherford, *Mr Rutherfoord's Letters. The Third Edition now Divided in Three Parts* (1675) more closely than they do any other edition we have been able to locate. This edition, as sighted in New College Library, Edinburgh, contains no publishing details. Keith refers to Rutherford's Epistles, part one: 2, 7, 9, 55, 120, 154, 120; part two: 2, 8, 22, 49, 56, 57; and part three: 13, 27, 56. See Keith, The *Way Cast Up*, 183, where he lists examples of Rutherford's alleged claims to immediate revelation. The numbering of the letters is a little different in the edition (held in New College Library, Edinburgh) we have consulted. An example of Rutherford's alleged claim to prophecy is Epistle 7 in part one of Rutherford's Letters. The edition we have consulted numbers the same epistle to Lady Kenmure as Epistle 6 (Rutherford, *Mr Rutherfoord's Letters,* 23): Rutherford writes: "A dry wind upon *Scotland*, but neither to fan nor to *cleanse*: but out of all question when the Lord hath cut down his *forrest*, the after-growth of *Lebanon* shall flourish, they shall plant *vines* in our *mountains*, and a cloud shall plant vines in our mountains, and a cloud shall fill the *Temple*". This is an application of Ezek. 7:10, which Rutherford has just cited. It is not necessary to interpret any of the examples Keith brings as immediate revelation or as extra-biblical prophecy.

inspired and uninspired preachers. He applies the term "prophet" from 1 Corinthians 12 and 1 Corinthians 14 to ordinary ministers,[35] while at the same time acknowledging that prophecies of the apostolic age were infallible.[36]

Rutherford also vigorously opposes any contemporary claims to extra-biblical revelation when he locks horns with the Antinomians. In his *Survey of the Spirituall Antichrist*, he confronts Antinomianism, a position which the Westminster Assembly also deliberately addressed in its literary productions.[37] For Rutherford, Antinomian John Saltmarsh epitomises the errors of both the "papacy" and "enthusiasm". Rutherford labels Saltmarsh as one who

> maketh the Scriptures as unperfect as the *Papists* doe, the one dreaming of a Spirit in the breast of the *Pope* and cursed Clergie to be the master of one faith, the *Anabaptisticall* Spirit of unwritten revelations to be our leader; and they reproach the word of God.[38]

In this engagement, Rutherford gives a technical explanation of how the Holy Spirit relates to the spirits of human beings when God brings revelations. Rutherford takes issue with the Schwenkfeldians, Familists and Antinomians who held in common claims to "immediate inspirations, revelations, without scripture, or indeavours or studying, or bookes or reading".[39] Rutherford, who maintains that his views are the orthodox ones because he is writing in submission "to the Learned and the Godly",[40] delineates his classification of "revelation". One type of revelation is the outward form of Scripture which may be "revealed to all within the vissible Church".[41] He also describes an internal fourfold revelation, of which the first "immediate" type is obsolete:

> [It is a] *Propheticall Revelation* [which] is that irradiation of the minde that the *Holy Ghost* makes on the minde and judgement of the penmen of holy scripture, whether *Prophets* or *Apostles* and that by an immediate in-breathing of the minde and will of *God* on them, whether in *visions, dreames*, or any other way, without the ministery or teaching of men [...]".[42]

---

[35] Samuel Rutherford, *The Due Right of Presbyteries or, A Peaceable Plea for the Government of the Church of Scotland* (London: Richard Whittaker and Andrew Crook, 1644), 297- 98.

[36] Rutherford, *The Due Right of Presbyteries*, 303.

[37] For a repudiation of Antinomian claims to extra-biblical revelation for assurance, see *WCF* 18:1-3.

[38] Rutherford, *A Survey of the Spirituall Antichrist*, 249.

[39] Rutherford, *A Survey of the Spirituall Antichrist*, 38.

[40] Rutherford, *A Survey of the Spirituall Antichrist*, 39

[41] Rutherford, *A Survey of the Spirituall Antichrist*, 39.

[42] Rutherford, *A Survey of the Spirituall Antichrist*, 39-40.

This revelation is a divine "inspiration", restricted to the authors of Scripture, as "none were inspired of *God*, but writers of Canonnick scripture, and Scripture onely is given by *divine inspiration*".[43] This now-superseded manner of revelation includes the "immediate" speaking of the Spirit.[44] Therefore, Rutherford taunts, if the Familists and others actually see visions of God, then miracles, speaking in tongues and "foretelling things contingent" will accompany such revelations and will place them on an equal footing with Scripture.[45]

At this point, Rutherford uses the word "propheticall" in a limited sense: to describe the process whereby God reveals such information as will be inscripturated. Such a "propheticall rapture", he later explains, removes free will from those prophets who are experiencing a vision.[46] At the same time, he describes this state as an "immediately inspiring impulsion of an actual extasie".[47] Precisely this was what the Antinomians, according to Rutherford, actually claimed to be the experience of every true Christian, something Rutherford vehemently denies.

"Visions and dreams", which are examples of inspiration, are therefore outlawed because they are "formally the express word, sense and minde of God".[48] It follows that if the various enthusiasts and Antinomians have "such *Revelations*. 1. they see the *Visions of God*. 2. They speake as acted by the *Spirit* immediately[...]".[49] Rutherford adds that all immediate revelation from God in the Old Testament was in the place of Scripture. It is of that order of importance, for

> what God spake in visions, dreams, and apparitions to the Patriarchs, was as binding and obliging a pattern interditing men [...] as the written word is to us.[50]

Furthermore, all these experiences were recorded in Scripture:

> God himself immediately spake by the Patriarchs, and to *Moses*, nothing but what after was committed to writing by *Moses* and the *Prophets* at Gods speciall Commandment.[51]

---

[43] Rutherford, *A Survey of the Spirituall Antichrist*, 39.

[44] Rutherford, *A Survey of the Spirituall Antichrist*, 40.

[45] Rutherford, *A Survey of the Spirituall Antichrist*, 40. In another work, Rutherford reiterates the idea that the apostles and prophets did not write "Canonick Scripture out of their own head". Instead there was "an immediate inspiration, which essentially did include every syllable and word that the *Apostles* and *Prophets* were to write[...]": Samuel Rutherford, *The Divine Right of Church Government and Excommunication* [...]" (London: Christopher Meredith, 1646), 66.

[46] Rutherford, *A Survey of the Spirituall Antichrist*, 298.

[47] Rutherford, *A Survey of the Spirituall Antichrist*, 298.

[48] Rutherford, *A Survey of the Spirituall Antichrist*, 40.

[49] Rutherford, *A Survey of the Spirituall Antichrist*, 40.

[50] Rutherford, *The Divine Right of Church Government*, 40.

This stance denied the likelihood of any non-canonical guidance by immediate revelation via dreams, visions and other means, for God intended his revelations to be recorded as Scripture.[52]

Rutherford also elucidates his cessationist views when he opposes the claims of another Antinomian, William Dell, in his *Survey of Antinomianisme*. Dell held that the Spirit works immediately, which provoked Rutherford to exclaim that Dell and the Familists

> juggle with *David Georgius* and *Henry Nicholas*, who understood by the word, *Verbum internum*, the *Enthusiasticall* inward word of the minde, and the Spirit[...]".[53]

In Rutherford's opinion contemporary foretelling was something quite distinct from the New Testament gift of extraordinary prophecy. In his 1646 book, *Divine Right of Church Government*, Rutherford avers that claims to a contemporary gift of New Testament prophecy are invalid. There he opposes "Popish and Ceremoniall additions", asserting not only that offices of evangelists and prophets "extraordinarily inspired" have ceased, but so have the gifts which accompanied them:

> When God commandeth such Offices to be in his house, which dependeth immediately upon his own immediate will of giving gifts essentially required to these Offices, then these offices are so long in his Church, as God is pleased by his immediate will to give these gifts; and when God denyeth these gifts essentially requisite, sure it is, his immediate wil hath altered and removed the office, not the will of the Church, so the Lord hath alterd and removed these Offices and gifts of Apostles, who could *speak with tongues*, and seal their doctrine with *Miracles, Evangelists, Prophets extraordinarily inspired, gifts of healing*, &c.[54]

It was not just the *offices* of apostle, evangelist and prophet which God caused to cease, therefore, but the revelatory gifts themselves, including the gift of extraordinary inspired prophecy used in these offices.

Rutherford, who ties the gifts to the offices of apostle and prophet, consistently teaches that biblical prophets in both Testaments were office-

---

[51] Rutherford, *The Divine Right of Church Government*, 40.

[52] Rutherford would have agreed with the deduction of Scott Thomas, "The Doctrine of Scripture in the Westminster Assembly" (unpublished PhD thesis, Drew University, 1984), who concludes in his study of the Westminster doctrine of Scripture that since Christ has ascended and God no longer communicates through dreams and visions, for the divines, Scripture is now the only special revelation available to the church (70).

[53] Samuel Rutherford, *A Modest Survey of the Secrets of Antinomianisme* (London: Andrew Crooke, 1648), 210.

[54] Rutherford, *The Divine Right of Church Government*, 64.

bearers,[55] a claim he supports by citing a number of texts from the New Testament.[56] Rutherford also limits prophets to two basic types, leaving no possibility that contemporary inspired prophets may be raised up:

> All Prophets are either ordinary or extraordinary, as is cleare in *Gods Word*; extraordinary now are not in the Church, and the ordinary Prophets now are not gifted to preach the Word, except as *Timothy*, from their youth they have beene trained up in the Scriptures[...]".[57]

He also challenges the arguments of an opponent who claims that the "two witnesses" of Rev. 11:3 represent the Scriptures and the assemblies of the faithful.[58] His opponent understands that the prophecy of the witnesses was *"no extraordinary and miraculous gift of prophecying*[...]".[59] While agreeing on this point, Rutherford nevertheless teaches that these witnesses were ministers, thus eliminating another text that could be appealed to as a precedent for claiming the possibility of contemporary inspired prophets.[60] Rutherford, therefore, denies the existence of contemporary, post- apostolic "propheticall" revelation, though for him, as we have already seen in Chapter Three, believers have mediate Scripture-revelations in the sense allowed in Eph. 1:17.

We have been at some pains to underscore that Rutherford was an earnest cessationist, because his writings selectively quoted, as we saw in Keith, can easily obscure the real Rutherford. Rutherford certainly proposes a third category of divine disclosure, distinct from "immediate" and Scripture revelations, which bears some resemblance to extraordinary inspired prophecy, but he carefully distinguishes it from the extraordinary and immediate prophetic gifts of the New Testament. While he allows for this special legitimate post-apostolic prophecy, he makes it abundantly clear in a marginal gloss that he is describing a type of prophecy quite different from that uttered by the apostles and prophets of the apostolic age: "Of revelations extraordinary of men in our ages *not immediately inspired*

---

[55] Rutherford, *The Due Right of Presbyteries*, 279 (irregular numbering - should be 579).

[56] Eph. 4:11, 1 Cor. 12:28, 2 Tim. 3:2, and Acts 20:28. He includes Acts 2:17, and Joel 2:28. Rutherford, *The Due Right of Presbyteries*, 279.

[57] Rutherford, *The Due Right of Presbyteries*, 280 [580].

[58] Rutherford is engaging John Robinson's, *The Peoples Plea for the Exercise of Prophecy against Master J. Yates His Monopolie* ([Leyden?], 1641) [no other details are available].

[59] Rutherford, *The Due Right of Presbyteries*, 295 [595].

[60] He cites Junias, Couper, Paraeus, Hus, Jerome of Prague, Luther, Melancthon, Bucer, Cariton, Zwinglius, Oecolampadius and Calvin who, he alleges, all believed that these witnesses were ministers of the gospel. Rutherford, *The Due Right of Presbyteries*, 295 [595].

[emphasis added][...]".[61] He lists Hus, Wycliffe, Luther, Wishart, Knox, and Davidson, and "diverse Holy and mortified preachers in *England* have done the like".[62]

Contrasting these foretellers with the agents of a fourth type of prophecy, revelations which have a Satanic origin, Rutherford reinforces the differences between modern prophets and the inspired prophets of old:

1. Genuine modern prophesiers "never gave themselves out as organs immediately inspired by the *Holy Ghost*".

2. They never denounced those who did not believe their predictions.

3. The events were revealed to "Godly and sound witnesses of Christ", and were not contrary to the Scriptures.

4. Although they predicted tragic ends for individuals, they never involved themselves in bringing about their deaths nor did they approve of those who killed them.

5. Most important of all:

> They had a generall rule going along that *Evill shall hunt the wicked man*: onely a secret harmlesse, but an extraordinary strong impulsion, of a Scripture-spirit leading them, carried them to apply a generall rule of divine justice, in their predictions, to particular Godlesse men, they themselves onely being foretellers not copartners of the act.[63]

These distinctions harmonise with the views of the English divines and with the Reformed orthodox position on the inseparability of Word and

---

[61] Rutherford, *A Survey of the Spirituall Antichrist*, 42. Martin Luther distinguishes two types of prophecy. The first has to do with "secular government and earthly affairs", and was more common in the Old Testament than the New. The second type concerns itself with the Kingdom of Christ. This second category "is still present in Christendom, but not so markedly as in the apostles. We, too, can predict and know such things, but only if we have learned this from the books of the apostles". Martin Luther, *Luther's Works*, ed. Jaroslav Pelikan (Saint Louis: Concordia Publishing house, 1970), vol. 24, 365-66.

[62] Rutherford, *A Survey of the Spirituall Antichrist*, 42. These men, of course, were among the most illustrious of the Reformation to which Rutherford was heir and were no doubt considered by him to be above criticism.

[63] Rutherford, *A Survey of the Spirituall Antichrist*, 44. See similar ideas expressed in Samuel Rutherford, *Christ Dying and Drawing Sinners to Himself, Or, a Survey of Our Saviour in His Soule-suffering: His Lovelynesse in His Death, and the Efficacie Thereof* (London: Andrew Crooke, 1647), 279-80. See also David Strickland's PhD thesis where he discusses an experience of God analogous to the impressions of the Holy Spirit granted Reformation prophets; namely the sensual intimations of the Spirit evident in Rutherford's doctrine of union with God through Christ. Strickland acknowledges: "Since these are not revelations of God or of His will, but merely revealed gifts of God, they can never be a rule for obedience". David Strickland, ""Union with Christ in the Theology of Samuel Rutherford: An Examination of His Doctrine of the Holy Spirit", unpublished PhD thesis (University of Edinburgh, 1972), 144.

Spirit. Furthermore, that Rutherford's examples all apply to ministers of the gospel is in accord with the Puritan view that post-apostolic "prophecy" usually came through ordained preachers. From Rutherford's perspective, had the revelations of these Reformation prophets come by immediate inspiration, these "prophets" ought to have rebuked those who failed to acknowledge them, because any such prophecies, in Rutherford's opinion, were on a par with Scripture. For Rutherford, modern foretelling always involves the general rule of the Word of God, and is accompanied by a motion or impulse from the Holy Spirit which assists preachers to predict God's temporal judgement on wicked individuals.

Such an experience of prophetic insight seems analogous to the way in which some theologians of the time thought that personal assurance of salvation was conveyed. In assurance of salvation, it was held, the Spirit applies the Word to the heart of the individual, conveying information from the Word which is particularly applicable to that person's circumstances.[64] The only difference between the two processes is the subject-matter to which the Spirit witnesses. Instead of an assurance of one's own salvation as a Scripture-promise based upon evident sanctification, it is an assurance of the judgement that will come upon others in return for their evident wickedness in terms of the principles of justice found in Scripture. For Rutherford, the role of the minister of the Word and Sacrament was "prophetic" in this uninspired sense. God enabled the minister to apply the Word in a meaningful way, making a specific application of doctrine to a particular circumstance by the leading of the Spirit.

This hermeneutic lay behind the whole justification of the jeremiad - a denunciation of a society or individual which was believed to have the force of God's intentions.[65] In this tradition, the minister was believed to speak with the lips of Christ, and so had the right to demand attention, or the acknowledgement that it was the Word of God which was conveyed through his preaching. As English divine Henry Scudder reminded the House of Commons in 1644:

> And *ordinary Ministers of the Gospel* are in the Scripture said to *speak to men by the word of the Lord*, and to *speak the word of the Lord*, as well as the Prophets, who were immediately inspired of God [1 Thess. 4:15; Heb.

---

[64] See, for example, Samuel Rutherford, *The Covenant of Life Opened or a Treatise of the Covenant of Grace* (Edinburgh: Robert Broun, 1655), 65-66. Or see Henry Scudder, *The Christian's Daily Walk* (Harrisburg, Va.: Sprinkle Publications, 1984), 338-42.

[65] For an extended discussion on the jeremiad, see Perry Miller, *The New England Mind. From Colony to Province* (Cambridge: Harvard University Press, 1953), vol. 2, 27-39.

13:7][...][W]hat they[ordinary ministers] speak according to his Word[written], is to be received as if God himself spake unto you.[66]

6.3.2 Alexander Henderson and Robert Blair[67]

A second category of Scottish commissioners presents a more complex picture. In Alexander Henderson's case, this in part because we have very little from his pen. Even if the New Testament gift had ceased, as the majority of the Reformed orthodox supposed, Alexander Henderson can still write in his brief *Reformation of Church Government in Scotland* that the Scottish Reformers were commonly believed to have possessed a "propheticall Spirit":

> They were not onely learned and holy men, but had somewhat in their calling, gifts and zeale to the glory of God, more then ordinary: Their Adversaries were not able to resist the wisdome and Spirit by which they spoke, some of them had a propheticall Spirit manifested in diverse particular and wonderfull predictions, and some of them were honoured to be Martyrs, & sealed the truth with their blood.[68]

Afterwards, "men of the same spirit" were also raised up and kept in contact with the divines of other nations,[69] though Henderson does not explain this as an instance of the gift of prophecy in a New Testament sense. An analysis of his use of the word "Propheticall", sometimes used by others to mean immediate inspirations, is of little help. Occasionally the Reformed orthodox used the term as a synonym for immediate inspiration,

---

[66] Henry Scudder, *Gods Warning to England by the Voyce of His ROD* (London: Philemon Stephens and Edward Blackmore, 1644), 7. Or, as Ronald Wallace says of Calvin's perspective on preaching, "The word preached by man can become 'God speaking'". Ronald S. Wallace, *Calvin's Doctrine of the Word and Sacrament* (Tyler: Geneva Divinity School Press, 1982), 83.

[67] See John Dick (1764-1833) for a later Scottish theologian who seems to allow for extra-biblical revelations, though the disclosures in question might conceivably fall within Rutherford's definition: "Whether God may not, for some important purpose, make known to individuals by his Spirit things secret and future, is a question which we presume not to decide; but such revelations are appropriated to the use of those individuals, and have no claim to the attention of others, unless they were authenticated by miracles, and wanting this attestation, are no more a part of the rule of faith and obedience than any mere human speculation". John Dick, *Lectures on Theology* (Edinburgh: Oliver and Boyd, 1838), vol. 3, 70. On Dick's life and ministry, see John McIntosh, "John Dick", *DSCHT*, 242.

[68] Alexander Henderson, *Reformation of Church-Government in Scotland, Cleered from Some Mistakes and Prejudices* (London: Robert Bostock, 1644), 3-4.

[69] Henderson, *Reformation of Church-Government in Scotland Cleered*, 4.

but not always. Samuel Rutherford, for example, uses it in both senses.[70] What we can say, though, is that Henderson makes no claims here that could not easily fit into Rutherford's explanation of contemporary foretelling.

While we have insufficient data from Henderson to conclude whether or not he relates modern prediction to a spiritual gift defined in the New Testament, other colleagues yield a potentially richer vein of argument. Robert Blair (1593-1666), moderator of the General Assembly in 1646, had been appointed a royal chaplain because he found favour with Charles I. Blair took something of a mediating role in the later dispute between the Resolutioners and Protesters, which resulted in both sides mistrusting him.[71] He is also one of two commissioners who expressed views that are not so easily reconciled with Rutherford's perspective on prophecy and with a cessationist interpretation of the *WCF*.

Like John Knox, Blair was another Scot whose alleged prophetic powers were accepted as authentic and his exercise of them was also recorded for subsequent generations through the work of Robert Wodrow. Wodrow recounts a story of Blair and others en route to New England by ship, when a storm threatened to overwhelm them:

> Mr Blair continoued still pleasant and merry, and said, 'Sirs, there is noe fear. It's born in on me, that I shall preach befor ane army that shall rise in Scotland for the Covenant and covenanted work of Reformation!' Which accordingly came to passe.[72]

According to Wodrow, Blair had also prophesied Scotland's deliverance by the Prince of Orange when the Prince was still only seven years old.[73]

Blair's mystical streak is confirmed in his own autobiographical account of a prophetic dream he experienced concerning the death of his wife. When Blair gives an explanation of his prophetic insights from 1632, he feels the need to clarify his unusual claims to his relatives:

---

[70] For "Propheticall" defined as "inspired", see Rutherford, *A Survey of the Spirituall Antichrist*, 39-40; as "uninspired" prophecy, see Rutherford, *Christ Dying and Drawing Sinners to Himself*, 279.

[71] David Lachman, "Robert Blair", *DSCHT*, 81-82. See also David Lachman, "Protesters", *DSCHT*, 681. In 1650, the Protesters complained of Charles II's admission to the Covenants. For the Resolutioners, see David Lachman, "Resolutioners", *DSCHT*, 710. The Resolutioners favoured repealing laws that prevented Charles II from raising an army to fight Cromwell.

[72] Wodrow, *Analecta: Or Materials for a History of Remarkable Providences; Mostly Relating to Scotch Ministers and Christians*, vol. 1, 24.

[73] Wodrow, *Analecta: Or Materials for a History of Remarkable Providences; Mostly Relating to Scotch Ministers and Christians*, vol. 1, 25. Blair was also credited with effecting a miraculous healing: Wodrow, *Analecta: Or Materials for a History of Remarkable Providences; Mostly Relating to Scotch Ministers and Christians*, vol. 1, 26.

> If any of my relations, reading these things, shall stumble, that both now and heretofore I have mentioned what hath been revealed to me of events to come, seeing revelations are now ceased, and we are to stick close to the revealed will of God in the Scriptures, for their satisfaction I answer as follows: That if an angel from heaven should reveal anything contrary to the Scriptures, or offer to add anything to that perfect rule of faith and manners, he ought to be accursed, and much more if any man on earth should offer to do the same. This accursed way of revelation we leave to papists and other sectaries. But, in the meantime, it ought not to be denied that the Lord is pleased sometimes, to his servants, especially in a suffering condition, to reveal some events concerning themselves and that part of the Church of God wherein they live.[74]

There are a number of factors in Blair's statement which should make us cautious in evaluating this as a claim to immediate prophetic revelation, because together they demonstrate that Blair's experiences can still be reconciled with the kind of cessationism evinced by Rutherford, Baillie or Johnston.

First, in his account of his dream, Blair is careful to record a Scriptural text which confirms the imminent loss of his wife (Ezek. 24:16). This indicates, at least on that occasion, that he does see a need to tie Scripture to such "revelations".[75]

Secondly, though Blair's clear distinction between revelation for matters of doctrine and revelation for the purpose of personal guidance suggests that both prophetic insights might be "immediate", Blair makes no claims to possess the New Testament spiritual gift of prophecy with "immediate" revelation.

Thirdly, his prophecy in his autobiographical account occurs many years before the deliberations on the *WCF*, and the reference to his relatives may indicate that he was not anticipating that his comments would be published widely. Although we can only speculate at this point, it is perhaps the case that had he realised how many people would read what he had written, he might have been more timid in expressing his views, or explained them more fully.

Fourthly, and most significantly, he recognizes the standard view of the day, which was that the cessation of revelation precluded prophetic

---

[74] Thomas M'Crie (ed.), *The Life of Mr Robert Blair, Minister of St Andrews, Containing his Autobiography, from 1593 to 1636* (Edinburgh: Wodrow Society, 1848), 97-98. English divine William Greenhill takes the view that Paul is speaking hypothetically in Gal. 1:8, the text to which Blair refers. Greenhill says that no angel has ever preached any other gospel or ever will: "Hypothetical propositions, according to logicians, produce no effects, but they prove the necessity of a consequent". William Greenhill, *An Exposition of Ezekiel* (Edinburgh: Banner of Truth Trust, 1994), 116.

[75] M'Crie (ed.), *The Life of Mr Robert Blair, Minister of St Andrews, Containing his Autobiography, from 1593 to 1636*, 96-97.

revelation for personal guidance as well. That he feels the need to give an explanation to his relatives makes this clear and suggests that he was concerned that he could have been seen to contradict the official view of the church.

Furthermore, nothing that Blair claims falls outside the ambit of Rutherford's explanation for modern foretelling as an application of Scripture to providence. Nor does Blair's position contradict the view that premonitions were still possible.[76] Because God governs all providence, a premonition can be said to be a revelation from God without needing to be "immediate". Blair conceivably could maintain the authenticity of his revelatory experiences and still subscribe to a cessationist reading of the *WCF*.

6.3.3 George Gillespie

The views of Blair's colleague George Gillespie cannot, at first sight, be easily reconciled with a consistent cessationism.[77] Willem Berends appeals to Gillespie as one who expressly "believed the [contemporary] prophets to be directly inspired by God's Spirit".[78] On the face of it, this conclusion is, however, questionable. A closer examination of the evidence does not give us much confidence to conclude that Gillespie believed Reformation prophets were directly inspired by the Spirit.

Gillespie was a controversial figure in his own day, esteemed by some but heartily disliked by others. His death grieved Robert Baillie's cousin, William Spang, who wrote to Baillie on 7 March 1649 eulogising Gillespie as one who was as "able a man as our Kirk had; of a clear judgement".[79] Although Baillie had once considered him "too rash a youth in his determinations",[80] he later regarded him as "a singular ornament of our Church".[81] Though Spang is of the opinion that experience and age would have amended his faults, Gillespie was also "mislyked" by some, even up

---

[76] On the difference between revelations and premonitions, see Chapter Four above, 148. See also David Mullan, *Scottish Puritanism, 1590-1638* (Oxford: Oxford University Press, 2000), 53-55, on the Scottish belief that premonitions in dreams were warnings, which coexisted, nonetheless, with a fair degree of scepticism by some Scots towards the revelatory nature of dreams. See 221, n14 above for Thomas M'Crie's attribution of such premonitions to John Knox. See also 256 below for Kennedy's similar allowance for premonitions in his own day.

[77] See Louis Hodges, "George Gillespie", *DSCHT*, 359-60.

[78] William Berends, "Prophecy in the Reformation Tradition", *Vox Reformata* 60 (1995), 30-43, at 39.

[79] Baillie, *The Letters and Journals of Robert Baillie*, vol. 3, 68.

[80] Baillie, *The Letters and Journals of Robert Baillie*, vol. 1, 189.

[81] Baillie, *The Letters and Journals of Robert Baillie*, vol. 2, 129.

to the point of his death.[82] Even after his death and the posthumous publication of his *Miscellany Questions*, as the *Records of the Kirk of Scotland* show, Samuel Rutherford believed that Gillespie had erred in the *Miscellany Questions* with regard to the way in which ministers should be elected.[83] This at least shows that not all of Gillespie's views were considered orthodox by everyone in Scottish ecclesiastical circles. Undoubtedly, one of the reasons why others reacted strongly to him was Gillespie's brilliance in debate and his ability to analyse the arguments of his opponents and to answer them with brutally efficient and incisive rhetoric.

Spang does not explain in his letter why Gillespie was "mislyked", but it is possible that he has in mind Gillespie's views on contemporary prophecy. Gillespie apparently believed that God had raised up extraordinarily gifted prophets in the post-apostolic church. His views, however, need to be explored within the broader context of his theological writings. Therefore, we will first outline his position on the continuance of New Testament prophecy and then discuss several points of tension which arise from a consideration of his wider thought.

Gillespie wrote two essays in his *A Treatise of Miscellany Questions* which discuss the subject of prophets and prophecy.[84] In both of these he is writing to oppose the view of some Independents that men out of office could preach in the church. As we have already seen, this matter had used up much ink in the seventeenth century.[85] In his first essay, Gillespie calls upon the authority of Peter Martyr and John Calvin who, he believes, shared his views on the existence of modern prophets and prophecy. Gillespie defines prophets as those who receive extraordinary revelations from the Holy Spirit.[86] Two sections later, he appeals to 1 Cor. 12:28 and

---

[82] Baillie, *The Letters and Journals of Robert Baillie*, vol. 3, 68.

[83] Alexander Peterkin, *Records of the Kirk of Scotland, Containing the Acts and Proceedings of the General Assemblies, from the Year 1638 Downwards [...]*" (Edinburgh: John Sutherland, 1838), 565.

[84] "Whether these prophets and prophesyings in the primitive church, 1 cor. 14; 12:28; eph. 4:11, were extraordinary, and so not to continue; or whether they are precedents for the preaching or prophesying of such as are neither ordained ministers nor probationers for the ministry": George Gillespie, "Miscellany Questions", *The Works of George Gillespie*, ed. David Meek (Edmonton: SWRB, 1991), vol. 2, 27; and "Of prophets and evangelists: in what sense their work and vocation might be called extraordinary, and in what sense ordinary": Gillespie, "Miscellany Questions", *The Works of George Gillespie*, vol. 2, 38.

[85] See Chapter Three, 112 above.

[86] Gillespie, "Miscellany Questions", *The Works of George Gillespie*, vol. 2, 29. He quotes "Peter Martyr, *Loci Communes* Part 4 chapter 1". See Peter Martyr Vermigli, Anthonie Marten (translator) *The Common Places, of the Most Famous and Renowned Divine Doctor Peter Martyr[...]Translated and Partlie Gathered by Anthonie Marten*

Eph. 4:11 to explain the presence of extraordinary prophets in the Scottish church at the time of the Reformation and beyond. Thus John Knox, John Welsh and others were:

> holy prophets receiving extraordinary revelations from God, and foretelling diverse strange and remarkable things, which did accordingly come to pass punctually, to the great admiration of all who knew the particulars.[87]

This statement is in itself unremarkable in the light of the cessationist Rutherford's similar description of the Reformed prophets in Scottish Reformation history. What sets Gillespie apart is his appeal to texts, without qualification, that others applied to "immediately" inspired prophets, those who Rutherford and others claimed had long since ceased to exist in the church.

Before he remarks on Knox and others as extraordinary prophets, Gillespie spends some time describing New Testament prophets in the primitive church. They were immediately inspired; usually in an office;[88] had greater gifts for expounding difficult Scripture texts; and interpreted the Scriptures with the same "Propheticall Spirit" by which it was written.[89] Gillespie's overall analysis of the status of New Testament prophecy also implies that Reformation "prophets" could be immediately inspired when he discusses the meaning of the word "prophesying", for he only sees three possible meanings of the word in the New Testament. One is the speaking with tongues which was fulfilled on the day of Pentecost. Ordinary preaching by a minister is another, although he sees no clear Scripture for this. His third category is "extraordinary prophesying from immediate and miraculous inspiration".[90] Such New Testament Prophets were also infallible.[91]

Thus, the conundrum Gillespie's position raises can be posed like this: if the texts just cited apply to the immediately-inspired prophets of the New Testament and also to a John Knox in the sixteenth century, can we assume that Gillespie wants us to see Knox as immediately inspired? Gillespie nowhere says in so many words that modern prophets receive "immediate revelations" from God or that they are "immediately inspired", but by appealing to the same texts to justify the prophecies of Agabus and Knox, Gillespie's stance is certainly open to that interpretation. Furthermore, even

---

[...]" (London: 1583) [no other publishing details are given], part 4: chapter 1, 6. Gillespie also cites "John Calvin, *Institutes* 4:3:4". John Calvin, *Institutes of the Christian Religion*, ed. John McNeill (Philadelphia: The Westminster Press, 1960).

[87] Gillespie, "Miscellany Questions", *The Works of George Gillespie*, vol. 2, 30.
[88] Gillespie, "Miscellany Questions", *The Works of George Gillespie*, vol. 2, 28.
[89] Gillespie, "Miscellany Questions", *The Works of George Gillespie*, vol. 2, 29.
[90] Gillespie, "Miscellany Questions", *The Works of George Gillespie*, vol. 2, 30.
[91] Gillespie, "Miscellany Questions", *The Works of George Gillespie*, vol. 2, 35.

though the *Miscellany Questions* were published posthumously with an acknowledgement by Gillespie's brother Patrick that they were imperfect, Patrick still had "the author's leave" to publish.[92]

Nevertheless, six points of tension arise within Gillespie's overall thought which militate against definitively using these essays to set him in conflict with a cessationist interpretation of *WCF* 1:1.

6.3.3.1 INTERNAL CONTRADICTIONS

First, Gillespie's views are often inconsistent or fluid. He debates by overwhelming the opposition with massive and detailed argumentation. As well as producing inconsistencies or even outright contradictions, this style of argument also illustrates his willingness to bend the data to fit the argument. For example, in one essay he obviously understands "prophecy" from 1 Cor. 13:8 and "prophesying" from 1 Thess. 5:20 to refer to ordinary preaching,[93] but in one of his essays on prophecy he allows only the text of Rev. 11:3 to possibly refer to ordinary preaching. In the latter essay, because it suits his purpose, he states that there are no other texts that "without controversy" prove that ordinary preaching is prophesying.[94]

Such an inconsistency is not only to be found within the *Miscellany Questions*. Gillespie also puts forward quite a different argument in the *Miscellany Questions* from the one he presents in an earlier published work, *An Assertion of the Government of the Church of Scotland*.[95] A comparison of these two treatises reveals other contradictions in Gillespie's writing. First, in *An Assertion*, he teaches that Rom. 12:6-8 subsumes the expounding of Scripture under prophecy as ordinary preaching, but all other "imployments" under ministry.[96] However, in his *Miscellany Questions* he exegetes the reference to "prophecy", in the same text, to denote the extraordinary gift.[97] Secondly, in *An Assertion*, he interprets the judgement of the prophets in 1 Cor. 14:29-32 to teach that there must be order in the

---

[92] Gillespie, "Miscellany Questions", *The Works of George Gillespie*, vol. 2, iii.

[93] Here Gillespie also denies that there can be any "immediate" enjoyment of God in this world without ordinances, thereby confirming that immediate dialogue with God is impossible in his view, a position which would categorically deny the possibility of immediate prophecy as well. Gillespie, "Miscellany Questions", *The Works of George Gillespie*, vol. 2, 2.

[94] Gillespie, "Miscellany Questions", *The Works of George Gillespie*, vol. 2, 2 and 30.

[95] George Gillespie, *An Assertion of the Government of the Church of Scotland, in the Points of Ruling-Elders, and of the Authority of Presbyteries and Synods* (Edinburgh: James Bryson, 1641).

[96] Gillespie, *An Assertion of the Government of the Church of Scotland*, 35.

[97] Gillespie, "Miscellany Questions", *The Works of George Gillespie*, vol. 2, 35 and 37.

church, not a trying of the spirits.[98] But in the *Miscellany Questions*, he teaches the opposite, that the prophets were to judge one another's prophecies.[99]

6.3.3.2 ON THE CESSATION OF THE OTHER MIRACULOUS GIFTS

If we accept that Gillespie intends to admit that contemporary extraordinary prophets prophesy by immediate revelation, we can identify a second point of tension in his arguments. With regard to other miraculous gifts, he adopts an essentially conservative position. For example, Gillespie considers that the miraculous gift of healing has ceased.[100] He also holds that the gift of miracles was given to confirm doctrine.[101] Consistency would presumably require him to hold that all miraculous gifts which had the purpose of confirming doctrine had also ceased.

6.3.3.3 A DISTINCTION BETWEEN MODERN AND BIBLICAL PROPHETS

A third point of tension is the clear distinction drawn by Gillespie between the prophets of apostolic times and those of the post-apostolic church. Gillespie does indeed differentiate between the prophets and prophecies of the two eras. This differentiation comes to light in a number of ways. While he accepts that the spiritual gift of the early prophets involved bringing a miraculous revelation for edifying the church,[102] the opening of "hard scriptures" by revelation and the interpreting of Scripture with "the same propheticall spirit by which it was dictated and written",[103] Gillespie's modern prophets are only described as "foretellers".[104] In addition, elsewhere he posits the cessation of the immediate call to the office of prophet. In his essays on prophecy, he argues that the early church prophets and evangelists did receive an extraordinary call and mission,[105] yet he is also convinced that the immediate vocation and mission has now ceased.[106] He confirms this position in the essay, "Whether Ordination be Essential to

---

[98] Gillespie, *An Assertion of the Government of the Church of Scotland*, 102.

[99] Gillespie, "Miscellany Questions", *The Works of George Gillespie*, vol. 2, 35. In the same text in his *Aarons Rod Blossoming*, Gillespie believes that the apostle gave "rules and directions concerning prophecying or interpretation of Scripture", for both good order and to be "examined, judged, and censured by the other Prophets". George Gillespie, *Aarons Rod Blossoming[...]"* (London: Richard Whitaker, 1646), 279. "Prophecying" in this latter work is the interpretation of Scripture rather than the imparting of revelation.

[100] Gillespie, "Miscellany Questions", *The Works of George Gillespie*, vol. 2, 83.

[101] Gillespie, "Propositions", *The Works of George Gillespie*, vol. 1, 5.

[102] Gillespie, "Miscellany Questions", *The Works of George Gillespie*, vol. 2, 34.

[103] Gillespie, "Miscellany Questions", *The Works of George Gillespie*, vol. 2, 29.

[104] Gillespie, "Miscellany Questions", *The Works of George Gillespie*, vol. 2, 30.

[105] Gillespie, "Miscellany Questions", *The Works of George Gillespie*, vol. 2, 40-41.

[106] Gillespie, "Miscellany Questions", *The Works of George Gillespie*, vol. 2, 41.

the Calling of a Minister", in which he disagrees with an Erastian appeal to Rom. 10:15. His opponents provided an exegesis that held that the sending and calling mentioned in the text is extraordinary, and that modern pastors do not have the extraordinary mission since it has ceased. In his response, Gillespie acknowledges that the *extraordinary* mission has ceased but maintains that the same text teaches that an *ordinary* mission is now essential:

> This text doth certainly hold forth the necessity of an ordinary and mediate mission when the extraordinary and immediate mission is ceased.[107]

Gillespie shows his consistency on this point later when he affirms that a minister "cannot be immediately and extraordinarily [sent] in the reformed churches".[108]

Furthermore, not only has the immediate mission ceased, but Gillespie also insists that "extraordinary preachers, apostles, evangelists, prophets, must have an extraordinary mission", in order to qualify as extraordinary officers.[109] Logic suggests that if there is no extraordinary mission, neither can there be extraordinary prophets of the pure New Testament classification of office bearer.

Gillespie's ambiguity about the prophetic office adds to the confusion. In his first essay on prophets, he attempts to establish that the New Testament prophets were in an office,[110] whereas in his second essay, he allows that prophecy may function out of office.[111] Although he calls Knox and others "more than ordinary pastors and teachers, even holy prophets[...]", he neither claims that modern "prophets" are ordained to the office of prophet nor that they should be.[112] Moreover, although the modern prophets receive "extraordinary revelations", Gillespie does not attribute "immediate inspiration" directly to them. In an earlier essay he even appears to deny the possibility of any resurgent prophecy:

> What those prophets were, and what is meant by prophesying there, all are not of one opinion. I hold that these prophets were immediately and extraordinarily inspired, and I reckon them among these other administrations, which were not ordinary *or ever* to continue in the church, apostles, evangelists, workers of miracles [emphasis added].[113]

---

[107] Gillespie, "Miscellany Questions", *The Works of George Gillespie*, vol. 2, 18.
[108] Gillespie, "Miscellany Questions", *The Works of George Gillespie*, vol. 2, 18.
[109] Gillespie, "Miscellany Questions", *The Works of George Gillespie*, vol. 2, 19.
[110] Gillespie, "Miscellany Questions", *The Works of George Gillespie*, vol. 2, 31.
[111] Gillespie, "Miscellany Questions", *The Works of George Gillespie*, vol. 2, 40. Here he has in mind New Testament prophetesses.
[112] Gillespie, "Miscellany Questions", *The Works of George Gillespie*, vol. 2, 30.
[113] Gillespie, "Miscellany Questions", *The Works of George Gillespie*, vol. 2, 25.

Is the phrase "or ever" a synonym for "always", or does Gillespie believe at this point that prophets were not to continue at all? Perhaps we have here further evidence that his *Miscellany Questions* had not yet been "perfected". The discrepancies make it difficult to conclude whether or not Gillespie intends in his *Miscellany* an absolute identification of modern Reformation prophets with New Testament prophets; or whether he has in mind that since there is no more immediate call to office, there is no more immediate revelational prophecy either.

6.3.3.4 A CONTINUATIONIST GILLESPIE IN A CESSATIONIST ASSEMBLY?

A fourth tension is perhaps the most compelling argument for interpreting Gillespie as a cessationist. William McKay's suggestion, in his comprehensive analysis of Gillespie's ecclesiology, that Gillespie's views on modern prophecy "do not fit comfortably into any 'camp'" is poorly founded.[114] If we interpret Gillespie as a continuationist, we set him at odds with the majority of his colleagues at Westminster. Such a deviation would have made it hard for Gillespie even to stand by the Assembly's conclusions on church government. For example, if Gillespie maintained that modern prophets occupied an identical office to that described in the New Testament, his position would contradict the *FPC* which was part of the uniformity of religion and which plainly declares that the offices of prophet and evangelist have ceased.[115] We have no other evidence to indicate that Gillespie did contradict the *FPC*. Additionally, to interpret Gillespie as a continuationist would also set him at odds with the *FPC's* exegesis of proof-texts, because the *FPC* uses the same texts to warrant ordinary preaching which Gillespie thought referred to inspired prophecy. 1 Cor. 14:3 is a text in point. For the *FPC*, the prophesying spoken of here belongs to the minister of the Word, whether teacher or pastor.[116] For Gillespie in *Miscellany Questions,* it is purely the prophesying of an extraordinary prophet.[117] Had the highly esteemed Gillespie dissented from the position of the *FPC*, this would have been additional evidence that he was indeed a continuationist, although such a case cannot be made from the literature available to us.

---

[114] William McKay, *An Ecclesiastical Republic: Church Government in the Writings of George Gillespie* (Carlisle: Paternoster Press, 1997), 182-86. McKay discusses Gillespie's views in the light of the modern debate between cessationism and continuationism, but gives no proof for his assertion.

[115] "*Of the Officers of the Church.* The officers which Christ hath appointed for the edification of his church, and the perfecting of the saints, are, some extraordinary, as apostles, evangelists, and prophets, which are ceased". *FPC*, 172.

[116] *FPC*, 174.

[117] Gillespie, "Miscellany Questions", *The Works of George Gillespie*, vol. 2, 34.

6.3.3.5 LINKING THE "MISCELLANY" TO THE ASSEMBLY DEBATES

Since we cannot link Gillespie's views expressed in these essays to the debates over the *WCF* 1:1, it would be wrong to attempt too quickly to reconcile a continuationist reading of Gillespie with the cessationist clause in the *WCF*. As both titles of his key essays in the *Miscellany Questions* show, his primary aim there is not to prove the existence of contemporary prophecy. In the first essay, his purpose is to deny that certain texts allow promiscuous preaching in the church by the unordained,[118] and in the second he argues for the necessity of ordination and commission by the church.[119] At the same time these writings do not seem to coincide with relevant debates over the status of church offices in the Westminster Assembly, debates which occurred in 1643.[120] Gillespie cites the Annotations first published in 1645 in his first and most comprehensive essay on continuing prophecy.[121] If the essays contained in the *Miscellany Questions* were published in chronological order, they were probably written following the composition and acceptance of the *WCF*. Gillespie cites the *WCF* in the essay bracketed by his two essays on prophets and prophecy.[122] Even if we are wrong in our inference concerning the chronology of their composition, it remains the case that the context of his essays is certainly not that of the debates over special revelation in the Assembly.

6.3.3.6 GILLESPIE'S COMMITMENT TO WESTMINSTER ORTHODOXY

A sixth tension arises if we suppose that Gillespie taught the continuance of "immediate" prophecy in the church. He demonstrates a strong commitment to the Westminster documents and has a high view of subscription, for he approves the English Parliament's order to punish those who had taken the covenant and then wrote or preached against the *DPW*.[123] It is also very unlikely that Gillespie would have wanted to provoke dissatisfaction with the *WCF* in the light of his important position in the Scottish church and his vocal commitment to uniformity of religion among the three kingdoms. William Berends' conclusions, therefore, jar somewhat with what we know of Gillespie's dedication to Reformed orthodoxy. In an essay, *Prophecy in the Reformation Tradition,* Berends claims:

---

[118] Gillespie, "Miscellany Questions", *The Works of George Gillespie*, vol. 2, 27.

[119] Gillespie, "Miscellany Questions", *The Works of George Gillespie*, vol. 2, 38.

[120] Gillespie, "Notes of Proceedings of the Assembly of Divines at Westminster", *The Works of George Gillespie,* vol. 2, 3.

[121] Gillespie, "Miscellany Questions", *The Works of George Gillespie*, vol. 2, 5.

[122] Gillespie, "Miscellany Questions", *The Works of George Gillespie*, vol. 2, 37.

[123] Gillespie, "Miscellany Questions", *The Works of George Gillespie*, vol. 2, 86.

as far as Gillespie was concerned, the inscripturation of God's Word and the closure of the canon did not preclude the possibility that God continues to give prophetic guidance in extraordinary situations through the words of present day prophets.[124]

Gillespie, however, does not clearly state that he has "immediate" prophecy in view, if this is what Berends is implying. We are obliged to question an argument which rests such a conclusion on a work which is both incomplete and published posthumously. After all, we must ask why Gillespie himself did not publish these essays in London during the sitting of the Assembly. Does the fact that he did not suggest that he was aware of the controversial nature of his work, or that he even considered it might be misconstrued as contradicting the majority view of the Assembly?

In his second essay on prophets in the *Miscellany Questions*, Gillespie is demonstrably aware that contemporary prophecy and the contemporary calling and office of evangelist and prophet are difficult subjects:

> This question appeareth to be very perplexed and thorny, yet I am led upon it both by the controversies of the times, concerning the necessity of mission and ordination unto all the ministers of holy things, and likewise by occasion of that which is maintained by some men of learning, that there are still, or may be, evangelists in the church.[125]

Gillespie's arguments in the *Miscellany Questions* should be considered as speculative and tentative attempts where the author is thinking through the implications of the claims of the Independents (concerning promiscuous preaching of the unordained) in the light of Scripture.

Moreover, an important opponent of Westminster orthodoxy, who, as we have seen, vigorously contested the Reformed orthodox epistemology,[126] believed that Gillespie denied the possibility of immediate objective revelation, the manner of revelation usually associated with inspired prophets. Quaker George Keith, disputing with the *WCF* which he claims denies the possibility of immediate or objective revelation, finds George Gillespie in accord with the *WCF* on the cessation of immediate revelation:

> But also I find it [the cessation of objective revelation] made use of by George Gillespie a man most famous in the Presbyterian way, in his book of Miscellanies, cap. 21. pag. 261.[127]

---

[124] Berends, "Prophecy in the Reformation Tradition", at 40.

[125] "Of prophets and evangelists: in what sense their work and vocation might be called extraordinary, and in what sense ordinary". Gillespie, "Miscellany Questions", *The Works of George Gillespie*, vol. 2, 38.

[126] See Chapter Four, 169-175 above.

[127] George Keith, *Immediate Revelation (or Jesus Christ the Eternal Son of God, Revealed in Man. Revealing the Knowledge of God, and the Things of his Kingdom, Immediately) Not Ceased, but Remaining a Standing and Perpetual Ordinance in the Church of Christ, and being of Indispensable Necessity, as to the Whole Body in*

6.3.3.7 GILLESPIE AS PROPHET

As Gillespie lay dying, he seems to have believed that he too was a prophet in the Rutherfordian sense of one who binds his predictions to an application of Scripture – a view that did not contradict the cessationist position. On his death-bed, Gillespie uttered a prophecy which was sent in a letter to a commission of the General Assembly. The letter was written on 7 September 1648, and in it he urges no compromise with those who were involved in the *Engagement* - a treaty between Charles I and Scottish nobles:[128]

> I must here apply to our present situation the words of Ezra: 'And after that is come upon us for our evil deeds and for [our] great trespass, seing that thou, our God, hast punished ws lesse than our iniquities deserve, and hast given ws such deliverance as this, Should wee againe breake thy commandements and joyne in affinitie with the people of these abominations, wouldst thou not be angry with ws till thou hadst consumed ws, so that there should be no remnant nor escaping?' O happy Scotland, if thow canst now improve aright and not abuse this golden opportunitie! But if thow wilt help the vngodly, and love them that hate the Lord, wrath vpon wrath, and woe vpon woe shall be vpon thee from the Lord.[129]

On one hand, Gillespie identifies Knoxian prophecies with the New Testament prophecies of Agabus; on the other, he qualifies Reformation and post-Reformation prophets in a manner not applicable to Agabus and other biblical prophets.

What can we conclude from such disparate evidence? The differences between the two types of prophets which we have gleaned from Gillespie's own writings may be summarised briefly:

1. In spite of being closely identified, biblical prophets and Reformation prophets differ in several essentials. Biblical prophets prophesied by extraordinary "immediate" revelation, whereas modern prophets prophesy by extraordinary though not immediate revelation. The biblical prophets were usually in office, whereas the modern prophets do not hold the office of prophet.

2. Biblical prophets could not only predict the future, but also had greater gifts than post-apostolic prophets do for opening up obscure Scripture texts;

General, so to Every Member thereof: Every True Believer in Particular, Asserted and Demonstrated. And the Objections that Have any Seeming Weight Against it Answered (London: 1675) [no further publishing details are given], 31. See Gillespie, "Miscellany Questions", *The Works of George Gillespie*, vol. 2, 110.

[128] See David Lachman, "The Engagement", *DSCHT*, 293.

[129] Alexander Mitchell and James Christie (eds.), *The Records of the Commissions of the General Assemblies of the Church of Scotland Holden in Edinburgh the Years 1648-1649* (Edinburgh: Scottish Historical Society, 1896), 54-55.

they interpreted the Scriptures with the same "propheticall Spirit" by which they were written. Modern prophets, by contrast, are only foretellers.

3. Biblical prophets had an immediate call to office, whereas the modern prophet has no such immediate call because this has been taken away.

4. Biblical prophets, such as the apostle Paul, had other extraordinary gifts like the gift of healing and the gift of speaking in previously unlearnt languages. For Gillespie, these further gifts and the miracles for confirming the apostles' doctrine have ceased.

Thus, a careful analysis of Gillespie's wider thought brings Gillespie far more nearly into line with his cessationist colleagues at the Assembly than may have been supposed by recent scholars such as Berends. Nothing that Gillespie concludes necessarily separates him from the majority view of the Reformed orthodox. He appeals to the same texts which others applied earlier to immediately-inspired prophets, but these texts, as we have seen, can also be used to justify a later non-miraculous though otherwise analogous gift of the Holy Spirit, as John Owen and other Westminster divines maintained.[130] Neither does anything Gillespie says preclude an explanation like Rutherford's of the Knoxian foretellers- namely that modern "prophets" were applying Scripture principles to providential circumstances under the leading of the Holy Spirit.

None of the Scottish commissioners, including Blair and Gillespie, therefore, needs to be understood as a proponent of a continuing immediate revelation. Indeed, there is insufficient evidence to allow that conclusion concerning any of them.

6.4. An Enduring Legacy

6.4.1 James Durham

The strength of a theological tradition is illustrated by its longevity. The durability of the view that Reformation and post-Reformation "prophecy" was mediate revelation as an application of Scripture to providence by the leading of the Spirit is seen most clearly where Westminster theology took hold and had its greatest success. The witnesses to this Scripture-providence-Spirit paradigm continued through the seventeenth into the eighteenth and nineteenth centuries among Scottish Presbyterians.

James Durham (1622-1658), co-author with David Dickson of the *Sum of Saving Knowledge*, was a significant seventeenth-century Scottish theologian in his own right.[131] Durham represents the continuity of

---

[130] See Chapter Five, at 203 above.

[131] David Lachman, "James Durham", *DSCHT*, 265-66. The *Sum of Saving Knowledge* was often bundled with the *WCF*: *The Confession of Faith and the Larger*

Reformed orthodoxy in an age when the Scottish church had embraced the Westminster symbols, so he is important for that reason alone.[132] Durham echoes the same sentiments as his contemporary, Samuel Rutherford, when he digresses to discuss prophecy in his monumental commentary on the book of Revelation.

Describing modern claims to extraordinary prophecy, Durham lists six points of definition and distinction. First:

> Their [There] is now no gift of prophesy, either for the bringing forth of any truth not formerly delivered, nor any gift to warrand one in a particular, simply condemned in the word, as to take other goods [...]".[133]

Secondly, there is prophecy in a certain sense, although speaking prophecy does not make one a biblical prophet. There may be:

> some particular neither formerly revealed nor yet in itself contrary to the world [should be "Word"], but that which concerneth some particular event or personal duty allenarly.[134]

However, such an ability "will not denominate one to be a prophet, although in some singular events God maketh this use of him".[135] This is a particularly striking stance, because like George Gillespie, Durham ranks Agabus with modern prophets. His examples include Agabus, Athanasius, Huss, Savonarola, Wishart and Knox. Yet obviously, there is at least one transparent qualitative distinction between an Agabus and a Knox because the former was designated a prophet in Scripture (Acts 21:10).

Thirdly, Durham concludes that both the gifts and the office of the prophets of 1 Corinthians 14 have ceased,[136] but helpfully he does clarify in what sense the ability of the modern prophet should be understood, if it is not the same as the extraordinary biblical gift and office of 1 Cor. 14:1-3 and 32:

> Yet if we take prophesy for the understanding of God's mind, and for attaining to be well acquainted with the mysteries of God, by a mediate way; yea, and that beyond the applied means, or to have a gift and capacity for discerning of these things with little pains and that beyond

---

and Shorter Catechism, First Agreed upon by the Assembly of Divines at Westminster. And now Appointed by the General Assembly of the Kirk of Scotland, etc. [With "The Summe of saving knowledge," by David Dickson and James Durham.] (London: Thomas Malthus, 1683).

[132] James Durham, *A Complete Commentary upon the Book of the Revelation, Delivered in Several Lectures, By that Learned, Laborious, and Faithful Servant of Jesus Christ [...]"* (Falkirk: 1799) [no further publishing details are given], vol. 2, 219.

[133] Durham, *A Complete Commentary upon the Book of the Revelation*, vol. 2, 220.

[134] Durham, *A Complete Commentary upon the Book of the Revelation*, vol. 2, 219.

[135] Durham, *A Complete Commentary upon the Book of the Revelation*, vol. 2, 221-22.

[136] Durham, *A Complete Commentary upon the Book of the Revelation*, vol. 2, 222.

what some others can attain unto by any labour, we conceive that in this sense prophesy and prophets may be said to be continued in the church[...]".[137]

Although such a foreteller will go "beyond the applied means", his facility is still "mediate" rather than "immediate". Moreover, when Durham asserts that prophets such as those of 1 Corinthians 12 and 14 have ceased, along with healing, tongues and interpretation of tongues, he affirms the usual cessationist position. [138]

Fourthly, Durham denies that God may appoint a modern prophet by an immediate call.[139] This, though consistent, is an interesting admission, because it limits God in a way that did not apply in the apostolic age. It also further reinforces Durham's statement that he does not wish to see any individuals called "prophets" in his own day.

Fifthly, Durham's explanation of the way in which God uses such a person in the church is reminiscent of Rutherford in his *Survey*:

> Yet we may say, that as God by gifts may furnish some in a more than ordinary way; so may he, and useth he to thrust them out in a mixed way, to the exercise of these for the edification of his church, and make the seal of his call extraordinarily ratify his sending of them, that is, as he may furnish men partly by means, and especially by his blessing extraordinarily accompanying them out partly in a mediate way by mens opening of the door, partly by his more than ordinary thrusting of them out, making up to what was defective in the mediate call by some extraordinary concurrences of impulse and gifts within, of circumstances of providence without, and efficacy upon, and acceptation of it amongst others, whereby it cometh to be ratified.[140]

Durham's "mediate" way is supported by other circumstances, but it still does not produce "immediate" revelations. One gets the feeling that Durham is trying very hard to avoid calling the divine disclosures "immediate" and experiences real difficulty in finding the language to explain how mediated prophecy can occur without God's thoughts being directly and immediately implanted. His solution is to resort to rather clumsy and vague language.

Durham also makes it plain that the people in question are indeed ministers of the gospel, though he does allow that some might receive extraordinary communications and yet not be in office. However, modern access to otherwise secret events does not give a person the right to use impulses to choose a preaching text. Moreover, since God no longer enables people to preach from "immediate" knowledge, to rely on such

---

[137] Durham, *A Complete Commentary upon the Book of the Revelation*, vol. 2, 223.
[138] Durham, *A Complete Commentary upon the Book of the Revelation*, vol. 2, 222.
[139] Durham, *A Complete Commentary upon the Book of the Revelation*, vol. 2, 224.
[140] Durham, *A Complete Commentary upon the Book of the Revelation*, vol. 2, 224.

impulses is to tempt God and to give Satan a chance to deceive.[141] Nevertheless, there may be an "inward leading of the mind", or "outward circumstances" which should not be despised when the preacher comes to apply his doctrine. Any supposed extraordinary leading must be tested, though, with the caveat that if such impulses can be dangerous in private, they can be equally damaging in public.[142] Still, if circumstances are different from those which prevailed when the preacher originally composed his sermon, it is possible for God to direct a preacher to make some "suggested" application:

> [Y]et where some outward providence, changeth the case from what it was in the speakers apprehension before his coming to public or where the matter suggested is pertinent both to the place of scripture and pressing of the same purpose which the preacher aimeth at, so as if it had offered in private, he would have embraced it before some things he had thought of[...]".[143]

Durham's carefully nuanced position is in accord with Rutherford's cautious view. His exposition also contain points of contact with Gillespie's position. Agabus and Knox can be united in their exercise of prophecy, yet unlike Agabus, Knox cannot be designated an extraordinary New Testament "prophet". Furthermore, the New Testament office and gift of prophecy, exercised by Agabus, have ceased in Durham's view, which means that a straightforward, unqualified identity of Agabus and Knox is not possible. Like Gillespie, he concludes that there is now no immediate call from God to the role of Prophet. Durham's emphasis on the mediate element in the modern prophet is also a feature that does not presumably apply to the biblical prophets who existed at the founding of the church.

6.4.2 Robert Fleming

Another contemporary Scottish minister, Robert Fleming (1630-94), who lived in a time of persecution, accepted a call to the Scottish church in Rotterdam but became one of the suffering Covenanters when he was imprisoned while on a visit to Scotland.[144] His most famous work is a three-

---

[141] Durham, *A Complete Commentary upon the Book of the Revelation*, vol. 2, 225.
[142] Durham, *A Complete Commentary upon the Book of the Revelation*, vol. 2, 226.
[143] Durham, *A Complete Commentary upon the Book of the Revelation*, vol. 2, 228.
[144] David Lachman, "Robert Fleming", *DSCHT*, 325. See also Thorbjorn Campbell, *Standing Witnesses* (Edinburgh: The Saltire Society, 1996), especially 18-25 for the "killing times"; James Douglas, *Light in the North* (Exeter: Paternoster, 1964), especially 98-110 for the outlawing of Presbyterianism, which ultimately led to the persecutions; Alexander Smellie, *Men of the Covenant* (Edinburgh: Banner of Truth, 1975), especially 485-87 for James Renwick's "miraculous" escapes; Hewison, *The*

part volume, *The Fulfilling of Scripture*, published in 1669, in which he endeavours to show that all providence is really just "fulfilling of Scripture".[145] He understood and interpreted history and eschatology in a fashion akin to the classical Puritan historicist. As a result, Fleming's explanation of modern prophecy bears a remarkable similarity to that of the English Puritans and Samuel Rutherford. Fleming's willingness to echo the explanation of his former teacher, the great Rutherford, is evidence of a common strand of teaching linking the Reformation with the second Reformation in the British Isles and with subsequent Covenanter history.

While Fleming does concede that modern prophets have "a more special discovery, and immediate inbreathing of God's mind as to the application thereof [of Scripture] in particular cases", the language of immediacy is tempered when he later gives a fuller explanation:[146]

> As it cannot be denied what extraordinary discoveries some in these last times have had of future things, and remarkable exigencies of the church, whose eminent holiness and sobriety made it the more convincing to others: yet even there did the general rule of the word still go along with them, and had no new things revealed but what was contained there, though carried therein by singular impulse of *a scripture-spirit* to apply the rule to particular cases and persons [emphasis added][…]".[147]

We recognize the unusual phrase "scripture-spirit" as exactly the same term used by Rutherford in his *Survey*. Furthermore, Fleming can hardly be implying that the "impulse of a scripture-spirit" is an extra-biblical immediate revelation because he has just ruled that possibility out:

> Though extraordinary ways of revealing Gods mind are now ceased, yet are they still the same in the scripture as to the substance thereof, to which as a great height a christian may get up in a serious enquiry after the truth, so as not only to discern present duty but things in their approach when at a distance, which the word is yet to bring forth, without any thing of that *Lumen Propheticum*, which in former times was known.[148]

Fleming denies extra-biblical inspired prophecy, but, on the other hand, he accepts angelic visitations,[149] healing miracles[150] and the revelation of

---

Covenanters, especially vol. 2, 312 for Alexander Peden's prophetic vision of impending suffering and death.

[145] Robert Fleming, *The Fulfilling of the Scripture Complete; in Three Parts* (London: J. and B. Sprint, Aaron Ward, Richard Ford, and John Oswald, 1726), 135.

[146] Fleming, *The Fulfilling of the Scripture*, 188.

[147] Fleming, *The Fulfilling of the Scripture*, 322-23.

[148] Fleming, *The Fulfilling of the Scripture*, 322.

[149] Fleming, *The Fulfilling of the Scripture*, 195.

[150] Fleming, *The Fulfilling of the Scripture*, 191.

secrets through dreams.[151] Yet he insists that not only are the Scriptures a necessary component of these revelations but also apostolic miracles have ceased.[152] Furthermore, Fleming seems to confirm that Robert Blair's prophetic experiences should be seen as an application of Scripture to providence, for he appears to paraphrase Blair's own explanation:

> we may see how these great servants of Christ were led in no other path than that of the written word, though they had some more extraordinary and immediate inbreathings of God's mind, as to the application thereof in particular cases, and with respect to that part of the church where they lived, which also with great caution, and much humble sobriety they did own.[153]

Here the "immediate inbreathings of God's mind" are not an extra-biblical revelations, but an impulse to apply Scripture to providential circumstances.

It is very difficult to reconcile Fleming's appeal to the miraculous on the one hand and his cessationist stance on the other. The tension evident in his thought makes his attempts to deny the immediacy of the Spirit's revelation, other than as an application of Scripture, all the more striking. It was plainly no easy task for Fleming to try to reconcile his view that history was the outworking or fulfilling of Scripture, with his other conviction that "extraordinary ways of revealing Gods mind are now ceased".

6.4.3 James Hog

James Hog (1658-1734), minister of Carnock in Fife from 1699 until his death, was also the leader of the Scottish ministers who were proponents of the soteriology articulated in the *Marrow of Modern Divinity* which had been written by English Presbyterian Edward Fisher.[154] Hog was also involved in the controversy over Antonia (or Antoinette) Bourignon (1616-1680), the Flemish mystic who claimed revelations of new teaching and whose position was considered by the 1711 Scottish General Assembly to be heresy.[155]

---

[151] Fleming, *The Fulfilling of the Scripture*, xxiii-xxiv.

[152] Fleming, *The Fulfilling of the Scripture*, 332.

[153] Fleming, *The Fulfilling of the Scripture*, 334. Fleming precedes his conclusion with words very similar to those with which Blair describes his own experience, including "yet it cannot to be denied [...] he hath been pleased to reveal[...]especially in a suffering condition" (334).

[154] For the Marrow controversy see David Lachman, "Marrow Controversy", *DSCHT*, 546-48. For a biographical account of Hog, see also David Lachman, "James Hog", *DSCHT*, 409-10.

[155] For an account of the teaching of Antoinette Bourignon and Bourignianism, see Nicholas Needham, "Bourignianism", *DSCHT*, 90-91.

The conjunction of the Word and providence provides the explanation for James Hog in his opposition to Bourignon: "Discoveries of things to come [...] are no additions to the Word, but applications thereof to particular cases contained in the same [...]".[156] Hog concludes that if Bourignon's alleged prophecies and warnings are genuine they must be placed on a par with Scripture:

> New light pretended, which is solely founded on the authority of the Revealer, they do not so much as attempt to apply the written word, to the respective cases[...]but if these Prophecys or prophetical warnings be what is pretended, they must be received as so much of new scripture given by immediate inspiration.[157]

While Hog is anxious not to limit God's ability to do something extraordinary in the future, he does warn against "extra-scriptural" impressions through dreams, visions and voices,[158] and insists that "leading of the Spirit and evidence of the Word go inseparably together, and the more clearly the better".[159]

In the nineteenth century, the same explanation of foretelling persisted, because claims to predictive prophecy were still being made and were still controversial in the Church of Scotland.

6.4.4 Edward Irving and the London Scottish Presbytery

It is not surprising, in view of the traditional explanation of foretelling, that nineteenth-century Scottish church courts looked unfavourably on the popular preacher and minister Edward Irving (1792-1834)[160] when they were called upon to rule in the controversy over his claims that miraculous charismatic gifts continued in the church.[161] Irving's views proved

---

[156] James Hog, *Notes about the Spirit's Operations, for Discovering from the Word, their Nature and Evidence, Together with Diverse Remarks for Detecting the Enthusiastical Delusions of the Cevennois, Antonia Bourignon, and Others[...] Being the Substance of Several Private Discourses on Gal. 3.2* (Edinburgh:1709) [no other publishing details are given], 29-30.

[157] Hog, *Notes about the Spirit's Operations*, 44.

[158] Hog, *Notes about the Spirit's Operations*, 74.

[159] Hog, *Notes about the Spirit's Operations*, 29-30.

[160] Irving was a member of the Scottish presbytery in London, which was part of the Church of Scotland in the early nineteenth century. For a summary of Irving's life, see Nicholas Needham, "Edward Irving", *DSCHT*, 436-37. For a recent unsympathetic biography, see Arnold Dallimore, *The Life of Edward Irving: Fore-runner of the Charismatic Movement* (Edinburgh: Banner of Truth Trust, 1983).

[161] See William Goode, *The Modern Claims to the Possession of the Extraordinary Gifts of the Spirit [...]*(London: J. Hatchard and Son, 1834), especially 1-49 for an account of the charismatic gifts that Irving and his followers claimed were functioning in his London congregation.

particularly controversial in a variety of matters, but his willingness to allow prophecy and tongues-speaking[162] in his congregation resulted in charges being laid against him.[163]

The proceedings of the trial show how novel Irving's position was believed to be by his critics, and in the end the presbytery itself considered that it, not Irving, was in step with Westminster orthodoxy. At the trial, Irving claimed support from the *Second Book of Discipline* for his stance on resurgent prophecy, but the London presbytery responded that the *DPW* taught that prophecy had ceased,[164] and gave an explanation of the clause in the *Second Book of Discipline* which allowed for the "stirring up" again of the gift. Luther, Calvin and Zwingli, it was said, were examples of apostles, prophets and evangelists, "but not in the strict sense, but as, in some measure discharging the same duty [...]".[165] Irving argued from 1 Cor. 13:10 that prophets remain till the end of the age,[166] but was contradicted by J. Mann who countered that 1 Cor. 13:8 proved that tongues-speaking had ceased.[167]

The proceedings reveal that Dr. Crombie added that Irving's claims to prophecy are contrary to the *First Book of Discipline*, which taught that

---

[162] Dallimore, *The Life of Edward Irving: Fore-runner of the Charismatic Movement*, especially 109-17. See also Gordon Strachan, *The Pentecostal Theology of Edward Irving* (London: Darton, Longman and Todd, 1973), especially 173-81 for the London trial; for Irving's controversial Christology, see Graham McFarlane, *Christ and the Spirit. The Doctrine of the Incarnation According to Edward Irving* (Carlisle: Paternoster, 1996), especially 125-83.

[163] For a discussion of the connections between the English Scottish churches and the national Church of Scotland, see Kenneth Black, *The Scots Churches in England* (London: William Blackwood, 1906), 279.

[164] W. Harding, *The Trial of the Rev. Edward Irving, M.A. before the London Presbytery* (Edinburgh: W. Harding, 1832), 78. The record in fact gives a citation from the *FPC* and not the *DPW*. The reason for this mistake is not clear.

[165] Harding, *The Trial of the Rev. Edward Irving*, 78. See also James Kirk (ed.), *The Second Book of Discipline* (Edinburgh: The Saint Andrew Press, 1980), 175-76. "Thair beand thrie extraordinar functionis: the office of the apostle, of the evangelist, and the propheit, quhilk ar not perpetuall and have now ceissit in the kirk of God except quhen he pleased [or it pleasit God] extraordinarlie for ane tyme to steir up sum of thame agane". That the framers of the *Second Book* (some thirty individuals were likely involved in its composition) did not have in mind prophets prophesying by immediate revelation is demonstrated when they make the office of doctor synonymous with "propheit, bischop, eldar, [and] catechesar" (187). For a briefer history and description of the *Second Book*, see James Kirk, "Second Book of Discipline", *DSCHT*, 765-66. See also George David Henderson (ed.), *The Scots Confession 1560* (Edinburgh: The Saint Andrew Press, 1960), especially 21-22, for discussion of Irving's attachment to and use of the "Second Book".

[166] Harding, *The Trial of the Rev. Edward Irving*, 23.

[167] Harding, *The Trial of the Rev. Edward Irving*, 56.

miraculous illumination had ceased;[168] while Rev. J. Miller charged that the claim for these manifestations runs counter to the *WCF* 1:6. Rev. W. McLean asserted that the cessationist clause in *WCF* 1:1 similarly excludes prophecy.[169] It is significant that the Presbytery was using *WCF* 1:1 and 1:6 against Irving's position, because Irving was not claiming new revelations for doctrine. Plainly Irving's fellow Scots believed that *all* extra-biblical revelations were excluded by the Westminster symbol. The presbytery delegates were united in their judgement that Irving's continuationist claims were inconsistent with the standards of the church.[170]

6.4.5 John Kennedy

From a later period, another figure, the celebrated John Kennedy of Dingwall (1819-1884), discussed claims to prophetic insight in his classic work, *The Days of the Fathers in Ross-shire*. Kennedy accepted that such ability could exist and this elicited opposition in his own day.[171] Alexander Auld considers the controversy in his biography of Kennedy:

> That the fathers of Ross-shire should be said to possess the secret of the Lord, in the way of receiving intimations of His mind as to events in providence, excited much censure.[172]

Auld's interpretation of Kennedy's claims echoes the tradition we have traced from the time of John Knox:

> These men, like other Scottish worthies of former days, sought to know the Lord's mind as to events that deeply interested them, and obtained it in connection with revealed truth; for we contend that there is no event of

---

[168] Harding, *The Trial of the Rev. Edward Irving*, 73. See James Cameron (ed.) *The First Book of Discipline* (Edinburgh: The Saint Andrew Press, 1972), especially "For the Schools", 129. See also 187-89, where the prophesying of 1 Cor. 14:29-32 is interpreted as the expounding of Scripture. See also James Kirk, "First Book of Discipline", *DSCHT*, 321-22. The First Book was the composition of the "six Johns" – Winram, Spottiswoode, Wilcock, Douglas, Row and Knox.

[169] Harding, *The Trial of the Rev. Edward Irving*, 77.

[170] We have been unable to identify the figures at the trial conclusively, so we refer to them by their initials as they are recorded. Dr. Crombie is possibly Rev. John Crombie of St Andrew's Stepney: Black, *The Scots Churches in England*, 39; J. Miller is possibly Rev. James Miller of the Southwark congregation: Black, *The Scots Churches in England*, 112.

[171] For an account of Kennedy's ministry and life, see Alan Sell, "John Kennedy", *DSCHT*, 455-56.

[172] Alexander Auld, *Life of John Kennedy, D.D.* (London: T. Nelson and sons, 1887), 75-76.

Providence - as there is nothing in the sphere of grace - that the principle on which it proceeds is not laid down in the chart of Scripture.[173]

In this he follows Kennedy himself, who wrote:

> That premonition [...] is something very different from the inspiration of the prophet. It results entirely from an adaptation of God Himself of His own written word.[174]

6.5 Conclusion

From the days of the Reformation in Scotland, an older tradition of second sight fused with a belief that godly ministers could predict the future. John Knox himself, the archetypal Protestant prophet, explained his abilities as foreteller by saying that he applied a Scripture principle to providential circumstances. The generation of the second Reformation presents a more complex picture. There are those who are obviously cessationist in their views and others such as Gillespie and Blair who present us with a certain amount of ambiguity. Knox's cessationist legacy offered a way to explain such prophets in the writings of such figures as Samuel Rutherford. The little we have from Archibald Johnston and Alexander Henderson on the subject does not contradict the tradition which explains post-apostolic prophecy as an application of Scripture-principle to providence under the leading of the Holy Spirit. Even the views of persons such as Blair and Gillespie, whose positions seem much more ambiguous at first glance, can still be reconciled with the view of their compatriot Rutherford. Representative explanations through the seventeenth and into the nineteenth centuries, including those of James Durham, Robert Fleming, James Hog, the London presbytery of the Scots Kirk which tried Edward Irving, and John Kennedy, reflect a consensus in clarifications of claims to post-apostolic prophecy, and in the Irving case the relevant clauses of *WCF* 1 were specifically given a strictly cessationist interpretation. The Knoxian/Rutherfordian explanation for contemporary foretelling, reflected in this tradition, is consistent with the burden of evidence from the English authorities at whom we looked in Chapter Five. These later Scottish Presbyterians lived in a confessional age, when subscription to the *WCF* was a matter of some importance for church office-bearers. In the next chapter we shall discuss the subject of subscription in an endeavour to discern whether subscription requirements in their own ways may shed further light on the precise meaning of the "cessationist clause" from *WCF* 1:1.

---

[173] Auld, *Life of John Kennedy*, 76.

[174] John Kennedy, *The Days of the Fathers in Ross-shire* [originally publishing in 1861](Inverness: Christian Focus, 1979), 208.

Chapter 7

Subscription and the Westminster Confession of Faith

7.1 Introduction

The question of subscription may be relevant for understanding the intended meaning of the cessationist clause in *WCF* 1:1. Depending on the terms of subscription to the *WCF* envisaged by its authors, adherence to a strictly cessationist position may not necessarily have been required. If a "loose" subscription, or one that acknowledged the *WCF* to be a standard of teaching only and not a test of heresy was in view, deviation from the precise formulations of the *WCF* may have been permissible.[1] This would keep the cessationist clause intact as a statement that extra-biblical revelation no longer occurred, while allowing someone like William Bridge to subscribe to the *WCF*. Alternatively, if a "strict" subscription to all clauses was required, this would more likely motivate the Assembly, who were after all seeking ecclesiastical unity, to prepare their confessional formulations with a degree of ambiguity. To resolve this question, we will firstly consider whether the cessationist clause shows any signs of being deliberately ambiguous, and secondly, examine the seventeenth-century

---

[1] Thomas Schafer, "The Beginnings of Confessional Subscription in the Presbyterian Church", *McCormick Quarterly* 19 (January 1966), has suggested four reasons why churches may officially recognise or approve a confession of faith: 1. as a confession of a body's beliefs; 2. as a manifesto stating its position on some particular controversy; 3. as a test of heresy whereby the confession becomes a standard forbidding contradictory teaching; or 4. as a preventive to "forestall future deviation from the church's official position"(102-19). On subscription, see also David Wright and Ian Hamilton, "Confessions of Faith", *DSCHT*, 203, for a similar list: confessions provide a faithful account of doctrine to the world; they serve as a standard of orthodoxy and as a test for office-bearers; they provide a useful summary of the faith for church members; they guard against false doctrine and practice and they provide a means of confirming the unity of the church; John Leith, *Creeds of the Churches* (Chicago: Aldine Publishing Company, 1963). Leith believes that creeds were written to exclude others (4); as a guide for preaching (6); to prepare candidates for baptism or catechising (7); to provide hermeneutical principles (8); to counter heresy (9); as a testimony to the world (9). See also Cornelius Plantinga, *A Place to Stand* (Grand Rapids, MI: Christian Reformed Church, 1979), 5, on the uses to which creeds have been put historically for fighting heresy, defying persecution, teaching new converts, and shaping public worship.

perspectives on confessional subscription among both the English and the Scots.

7.2 An Ambiguous Cessationist Clause?

The divines did compose some of the articles of the *WCF* in a form that allowed them to be interpreted according to different viewpoints. There were two ways in which this tolerance was intentionally built into the *WCF*. The first was simply through the omission of controversial points of theology. Thus a supralapsarian like William Twisse could subscribe to the *WCF*, alongside the majority of his fellow-members of the Assembly who were infralapsarians, simply by virtue of the fact that distinctions about the order in which the divine decrees were made were entirely excluded.[2] Similarly, the Assembly did not formally write into its confession of faith a particular scheme of eschatology specifying the timing of the parousia in relation to a millennium.[3]

A second way in which the principle of inclusion operated was by the introduction into the *WCF* of a doctrinal concept which was left open to different interpretations within agreed boundaries. To take just one

---

[2] On Twisse's supralapsarianism and the Assembly's desire not to define the order of decrees too closely, see Alex F. Mitchell and John Struthers (eds.), *Minutes of the Sessions of the Westminster Assembly of Divines* (Edmonton: SWRB, 1991), liv-lvi; and for the discussion in the Assembly itself, see Mitchell and Struthers (eds.), *Minutes of the Sessions of the Westminster Assembly of Divines*, 151. Nevertheless, the divines were willing to be exclusive on some controversial matters. For example, they reinterpreted the original intent of the statement in the Apostles' Creed that Christ had descended into hell. *LC* Q & A 50 interprets it to refer to Christ's burial and his being under the "power of death". Thus they excluded the traditional interpretation that Christ had literally descended into the realm of the dead to preach the gospel to them. This changed interpretation may be evidence that when they framed the *WCF*, *LC* and *SC*, the divines always wanted their statements to be evaluated in the light of Scripture rather than in the light of church tradition.

[3] The Assembly divines were plainly not of one mind over what comprised a biblical eschatology. See Baillie's rejection of the pre-millennial views of his Assembly colleagues, Thomas Goodwin and Jeremiah Burroughs, in Robert Baillie, *A Dissuasive from the Errours of the Time: Wherein the Tenets of the Principall Sects, Especially of the Independents, are Drawn Together in One Map, for the Most Part, in Words of Their own Authours, and Their Maine Principles are Examined by the Touch-stone of the Holy Scriptures* (London: Samuel Gellibrand, 1645), published during the sitting of the Assembly. See especially 234 for the views of Goodwin and Burroughs, and 229-34 for Baillie's post-millennialism. On the Puritans' eschatology, see Peter Toon (ed.), *Puritans, the Millennium and the Future of Israel: Puritan Eschatology 1600-1660* (Greenwood: Attic Press, 1970). See also William M. Lamont, *Godly Rule* (London: Macmillan, 1969), especially 21 on the various interpretations of the book of Revelation.

example: the manner in which the "testimony of the Spirit" was understood to function was left unspecified. As Joel Beeke points out, this occurred for two reasons. One was to protect the freedom of the Spirit, but the other was because

> the assembly wanted to allow freedom of conscience to those who differed among themselves about the details of the Spirit's testimony.[4]

We see the same tolerance at work in a debate over whether God handed down only one or several decrees. George Gillespie suggested that leaving a word out of the clause that could decide the disputed point did not alter the truth of the proposition, but it did allow that "every one may enjoy his own sense".[5] His English colleague, Edward Reynolds, immediately endorsed Gillespie's magnanimity, exclaiming: "Let not us put in disputes and scholastical things into a Confession of Faith".[6]

Underlying this show of unity was a genuine willingness to try to achieve unanimity before voting on a matter that might have easily been carried by a clear majority. Robert Baillie, in a letter to William Spang in 1643, writes that on one occasion the Assembly tried strenuously to avoid forcing a vote but instead took the option of sending the matter to committee so that they might resolve differences in the smaller forum:

---

[4] Joel Beeke, *The Quest for Full Assurance* (Edinburgh: Banner of Truth, 1999), 142. For the witness of the Spirit making use of inward evidences of God's grace, see George Gillespie, "A Treatise of Miscellany Questions", *The Works of George Gillespie*, ed. David Meek (Edmonton: SWRB, 1991), vol. 2, 104-109; for the view that the Spirit witnesses directly by applying Scripture to the soul, see Samuel Rutherford, *The Covenant of Life opened, or a Treatise of the Covenant of Grace* (Edinburgh: Robert Broun, 1655), 65-66.

[5] Mitchell and Struthers (eds.), *Minutes of the Sessions of the Westminster Assembly of Divines*, 151, also cited in Sinclair B. Ferguson, "The Teaching of the Confession", Alasdair I. C. Heron (ed.), *The Westminster Confession in the Church Today* (Edinburgh: St Andrew Press, 1982), 28-39, at 38.

[6] Mitchell and Struthers (eds.), *Minutes of the Sessions of the Westminster Assembly of Divines*, 151. See also Alexander G. Mitchell, *The Westminster Assembly: Its History and Standards* (Edmonton: SWRB, 1992), 151-55. This desire for unity was evident in the way Thomas Gataker handled his dissent from the Assembly on the matter of Christ's active and passive obedience. Simeon Ashe writes: "And in his study of Peace with modesty was in this remarkable, that when his Reasons delivered concerning Christs obedience in order to our Justification (wherein he differed from his brethren) could not obtain assent from the majority part which determined the Question contrary to his sense, his own love of unity imposed upon him silence; and wrought him likewise unto resolutions, not to publish his discourses of that subject from Rom. 3.28. that he might not publikly discover his dissent from the Votes of that Reverend Assembly". Simeon Ashe, *Gray Hayres Crowned with Grace: A Sermon Preached at Redriff near London, Aug. 1, 1654. at the Funerall of that Reverend [...] Mr. Thomas Gataker* (London: George Sawbridge, 1655), 52.

There was no doubt but we would have carried it by far most voices; yet because the opposites were men verie considerable, above all gracious and learned little Palmer, we agreed upon a committee to satisfie, if it were possible, the dissenters.[7]

There is no evidence, however, either in the extant records of the debates or in other works of Assembly members, that the cessationist clause was a candidate for deliberate ambiguity. It cannot be assessed under either of the two methods outlined above. Obviously reference to any hint of cessationism was not simply excluded. The only way in which the cessationist clause could have been interpreted as applying to "Scripture-producing revelation" alone, thus leaving open the possibility of inspired immediate prophecy for personal or corporate guidance, was if the concept of "salvation" in *WCF* 1:1 was supposed to be restricted to personal eschatological salvation.

As we have argued at length in Chapter Two, such a construal of the reference to "salvation" is untenable.[8] While the cessationist clause delimited the "former ways" of supernatural immediate revelation "unto salvation", that "salvation" included, for the framers of the *WCF*, the experiences of divine guidance, prophetic prescience and the revelation of secrets for both the Old Testament believer and the seventeenth-century Christian. The great difference between the two was that revelation was considered to function "immediately" in the Old and "mediately" in the post-apostolic era. Salvation as personal redemption from sin, or as a

---

[7] Robert Baillie, *The Letters and Journals of Robert Baillie, A. M. Principal of the University of Glasgow M.DC.XXXVII.-M.DC.LXII.*, ed. David Laing (Edinburgh: Bannatyne Club, 1841-1842), vol. 2, 111. This particular debate was over appointing ruling elders. Robert Lewis Dabney also sees this conciliatory spirit in the Assembly: "The Assembly, therefore, was too wise to attempt the conciliating of opposites by the surrender of any essential member of the system of revealed truth [...] on the other hand, they avoid every excess, and every extreme statement. They refrained, with a wise moderation, from committing the church of God on either side of those 'isms' which agitated and perplexed the professors of the Reformed Theology". Robert Lewis Dabney, "The Doctrinal Content[s] of the Confession", David W. Hall (ed.), *The Practice of Confessional Subscription* (Lanham: University Press of America, 1995), 173. Benjamin B. Warfield has a similar assessment: "The differences that existed between the members were not smoothed over in ambiguous language. They were fully ventilated. Room was made for them when they were considered unimportant and a mere *apices logici*: but when they contained matters of moment, after full discussion, the doctrine of the Assembly - well-reasoned and fully thought out - as distinguished from that of individuals, was embodied clearly and firmly in the document". Benjamin Warfield, *The Works of Benjamin B. Warfield* (Grand Rapids, MI: Baker, 1991), vol. 6, 146-47.

[8] See Chapter Two, 83-107 above.

process of forensic justification, did not exhaust the Assembly's definition of salvation in *WCF* 1:1.

Nonetheless, even if the divines did intend the cessationist clause to be unambiguous, this did not necessarily mean that they were demanding a strict subscription to it. The divines, the civil government and the churches may have intended that the *WCF* should be used as a standard of teaching, not as a definitive or non-negotiable replica of Scriptural truth for testing heresy. In that case they may have permitted deviation from its tightly argued clauses, thus tolerating dissenting views on some subjects. If, on the other hand, the authorities demanded strict subscription to a comprehensive cessationism, it is difficult to imagine how a continuationist could have continued in the ministry.

Thomas Schafer's study of subscription to the *WCF* suggests that the English and the Scots approached confessional subscription differently. The positions he identifies can also be contrasted as "loose" and "strict" subscription. Schafer concludes that English divines, though at odds over church government, were nonetheless all united, whether as Erastians, Presbyterians or Independents, in their view of uniformity of religion. Their submission to Scripture was part of that uniformity, but a personal or strict subscription to the *WCF* was not. Schafer also argues that the English Parliament adopted the *WCF* only as a standard of teaching, and that similarly the Independents who wrote the *Savoy Declaration* stated explicitly that their confession of faith should not be imposed on anyone.[9] It was accepted that subscription to a confession implied acceptance of the document as a standard of teaching, but that it did not expose individuals to sanctions if they departed from this confession at specific points.

The Scottish Presbyterians, on the other hand, came to the Assembly with the *National Covenant* of 1638 still vivid in their memories. Those who subscribed to this document agreed that Puritan worship, Presbyterian polity and Calvinist theology were "identified with Scottish nationalism", and that Scots were free to have uniform faith and practice.[10] Whereas the English understood liberty to mean toleration, and therefore assumed the principle of a loose subscription if any at all, the Scots identified liberty with a freedom to be Presbyterian, Puritan and Calvinistic, and were therefore more concerned to enforce strict subscription. A comparison of attitudes to subscription in England and Scotland suggests that Schafer is substantially correct in his conclusions.

---

[9] Schafer, "The Beginnings of Confessional Subscription in the Presbyterian Church", 102-104.

[10] Schafer, "The Beginnings of Confessional Subscription in the Presbyterian Church", 107.

7.3 Subscription in England

The English Puritans were bound to have scruples about subscription in the light of their recent past. Anthony Tuckney speaks for many who could recall ecclesiastical persecution against non-subscribers:

> In the Assemblie, I gave my vote with others that the Confession of Faith, put outt by Authority, should not bee eyther required to bee sworn or subscribed too; wee having bin burnt in the hand in that kind before, but so as not to be publickly preached or written against.[11]

Thomas Schafer comments: "By 'burnt in the hand,' Tuckney doubtless means by Prayer-Book uniformity and subscription to the Thirty-nine Articles".[12] Shafer adds: "There is no evidence that any of the English members of the Assembly ever subscribed the Confession or intended that others should".[13]

A lively appreciation of the fallibility of human beings is consistent with the looser subscription requirement. Edward Reynolds, preaching to the Westminster Assembly on the subject of self-denial, urges his colleagues to humility and submission when they feel the need to bring their own opinion or sense in the Assembly. Reynolds reminds his audience of the tentative nature of human conclusions, because they do not speak in "oracles", but rather have personal opinions.[14]

It is also very likely that the English Puritans saw the clause in *WCF* 31:4 as a necessary qualification for the very documents they produced at the Westminster Assembly.[15] Certainly that is how John Ley understood the

---

[11] Benjamin Whichcote, *Moral and Religious Aphorisms: Collected from the Manuscript Papers of the Reverend and Learned Doctor Whichcote; and Published in MDCVIII, by Dr. Jeffery. Now Re-published, with Very Large Additions, from the Transcripts of the Latter, by Samuel Salter[...] to which are Added, Eight Letters: which Passed between Dr. Whichcote[...] and Dr. Tuckney[...] on Several Very Interesting Subjects* [Held in the British Library's London reading rooms]. From a letter to Benjamin Whichcote, cited in C. A. Briggs, *Whither?* (New York: 1889) [no further publishing details are given], 28, reproduced by Schafer, "The Beginnings of Confessional Subscription in the Presbyterian Church", 104. Shafer observes: "Tuckney does not say that he was voting with the majority, but this is his probable meaning in light of Parliament's subsequent action" (104, n3).

[12] Schafer "The Beginnings of Confessional Subscription in the Presbyterian Church", 104.

[13] Schafer "The Beginnings of Confessional Subscription in the Presbyterian Church", 104.

[14] Edward Reynolds, *Self-Deniall* (London: George Thomason, 1659), 38-39.

[15] "All synods or councils, since the Apostles' times, whether general or particular, may err; and many have erred. Therefore they are not to be made the rule of faith or practice; but to be used as a help in both". *WCF* 31:4.

twenty-first of the *Thirty-Nine Articles*,[16] "Of the Authority of General Councils", for he interpreted that article to mean that bishops who subscribed to it were admitting that their canons could not be received as infallible decrees.[17]

The aversion of the English to subscription was a reaction to ecclesiastical intolerance, especially that directed against personal convictions. The antipathy towards subscribing to someone else's agenda was evident to a greater or lesser degree across the broad spectrum of ecclesiastical preference.[18] Ironically, the suspicion among Episcopalians arose because they believed that Puritans, having styled themselves champions of tolerance who had been compromised by a required subscription to the Book of Common Prayer, wanted now to impose strict subscription on non-Puritans.

7.3.1 Episcopalians

When the Puritan-dominated state required Episcopal scholars at Oxford University to subscribe to the *Solemn League and Covenant* and therefore to a Puritan social and ecclesiological programme they despised, these scholars were quick to voice their objections. In an elaborate apology, they rejected the document, along with the *Negative Oath* and the *DPW*. They took exception in three different ways. First, they question the ambiguous and vague language of the *Solemn League and Covenant* they are meant to sign:

> [W]e find in the Covenant, sundry expressions of dark or doubtfull construction: Whereunto we cannot sweare in judgement, till their sense

---

[16] "*Generall Counsels may not be gathered together without the commaundement and wyll of princes. And when they be gathered together, (forasmuche as they be an assemblie of men, whereof all be not governed with the spirite and word of God) they may erre, and sometym have erred, even in thinges parteynyng unto God. Wherefore, things ordayned by them as necessary to salvation, have neyther strength nor aucthoritie, unlesse it may be declared that they be taken out of holy Scripture*": For the *Thirty-Nine Articles*, see Philip Schaff (ed.), *The Creeds of Christendom* (Grand Rapids, MI: Baker, 1985), vol. 3, 500-501. It is transparent that this Article lies behind *WCF* 31:4, which includes the sentence "All synods or councils,[...]may err; and many have erred".

[17] John Ley, *An Acquittance or Discharge [...]* (London: K. Brewster, 1655), epistle dedicatory.

[18] The Erastian John Selden believed that only "matter of Faith" should be in the *Thirty-Nine Articles* and presumably in any subscribable confession of faith. He did not see church government or the baptism of infants as such a "matter of Faith": John Selden, *Table-Talk: Being the Discourses of John Selden Esq; or His Sence of Various Matters of Weight and High Consequence Relating Especially to Religion and State* (London: E. Smith, 1689), 2.

be cleared and agreed upon. As, Who are the *Commons Enemies?* and which *be the best Reformed Churches?* mentioned in the first Article. Who (in the fourth Article) are to be accounted *Malignants*? How far that phrase of *hindring Reformation* may be extended? What is meant by *the supreme judicatory of both Kingdomes?* and sundry other.[19]

Of course, the scholars had a point, for many of the statements were not clear and their objections were valid on that count at least. Furthermore, the *DPW* in particular was an obstacle, because in their view owning the *DPW* meant the taking away of the *Book of Common Prayer*.[20] Another perceived problem was the negative effect that subscription to the *Solemn League and Covenant* would have on the stability of the social order. To require these subscription commitments will, they contend, be:

> a ready way, to Children that are sick of the Father, Husbands that are weary of their Wives, &c. by appealing such, as stand between them and their desires, of Malignancy, the better to effectuate their unlawfull intentions and designs.[21]

The overriding Episcopal suspicion of Puritan aspirations, which Parliament codified in the *Solemn League and Covenant,* was understandable. The Oxford men recognized clearly enough that subscription required them personally to own propositions with which they were at odds. At the very least, they thought that the Puritans were imposing a strict subscription; dissenting from that position, Episcopalians preferred to be loose subscriptionists if subscribers at all. However, these churchmen were probably being over-scrupulous; for a strict subscription was hardly what the generality of Puritan divines would accede to themselves.

7.3.2 Non-conformists

Non-conformists such as Richard Baxter shared the deep suspicion held by Episcopalians. Nonetheless, Baxter's evident sympathy towards Westminster is illustrated by the way he both elucidates his own confession of faith and expresses his approval of the *SC, LC* and *WCF:*

---

[19] *Reasons of the Present Judgement of the University of Oxford, Concerning the Solemne League and Covenant. The Negative Oath. The Ordinances Concerning Discipline and Worship* (Oxford: 1647) [no further publishing details are given], 19.

[20] *Reasons of the Present Judgement of the University of Oxford,* 33.

[21] *Reasons of the Present Judgement of the University of Oxford,* 15.

I truly profess, I take the labours of the Assembly, especially these three pieces now mentioned [The *WCF* and the two catechisms], for the best Book, next [to] my Bible, in my Study.[22]

This quotation raises an interesting question because, while Baxter records that he dissents on some points from the *LC* and the *WCF*, he does not object to the cessationist clause in *WCF* 1:1 in spite of his continuationist stance on visions and dreams.[23]

A likely explanation for Baxter's avowed continuationism on the one hand, and his apparent approval of the *WCF* cessationist clause on the other, appears in three ways. First, in his own confession of faith in which he discusses the Assembly documents, Baxter makes it clear that confessions of faith should be brief and should contain only those doctrines which are necessary for personal redemption. He thereby implies that supporting argumentation should be kept to a minimum.[24] Thus, in his reluctant attempt to confess his own faith in writing, he "descend[s] to such particulars" which are necessary for salvation.[25] His whole discussion deserves to be seen in that light. Since contrasting views of the cessationist clause do not necessarily impinge directly on the issue of personal redemption, Baxter would likely have seen the clause as an unnecessary detail.

Secondly, Baxter appears to accept that confessions should not be for the purpose of contradicting the errors of heretics.[26] If the cessationist clause was designed to oppose those "enthusiasts" who still claimed immediate revelation, Baxter by implication would not have accepted it as a legitimate part of a confession of faith. We have already developed the theory in this thesis that much of the *WCF* was understood as a reaction to perceived contemporary heresies or errors. Baxter's desire to restrict the content of confessions and catechisms to doctrines strictly necessary for salvation therefore explains why he restricts his exceptions to the Westminster documents to what he considers non-negotiable doctrines for personal redemption. The matters he disputes in the *LC* concern only the parties to

---

[22] Richard Baxter, *Rich: Baxter's Confession of His Faith, Especially Concerning the Interest of Repentance and Sincere Obedience to Christ, in Our Justification & Salvation* (London: Tho. Underhil, and Fra. Tyton, 1654), 22.

[23] See Chapter Four, 160-161 above for Baxter's continuationism.

[24] Baxter, *Rich: Baxter's Confession of His Faith, Especially Concerning the Interest of Repentance and Sincere Obedience to Christ, in Our Justification & Salvation*, especially 11-13, where he adopts the very brief "*Worcester-shire* Profession of faith".

[25] Baxter, *Rich: Baxter's Confession of His Faith, Especially Concerning the Interest of Repentance and Sincere Obedience to Christ, in Our Justification & Salvation*, 11.

[26] Baxter, *Rich: Baxter's Confession of His Faith, Especially Concerning the Interest of Repentance and Sincere Obedience to Christ, in Our Justification & Salvation*, 16.

the Covenant of Grace, the nature of saving faith and the identity of those entitled to preach the gospel.[27]

Similarly his areas of difference with the *WCF* include doctrines pertaining to personal redemption. His exceptions are respectively:
1. Chapter 3 on the explanation of redemption;
2. Chapter 11 on faith as an instrument;
3. Chapter 18 on assurance as an article of faith;
4. Chapter 19, in which he denies that the promise of life is still held out if one obeys the moral law;
5. Chapter 21, in which he dissents from the view that the keeping of the Sabbath is a moral obligation;
6. Chapter 25, where he has two objections: he understands the term "Catholic Church" to refer only to the church at the end of time, and he objects to the divines' explanation of how the invisible church is constituted. Baxter is primarily interested in truths that are expressed as articles of faith, or, in the case of "assurance of salvation", in whether a purported article of faith should be accepted as such.[28]

Thirdly, Baxter is reluctant to affirm that he fully understands the intentions of the Assembly in some of its wording, which suggests that there may be other ambiguous matters on which he also reserved his opinion.[29] In his fulsome praise of the *WCF*, Baxter adds:

> I Have perused oft the Confession of the Assembly and verily judge it the most excellent for fullness and exactness that I have ever read from any Church; And though the truths therein being of several degrees of Evidence and Necessity, I do not hold them with equal clearness, confidence or certainty; and though some few points in it are beyond my reach, yet I have observed nothing in it contrary to my judgement, if I may be allowed these Expositions following.[30]

The "expositions" in question are those we have just noted. Baxter dissented from some of the conclusions of Westminster, but it is important to reiterate that Baxter here again concerns himself with matters as articles of faith. There are "truths therein" of which he is not fully confident or certain, let alone clear about. He chooses not to explore these lesser matters, but only highlights those points which he believes are necessary to faith.

---

[27] Baxter, *Rich: Baxter's Confession of His Faith, Especially Concerning the Interest of Repentance and Sincere Obedience to Christ, in Our Justification & Salvation*, 10 and 18.

[28] Baxter, *Rich: Baxter's Confession of His Faith, Especially Concerning the Interest of Repentance and Sincere Obedience to Christ, in Our Justification & Salvation*, 20-23.

[29] Baxter, *Rich: Baxter's Confession of His Faith, Especially Concerning the Interest of Repentance and Sincere Obedience to Christ, in Our Justification & Salvation*, 19.

[30] Baxter, *Rich: Baxter's Confession of His Faith, Especially Concerning the Interest of Repentance and Sincere Obedience to Christ, in Our Justification & Salvation*, 20.

Possibly Baxter understands the cessationist clause of *WCF* 1:1 to refer to matters of personal redemption only, but more likely he sees it as one of those points of supporting argumentation concerning which he is not fully certain in his own mind, and which he did not want to call into question in this treatise.

The chronology of Baxter's two apparently contradictory opinions may also explain the paradox. His approval of the *WCF* was published in 1655, but it was not until 1673, almost twenty years later, that his *Christian Directory* appeared. In spite of his clarifications of and warm appreciation for the *WCF*, Baxter has a practical aversion to subscription. He does not believe that subscription to these or any human documents should be required of ministers, unless the documents are "clearly Rational or Scriptural, as no Sober, Studious, Competent, Godly Divine shall scruple", and considerably abbreviated.[31] By "Rational and Scriptural", he probably means containing statements that do not contradict the law or light of nature, or the clear teaching of Scripture.

While Baxter admits that confessions are useful for teaching young ministers, he rejects Shafer's third use for confessions, namely the treatment of them as a test for heresy, because heresy cannot adequately be prevented by subscription to a form of words designed by humans.[32]

7.3.3 The Westminster Divines

When we turn to examine the views of the Westminster divines to subscription, we soon see that Baxter was not alone in his views. Opinions like Baxter's were evident when the Assembly debated the *Solemn League and Covenant* at its very beginning. The *Solemn League* had already been agreed to by the Scots and, on 18 August Stephen Marshall and Philip Nye sent a letter confirming the Scottish church's support which was read in Parliament. Parliament in turn promptly sought the advice of the Assembly. On 28 August, the Assembly began a spirited discussion on the lawfulness of the document. The clause that "bred all the doubting", as Lightfoot puts it, took a whole day to debate:

> 'I will endeavour the preservation of the true reformed Protestant religion, in the church of Scotland, in doctrine, discipline, worship, and government, according to the word of God'.[33]

---

[31] Baxter, *Rich: Baxter's Confession of His Faith, Especially Concerning the Interest of Repentance and Sincere Obedience to Christ, in Our Justification & Salvation*, 27.

[32] Baxter, *Rich: Baxter's Confession of His Faith, Especially Concerning the Interest of Repentance and Sincere Obedience to Christ, in Our Justification & Salvation*, 27.

[33] John Lightfoot, *The Whole Works of the Rev. John Lightfoot, D.D.*, ed. J. R. Pitman (London: Printed by J. F. Dove, 1822), vol. 13, 10.

The last phrase "according to the word of God", had two possible meanings. Either it set a "limitation, viz. to preserve it, as far as it was according to the word", or it meant "approbation, viz. as concluding that the Scottish discipline was undoubtedly according to the word".[34] Significantly, the former meaning was sustained. This was the position of Henry Vane and Philip Nye, who had negotiated the clause with the Scots. The majority of the Assembly agreed that there was still work to do if doctrinal and ecclesiastical uniformity would be achieved, and therefore the Assembly should not accept a Scottish definition of what "reformed" meant without careful recourse to the "rule" – the Bible.

Even once uniformity had been achieved, the English divines were clear that they did not intend to advise the Parliament to require a full subscription to any of the Assembly's documents. Their abhorrence of an imposed subscription was underscored by the fact that they included a "declaratory" statement, which was appended to the foundational document– the *Solemn League and Covenant* itself.

The attempt to add this qualification: "'As far as in my conscience, I shall conceive it to be according to the word of God'",[35] was ultimately unsuccessful as a written condition, because apparently Parliament did not approve the addition.[36] Perhaps they were concerned that such a condition would be unacceptable to the Scots and would jeopardise the crucial military support upon which the English Parliament was relying.

Nonetheless, such an attempt to nullify a subscription requirement exposes the underlying resistance of the English Puritan clergy to subscription to a human composition, no matter how noble or beneficial the document in question might be. There is every reason to believe that the same attitude towards subscription prevailed in the case of the *WCF* itself. The principle that the conscience was subject only to the Lord was a concept intimately connected with the Protestant doctrine of the right of private judgement, and it was enshrined in Chapter 20 of the *WCF*:

---

[34] Lightfoot, *The Whole Works of the Rev. John Lightfoot, D.D.*, vol. 13, 10.

[35] Lightfoot, *The Whole Works of the Rev. John Lightfoot, D.D.*, vol. 13, 10.

[36] While the safest conclusion would be that the Parliament must have rejected it because the clause did not make its way into the completed document, *The Parliamentary History of England* implies that Parliament did accede to the divines' petition. Parliament having listened to the divines' request (probably by the prolocutor Twisse) to add a conscience clause, we are told: "Matters being thus settled *in Foro Conscientiae*, this new Oath went smoothly down: It was first taken by all the Lords and Commons then in Town; all the Officers in their Army were strictly enjoined to do the same; and afterwards it was ordered to be taken throughout the Kingdom". See *The Parliamentary or Constitutional History of England from the earliest times to the restoration of King Charles 2nd* (London: 1751-62) [no further publishing details are given], vol. 12, 400-401. The implication is that the Parliament acceded to the use of this oral declaratory statement.

God alone is Lord of the conscience, and hath left it free from the doctrines and commandments of men, which are in anything, contrary to His Word; or beside it, if matters of faith or worship. So that, to believe such doctrines, or to obey such commands, out of conscience, is to betray true liberty of conscience: and the requiring of an implicit faith, and an absolute and blind obedience is to destroy liberty of conscience, and reason also.

On 15 September, the House of Commons and the Assembly jointly consented to the *Solemn League and Covenant* by raised hand and by written subscription.[37] However, for the reasons we have outlined, there is every reason to believe that most members did not believe that their subscription was "strict", that is, that they were not being held to a particular and precise interpretation of the words of the *Solemn League*.

All of this, though, should not obscure a significant difference that existed between the Independents and some Presbyterians over the matter of subscription. In 1646, the Presbyterian John Vicars denounced what he saw as a weak attitude towards subscription among the Independents:

[They make] our solemne League and most sacred Covenant that happy & heavenly tie upon our consciences to Almighty God himself to be (if possibly it may be) a mayn snare and most dangerous Dilemma [(]or nose of wax) to undo us all [...] Telling us that the Parliament intended not the sense and acceptation of it, thus and thus, according to the Letter of it as we the *Presbyterians* take it.[38]

One person whom he had in mind may well have been that most vocal of Independents divines, Philip Nye. Nye was outspoken on several issues, but not least on the subject of subscription. Nye's views remained unchanged over the years, and he hints strongly that the Assembly composed its documents without intending to require strict subscription to them.

Nye's anti-subscription views were most clearly expressed in a 1659 treatise against enforced subscription. He presents several arguments to support his position, but his main concerns were these:

1. Parliament did not require the *SC* to be used, nor did it disallow the use of other catechisms;[39]
2. The *Solemn League and Covenant* did not bind anyone to contravene his or her conscience in matters of worship;[40]

---

[37] Lightfoot, *The Whole Works of the Rev. John Lightfoot, D.D.*, vol. 13, 10 and 15.

[38] John Vicars, *The Schismatick Sifted. Or the Picture of Independents, Freshly and Fairly Washt-over Again* (London: Nathanael Webb, and William Grantham, 1646), 26.

[39] Philip Nye, *Beames of Former Light, Discovering how Evil it is to Impose Doubtfull and Disputable Formes or Practises upon Ministers; Especially under the Penalty of Ejection for Non-conformity unto the Same. As also Something about Catechizing* (London: Adoniram Byfield, 1660), 11.

[40] Nye, *Beames of Former Light*, 54.

3. A modern covenant cannot annul an older covenant and thus the *Solemn League* adds "*according to the Word of God*";[41]
4. The Scots did not identify uniformity in "a sameness of words";[42]
5. Since most of the catechism is commentary on the Bible:

> To enjoyn Ministers to receive into their Congregations for publike use Commentaries composed by men subject to errour, and *ex animo* to subscribe to them (or that which is equivalent) to own them and teach them to others, not only as truths, but the true meaning of the Spirit in such or such a text, is such an imposing as in the worst of times the Ministers of *England*, or any reformed Church hath not yet been acquainted with.[43]

Nye clearly opposes Schafer's third reason for subscribing a confession, namely treating it as a test of heresy. For Nye, such subscription was too restrictive, because the requirement to own human compositions as the true meaning of Scripture, in his view, was a return to the dark days of enforced subscription.

6. The Assembly did never intend such a "stinted [strict adherence] stated use of it [the *DPW*] in the solemn Worship of God";[44]
7. The Westminster Assembly condemned such a notion;[45]
8. The Scots likewise received the *DPW* for catechising only;[46]
9. Finally, the English Presbyterians at the Assembly never intended uniformity to require a strict subscription to the *DPW*, the *FPC*, *WCF* and *Catechism*.[47] All the documents were to be treated similarly, and strict subscription and use of any of them was not intended by any of the official bodies connected with them.

Whether Philip Nye is totally correct or not in all his claims, other Puritans certainly echo his views. If things had been otherwise among the Independents at least, John Owen could hardly have expressed himself as he did in his preface to the 1658 *Savoy Declaration*, where he writes:

> *Confessions*, when *made by a company* of professors of Christianity joyntly meeting to that end, the most genuine and natural use of such *Confessions* is, That under the same form of words, they express the substance of the same *common salvation*, or *unity of their faith*, whereby *speaking the same things, they shew themselves perfectly joyned in the same minde and in the same judgement*[...]and no way to be made use of

---

[41] Nye, *Beames of Former Light*, 55.
[42] Nye, *Beames of Former Light*, 58.
[43] Nye, *Beames of Former Light*, 77.
[44] Nye, *Beames of Former Light*, 217.
[45] Nye, *Beames of Former Light*, 217. Here he refers to the preface of the *DPW* where it criticises the past use of set liturgical forms. See *DPW* 135, for example.
[46] Nye, *Beames of Former Light*, 220.
[47] Nye, *Beames of Former Light*, 221.

as an *imposition* upon any: Whatever is of force or constraint in matters of this nature, causeth them to degenerate from the *name* and *nature* of *Confessions*, and turns them from being *Confessions of Faith*, into *exactions* and *impositions of Faith*.[48]

The Independents were clear about their rejection of a strict subscription, although they agreed with Schafer's first purpose of it as an adherence to a body's statement of belief.

7.3.4 Presbyterians

However, some Presbyterians at the Assembly also evinced wariness towards imposing strictures as much as Nye or Owen did. Presbyterian Thomas Hill took an equally firm line on liberty of conscience. On one occasion, Hill warns his audience against making a *Jus Divinum* of their every opinion, unless they are sure they stand on "Scripture-grounds".[49] In the same sermon, he expressed the very sentiments that seem to be representative of English divines in general:

> Take heed of *being too far engaged in a party*; it is the way to *fell a mans judgement*: for if I be one of a party, I must *strain hard* to say as they say, and subscribe as they subscribe, else I shall be an *Apostate*; this is dangerous, then all must be proclaimed Heretical that differ. *Many a man hath broke his Conscience, violated his peace, by this Engagement, because he must not break with his Party.*[50]

Since Hill and the Presbyterian majority were a part of the Assembly, they too must have desired the "declaratory" statement in the debate over the *Solemn League and Covenant*. Nonetheless, a number of representative groups of Presbyterian ministers endorsed the Assembly documents by subscribing to joint "Testimonies", which suggests a firmer commitment to subscription by the wider body of Presbyterian Puritans. Thirty-nine London ministers, for example, willingly subscribed to the Assembly documents and affirmed their endorsement of the *Solemn League and Covenant* with a strong assertion of the soundness of the *WCF* and its agreement with Scripture:

---

[48] *A Declaration of the Faith and Order Owned and Practised in the Congregational Churches in England; Agreed upon and Consented unto by Their Elders and Messengers in Their Meeting at the Savoy, October 12. 1658* (London: John Allen, 1659), preface. John Owen is believed to be the author of the preface. See Arnold Gwynne Matthews (ed.), *The Savoy Declaration of Faith and Order 1658* (London: Independent Press, 1959), 21.

[49] Thomas Hill, *Truth and Love Happily Married in the Saints, and in the Churches of Christ* (London: Peter Cole, 1648), 32-33.

[50] Hill, *Truth and Love Happily Married in the Saints, and in the Churches of Christ*, 33.

Hereupon we embrace and assent unto the whole, and with the *Reverend Assembly* concurr in our humble and hearty desires that it may receive the approbation and Sanction of Authority, as the joynt Confession of Faith, for these three Kingdomes, in pursuance of our *Covenant*.[51]

There is, however, a hint that arises within this document which proposes that the ministers did not mean to imply by their subscription that they were adopting it as a personal confession of faith. Although there is nothing to suggest that they did not embrace the *WCF* in the same terms as did other London ministers, thirteen Westminster divines also appended their names to this document but would not subscribe to the *WCF* or to the *FPC* (which they called the *Directory for Church Government* in this document). Their stated reason was that they still "waited upon their [Parliament's] pleasure" for its final approbation.[52] Had they wanted to affirm it as their personal confession of faith, there would seem to be little to hold them back at this point. Possibly they were merely following some formal convention, but their scruple may be best explained as an unwillingness to pre-empt Parliament's decision on the matter. The divines saw the *WCF* as the joint confession of faith which was part of a standard of uniformity, rather than as a personal confession requiring a strict commitment to all its clauses.

Edward Reynolds also underscores the same Presbyterian reluctance to strict subscription in his *Brotherly Reconciliation*, significantly a sermon preached before the Westminster Assembly. When he makes Scripture the final authority for resolving differences of doctrine, he also raises an objection to subscription requirements:

> The Church by her Ministers hath the ordinary publick power of expounding Scriptures; but not power to lead the people to subscribe to

---

[51] *A Testimony to the Truth of Jesus Christ, and to our Solemn League and Covenant; as also Against Errours, Heresies and Blasphemies of These Times, and the Toleration of Them* (London: Tho. Underhill, 1648), 3.

[52] *A Testimony to the Truth of Jesus Christ*, 36-38. The divines were William Gouge, Thomas Gataker, George Walker, Daniel Cawdrey, Nicholas Proffet, Anthony Tuckney, Edmund Calamy, Simeon Ashe, Thomas Case, Lazarus Seaman, Stanley Gower, Henry Wilkinson, and Anthony Burgess. A similar testimony from the ministers of Lancaster province, headed by Westminster divine Richard Heyrick, taught that confessions of faith served several purposes. They were to confirm for the ignorant the main points needed to be known for salvation; for the preservation of truth; for detecting heretics; and finally to serve as a unifying symbol of agreement in the one "Faith". *The Harmonious Consent of the Ministers of the Province within the County Palatine of Lancaster* (Edinburgh: Printed by Evan Tyler, 1648), 8. They therefore subscribed their "Testimony" approving the *WCF*, which was effectively a subscription to the *WCF* itself (8).

such expositions as peremptory and infallible, for they have a spirit of *discerning* to prove all things, and hold fast that which is good.[53]

Confessions of faith are not sermons, but it is difficult to see how Reynolds' commitment to such a Berean spirit (cf. Acts 17:11) could happily co-exist with enforced subscription to a confession of faith in the case of either congregational members or ministers.

Another moderate Presbyterian, Cornelius Burgess, overtly pleads for looser subscription in his *Reasons Shewing the Necessity of Reformation*.[54] He contends that the earlier English church bound ministers to a strict subscription to the *Thirty-Nine Articles*, although she had given the "Bishops and Clergy in Convocation" the right to put their own sense on the doctrines in the Articles.[55] Burgess complained that insufficient leeway was given for limited or qualified subscription and, like Baxter, appealed to

---

[53] Edward Reynolds, "Brotherly Reconciliation", *Twenty Sermons Preached upon Several Occasions* (London: George Thomason, 1660), 29. Samuel Rutherford has a stronger view of the authority of ministerial expositions. He explains that there is an authority structure in the church which requires that the church members honour the judgement of their ministers. What the minister teaches is not an opinion to be placed on the same level as the member's own reading of the Bible. There is a judgement [other than that of a private Christian] that is "ministeriall, officiall, and authoritative, and this is terminated not on Christian beleeving, but supposeth a ministeriall beleeving; that what the shepheard teacheth others *God* revealed to him first, and is put forth in a ministeriall and officiall judging either in Synods, or in publick Pastorall Sermons and authoritative, but in ministeriall publishing the will and mind of *Christ. Mal 2.7. They shall seeke the Law from his mouth. Heb. 13.7.17.* That way the people depends upon the Ministeriall judgement of Synods and Pastors: but its most false that Pastors depends on their Ministeriall judgement who are sheepe, and that there is a like and equall power in shepheards and sheepe [...]. For Pastors and Synods teach fundamentals of faith ministerially to the people, and by hearing of them is faith begotten in the hearers, and they *may command, exhort, rebuke with all long suffering, 2 Tim. 4. 1.2. 2. Tim. 2.14.* stop their mouthes, *Tit.*1.11 and authoritatively enjoyne them silence. *Act.* 15.22.23,24,25. *Act.* 6.4". Samuel Rutherford, *A Free Disputation against Pretended Liberty of Conscience Tending to Resolve Doubts Moved by Mr John Goodwin, John Baptist, Dr. Jer. Taylor, the Belgick Arminians, Socinians, and Other Authors Contending for Lawlesse Liberty, or Licentious Toleration of Sects and Heresies* (London: Andrew Crook, 1650), 26.

[54] Cornelius Burges, *Reasons Shewing the Necessity of Reformation [...]"* (London: 1660) [no further publishing details are given]. For a critique of Burges's views of the *Thirty-Nine Articles* by an Episcopalian, see John Parson, *An Answer to Dr. Burges His Word by Way of Postscript* (London: Nathaniel Brook, 1660), especially 7-9 for Burges's view that all necessary doctrines should be added to the *Thirty-Nine Articles*, and Parson's response that the Articles only focus on those truths in Scripture presently under attack.

[55] Burges, *Reasons Shewing the Necessity of Reformation*, 5.

tender consciences.[56] Moreover, in his view, full subscription to the *Thirty-Nine Articles* meant being bound to defective statements of doctrine.[57] Burgess also distinguished between subscription and assent. Subscription meant a less firm commitment to the Articles, and on its own did not mean a full acceptance of the matter subscribed:

> [T]he Statute doth require belief of every one of these Articles [the *Thirty Nine Articles*], when it enjoyns not only *subscription*, but an *assent* unto them [...]".[58]

He is in favour of something like a declaratory act, but denies that there is one for the Articles:

> [I]f we may not subscribe with such an addition (*so far forth as the same Articles are agreeable to Gods Word*) it must needs be granted, that the Composers of them are admitted to be *infallible*; and their *Articles*, of equal Authority with Canonical Scripture.[59]

The statement in parenthesis implies that the final responsibility should rest with the individual's conscience with regards to Scripture teaching. In Burgess' eyes, a requirement to subscribe and assent to the Articles elevates them to the status of Scripture.

We have seen in their wider writing that English Puritans were unhappy with enforced subscription, but that the stipulations in the *FPC* produced by the Assembly suggest that subscription to that document did not emasculate liberty of conscience. When the English Parliament issued the *Form of Church Government*, in what might perhaps be described as an attempt to "presbyterianise" England and Ireland, it incorporated a portion of the *FPC* that had been composed by the august Assembly.[60] The *Form* requires ruling elders to take the covenant,[61] but requires something additional in the case of the minister. Unlike ruling elders in general, the minister must show proficiency in his study and bring his degrees. However, he is not required to subscribe to the *WCF*. The rules of examination, also incorporated into the Anglo-Irish *Form of Church Government*, require that the congregation inquire "concerning his faith in Christ Jesus, & his perswasson of the truth of the reformed Religion according to the Scriptures".[62] Again, subscription

---

[56] Burges, *Reasons Shewing the Necessity of Reformation*, 6.

[57] Burges, *Reasons Shewing the Necessity of Reformation*, 6-7.

[58] Burges, *Reasons Shewing the Necessity of Reformation*, 6.

[59] Burges, *Reasons Shewing the Necessity of Reformation*, 5.

[60] *The Form of Church-Government to be used in the Church of England and Ireland: Agreed upon by the Lords and Commons Assembled in Parliament, After Advice had with the Assembly of Divines* (London: John Wright, 1648).

[61] *The Form of Church-Government to be used in the Church of England and Ireland*, 2.

[62] *The Form of Church-Government to be used in the Church of England and Ireland*, 23.

to a confession of faith is not demanded. Schafer could be speaking for the generality of English Westminster divines when he notes correctly concerning the English Parliament of 1648: "It was evidently not their intention to go beyond the adoption of the Confession as a manifesto and as a standard of teaching".[63]

7.4 Subscription in Scotland

Scots approached the issue of subscription quite differently from the English, although historians adopt two different positions on the history of subscription to the *WCF* in Scotland. Earlier generations of historians tended to assume that subscription to the *WCF* was required at the time of its acceptance by the General Assembly. The seventeenth-century author James Kirkton in his *History of the Church of Scotland*, for example, implies that the *WCF* was subscribed to by ministers prior to the Restoration:

> Every minister was a very full professor of the reformed religion according to the large confession of faith framed at Westminster by the Divines of both nations.[64]

If by this he means that subscription was a requirement of pre-Restoration clergy, Kirkton offers no evidence in support of his claim. Charles Greig M'Crie, again without citing an authority, states that prior to 1690, "[i]n the case of the Westminster Confession individual acceptance was indicated for a time by adhibiting the signature to a copy of the symbol".[65]

Some modern historians appear to accept this older tradition uncritically. Jennings Ligon Duncan, in his essay "Owning the Confession: Subscription in the Scottish Presbyterian Tradition", for example, assumes that the Scottish General Assembly required subscription to the *WCF* directly after its initial acceptance and political ratification:

> With the approval of the *Westminster Confession* by the General Assembly on August 27, 1647 and its ratification by Parliament on February 7, 1649, unqualified verbal subscription was required of all ministers.[66]

---

[63] Schafer, "The Beginnings of Confessional Subscription in the Presbyterian Church", 104-105.

[64] James Kirkton, *The Secret and True History of the Church of Scotland, from the Restoration to the Year 1678* (Edinburgh: John Ballantyne, 1817), 64.

[65] C. G. MCrie, *The Confessions of the Church of Scotland* (Edinburgh: MacNiven & Wallace, 1907), 227.

[66] Jennings Ligon Duncan, "Owning the Confession: Subscription in the Scottish Presbyterian Tradition", David W. Hall (ed.), *The Practice of Confessional Subscription* (Lanham: University Press of America, 1995), 81.

Duncan provides no reference to documentary sources to substantiate this claim. Schafer also makes assumptions about early subscription requirements to the *WCF*:

> While nothing is said of subscription [following Parliament's ratifying of the *WCF*], this may be regarded as assumed, insofar as the new document supplanted the old Scots Confession as the doctrinal core of the National Covenant.[67]

He goes on to quote the subscription requirements of 1638, citing the Act of General Assembly of that year:

> 'that all Ministers, Masters of Universities, Colledges, and Schooles, and all others who have not already subscribed the said Confession and Covenant, shall subscribe the same' -with an added abjuration of the Five Articles of Perth and episcopal government-and that 'the said Covenant, with this declaration, to be insert in the registers of the Assemblies of this Kirk, General, Provinciall, and Presbyteriall.'[68]

But it was the *Solemn League and Covenant* of the three kingdoms which could claim the *WCF* as its doctrinal core, not the *National Covenant*. Furthermore, we would expect to see in it some formal acknowledgement that the *WCF* replaced the *Scots Confession*, if indeed the intention was to amend the 1638 *National Covenant* in this way.

There is, however, modern dissent to the received view. John Reid, who contends that there was no subscription requirement to the *WCF* between the years 1647 and 1690, suggests a second analysis of historical requirements to subscription to the *WCF*. His findings can be summarised briefly: in 1560 subscription was required only of superintendents and ministers; in 1581 and 1638 of all; and in 1707 of ministers and office bearers. The objects of subscription in 1560 were "doctrines contained in the Scriptures"; in 1638 the Scots' Confession; and in 1690 "approbation" to the *WCF*. The latter approval, he says, was equivocal, and it was only in 1711 that subscription came to mean to "'own and believe the whole doctrine of the [Westminster] Confession of Faith to be the truth of God contained in the Scriptures'".[69]

---

[67] Schafer, "The Beginnings of Confessional Subscription in the Presbyterian Church", 108.

[68] Schafer, "The Beginnings of Confessional Subscription in the Presbyterian Church", 108.

[69] John K. S. Reid, "Confessional Subscription: A Personal View", Alasdair I. C. Heron (ed.), *The Westminster Confession in the Church Today*, 132-40, at 134-35. For a discussion of subscription to the *WCF* in Scotland, see also Ian Hamilton, *The Erosion of Calvinist Orthodoxy: Seceders and Subscription in Scottish Presbyterianism* (Edinburgh: Rutherford House Books, 1990). Hamilton's work is useful, but does not deal in any substantial way with subscription in relation to the 1647 approval of the

Most historians continue to make the assumption - one that is not without some merit, but an assumption nevertheless - that the adoption of the *WCF* by the Scottish church automatically implied that the clergy at least were required to subscribe to it. However, it does seem odd that the Scots did not endorse a subscription formula when they gave their official sanction to the *WCF*, in view of the longstanding culture of subscription to religious documents. In order to understand the Scots' attitude towards subscribing to the *WCF*, we need to survey more closely the Scottish history of subscription.

7.4.1 The Use of Subscription Formulas

Subscription formulas were not an innovation when the 1638 *National Covenant* was enthusiastically and publicly subscribed. The Glasgow Assembly had met in December of that year and produced a subscription formula which embraced both the *National Covenant* and the 1560 *Scots Confession*, abjuring the *Five Articles of Perth* and Episcopacy, but subscription formulas had already appeared much earlier than the seventeenth century.

In 1578, the General Assembly, meeting in the Magdalene Chapel, Edinburgh, listed several articles established by the previous Assembly,[70] including a subscription requirement:

> That none be admitted to publick office, or Counsell, but such as have given confession of their faith, subscribed the articles of religion, and communicat at the Lord's Table, conforme to the Act of Parliament made at Edinburgh, the 15 December 1567.[71]

By 1580, all classes of society including the king himself had subscribed officially to a formula which both authorised the 1560 confession and added anti-papal heads.[72] The strict nature of this subscription requirement is self-evident:

> To the quhilk confession [1560 Scots Confession] and Forme of Religion we willingly agree in owre conscience in all poyntis, as unto Gods undoubted trueth and veritie, grounded onely upon his written Worde.[73]

James VI required that all parishioners subscribe, just as he and his household had done. Failure to do so meant a hefty fine.[74] Refusal to

---

WCF by the Scots' Assembly. For a more general overview by the same author, see Ian Hamilton, "Subscription, Confessional", *DSCHT*, 805-806.

[70] These had not gained political approval.

[71] *The Book of the Universall Kirk of Scotland*, ed. T. Thomson (Edinburgh: The Maitland Club, 1840), vol. 2, 405.

[72] *The Book of the Universall Kirk of Scotland*, vol. 2, 515.

[73] *The Book of the Universall Kirk of Scotland*, vol. 2, 515-16.

[74] *The Book of the Universall Kirk of Scotland*, vol. 2, 518.

subscribe was still frowned upon in 1592 when one Alexander Dicksone "differit from them in all the substantiall heids and points of religion quherin the Papists contraverts with them". Session 17 on 3 June required him "either to subscryve the Confessioun of Faith, or within lx dayes to passe out of the realme [...]".[75]

The 1638 *National Covenant* notably embraced the 1560 *Scots Confession,* which was still at the heart of the nation's faith. When the Scots approved the *WCF* in 1647 the new confession was measured against the benchmark of their existing confession, for when the General Assembly accepted the *WCF* "as to the truth of the matter", they added that it was "most agreeable to the Word of God, and in nothing contrary to the received Doctrine, Worship, Discipline, and Government of this Kirk[...]".[76] James Cooper in his *Confessions of Faith and Formulas of Subscription* contends that the old confession had not yet been cast off as an obsolete form, for the simple reason that "if any difficulty were to arise as to what the Westminster Confession means, recourse should be had to that of 1560".[77] As George Henderson affirms, the influence and status of the *Scots Confession* in both the Covenanting and Episcopalian camps of the Scottish church continued after the adoption of the *WCF* in 1647.[78]

In 1647 there was an obvious opportunity for the General Assembly to legislate for subscription to the *WCF* when its passed another act which reaffirmed the rules for admission by "Expectants to the Ministerie".[79] This would have been an ideal time to introduce a new subscription formula. However, the articles especially renewed were those of 1596 (probably meant to be 1590) which had been approved in Glasgow in 1638 and again in 1642 at the St Andrews General Assembly.[80] The Twenty-third Article from 1638 is specifically referred to. It reads:

> Anent the tryall of *Expectants* before their entrie to the ministerie, it being notour that they have subscribed the confession of Faith now declared in this Assembly[...]".[81]

---

[75] *The Book of the Universall Kirk of Scotland*, vol. 2, 789.

[76] Alexander Peterkin, *Records of the Kirk of Scotland, Containing the Acts and Proceedings of the General Assemblies, from the Year 1638 Downwards [...]"* (Edinburgh: John Sutherland, 1838), 475.

[77] James Cooper, *Confessions of Faith and Formulas of Subscription in the Reformed Churches of Great Britain and Ireland Especially in the Church of Scotland* (Glasgow: James Maclehose and Sons, 1907), 37.

[78] George David Henderson, *The Scots Confession 1560* (Edinburgh: The Saint Andrew Press, 1960), 19.

[79] Peterkin, *Records of the Kirk of Scotland*, 476-77.

[80] Peterkin, *Records of the Kirk of Scotland*, 477.

[81] Peterkin, *Records of the Kirk of Scotland*, 37.

No statement was made at this 1647 Assembly about replacing the 1560 *Scots Confession* with the *WCF* in respect of this formula. The implication was that anyone who reaffirmed it also subscribed to the old confession. Such a clarification would surely have been made if the Assembly had indeed intended subscription to the newly-received *WCF*.

Since the 1560 *Scots Confession* was the specific document embraced by the renewed articles, it is evident that the *WCF*, though approved at the same Assembly, was not yet the standard to which ministers had to subscribe in their presbyteries. It seems unlikely that the *WCF* could be imported into this "renovation Act" in any case, since the Scottish Parliament did not ratify the *WCF* until 7 February 1649. It was at that time that the *WCF* was ordained "to be recorded, published, and practised", but with no explicit mention of subscription,[82] although the order to "practice" might imply a level of subscription-like commitment.

Furthermore, it was the standard practice of the General Assembly to send important matters for consideration by presbyteries. In the same 1647 synod, for example, the Assembly charged Zachary Boyd with putting songs from Scripture into meter and then to make them available for presbytery consideration before they were accepted.[83] More important was the way in which the *LC* was treated on 20 July 1648. It was only after a trial in presbyteries that the Assembly would accept it. Therefore, it is highly likely that the General Assembly would have wanted all ministers and other ruling elders in presbyteries to become fully acquainted with the *WCF* before the church would impose a stringent requirement of subscription even if, as a national body, they had accepted the document as a part of the uniformity of religion in the three kingdoms. Writing of this early period, Cooper draws a similar conclusion:

> It was to the Covenants that subscription continued to be enforced: it may be doubted if, at this period, the Westminster Confession was subscribed at all: I have not met with any *Formula* of subscription to it; and it is not so much as mentioned in the Ordination Questions put forth by the Westminster Divines.[84]

---

[82] Peterkin, *Records of the Kirk of Scotland*, 569; and *The Confession of Faith; the Larger and Shorter Catechisms[...]"* (Glasgow: Free Presbyterian Publications, 1988), 16. Hewison notes that in the original statute book the words "and practised" were in parentheses. Hewison comments that these were "essential words apparently omitted": James Hewison, *The Covenanters* (Glasgow: John Smith and Son, 1908), vol. 1, 400. The records, included in the same note of proceedings, require a subscription to the covenant especially required on January 26 of 1649: "Act ratifying and containing the tenor of the band for securing the peace of the kingdom and injoining the same to be subscribed, p. 348". Peterkin, *Records of the Kirk of Scotland*, 569.

[83] Peterkin, *Records of the Kirk of Scotland*, 475.

[84] Cooper, *Confessions of Faith and Formulas of Subscription*, 37.

Moreover, in the Synod of 1648, the adoption of the *Act against sudden admitting deposed Ministers to particular Congregations* implies that uniformity to the *Solemn League and Covenant* could not be enforced nationally until it was secured in the three kingdoms. This seems the most likely background to the clause in the legislation which reads:

> Therefore finding it necessary untill the ends of the Solemn League and Covenant be setled and secured to restrain the suddenness of admitting deposed Ministers to particular charges[...][etc].[85]

We have, however, one clear case of a requirement to subscribe to the *WCF* in this period. The General Assembly pronounced in 1649 that the king was charged with responsibility to conform to both the *National Covenant* and the *Solemn League and Covenant*. This also included swearing by oath to own the *WCF* and to practise it in his family.[86] Logically, this case seems to establish political adherence by the royal family to the Reformed orthodox agenda, but it is plainly distinguishable from clerical subscription. The same Assembly passed another act requiring the church to distribute the *WCF*, the *Directory for Family Worship* and the *Larger* and *Shorter Catechisms* to every family in which someone was literate, but there was no mention of a subscription requirement as there had been in the case of the king.[87]

The reversal of fortune for the Presbyterians soon nullified any hope for enforcement of Westminster orthodoxy in Scotland. From 1660, during the time of the Covenanter persecutions which continued until 1690, the Restoration church in Scotland shunned the *Solemn League and Covenant* and embraced Episcopacy. Acts legalising the Westminster symbols were annulled, and it was only in 1690 that the estates again ratified the *WCF* and the General Assembly made subscription obligatory.[88]

Nevertheless, it would be thoroughly misleading to suggest that even if subscription was not required, the outlawed Covenanters did not preserve an exalted place for the Westminster doctrine. They had the highest regard for the *WCF,* which functioned for them as the pre-eminent subordinate standard. During their time of persecution, the Covenanters pleaded for toleration from the civil authorities in a document they wrote to the Lords Temporal in 1677 – *"An Apology for or Vindication of the Oppressed persecuted Ministers & Professors of the Presbyterian Reformed Religion in the Church of Scotland[...]"*. In it they sought to link their ecclesiastical position with the Reformed tradition, making it clear that the *WCF* was their confession of choice:

---

[85] Peterkin, *Records of the Kirk of Scotland*, 496.
[86] Peterkin, *Records of the Kirk of Scotland*, 547.
[87] Peterkin, *Records of the Kirk of Scotland*, 549.
[88] Cooper, *Confessions of Faith and Formulas of Subscription*, 49.

[We] resolve[...]to maintaine the reformed Protestant Religion[...]as it is contained in the holy Scriptures, summed up, and briefly comprehended in the Confessions of faith of the reformed Churches; especially in the Confession of faith, Larger & shorter Catechismes of this Church[...]".[89]

The Covenanters also believed that Reformed confessions of faith in general had an important role in opposing error.[90] Notwithstanding the Covenanters' loyalty to Westminster, John Reid reminds us that it was not until 1690 that an equivocal "approbation" of the *WCF* was required of ministers, and that it was only in 1711 that subscription came to mean to "'own and believe the whole doctrine of the [Westminster] Confession of Faith to be the truth of God contained in the Scriptures'".[91]

The reaction of the Episcopalians to such a new sanction is clear evidence that they believed that more than "approbation" was being sought. In 1691, in his *Presbyterian Inquisition,* Episcopalian scholar Alexander Monro records what some of the Presbyterian commission were themselves demanding by subscription to the *WCF*:

[B]y the *Acknowledging* and *Subscribing* the *Westminster Confession Faith* [...]imports, an absolute owning of every particular Article thereof, as the *only* and *most perfect Confession*, that hath been or can yet be composed; and that therefore it was to be *Acknowledged, Professed*, and, *Subscribed*, without any Limitation, Restriction or Reservation whatsoever.[92]

An observer reported that when Munro was asked to subscribe, he refused, exclaiming:

---

[89] They add that there are no revelations for doctrine, worship and government, but only illumination: "We hold the teaching of the Spirit necessare to the saving knowledge of Christ; but absolutely deny, that the Spirit bringeth new revelations in matters of doctrines, worship & Government; but only that he opens the eyes, and enlightens the understanding, that we may perceive and rightly take up, what is of old revealed in the word by the same Spirit": Hugh Smith, *An Apology for or Vindication of the Oppressed Persecuted Ministers & Professors of the Presbyterian Reformed Religion in the Church of Scotland* [...]" (London? 1677) [no further publishing details are given], pages not numbered.

[90] Smith, *An Apology for or Vindication of the Oppressed Persecuted Ministers & Professors of the Presbyterian Reformed Religion in the Church of Scotland* [not paginated].

[91] John K. S. Reid, "Confessional Subscription: A Personal View", Alasdair I. C. Heron (ed.), *The Westminster Confession in the Church Today*, 134-35.

[92] Alexander Munro, *Presbyterian Inquisition; As it was Lately Practised against the Professors of the Colledge of Edinburgh. August and September. 1690. In Which the Spirit of Presbytery and Their Present Method of Procedure, is Plainly Discovered, Matter of Fact by Undeniable Instances Cleared, and Libels against Particular Persons Discussed* (London: J. Hindmarsh, 1691), 4.

nor are Confessions thus imposed in any Protestant Church upon Earth; they look upon them as Secondary Rules, and consequently to be Examined by the Word of God.[93]

Munro claimed that his understanding of a less stringent subscription was faithful to both the record of history and the practice of the universal Reformed church, and that it was equally the position of the Scottish kirk up to his time.

However, the same is unlikely to have been the historical understanding of Presbyterians like Samuel Rutherford. When the 1647 Assemblymen approved the *WCF* as to its "matter", they claimed in essence that the *WCF* faithfully represents the true teachings of Scripture in all points, whether fundamental or non-fundamental. By "matter" Rutherford intends the meaning or sense of Scripture, for he identifies "matter" directly as Scripture: "*A Confession of faith, is to be respected in regard of the matter which is Divine Scripture*",[94] later explaining that "the *Word of God*" and its "sense and meaning [...] are one".[95]

Scripture is composed of "matter" and "form". "Matter" is the meaning or sense of the content of Scripture, while "form" is the grammar, language and style in which it is cast. The Scriptures, considered as both matter and form, are "the express written word" of God,[96] though the original form must be distinguished from a translation.[97] Because the translation is not the original form, which of course entailed the original languages, the swearing of a human confession of faith is somewhat analogous to swearing and subscribing to the Bible in translation:

> [We] do not sweare to the translation, characters, and humane expression; but to the **matter** contained in the translation; and that because *Jehovah our Lord* hath spoken it in his Word [bold emphasis added].[98]

Thus in human covenant or confession:

---

[93] Munro, *Presbyterian Inquisition; As it was Lately Practised against the Professors of the Colledge of Edinburgh*, 49.

[94] Samuel Rutherford, *The Due Right of Presbyteries or, A Peaceable Plea for the Government of the Church of Scotland* (London: Richard Whittaker and Andrew Crook, 1644), 131.

[95] Samuel Rutherford, *The Due Right of Presbyteries*, 133.

[96] Samuel Rutherford, *The Due Right of Presbyteries*, 133.

[97] Samuel Rutherford, *The Due Right of Presbyteries*, 135.

[98] Samuel Rutherford, *The Due Right of Presbyteries*, 135. Richard Muller also recognises that the *WCF* teaches that it is the Bible in its original languages that is immediately inspired, and to which final appeal is to be made when deciding controversies, rather than to translations: Richard Muller, *Post-Reformation Reformed Dogmatics* (Grand Rapids, MI: Baker, 2003), vol. 2, 90.

We also sweare a National covenant, not as it is mans word, or because the Church or Doctors, at the Churches direction, have set down in such and such words, such an order or method, but because it is *Gods Word*, so that we sweare to the sense, and meaning of the plat-forme of confession, as to the *Word of God*.[99]

However, has Rutherford not elevated a confession of faith or a national covenant to the status of Scripture? We must conclude that he seems to have done so– at least to the status of a translation of Scripture, albeit with the assumption that a confession must always be checked against Scripture. The "matter" of both is the Word of God, although the Scriptures are the primary and ultimate source of truth. For Rutherford, though a confession or human covenant is not in its "form" the Word of God, that does not mean that it cannot be subscribed to as though it were the Word of God:

> Because confessions are to be believed in so far, as they are agreable to *Gods* Word, and lay upon us an obligation secondary onely, yet are they not so loose, as that we may leap from poynts of faith, and make the doctrine of faith *arena gladiatoria* a fencing field for Gamesters and Fencers.[100]

Because "matter" is the sense of Scripture, when that sense is framed in words other than those set down in Scripture in the original languages, it is still the Word of God. This applies not only to fundamentals but also to non-fundamentals, and thus both are subscribed to as the teaching or meaning of Scripture paraphrased in a confession of faith.[101] There seems little doubt that if a church body or an individual subscribed to a confession of faith whose "matter" could be found in Scripture, then their appended signature was an affirmation that the document in all its clauses and chapters contained an accurate statement of the Word of God.

7.5 Conclusion

In his *English Popish Ceremonies*, George Gillespie contends that the Scottish kirk required the severest form of subscription: "No Reformed Church in Europe is so strictly tied by the bond of an oath and subscription

---

[99] Samuel Rutherford, *The Due Right of Presbyteries*, 133. See also 132, where Rutherford compares subscription to the taking of a religious oath. Furthermore, in the light of *WCF* 22 (*Of lawful Oaths and Vows*), and the use of the term "swear" being synonymous with "subscribe", as we have it both here with Rutherford and with taking a lawful oath (*WCF* 22:1), subscription can be synonymous with making a religious oath or vow.

[100] Rutherford, *The Due Right of Presbyteries*, 139.

[101] Rutherford, *The Due Right of Presbyteries*, 139.

[...]".[102] Thus Scots acknowledged themselves that they differed from others in the strictness of their subscription requirements. Although there is limited evidence to suggest that some English Presbyterians held a firmer view of subscription than other English Puritans did, the English aversion to strict subscription probably meant that the majority of Westminster divines and the English Parliament intended to see the *WCF* as a standard of teaching only. The Scots, in spite of their stricter view of subscription, most probably did not subscribe to the *WCF* until 1690, following the "glorious Revolution", even though it was the confession of choice for the persecuted Covenanters after the Restoration.

All of this need not imply that the majority of the English Puritans and Scots could not have strictly subscribed the *WCF* if such a strict subscription had been considered desirable. But non-subscription to the *WCF* between 1647 and 1690 could mitigate the view that Scottish mysticism and acceptance of dreams, visions and other revelatory operations of the Spirit give evidence that the cessationist clause of the *WCF* still allowed for such things. The Covenanter hagiographical tradition in particular seems to challenge the epistemic boundaries of the *WCF*. Yet, as we saw in the previous chapter, at least some of these mystical experiences and romantic stories of divine intervention among the persecuted Covenanters can be accounted for by the explanation of a John Knox or a Samuel Rutherford – that the conjunction of Word, Spirit and providence grants a mediate prophetic insight to God's faithful people.

Although the English Independents and Presbyterians would not have required a continuationist such as William Bridge to subscribe the *WCF* strictly, it is likely that all of the Scottish commissioners to the Assembly, including George Gillespie and Robert Blair, fully embraced the *WCF*. If, along with the rest of the 1647 General Assembly, the commissioners were required to subscribe to it as a comprehensive confession of their own faith, one might speculate that they would have willingly acceded and thus would have fully accepted a cessationist construal of *WCF* 1:1.

---

[102] Gillespie, "A Dispute Against the English Popish Ceremonies", *The Works of George Gillespie*, vol. 1, 209.

Conclusion

In many ways the modern debate over the likelihood of new divine revelation and the possibility of contemporary manifestations of miraculous New Testament spiritual gifts echoes the same debate which took place in seventeenth-century Britain. Whether God still uses dreams and visions and grants prophecies to the contemporary church is as controversial now as it was then. Modern continuationists commonly affirm that no further revelation will be given to show the way of salvation, as all that God intended to impart for that purpose is fully contained in Scripture. At the same time they suggest that God may also, either with or without the help of Scripture, reveal information for individual or corporate guidance in other matters.

Usually, although not always, going hand in hand with this position is an assumption that all or most of the miraculous New Testament spiritual gifts have re-emerged in the twentieth century and that these remain normative for the contemporary church. Thus continuationists affirm that visions and dreams contain revelations which are valid for today and assume that tongues-speaking and prophecy are gifts widely available in the modern church. What this thesis has endeavoured to discover is the view or views of the seventeenth-century Westminster Assembly concerning a similar continuationism espoused in their day.

In composing their various documents, the Westminster divines on behalf of their political masters sought doctrinal unity and a common ecclesiastical government in the three kingdoms of England, Scotland and Ireland while striving both to appeal to and reflect wider international Reformed orthodoxy. The linchpin of that orthodoxy was a belief in the unity of Word and Spirit, a doctrine that was thoroughly entrenched in the seventeenth century. Moreover, it was a doctrine which had been honed in debate with the two main parties of opposition, the Catholics and those sects that traced their genesis to the Radical Reformation. Both of these groupings appeared to grant the Spirit greater freedom in their religious epistemology than the Reformed orthodox did, allowing degrees of liberty that, to their Reformed theological adversaries, led ultimately to heresy and to the shipwreck of souls. Englishman William Whitaker had articulated the Reformed orthodox response to both sets of opponents, and his legacy was still influential among the authors of Westminster theology. As a result, Westminster theologians strongly affirmed a Protestant religious epistemology which held tenaciously to the unity of Word and Spirit. Indeed, the Westminster divines made it an article of faith in *WCF* 1:1 that the former means by which God revealed his will unto salvation had now ceased and that that cessation was what rendered Scripture necessary in order to know the way of salvation.

However, the question that arises from the consideration of this "cessationist clause" is whether the divines intended by their statement to uphold a unity of Word and Spirit only for matters of personal redemption. Did they perhaps not intend to deny that the Spirit could still bring revelation for other purposes directly from God, using the former modes of divine disclosure?

There is, in the view of some modern scholars, evidence to demonstrate that the Westminster Puritans did leave room for God to reveal his will for non-redemptive matters using such former modes as dreams and visions; so that extra-biblical prophecy was still considered not only possible but evident in the ministries of some of the Reformation notables such as John Knox. This evidence includes the writings of Westminster divine William Bridge, who argues for the continuance of the Old Testament ordinances of dreams and visions and the like in his own day. In addition there was almost universal agreement that Luther, Knox and many others had predicted contingent occurrences to such a degree that they were called prophets by many of their admirers. Luther was even described as an "apostle". George Gillespie, Scottish commissioner to the Westminster Assembly, had also written that Knox and others were prophets in the line of the biblical prophet Agabus (Acts 11:28 and 21:10) and therefore messengers of extraordinary prophecies. Moreover, Gillespie's colleague Robert Blair in his autobiography claimed to have received extraordinary revelations. If these important figures, either connected to the Westminster Assembly themselves or among those who endorsed the adoption of the *WCF* as their confession of faith, held to continuing revelation on the one hand and presumably subscribed to the *WCF* on the other, the cessationist clause cannot have been meant to proscribe all extra-biblical revelations. Therefore, the argument goes, the cessationist clause in context must only relate to matters of spiritual salvation and not to temporal guidance or to the foretelling of contingent events by Reformation and post-Reformation prophets.

Our investigation has shown that this is a simplistic analysis of the likely meaning of the cessationist clause. There are several missing elements to this argument which, when taken into consideration, present a quite different conclusion concerning the intended meaning of the clause.

Firstly, the divines understood "salvation" to be a concept that transcended the limits of personal redemption or eschatological salvation. They understood the term to embrace temporal mercies, temporal guidance and temporal deliverances. These blessings were experienced by individuals, the church or nations and all were appropriately listed under the rubric "salvation". Therefore when the divines wrote that the knowledge of the way of salvation was now preserved in the Scriptures, and no longer came through the former various vehicles of revelation such as visions and dreams, Urim and Thummim, prophetic inspiration and angelic visitations, they meant that these ways had ceased to convey God's mind for salvation in its broadest scope.

Secondly, when the divines penned their cessationist clause, they were operating with a conscious distinction between two types of revelations, one of which they deemed had ceased and one of which continued, and always would continue until the end of time. That which had ceased was "immediate" revelation in the sense of a direct conveyance by the Holy Spirit through visions, dreams, angelic action or by an impression of the Spirit upon the faculty of the understanding. The key features of this "immediate" revelation were that it was equal to Scripture in authority and that it contained new extra-biblical revelation of either doctrine, ethics or other forms of divine guidance. The divines argued that this type of divine disclosure had ceased and therefore the modes of its conveyance were now obsolete. The Quakers from the middle of the seventeenth century took issue with the Westminster epistemology and stridently argued that immediate revelation continued. Their polemic helpfully provoked a clearer explanation from those who had adopted the *WCF* as a subordinate standard and who asserted that the Quakers were in error in their continuationism, although the Quaker apologists had correctly understood the *WCF* cessationist clause to be a denial that such "immediate" revelation continued. The only firm evidence of a belief in continuing *immediate* revelation was in the superstition that a dying person could prophesy future events as his or her soul began to leave the body. This ability was not considered to be a resurgence of a spiritual gift, but a natural propensity which relied upon a Platonic idea that the body restricted the soul's communication with other spirits. Yet our analysis of Edmund Calamy's discussion of this subject in *The Godly Mans Ark* gives us cause to conclude that he considered this phenomenon to be equivalent to "mediate" revelation.

Thirdly, the divines allowed that dreams, angelic visitations and prophetic impulses or motions might have a role in the only legitimate revelation that now remained, "mediate" revelation. "Mediate" revelation, as its name implies, was revelation mediated through some intermediary: in this case, the Scriptures. The Scriptures were an essential means whereby God imparted this revelation. What was thus conveyed was a greater understanding of the meaning of God's mind in the Scriptures, not merely a greater grammatical or contextual understanding of the biblical text. "Mediate" revelation was considered to be an application of the divinely inspired written Word of God to the life of an individual, nation or church.

An analogous use of the former modalities of "immediate" revelation was not, therefore, denied. Dreams were widely considered to be sometimes used by God in concurrence with some text of Scripture to give guidance to a believer. These dreams operated quite differently than they had usually done as channels of "immediate" revelation, for in the days when such revelation was still given, God used dreams to convey extra-biblical ideas to the mind of the recipient. The Reformed orthodox of the seventeenth century believed that a dream might now have a purely human origin and yet be used by God "providentially" to confirm some event whose primary revelation was to be sourced in Scripture. These "mediate" revelations could also occur simultaneously with an impulse of the Holy Spirit giving (usually to a godly preacher) confidence that God was going to perform some event in the future which was in line with his revealed will in Scripture. A case in point might be God's punishment of an evildoer, an historical example often associated with the ministry of John Knox. Angels too were considered to be able to impress the faculty of the imagination and move the thought processes in such a manner that secrets could be discovered concerning contingent events. The 1605 Gunpowder Plot was believed to be providentially uncovered through the means of an angelic agency putting it into the mind of Francis Tresham to warn his Catholic brother-in-law Lord Monteagle by letter, advising him not to attend Parliament on 5 November of that year. Lord Monteagle subsequently revealed the plot to the government and so a disaster was thwarted. The Scriptures were relevant in these sorts of cases as the source of the mediated revelation, because they contained promises of deliverances for God's people, covenanted nations and churches, in a variety of contexts.

While the scope of the concept of "salvation", together with this "immediate"/ "mediate" distinction, are important elements of which we need to take cognizance if we are to understand the extent of the cessationist clause of *WCF* 1:1, another factor external to the wording of the *WCF* itself is the clear opinion of most Westminster divines, Scottish commissioners and other Reformed contemporaries that God had ceased to impart miracles, miraculous gifts and extra-biblical revelations in the post-apostolic era. The Reformed orthodox consistently dismissed the idea that miraculous gifts of the Spirit, of which immediately inspired prophecy was considered to be one, continued after the foundational period of the Christian church. These gifts and other miraculous powers, claimed for the early church, were deemed to have ceased, because their purpose of authenticating the apostles' doctrine had now been fulfilled. It would have been highly controversial for the Westminster Assembly to allow for "immediate" revelation which had no reference to Scripture, or to condone a power to perform modern miracles, because always close to the consciousness of the Protestant divine were the assertions of both the Catholic and radical Reformation opposition who laid claim to continuing extra-biblical revelations and miracles. Had the divines undermined the long-established polemic against Rome and the sects that modern miracles were either delusions or of satanic origin, they would have been overturning a key plank of Protestant orthodoxy that dated from the earliest days of the Reformation.

When it came to the cessation of the New Testament gift of prophecy, John Owen represented a common perspective among the English and Scottish divines, that God still imparted spiritual gifts *analogous* to the miraculous gifts of the Spirit. Thus a prophetic function continued, though it was not prophesying by immediate revelation or divine inspiration and therefore not in a manner that bypassed Scripture.

In the few cases of those Westminster English Puritans or Scottish Presbyterians in whom we see evidence that might imply the continuance of immediate revelation, we have noticed that the data are far from conclusive. In the case of William Bridge, while he accepts the possibility of dreams and visions continuing, the "most sure light" is still the light of Scripture; so that there is a profound difference between the revelations of the apostolic era and those of his own day. Scripture is still for Bridge the arbiter of the authenticity of any claimed modern revelation. Although he may have posited ongoing "immediate" revelation through the modalities of dreams and visions, he does not admit to it in so many words. In the case of George Gillespie, he too does not directly ascribe "immediate" revelation to the Reformation "prophets", but he can also be understood to mean that the revelations of John Knox and others were "mediated" through the Scriptures.

However, while the Reformed orthodox at the Assembly probably meant to allow a place for at least dreams and angelic "motions" in providence, it is clear that such phenomena were considered part of the process of "mediate" revelation. Westminster orthodoxy did not reject the principle that God could still use such modalities to speak in a mediate way and to grant revelations concerning matters of duty to the godly or to warn of imminent danger. *In this sense*, Westminster religious epistemology was indeed "continuationist". The divines believed that God "continued" to speak in surprising and extraordinary ways, albeit not as directly as he had in biblical times. They rarely considered themselves to be disadvantaged in their access to the will of God for their own day in comparison with those who lived in the days when immediate revelation was still given, because the Scriptures spoke not only to *all of life*, but also to *all of history*. For every providence, there was a concurrent Scripture principle or text to speak to it, sometimes clearly and sometimes more darkly, but the point was that God had not forgotten to address his people in any extremity. The Assembly would surely have concurred with the fifth stanza of William Cowper's famous hymn concerning the God of providence:

Blind unbelief is sure to err and scan His work in vain; God is His own Interpreter and He will make it plain[1]

It remains to ask: can the Puritans help us in the modern debate over the same questions and perhaps point to how the modern continuationist and cessationist may be able to draw more closely together in a united witness?

Our analysis of the Puritan view of revelation critiques the two standpoints evident in the Protestant church today. Where the contemporary continuationist claims that God may still reveal hidden and future events to the church, he or she stands in line with Reformed orthodoxy as represented at the Westminster Assembly. Where the modern cessationist denies any God-given ability to discern such matters, he or she is at odds with the pneumatology and the doctrine of Scripture of the Westminster Assembly. Conversely, the continuationist who precludes the mediation of Scripture in *any* modern "prophecy" has entered the lists of those "enthusiasts" whom the Reformed orthodox sternly resisted. It is equally probable that the cessationist who is open to God's granting extraordinary revelations in a "mediate" way which will always require a primary role for Scripture, will feel very comfortable with the Puritan and Scottish Presbyterian notion that God's immanence is as evident in the guidance of the contemporary church as it was in the days of the Apostles.

---

[1] "God Moves in a Mysterious Way", 1772.

Appendix

Private Spirits

The authors of the *WCF* deliberately set out to expose and oppose the claims of their theological opponents on a wide range of topics[1] including the work of the Holy Spirit.[2] The precise boundaries within which the Holy Spirit functions were addressed by the Assembly, because threats to orthodoxy were perceived from Catholicism on the one hand and from "enthusiasm" in its various manifestations on the other. As we have seen in William Whitaker's *Disputation*, one criticism from Catholic theologians was that the Protestant claim to authority was misguided and false.[3] Robert Bellarmine had asserted that "all who are in doubt on any matter, are [viz. should be] sent to a living judge, not to their own private spirits".[4] This debate, and Whitaker's retort that Protestants do not send people to a private spirit, "but to the scripture itself, and the Spirit of God speaking clearly in the scripture," has its echo in *WCF* 1:10.[5] Following Whitaker, the *WCF* holds that:

> The supreme judge by which all controversies of religion are to be determined, and all decrees of councils, opinions of ancient writers, doctrines of men, and private spirits, are to be examined; and in whose

---

[1] Other examples include Arminianism, countered in Chapter 3 (*Of God's Eternal decree*) and Chapter 10 (*Of Effectual Calling*); Pelagianism in Chapter 9 (*Of Free Will*); works' righteousness in Chapter 11 (*Of Justification*) and Chapter 16 (*Of Good Works*); Antinomianism in Chapter 18 (*Of Assurance of Grace and Salvation*) and Chapter 19 (*Of the Law of God*); the Anabaptist rejection of oaths and vows, and Catholic monasticism in Chapter 22 (*Of Lawful Oaths and Vows*); and perhaps most obviously, Catholic sacramentalism in Chapters 27 to 29 (*Of the Sacraments, Of Baptism,* and *Of the Lord's Supper* respectively).

[2] The Holy Spirit's work is referred to in the following chapters and sections of the *WCF*: 1:5; 1:6; 1:10; 2:1; 3:6; 7:3; 7:5; 8:3; 8:5; 8:8; 10:1; 10:2; 10:3; 10:4; 11:4; 12:1; 13:1; 13:2; 13:3; 14:1; 6:3; 16:5; 17:1; 17:2; 17:3; 18:2; 18:3; 18:4; 19:7; 20:1; 21:3; 21:6; 25:3; 26:1; 27:3 and 32:3. It is also alluded to in others much more widely. For a recent discussion on the Holy Spirit in the *WCF*, see O. Palmer Robertson, "The Holy Spirit in the Westminster Confession", Ligon Duncan (ed.), *The Westminster Confession into the 21st Century* (Fearn: Christian Focus Publications, 2003), 57-99, especially 91-98 for the work of the Spirit within Christians.

[3] See Chapter 1, 55-56 above.

[4] William Whitaker, *Disputation on Holy Scripture* (Cambridge: The University Press, 1849), 418.

[5] Whitaker, *Disputation*, 418.

sentence we are to rest; can be no other but the Holy Spirit speaking in the Scripture.

While there is little question that *WCF* 1:10 seeks to answer Catholic criticisms against the Protestant notion of a private spirit, scholars dispute whether or not inclusion of the phrase "private spirits" in this article is also an endorsement of the idea that genuine extra-biblical revelations are still available. One writer on the subject, Byron Curtis, has suggested that the term in the *WCF* refers to authentic private revelations, even if they still need to be tested against Scripture. Curtis seeks to equate the private spirits of *WCF* 1:10[6] with genuine and sanctioned private revelations, concluding: "That recognized meaning denotes private revelation, not personal opinion".[7] In a response in the same journal, I have endeavoured to argue that the term "private spirits" does not refer to genuine or possible extra-biblical revelation, but either to the private opinions of human beings or to false revelations of "enthusiasts".[8]

Neither of these essays, though, examines the writings of the Assembly divines themselves. Study of the way in which the Westminster divines use the term elsewhere confirms our earlier conclusion that the designation "private spirit" is likely to refer either to opinions of human beings or to false claims to revelation by "enthusiasts".[9] A brief review of the divines' use of the term demonstrates that they frequently identified "private spirits" with personal opinion.

8.1 Private Spirits as Personal Opinion[10]

Most discussion of the designation "private spirit" in a seventeenth-century context occurs either in the matter of interpreting the Bible or of affirming that the Bible is the Word of God. Even a non-Puritan outside the circle of the Westminster Assembly, such as Charles I, could write to Alexander Henderson to warn him against the use of a "private spirit". Charles stresses

---

[6] *WCF* 1:10. The proof-texts for this sentence are Matt. 22: 29, 31; Eph. 2:20; Acts 28:25.

[7] Byron Curtis, "'Private Spirits' in Westminster Confession §1.10 and in Catholic-Protestant Debate (1588–1652)," 58/2 *WTJ* (Fall 96), 257-66, at 264.

[8] Garnet Milne, "'Private Spirits' in the Westminster Confession of Faith and in Protestant-Catholic Debates: A Response to Byron Curtis," 61/1 *WTJ* (Spring 1999), 101-10.

[9] Milne, "'Private Spirits' in the Westminster Confession of Faith and in Protestant-Catholic Debates: A Response to Byron Curtis," 110.

[10] See the Catholic diatribe against the alleged Protestant private spirit, which the author identifies as personal opinion. James Sharpe, *The Triall of the Protestant Private Spirit* (1630) [No further publishing details given], 20. Nonetheless, Sharp also argues that the Protestants equate their private spirit with the Holy Spirit or more accurately the testimony of the Holy Spirit (200 and 207-208).

the need to consult the Church Fathers when resolving conflicts concerning the interpretation of Scripture: "[F]or if this be not [i.e. consulting the Fathers] then of necessity the interpretation of private spirits must be admitted: the which contradicts St. Peter, (2 Pet. I.20) [...]". Charles assumes that the 2 Peter text warns against interpreting the Bible as an individual.[11]

The definition suggested by Charles is widely attested among Westminster divines. Commonly the term "private spirit" is used when deprecating personal opinion in contrast to divine revelation. William Greenhill, in his extensive commentary on Ezekiel, when commenting on Ezek. 43:7-9, warns:

> The scope of God in these words is this, that the worshippers in the new temple shall do nothing of their own private spirits, of their own heads [...]".[12]

Plainly, since Scripture performs *the* function of the rule, a "private spirit" cannot be a rule of faith and life. Protestants clarified that the understood the "private spirit" to be opinion in response to their critics. Anthony Burgess, for example, makes a distinction concerning the "private spirit", which he says the godly are accused of using when they claim to interpret Scripture. An individual may, as a private person, "gain-say the whole world, if he have a true interpretation of Scripture".[13] However, Burgess points out that it is wrong to arrive at an interpretation which does not appear publicly in the words of Scripture. A case in point might be when an individual interprets Scripture in such a way that his conclusions prove to be motivated by a desire for some personal advantage. "So then", Burgess concludes:

> a private spirit is then made a rule, when we take our own thoughts of the Scripture, and doe not found or establish our meaning upon the context.[14]

One is relying upon one's own spirit, whose subjective insights into the text prevail over the actual context of the passage – a context and an interpretation which is publicly available.

---

[11] John Fuller Russel (ed.), *The Judgement of the Anglican Church (posterior to the Reformation) on the Sufficiency of Holy Scripture and the Authority of the Holy Catholic Church in Matters of Faith* (London: A.H. Baily & Co, 1838), 73. John Owen, *The Works of John Owen* (Edinburgh: The Banner of Truth Trust, 1979), vol. 4, 77. Owen teaches that 2 Pet. 1:20 disclaims that the Scriptures were the product of a private spirit, meaning the private opinions of the apostles.

[12] William Greenhill, *An Exposition of Ezekiel* (Edinburgh: Banner of Truth Trust, 1994), 794.

[13] Anthony Burges[s], *The Difficulty of, and The Encouragements to a Reformation* (London: Thomas Underhill, 1643), 14.

[14] Burges, *The Difficulty of, and The Encouragements to a Reformation*, 14.

The "private spirit" was also identified with self-conceit or selfish ambition.[15] When Alexander Henderson, in a sermon preached to the House of Lords, discusses hindrances that might cause the peers to stumble in their duty to prosecute reformation, he clearly uses the term "private spirits" to mean self-promotion. Thus, he concludes: "Private spirits are evill spirits, whether they be in Church or Parliament [...] they are foolish spirits".[16]

It also became a commonplace to contrast "private spirit" as opinion with the inner testimony of the Holy Spirit,[17] or in distinction from the work of the Holy Spirit more generally.[18] It was a natural progression, therefore, to label the alleged revelations of the "enthusiasts" "private spirits", and thus to regard them as an expression of human opinion only.

8.2 Private Spirits as the Private Revelations of the "Enthusiasts"

The Westminster Puritans argued that a private spirit was not the Holy Spirit, because the private spirit is something *internal,* while the Holy Spirit is of *external* origin. The Reformed orthodox were themselves charged with claiming personal revelation through a private spirit, but their strident denials make one thing obvious: any implication that they intended the term "private spirits" to mean genuine revelation in *WCF* 1:10 is quite implausible.

Edward Reynolds, for example, rejects the charge that the Holy Spirit who was believed to illuminate Scripture is in fact a private spirit. Having described the Holy Spirit's work, he answers the objection: "That we make all Religion hang upon a private spirit".[19] Reynolds' answer is that the

---

[15] See, for example, William Goode, *The Discoverie of a Publique Spirit* (London: Christopher Meredith, 1645), 17-18.

[16] Alexander Henderson, *A Sermon Preached before the Right Honourable House of Lords* (London: Robert Bostock, 1645), 25. See also Westminster divine Daniel Cawdrey's *The Good Man A Publick Good* where he contrasts men of a public selfless spirit with "a narrow or private spirit: one that is either covetous, or ambitious, or voluptuous, that seekes himselfe and his own ends, and not the things of Jesus Christ". Daniel Cawdrey, *The Good Man A Publick Good* (London: Charles Greene, 1643), 33. Cawdrey (1599-1664), was the son of a non-conformist minister himself. He was educated at Cambridge later becoming minister at Little Ilford, Essex. Following the Act of Uniformity, he was cast out of his charge at Great Billing, Northampton. Cawdrey had been a later addition to the originally appointed Westminster divines. James Reid, *Memoirs of the Westminster Divines* (Edinburgh: Banner of Truth, 1982), vol. 1, 219-20.

[17] William Twisse, *The Scriptures Sufficiency To Determine All Matters of Faith, Made Good against the Papist: OR, That a Christian May be Infallibly Certain of His Faith and Religion by the Holy Scriptures* (London: Matthew Keynton, 1656), 134.

[18] Stephen Marshall, *Meroz Cursed* (London: Samuel Gellibrand, 1641), 5.

[19] Edward Reynolds, "Brotherly Reconciliation", *Twenty Sermons Preached upon Several Occasions* (London: George Thomason, 1660), 29.

Spirit who dwells in all believers is not a private spirit, because he comes from *outside* them: "That this spirit, though in a private man, yet is *not a private spirit* [...]".[20]

When he contrasts the public spirit with the private spirit, William Lyford adds his voice to those who reject the private spirit understood as a spirit of revelation apart from the Word:

> The Spirit of God speaking in Scripture is the Publick Spirit [...]. A private Spirit is that which one man hath, and not another; and therefore it is but the figment of mens brains.[21]

Richard Capel similarly dismisses the accusation that Protestants rely on a private spirit as revelation:

> But is not this to fall upon private revelations? No such matter: for we call not in for the Testimony of revealing of the Spirit to teach us any thing but what is revealed in the word; that were to bring in private revelations[...]. *A private spirit is to lead us from, this is to lead us to the Word.*[22]

The inner testimony of the Spirit illuminating Scripture is contrasted with the private spirit here.

What was true of the Westminster divines was also true of the Reformed orthodox in general. Joseph Caryl gave his imprimatur in 1651 to a sermon by the Puritan William Ames. Preaching on 1 Jn. 2:20, where Christians are described as possessing an "anointing from the Holy One", Ames rejects the idea that such anointing can be identified with a private spirit:

> *The Holy Spirit, which is understood by this anointing, is no private spirit, or particular impulse, no singular perswasion or extraordinary inspiration, but a generall and universall sense in all regenerate minds.*[23]

While Protestantism had been charged with relying upon a private spirit as a source of revelation, Protestant apologists rejected the charge vehemently and argued forcefully against any claim to new revelation, themselves using the term "private spirits" dismissively and pejoratively. Furthermore, they not only dismiss the accusation that they claim to receive

---

[20] Reynolds, "Brotherly Reconciliation", 29.

[21] William Lyford, *The Plain Mans Senses Exercised to Discern Both Good and Evil: Or, A Discovery of the Errors, Heresies, and Blasphemies of These Times, and the Toleration of Them as They are Collected and Testified Against by the Ministers of London [...]"* (London: Richard Royston and Edward Forrest, 1655), 21.

[22] Richard Capel, *Capel's Remains, Being An Useful Appendix to His Excellent Treatise of Tentations. Concerning the Translations of the Holy Scriptures* (London: John Bartlet, 1658), 87-89.

[23] William Ames, *The Saints Security, against Seducing Spirits. Or the Anointing from the Holy One the Best Teaching* (London: William Adderton, 1652), 11.

revelation by a private spirit, but also use the term when they accuse others of false claims to immediate and extra-biblical revelation.

The Westminster divines were greatly concerned by the claims of the Antinomian and Familist sects to private revelation of either new truths or new interpretations of Scripture. Rutherford, in his *Survey of the Spirituall Antichrist*, describes the sorts of claims such enthusiasts made:

> Since Familists deny that they are infallible in exponing any Scripture, and yet the Spirit doth suggest these spirituall senses, that *Antinomians* and *Familists* boast off, and that immediately acting on our soules as dead, passive organs without discoursing, reasoning and arguing, which to me is the very Propheticall immediately inspiring Spirit that carried the *Prophets* and *Apostles* in seeing the visions of *God*.[24]

Since private claims to revelation by such mystical sects were very much on the minds of the Westminster Assembly, it is very likely that the clause in *WCF* 1:10 was intended to oppose such assertions as well. The supposition that the term "private spirits" was intended to identify and reject an *illegitimate* source of authority fits well with the status of other categories mentioned in the clause, creating a balance between two legitimate and two illegitimate sources of knowledge. While the first two, "decrees of councils [and] opinions of ancient writers", are legitimate and useful, the third category consist of the "doctrines of men", which are to be tested by Scripture. The latter phrase is derived from Col. 2:22, which teaches that such "doctrines" are to be rejected, because they are set in opposition to revealed truth. It is most likely that the phrase "private spirits" carries the same negative connotation. David Dickson certainly understood the phrase this way in his commentary on *WCF* 1:10. Not only does he engage the "Papists [who err] who maintain that the Church of Rome, and the Pope, are the supreme judges of all controversies of faith", but he also rejects the Quaker doctrine of "light within":

> Do not likewise the Quakers err who maintain, That the light within, which teacheth the elect, is the only judge of all controversies of faith.[25]

---

[24] Samuel Rutherford, *A Survey of the Spirituall Antichrist.[...]"* (London: Andrew Crooke, 1648), 311.

[25] David Dickson, *Truth's Victory over Error: Or, the True Principles of the Christian Religion, Stated and Vindicated Against the Following Heresies, viz. Arians, Arminians, Anabaptists, Antinomians, Brownists, Donatists, Epicureans, Eutychians, Erastians, Familists, Jesuits, Independents, Libertines, Manicheans, Pelagians, Papists, Quakers, Socinians, Sabellians, Sceptics, Vaninians, &c. The Whole being a Commentary on All the Chapters of the Confession of Faith, by Way of Question and Answer: In which, the saving Truths of our Holy Religion are Confirmed and Established; and the Dangerous Errors and Opinions of its Adversaries Detected and Confuted* (Kilmarnock: Printed by John Wilson, 1787), 36-37.

He obviously identifies the Quaker light within as a private spirit, rejecting that "light", "because we are commanded to prove all things, and to try the spirits [...]".[26] Quaker claims to immediate revelation were examples of the use of "private spirits" to establish religious truth. Dickson rightly recognises that this was the intended use of the expression "private spirits". There is no evidence to suggest that the supporters of Westminster orthodoxy considered that "private spirits" was a phrase which described a source of genuine, immediate divine revelation.

Moreover, the affirmation by the Westminster divines in *WCF* 1:1 that former modes of revelation had ceased, together with their acknowledgement that the "illumination" of the Holy Spirit was sufficient for the contemporary Christian (*WCF* 1:6), is further confirmation of their desire to reject any extra-biblical immediate revelation by the Spirit.

The traditional interpretation of the term "private spirits", as we have outlined it, was influential and enduring. Two centuries later, we find a Scottish Reformed theologian, William Cunningham, in his *Theological Lectures,* deriving the same meaning from *WCF* 1:10. For Cunningham, the reference to private spirits is a claim to false revelation by "enthusiasts and fanatics":

> The private spirits here spoken of are impressions which enthusiasts and fanatics have sometimes had of views of doctrine and duty which they imagined or professed to have been communicated to them by the Spirit, apart from the statements of the written word, by the Spirit speaking to them individually through some other channel than the Scriptures[...]. [W]e have no ground to believe that the Spirit communicates to men any views of doctrine or duty, but what are contained in or may be deduced from the statements of Scripture critically understood.[27]

"Private spirits" are not genuine revelation but the opinions of individuals, which may also be false claims to supernatural extra-biblical immediate revelation. The use of the term in *WCF* 1:10 cannot be an argument for limiting the cessationist clause of *WCF* 1:1 to revelations for doctrinal purposes only.

---

[26] Dickson, *Truth's Victory over Error*, 37.

[27] William Cunningham, *Theological Lectures on Subjects Connected with Natural Theology, Evidences of Christianity, the Canon and Inspiration of Scripture* (London: James Nisbet, 1878), 611-12.

Bibliography

Primary Sources

A Declaration of the Faith and Order Owned and Practised in the Congregational Churches in England; Agreed upon and Consented unto by Their Elders and Messengers in Their Meeting at the Savoy, October 12. 1658. London: John Allen, 1659.

A Declaration of the Lords and Commons in the Parliament of England, to the Generall Assembly of the Church of Scotland. London: 1643.

A Solemne League and Covenant. London: Edw. Husbands, 1643.

A Testimony to the Truth of Jesus Christ, and to our Solemn League and Covenant; as also Against Errours, Heresies and Blasphemies of These Times, and the Toleration of Them. London: Tho. Underhill, 1648.

Ambrose, Isaac, *Ministration of and Communion with Angels.* London: Rowland Reynolds, 1673.

Ames, William, *The Saints Security, against Seducing Spirits. Or the Anointing from the Holy One the Best Teaching.* London: William Adderton, 1652.

Amyraldus, Moses (Moïse or Moisé), *A Discourse Concerning the Divine Dreams Mention'd in Scripture, Together with the Marks and Character by which They Might be Distinguished from Vain Delusions. In a Letter to Monsieur Gaches by Moses Amyraldus,* Lorrde. Ja. (translator). London: Walter Kettilby, 1676.

Annotations upon All the Books of the Old and New Testament: This Third, above the First and Second, Edition so Enlarged, As They Make an Entire Commentary on the Sacred Scripture: The Like Never before Published in English. Wherein the Text is Explained, Doubts Resolved, Scriptures Parallel'd, and Various Readings Observed; By the Labour of Certain Learned Divines Thereunto Appointed, and Therein Employed, As is Expressed in the Preface, 2 vols [vol. 2 starts at Isaiah]. London: Evan Tyler, 1657.

Aquinas, Thomas, *Commentary on Saint Paul's Epistle to the Ephesians.* Albany: Magi books, 1966.

—, *Summa Theologiae,* 60 vols. London: Blackfriars; and Eyre & Spottiswoode; New York: McGraw-Hill, 1964-1976.

Arrowsmith, John, *Armilla Catechetica. A Chain of Principles; Or, An Orderly Concatenation of Theological Aphorismes and Exercitations*[...]". Cambridge: Cambridge University, 1659.

— *Englands Ebenezer or Stone of Help*[...]". London: Samuel Man, 1645.

— *ΘΕΑΝΘΡΩΠΟΣ; or, God-Man.* London: Humphrey Moseley and William Wilson, 1660.

— *The Covenant Avenging Sword Brandished.* London: Samuel Man, 1642.

Ash, Simeon, *The Best Refuge, for the Most Oppressed*. London: Edward Brewster and John Burroughs, 1642.
— *Gray Hayres Crowned with Grace: A Sermon Preached at Redriff near London, Aug. 1, 1654. at the Funerall of that Reverend [...] Mr. Thomas Gataker*. London: George Sawbridge, 1655.
— *The Church Sinking, Saved by Christ*. London: Edward Brewster, 1645.
Augustine, Henry Chadwick (tr.), *Saint Augustine: Confessions*. Oxford: Oxford University Press, 1992.
Baillie, Robert (or Baylie), *A Dissuasive from the Errours of the Time: Wherein the Tenets of the Principall Sects, Especially of the Independents, are Drawn Together in One Map, for the Most Part, in Words of Their own Authours, and Their Maine Principles are Examined by the Touch-stone of the Holy Scriptures*. London: Samuel Gellibrand, 1645.
— *Anabaptism, the True Fountaine of Independency, Antinomy, Brownism, Familisme, and Most of the Other Errours, which for the Time doe Trouble the Church of England, Unsealed*. London: Samuel Gellibrand, 1647.
— *The Letters and Journals of Robert Baillie, A. M. Principal of the University of Glasgow M.DC.XXXVII.-M.DC.LXII.*, 3 vols., ed. David Laing. Edinburgh: Bannatyne Club, 1841-1842.
Ball, John, *A Short Treatise Contayning all the Principall Grounds of Christian Religion*. London: Edward Brewster and Robert Bird, 1633.
— *A Treatise of the Covenant of Grace: Wherein the Graduall Breakings out of Gospel-grace from Adam to Christ are Clearly Discovered, the Differences Betwixt the Old and New Testament are Laid Open, Divers Errours of Arminians and Others are Confuted; the Nature of Uprightnesse, and the Way of Christ in Bringing the Soul into Communion with Himself, Together with Many Other Points, both Doctrinally and Practically Profitable, are Solidly Handled*. London: Simeon Ash, 1645.
Barclay, Robert, *An Apology for the True Christian Divinity*. Glasgow: R. Barclay Murdoch, 1886.
Baron [or Barron], Robert, *Ad Georgii Turnebulli Tetragonismum Pseudographum Apodixis Catholica, Sive Apologia pro Disputatione de Formali Objecto Fidei*. Aberdeen: 1631.
Baxter, Richard, *A Christian Directory: Or, A Summ of Practical Theologie and Cases of Conscience*. London: Nevil Simmons, 1678.
— *Fair Warning: The Second Part. Or XX Prophesies Concerning the Return of Popery*. London: H. Marsh, 1663.
— *Reliquiae Baxterianae: or, Mr. Richard Baxter's Narrative of the Most Memorable Passages of His Life and Times. Faithfully Publish'd from His Own Original Manuscript by Matthew Sylvester*. London: printed for T. Parkhurst, J. Robinson, J. Lawrence, and J. Dunton, 1696.

Bibliography 301

— Rich: Baxter's Confession of His Faith, Especially Concerning the Interest of Repentance and Sincere Obedience to Christ, in Our Justification & Salvation. London: Thos. Underhil and Fra. Tyton, 1655.

Bellarmino, Robert, *Disputationum Roberti Bellarmini [...] de Controuersiis Christianae Fidei, Aduersus Huius Temporis Haereticos, Tomus Secundus (tertius)[...]"*. Ingolstadii: Dauidis Sartorii, 1588.

Bond, John, *Ortus Occidentalis: Or, A Dawning in the West*. London: Fr. Eglesfield, 1645.

— *Salvation in a Mystery: Or A Prospective Glasse for Englands Case*. London: Francis Eglesfeild, 1644.

Bridge, William, *The Works of the Rev. William Bridge M.A.*, 5 vols. London: Thomas Tegg, 1845.

Briggs, C. A., *Whither?* New York: 1889.

Brown, John [of Haddington], *Help for The Ignorant Being an Essay Towards an Easy Explication of The Westminster Confession of Faith and Catechisms*. Edinburgh: William Gray, 1758.

Brown, John, *Quakerisme the Path-way to Paganisme. Or a View of the Quakers Religion: Being An Examination of the Theses and Apologie of Robert Barclay [...]*. Edinburgh: John Cairns, 1678.

Brownrig, Ralph, *Fourty Sermons*. London: John Martyn, James Allestry, and Thomas Dicas, 1661.

Burges[s][e], Anthony, *Vindiciae Legis: Or, A Vindication of the Morall Law and the Covenants, from the Errours of Papists, Arminians, Socinians, and More Especially, Antinomians*. London: Thomas Underhill, 1647.

— *The Scripture Directory, for Church-Officers and People or, a Practical Commentary Upon the Whole Third Chapter of the First Epistle of St Paul to the Corinthians[...]"*. London: Thomas Underhill, George Calvert and Henry Fletcher, 1659.

— *A Demonstration of the Day of Judgment, Against Atheists & Hereticks*. London: T. Underhill, 1657.

— *CXLV Expository Sermons Upon the Whole 17th Chapter of the Gospel According to St John: or Christ's Prayer Before His Passion Explicated, and Both Practically and Polemically Improved*. London: Thomas Underhill, 1656.

— *Spiritual Refining: Or, a Treatise of Grace and Assurance, The Use of Signs in Self Examination [...]"*. London: T[homas] U[nderhill], 1658.

— *The Difficulty of, and The Encouragements to a Reformation*. London: Thomas Underhill, 1643.

Burges, Cornelius, *Reasons Shewing the Necessity of Reformation[...]"*. London: 1660.

Burroughs, Jeremiah, *A Sermon Preached [...] 26. Novemb. 1645*. London: R. Dawlman, 1646.

— *An Exposition of the Prophecy of Hosea*. Edinburgh: James Nichol, 1865.

— *Irenicum, to the Lovers of Truth and Peace*. London: Robert Dawlman, 1645.

— *Sions Joy*. London: R. Dawlman, 1641.

— *The Saints' Treasury*. Ligonier, PA: Soli Deo Gloria, 1991 [reprint from 1656].

Byfield, Richard, *The Power of the Christ of God, Or a Treatise of Power, as It is Originally in God the Father, and by Him given to Christ His Sonne*. London: Jo. Bellamie, and Ralph Smith, 1641.
— *Zion's Answer to The Nations Ambassadors, According to Instructions Given by Isaiah From God's Mouth*. London: Ralph Smith, 1645.
Calamy, Edmund, *Englands Antidote, Against the Plague of Civil Warre*. London: Christopher Meredith, 1645.
— *Englands Looking-Glasse*. London: Chr. Meredith, 1642.
— *The Godly Mans Ark, or City of Refuge in the Day of His Distress*. London: Thomas Parkhurst and John Hancock, 1693.
Calov, Abraham, *Systema Locorum Theologicorum*. Witebergea: Sumptibus A Hartmanni, 1655-1677.
Calvin, John, *Calvin: Institutes of the Christian Religion*, 2 vols., ed. John T. McNeill. Philadelphia: The Westminster Press, 1960.
— *Calvin's Commentaries*, 22 vols. Grand Rapids, MI, MI: Baker, 1993.
— *Calvin's New Testament Commentaries*, 12 vols., eds. David Torrance, and Thomas Torrance. Grand Rapids, MI, MI: Eerdmans, 1989-93.
— *Letters of John Calvin Compiled from The Original Manuscripts and Edited with Historical Notes by Dr. Jules Bonnet*, 4 vols. Philadelphia: n.d.
— *Treatises Against The Anabaptists and Against The Libertines*. Grand Rapids, MI, MI: Baker, 1982.
Cameron, James (ed.), *The First Book of Discipline*. Edinburgh: The Saint Andrew Press, 1972.
Capel, Richard, *Capel's Remains, Being An Useful Appendix to His Excellent Treatise of Tentations. Concerning the Translations of the Holy Scriptures*. London: John Bartlet, 1658.
Carter, Thomas, *Prayers Prevalencie for Israels Safety*. London: John Bellamie and Ralph Smith, 1643.
Carter, William, *The Covenant of God with Abraham Opened [...] Together with A Short Discourse Concerning the Manifestations of God unto His People in the Last Dayes. Wherein is Shewed the Manner of the Spirits Work Therein to be in the Use of Ordinary Gifts, not by Extraordinary Revelations*. London: John Rothwell, 1654.
Cartwright, Thomas, *A Confutation of the Rhemists Translation*. Amsterdam: Theatrum Orbis Terrarum Ltd, 1971.
Caryl, Joseph, *An Exposition with Practicall Observations Continued upon the Fourth, Fifth, Sixth and Seventh Chapters of the Booke of Job*. London: H. Overton, L. Fawne, I. Rothwell, and G. Calvert, 1645.
— *The Arraignment of Unbelief, as the Grand Cause of our Nationall Non-establishment*. London: Giles Calvert, 1645.
— *The Saints Thankfull Acclamation at Christs Resumption of His Great Power and the Initials of His Kingdome*. London: Giles Calvert, 1644.
Casaubon, Meric, *A Treatise Concerning Enthusiasme, as It is an Effect of Nature: But is Mistaken by Many for Either Divine Inspiration, or Diabolical Possession*. London: Thomas Johnson, 1656.

Case, Thomas, *A Model of True Spiritual Thankfulnesse*. London: Luke Fawne, 1646.
— *A Sermon Preached before the Honourable House of Commons at Westminster, August 22. 1645*. London: Luke Fawne, 1645.
— *Gods Rising, His Enemies Scattering*. London: Luke Fawne, 1644.
— *Jehoshaphats Caveat to His Judges*. London: Luke Fawn, 1644.
— *Spirituall Whordome*. London: Luke Fawne, 1647.
Cawdrey, Daniel, *The Good Man A Publick Good*. London: Charles Greene, 1643.
Cheynell, Francis, *An Account Given to the Parliament by the Ministers Sent by Them to Oxford [...] The Chief Points Insisted on in Those Conferences are, 1. Whether Private Men might Lawfully Preach. 2. Whether the Ministers of the Church of England were Antichristian. Both which Questions were Disputed, Objections Answered, and the Truth Confirmed. 3. And Lastly, Divers of M. Erbury's Dangerous Errours which He hath Broached and Maintained, are Recited and Refuted*. London: Samuell Gellibrand, 1647.
— *A Plot for the Good of Posterity*. London: Samuel Gellibrand, 1646.
Christmas, Henry, *Preachers and Preaching in Ancient and Modern Times*. London: Ward, Lock, & co., 1878.
Church of Scotland General Assembly, *An information to all good Christians within the kingdome of England, from the noblemen, barrons, borrows, ministers, and commons of the kingdome of Scotland, for vindicating their intentions and actions from the unjust callumnies of their enemies*. Edinburgh: Printed by James Bryson, 1639.
Clarke, Samuel, *A General Martyrologie*. London: 1677.
Coleman, Thomas, *The Christians Course and Complaint, Both in the Pursuit of Happinesse Desired, and for Advantages Slipped in that Pursuit*. London: Christopher Meredith, 1643.
Conant, John, *Sermons Preach'd on Several Occasions. The Third Volume*. London: Thomas Cockerill and H. Walwyn, 1698.
Corbett, Edward, *Gods Providence*. London: Robert Bostock, 1642.
de La Marche, John, *A Complaint of the False Prophets Mariners upon the Drying up of Their Hierarchicall Euphrates. As it was Preached Publickly in the Island of Garnezey before a Sett Order of Ministers*. London: Thomas Payne, 1641.
Dell, William, *The Tryal of Spirits Both in Teachers and Hearers, Wherein is Held Forth the Clear Discovery, and Certain Downfal of the Carnal and Antichristian Clergie of These Nations. Testified from the Word of God to the University-Congregation in Cambridge. Whereunto is Added A Plain and Necessary Confutation of Divers Gross Errors Delivered by Mr Sydrach Simpson in a Sermon Preached to the Same Congregation at the Commencement, Anno 1653[...]"*. London: Giles Calvert, 1660.
Dick, John. *Lectures on Theology*, 4 vols. Edinburgh: Oliver and Boyd, 1838.
Dickson, David, *Truth's Victory over Error: Or, the True Principles of the Christian Religion, Stated and Vindicated Against the Following Heresies, viz. Arians, Arminians, Anabaptists, Antinomians, Brownists, Donatists, Epicureans, Eutychians, Erastians, Familists, Jesuits, Independents, Libertines, Manicheans, Pelagians, Papists, Quakers, Socinians, Sabellians, Sceptics, Vaninians, &c. The Whole being a

Commentary on All the Chapters of the Confession of Faith, by Way of Question and Answer: In which, the saving Truths of our Holy Religion are Confirmed and Established; and the Dangerous Errors and Opinions of its Adversaries Detected and Confuted. Kilmarnock: printed by John Wilson, 1787.

Diodati, John [or Giovanni], *Pious and Learned Annotations upon the Holy Bible.* London: Nicholas Fussell, 1664.

Durham, James, *A Complete Commentary upon the Book of the Revelation, Delivered in Several Lectures, By that Learned, Laborious, and Faithful Servant of Jesus Christ[...]"*, 2 vols. Falkirk: 1799.

Dury [or Durye], John, *Israels Call to March out of Babylon unto Jerusalem.* London: Tho. Underhill, 1646.

Edwards, Thomas, *The First and Second part of Gangraena: or a Catalogue and Discovery of Many of the Errors, Heresies, Blasphemies and Pernicious Practices of the Sectaries of this Time, Vented and Acted in England in these Four Last Years.* London: Ralph Smith, 1646.

— *The Third Part of Gangraena or, a New and Higher Discovery of the Errors, Heresies, Blasphemies, and Insolent Proceedings of the Sectaries of these Times; with Some Animadversions by Way of Confutation upon Many of the Errors and Heresies Named.* London: Ralph Smith, 1646.

Eight Letters of Dr. A. Tuckney and Dr. B. Whichcote. [Held in the British Library's London reading rooms] cited in C. A. Briggs, *Whither?* New York, 1889.

English House of Commons, *A remonstrance of the state of the kingdom. Die mercurii 15 Decemb. 1641. It is this day resolv'd upon the question, by the House of Commons; that order shall be now given for the printing of this remonstrance, of the state of the kingdom.* London: printed for Ioseph Hunscutt, 1641.

English House of Commons, *Commons Debates for 1629*, eds. W. Notestein and F. H. Relf. Minneapolis: 1921.

Fairbairn, Patrick, *The Typology of Scripture,* 2 vols. Grand Rapids, MI: Kregel, 1989 [2 vols. are bound as one, but retain separated pagination].

Flavel, John, *The Works of John Flavel,* 6 vols. London: Banner of Truth Trust, 1968.

Fleming, Robert, *The Fulfilling of the Scripture Complete; in Three Parts.* London: J. and B. Sprint, Aaron Ward, Richard Ford, and John Oswald, 1726.

Ford, Thomas, *Singing of Psalmes the Duty of Christians under the New Testament or a Vindication of that Gospel-Ordinance.* London: F. Eaglesfield, 1659.

Fox, George, *Gospel Truth Demonstrated, in a Collection of Doctrinal Books[...]".* New York: Isaac T. Hopper, 1831.

— *Something in Answer to that Book Called the Church-Faith Set Forth by Independents and Others; Agreed upon by Divine Messengers, Meeting at the Savoy in London. And also, to that Book, Intituled, the Confession of Faith, Approved on by the Church of Scotland.* London: Robert Wilson, 1660.

Foxe, John, *Actes and Monuments of these Latter and Perilous Dayes, Touching Matters of the Church,* 8 vols. London: R.B. Seeley and W. Burnside, 1839.

Fuller, Thomas, *Truth Maintained.* Oxford: 1643.

Gataker, Thomas, *A Sparke Towards the Kindling of Sorrow for Sion.* London: William Sheffard, 1621.

— *His Vindication of the Annotations by Him Published Upon these Words, Thus Saith the Lord, Learn not the Way of the Heathen, and be not Dismayed at the Signes of Heaven, for the Heathen are Dismayed at them. Jer. 10.2.* London: Richard Thrayle, 1653.

— *Of the Nature and Use of Lots; a Treatise Historicall and Theologicall.* London: William Bladen, 1619.

— *Shadowes without Substance, or, Pretended New Lights.* London: Robert Bostock, 1646.

Gillespie, George, *A Sermon Preached[...]27th. of August, 1645.* London: Robert Bostock, 1645.

— *Aarons Rod Blossoming[...]".* London: Richard Whitaker, 1646.

— *An Assertion of the Government of the Church of Scotland, in the Points of Ruling-Elders, and of the Authority of Presbyteries and Synods.* Edinburgh: James Bryson, 1641.

— "Notes of Debates and Proceedings of the Assembly of Divines and other Commissioners at Westminster. February 1644 to January 1645", *The Works of George Gillespie*, ed. David Meek. Edmonton: SWRB, 1991, vol. 2, 1-120.

— *The Works of George Gillespie*, 2 vols., ed. David Meek. Edmonton: SWRB, 1991.

Gillespie, Thomas, *An Essay on the Continuance of Immediate Revelations of Facts and Future Events.* Edinburgh: W. Gray, 1771.

Goode, William, *The Modern Claims to the Possession of the Extraordinary Gifts of the Spirit[...].*
London: J. Hatchard and Son. 1834. [to be distinguished from the Puritan and Westminster divine below]

Goode, William, *Jacob Raised: Or, the Means of Making a Nation Happy Both in Spiritual and Temporal Priviledges.* London: Nath. Webb and Will. Grantham, 1647.

— *The Discoverie of a Publique Spirit.* London: Christopher Meredith, 1645.

Goodwin, Thomas, *The Heart of Christ in Heaven, Towards Sinners on Earth. Or, a Treatise Demonstrating the Gracious Disposition and Tender Affection of Christ in His Humane Nature Now in Glory, unto His Members under all Sorts of Infirmities, Either of Sin or Misery.* London: R. Dawlman, 1642.

— *The Works of Thomas Goodwin, D.D.*, 12 vols. Edinburgh: James Nichol, 1861-63.

Gouge, William, *A Learned and Very Useful Commentary on the Whole Epistle to the Hebrewes.* London: Joshua Kirton, 1655.

— *Gods Three Arrowes: Plague, Famine, Sword, In Three Treatises.* London: Edward Brewster, 1631.

— *The Extent of Gods Providence.* London: Edward Brewster, 1631.

— *The Progresse of Divine Providence.* London: Joshua Kirton, 1645.

Greenham, Richard, *The Workes of the Reverend and Faithfull Servant of Jesus Christ M. Richard Greenham.* London: Cuthbert Burbie, 1605.

Greenhill, William, *An Exposition of Ezekiel.* Edinburgh: Banner of Truth Trust, 1994.

Guild, William, *The Throne of David.* Oxford: Rob. Blagrave, 1659.

Haak, Theodore (translator), *The Dutch Annotations upon the Whole Bible: Or, All the Holy Canonical Scriptures of the Old and New Testaments, Together with, and According to Their Own Translation of All the Text: As Both the One and the Other were Ordered and Appointed by the Synod of Dort, 1618. and Published by Authority, 1637,* 2 vols. [vol. 2 starts at Jeremiah]. London: John Rothwell, Joshua Kirton, and Richard Tomlins, 1657.

Hacket, John, *A Century of Sermons upon Several Remarkable Subjects.* London: Robert Scott, 1675.

Hall, Edmund, *Digitus Testium, or a Dreadful Alarm to the Whole Kingdom.* London: 1650.

Hammond, Henry, *A Brief Vindication of Three Passages in the Practical Catechisme, from the Censures Affixt on Them by the Ministers of London, in a Book Entitled, A Testimony to the Truth of Jesus Christ &c.* London: Richard Royston, 1648.

— *Sermons Preached by that Eminent Divine Henry Hammond, D.D.* London: Robert Pawlet, 1675.

Harding, W, *The Trial of the Rev. Edward Irving, M.A. before the London Presbytery.* Edinburgh: W. Harding, 1832.

Harris, John, *The Puritanes Impurity: Or the Anatomie of a Puritan or Seperatist, by Name and Profession, Wherein is Declared the Differences betwixt the True Protestant and a Puritane Made Manifest by the Sincerity of the One and Hypocrisie of the Other.* London: printed by T. Fawcet, 1641.

Henderson, Alexander, *A Sermon Preached before the Right Honourable House of Lords.* London: Robert Bostock, 1645.

— *A Sermon Preached[...]December 27. 1643.* London: Robert Bostock, 1644.

— *Reformation of Church-Government in Scotland, Cleered from Some Mistakes and Prejudices.* London: Robert Bostock, 1644.

Herle, Charles, *Ahab's Fall by His Prophet's Flatteries.* London: J. Wright, 1644.

Heyricke, Richard, *Three Sermons Preached at the Collegiate Church in Manchester.* London: L. Fawne, 1641.

Hill, Thomas, *Six Sermons, of Thomas Hill D.D. Master of Trinity Colledge in Cambridge.* London: Peter Cole and Richard Westbrook, 1649.

— *The Best and Worst of Paul and his Character in Both Conditions.* Cambridge: 1648.

— *The Good Old Way Gods Way, to Soule-refreshing Rest.* London: John Bellamie and Philemon Stephens, 1644.

— *The Militant Church Triumphant over the Dragon and His Angels.* London: John Bellamie and Ralph Smith, 1643.

— *The Trade of Truth Advanced.* London: John Bellamie, Philemon Stephens, and Ralph Smith, 1642.

— *Truth and Love Happily Married in the Saints, and in the Churches of Christ.* London: Peter Cole, 1648.

Hog, James, *Notes about the Spirit's Operations, for Discovering from the Word, their Nature and Evidence, Together with Diverse Remarks for Detecting the Enthusiastical Delusions of the Cevennois, Antonia Bourignon, and Others[...] Being the Substance of Several Private Discourses on Gal. 3.2.* Edinburgh: 1709.

Howe, John, *The Whole Works of John Howe*, 8 vols. London: F. Westley, 1822.
Howie, John, *The Scots Worthies*. Edinburgh: Oliphant, Anderson & Ferrier, n.d.
Hyde, Ed, *Christ and His Church: or, Christianity Explained, under Seven Evangelical and Ecclesiastical Heads*. Oxford: Rich Davis, 1658.
James I, *The Workes of the Most High and Myghtie Prince*. London: [printed by] Robert Barker and John Bill, 1616.
James I, *Political Works of James*, ed. Charles McIlwain. New York: Russell & Russell, 1965.
Jamison, William, *Verus Patroclus: Or, the Weapons of Quakerism, the Weakness of Quakerism*. Edinburgh: 1689.
Jenkyn, William, *Reformation's Remora; or Temporizing the Stop of Building the Temple*. London: Christopher Meredith, 1646.
Johnston, Archibald, *Diary of Sir Archibald Johnston of Wariston 1632-1639*, ed. George Morison Paul. Edinburgh: Scottish History Society, 1911.
Journal of the House of Commons. London: 1803. (The chronology is somewhat complicated by the Journal's use of Regnal years which did not necessarily coincide with calendar years.)
George Keith, *George Keith's Explications of Divers Passages Contained in his Former Books[...]"*. London: B. Alymer and Rich. Baldwin, 1697.
— *Help in Time of Need, from the God of Help. To the People of the (so called) Church of Scotland, Especially the Once more Zealous and Professing, Who Have so Shamefully Degenerated and Declined from that Which their Fathers the Primitive Protestants Attained unto [...] Being Certain Particulars Very Weighty, and of Great Concernment for Them to Consider Seriously[...]"*. Aberdeen: 1665.
— *Immediate Revelation (or Jesus Christ the Eternal Son of God, Revealed in Man. Revealing the Knowledge of God, and the Things of His Kingdom, Immediately) Not Ceased, butRemaining a Standing and Perpetual Ordinance in the Church of Christ, and being of Indispensable Necessity, as to the Whole Body in General, so to Every Member Thereof: Every True Believer in Particular, Asserted and Demonstrated. And the Objections that Have Any Seeming Weight Against It Answered*. London: 1675.
— *The Deism of William Penn and his Brethren, Destructive to the Christian Religion, Exposed and Plainly Laid Open, in The Examination and Refutation of His Late Reprinted Book[...]"*. London: Brab. Aylmer, 1699.
— *The Presbyterian and Independent Visible Churches in New England and Elsewhere, Brought to the Test, and Examined According to the Doctrine of the Holy Scriptures, in Their Doctrine, Ministry, Worship, Constitution, Government, Sacraments and Sabbath Day, and Found to be No True Church of Christ*. Philadelphia: Will. Bradford, 1689.
— *The Pretended Antido[t]e Proved Poysen*. Philadelphia: Will. Bradford, 1690.
— *The Way Cast Up, and the Stumbling-blocks Removed from Before the Feet of Those, Who are Seeking the Way to Zion, with Their Faces Thitherward: Containing an Answere to a Postscript, Printed at the End of Samuel Rutherford's Letters, Third Edition, by a Nameless Author[...]'*. Aberdeen: 1677.

Kirk, James (ed.), *The Second Book of Discipline*. Edinburgh: The Saint Andrew Press, 1980.

Kirkton, James, *The Secret and True History of the Church of Scotland, from the Restoration to the Year 1678*. Edinburgh: John Ballantyne, 1817.

Knox, John, *The Works of John Knox*, 6 vols., ed. D. Laing. Edinburgh: James Thin, 1895.

Langley, John, *Gemitus Columbae: The Mournfull Note of the Dove*. London: Philemon Stephens, 1644.

Leigh, Edward, *A Systeme or Body of Divinity: Consisting of Ten books. Wherein the Fundamentals and Main Grounds of Religion are Opened: The Contrary Errours Refuted[...]"*. London: William Lee, 1654.

Leslie, William, *Vindiciae Theoligicae pro Perseverantia Sanctorum in Gratia Salvifica*. Aberdeen: E. Rabanus, 1627.

Ley, John, *An Acquittance or Discharge [...]"*. London: K. Brewster, 1655.

— *Light for Smoke or a Cleare and Distinct Reply]...]to a Darke and Confused Answer in a Booke Made, and Intituled The Smoke in the Temple, by John Saltmarsh[...]"*. London: Christopher Meridith, 1646.

Lightfoot, John, "The Journal of the Proceedings of the Assembly of Divines, from January 1, 1643 [actually 1 July 1643], to December 31, 1644", *The Whole Works of the Rev. John Lightfoot, D.D.*, ed. John Pitman. London: Printed by J. F. Dove, 1824, vol. 13, 1-344.

— *The Whole Works of the Rev. John Lightfoot, D.D.* 13 vols., ed. J. R. Pitman. London: Printed by J. F. Dove, 1822-24.

Love, Richard, *The Watchmans Watchword*. Cambridge: Cambridge University, 1642.

Luther, Martin, *Luther's Works*, 55 vols., ed. Jaroslav Pelikan. Saint Louis: Concordia Publishing house, 1970.

Lyford, William, *An Apologie for our Publick Ministerie and Infant-Baptism*. London: Richard Royston, 1657.

— *The Plain Mans Senses Exercised to Discern Both Good and Evil: Or, A Discovery of the Errors, Heresies, and Blasphemies of These Times, and the Toleration of Them as They are Collected and Testified Against by the Ministers of London[...]"*. London: Richard Royston and Edward Forrest, 1655.

Manton, Thomas, *An Exposition of the Epistle of James*. London: The Banner of Truth Trust, 1962.

— *The Complete Works of Thomas Manton, D.D.*, 22 vols. London: James Nisbet, 1870-1873.

Marshall, Stephen, *A Peace-Offering to God*. London: Samuel Man, 1641.

— *A Sacred Record to be Made of Gods Mercies to Zion*. London: Stephen Bowtell, 1645.

— *A Sermon of the Baptizing of Infants*. London: Stephen Bowtell, 1644.

— *A Sermon Preached[...]November 17.1640, upon 2 Chron. 15.2..* London: Samuel Man, 1641.

— *Meroz Cursed*. London: Samuel Gellibrand, 1641.

— *Reformation and Desolation*. London: Samuel Gellibrand, 1642.

── *The Right Understanding of the Times*. London: Stephen Bowtell, 1647.
── *The Works of Mr Stephen Marshall*. London: printed by Peter and Edward Cole, 1661.
Mather, Cotton, Allen, James, Moody, Joshua and Willard, Samuel, *The Principles of the Protestant Religion Maintained, and Churches of New-England, in Profession and Exercise thereof Defended, Against All the Calumnies of One George Keith, a Quaker, in a Book Lately Published in Pensilvania, to Undermine Them Both.* Boston: Richard Pierce, 1690.
Maynard [or Mainard], John, *The Law of God Ratified*[...]". London: Francis Tyton, 1674.
── *The Beauty and Order of the Creation*. London: Henry Eversden, 1668.
M'Crie, Thomas (ed.), *The Life of Mr Robert Blair, Minister of St Andrews, Containing his Autobiography, from 1593 to 1636.* Edinburgh: Wodrow Society, 1848.
Mitchell, Alex F. and Struthers, John (eds.), *Minutes of the Sessions of the Westminster Assembly of Divines.* Edmonton: SWRB, 1991.
Mitchell, Alexander and Christie, James (eds.), *The Records of the Commissions of the General Assemblies of the Church of Scotland Holden in Edinburgh the Years 1648-1649.* Edinburgh: Scottish
Historical Society, 1896.
Mitchell, Alexander F., *Catechisms of the Second Reformation*. London: James Nisbet, 1886.
Munro, Alexander, *Presbyterian Inquisition; As it was Lately Practised against the Professors of the Colledge of Edinburgh. August and September. 1690. In Which the Spirit of Presbytery and Their Present Method of Procedure, is Plainly Discovered, Matter of Fact by Undeniable Instances Cleared, and Libels against Particular Persons Discussed.* London: J. Hindmarsh, 1691.
Neal, Daniel, *The History of the Puritans; or, Protestant Nonconformists; from the Reformation in 1517, to the Revolution in 1688*, 3 vols. London: Thomas Tegg and son, 1837.
Newcomen, Matthew, *A Sermon, Tending to Set Forth the Right Use of the Disasters that Befall Our Armies.* London: Christopher Meredith, 1644.
Nye, Philip, *Beames of Former Light, Discovering how Evil it is to Impose Doubtfull and Disputable Formes or Practises upon Ministers; Especially under the Penalty of Ejection for Non-conformity unto the Same. As also Something about Catechizing.* London: Adoniram Byfield, 1660.
── *A Case of Great and Present Use*. London: Jonathan Robinson, 1677.
Owen, John, *An Exposition of the Epistle to the Hebrews*, 7 vols. Edinburgh: Banner of Truth Trust, 1991.
── *The Correspondence of John Owen (1616-1683): with an Account of his Life and Work*, ed.
Peter Toon. Cambridge: James Clark, 1970.
── *The Works of John Owen,* 16 vols. Edinburgh: The Banner of Truth Trust, 1979.

Palmer, Herbert, *The Necessity and Encouragement of Utmost Venturing for the Churches Help: Together with the Sin, Folly, and Mischief of Self-Idolising.* London: John Bellamie, 1643.
— *The Glasse of Gods Providence towards His Faithfull Ones.* London: Th. Underhill, 1644.
Parker, W [William?]., *The Late Assembly of Divines Confession of Faith Examined. As it was Presented by Them unto the Parliament. Wherein Many of Their Excesses and Defects, of Their Confusions and Disorders, of Their Errors and Contradictions are Presented, Both to Themselves and Others.* London: 1651.
Parson, John, *An Answer to Dr. Burges His Word by Way of Postscript.* London: Nathaniel Brook, 1660.
Perkins, William, *A Commentarie or Exposition, upon the Five First Chapters of the Epistle to the Galatians [...] by [...] W. Perkins. Now Published for the Benefit of the Church, and Continued with a Supplement upon the Sixth Chapter, by Rafe Cudworth.* Cambridge: John Legat, 1604.
— *A Commentary on Hebrews 11.* New York: Pilgrim Press, 1991, [reprint of 1909 edition].
— *The Work of William Perkins,* ed. Ian Breward. Appleford: The Sutton Courtney Press, 1970.
— *The Workes of that Famous and Worthie Minister of Christ in the Universitie of Cambridge, M. W. Perkins,* 3 vols. Cambridge: University of Cambridge, 1609.
— *The Workes of that Famous and Worthy Minister of Christ in the Universitie of Cambridge, M. W. Perkins,* 3 vols. London: printed by John Haviland, 1631.
Perne, Andrew, *Gospell Courage, or Christian Resolution for God, and His Truth.* London: Stephen Bowtell, 1643.
Peterkin, Alexander, *Records of the Kirk of Scotland, Containing the Acts and Proceedings of the General Assemblies, from the Year 1638 Downwards*[...]". Edinburgh: John Sutherland, 1838.
Proffet, Nicolas, *Englands Impenitencie under Smiting, Causing Anger to Continue, and the Destroying Hand of God to be Stretched Forth Still.* London: Christopher Meredith, 1645.
Rathband, William, *A Briefe Narration of some Church Courses Held in Opinion and Practise in the Churches Lately Erected in New England.* London: Edward Brewster, 1644.
— *A Most Grave, and Modest Confutation of the Errors of the Sect, Commonly Called Brownists or: Separatists.* London: Edward Brewster and George Badger, 1644.
— *Reasons of the present judgement of the University of Oxford, Concerning the Solemne League and Covenant. The Negative Oath. The Ordinances Concerning Discipline and Worship.* Oxford: 1647.
Reyner, William, *Babylons Ruining-Earthquake and the Restauration of Zion.* London: Samuel Enderby, 1644.
Reynolds, Edward, *A Treatise of the Passions and Faculties of the Soul of Man. With the Several Dignities and Corruptions Thereunto Belonging.* London: Robert Boulter, 1678.

Bibliography

— *An Explication of the CX. Psalm [...] Being the Substance of Several Sermons Preached at Lincolns Inne*. London: R[obert?]. B[ostock?]., 1656.
— *Divine Efficacy without Humane Power*. London: George Thomason, 1660.
— *Self-Deniall*. London: George Thomason, 1659.
— *The First Sermon upon Hosea*. London: Robert Bostock, 1649.
— *Three Treatises of the Vanity of The Creature. The Sinfulnesse of Sinne. The Life of Christ*. London:
Rob. Bostocke and George Badger, 1642.
— *Twenty Sermons Preached upon Several Occasions*. London: George Thomason, 1660.
Robinson, John, *The Peoples Plea for the Exercise of Prophecy against Master J. Yates His Monopolie*. [Leyden?], 1641.
Rogers, John, *The Displaying of an Horrible Secte of Grosses and Wicked heretiques, and what Doctrine they Teach in Corners. Newely Set Foorth by J. R. 1578. Whereunto There is Annexed a Confession of Certain Articles, Which was Made by Two of the Familie of Love, being Examined before a Iustice of the Peace, the 28 of May 1561, Touching Their Errours Taught Amongest Them in Their Assemblies*. London: John Day, 1579.
Rollock, Robert, *A Treatise of Effectual Calling*. London: 1603.
— *Select Works of Robert Rollock*, 2 vols. ed. William Gunn. Edinburgh: 1849.
Ruchat, Abraham, *Histoire de la Réformation de la Suisse, où l'on voit tout ce qui s'est Passé de plus Remarquable, depuis l'An 1516. jusqu'en l'An 1556., dans les Églises des XIII. Cantons, & des États Confédérez qui Composent avec eux le L. Corps Helvétique*. Geneva: Marc-Michel Bousquet, 1727.
Russel, John Fuller (ed.), *The Judgement of the Anglican Church (posterior to the Reformation) on the Sufficiency of Holy Scripture and the Authority of the Holy Catholic Church in Matters of Faith*. London: A.H. Baily & Co, 1838.
Rutherford (or Rutherfurd), Samuel, *A Free Disputation against Pretended Liberty of Conscience Tending to Resolve Doubts Moved by Mr. John Goodwin, John Baptist, Dr. Jer. Taylor, the Belgick Arminians, Socinians, and Other Authors Contending for Lawlesse Liberty, or Licentious Toleration of Sects and Heresies*. London: Andrew Crook, 1649.
— *A Modest Survey of the Secrets of Antinomianisme*. London: Andrew Crooke, 1648.
— *A Sermon Preached [...].Janu. 31.1643*. London: Richard Whittakers and Andrew Crooke, 1644.
— *A Sermon Preached before the Right Honorable House of Lords,[...]Wednesday the 25. day of June, 1645*. London: Andrew Crook, 1645.
— *A Survey of the Spirituall Antichrist. [...]"*. London: Andrew Crooke, 1648.
— *Christ Dying and Drawing Sinners to Himself, Or, a Survey of Our Saviour in His Soule-suffering: His Lovelynesse in His Death, and the Efficacie Thereof*. London: Andrew Crooke, 1647.
— *Exercitationes apologeticae pro divina gratia, in quibus vindicatur doctrina orthodoxa adversus Jacobum Arminium & Jesuitas*. Amsterdam: 1636.

— *Influences of the Life of Grace. Or, a Practical Treatise Concerning the Way, Manner, and Means of Having and Improving of Spiritual Dispositions, and Quickning Influences from Christ the Resurrection and the Life.* London: Andrew Crook, 1659.

— *Mr Rutherfoord's Letters. The Third Edition now Divided in Three Parts.* 1675.

— *Rutherford's Catechism Containing the Sum of Christian Religion.* Edinburgh: Blue Banner Productions, 1998.

— *The Covenant of Life Opened or a Treatise of the Covenant of Grace.* Edinburgh: Robert Broun, 1655.

— *The Divine Right of Church-Government and Excommunication [...]".* London: Christopher Meredith, 1646.

— *The Due Right of Presbyteries or, A Peaceable Plea for the Government of the Church of Scotland.* London: Richard Whittaker and Andrew Crook, 1644.

Salnar, *An Harmony of the Confessions of the Faith of the Christian and Reformed Churches [...] of Europe. [with notes by S. Goulart.] [...] In the Name of the Churches of France and Belgia [...] Submitted to the [...] Judgement of All Other Churches [...]Newlie Translated out of [the] Latine [...]Also [...]the Confession of the Church of Scotland.* Cambridge: T. Thomas, 1586.

Saltmarsh, John, *An End of One Controversie: Being an Answer or Letter to Master Ley's Large Last Book Called Light for Smoke.* London: G. Calvert, 1646.

— *The Smoke in the Temple, Wherein is a Designe for Peace and Reconciliation of Believers[...]".* London: G. Calvert, 1646.

— *Twelve Strange Prophesies, besides Mother Shiptons. With the Predictions of John Saltmarsh.* London: 1648.

Schaff, Philip (ed.), *The Creeds of Christendom*, 3 vols. Grand Rapids, MI: Baker, 1985.

Scudder, Henry, *Gods Warning to England by the Voyce of His ROD.* London: Philemon Stephens and Edward Blackmore, 1644.

— *The Christians Daily Walk in Holy Security and Peace.* London: Henry Cripps and Lodowick Lloyd, 1652.

— *The Christian's Daily Walk.* Harrisburg, Va.: Sprinkle Publications, 1984.

Seaman, Lazarus, *A Glasse for the Times.* London: John Rothwell, 1650.

Sedgewick[e][or Sedgwick], Obadiah, *A Thanksgiving-Sermon [...]".* London: Samuel Gellibrand, 1644.

— *An Arke against a Deluge: Or Safety in Dangerous Times.* London: Samuel Gellibrand, 1644.

— *The Bowels of Tender Mercy Sealed in the Everlasting Covenant [...]".* London: Adoniram Byfield, 1661.

Selden, John, *A Prophecy, Lately Found Amongst the Collections of Famous Mr John Selden.* London: 1659.

— *Table-Talk: Being the Discourses of John Selden Esq; or His Sence of Various Matters of Weight and High Consequence Relating Especially to Religion and State.* London: E. Smith, 1689.

Several Choice Prophecyes of the Incomparable and Famous Dr Martin Luther, as also, the Remarkable Prophecy of the Learned and Reverend Dr Musculus. Collected by R.C. London: Edward Thomas, 1666.

James Sharpe, *The Triall of the Protestant Private Spirit* (1630)

Simpson, Sydrach, *Two Books of Mr Sydrach Simpson[...] I. Of faith, Or, Beleeving is Receiving Christ; And Receiving Christ is Believing. II. Of Covetousness.* London: Peter Cole, 1658.

— *Two Books of Mr Sydrach Simpson[...]I. Of Unbelief, or the Want of Readiness to Lay Hold on the Comfort Given by Christ, II. Not Going to Christ for Life and Salvation is an Exceeding Great Sin, Yet it is Pardonable.* London: Peter Cole, 1658.

Smith, Hugh, *An Apology for or Vindication of the Oppressed Persecuted Ministers & Professors of the Presbyterian Reformed Religion in the Church of Scotland [...]".* London?: 1677.

Spurstow[e], William, *The Spiritual Chymist: Or, Six Decad[e]s of Divine Meditations on Several Subjects.* London: 1666.

— *The Wels of Salvation Opened: Or, A Treatise Discovering the Nature, Preciousness, Usefulness of Gospel-Promises, and Rules for the Right Application of Them.* London: Ralph Smith, 1655.

ΣATANA NOHMATA: *Or, the Wiles of Satan in a Discourse upon 2. Cor.2.11.* London: 1666.

Stapleton, Thomas, *Principiorum Fidei Doctrinalium Demonstratio Methodica, per Controversias Septem in Librie Duodecim Tradita.* Paris: 1578.

Sterry, Peter, *England's Deliverance from the Northern Presbytery, Compared with its Deliverance from the Roman Papacy.* London: Peter Cole, 1652.

— *The Clouds in which Christ Comes.* London: R. Dawlman, 1648.

Strickland, John, *Immanuel, or The Church Triumphing in God with Us.* London: Henry Overton, 1644.

Strong, William, 'Ημερα' Αποκαλυψεως. *The Day of Revelation of the Righteous Judgement of God.* London: I. Benson, and I. Saywell, 1645.

— *A Discourse of the Two Covenants: Wherein the Nature, Differences and Effects of the Covenant of Works and of Grace are Distinctly, Rationally, Spiritually and Practically Discussed; Together with the Considerable Quantity of Practical Cases Dependent Thereon.* London: Francis Tyton, 1678.

— *A Treatise Shewing the Subordination of the Will of Man unto the Will of God.* London: Francis Tyton, 1657.

— *Communion with God in Ordinances[...]".* London: Fra. Tyton, 1656.

— *XXXI. Select Sermons, Preached on Several Occasions.* London: Francis Tyton, 1656.

Taylor, Francis, *Gods Glory in Mans Happiness: with the Freeness of His Grace in Electing us. Together with Many Arminian Objections Answered.* London: G. and H. Eversden, 1654.

Tesdale, Christopher, *Hierusalem: Or a Vision of Peace.* London: Phil. Stephens, 1644.

The Book of the Universall Kirk of Scotland, ed. T. Thomson, 3 vols. Edinburgh: The Maitland Club, 1839-1845.

The Confession of Faith and the Larger and Shorter Catechism, First Agreed upon by the Assembly of Divines at Westminster. And now Appointed by the General Assembly of the Kirk of Scotland, etc. [With "The Summe of saving knowledge," by David Dickson and James Durham.]. London: Thomas Malthus, 1683.

The Confession of Faith, Larger Catechism, Shorter Catechism, Directory of Public Worship, Presbyterian Church Government. Edinburgh: William Blackwood, 1949.

The Confession of Faith; the Larger and Shorter Catechisms[...]". Glasgow: Free Presbyterian Publications, 1988.

The Form of Church-Government to be used in the Church of England and Ireland: Agreed upon by the Lords and Commons Assembled in Parliament, After Advice had with the Assembly of Divines. London: John Wright, 1648.

The Generall Assemblies Answer and Declaration to the Parliament of England. Edinburgh: 1643.

The Harmonious Consent of the Ministers of the Province within the County Palatine of Lancaster. Edinburgh: Printed by Evan Tyler, 1648.

The Parliamentary and Constitutional History of England from the Earliest Times to the Restoration of King Charles 2nd, 24 vols. London: 1751-1762.

Tuckney, Anthony, *A Good Day Well Improved[...]to Which is Annexed a Sermon on 2 Tim. 1.13*. London: I. Rothwell, 1656.

— *Forty Sermons upon Several Occasions [...]"*. London: Jonathan Robinson and Brabazon Aylmer, 1676.

Twisse, William, *The Scriptures Sufficiency To Determine All Matters of Faith, Made Good against the Papist: OR, That a Christian May be Infallibly Certain of His Faith and Religion by the Holy Scriptures*. London: Matthew Keynton, 1656.

Usher (or Ussher), James, *A Body of Divinity, or The Summe and Substance of Christian Religion; Catechistically Propounded, and Explained, by Way of Question and Answer: Methodically and Familiarly Handled. Collected long since out of Sundry Authors, and Reduced unto One Common Method by James Usher B. of Armagh*. London: Tho. Downes and Geo. Badger, 1649.

— *Strange and Remarkable Prophesies and Predictions of the Holy, Learned, and Excellent James Usher, Late L. Arch-Bishop of Armargh, and Lord Primate of Ireland*. 1681.

— *The Strange and Remarkable Prophecies and Predictions of the Holy Learned and Excellent James Usher etc*. London: 1780.

Valentine, Thomas, *A Charge against the Jews, and the Christian World, for not Coming to Christ who would have Freely Given them Eternall Life*. London: John Rothwell, 1647.

Vermigli, Peter Martyr, *The Common Places, of the Most Famous and Renowned Divine Doctor Peter Martyr[...]Translated and Partlie Gathered by Anthonie Marten*. London: 1583.

Vicars, John, *The Schismatick Sifted. Or the Picture of Independents, Freshly and Fairly Washt-over Again*. London: Nathanael Webb, and William Grantham, 1646.

Vines, Richard, *The Happinesse of Israel[...]March 12th 1644*. London: Abel Roper, 1645.
Walker, George, *The Key of Saving Knowledge, Opening out of the Holy Scriptures, the Right Way, and Straight Passage to Eternal Life[...]"*. London: 1640.
Warfield, Benjamin, *Counterfeit Miracles*. London: Banner of Truth, 1972.
— *The Westminster Assembly and its Work*. Cherry Hill: Mack Publishing company, 1972.
— *The Works of Benjamin B. Warfield*, 10 vols. Grand Rapids, MI: Baker, 1991.
Whichcote, Benjamin, *Moral and Religious Aphorisms: Collected from the Manuscript Papers of the Reverend and Learned Doctor Whichcote; and Published in MDCVIII, by Dr. Jeffery. Now Re-published, with Very Large Additions, from the Transcripts of the Latter, by Samuel Salter[...] to which are Added, Eight Letters: which Passed between Dr. Whichcote[...] and Dr. Tuckney[...] on Several Very Interesting Subjects*. London: J. Payne, 1753.
Whitaker, William, *Disputation on Holy Scripture*. Cambridge: The University Press, 1849.
Whitakero, Guilielmo, *Disputatio de Sacra Scriptura*. Cantabrigia: 1588.
White, John, *A Way to the Tree of Life Discovered in Sundry Directions for the Profitable Reading of the Scriptures: Wherein is Described Occasionally The Nature of a Spirituall Man*. London: R. Royston, 1647.
— *The Troubles of Jerusalems Restauration, or, the Churches Reformation[...]*. London: 1646.
Whitehead, George, *The Law and Light Within, The most sure Rule or Light, which Sheweth the Right Use and End of the Scripture, Manifested in Opposition to Several False Principles Inserted in a Book Intituled Scripture Light the Most Sure Light, by William Bridge, the Great Pastor and Reverend Father, so Accounted, of the Church at Yarmouth in Norfolk*. London: 1662.
Wilkinson, Henry, *A Catechisme, Contayning a Short Exposition of the Points in the Ordinary Catechisme, with Proofes of the Same out of the Scripture[...]"*. London: Robert Birde, 1629 [Westminster divine Wilkinson Snr.].
Wilkinson, Henry, *Babylons Ruine, Jerusalems Rising*. London: Chr. Meredith and Sa. Gellibrand, 1644 [Westminster divine Wilkinson Jnr.].
Wilkinson, Henry, *Three Decad[e]s of Sermons Lately Preached to the University at St Mary's Church in Oxford*. Oxford: Thomas Robinson, 1660 [known as Dean Harry, and not a Westminster divine].
Wilson, Thomas, *Jerichoes Down-Fall*. London: John Bartlet, 1643.
Wodrow, Robert, *Analecta: Or Materials for a History of Remarkable Providences; Mostly Relating to Scotch Ministers and Christians*, 4 vols. Edinburgh: Maitland Club, 1834, 1842.
Woodcock, Francis, *The Two Witnesses*. London: Luke Fawne, 1643.

Manuscripts

Dr. Williams's Library, London

"Minutes of the Sessions of the Assembly of Divines, from August 4th, 1643, to March 25th, 1652", 3 vols. in folio Ms. are held in the Dr. Williams's Library, London. We have used the transcribed minutes, prepared by E. Maunde Thompson, 5 vols., "Minutes of the Sessions of the Assembly of Divines from August 4th, 1643 to April 24th 1652 ." The transcribed volumes are held at New College Library in Edinburgh. The original vols. 1 and 3 are both transcribed into two parts.

Edinburgh University, Central library

MS. Dc.2.68. "Westminster Assembly. Explication of the Westminster Confession of Faith. 1 vol.". Edinburgh University, 1719.

MS. Dc.6.64-66 (3 vols.). "Westminster Assembly. Sermons on the Westminster Confession 1716 to 1725". Edinburgh University.

Rutherford, Samuel, MS. Dc.S.30, "Sermon on Revelation 3:20". Edinburgh University.

— MS Dc.S.30, "Sermon on Genesis 28:10-15". Edinburgh University.

Edinburgh University, New College library

E. Maunde Thompson, "Minutes of the Sessions of the Assembly of Divines from August 4th, 1643 to April 24th 1652", 5 vols. [transcribed minutes of the 3 vols. folio, kept in Dr. Williams library, London.].

MS. Wes. 3.3. 1-2. "Exposition of the Westminster Confession of Faith". Quarto. 2 v. 1718. Edinburgh University.

National Library of Scotland

Johnston, Archibald, "The Diary of Archibald Johnston (1655-61)", MS.6247-6259. Edinburgh: National Library, 1940.

Secondary Sources

Acheson, Robert, *Radical Puritans in England*, 1550-1660. London: Longman, 1990.

Alexander, Henry Gavin, *Religion in England 1558-1662*. London: University of London Press, 1975.

Armstrong, Brian, *Calvinism and the Amyraut Heresy: Protestant Scholasticism and Humanism in Seventeenth-Century France*. Madison: University of Wisconsin Press, 1969.

Auld, Alexander, *Life of John Kennedy, D.D.* London: T. Nelson and sons, 1887.

Aune, David E., *Prophecy in Early Christianity and the Ancient Mediterranean World*. Grand Rapids, MI: Eerdmans, 1983.

Bailey, Richard, *New Light on George Fox and Early Quakerism: The Making and Unmaking of God*. San Francisco: Mellen Research University Press, 1992.

Barbour, Hugh, *The Quakers in Puritan England*. New Haven: Yale University Press, 1964.

Barker, William, *Puritan Profiles, 54 Personalities Drawn Together by the Westminster Assembly*. Fearn: Christian Focus, 1996.

Barlow, John, *George Whitehead: The Last of the Early Friends.* London: Headley Brothers, 1908.
Barnes, Robin, *Prophecy and Gnosis, Apocalypticism in the Wake of the Lutheran Reformation.* Stanford: Stanford University Press, 1988.
Beattie, Francis, *The Presbyterian Standards: An Exposition of the Westminster Confession of Faith and Catechisms.* Richmond: The Presbyterian Committee of Publication, 1896.
Beeke, Joel, *Assurance of Faith.* New York: Peter Lang, 1991.
— "Personal Assurance of Faith: The Puritans and Chapter 18.2 of the Westminster Confession", *WTJ* 55/1 (Spring 1993), 1-30.
— *The Quest for Full Assurance, The Legacy of Calvin and his successors.* Edinburgh: Banner of Truth, 1999.
Bell, Charles, *Calvin and Scottish Theology. The Doctrine of Assurance.* Edinburgh: Handsel Press, 1985.
Bellshaw, William G., "The Confusion of Tongues", *Bibliotheca Sacra* 120 (April 1963), 145-53.
Berends, Willem, "Cessationism", *Vox Reformata* 60 (1995), 44-54.
— "Prophecy in the Reformation Tradition", *Vox Reformata* 60 (1995), 30-43.
Beveridge, William, *A Short History of the Westminster Assembly.* Edinburgh: T. & T. Clark, 1904.
Black, Kenneth, *The Scots Churches in England.* London: William Blackwood, 1906.
Blethen, Tyler and Wood, Curtis (eds.), *Ulster and North America: Transatlantic Perspectives on the Scotch-Irish.* Tuscaloosa: University of Alabama Press, 1997.
Brett, Sidney Reed, *John Pym, 1583-1643. The Statesman of the Puritan Revolution.* London: John Murray, 1940.
Brown, Peter, *Augustine of Hippo, A Biography.* London: Faber and Faber, 1967.
— *The Cult of the Saints: Its Rise and Function in Latin Christianity.* London: SCM Press, 1981.
Burgess, Glenn, *The Politics of the Ancient Constitution. An Introduction to English Political Thought, 1603-1642.* London: Macmillan, 1992.
— *Absolute Monarchy and the Stuart Constitution.* New Haven: Yale University Press, 1996.
Burrell, Sydney, "The Apocalyptic Vision of the Covenanters", *The Scottish Historical Review* 135 (April 1964), 1-24.
Button, Clifford, "Scottish Mysticism in the Seventeenth Century. With Special Reference to Samuel Rutherford". Unpublished PhD thesis, University of Edinburgh, 1927.
Campbell, Thorbjorn, *Standing Witnesses.* Edinburgh: The Saltire Society, 1996.
Capp, Bernard, *The Fifth Monarchy Men. A Study in Seventeenth-Century English Millenarianism.* London: Faber and Faber, 1972.
Carden, Allen, "Biblical Texts and Themes in American Puritan Preaching, 1630-1700", *Andrews University Seminary Studies* 21/2 (Summer 1983), 113-28.

Carden, Allen, "The Word of God in Puritan New England: Seventeenth-Century Perspectives on the Nature and Authority of the Bible", *Andrews University Seminary Studies* 18, 1 (Spring 1980), 1-16.

Carlton, Charles, *Archbishop William Laud*. London: Routledge & Kegan Paul, 1987.

Carruthers, Samuel William, *The Everyday Work of the Westminster Assembly*. Philadelphia: The Presbyterian Historical Society (of America) *and* the Presbyterian Historical Society of England, 1943.

— *The Westminster Confession of Faith, Being An Account of the Preparation and Printing of its Seven Leading Editions to Which is Appended a Critical Text of the Confession with Notes Thereon*. Manchester: R. Aikman & Son, 1937.

Carson, Donald, *Showing the Spirit*. Grand Rapids, MI: Baker, 1987.

Carson, John and Hall, David (eds.), *To Glorify and Enjoy God*. Edinburgh: Banner of Truth, 1994.

Christianson, Paul Kenneth, "English Protestant Apocalyptic Visions c. 1536-1642". Unpublished PhD thesis, University of Minnesota, 1971.

Coffey, John, *Politics, Religion and the British Revolutions: The Mind of Samuel Rutherford*. Cambridge: Cambridge University Press, 1997.

Cohn, Shari Ann, "The Scottish Tradition of Second Sight and other Psychic Experiences in Families". Unpublished PhD thesis, University of Edinburgh, 1996.

Collinson, Patrick, *English Puritanism*. London: The Historical Association, 1987.

Cooper, James, *Confessions of Faith and Formulas of Subscription in the Reformed Churches of Great Britain and Ireland Especially in the Church of Scotland*. Glasgow: James Maclehose and Sons, 1907.

Cooper, Tim, *Fear and Polemic in Seventeenth-Century England*. Aldershot: Ashgate, 2001.

Cothener, Éduard, "Prophétisme dans le Nouveau Testament", Fulcran Vigouroux *Dictionnaire de la Bible: Supplément / Commencé par Louis Pirot et André Robert, Continué sous la Direction de Henri Cazelles et André Feuillet Tome 8: Pithom-Providentissimus*. Paris: Letouzey & Ané, 1972.

Cowan, Edward, "Prophecy and Prophylaxis: A Paradigm for the Scotch-Irish?", Tyler Blethen and Curtis Wood (eds.), *Ulster and North America: Transatlantic Perspectives on the Scotch-Irish*. Tuscaloosa: University of Alabama Press, 1997, 15-23.

Cressy, David, *Literacy and Social Order: Reading and Writing in Tudor and Stuart England*. Cambridge: Cambridge University Press, 1980.

Crone, Theodore M., *Early Christian Prophecy: A Study of its Origin and Function*. Baltimore: St. Mary's University Press, 1973.

Cunningham, William, *Theological Lectures on Subjects Connected with Natural Theology, Evidences of Christianity, the Canon and Inspiration of Scripture*. London: James Nisbet, 1878.

Curtis, Byron, "'Private Spirits' in Westminster Confession §1.10 and in Catholic-Protestant Debate (1588–1652)", 58/2 *WTJ* (Fall 1996), 257-66.

Dabney, Robert Lewis, "The Doctrinal Content[s] of the Confession", David W. Hall (ed.), *The Practice of Confessional Subscription*. Lanham: University Press of America, 1995, 171-83.

Dallimore, Arnold, *The Life of Edward Irving: Fore-runner of the Charismatic Movement*. Edinburgh: Banner of Truth Trust, 1983.

Daniels, Christopher, and Morrill, John, *Charles I*. Cambridge: Cambridge University Press, 1988.

Danner, Dan, "The Contribution of the Geneva Bible of 1560 to the English Protestant Tradition", *The Sixteenth Century Journal* 12/3 (Fall 1981), 5-18.

Davidson, Hilda (ed.), *The Seer in Celtic and Other Traditions*. Edinburgh: John Donald, 1989.

Davies, Horton, *The Worship of the English Puritans*. Westminster: Dacre Press, 1948.

— *Worship and Theology in England*. Grand Rapids, MI: Eerdmans, 1996.

de Witt, J. R., *Jus Divinum: The Westminster Assembly and the Divine Right of Church Government*. Kampen: J. H. Kok, 1969.

Deere, Jack, *Surprised by the Power of the Spirit*. Grand Rapids, MI: Zondervan, 1993.

Demerson, Geneviève et Dompnier, Bernard (eds.), *Les Signes de Dieu aux XVIe et XVIIe Siècles: Actes du Colloque Organisé par le Centre de Recherches sur La Réforme et La Contre-Réforme*. Clermont-Ferrand: Faculté des Lettres et Sciences humaines de l'Université Blaise-Pascal, 1993.

Denzinger, Heinrich, *The Sources of Catholic Dogma*, Roy J. Deferrari (trans.). St. Louis: Herder, 1957.

Donagan, Barbara, "Godly Choice: Puritan Decision-Making in Seventeenth-Century England", *Harvard Theological Review* 76/3 (1983), 307-34.

— "Providence Chance and Explanation: Some Paradoxical Aspects of Puritan Views of Causation", *Journal of Religious History* 9 (1982), 385-403.

Donald, Peter, "The Scottish National Covenant and British Politics, 1638-1640", ed. John Morrill, *The Scottish National Covenant in its British Context*. Edinburgh: Edinburgh University Press, 1990, 90-105

Douglas, James D., *Light in the North*. Grand Rapids, MI: Eerdmans, 1964.

Dowey, Edward, *The Knowledge of God in Calvin's Theology*, 3rd edn. Grand Rapids, MI: Eerdmans, 1994.

Dudley, Martin (ed.), *Like a Two-Edged Sword. The Word of God in Liturgy and History*. Norwich: The Canterbury Press, 1995.

Duncan, Ligon Jennings, "Owning the Confession: Subscription in the Scottish Presbyterian Tradition",

David W Hall (ed.), *The Practice of Confessional Subscription*. Lanham: University Press of America, 1995, 77-91.

— *The Westminster Confession into the 21st Century*. Fearn: Christian Focus Publications, 2003.

Ellis, Earle, *Prophecy and Hermeneutic in Early Christianity*. Grand Rapids, MI: Baker, 1993.

Erskine, Ebenezer and Fisher, James, *The Assembly's Shorter Catechism Explained*. Edinburgh: Oliver and Boyd, 1835.

Fee, Gordon, *God's Empowering Presence: The Holy Spirit in the Letters of Paul*. Peabody: Hendrickson Publishers, 1994.

Ferguson, Sinclair B., *John Owen on the Christian Life*. Edinburgh: Banner of Truth, 1987.

— *The Holy Spirit*. Leicester: IVP, 1996.

— "The Teaching of the Confession", Alasdair I. C. Heron (ed.), *The Westminster Confession in the Church Today*. Edinburgh: St Andrew Press, 1982, 28-39.

Fountain, David G., *John Wycliffe: the Dawn of the Reformation*. Southampton: Mayflower Christian, 1984.

Froom, Le Roy, *The Prophetic Faith of our Fathers*. Washington: Review and Herald, 1950.

Gaffin, Richard and White, Randall Fowler, "Eclipsing the Canon? The Spirit, the Word, and 'Revelations of the Third Kind'," Gary Johnston and Randall Fowler White (eds.), *Whatever Happened to the Reformation?* Phillipsburg: Presbyterian and Reformed, 2001, 133-57.

Gaffin, Richard, "A Cessationist View", Wayne A. Grudem (ed.), *Are Miraculous Gifts for Today?: Four Views*. Leicester: Inter-varsity Press, 1996, 25-64.

— *Perspectives on Pentecost. New Testament Teaching On the Gifts of the Holy Spirit*. Phillipsburg: Presbyterian and Reformed, 1979.

Gamble, Richard (ed.), *Articles on Calvin and Calvinism*, 14 vols. New York: Garland, 1992.

— "Calvin's Theological Method: Word and Spirit, A Case Study", Richard Gamble(ed.), *Articles on Calvin and Calvinism*. New York: Garland, 1992, vol. 7, 61-73.

Gentry, Kenneth, *The Charismatic Gift of Prophecy: A Reformed Response to Wayne Grudem*. Memphis: Footstool Publications, 1986.

Gerstner, John, Kelly, Douglas and Rollinson, Philip, *A Guide - The Westminster Confession of Faith*. Signal Mountain: Summertown Texts, 1992.

Gillespie, Thomas W., *The First Theologians. A Study in Early Christian Prophecy*. Grand Rapids, MI: Eerdmans, 1994.

Gomes, Alan, "De Jesu Christo Servatore: Faustus Socinus on the Satisfaction of Christ", *WTJ* 55 (Fall 1993), 209-31.

Greaves, Richard L., *Theology and Revolution in the Scottish Reformation*. Grand Rapids, MI: Christian University Press, 1980.

Green, Michael, *Baptism: Its Purpose, Practice and Power*. London: Hodder and Stoughton, 1987.

Greenspahn, Frederick, "Why Prophecy Ceased", *Journal of Biblical Literature* 108/1(1989), 37-49.

Gribben, Crawford, *The Irish Puritans: James Usher and The Reformation of The Church*. Darlington: Evangelical Press, 2003.

—, *The Puritan Millennium: Literature and Theology, 1550-1682*. Dublin: Four Courts Press, 2000.

Griffiths, Steve, *Redeem the Time: The Problem of Sin in the Writings of John Owen*. Fearn: Mentor, 2001.

Bibliography

Grudem, Wayne A. (ed.), *Are Miraculous Gifts for Today?: Four Views.* Leicester: Inter-varsity Press, 1996.
— *The Gift of Prophecy in 1 Corinthians.* Lanham: University Press of America, 1982.
— *The Gift of Prophecy in the New Testament and Today.* Eastbourne: Kingsway, 1988.
Guy, Harold, *New Testament Prophecy: Its Origin and Significance.* London: Epworth Press, 1947.
Hagendahl, Harald, *Latin Fathers and the Classics: A Study on the Apologists, Jerome, and other Christian Writers.* Gothenburg: Gothenburg University Press, 1958.
Hall, Basil, "Puritanism: The Problem of Definition", *Studies in Church History* 2 (1965), 283-96.
Hall, David D. and Allen, David Grayson (eds.), *Seventeenth-Century New England.* Boston: The Colonial Society of Massachusetts, 1984.
Hall, David D., "A World of Wonders: The Mentality of the Supernatural in Seventeenth-Century New England", David D. Hall and David Grayson Allen (eds.), *Seventeenth-Century New England.* Boston: The Colonial Society of Massachusetts, 1984, 239-74.
— (ed.), *The Antinomian Controversy, 1636-1638: A Documentary History.* Durham: Duke University Press, 1990.
Hall, David W. (ed.), *The Practice of Confessional Subscription.* Lanham: University Press of America, 1995.
Haller, William, *Foxe's Book of Martyrs and the Elect Nation.* London: J. Cape, 1963.
— *Liberty and Reformation in the Puritan Revolution.* New York: Columbia University Press, 1967.
Hamilton, Ian, *The Erosion of Calvinist Orthodoxy: Seceders and Subscription in Scottish Presbyterianism.* Edinburgh: Rutherford House Books, 1990.
Hart, Trevor A. (ed.), *The Dictionary of Historical Theology.* Grand Rapids, MI: Eerdmans, 2000.
Hetherington, William, *History of the Westminster Assembly.* Edinburgh: James Gemmell, 1890.
Helm, Paul, *Calvin and the Calvinists.* Edinburgh: Banner of Truth Trust, 1982.
Henderson, George (ed.), *The Scots Confession 1560.* Edinburgh: The Saint Andrew Press, 1960.
— *Religious Life in Seventeenth-Century Scotland.* Cambridge: Cambridge University Press, 1937.
Henderson, Robert, *The Teaching Office in the Reformed Tradition.* Philadelphia: Westminster Press, 1962.
Hendry, George, *The Holy Spirit in Christian Theology.* London: SCM Press, 1957.
— *The Westminster Confession for Today: A Contemporary Interpretation.* Richmond, VA: John Knox Press, 1960.
Heron, Alasdair I. C. (ed.), *The Westminster Confession in the Church Today.* Edinburgh: St Andrew Press, 1982.
Hewison, James, *The Covenanters,* 2 vols. Glasgow: John Smith and Son, 1908.
Hill, David, *New Testament Prophecy.* London: Marshall, Morgan and Scott, 1979.

Hodge, Archibald Alexander, *The Confession of Faith: A Handbook of Christian Doctrine Expounding the Westminster Confession.* Edinburgh: Banner of Truth Trust, 1978.

Hodge, Charles, *Systematic Theology,* 3 vols. Grand Rapids, MI: Eerdmans, 1993.

Hoekema, Anthony, *What About Tongue-speaking?* Exeter: Paternoster Press, 1966.

Holly, Larry, "The Divines of the Westminster Assembly: A Study of Puritanism and Parliament". Unpublished PhD thesis, Yale University, 1979.

Horton, Michael (ed), *Power Religion, the Selling Out of the Evangelical Church?* Chicago: Moody Press, 1992.

Howell, Wilbur S., *Logic and Rhetoric in England, 1500-1700.* Princeton: Princeton University Press, 1956.

Hunter, Harold, "Tongues-Speech: A Patristic Analysis", *The Journal of the Evangelical Theological Society* 23/2 (June 1980), 125-37.

Janton, Pierre, "Prophétie et Prophesying chez John Knox et dans La Tradition Puritaine", Geneviève Demerson et Bernard Dompnier (eds.), *Les Signes de Dieu aux XVIe et XVIIe Siècles: Actes du Colloque Organisé par le Centre de Recherches sur La Réforme et La Contre-Réforme.* Clermont-Ferrand: Faculté des Lettres et Sciences humaines de l'Université Blaise-Pascal, 1993, 37-44.

Johnson, Dale, "Prophecy, Rhetoric and Diplomacy: John Knox and the Struggle for the Soul of Scotland", unpublished PhD thesis. Georgia State University, 1995.

Johnston, Gary and White, Randall Fowler (eds.), *Whatever Happened to the Reformation?* Phillipsburg: Presbyterian and Reformed, 2001.

Johnston, O. R., "The Puritan Use of the Old Testament," *Evangelical Quarterly* 23/3 (July 1951), 183-209.

Kelly, Douglas F., "The Westminster Shorter Catechism", John L. Carson and David W. Hall (eds.), *To Glorify and Enjoy God.* Edinburgh: Banner of Truth, 1994, 101-26

Kelly, John Norman Davidson, *Jerome: His Life, Writings and Controversies.* London: Gerald Duckworth, 1975.

Kendall, Robert T., *Calvin and English Calvinism to 1649.* Carlisle: Paternoster, 1997.

Kennedy, John, *The Days of the Fathers in Ross-shire.* Inverness: Christian Focus, 1979.

Kenyon, John, *Stuart England.* Harmondsworth: Penguin, 1985.

— with Ohlmeyer, Jane, "The Background to the Civil War in the Stuart Kingdoms", eds. John Kenyon and Jane Ohlmeyer, *The Civil Wars, A Military History.* Oxford: Oxford University Press, 1998, 3-40.

— and Ohlmeyer, Jane (eds.), *The Civil Wars, A Military History.* Oxford: Oxford University Press, 1998

— (ed.) *The Stuart Constitution 1603-1688.* Cambridge: Cambridge University Press, 1966.

Kester, Aaron, "The Charismata in Crisis: The Gifts of the Holy Spirit in the Reformation Church of England". Unpublished PhD thesis, Miami University, 1990.

Knight III, George, *Prophecy in the New Testament.* Dallas: Presbyterian Heritage Publications, 1988.

Knott, John Jnr., *The Sword of the Spirit. Puritan Responses to the Bible*. Chicago: University of Chicago Press, 1980.

Knowles, Nigel, *Richard Baxter of Kidderminster*. Bewdley: Star and Garter, 2000.

Kuyper, Abraham, *The Work of the Holy Spirit*. Grand Rapids, MI: Eerdmans, 1975.

Laistner, M. L. W., "The Western Church and Astrology During the Early Middle Ages", *Harvard Theological Review* 34 (1941), 253-75.

Lamont, William M., *Godly Rule*. London: Macmillan, 1969.

Lane, Anthony, *John Calvin: Student of the Church Fathers*. Edinburgh: T. & T. Clark, 1999.

Langstaff, Beth, "Temporary Gifts: John Calvin's Doctrine of the Cessation of Miracles". Unpublished PhD thesis, Princeton Theological Seminary, 1999.

Lederle, Henry, *Treasures Old and New: Interpretations of "Spirit-Baptism" in the Charismatic Renewal Movement*. Peabody: Hendrickson, 1988.

Leith, John, *Creeds of the Churches*. Chicago: Aldine Publishing Company, 1963.

Loades, David (ed.), *John Foxe and the English Reformation*. Aldershot: Scolar Press, 1997.

Loewenstein, David, *Milton and the Drama of History: Historical Vision, Iconoclasm and the Literary Imagination*. Cambridge: C.U.P., 1993.

Logan, Samuel, "The Context and Work of the Assembly", John L. Carson and David W. Hall (eds.), *To Glorify and Enjoy God*. Edinburgh: Banner of Truth, 1994, 27-46.

M'Crie [or McCrie)], Thomas, *The Life of John Knox*. Caithness: Free Presbyterian Church of Scotland, 1960.

M'Crie, C. G., *The Confessions of the Church of Scotland*. Edinburgh: MacNiven & Wallace, 1907.

MacArthur, John, *Charismatic Chaos*. Grand Rapids, MI: Zondervan, 1992.

MacQueen, John, "The Saint as Seer: Adomnan's Account of Columba", Hilda Davidson (ed.), *The Seer in Celtic and Other Traditions*. Edinburgh: John Donald, 1989, 37-49.

MacPherson, John, *The Westminster Confession of Faith. With Introduction and Notes by the Rev. John MacPherson, M.A., Findhorn*. Edinburgh: T& T Clark, 1881.

Marsh, Christopher, *The Family of Love in English Society, 1550-1630*. Cambridge: Cambridge University Press, 1994.

Martin, Hugh, *The Westminster Doctrine of the Inspiration of Scripture*. London: J. Nisbet, 1877.

Mason, Roger A. (ed.), *John Knox and the British Reformations*. Aldershot: Ashgate, 1998.

Matthews, Arnold Gwynne (ed.), *The Savoy Declaration of Faith and Order 1658*. London: Independent Press, 1959.

McCoy, Florence, *Robert Baillie and the Second Scots Reformation*. Berkeley: University of California Press, 1974.

McFarlane, Graham, *Christ and the Spirit. The Doctrine of the Incarnation According to Edward Irving*. Carlisle: Paternoster, 1996.

McGregor, J. and Reay, Barry (eds.), *Radical Religion in the English Revolution*. Oxford: Oxford University Press, 1984.

McKay, William, *An Ecclesiastical Republic: Church Government in the Writings of George Gillespie*. Carlisle: Paternoster Press, 1997.

McKim, Donald, *Ramism in William Perkins' Theology*. New York: P. Lang, 1987.

Miller, Perry, *The New England Mind. The Seventeenth Century*. New York: Macmillan, 1939.

— *The New England Mind. From Colony to Province*. Cambridge: Harvard University Press, 1953.

Milne, Bruce, *Know the Truth*. Leicester: Inter-Varsity Press, 1982.

Milne, Garnet, "'Private Spirits' in the Westminster Confession of Faith and in Protestant-Catholic Debates: A Response to Byron Curtis", 61/1 *WTJ* (Spring 1999), 101-10.

Milton, Anthony, *Catholic and Reformed: the Roman and Protestant Churches in English Protestant Thought, 1600-1640*. Cambridge: Cambridge University Press, 1995.

Minutes of the Eighth General Assembly of the Presbyterian Church in America. Savannah, GA: 1980.

Mitchell, Alexander G., *The Westminster Assembly: Its History and Standards*. Edmonton: SWRB, 1992.

Morgan, John, *Godly Learning: Puritan Attitudes towards Reason, Learning and Education, 1560-1640*. Cambridge: Cambridge University Press, 1986.

Morison, William, *Johnston of Warriston*. London: Oliphant Anderson and Ferrier, 1901.

Morrill, John, "The Impact of Puritanism", ed. John Morrill, *The Impact of the English Civil War*. London: Collins and Brown, 1991, 50-66.

— (ed.) *The Impact of the English Civil War*. London: Collins and Brown, 1991

— "The National Covenant in its British Context", ed. John Morrill, *The Scottish National Covenant in its British Context*. Edinburgh: Edinburgh University Press, 1990, 1-30

— *The Nature of the English Revolution*. London: Longman, 1993.

— *The Scottish National Covenant in its British Context*. Edinburgh: Edinburgh University Press, 1990.

Morris, Edward, *Theology of the Westminster Symbols*. Columbus: 1900.

Mullan, David, *Scottish Puritanism, 1590-1638*. Oxford: Oxford University Press, 2000.

Muller, Richard A., *Christ and the Decree, Christology and Predestination in Reformed Theology from Calvin to Perkins*. Grand Rapids, MI: Baker, 1986.

— *Post-Reformation Reformed Dogmatics. The Rise and Development of Reformed Orthodoxy. Ca.1520 to ca. 1725*, 4 vols. Grand Rapids, MI: Baker, 2003.

Murphy, Scott Thomas, "The Doctrine of Scripture in the Westminster Assembly". Unpublished PhD thesis, Drew University, 1984.

Murray, Iain, *The Puritan Hope*. London: Banner of Truth Trust, 1971.

Murray, John, *Collected Writings of John Murray*, 4 vols. Edinburgh: Banner of Truth, 1977-82.

Niesel, Wilhelm, *The Theology of Calvin*. Grand Rapids, MI: Baker, 1980.

Norris, Robert M., "The Thirty-nine Articles at the Westminster Assembly". Unpublished PhD thesis, University of St. Andrews, 1977.

Oberman, Heiko, *Luther: Man between God and the Devil*. New Haven: Yale University Press, 1989.

Ong, Walter, *Ramus: Method and Decay of Dialogue: From the Art of Discourse to the Art of Reason*. Cambridge: Harvard UP, 1958.

Orme, William, *Memoirs of the Life, Writings, and Religious Connexions, of John Owen, D.D., Vice-Chancellor of Oxford, and Dean of Christ Church, during the Commonwealth*. London: T. Hamilton, 1820.

Packer, James, *Among God's Giants*. Eastbourne: Kingsway, 1991.

Parker, T. H. L., *The doctrine of the Knowledge of God: A Study in the Theology of John Calvin*. Grand Rapids, MI: Eerdmans, 1994.

Paul, Robert S., *The Assembly of The Lord*. Edinburgh: T. & T. Clark, 1985.

Payne, Gordon R., "Augustinianism in Calvin and Bonaventure", *WTJ* 44/1 (Spring 1982), 1-30.

Penny, Andrew, "John Foxe, the Acts and Monuments and the Development of Prophetic Interpretation", David Loades (ed.), *John Foxe and the English Reformation*. Aldershot: Scolar Press, 1997, 252-77.

Petersen, Rodney Lawrence, "Preaching in the Last Days: The Use of the Theme of 'Two Witnesses,' as Found in Revelation 11:3-13, With Particular Attention to the Sixteenth and Early Seventeenth Centuries". Unpublished PhD thesis, Princeton Theological Seminary, 1985.

Philip, James, *The Westminster Confession of Faith. An Exposition, Part 1 Chapters 1-8*. Edinburgh: Holyrood Abbey Church, 1966.

Pinnock, Clark (ed.), *The Grace of God, the Will of Man: a Case for Arminianism*. Grand Rapids, MI: Academie, 1989.

Plantinga, Cornelius, *A Place to Stand*. Grand Rapids, MI: Christian Reformed Church, 1979.

Poythress, Vern S., "Linguistic and Sociological Analyses of Modern Tongues-Speaking: Their Contributions and Limitations", *WTJ* 42/2 (Spring 1980), 367-88.

— "Modern Spiritual Gifts As Analogous to Apostolic Gifts: Affirming Extraordinary Works Of The Spirit Within Cessationist Theology", *Journal of the Evangelical Theological Society* 39/1 (March 1996), 71-102.

Reay, Barry, "Quakerism and Society", J. McGregor and Barry Reay (eds.), *Radical Religion in the English Revolution*. Oxford: Oxford University Press, 1984, 141-64.

Reid, James, *Memoirs of the Westminster Divines*. Edinburgh: Banner of Truth, 1982 [formerly a two vol. work, but now bound as one, but retaining individual volume numbering].

Reid, John K. S., "Confessional Subscription: A Personal View", Alasdair I. C. Heron (ed.), *The Westminster Confession in the Church Today*. Edinburgh: St Andrew Press, 1982, 132-40.

Reid, Stanford W., *Trumpeter of God*. Grand Rapids, MI: Baker, 1974.

Reymond, Robert, *"What About Continuing Revelation and Miracles in the Presbyterian Church Today?"* Philadelphia: Presbyterian and Reformed, 1977.

Robertson, O. Palmer, *The Final Word*. Edinburgh: Banner of Truth, 1993.

— "The Holy Spirit in the Westminster Confession", Ligon Duncan (ed.), *The Westminster Confession into the 21st Century*. Fearn: Christian Focus Publications, 2003, 57-99.

Rogers, Jack B., *Scripture in the Westminster Confession. A Problem of Historical Interpretation for American Presbyterianism*. Grand Rapids, MI: Eerdmans, 1967.

Russell, Conrad, *The Fall of the British Monarchies, 1637-1642*. Oxford: Clarendon Press, 1991.

Ruthven, John, "On the Cessation of the Charismata: The Protestant Polemic of Benjamin B. Warfield". Unpublished PhD thesis, Marquette University, 1989.

— *On the Cessation of the Charismata, The Protestant Polemic on Postbiblical Miracles*. Sheffield: Sheffield Academic Press, 1993.

Ryken, Leland, *Worldly Saints*. Grand Rapids, MI: Zondervan, 1990.

Ryken, Philip, "Scottish Reformed Scholasticism", Carl Trueman and Scott Clark (eds.), *Protestant Scholasticism: Essays in Reassessment*. Carlisle: Paternoster, 1999, 196-210.

Saucy, Robert, "An Open but Cautious View", Wayne Grudem (ed.), *Are Miraculous Gifts for Today?: Four Views*. Leicester: Inter-varsity Press, 1996, 97-148.

Schafer, Thomas A., "The Beginnings of Confessional Subscription in the Presbyterian Church", *McCormick Quarterly* 19 (January 1966), 102-19.

Schreiner, Susan E., " 'Through a Mirror Dimly': Calvin's Sermons on Job", *Calvin Theological Journal* 21/2 (1986), 175-93.

— *The Theatre of His Glory*. Grand Rapids, MI: Baker, 1991.

Scott, Jonathan, *England's Troubles: Seventeenth-century English Political Instability in European Context*. Cambridge: Cambridge University Press, 2000.

Sefton, Henry (ed.), *John Knox*. Edinburgh: Saint Andrew Press, 1993.

Shaw, Robert, *The Reformed Faith*. Inverness: Christian Focus Publications, 1973.

Sheppard, Gerald T. (ed.), *The Geneva Bible. The Annotated New Testament 1602 Edition*. Cleveland: The Pilgrim Press, 1989.

Shipps, Kenneth, "The 'Political Puritan'", *Church History* 45 (1976), 196-205.

Shogren, Gary Steven, "Christian Prophecy and Canon in the Second Century: A Response to B. B. Warfield", *The Journal of the Evangelical Theological Society* 40/4 (December 1997), 609-26.

Smellie, Alexander, *Men of the Covenant*. Edinburgh: Banner of Truth, 1975.

Smith, Dean, "The Scottish Presbyterians and Covenanters: A Continuationist Experience in a Cessationist Theology", *WTJ* 63 (2001), 39-63.

Smith, Thomas, *Select Memoirs of the Lives, Labours and Sufferings of Those Pious and Learned English and Scottish Divines [...] who Ultimately Crowned the Venerable Edifice with the Celebrated Westminster Confession of Faith*. Glasgow: D. Mackenzie, 1828.

Smout, Thomas, *A History of the Scottish people 1560-1830*. London: Fontana, 1985.

Spear, Wayne, "Covenanted Uniformity in Religion: The Influence of the Scottish Commissioners upon the Ecclesiology of the Westminster Assembly". Unpublished PhD thesis, University of Pittsburgh, 1976.

— "The Westminster Confession of Faith and Holy Scripture", John L. Carson and David W. Hall (eds.), *To Glorify and Enjoy God*. Edinburgh: Banner of Truth, 1994, 87-100.
— "Word and Spirit in the Westminster Confession", Ligon Duncan (ed.), *The Westminster Confession into the 21st Century*. Fearn: Christian Focus, 2003, vol. 1, 39-56.
Spinks, Bryan, "Brief and Perspicuous Text; Plain and Pertinent Doctrine: Behind 'Of the Preaching of the Word' in the Westminster Directory", Martin Dudley (ed.), *Like a Two-Edged Sword, the Word of God in Liturgy and History*. Norwich: The Canterbury Press, 1995, 91-112.
Strachan, Gordon, *The Pentecostal Theology of Edward Irving*. London: Darton, Longman and Todd, 1973.
Strickland, David, "Union with Christ in the Theology of Samuel Rutherford: An Examination of His Doctrine of the Holy Spirit". Unpublished PhD thesis, University of Edinburgh, 1972.
Strong, Augustus, *Systematic Theology*. Old Tappan, N.J.: Fleming H. Revell, 1907.
Subritzky, Bill, *Demons Defeated*. Chichester: Sovereign World, 1985.
Todd, Margo, "Providence, Chance and the New Science in Early Stuart Cambridge", *Historical Journal* 29/3 (1986), 697-711.
— *The Culture of Protestantism in Early Modern Scotland*. New Haven: Yale University Press, 2002.
Toon, Peter, *God's Statesman: The Life and Work of John Owen, Pastor, Educator, Theologian*. Exeter: Paternoster Press, 1971.
— (ed.), *Puritans, the Millennium and the Future of Israel: Puritan Eschatology 1600-1660*. Greenwood: Attic Press, 1970.
Trevett, Christine, *Montanism: Gender, Authority and the New Prophecy*. Cambridge: Cambridge University Press, 1996.
Trevor-Roper, Hugh Redwald, *Archbishop Laud*. London: Macmillan, 1940.
Trueman, Carl and Clark, Scott (eds.), *Protestant Scholasticism: Essays in Reassessment*. Carlisle: Paternoster, 1999.
Trueman, Carl, *The Claims of Truth: John Owen's Trinitarian Theology*. Carlisle: Paternoster Press, 1998.
Tyacke, Nicholas, *Anti-Calvinists: The Rise of English Arminianism c.1590-1640*. Oxford: Clarendon, 1987.
Underwood, Ted, "Early Quaker Eschatology", Peter Toon (ed.), *Puritans, the Millennium and the Future of Israel: Puritan Eschatology 1600-1660*. Greenwood: Attic Press, 1970, 91-103.
— *Primitivism, Radicalism, and the Lamb's War. The Baptist-Quaker Conflict in Seventeenth-Century England*. Oxford: Oxford University Press, 1997.
Van Dam, Cornelis, *The Urim and Thummim. A Means of Revelation in Ancient Israel*. Winona Lake: Eisenbrauns, 1997.
VanderMolen, Ronald, "Providence as Mystery, Providence as Revelation: Puritan and Anglican Modifications of John Calvin's Doctrine of Providence", *Church History* 47/1 (1978), 27-47.

Vigouroux, Fulcran, *Dictionnaire de la Bible: Supplément / Commencé par Louis Pirot et André Robert, Continué sous la Direction de Henri Cazelles et André Feuillet Tome 8: Pithom-Providentissimus.* Paris: Letouzey & Ané, 1972

Vos, Arvin, *Aquinas, Calvin, and Contemporary Protestant Thought.* Washington, D.C.: Christian University Press, 1985.

Wagner, Peter, "A Third Wave?", *Pastoral Renewal* (July-August, 1983), 1-5.

— *The Third Wave of the Holy Spirit.* Ann Arbor, MI: Vine Books, Servant Publications, 1988.

Walker, Eric C., *William Dell, Master Puritan.* Cambridge: Heffer, 1970.

Walker, Patrick, *Six Saints of the Covenant: Peden: Semple: Welwood: Cameron: Cargill: Smith,* 2 vols. London: Hodder and Stoughton, 1901.

Wallace, Ronald S., *Calvin's Doctrine of the Word and Sacrament.* Tyler: Geneva Divinity School Press, 1982.

Walsham, Alexandra, *Providence in Early Modern England.* Oxford: Oxford University Press, 2001.

Ward, Rowland, *The Westminster Confession for the Church Today: A Modernised Text and Commentary Commemorating the 350th Anniversary of the Westminster Assembly 1643-49.* Melbourne: Presbyterian Church of Eastern Australia, 1992.

Warfield, Benjamin, *The Westminster Assembly and its Work.* Cherry Hill: Mack Publishing company, 1972.

Wendel, Francois, *Calvin.* Glasgow: William Collins Sons and Co, 1976.

White, Randall Fowler, "Contrary to What You May Have Heard: On the Rhetoric and Reality of Claims of Continuing Revelation", Gary Johnston and Randall Fowler White (eds.), *Whatever Happened to the Reformation?* Phillipsburg: Presbyterian and Reformed, 2001, 159-84.

Whiting, Charles, *Studies in English Puritanism from the Restoration to the Revolution, 1660-1688.* London: Frank Cass by arrangement with the Trustees of the Society for Promoting Christian Knowledge, 1968.

Wilks, Michael, *Wyclif: Political Ideas and Practice.* Oxford: Oxbow, 2000.

Williams, George Huntson, *The Radical Reformation.* Kirksville: Sixteenth Century Journal Publishers, 1992.

Wilson, John F., *Pulpit in Parliament: Puritanism during the English Civil Wars 1640-1648.* Princeton: Princeton University Press, 1969.

Wimber, John and Springer, Kevin N., *Power Evangelism.* San Francisco: Harper and Row, 1986.

— *Power Healing.* London: Hodder & Stoughton, 2001.

Winship, Michael P., *Seers of God. Puritan Providentialism in the Restoration and Early Enlightenment.* Baltimore: John Hopkins University Press, 1996.

Wood, Douglas C., *The Evangelical Doctor: John Wycliffe and the Lollards.* Welwyn: Evangelical, 1984.

Young, John, *The Scottish Parliament 1639-1661.* Edinburgh: John Donald, 1996.

Index

Agabus, 5, 179, 180, 239, 246, 248, 250, 286
Amyraldianism, 42, 135
Amyraut, Moisé (Moïse or Moses), 135
Angels, 3, 1, 43, 44, 47, 48, 50, 153, 154, 168, 170, 180, 184, 185, 186, 187, 217, 236
Antinomianism, 41, 63, 116, 117, 118, 122, 157, 160, 205, 209, 228, 230, 291, 296
Apocrypha, 31, 168
Apparitions, 127, 140, 148, 159, 229
Aquinas, Thomas, 44, 45
Aristotle, 171, 183
Arminianism, 18, 24, 25, 31, 61, 167, 313
Arrowsmith, John, 63, 74, 148, 182, 187, 210
Ash[e], Simeon, 61, 62, 84, 259, 272,
Atonement, 42, 86, 89, 135, 159
Audible voice from heaven, 1, 6, 58, 61, 92, 125, 170, 221
Augustine, 42, 43, 44, 45, 46, 48, 57, 66, 142, 152, 157
Baillie, Robert, 12, 28, 40, 64, 72, 111, 112, 126, 134, 136, 224, 225, 237, 238, 258, 259, 260
Ball, John, 60, 61, 125, 275
Barclay, Robert, 126, 169
Baxter, Richard, 34, 37, 61, 66, 135, 159, 167, 168, 176, 209, 211, 264, 265
Bellarmine, Robert, 53, 291
Berends, Willem, 3, 4, 5, 7, 8, 46, 237, 244, 245, 247
Berends, William, 3, 4, 5, 7, 8, 46, 237, 244, 245, 247
Blair, Robert, 191, 224, 234, 235, 236, 252, 284, 286
Bond, John, 95, 96
Book of Common Prayer, 25
Book of Sports, 24, 88, 97, 140, 193, 195
Bourignianism, 252

Boyd, Zachary, 279
Bridge, William, 1, 8, 41, 49, 73, 83, 85, 125, 160, 161, 162, 163, 164, 165, 176, 194, 210, 257, 284, 286, 289
Bullinger, Henry, 42
Burgess, Anthony, 38, 69, 98, 105, 114, 137, 140, 142, 143, 184, 192, 196, 272, 293
Burgess, Cornelius, 13, 100, 273
Burgess, Glenn, 19, 20, 35
Burroughs, Jeremiah, 67, 88, 89, 104, 203, 258
Byfield, Adoniram, 11, 84, 195, 214, 269
Byfield, Richard, 97, 192
Calamy, Edmund, 25, 87, 141, 154, 155, 211, 272, 287
Calvin, John, 4, 5, 18, 42, 44, 45, 46, 47, 48, 53, 82, 136, 137, 198, 211, 238, 239
Capel, Richard, 192, 295
Carruthers, Samuel, 2, 6, 11, 136
Carter, Thomas, 106, 107, 213
Carter, William, 129, 130, 138, 148, 184, 186, 205
Cartwright, Thomas, 206
Caryl, Joseph, 38, 39, 105, 186, 199, 200, 295
Casaubon, Meric, 78, 208
Case, Thomas, 89, 93, 97, 117, 118, 150, 272
Cawdry, Daniel, 63
Cessationism, 1—9, 22, 48, 53, 57, 58, 60, 65, 66, 67, 68, 77, 94, 109—114, 124, 125, 129—138, 143, 145—148, 153, 154, 156, 164—176, 183, 186, 188, 192—196, 199, 207, 209, 211, 223—227, 230, 231, 235—257, 260, 261, 265, 267, 284—290, 297
Charismatic, 1, 2, 3, 4, 178, 189, 253
Charles I, 13—23, 26, 27, 32, 35, 62, 150, 205, 209, 235, 246, 292
Cheynell, Francis, 144, 187, 195

Coleman, Thomas, 120, 153
Conant, John, 195, 216
Confessional Subscription, 2, 8, 27, 100, 116, 156, 214, 244, 256, 257, 261, 262, 263, 264, 267, 268, 269, 270, 271, 272, 273, 274, 275, 276, 277, 278, 279, 280, 281, 282, 283, 284
Continuationism, 1—6, 44, 48, 66, 133, 146, 153—160, 166, 172, 176, 178, 194, 224, 226, 227, 243, 244, 255, 261, 265, 284—289, 290
Counter-Reformation, 15, 17, 18, 34
Covenant of Grace, 61, 131, 233, 259, 266
Covenanters, 7, 19, 27, 28, 29, 219, 223, 224, 226, 250, 251, 278, 279, 280, 281, 284
Crisp, Tobias, 116
Cromwell, Oliver, 10, 27, 49, 150, 188
Cunningham, William, 55, 297
Curtis, Byron, 8, 292
de La Marche, John, 199
Dell, William, 41, 205, 230
Demons, 43, 44, 125
Dick, John, 234
Dickson, David, 82, 125, 133, 247, 248, 296
Diodati Annotations, 134
Diodati, John, 134
Divination, 45, 157, 208
Douglas, Robert, 224
Downame, John, 60
Durham, James, 247, 248, 256
Dury, John, 89, 90
Dutch Annotations, 72, 133, 134
Earl, John, 224
Edwards, Thomas, 40, 111
Elizabeth, 16, 37, 39, 154, 223
England as Israel, 90
English Annotations, 16, 72, 73, 134, 135, 136
English Civil War, 14—35, 70, 87
Enthusiasm, 12, 55, 56, 65, 109, 112, 120, 125, 133, 151, 166, 194, 198, 208, 215, 228, 229, 265, 290, 291, 292, 294, 296, 297

Episcopacy, 24, 26, 28, 32, 64, 73, 92, 131, 156, 187, 263, 264, 273, 277, 278, 280, 281
Epistemology, 9, 19, 42, 52, 53, 65, 67, 68, 71, 75, 108, 110, 126, 133, 166—169, 207, 245, 285, 287, 289
Erastianism, 7, 242, 263
Erskine, Charles, 224
Eschatology, 35, 126, 258
European Context, 14—15
Familists, 40, 82, 125, 167, 228, 229, 230, 296
Family of love, 40
Featley, Daniel, 72, 78
Ferguson, Sinclair, 1, 189
Fifth Monarchy men, 83
First Book of Discipline, 254, 255
Fisher, Edward, 252
Five Articles of Perth, 276, 277
Five Knights' case, 22
Flavel, John, 124, 125, 206
Fleming, Robert, 49, 250, 251, 256
Ford, Thomas, 195
Foretelling, 182, 198, 200, 202, 206, 207, 220, 224, 229, 230—239, 253, 256, 286
Fox, George, 126, 167
Foxe, John, 36, 37, 38
Fuller, Thomas, 41
Fundamentals, 101, 102, 103, 273, 283
Gaffin, Richard, 1, 177
Gangraena, 40, 111, 112
Gataker, Thomas, 16, 41, 63, 78, 142, 181, 182, 259, 272
Geneva Bible, 127, 135
Gentry, Kenneth, 6, 8, 77
Gillespie, George, 4, 7, 8, 12, 32, 41, 86, 120, 137, 171, 224, 237—246, 248, 259, 283, 284, 286, 289
Gillespie, Patrick, 240
Gillespie, Thomas, 147, 206, 211, 212
Goode, William, 81, 253, 294
Goodwin, John, 103, 273
Goodwin, Thomas, 49, 73, 86, 104, 110—113, 119, 122, 129, 194, 205, 258

Index 331

Gouge, William, 16, 63, 75, 94, 131, 140, 147, 156, 184, 185, 191, 192, 196, 212, 272
Gower, Stanley, 11, 272
Grand Remonstrance, 18
Greenham, Richard, 163
Greenhill, William, 186, 193, 236, 293
Grudem, Wayne, 1—6, 77, 177, 178, 179, 180, 189
Gunpowder Plot, 24, 187, 217, 288
Haak(or Haake),Theodore, 72, 133, 134
Hacket, John, 156
Hall, Edmund, 120
Hammond, Henry, 197
Harris, Robert, 63, 197
Henderson, Alexander, 27, 34, 107, 149, 224, 234, 256, 292, 294
Herle, Charles, 63, 182, 183
Hetherington, William, 33
Heyrick, Richard, 32, 272
Hill, Thomas, 39, 53, 123, 144, 145, 214, 215, 271
Hodge, Charles, 4
Hog, James, 252, 253, 256
Holy Spirit, 1, 2, 3, 1, 2, 3, 4, 5, 6, 9, 35, 40, 41, 45, 49, 51, 54, 55, 56, 57, 58, 65, 74, 75, 79, 80, 98, 105, 107, 110, 111, 113, 115, 117, 118, 122, 153, 161, 164, 169, 170, 171, 177, 182, 183, 189, 195, 198, 207, 216, 217, 222, 223, 228, 232, 233, 238, 247, 256, 287, 288, 291, 292, 294, 295, 297
Hoyle, Joshua, 63, 193
Human reason, 203
Hus, John, 201, 207, 210
Immediate inspiration, 115, 140, 145, 148, 216, 217, 228, 229, 233, 234, 242, 253
Independentism, 72, 273
Inner testimony of the Holy Spirit, 54, 55, 56, 57, 58, 59, 65, 294, 295
Irish Articles, 50, 59, 60, 69, 73
Irving, Edward, 253, 254, 255, 256
James I (James VI of Scotland), 19, 20, 22, 110, 111
Jerome, 157, 158, 231

Johnston, Archibald (Lord Warriston), 27, 149—152, 224—226, 256
Keith, George, 169, 170, 174, 175, 206, 207, 227, 245
Kennedy, John, 255, 256, 316
Kirk, Robert, 220
Knox, John, 17, 70, 201, 206, 207, 214, 219, 221—223, 224, 235, 237, 239, 246, 247, 255, 256, 284, 286, 288, 289
Kuyper, Abraham, 198
Langely, John, 26
Larger Catechism, 1, 2, 10, 78, 94, 105, 112, 113, 124, 185, 258, 264, 265, 279
Last days, 92, 113, 131, 132, 133, 139
Laud, William, 17, 24, 25, 26, 27, 30, 33, 35, 186, 188, 195, 209
Leigh, Edward, 67, 131, 132, 171
Ley, John, 41, 78, 92, 157, 262, 263
Libertines, 46, 48, 54, 82, 125, 167, 296,
Light of nature, 6, 68, 69, 71, 72, 74, 77, 267
Lightfoot, John, 12, 120, 121, 128, 129, 132, 138, 145, 180, 181, 190, 200, 201, 202, 267, 268, 269
Love, Richard, 204, 205
Luther, Martin, 42, 46, 161, 164, 201, 209, 210, 214, 232
Lyford, William, 84, 85, 191, 192, 197, 295
Maitland, John, 224
Malignants, 264
Manton, Thomas, 137, 138, 194, 216
Marshall, Stephen, 13, 24, 25, 34, 37, 89, 105, 106, 143, 181, 194, 200, 203, 204, 267, 294
Mather, Cotton, 174
Maynard, John, 69, 70, 185
Michelson (or Mitchell), Margaret, 225
Miracles, 1, 4, 5, 7, 8, 9, 41—50, 71, 110—112, 125, 135, 141, 142, 145, 152, 157, 163, 170, 192, 193, 194, 195, 196, 197, 203, 216, 219—221, 229, 234, 241, 242, 247, 251, 288

Miraculous gifts, 1—5, 9, 41, 47, 48, 133, 136, 189, 192—196, 226, 241, 288, 289
  Dreams, 1, 3, 6, 7, 8, 9, 41, 43, 44, 51, 54, 60, 61, 92, 93, 94, 108, 120, 125, 127, 128, 129, 130, 133, 134, 135, 138, 139, 140, 142, 145, 146—165, 166, 170, 173, 176, 183, 206, 219, 226, 229, 230, 237, 252, 253, 265, 284—289
  Healing, 2, 3, 4, 43, 47, 195, 219, 220, 230, 235, 241, 247—251
Prophecy
  extraordinary, 1, 137, 176, 188, 190, 192, 199, 207, 225, 226, 230, 248
  and the Westminster divines, 177—218
  and the Scots, 219—256
  Tongues, 2, 3, 4, 47, 137, 178, 206, 229, 230, 239, 249, 254, 285
  Visions, 1, 3, 6, 7, 8, 9, 41, 43, 45, 47, 48, 54, 60, 61, 62, 92, 93, 94, 106, 108, 111, 119, 123, 125, 127, 128, 129, 130, 133—148, 156—166, 170, 173, 183, 186, 214, 226, 228, 229, 230, 253, 265, 284—287, 289, 296
Mitchell, Alexander G., 10, 99, 224, 259
Mitchell, Alex F. and Struthers, John, 11, 12, 258
Monro, Alexander, 281
Montagu, Richard, 23
Morrill, John, 15, 18, 23, 26, 29, 32
Muller, Richard, 13, 56, 67, 76, 109, 114, 282
Musculus, Andreas, 209
Muslims, 168, 210
National Covenant, 7, 18, 26, 27, 28, 29, 73, 149, 261, 276—280
necessitas medii, 102, 103
necessitas praecepti, 101, 103
Negative Oath, 263—264

New England, 174
Newcomen, Matthew, 25, 63
Norris, Robert M., 10
Nuttall, Geoffrey, 74, 153
Nye, Philip, 34, 49, 205, 213, 267—269, 270
Ordinances, 23, 80, 81, 95, 99, 143, 160, 164, 204, 240, 286
Owen, John, 1, 8, 37, 39, 49, 132, 150, 154, 188, 189, 191, 247, 270, 271, 289, 293
Palmer, Herbert, 16, 32, 33, 38, 107, 191
Parker, William, 167, 168, 208
Parliament, 10, 11, 13, 14, 18—38, 62, 64, 65, 70, 72, 74, 81, 83, 84, 87, 89, 90, 93, 95, 100, 106, 107, 111, 117, 123, 124, 127, 134, 144, 167, 168, 181, 187, 188, 195, 199, 208, 210, 211, 244, 261, 262, 264—284, 288, 294
Paul, Robert S., 14
Peden, Alexander, 219, 251
Pentecostalism, 1, 2, 3, 4, 178, 254
Perkins, William, 4, 8, 49, 50, 51, 65, 213
Perne, Andrew, 70
Personal Rule, 18, 24
Pighius, Albert, 46
Plague, 88, 212
Prayer Book, 25, 26, 27, 156
premonitions, 237, 256
Presbyterianism, 2, 6, 8, 9, 13, 16, 17, 19, 24, 25, 26, 27, 28, 29, 32, 37, 49, 60—69, 74, 77, 81, 84, 87, 89, 90, 92, 100, 106, 109, 111, 115, 121, 123, 127, 136, 147, 155, 166—183, 206, 213, 219, 220, 222, 223, 227, 245, 247, 250, 252, 256—290
Private Spirits, 8, 35, 59, 107, 291—297
Proof-texting, 6, 11—13, 68, 76, 79, 80, 82, 94, 113, 124, 175, 189, 243, 292
Prophet, Nicholas, 63
Protestant Scholasticism, 99, 135

Index 333

Providence, 5, 6, 7, 32, 38, 52, 59, 68, 69, 71, 77, 84, 93, 147—161, 171, 180, 185—187, 202, 210, 211, 214, 216, 217, 237, 247, 249—256, 284, 289
Puritans, definition 31—33
Pym, John, 23, 29
Quakers, 40, 82, 125, 126, 146, 150, 152, 165—176, 206, 225—227, 245, 287, 296, 297
Radical Reformation, 40, 199, 285
Ramism, 213, 214
Restoration, 13, 24, 27, 38, 39, 49, 76, 87, 95, 97, 126, 149, 150, 156, 197, 205, 211, 275, 280, 284
Revelation
　general revelation, 68—73
　immediate revelation, 40, 50, 55—59, 65, 94, 111, 113—145, 297
　mediate revelation, 1, 2, 3, 55, 113—123, 172, 175, 210, 214—217, 231, 242, 247—250, 284, 287—290
　special revelation, 1, 67, 74, 109, 123
Reyner, William, 38, 107
Reynolds, Edward, 63, 87, 100, 101, 110, 119, 139, 143, 183, 209, 211, 259, 262, 272, 273, 294
Robertson, O. Palmer, 1, 9, 111, 291
Rogers, Jack, 60, 62, 69, 74
Rollock, Robert, 115
Roman Catholicism, 17, 18, 19, 28, 162, 209, 291
Rous, Francis, 24
Royalists, 14
Russell, Conrad, 23, 26, 29, 30
Rutherford, Samuel, 25, 41, 71, 78, 85, 101, 102, 118, 144, 148, 149, 152, 163, 184, 190, 191, 219—238, 248, 251, 256, 259, 273, 282, 283, 284, 296
Saltmarsh, John, 41, 157, 209, 228
Salvation, 77—108, 116, 141, 168, 175, 260, 265, 266, 267, 291
　holistic and temporal, 79-84

Satan, 6, 67, 78, 117, 124, 141, 154, 161, 162, 166, 182, 183, 185, 250, 313, 325
Saving faith, 78, 80, 81, 266
Savoy Declaration, 160, 188, 261, 270, 271
Schaff, Philip, 1, 11, 59, 68, 73, 263
Schwenkfeldians, 40, 228
Scots Confession 1560, 254, 276, 277, 278, 279
Scott, Jonathan, 15, 17
Scripture, 1—13
　and dreams, 151
　and providence, 52, 59, 237, 246, 252
　as authority for Reformation, 22
　as rule of faith and life, 60, 65, 76, 82, 100, 105-107, 112, 151, 163, 185, 201, 236, 253, 268, 293
　as voice of Christ, 55, 115, 199
　as Word of God, 106—108, 141—144
　confirmed by miracles, 142
　Geneva Bible, 127, 135
　necessity of, 52—54, 98—108, 122
　prophecy linked to, 47, 221, 226, 233, 245
　promises in, 106, 108, 139, 200, 253
　replaces Urim and Thummim, 61, 92—95, 108, 125, 143, 199, 203, 287
　special revelation confined to, 113, 123-133
　sufficiency of, 101, 199, 293, 294
　unity with Holy Spirit, 1—3, 13, 14, 16, 30, 33, 45, 49, 59, 65, 123, 150, 167, 176, 257, 259, 270, 285, 286
Scripture-spirit, 232, 251
Scudder, Henry, 37, 205, 233, 234
Seaman, Lazarus, 196, 197, 272
Second Book of Discipline, 254, 308
Second Helvetic Confession, 11, 73
Sedgewick, Obadiah, 84, 100

Seekers, 40
Selden, John, 7, 16, 99, 120, 209, 263
Shipmoney, 29
Shorter Catechism, 1, 2, 10, 19, 59, 93, 105, 122, 124, 206, 248, 258, 264, 269, 279, 280
Simpson, Sydrach, 49, 83, 84, 133, 142, 143, 205
Smectymnuus, 24, 63, 81, 87
Socinianism, 31, 41
Solemn League and Covenant, 19, 34, 269
Spang, William, 12, 136, 237, 259
Spear, Wayne, 49, 52, 64, 160
Spiritual Babylon, 90, 91
Spiritual gifts, 3, 4, 5, 8, 44, 148, 194, 223, 226, 285, 289
Spiritual Jerusalem, 91
Spurgeon, Charles, 215
Spurstowe, William, 25, 81, 141, 183, 185
Stapleton, Thomas, 53
Sterry, Peter, 37, 154
Strong, Augustus, 4
Strong, William, 152, 184, 198, 200
Temple, Thomas, 63
Temporal salvation, 1, 78, 81, 84, 85, 86, 87, 88, 89, 90, 94, 96, 97, 98, 104, 105, 106, 107, 108, 286
Tesdale, Christopher, 196
The Directory for the Public Worship of God, 1, 2, 10, 213, 244, 254, 263, 264, 270
The Form of Church Government, 1, 2, 10, 111, 189, 243, 254, 270, 272, 274
Third Wave, 2, 3
Thirty-nine Articles, 10, 13, 99, 262
Thompson, E. Maunde, 12, 193
Tuckney, Anthony, 63, 98, 122, 123, 141, 215, 216, 262, 272
Twisse, William, 101, 183, 258, 294
Two witnesses, 38, 231

Tyacke, Nicholas, 18, 23
Typology, 86, 89, 90, 93, 129, 133, 136, 138, 148
Urim and Thummim, 61, 92, 93, 94, 108, 143, 199, 203, 287
Usher, James, 16, 50, 59—60, 69, 71, 75, 114, 125, 130, 191, 197, 206, 209, 211
Valentine, Thomas, 140
Vane, Henry, 34, 268
Vermigli, Peter Martyr, 42, 48, 238
Vines, Richard, 90
Walker, George, 127, 272
Warfield, Benjamin, 2, 4, 11, 60, 71, 260
Welsh, John, 239
Westminster Abbey, 10, 39, 101, 144
Westminster Assembly, 1—27, 31, 33, 34, 39, 41, 42, 50, 59—70, 74, 75, 76, 108—114, 116, 120, 121, 127, 129, 131, 135, 136, 140, 149, 160, 181, 195, 199, 219, 224—230, 244, 258—262, 270, 272, 285, 286, 288, 290, 292, 296
Westminster Confession of Faith 1, 2, 6, 9, 10, 11, 52, 65, 80, 82, 109, 115—117, 156, 167, 194, 257, 292,
Whitaker, Jeremiah, 63
Whitaker, William, 52—59, 65, 76, 285, 291
White, John, 32, 95, 100, 210
Whitehead, George, 165, 176
Wilkinson Sr, Henry, 76
Wilkinson Jr, Henry, 201
Wilkinson, Henry of St Mary's Oxford, 106
Wilson, Thomas, 11, 195
Witchcraft, 51
Wodrow, Robert, 7, 219, 235
Woodcock, Francis, 39
Wycliffe, John, 15, 42
Zwingli, Huldrich, 42

Studies in Christian History and Thought
(All titles uniform with this volume)
Dates in bold are of projected publication

David Bebbington
Holiness in Nineteenth-Century England
David Bebbington stresses the relationship of movements of spirituality to changes in their cultural setting, especially the legacies of the Enlightenment and Romanticism. He shows that these broad shifts in ideological mood had a profound effect on the ways in which piety was conceptualized and practised. Holiness was intimately bound up with the spirit of the age.
2000 / 0-85364-981-2 / viii + 98pp

J. William Black
Reformation Pastors
Richard Baxter and the Ideal of the Reformed Pastor
This work examines Richard Baxter's *Gildas Salvianus, The Reformed Pastor* (1656) and explores each aspect of his pastoral strategy in light of his own concern for 'reformation' and in the broader context of Edwardian, Elizabethan and early Stuart pastoral ideals and practice.
2003 / 1-84227-190-3 / xxii + 308pp

James Bruce
Prophecy, Miracles, Angels, *and* Heavenly Light?
The Eschatology, Pneumatology and Missiology of Adomnán's Life of Columba
This book surveys approaches to the marvellous in hagiography, providing the first critique of Plummer's hypothesis of Irish saga origin. It then analyses the uniquely systematized phenomena in the *Life of Columba* from Adomnán's seventh-century theological perspective, identifying the coming of the eschatological Kingdom as the key to understanding.
2004 / 1-84227-227-6 / xviii + 286pp

Colin J. Bulley
The Priesthood of Some Believers
Developments from the General to the Special Priesthood in the Christian Literature of the First Three Centuries
The first in-depth treatment of early Christian texts on the priesthood of all believers shows that the developing priesthood of the ordained related closely to the division between laity and clergy and had deleterious effects on the practice of the general priesthood.
2000 / 1-84227-034-6 / xii + 336pp

Anthony R. Cross (ed.)
Ecumenism and History
Studies in Honour of John H.Y. Briggs

This collection of essays examines the inter-relationships between the two fields in which Professor Briggs has contributed so much: history—particularly Baptist and Nonconformist—and the ecumenical movement. With contributions from colleagues and former research students from Britain, Europe and North America, *Ecumenism and History* provides wide-ranging studies in important aspects of Christian history, theology and ecumenical studies.

2002 / 1-84227-135-0 / xx + 362pp

Maggi Dawn
Confessions of an Inquiring Spirit
Form as Constitutive of Meaning in S.T. Coleridge's Theological Writing

This study of Coleridge's *Confessions* focuses on its confessional, epistolary and fragmentary form, suggesting that attention to these features significantly affects its interpretation. Bringing a close study of these three literary forms, the author suggests ways in which they nuance the text with particular understandings of the Trinity, and of a kenotic christology. Some parallels are drawn between Romantic and postmodern dilemmas concerning the authority of the biblical text.

2006 / 1-84227-255-1 / approx. 224 pp

Ruth Gouldbourne
The Flesh and the Feminine
Gender and Theology in the Writings of Caspar Schwenckfeld

Caspar Schwenckfeld and his movement exemplify one of the radical communities of the sixteenth century. Challenging theological and liturgical norms, they also found themselves challenging social and particularly gender assumptions. In this book, the issues of the relationship between radical theology and the understanding of gender are considered.

2005 / 1-84227-048-6 / approx. 304pp

Crawford Gribben
Puritan Millennialism
Literature and Theology, 1550–1682

Puritan Millennialism surveys the growth, impact and eventual decline of puritan millennialism throughout England, Scotland and Ireland, arguing that it was much more diverse than has frequently been suggested. This Paternoster edition is revised and extended from the original 2000 text.

2007 / 1-84227-372-8 / approx. 320pp

Galen K. Johnson
Prisoner of Conscience
John Bunyan on Self, Community and Christian Faith

This is an interdisciplinary study of John Bunyan's understanding of conscience across his autobiographical, theological and fictional writings, investigating whether conscience always deserves fidelity, and how Bunyan's view of conscience affects his relationship both to modern Western individualism and historic Christianity.

2003 / 1-84227-223-3 / xvi + 236pp

R.T. Kendall
Calvin and English Calvinism to 1649

The author's thesis is that those who formed the Westminster Confession of Faith, which is regarded as Calvinism, in fact departed from John Calvin on two points: (1) the extent of the atonement and (2) the ground of assurance of salvation.

1997 / 0-85364-827-1 / xii + 264pp

Timothy Larsen
Friends of Religious Equality
Nonconformist Politics in Mid-Victorian England

During the middle decades of the nineteenth century the English Nonconformist community developed a coherent political philosophy of its own, of which a central tenet was the principle of religious equality (in contrast to the stereotype of Evangelical Dissenters). The Dissenting community fought for the civil rights of Roman Catholics, non-Christians and even atheists on an issue of principle which had its flowering in the enthusiastic and undivided support which Nonconformity gave to the campaign for Jewish emancipation. This reissued study examines the political efforts and ideas of English Nonconformists during the period, covering the whole range of national issues raised, from state education to the Crimean War. It offers a case study of a theologically conservative group defending religious pluralism in the civic sphere, showing that the concept of religious equality was a grand vision at the centre of the political philosophy of the Dissenters.

2007 / 1-84227-402-3 / x + 300pp

Byung-Ho Moon
Christ the Mediator of the Law
Calvin's Christological Understanding of the Law as the Rule of Living and Life-Giving

This book explores the coherence between Christology and soteriology in Calvin's theology of the law, examining its intellectual origins and his position on the concept and extent of Christ's mediation of the law. A comparative study between Calvin and contemporary Reformers—Luther, Bucer, Melancthon and Bullinger—and his opponent Michael Servetus is made for the purpose of pointing out the unique feature of Calvin's Christological understanding of the law.

2005 / 1-84227-318-3 / approx. 370pp

John Eifion Morgan-Wynne
Holy Spirit and Religious Experience in Christian Writings, c.AD 90–200

This study examines how far Christians in the third to fifth generations (c.AD 90–200) attributed their sense of encounter with the divine presence, their sense of illumination in the truth or guidance in decision-making, and their sense of ethical empowerment to the activity of the Holy Spirit in their lives.

2005 / 1-84227-319-1 / approx. 350pp

James I. Packer
The Redemption and Restoration of Man in the Thought of Richard Baxter

James I. Packer provides a full and sympathetic exposition of Richard Baxter's doctrine of humanity, created and fallen; its redemption by Christ Jesus; and its restoration in the image of God through the obedience of faith by the power of the Holy Spirit.

2002 / 1-84227-147-4 / 432pp

Andrew Partington,
Church and State
The Contribution of the Church of England Bishops to the House of Lords during the Thatcher Years

In *Church and State*, Andrew Partington argues that the contribution of the Church of England bishops to the House of Lords during the Thatcher years was overwhelmingly critical of the government; failed to have a significant influence in the public realm; was inefficient, being undertaken by a minority of those eligible to sit on the Bench of Bishops; and was insufficiently moral and spiritual in its content to be distinctive. On the basis of this, and the likely reduction of the number of places available for Church of England bishops in a fully reformed Second Chamber, the author argues for an evolution in the Church of England's approach to the service of its bishops in the House of Lords. He proposes the Church of England works to overcome the genuine obstacles which hinder busy diocesan bishops from contributing to the debates of the House of Lords and to its life more informally.

2005 / 1-84227-334-5 / approx. 324pp

Michael Pasquarello III
God's Ploughman
Hugh Latimer: A 'Preaching Life' (1490–1555)

This construction of a 'preaching life' situates Hugh Latimer within the larger religious, political and intellectual world of late medieval England. Neither biography, intellectual history, nor analysis of discrete sermon texts, this book is a work of homiletic history which draws from the details of Latimer's milieu to construct an interpretive framework for the preaching performances that formed the core of his identity as a religious reformer. Its goal is to illumine the practical wisdom embodied in the content, form and style of Latimer's preaching, and to recapture a sense of its overarching purpose, movement, and transforming force during the reform of sixteenth-century England.

2006 / 1-84227-336-1 / approx. 250pp

Alan P.F. Sell
Enlightenment, Ecumenism, Evangel
Theological Themes and Thinkers 1550–2000

This book consists of papers in which such interlocking topics as the Enlightenment, the problem of authority, the development of doctrine, spirituality, ecumenism, theological method and the heart of the gospel are discussed. Issues of significance to the church at large are explored with special reference to writers from the Reformed and Dissenting traditions.

2005 / 1-84227-330-2 / xviii + 422pp

Alan P.F. Sell
Hinterland Theology
Some Reformed and Dissenting Adjustments

Many books have been written on theology's 'giants' and significant trends, but what of those lesser-known writers who adjusted to them? In this book some hinterland theologians of the British Reformed and Dissenting traditions, who followed in the wake of toleration, the Evangelical Revival, the rise of modern biblical criticism and Karl Barth, are allowed to have their say. They include Thomas Ridgley, Ralph Wardlaw, T.V. Tymms and N.H.G. Robinson.

2006 / 1-84227-331-0 / approx. 350pp

Alan P.F. Sell and Anthony R. Cross (eds)
Protestant Nonconformity in the Twentieth Century

In this collection of essays scholars representative of a number of Nonconformist traditions reflect thematically on Nonconformists' life and witness during the twentieth century. Among the subjects reviewed are biblical studies, theology, worship, evangelism and spirituality, and ecumenism. Over and above its immediate interest, this collection provides a marker to future scholars and others wishing to know how some of their forebears assessed Nonconformity's contribution to a variety of fields during the century leading up to Christianity's third millennium.

2003 / 1-84227-221-7 / x + 398pp

Mark Smith
Religion in Industrial Society
Oldham and Saddleworth 1740–1865

This book analyses the way British churches sought to meet the challenge of industrialization and urbanization during the period 1740–1865. Working from a case-study of Oldham and Saddleworth, Mark Smith challenges the received view that the Anglican Church in the eighteenth century was characterized by complacency and inertia, and reveals Anglicanism's vigorous and creative response to the new conditions. He reassesses the significance of the centrally directed church reforms of the mid-nineteenth century, and emphasizes the importance of local energy and enthusiasm. Charting the growth of denominational pluralism in Oldham and Saddleworth, Dr Smith compares the strengths and weaknesses of the various Anglican and Nonconformist approaches to promoting church growth. He also demonstrates the extent to which all the churches participated in a common culture shaped by the influence of evangelicalism, and shows that active co-operation between the churches rather than denominational conflict dominated. This revised and updated edition of Dr Smith's challenging and original study makes an important contribution both to the social history of religion and to urban studies.

2006 / 1-84227-335-3 / approx. 300pp

July 2005

Martin Sutherland
Peace, Toleration and Decay
The Ecclesiology of Later Stuart Dissent
This fresh analysis brings to light the complexity and fragility of the later Stuart Nonconformist consensus. Recent findings on wider seventeenth-century thought are incorporated into a new picture of the dynamics of Dissent and the roots of evangelicalism.
2003 / 1-84227-152-0 / xxii + 216pp

G. Michael Thomas
The Extent of the Atonement
A Dilemma for Reformed Theology from Calvin to the Consensus
A study of the way Reformed theology addressed the question, 'Did Christ die for all, or for the elect only?', commencing with John Calvin, and including debates with Lutheranism, the Synod of Dort and the teaching of Moïse Amyraut.
1997 / 0-85364-828-X / x + 278pp

David M. Thompson
Baptism, Church and Society in Britain from the Evangelical Revival to *Baptism, Eucharist and Ministry*
The theology and practice of baptism have not received the attention they deserve. How important is faith? What does baptismal regeneration mean? Is baptism a bond of unity between Christians? This book discusses the theology of baptism and popular belief and practice in England and Wales from the Evangelical Revival to the publication of the World Council of Churches' consensus statement on *Baptism, Eucharist and Ministry* (1982).
2005 / 1-84227-393-0 / approx. 224pp

Mark D. Thompson
A Sure Ground on Which to Stand
The Relation of Authority and Interpretive Method of Luther's Approach to Scripture
The best interpreter of Luther is Luther himself. Unfortunately many modern studies have superimposed contemporary agendas upon this sixteenth-century Reformer's writings. This fresh study examines Luther's own words to find an explanation for his robust confidence in the Scriptures, a confidence that generated the famous 'stand' at Worms in 1521.
2004 / 1-84227-145-8 / xvi + 322pp

Carl R. Trueman and R.S. Clark (eds)
Protestant Scholasticism
Essays in Reassessment

Traditionally Protestant theology, between Luther's early reforming career and the dawn of the Enlightenment, has been seen in terms of decline and fall into the wastelands of rationalism and scholastic speculation. In this volume a number of scholars question such an interpretation. The editors argue that the development of post-Reformation Protestantism can only be understood when a proper historical model of doctrinal change is adopted. This historical concern underlies the subsequent studies of theologians such as Calvin, Beza, Olevian, Baxter, and the two Turrentini. The result is a significantly different reading of the development of Protestant Orthodoxy, one which both challenges the older scholarly interpretations and clichés about the relationship of Protestantism to, among other things, scholasticism and rationalism, and which demonstrates the fruitfulness of the new, historical approach.

1999 / 0-85364-853-0 / xx + 344pp

Shawn D. Wright
Our Sovereign Refuge
The Pastoral Theology of Theodore Beza

Our Sovereign Refuge is a study of the pastoral theology of the Protestant reformer who inherited the mantle of leadership in the Reformed church from John Calvin. Countering a common view of Beza as supremely a 'scholastic' theologian who deviated from Calvin's biblical focus, Wright uncovers a new portrait. He was not a cold and rigid academic theologian obsessed with probing the eternal decrees of God. Rather, by placing him in his pastoral context and by noting his concerns in his pastoral and biblical treatises, Wright shows that Beza was fundamentally a committed Christian who was troubled by the vicissitudes of life in the second half of the sixteenth century. He believed that the biblical truth of the supreme sovereignty of God alone could support Christians on their earthly pilgrimage to heaven. This pastoral and personal portrait forms the heart of Wright's argument.

2004 / 1-84227-252-7 / xviii + 308pp

Paternoster
9 Holdom Avenue,
Bletchley,
Milton Keynes MK1 1QR,
United Kingdom
Web: www.authenticmedia.co.uk/paternoster

www.ingramcontent.com/pod-product-compliance
Lightning Source LLC
Chambersburg PA
CBHW071150300426
44113CB00009B/1158